THE PRINCIPLES OF BUSINESS COMPUTING

THE PRINCIPLES OF BUSINESS COMPUTING

by

P.M.Q. Lay

M Com (Cape Town) Ph D (Cape Town)

Researcher and Consultant

M.G. Eccles

B Com (Hons) BDP (Cape Town) M Com (Cape Town)

Senior Lecturer, Information Systems Section,
Department of Accounting, University of Cape Town

F.W. Julyan

B Sc (PU for CHE), D Compt (Unisa), NED (DEAS), CFA (SA)

Professor, Department of Accounting,
University of South Africa

G. Boot

B Sc (Hons) (Unisa), D Com (Unisa), FIMTA (SA), MCSSA

Professor, Department of Accounting
University of South Africa

Juta & Co. Ltd
1993

First published 1984
Second edition 1985
Third edition 1988
Second impression 1990
Fourth edition 1993

PO Box 14373, Kenwyn 7790

Edited by David Michael, Cape Town
Cover design by Joy Wrench, Cape Town
Typeset by Mixed Media, Cape Town, in 10½ on 12½ pt Times
Printed and bound by Creda Press, Eliot Avenue, Epping 2

ISBN 0 7021 2837 6

Preface

It is now 10 years since the first edition of *The Principles of Business Computing* was published. To put this new edition into perspective it is interesting to consider the nature of business computing in those days — the early 1980s — and to reflect on the extent of change that has taken place since that time.

In the first place microcomputers had yet to make a real mark. The IBM PC, announced late in 1981, was only just finding its way into the corporate arena, and by today's standards the technology was slow and cumbersome. It certainly did not have the power to perform any of the applications that are now commonplace in the business world. Application packages that are almost taken for granted today, such as wordprocessing, spreadsheets, database manipulation, were also only just appearing, some in a very rudimentary form. The main language was BASIC — so simple, yet so crude.

Secondly, local area networks (LANs), so commonplace today, were unheard of then. The power of networking is now being felt in most businesses, linking hardware and applications into cohesive units, bringing data access to users in a form that in the early 1980s would only have been a dream.

The topic of user-friendly systems was lectured, taught, discussed and debated in those days, but the systems being installed were clumsy, unfriendly and difficult to maintain. Now, thanks mainly to the personal computer, with all the trimmings of colour screens, touch pads, sound and graphics, systems are being used at all levels of the organization by all manner of people, from the lowliest right up to the chief executive.

Despite all this, what has *really* changed in the information systems world? The systems that were developed ten, fifteen, twenty years ago are still with us, with their high costs of maintenance. These systems probably make up 70 to 80 % of a large organization's portfolio. Many such organizations are being placed in a catch-22 situation: the cost of re-development of systems is too high, so they are forced to modify, modify, modify — yet they are working with old-fashioned, ungainly systems so the cost of modification outstrips that of current systems. *Re-engineering* and *reverse engineering* are buzzwords that are heard more and more often, implying the need to introduce current design methods and technologies into previously developed systems.

So, considering these and all the other changes that have taken place in information systems in the last 10 years, there is little that is revolutionary, there is no wondrous new hardware, and no dramatic systems design technique. Yet if you add up all the little changes that have taken place, then the face is a very different one from that which organizations were seeing in the 1980s. And that is what the reader will see in this book if it is compared to the first edition: the structure is very different. The reason for the change is simple: research by academics and practitioners has developed proven methods, procedures, techniques and methodologies for working with information systems hardware and its users. These are based on a structured approach to analysing, designing, implementing, controlling and managing the technology and the people involved with that technology. Whereas before, technology was something mystical and knowledge of it belonged to an élite few, it is now in the domain of the workplace with everybody using it and developing systems for it. Under these circumstances those techniques had better be proven, or there will be a lot of very unhappy users in the workplace!

With this in mind, the technology sections have been re-written to accommodate the changes that have taken place in the market. Module 3 — Systems Development — has been re-written along modern systems development lines, integrating such procedures as Strategic Systems Planning, Joint Application Design and Prototyping into the process. The most extensive changes in this new edition have been made in the applications module. Previously this module assumed a basic knowledge of the structure and implementation of accounting systems in the South African environment and focused on the technical aspects of their computerization. The module has been completely rewritten and provides the reader with a strong foundation as to the nature and functionality of common accounting applications prior to discussion of their computer implementation. The module also provides additional application-related audit and control information. Modules 1, 4 and 5 have been extensively re-worked to make them more reader or student-friendly.

No preface would be complete without acknowledgements. It is therefore with grateful thanks that we acknowledge the contributions of Des Walker and Gavin Stanford of Juta for their encouragement and enthusiasm, our colleagues Steve Erlank, Raoul du Plessis and Derek Smith for their comments and criticisms, Graham McLeod for his contribution of the chapter on the Graphic User Interface, and all the institutions who have supported us by prescribing this book, for their feedback.

Contents

MODULE 1

Information processing concepts

OBJECTIVES

In order to appreciate the role that the information system plays in business, every student must have an understanding of the importance of information processing, controls and management reporting.

On completion of this module students should be able to:

- Explain the role and significance of information processing in the business organization.
- Describe the uses to which management and other users put this information.
- Understand the importance, place, and nature of information technology and the various components of information systems necessary to provide suitable management information.
- Describe the impact of the computer on the gathering and recording of information.
- Explain the need for controls over information processing.
- Describe the advantages and risks in using the computer for information processing.

CHAPTER 1 The business environment

1.1 INTRODUCTION

In order to stay competitive, modern business organizations must be productive and effective. Productivity and effectiveness in any organization can be attained through proper management. Allen[1] describes business as 'the development of strategic objectives based on the odds attending various alternatives.'

In this chapter, we shall discuss information processing in business from a management and decision-making point of view. We shall look into business organizations' need for management and examine theories concerning the management process related to the decision-making functions.

We shall then look at management's need for information and for an information system based on the organizational structure of the enterprise.

1.2 THE NEED FOR MANAGEMENT

Management, as we know it today, is essential in all walks of life. Especially in modern business organizations, a lack of proper management would result in operational losses and such organizations would probably cease to exist. Without proper management standards of living would drop considerably.

Any organization's success depends on its management's selection of goals and objectives, and the ways in which resources are used to attain these goals and objectives. Management, therefore, determines the effectiveness and efficiency of organizational activities. Effectiveness refers to the accomplishment of an organization's goals and objectives, while efficiency is related to the quantity of resources used in producing the desired results.

Since resources are needed to create goods and services, it is clear that the role of management is vital, not only for each organization, but also for the country as a whole.

1.3 MANAGEMENT THEORY

For our purposes, management can be defined as:

> The process of seeking desired outcomes by utilizing the available resources and influencing the human relationships of the organization.[6]

In business organizations, management is involved in seeking goals and objectives. It does this by using resources in various ways. This requires managers to make decisions and influence other people's behaviour in order to 'get things done'.

Davis[5] identifies six management functions to be performed in an organization which pursues goals and objectives. These cannot be achieved without managing material and human resources. The management functions are:

- *Planning.* Selecting goals and objectives, and defining policies, procedures, and programs for achieving them. These activities should guide future decision-making.
- *Organizing.* Grouping the activities to be performed, and establishing organizational structures and relations to carry out these activities.
- *Staffing.* Selecting and training people to work within the organizational structures.
- *Directing.* Leading, guiding, directing, and motivating people in the organization.

- *Co-ordinating*. Scheduling activities in proper sequence and communicating information to and from various levels within the organization.
- *Controlling*. Measuring performance and reporting deviations from planned results. Regulation and correction of activities or adjustments to policies, procedures and programs, where necessary.

All management functions involve decision-making on the part of the manager. Decision-making is, in fact, the most important contribution that a manager makes to an organization.

Decision-making by management takes place at three levels: *strategic planning*, *management control* and *operational control*.[5]

- Strategic planning develops a strategy with which a business organization will attempt to achieve its objectives. The time range for strategic planning tends to be fairly long and does not necessarily have to occur on a regular basis. Some strategic planning will, however, be scheduled into the annual planning and budgeting cycle.
- Management control (which includes tactical planning) involves the measuring of performance, deciding on control actions, formulating new decision rules to be applied by operating personnel, and allocating resources. The time range for management control is shorter than that of strategic planning and decisions have to be made on a more regular basis.
- Operational control is the process of ensuring that operational activities are carried out effectively and efficiently. It utilizes predetermined procedures and decision-rules and therefore a large percentage of the decisions can be programmed. The operating decisions and resulting actions generally cover short periods and tend to be very regular.

1.4 DECISION-MAKING BY MANAGERS

Decision-making should be seen as a process and not as something that happens in a passing moment. In many cases decision-making can take a considerable amount of time. Bodnar and Hopwood[2] recognize a number of steps that managers normally follow systematically when making decisions. These are:

- recognizing and defining a particular problem;
- determining alternative courses of action for solving the problem;
- evaluating the available courses of action and selecting the best one for solving the problem;
- using the selected course of action in solving the problem; and
- monitoring the activity to ensure that the desired results are obtained.

In short, decision-making involves *intelligence* (knowledge or information regarding a problem), *design* (inventing, developing and analysing possible courses of action), and choice (selecting and implementing a particular course of action).

All steps involved in decision-making require information. No decisions can be taken without timely, accurate and meaningful information. The discussion in the remainder of this chapter deals with the provision of information and related data for management, decision-making, and operational activities.

Before going into systems and processes for the provision of management information, it is necessary to look at the organizational structure of a business enterprise.

1.5 ORGANIZATIONAL THEORY

A business organization is a collection of decision-making units that exist to pursue certain business objectives. Every business organization operates as a system which accepts *inputs* (resources) and transforms them into *outputs* (goods and services). A manufacturing concern, for instance, uses raw material, labour and other scarce resources and transforms them into items such as motor cars and other consumer products that are subsequently sold in order to make a profit.

Any organization is made up of at least three kinds of interrelated elements. First, there are the resources or productive factors which have to be controlled. In business organizations these are normally *people, materials, machines* and money. Second, there are the specific activities that an organization carries out in order to attain required results. In business organizations these might be *manufacturing, marketing, personnel management* and *financial management*. Finally, there are management activities which include *setting objectives, developing and executing plans*, and *evaluating the results*.[4]

All activities of an organization are normally carried out under the direction of managers. Organizational theory adopts a broad perspective of how management fits into an organization. Max Weber identified numerous properties that an ideal organization should have, including the structural relationships among operational functions (such as the division of work and the hierarchy of authority), personnel management, and processes for communicating information in order to get unified actions from specialist employees.[6]

Wilkinson[7] describes a formal organizational structure as a hierarchical arrangement of the various functions within the organization. It specifies the relationships among these functions as well as the authority delegated to management at the various levels.

The principles related to a traditional organizational structure can be described as follows:

- *Division of work.* This refers to the segmentation of tasks or operations and includes the division of managerial tasks. This enables managers and employees to specialize and helps to achieve more effective control over a variety of operations and activities.
- *Authority and responsibility*. This refers to a manager's power to get things done. Authority is delegated to lower levels of management and the degree of such authority should be related to the manager's assigned responsibility for achieving specific objectives.
- *Unity of command and direction*. This refers to clear lines of authority, with each employee or group that shares the same objectives being directed by one manager.
- *Span of control*. This refers to the number of subordinate managers or supervisors reporting to a superior manager.

Organizational structure can therefore be regarded as the configuration of positions, the allocation of authority and responsibility, as well as the relationships between functions and employees for handling the overall work load.

1.6 MANAGEMENT'S NEED FOR INFORMATION

In order to make meaningful decisions, managers need timely, accurate, and meaningful information. The identification of the information requirements for managerial decision-making is one of the most important factors in setting up a modern business enterprise.

The information needs of managers are identified according to their responsibilities, the way in which they are evaluated, the types of problems they face, the means by which they evaluate personal output, and the types of decisions they have to make.

The provision of information is part of the communication function of an organization. This means that information must be in a form the manager can clearly understand and interpret. Furthermore, if communication is to be effective, the information received by managers should have value and stimulate them to make decisions that will assist in achieving the organization's objectives.

As stated by Wilkinson,[7] management's needs for information can be analysed according to information content, information characteristics, dimensions of information needs, and each manager's individual information needs.

1.6.1 Information content

Information should have some substance: for instance, number of units sold during the previous week, or the number of units expected to be sold the following week. The content of information can be valued relative to its usefulness in making specific decisions.

1.6.2 Information characteristics

In addition to specific content, information has certain characteristics which influence the quality of decision-making. Significant information characteristics include the following:

- The relevance of the information to the decision situation or to the organization's goals and objectives.
- The reliability and precision of the information.
- The currency of the information.
- The scope of the information.
- The degree to which numeric values can be assigned to the information.
- The degree to which the information is summarized or aggregated.

1.6.3 Dimensions of information needs

The dimensions of information needs vary considerably in relation to managerial activities, managerial levels, organizational structures and operational functions. By analysing information needs along these lines, one can obtain a better understanding of the requirements of individual managers.

Managerial activities

Planning relates to the comparison of alternative options, whereas control highlights the comparison of actual results against planned results. Because of these differences, the information content necessary for planning decisions will be different from the information content necessary for control decisions.

In addition to information content, the characteristics of information necessary for strategic planning would differ from those needed for tactical planning. Similarly, the characteristics of information needed for making decisions regarding management control would differ from those needed for making decisions regarding operational control.

Managerial levels

Managers at different managerial levels have varying needs for information. Managers at higher levels make decisions regarding strategic planning and therefore they need information that has been summarized or aggregated, with a broad scope and a long-range perspective. They need many different kinds of information, including qualitative, quantitative, internal, and external information.

Middle management may need both summarized and detailed information, depending on the situation at hand. For instance, in making decisions regarding management control a sales manager may need summarized and quantitative weekly reports concerning the performance of branch managers. On the other hand, in making decisions regarding tactical planning, a plant manager may need information concerning the coming week's production workload together with the availability of labour and money.

At the lower levels, managers make decisions regarding operational planning and control and therefore they need detailed, accurate, timely, and quantitative information.

Organizational structures

Business organizations are usually structured according to operational functions, product lines, etc. Information needs may vary in accordance with such structures, especially at middle-management levels.

Operational functions

Each operational function will need its own distinctive information in accordance with its assigned responsibilities. The financial manager, for instance, needs information regarding cash flow, financial status, and operating results.

It can also happen that two or more operating functions share certain information needs. The sales forecast which contains the basic information for preparing budgets, for instance, can also be used in decision-making concerning production scheduling and the acquisition of materials.

1.6.4 Information needs of individual managers

The unique needs of individual managers will depend largely on the types of decisions to be made, the level on which they operate, and the operational functions they perform. A manager's personal background (such as education and experience) will also influence the type of information needed.

1.7 THE NEED FOR INFORMATION SYSTEMS

Every business organization needs information to support its management functions. In an uncertain and demanding society, the managers of modern business organizations need new and improved ways of managing human and economic resources. They do not need more data; they need better information which consists of data that have been filtered, analysed and compared.

As managers face new problems, their information requirements change accordingly. They also have personal differences. Whether managers ask for new information or better access to existing information, the information system should be able to respond quickly to changing requirements. Different presentations, associations, and summaries of data can sometimes lead to new insights for management.

According to Bower, Schlosser and Newman,[3] a business information system must be able to fulfil three basic information needs. First, the system must provide for the internal information needs of management. Second, the system must provide management with information for controlling business activity. Finally, the system must provide information for external reporting to various individuals and organizations.

1.7.1 Internal information needs of management

Management needs an information system that can provide information regarding the past, the present, and the future. Historical information relates closely to the need to record and process routine business events. Regarding the present, management needs to know who is responsible for the various assets, where each asset is located, what should be on hand, and also the events that are taking place. Current information may prove especially meaningful when compared with information from previous periods, budgets or standards. Current and historical information can also be used to project future events or outcomes and to perform meaningful planning.

1.7.2 Information for controlling business activity

An important aspect of any information system should be its ability to provide management with information for effectively controlling business activities. Although the need for information for control purposes is part of management's internal information need, it differs since control depends on factors such as the assignment of duties and organizational relationships. In order to operate the business effectively on a day-to-day basis, timely, accurate, and meaningful information must flow from the information system.

An information system that enables management to control performance, and at the same time measure and motivate it, will always be very important for managers. Most respectable information systems contain a reporting system known as *responsibility accounting*. This enables expenditure at all levels of management to be controlled and related to the individuals responsible for it.

1.7.3 Information for external reporting

The information system should also provide information to individuals outside the organization. Much of the information for external needs can be derived from data used for internal information needs. The needs of external users such as stockholders, investors, creditors and government impose a major burden on South African businesses.

REVIEW QUESTIONS

1. Explain why managers depend on the right kind of information.
2. Discuss decision-making in the context of the various management levels of an organization.
3. Explain how an organization's information needs relate to its organizational structure.
4. Discuss the characteristics of good quality information for decision-making.
5. Discuss the qualities that a good information system for the provision of management information should possess.

SELECTED REFERENCES AND RECOMMENDED READING

1. Allen, L. A. 1964. *The Management Profession.* New York: McGraw-Hill Book Company.
2. Bodnar, G. H. and Hopwood, W. S. 1987. *Accounting Information Systems.* Third edition. Newton, Massachusetts: Allyn and Bacon, Inc.
3. Bower, J. B., Schlosser, R. E. and Newman, M. S. 1985. *Computer-Oriented Accounting Information Systems.* Cincinnati: South-Western Publishing Co.
4. Brabb, G. J. 1980. *Computers and Information Systems in Business.* Second edition. Boston: Houghton Mifflin Company.
5. Davis, G. B. 1974. *Management Information Systems: Conceptual Foundations, Structure, and Development.* Tokyo: McGraw-Hill Kogakusha, Ltd.
6. Greene, C. N., Adam, E. E. Jr. and Ebert, R. J. 1985. *Management for Effective Performance.* Englewood Cliffs: Prentice-Hall, Inc.
7. Wilkinson, J. W. 1986. *Accounting and Information Systems.* Second edition. New York: John Wiley and Sons.

CHAPTER 2 Business information systems

2.1 INTRODUCTION

This chapter deals with information and information systems. After defining an information system and distinguishing between data, information and knowledge, the basic elements of an information system are highlighted. The principles for the design of an efficient and effective information system are extremely important because all discussions in this book regarding the purposes, nature, role, development, implementation and control of information systems in business will be based on them.

The important role of information systems in business will be explained by looking into the organizational structure, the specific information needs of managers, and the value and usefulness of information and management reports. The importance of user involvement in the design and development of an information system is also emphasized because it is the users who will ultimately determine whether the system is successful or not.

Over the past several years a new concept, information technology (IT), has emerged. This concept is the outgrowth of the micro-electronics revolution and has a much wider scope than the term information systems. It comprises all kinds of computers, other automation technologies, and communication.[2] In this chapter the managerial and strategic importance of information technology will be touched upon.

2.2 INFORMATION TECHNOLOGY

Some confusion still exists on the actual meaning of this concept. Different people give different meanings to it. From a technical perspective it comprises computing, automation technologies, and all types of telecommunications. As an activity it comprises the various acquisition, development and operational activities involved when these technologies are used to an organization's advantage. As a philosophy, the new information technology era represents aims, means, and responsibilities that are different from those of the old data processing era where there was little management involvement.[7]

In general IT represents the convergence of all types of computer equipment, certain electronic (audio and video) equipment, all types of software developed for use with computers, telecommunications equipment and software, and other automation techniques. Computer software includes word processing, other processing and application packages, database systems, fourth-generation programming languages, knowledge-based systems and artificial intelligence.

The changes from the old data-processing environment to a new information technology environment require a new approach to management. In most cases IT is regarded as being a strategic resource that must be managed accordingly. The case for strategically managing IT can be founded on a number of statements:[7]

- IT is critical to most organizations and is becoming a strategic weapon.
- IT affects all functions and levels of management.
- IT brings new possibilities and new pressures for management information systems.
- IT involves more stakeholders.
- IT is a high expenditure activity.

The management and other information systems dealt with in the remainder of this book, all form part of the information technology described above.

2.3 INFORMATION SYSTEMS DEFINED

Systems that process a business organization's data and provide information to management, are known under various names; for example, data processing systems, management information systems, business information systems, accounting information systems, and others. The objective of an information system is to transform all types of data into information and to provide management with the information they need for decision-making.

Among various definitions of information systems, there is consensus that the purpose of an information system is to provide information that supports management and to add value to the business organization. An information system is therefore an orderly way of providing the information that business organizations need to operate successfully and make a profit. For our purposes we adopt the following definition of an information system:

> An information system is an integrated man/machine system for providing information to support the operations, management and decision-making functions in an organization. The system utilizes computer hardware and software, manual procedures, management and decision models, and a database.[5]

Because information costs money to create, maintain, and use, the information system should justify that cost by providing specific, identifiable benefits to the organization.

2.4 MANAGEMENT INFORMATION SYSTEMS

Although a management information system (MIS) will involve all elements contained in the above definition, and will form part of the comprehensive information system, its main function is to provide information for strategic management and decision-making purposes. A MIS is not purely data processing, although it encompasses certain processing activities; it is not computer science, even though database structure and design require knowledge drawn from computer science; it is not management science, although decision and optimization models are used for decision support; and it is not management of human behaviour, although MIS designers need a background in organization behaviour for a successful system installation. Management information systems draw from all these areas and, together with information technology, they are changing the shape and behaviour of most organizations. A MIS may also be described in terms of *physical components* (hardware, software, personnel), *managerial components* (strategic planning, tactical planning and management control, and operational control), or *management support for decision-making*.[1]

Providing management information on a higher level requires much more than simple data processing. For this reason decision support systems (DSS) were introduced to support, but not replace, the decision-making process. Where DSSs are closely related to decision-making, they depend on information management as well as data processing.

Over the years there has been a progression from *data processing* to *information management* to *decision support* to *expert systems*.[1] The latter two systems will be discussed in more detail in chapter three of this module.

Another issue associated with management information is the use of knowledge bases. A knowledge base contains facts, rules, inferences and procedures. Through the use of a knowledge base, managers are able to make decisions related to a particular domain or expertize; eg. authorization of credit card purchases.[1]

2.5 DATA, INFORMATION AND KNOWLEDGE

It is important to point out that there is a widely accepted distinction between the concepts *data*, *information* and *knowledge*. Although there are various definitions, we will use the following:

Data can be defined as *content or descriptions of objects and events*. If data are already known, or if they are of no concern to the person who receives them, they cannot be information.[9]

Information is obtained *when meaning and usefulness have been added to the data*. Information, therefore, results from data that have been processed and transformed, and that mean something to the receiver. It should reduce uncertainty, convey a message to the decision-maker, and possess the potential to evoke some response.[9]

Knowledge involves the collection of interpreted information from various sources into one related unit, serving as a single source of information for specific purposes (a certain field of expertise).[8]

2.6 BASIC ELEMENTS OF AN INFORMATION SYSTEM

Based upon the definition given above, one can identify five basic elements of information systems: *people*, *machines*, *procedures*, *databases* and *control*.[9]

2.6.1 People

People, the most important element in an information system, play many roles at various levels within the system. Managers and other personnel should be the prime beneficiaries because information systems are designed to meet their information needs.

2.6.2 Machines

Modern information systems are distinguished by the presence of computers. Although people are still as necessary to computer-based systems as they were before, their roles have changed from doing routine work to making decisions based on system inputs and outputs.

2.6.3 Procedures

Procedures in the information system use both computer-based and non-computer-based knowledge, models, and personnel to ensure that the correct data are entered into the computer, and that they are then properly transformed, communicated and used.

Procedures include all processing and information flow activities, computer programs, and program specifications.

2.6.4 Database

The processes of collecting, storing, processing and transforming data into meaningful information for use in making decisions are central to the information system. In a computer-based system, data must be accessible to, and compatible with the computer system. A formalized database is the foundation upon which such an information system should be built.

2.6.5 Control

Each information system requires an element of control which relates to the interaction between all the other basic elements (people, machines, procedures and the database). Information systems require measurement, feedback and adjusting mechanisms for cost-effective performance.

2.7 PRINCIPLES FOR THE DESIGN OF INFORMATION SYSTEMS

A system principle is the basis for the design of an information system that will produce the required results. If an information system is to provide management with timely, accurate and meaningful information as well as a means of planning, organizing, directing, co-ordinating and controlling effectively, the applicable systems principles will serve as a guide to designing, developing and operating such a system.[4]

Systems principles can, in many respects, be compared to accounting principles. Whereas accountants have for many years devoted attention to the statements of accounting principles, systems practitioners have over the years worked on developing systems principles.

Nine principles of information system design have been proposed. Each of them has a significant impact on the major aspects of systems analysis, design, development and implementation, and operation.[4]

- *Reasonable cost.* The system should provide information and internal control, consistent with the needs of management, at a reasonable cost.
- *Effective reporting.* The system should provide for effective and extensive reporting, both internally and externally, since reports are a primary systems product.
- *Human factors.* The system should take into account human factors, requirements, and priorities, since people are responsible for the effectiveness and ultimate success of the system.
- *Organization structure.* The system should function in a specific, clearly defined, organizational structure. It should be developed according to the structure of the business in order to satisfy its particular information and control needs.
- *Reliability.* The system should be able to check the reliability and accuracy of financial and other data, minimize error, safeguard assets, and prevent fraud or other irregularities.

- *Flexibility*, *uniformity* and *consistency*. The system should be flexible, yet ensure reasonable uniformity and consistency of application in order to allow business operations to run smoothly.
- *Auditability*. The system should facilitate the tracing of procedural steps in order to permit the analysis and scrutiny of detailed data underlying summarized information.
- *Database*. The system should enable the rapid and efficient recording and classification of data so that they can be transformed into meaningful information for planning, control, and administration.
- *Data processing*. The system should provide for meaningful, continuous and controlled processing of data in order to produce reliable information and facilitate control.

The reasonable cost principle is probably the most important one. The principles of flexibility, uniformity, consistency and auditability are related to the actual design of the system. The principles of reliability, organization structure, and human factors serve as the primary basis for internal control. The database, data processing, and reporting principles govern data and information flow throughout the organization. The proper application of these systems principles should produce an optimum business information system.

2.8 FOUNDATIONS FOR DESIGN AND DEVELOPMENT

The design and development of an information system that will satisfy the needs of all users seems to be a complicated task. It is clear that during the design and development processes various disciplines and other issues come into play. If, however, the different foundations on which a successful comprehensive information system should be built are taken into account during the design phase, this task should not be too difficult.

The following factors (foundations) should be considered when designing a comprehensive information system:[3]

- Management functions
- Quality of information
- Design principles
- Financial accounting principles and practices (based on generally accepted accounting practices — GAAP)
- Management accounting practices (which include cost accounting and management accounting models)
- Audit and security principles.

The relationships between these factors are important. These relationships can best be explained by way of a diagram (Figure 2.1) in which the hierarchy of information provision is shown in the context of strategic management.[3]

2.9 THE NATURE AND PURPOSES OF INFORMATION SYSTEMS

Managers maintain information systems for a number of reasons which include the following:[4]

- They allow interested parties to tell what has happened in the past, what the current situation is, and the direction in which things are going.
- They facilitate management; it is impossible to manage or control without information expressed in monetary or quantitative terms.
- Records can be maintained, reports can be produced, and data and information can be audited.
- Routine accounting activities such as billing, paying and receiving can be executed.

FIGURE 2.1. Relationships between the different foundations for the provision of management information.

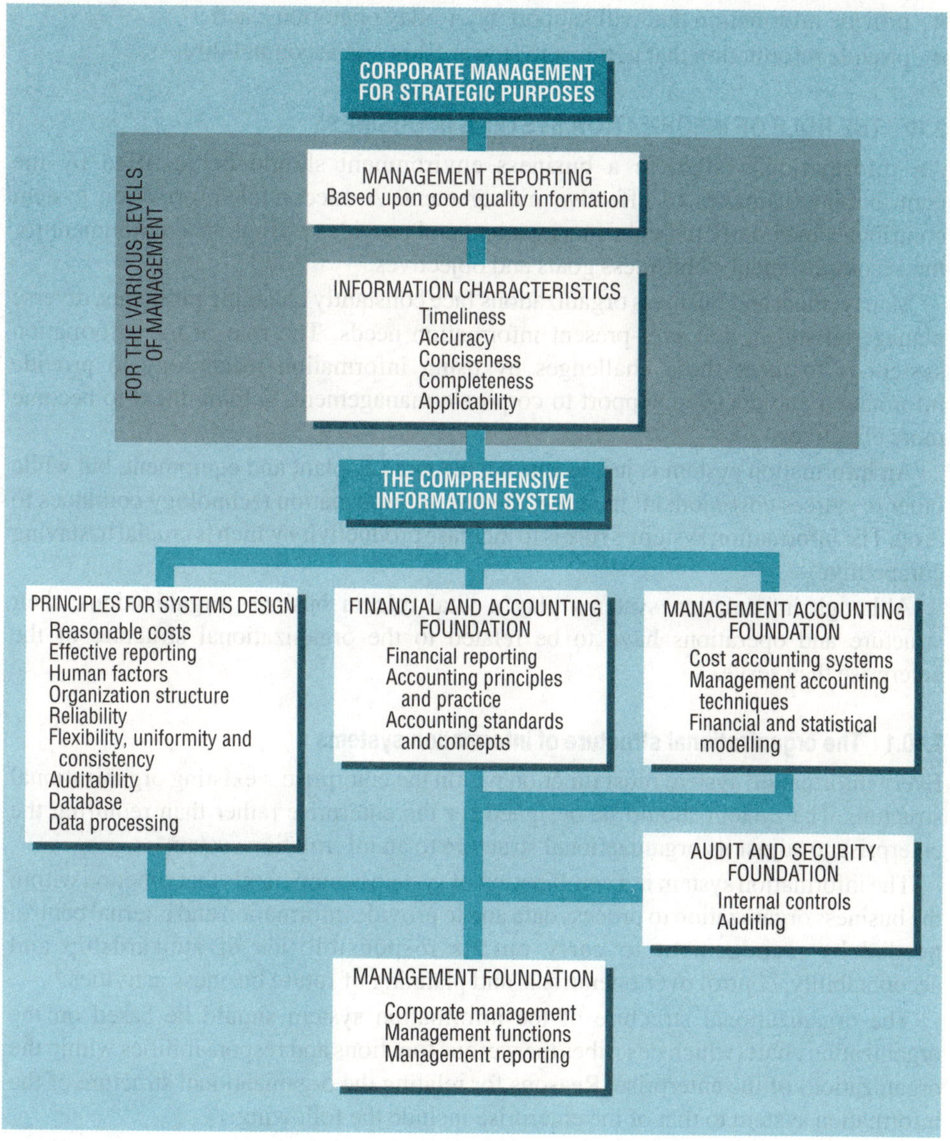

- Those responsible for the custody of property can discharge their custodianship because they are aware of the value associated with assets, their quantities and their location.

The information system includes the records and processing structure by which goals and objectives requiring quantitative information can be accomplished. A well-designed information system is essential for successful management planning and control since these functions require a steady flow of accurate and reliable information.

In short, the purposes of information systems in business are to:

- provide information that will support decision-making;
- provide information that will support day-to-day operations; and
- provide information that pertains to stewardship and accountability.

2.10 THE ROLE OF INFORMATION SYSTEMS IN BUSINESS

An information system in a business environment should be justified by the contributions it makes to effective management. A successful information system contributes materially to better management and provides a vigorous environment for the accomplishment of business goals and objectives.

Management and business organizations face constantly changing problems, diverse managerial styles, and ever-present information needs. The role of the information system is to meet these challenges by using information technology to provide information and decision support to corporate management, helping them to become more effective.

An information system is just as much a resource as plant and equipment, but while other resources cost more all the time, the cost of information technology continues to drop. The information system's role is to increase productivity which is crucial to staying competitive.

Although information systems play a vital role in business organizations, their structure and operations have to be related to the organizational structure of the enterprise they serve.

2.10.1 The organizational structure of information systems

Every information system must function within the enterprise's existing organizational structure. The system should be designed for the enterprise rather than requiring the enterprise to adjust its organizational structure to an information system.

The information system is a combination of systems components that function within the business organization to process data and to provide information and internal control needed by management to carry out its responsibilities of stewardship and accountability, control over operations, and planning of future business activities.[4]

The organizational structure of the information system should be based on the organization chart (which describes the various functions and responsibilities within the organization) of the enterprise. Reasons for relating the organizational structure of the information system to that of the enterprise include the following:

- Both are guided by the goals and objectives of the enterprise.
- The organization chart defines the structure of the responsibility centres and therefore the positions of the decision-makers. Since these managers need reports to aid decision-making, the organizational structure determines to a large extent the routing of information within the enterprise.
- Much of the key information in an enterprise flows vertically upward to the various managerial levels of the respective functions.
- The responsibilities that have been assigned to each responsibility centre in the organization determine the content of many of the reports that an information system has to provide.
- The information system should also help to co-ordinate the respective operational activities of the enterprise. This can only be achieved through the processing of transactions, during which data and information flow laterally among organizational units.

Usually an information system is made up of various subsystems that relate to the business organization's managerial and operational activities. A subsystem includes the procedures, methods and operations designed to accomplish specific objectives within a specified segment of business. *Procedures* reflect what is to be done and why. *Methods* and *operations* relate to how things should be done.

For a business organization these segments can, for example, be marketing, production, inventory control, personnel, finance and accounting, and information

FIGURE 2.2. The organizational relationships of an information system.

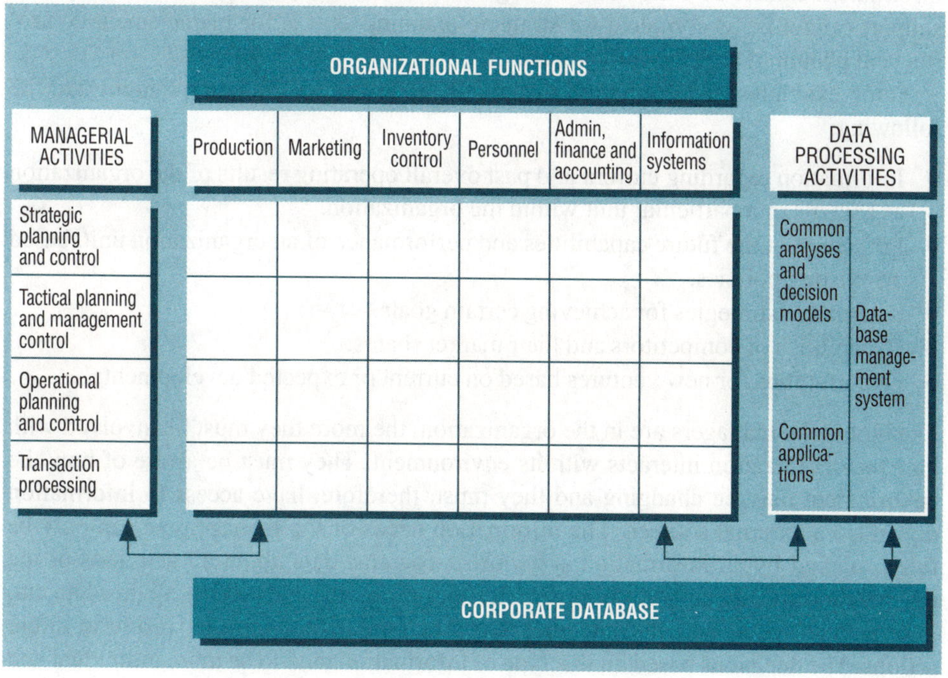

systems. In an integrated system, each subsystem has facilities to perform all processing related to its function, based upon a common database with its applications programs. There will be applications for transaction processing, operational control, managerial control, and strategic planning. These relationships are depicted in Figure 2.2.[5]

2.10.2 The information needs of managers

There are relationships between the hierarchical position of managers in the organization and the type, form, and amount of information they require for the effective and efficient execution of their functions.

Anthony[10] has proposed a systems framework based on the level of planning and control activities in an organization. Anthony's hierarchy consists of strategic planning, management control, and operational control.

Strategic planning

Strategic planning is the process of deciding on objectives for the organization, on changes in these objectives, on the resources used to attain them, and on the policies that are to govern the acquisition, use, and disposition of these resources.[10]

Managers at the higher levels of the organization are more involved in setting goals and objectives and making plans to attain them, but not so much in the execution of plans. They have the responsibility for strategic planning; ie. deciding on what should be done. Strategic planning generally needs information in the form of processed, analysed and summarized data from a variety of sources. Senior managers also need a considerable amount of external information (from the environment). Much of this information cannot be collected on a regular basis, and therefore information system support cannot be as complete for strategic planning as it is for management control (tactical planning) and operational control.

Some examples of information that might be useful in strategic planning are the following:

- Information regarding current and past overall operating results of the organization as a whole or a particular unit within the organization.
- Projection of the future capabilities and performance of an organization unit, based on existing policies.
- Alternative strategies for achieving certain goals.
- Capabilities of competitors and their market shares.
- Opportunities for new ventures based on current or expected developments.

The higher the managers are in the organization, the more they must be involved with how the organization interacts with its environment. They must be aware of how the environment may be changing and they must, therefore, have access to information drawn from external sources. The information needs of top management can only be fully satisfied by an information system that contains data about all activities of the organization and about its environment. It should combine and process all this data into information to show both the outcomes of past actions and the expected results of future actions. The decisions based on this type of information tend to be more individual and unique, and therefore related information requirements are more difficult to predict. Examples of these types of decisions are:

- How can the quality of existing products be improved?
- How should the prices for products be determined?
- What new products should be introduced?
- How should the actions of competitors be counteracted in order to retain or increase our share of the market?

Management control and tactical planning

Management control is the process by which managers assure that resources are obtained and used effectively in the accomplishment of an organization's objectives.[10]

Managers at the middle levels of the organization are responsible for management control and tactical planning; ie. how things should be done. They need summaries of information (and exception reports) — processed so that trends may be observed, reasons for performance variances may be understood, and solutions may be suggested. These managers attempt to optimize relationships between resource inputs and product or service outputs. They deal with problems such as scheduling of tasks, determining optimal inventory levels, allocation of resources, and cost control. The management control process requires more detailed information about results of past actions. These needs are, however, more predictable than the information needs of top management. The following types of information are needed by this level of management:

- Planned performance (budgeted, expected and standard)
- Variances from planned results
- Possible reasons for such variances
- Analysis of possible solutions or courses of action

The database for management control should contain data provided by operations, as well as plans, standards and budgets which define management's expectations regarding performance. There may also be external data such as cost indices. Information system support for managerial control and tactical planning should include the following:

- Planning/budgeting models to assist managers in preparing and revising plans and budgets.
- Exception reporting programs to process scheduled reports showing variances from planned results.
- Problem analysis models to analyse data in order to provide input for decision-making purposes.
- Decision models to analyse a problem situation and provide a satisfactory solution for management approval.
- Inquiry models to assist in responding to inquiries in an efficient way.

The outputs from the information system for management control and tactical planning include plans and budgets, scheduled reports, analyses of problem situations, decisions for review, and inquiry responses.

Operational control

Operational control is the process of assuring that specific tasks are carried out efficiently. At this level, goals have been set and methods of attaining them determined.[10]

Managers at the lower levels of the organization have the responsibility of operational control; ie. supervising day-to-day tasks and ensuring that plans are carried out properly. In this case planning is minimal and the focus is on individual tasks and the techniques for performing those tasks.

At this level, individual transactions are important. The transaction processing part of the system must therefore be able to respond to both individual transactions and summaries of transactions. The information system's processing support for operational control is based on data generated from transactions and must include:

- transaction processing;
- report processing; and
- enquiry processing.

These three types of processing contain various decision-making modules which utilize decision rules that have been agreed upon or provide descriptions on how a decision should be taken.

FIGURE 2.3. An information system as a pyramid of information levels.

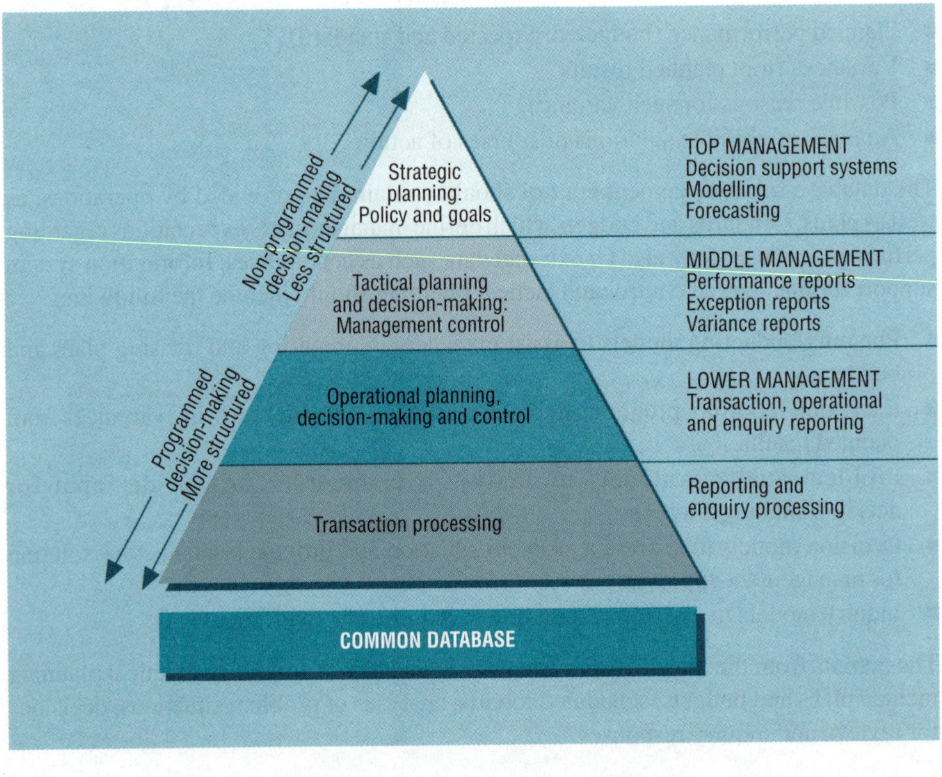

Taking into account the information needs of management, the information system in organizational context can be seen as a pyramid of information levels (see Figure 2.3).

2.10.3 Usefulness and value of information

As discussed above, information differs from data in that information is useful to the decision-maker. The usefulness of information stems from its impact on the manager's beliefs regarding events relevant to the decision-making process.

With regard to planning, information is useful if it aids the manager in predicting future results of various alternative courses of action. Any information that improves the accuracy of these predictions or increases their certainty will be useful to the manager.

Information derives value from its effect on decisions. It requires resources like data storage, preparation and presentation. The provision of information costs money and if it does not improve or affect decision-making, it has negative value. The value or quality of information therefore depends on its attributes which can be summarized as follows:

- *Timeliness.* The timeliness of information is important for control purposes. It is important to detect and solve problems before they get out of hand.
- *Accuracy.* This relates to the information's correctness. One obvious source of inaccuracy is errors in the data used to generate information. Another less obvious source of inaccuracy relates to using the wrong data to generate information.
- *Conciseness.* This refers to the degree of detail in the information. In general, a concise report will be brief and to the point. The level of summarization or aggregation will also be high.
- *Completeness.* This refers to the scope of informational representation. Although reports should be concise, they must provide all the relevant information required to allow the user to reach a conclusion.
- *Relevance.* This refers to how well given information relates to a particular problem that demands decision-making.

2.10.4 Reporting to management

One of the functions of management is communication. No information system is complete unless the outputs produced are fully and effectively communicated to management. This means that information systems must be designed to develop outputs in response to managers' needs and not just for data processing convenience. Reports provide the interface between the information system and the users of the system. Reporting can therefore be seen as the formal communication link between the information system and managers.

In most business organizations there are various types of reports. Davis, Alderman and Robinson[6] identify these reports as *status reports*, *activity reports*, *management exception reports* and *analytical reports*. The various types of reports are related to the information needs of managers at different levels.

- *Status reports*. These reports define the condition of a particular organizational unit at a given point in time. Status reports are accurate only on the date for which they were prepared.
- *Activity reports*. Activity or transaction reports describe the activities that have taken place during a given period of time. Managers should not become involved in the routine activities of their operational units. They therefore require activity reports and listings that constitute an essential link between status reports. When combined with standards and budgets, these reports provide the necessary documentation of organizational activity.
- *Management exception reports*. These reports are analyses of operational results. They report on variances from planned standards and therefore suggest a need for particular managerial attention. Conditions and circumstances that caused these variances often require special investigation and remedial action.
- *Analytical reports*. These reports are designed to examine or highlight certain trends, directions, conditions and relationships in the operation of an organizational unit. Their purpose is to provide managers with a clearer understanding of departmental behaviour and so to enable better planning and control.

Each of these types of reports can be categorized according to its purpose. *Planning* reports usually take the form of budgets and are useful in helping managers to allocate and acquire resources for future operations. *Control* reports assist managers to ensure that operations take place according to plan. *Operational* reports focus on the current status of operations. Their most important purpose is to provide support for individuals in carrying out their day-to-day operational activities.

The adequate communication of data and information depends on good reporting. Reports present facts, provide the basis for decision-making, direct attention to efficiencies and inefficiencies, and provide management with a basis for planning and control.

2.10.5 Involvement of management and other users

A user-oriented approach to the design of an information system is important because it provides for user interaction through the system. Managers and users should be actively involved in determining the required information needs, in the design and development of the system, and in the ultimate operation of the system. This will prevent a situation where a system works 'satisfactorily', is well documented, was developed and implemented within budget and time limits, but fails to fulfil managers' and users' information needs because managers, users and systems developers held different views of what was to be done.[2]

Managers play informational roles by monitoring the organization's information flow, distributing information to other people within their organizational units, and serving as spokesmen to people outside their organizational units. To be able to do this and have the right information at hand at the right time, they must be involved when information needs are established.

User co-operation is required continually once the information system has been implemented. Such co-operation should be fostered during the design of the system and not afterwards. A philosophy of user-oriented design and operation encourages a set of attitudes and an approach to systems design that consciously considers the organizational context. Careful attention to the quantity and format of output during the design phase will prevent managers and other users having to rework data or request new reports once the system is in operation. Outputs should be designed to facilitate management decisions, and users must understand the nature and purpose of outputs to be able to use them.

Finally, the system must be able to make and accept changes once it has been put into operation. The fact that users normally require the system to respond to their changing needs must be borne in mind during the design phase.[2]

REVIEW QUESTIONS

1. Distinguish between information technology and information systems.
2. Distinguish between a comprehensive information system (IS) and a management information system (MIS).
3. Distinguish between data, information and knowledge.
4. Describe the basic elements of an information system and relate these to the principles for the design of such a system.
5. Discuss the different foundations to be taken into account when designing a comprehensive information system.
6. Explain the relationship between the different foundations for the provision of information from a strategic management point of view.
7. Discuss the role of information systems in business from an organizational and management point of view.
8. Discuss the different ways in which information can be communicated by management reporting.

SELECTED REFERENCES AND RECOMMENDED READING

1. Awad, E. M. 1988. *Management Information Systems — Concepts, Structure and Applications*. Menlo Park, California: The Benjamin Cummings Publishing Company, Inc.
2. Bodnar, G. H. and Hopwood, W. S. 1987. *Accounting Information Systems*. Third edition. Newton, Massachusetts: Allyn and Bacon, Inc.
3. Boot, G. 1990. *Inligtingstelsels vir Plaaslike Owerhede*. Brits: Aquarius Uitgewery.
4. Bower, J. B., Schlosser, R. E. and Newman, M. S. 1985. *Computer-Oriented Accounting Information Systems*. Cincinnati: South-Western Publishing Co.
5. Davis, G. B. 1974. *Management Information Systems: Conceptual Foundations, Structure, and Development*. Tokyo: McGraw-Hill Kogakusha, Ltd.
6. Davis, J. R., Alderman, C. W. and Robinson, L. A. 1990. *Accounting Information Systems — A Cycle Approach*. Third edition. New York: John Wiley and Sons.
7. Earl, M. J. 1989. *Management Strategies for Information Technology*. London: Prentice-Hall International (UK) Ltd.
8. Ernst, C. J. 1988. *Management Expert Systems*. Workingham, England: Addison-Wesley Publishing Company.
9. Greene, C. N., Adam, E. E. Jr. and Ebert, R. J. 1985. *Management for Effective Performance*. Englewood Cliffs: Prentice-Hall, Inc.
10. Rahman, M. and Halladay, M. 1988. *Accounting Information Systems — Principles, Applications, and Directions*. Englewood Cliffs: Prentice-Hall, Inc.

CHAPTER 3 System taxonomies

3.1 INTRODUCTION

A business information system will usually consist of a number of subsystems. These will work together in achieving a common goal, namely the provision of data and information for a business organization's operations and for decision- making functions at all management levels. This chapter describes the various subsystems that can make up an overall information system. Although these subsystems will vary from business to business, the data processing system, accounting system, some support systems, and control systems are usually part of the total information system.

Subsystems may take on many forms. We have already identified and discussed organizational and managerial subsystems, for example. *Although subsystems may be distinguished from each other, they should never be separated.* They should interact and, to a certain extent, overlap.

The nature and purposes of the different subsystems will vary from organization to organization. There are, however, a few systems that are worth mentioning here because they are normally part of the total information system of a business organization.

3.2 DATA PROCESSING SYSTEMS

Data processing is the capture, storage and processing of data so that they become information. It therefore involves recording, summarizing, analysing and reporting data and information concerning the activities of an organization. Data processing forms a major part of any information processing system. Any processing that takes place must be handled by the data processing functions of the system.[3]

Integrated data processing attempts to record each data item only once, to record it correctly, and to use it in the same form to provide information for the planning and control purposes of the organization. This concept of recording, storing, and retrieving data and information relates to the database principle of systems design and prevents the duplication of data as far as possible.

3.2.1 The nature and purpose of data processing

The reasons for capturing the facts associated with business transactions and processing them, can be grouped into three general categories:

- Some data must be collected and analysed to provide information for management planning and control activities.
- Some data must be collected as a basis for the custodial processing activity.
- Data must be collected and retained to provide historical facts relating to the other two types of activity.

3.2.2 Data processing operations

Regardless of how the data processing is accomplished, certain basic activities have to be performed. Each of these is designed to increase the usefulness of the data by adding time, place and form utility. *Time utility* refers to giving the data value by making them available when they are needed. *Place utility* refers to making the data available where they are needed. *Form utility* refers to providing data in the desired form.

Brabb[3] recognizes the following data processing activities that have to be performed by any data processing system:

Input
Recording. Data describing a transaction or a condition must be captured in some form for processing (time utility).

Processing
Classification and sorting. Recorded data must be classified into different types and then be arranged into particular sequences or groups in order to be useful in guiding management decisions (form utility).
Storage and retrieval. Data must be retained in some accessible form after their initial recording (time utility).
Summarization. The reduction of large amounts of data into a concise, usable form (form utility).

Output
Communication. After the various data processing operations have been completed, the results must be communicated in a meaningful form to appropriate individuals or groups. Results are worthless if they are not accepted by someone who can use them (place utility).

3.3 ACCOUNTING SYSTEMS

Accounting has long been regarded as the principal information discipline in business, providing the necessary information for a wide variety of decisions. The expanding use of computers in management and decision-making, however, requires one to look at accounting systems in the context of the overall information system.[5]

Accounting and information systems are closely related.[9] Accounting is essentially an information system. More precisely, it is an application of the general theory of information to the problem of efficient economic operations. It also produces a large part of a business's quantitative information, however. This means that it is part of the total information system.

This close relationship is acknowledged by the widespread use of the term *accounting information systems*. An accounting information system can be regarded as a formal information system because it embraces all of the characteristics of an information system. It covers all the organization's activities and provides financial and non-financial data to all the users of the system.

An accounting information system is actually one major component of the total information system. The difference lies in the scope of coverage. Whereas an accounting information system accumulates, classifies, processes, analyses, and communicates relevant financial information, the total information system performs these functions for all types of information affecting an organization's operations.

An appreciation of the role of an accounting information system and its accounting data requires an understanding of accounting techniques and accounting principles, and also of underlying accounting theory. This is because, when designing accounting information systems, all applicable accounting principles and practices must be considered.[5]

Accounting information systems (apart from financial accounting applications) should also include the necessary management accounting applications. These will include applicable cost accounting models, based on the underlying financial accounting data, as well as models supporting quantitative techniques such as network analysis and linear programming. When such applications are used to support decision-making at higher levels of management, they should be viewed as decision support systems.[2]

3.4 SUPPORT SYSTEMS

Some business organizations introduce support systems into the structures of their information systems in an attempt to increase the efficiency and effectiveness of their managerial planning and controlling activities.

Although the accounting function is one of the most important functions in a business organization, it is not a complete information system. Another very important part of the overall information system is the provision of management information. The purpose of this component of the system is to provide managers with decision-making and attention-directing information, both financial and non-financial. Again, it must be stressed that the various functions or functional subsystems overlap to a large extent because they supply data to — and receive information from — each other. In reality these overlapping systems comprise only one formal integrated and co-ordinated system.

For the purpose of providing management information, the information system can be seen as consisting of a number of major subsystems (depending on local circumstances). These might include transaction support systems, operational support systems, decision support systems, and expert systems.

3.4.1 Transaction support system

The transaction support system resides at the operational level of the information system. Its primary function is not to aid managerial decision-making as such, but to provide a framework through which routine data processing operations are performed.

3.4.2 Operational support system

The operational support system's purpose is to supply information for operational and management planning and control. It is mainly concerned with structured tasks and with problem situations in an organization. It focuses on short-term tactical planning and operational control decisions made by middle- and lower-level managers. Many of the decisions involving operational support (such as product scheduling and credit control) are made mainly or solely by the system itself. This results in increased operating efficiency and possible lower costs.

Some examples of problem-solving questions that the tactical planning process would attempt to answer are:

- What should the production schedule be for the current month?

- What specific steps should be implemented to improve production efficiency next month?
- How can the flow of cash resources be improved?
- How should the working capital needs of the next quarter be met?

Operational control decisions are therefore concerned with the establishment of processes that provide efficiency in operational or technical activities.

3.4.3 Decision support systems

Decision support systems (DSSs) are specialized systems that aid higher- and middle-level managers in making decisions that extend beyond routine operations. These systems are concerned with decisions involving long-term and relatively unstructured problem situations. The decisions concern strategic planning and always require active managerial participation.[5]

A decision support system requires the availability of extensive and sophisticated computer hardware and software. The managers involved must have terminals or microcomputers readily available so that they can quickly access relevant decision models and databases. A powerful means of conversing with the system must be provided, so that managers can easily specify desired information or changes to the models they are using. Recent developments in information technology and decision science have extended the capabilities of information systems to fulfil this requirement. These include interactive and high-powered computer-based systems as well as business-oriented planning models.[6]

A decision support system improves the effectiveness of management decision-making at the middle and higher levels of the organization. It achieves this by providing managers with more than just structured reports. While structured information is important, it is not sufficient. A useful decision support system provides managers with a set of information-processing tools which they can use to model the relevant data and experiment with them easily. In this way they can better understand the unstructured problem situations that require strategic and tactical decisions because they can discover and evaluate the various alternative courses of action. Some examples of questions that decision support systems would attempt to answer are:

- Should an existing product be discontinued or should a newly-developed product be marketed?
- Where should the new production facilities be located?
- What new manufacturing equipment should be acquired and when?
- What should be the budgeted net income and return on investment for each of the operating divisions?
- How should products be priced for maximum sales and profits?

The various levels at which management decisions are made, together with the system support they can depend on, have been shown in Figure 2.3.

3.4.4 Expert systems

Although decision support systems are developed to support managerial decision-making, they are sometimes found to be restrictive in the sense that most of the 'intelligence' has to be supplied by the user. Formal computer languages are however, frequently a barrier to non-technical users.[1]

There seems, therefore, to be a need for more intelligence in decision support systems and also for a 'natural' language with which one can access such intelligence.

Since the 1960s, researchers have been working to expand the normal capabilities and power of computers by developing hardware and software that can imitate intelligent human behaviour, ie. systems that have the ability to reason, to learn, to accumulate knowledge, to strive for self-improvement, and to simulate human sensory and mechanical capabilities. This area of research is known as *artificial intelligence* (AI).[6]

Artificial intelligence can be defined as *the science of making machines behave in a way that would generally be accepted as requiring human intelligence.*[7]

Research in the field of artificial intelligence can be divided into *natural languages* and *knowledge-based and expert systems*. A natural language, which makes it possible to manipulate a database without possessing a technical understanding of its functions, can be used to specify the input to a DSS and pose questions using plain English.

An expert system (also called a knowledge-based system) is an interactive system that responds to questions, asks for clarifications, makes recommendations, and generally aids in the decision-making process.

Expert systems (ESs) are used for solving difficult problems in a particular field called a *domain* (eg. income tax). Although knowledge-based systems rely on factual knowledge, they also utilize heuristic knowledge such as intuition, judgment and inference. These systems use this human-supplied knowledge to model the human thought process within a particular area of expertise and to simulate the logic of a well-informed human decision-maker.[6]

An expert system has two components: an *inference engine* and a *knowledge base.* An inference engine is the software configuration that manipulates knowledge provided by the knowledge base. The knowledge base captures and contains concepts, intuition, and rules that form an expert domain in a problem area.[8]

Applications of expert systems include medical diagnoses, credit card authorizations, credit control, troubleshooting when machines malfunction, auditing, accounting, and investment.

3.5 CONTROL SYSTEMS

A control and security system usually forms an integral part of an information system. Such a system contains all transaction cycles, together with a wide variety of controls and security measures. It also extends to the structure, physical facilities, operations, management practices, and other aspects of the business organization.[9]

The primary objective of control is to accomplish the directives of management and provide assurances that management's plans and objectives are being properly attained. Without adequate built-in controls most information systems cannot survive.

A control and security system, also known as an *internal control system*, has four broad purposes:[9]

- To safeguard the assets of the organization.
- To ensure the accuracy and reliability of data and information.
- To promote efficiency in all the operations.
- To encourage adherence to management's prescribed policies and procedures.

From a management point of view, these are very important. Managers must be able to rely on the information in the reports they receive since they are responsible for resources such as cash and inventory. Today's managers feel particularly vulnerable to inadequate internal control systems because of increased risk exposures which will be discussed later.

3.5.1 Feedback control systems

A different but equally instructive view of the information system is provided by cybernetics. Each organization or part of an organization is seen as an operating feedback and control system. Each system consists of three elements: the *planning and control system*, the *operating element* performing the activity, and an *evaluation element* monitoring the results of the operation and reporting back to the planning and control element.[3]

Planning and control receives input from outside the organization (economic conditions and market trends) as well as information from within the organization by way of the evaluation element. On the basis of this information, management planning and control sets goals, develops policies and operating guidelines, and issues directives to the operating element. The resulting activity is monitored by the evaluation element and matched against the goals, plans, and directives established by management planning and control. Deviations from desired results are reported back to management planning and control so that corrective action can be formulated and undertaken.

Every function of an organization has certain elements that must be controlled, and management must select the proper control device and set standards with which to control each function. Examples of feedback control systems include standard cost accounting and inventory control.

3.5.2 Feedforward control systems

Some feedback controls may lag behind the information system by varying periods of time.[4] To overcome the time lag in controlling critical functions, many organizations have developed feedforward systems in order to prevent delays in reporting. This is accomplished by predicting outcomes based on the inputs used in a particular situation and also by predicting outcomes if inputs continue to display certain trends. As predictions are made from the system, inputs can be changed to correct or improve remaining outputs. Examples of feedforward systems are *cash flow systems*, *budgeting systems*, and *inventory control systems* (for storage and reordering purposes).

3.5.3 Preventive controls

From a management point of view, preventive controls are also very important. These are more general in nature and are applied as and when needed. They act as guidelines to effect desired results and avert potential problems. Preventive controls should be incorporated into the system during its design phase and should apply to every systems function in the organization. They include the following:[4]

- System, program and operating documentation, which serve as a prime communication link between many systems within the organization.
- Separation of duties provides for a checking system by requiring each major function to be performed by more than one individual. This is a very important control tool, allowing management to prevent problem situations.
- The proper placement of well-trained personnel with integrity is very important, especially in computerized operations.
- Physical controls, including items such as fire protection, temperature, humidity, and static electricity control, security devices and personnel to control unauthorized access to hardware, software and data files, and screening devices to prohibit people from taking unauthorized items from the processing centre.

REVIEW QUESTIONS

1. Explain why data processing systems still perform an important function within total information systems.
2. Explain the relationship between the overall information system and the accounting information system.
3. Distinguish clearly between the following:
   (a) Data processing (DP) and accounting information systems (AIS);
   (b) Management information systems (MIS) and accounting information systems;
   (c) Management information systems, decision support systems (DSS) and expert systems (ES).
4. Discuss the functions of the different support systems within a business organization.
5. Explain the difference between feedback and feedforward control systems.

SELECTED REFERENCES AND RECOMMENDED READING

1. Awad, E. M. 1988. *Management Information Systems —Concepts, Structure and Applications.* Menlo Park, California: The Benjamin Cummings Publishing Company, Inc.
2. Boot, G. 1990. *Inligtingstelsels vir Plaaslike Owerhede.* Brits: Aquarius Uitgewery.
3. Brabb, G. J. 1980. *Computers and Information Systems in Business.* Second edition. Boston: Houghton Mifflin Company.
4. Davis, J. R., Alderman, C. W. and Robinson, L. A. 1986. *Accounting Information Systems —A Cycle Approach.* Third edition. New York: John Wiley and Sons.
5. Heymann, H. G. and Bloom, R. 1988. *Decision Support Systems in Finance and Accounting.* New York: Quorum Books.
6. Long, L. 1989. *Management Information Systems.* Englewood Cliffs: Prentice-Hall, Inc.
7. Prerau, D. S. 1990. *Developing and Managing Expert Systems: Proven Techniques for Business and Industry.* Reading: Addison-Wesley Publishing Company, Inc.

8. Rahman, M. and Halladay, M. 1988. *Accounting Information Systems — Principles, Applications, and Directions.* Englewood Cliffs: Prentice-Hall, Inc.
9. Wilkinson, J. W. 1986. *Accounting and Information Systems.* Second edition. New York: John Wiley and Sons.

CHAPTER 4 The significance of computers in business

4.1 INTRODUCTION

In this chapter a description of the impact of computers on information systems, management and controls is followed by an indication of the risks and exposures business organizations have to face when they become computerized. The chapter concludes by highlighting the advantages of computerizing business information systems.

Before computers became popular in business, many organizations were decentralized in terms of both information processing and decision-making. Under a decentralized structure, top management delegates decision-making authority and the responsibility for decisions to lower operating levels. Decentralized decision-making usually causes positive motivational responses from employees. People will normally have higher morale and greater loyalty to their subsystem's goals if they have participated in making organizational decisions.[2]

With the advent of electronic data-processing techniques, a new and powerful data-processing function emerged, usurping some of the functions and operations previously performed by accountants. A new breed of information system specialist began to assume the responsibility for information system analysis and design.

Computerized information systems have had a significant impact on the structure of the organization and its information system, and also on the control systems incorporated in the overall organizational structure.

4.2 THE IMPACT OF COMPUTERS ON MANAGEMENT AND INFORMATION SYSTEMS

The computerization of a business organization usually centralizes the information-processing functions within the electronic data-processing system. Centralization of information processing does not, however, necessarily centralize decision-making. For those organizations with computerized data-processing systems, the ideal organizational structure may be a mixture of centralization and decentralization. This would vastly increase the speed of the data-processing activities. Centralized information processing would allow employees more opportunities for creative activities by eliminating much time-consuming and non-creative data-processing work from their jobs. Information can be communicated by top management to subsystem managers, enabling decentralized decision-making to continue within an organization. As a result of top management continuing to delegate decision-making authority to subsystem managers, these managers should be positively motivated to achieve their organization's goals.

Computers affect management in three areas. First, they affect the ways in which managers perform their duties; in other words, they have operational effects. Second, there are effects on the organization of the management function, particularly with respect to the placement of the information system function. Finally, the computer has brought general management the special problems associated with the management of a highly creative and technically oriented work force — the information specialists — and the information system they create and operate.

The way management performs and the effects of computers on the content of managerial jobs are due primarily to the relatively new capabilities of computers as suppliers of management information. This has led to the development of new management tools.

Three specific capabilities of computers have had an impact on managerial practice. These are the *speed* and *accuracy* with which computers perform and the *complexity of analysis* that they make possible. The implications of these new capabilities are obvious. To compete effectively with their counterparts in other businesses and industries, today's managers must be able to utilize the results of the analyses referred to above. They must ensure that information systems take advantage of the new techniques made available by the computer. Although managers do not need to become mathematicians, statisticians, or operations researchers, they do need to become aware of the new tools that are available and they should know how to use them. They must assure themselves that they are receiving competent technical advice and assistance in applying and interpreting these new analytic techniques.

All managers perform the functions of planning, organizing, staffing and controlling. The computer is expected to take over more of the controlling function, primarily by applying the concept of control by exception. Responses to many exceptions can be predetermined and left to the computer. As a result, managers have more time to recognize opportunities and to plan to capitalize on them. More time can be devoted to personnel relations and communication, and improving morale and productivity.

Using computers to guide management decisions should do three things:

- Assist managers to make decisions where decision procedures are only partly structured, ie. where complete decision algorithms are unavailable.
- Support (rather than replace) managerial judgement in decision-making.
- Improve effectiveness and efficiency of decisions.

4.3 THE IMPACT OF COMPUTERS ON CONTROLS

Two things that distinguish manual and computerized data processing are the increased speed and the increased processing capabilities gained through integrated data processing. Each element of transactional data may be used for a variety of reports and purposes. As an organization moves toward integrated data processing, numerous manual procedures may be subsumed in, or eliminated by, machine operations. Although this elimination of human processing increases speed, one problem is that controls and checking mechanisms associated with manual procedures are eliminated along with the procedures themselves. It is important, therefore, to ensure that similar controls are an integral part of a computer processing system.

The controls needed for computer-based information systems are general controls and specific (application) controls. These will be discussed more fully in later chapters of this book.

The introduction of a computer into an organization's data processing system can create problems regarding the audit trail. In a manual data processing system, following the audit trail of an accounting transaction is normally not difficult. In a computerized system, however, the transaction trail becomes more difficult to follow because the processing is performed within the computer.

As a result of computerization, auditors have lately taken an approach whereby they audit 'through' the computer (using the computer in the auditing process) instead of 'around' it (using manual procedures to audit computer output). By doing this, auditors become more familiar with the organization's hardware and software, they help establish the preventive control system, and periodically review the control systems to make sure they are functioning properly.

The introduction of computer-based data processing systems usually requires additional controls in respect of the following:

- Segregation of duties
- Recording of transactions
- Execution of transactions
- Access to assets
- Comparison of recorded accountability with assets

4.4 RISKS AND EXPOSURES

The rapid growth of computerized operations in business has brought about certain new dangers and threats. Lay and Still[1] divide potential threats to a business organization into four categories, namely *natural disasters* (like fire, floods and earthquakes), *man-made disasters* (such as war and terrorism), *fraud* (such as theft and the unlawful manipulation of data), and *operator error*.

In today's computer environment, fraud may be committed without leaving a single shred of tangible evidence that can be traced to a specific person.

These problems arise in spite of the fact that computers manipulate and transcribe data with impeccable accuracy. Control and security problems that accompany computerization stem from the following factors:[3]

- The concentrated nature of processing.
- The machine-oriented nature of stored data.
- The fragmentation of the audit trail.
- The substitution of machine obedience for human judgement.
- The introduction of added complexity.
- The vulnerability of stored data.
- The vulnerability of computer equipment.

The problems that increase when computerization occurs are:

- Unauthorized access to confidential data.
- Unauthorized manipulation of data, files and/or programs in order to benefit one or more persons unlawfully.
- Intentional or unintentional destruction of data and files.
- Intentional or unintentional interruption of business operations.
- Unintentional entry of errors in data inputs or creation of errors through processing.

Achieving the objectives of control is particularly important when computer-based processing is introduced in an information system. The presence of computers heightens the exposure to errors and losses of various types. The impact of fraud and errors, moreover, tends to be much larger than before computerization.

4.5 ADVANTAGES OF COMPUTER PROCESSING

The advantages of computer processing can be related to the principles for the design of an information system. If these principles are built into the system in a responsible manner, the computerization of a business organization's information system will yield the following advantages:

- *Reasonable cost.* Because computers can process and store vast numbers of transactions and events more efficiently than humans, the cost per transaction could, under certain conditions, be less expensive than by any other means of processing and storage.
- *Effective reporting and management.* Computers, when working together with humans, can meet the needs of managers better than humans alone. Computers can help to provide reports in a more timely manner. Because of their computational power, computers can prepare reports that are as detailed or as selective as desired.
- *Human factors.* In the case of on-line and real-time systems, users are brought into direct contact with computer systems. They can enter data and receive output directly via a terminal. This makes the interface between the user and the computer much more meaningful because the user is, in many instances, no longer dependent on a third party for his or her information needs.
- *Organization structure.* Computer-based information systems can provide horizontal and vertical integration in the business organization. They change relationships between people and their functions, and they improve the organization's climate by facilitating better communication routes between organizational units.
- *Reliability and consistency.* Computer systems are usually more dependable because they automatically follow sets of detailed coded instructions (programs) in an exact and consistent manner. They can flawlessly execute complex programs involving computations, comparisons and choices.
- *Accounting and auditability.* The computer's ability to handle an organization's routine accounting functions has been a major reason for the growth of managerial accounting. The computer has taken over routine work and accountants can now concentrate on the design of the system, the management of their own departments, and the recommendation of future managerial actions in a wide variety of operational areas. The computer can also assist the auditing function by facilitating computer-assisted auditing techniques.
- *Databases.* By utilizing databases and database management systems, computers can store and retrieve data much more efficiently than any other means. They also help management cope with the increasing problem of handling paper. Paper needs are

eliminated through the storage of data in elaborately constructed databases and files where they can be retrieved when needed.

- *Data processing*. Computers are the most efficient and effective means of processing data. A computer can process transactions all day without making a single error and it can process complex transactions or problems at a very high speed without interruption.

Computers are also able to integrate transaction-processing cycles and files. Together with communication networks they can tie together data and files at physically distant locations.

The positive effects of computerization tend to offset any negative factors that may exist. Future results can be positive if accountants rise to the challenge and opportunity of information technology and take the lead in information management. To become leaders in information management, accountants must become knowledgeable in the analysis and design of computer-based information systems.

4.6 CONCLUSION

Although the first module of this book has emphasized the overall information system from a management point of view, the remaining modules will concentrate more on the accounting attributes of such a system. The principles are, however, the same and the reader must bear in mind that the accounting information system is part of the total information system of a business enterprise.

REVIEW QUESTIONS

1. Discuss the impact of modern information technology (IT) on management and its information systems.
2. Explain the impact computerized data processing has on the control of information systems.
3. Describe the risks and exposures that computerized operations have brought about.
4. Discuss the advantages of business data processing in the context of the principles for the design of good information systems.

SELECTED REFERENCES AND RECOMMENDED READING

1. Lay, P. M. Q. and Still, R. G. 1987. *Control and Audit of Accounting Information Systems.* Cape Town: Juta and Co. Ltd.
2. Moscove, S. A. and Simkin, M. G. 1987. *Accounting Information Systems -Concepts and Practice for Effective Decision-Making.* Third edition. New York: John Wiley and Sons.
3. Wilkinson, J. W. 1986. *Accounting and Information Systems.* Second edition. New York: John Wiley and Sons.

MODULE 1 KEY POINT SUMMARY

- Proper management is a prerequisite for the success of any business enterprise. To be able to plan, organize and control organizational activities, managers have to make important decisions.
- Managerial decision-making requires timely, accurate and meaningful information that relates to the various management levels and activities, and to the organization's structures.
- The only way to provide management with the information it requires, is to develop and maintain an effective and efficient information system based on a sound foundation, which would include sound organizational structure, management functions, quality of information, systems design principles, financial and management accounting principles, as well as sound auditing and security principles.
- The type and format of information needed is directly related to each manager's level of activity. The higher the level, the more the information will be analysed and summarized.
- Information systems are not single entities, but consist of subsystems such as functional subsystems (eg. production and marketing), managerial subsystems (eg. tactical planning and management control) and information processing subsystems (eg. data processing and decision support systems).
- In any business organization, various types of controls are needed. Although information systems should provide the required controls at all levels, they should also contain their own internal controls to minimize risks and exposures which result from the use of electronic computer systems.

MODULE 2 Computer concepts

OBJECTIVES

In order to appreciate the role of computers in business, every student must have a basic understanding of how a computer functions.

On completion of this module you should be able to:

- Identify important events in the history of computing.
- Describe the principal components of computer hardware and software.
- Outline the major differences between micro, mini and mainframe computers.
- Differentiate between the various categories of programming languages.
- Outline the major functions of system and applications software.
- Differentiate between the various file organization methods.
- Explain the database concept highlighting the advantages and disadvantages it has over traditional file processing methods.
- Discuss the alternative methods of computer processing.
- Discuss the evolution of the user interface from command-based systems to the graphical user interface.

CHAPTER 5 The history of computing

5.1 INTRODUCTION

Why is it important to study the history of computing when things are changing so fast that many machines and concepts that were in vogue ten years ago are already obsolete? The answer is that rapid technological change is really the best reason for teaching the topic. Students introduced to computers for the first time are not normally aware that things were different last year and will change again in the near future.

It is important that each individual:

- understands that the computer industry is young and dynamic;
- can apply an appreciation of what has happened in the past in order to anticipate the future.

5.2 THE EARLY YEARS

The origins of computing date back to the development of systems for counting and measuring. The term 'digit' derives from the use of fingers for counting, as does the decimal system where numbers are manipulated in groups of ten. Several forms of notation were developed in order to record the manipulation of numbers. These include the Egyptian, Roman, and Arabic notations, the latter becoming a standard in the Western world by the fifteenth century.

Initially mathematical problems were solved manually. The earliest form of mechanization was the *abacus* which underwent several changes during its history. The abacus used in schools today is usually the Roman variety, with beads threaded on wires in groups of ten.

With the growth of science, particularly in the field of astronomy, large numbers of complex calculations were necessary. Performing these calculations was a process that was both slow and susceptible to error. John Napier, a Scot, was fascinated by mathematics and in 1614 he developed a table of logarithms which enabled multiplication and division to be performed by simple addition or subtraction. The system was immediately accepted.

An English clergyman by the name of William Oughtred developed the slide rule based on Napier's logarithms, and both systems remained in use until the introduction of the electronic calculator. Napier also invented *Napier's bones*, consisting of a series of rods, as a device for multiplication.

In 1642 a Frenchman, Blaise Pascal, developed a device that could add and subtract using a series of pin-wheels and cylinders. Gottfried von Leibnitz, a German, followed with a similar machine that could also multiply and divide.

By the beginning of the seventeenth century an event unrelated to the automation of calculation but of great impact on the design of future computers occurred — the invention of the automatic weaving loom. Using a series of needles that passed through holes in punched cards, Joseph Jacquard was able to control the weaving pattern on the loom below. The cards could be used repeatedly, providing a consistent product and reducing the manual labour required to operate the loom. In computer terms these cards represented a *program* that controlled the machine.

5.3 THE BIRTH OF THE COMPUTER

It was left to an inventive but eccentric English mathematician by the name of Charles Babbage to pull the ideas from previous developments together to produce the notion of a programmable calculator. His final invention, the *analytical engine*, was too complex to be built using the tools and materials of the day but is recognized as the first device that could be termed a computer. It included a *storage or memory area* to hold instructions or data, and a *mill* or *processor* capable of performing arithmetical and logical functions. The most important innovation was that the machine could be programmed to perform different calculations by instructions on punched cards. Cards were also used to input data.

Countess Ada of Lovelace, daughter of Lord Byron, was a brilliant mathematician and was fascinated by Babbage's work. She is best remembered for her descriptive notes on the 'analytical engine'.

5.4 ELECTROMECHANICAL COMPUTING DEVICES

In the United States a population census was held every ten years. This task was becoming increasingly difficult because of the rapid population growth and the need for more detailed statistics. The 1880 census handled the details of 50 million people and took 7½ years to process. The United States government, aware that a number of engineers and inventors were working on devices to mechanize the handling of data, invited the submission of data processing systems to analyse the 1890 census.

In Herman Hollerith's solution, the data were represented by holes in punched cards. Using the same principle as the Jacquard loom, needles detected the holes in the cards and an electric current opened the lid of a box or shifted a dial by one digit. The machine was therefore able to sort, classify and count the cards. To set up the device for a particular task the operator had to change a series of wires on a plug board.

The Hollerith tabulator was far superior to the other devices that had been proposed and it was adopted by the census bureau. The tabulator enjoyed considerable success over the next half-century, firstly as a census machine and, later, in the larger manufacturing and retailing companies, to process applications such as payrolls, debtors, and stock.

Hollerith's invention was important in two respects:

- It was electromechanical and therefore far superior to the slow, heavy mechanical devices that came before it.
- The device concentrated not on complex calculation (so important in scientific fields) but rather on the efficient processing of large volumes of data (the major requirement in business applications).

In 1924, Hollerith's tabulating machine company was renamed International Business Machines (IBM). It grew to become the largest computer manufacturer in the world.

Although the computer age was still 50 years away, most of the basic concepts were understood and the first half of the twentieth century saw a flurry of activity — much of it motivated by the two world wars.

James Powers (founder of UNIVAC) improved on the tabulator to make it automatically print results.

William Burroughs (founder of Burroughs computers, now amalgamated with UNIVAC to form UNIDATA) invented a calculator that also produced printed output. Burroughs was a perfectionist and when the first machines that were manufactured did not come up to expectation he personally hurled all fifty of them out of his office window onto the pavement two stories below.

The first serious attempt to build a computer for scientists was made by an American engineer, Vannevar Bush. Between 1930 and 1940 he built a series of electromechanical programmable analog calculators termed *differential analysers*. The most powerful of these contraptions weighed 100 tons, and contained 2000 vacuum tubes, several thousand relays, 150 motors and about 200 miles of wire.

At the same time, research on digital devices at Bell telephone laboratories confirmed that binary counting systems had advantages for the design of automatic switching circuitry. Problems in representing the ten numeric symbols in the decimal system using electrical current led to the idea of a system with only two symbols representing on or off — the *binary* system. Nearly 100 years earlier, George Boole had proposed a system of algebra and logic based on the binary approach.

George Stibitz developed a binary calculator known as the *complex number computer* using electromechanical relays (known as *flip-flops*) to detect the presence or absence of a current, and making use of Boolean algebra.

During the Second World War, a number of countries invested heavily in computer research. In 1941 a German by the name of Konrad Zuse built the Z3, the last and most powerful of a series of electromechanical digital computers.

The idea of an electromechanical digital computer also occurred to a Harvard student by the name of Howard Aiken. His machine was essentially a marriage of the ideas of Babbage and Hollerith — an electromechanical analytical engine using IBM punch card technology. Aiken obtained assistance from IBM and his *automatic sequence controlled calculator* (ASCC), often referred to as the Mark 1, was completed in 1944. The finished product was 51 feet long and 8 feet high. It took 0.3 seconds to add, 6 seconds to multiply, and 12 to divide. Input was by punched card, output was to a typewriter, and the program was read in from paper tape.

Weighing 5 tons and containing more than 800 000 parts, the Mark 1 could not have been described as elegant. Someone once remarked that it sounded like a roomful of ladies knitting. Despite its physical appearance, the Mark 1 was the most famous machine of its time and was described in the press as the 'Harvard robot' and the 'super brain'. By the time the machine had been completed, however, it was obsolete since plans to build the first fully electronic machine were well advanced.

5.5 ELECTRONIC COMPUTING DEVICES

One of the major problems in ballistics is that every gun requires a set of firing tables. To construct a table requires the calculation of many thousands of trajectories, each needing approximately 750 multiplications. In 1941 John Mauchly, a physicist with an interest in calculating machines, and Presper Eckert, a science graduate researching vacuum tube (valve) technology, joined forces at the University of Pennsylvania to develop an electronic calculator to generate ballistics tables. Although notoriously unreliable, the switching speeds of vacuum tubes were far superior to electromechanical relays and the resulting device, code-named ENIAC, was about 500 times faster than the Mark 1. However, by today's standards it was still a dinosaur weighing 30 tons and requiring 160 kilowatts of power. It was jokingly said that the lights of Philadelphia dipped when ENIAC was switched on. While the ENIAC was being constructed, the team of Eckert, Mauchly, and a brilliant mathematician by the name of John von Neumann, proposed a new machine, the EDVAC, that embodied — among other things — the concept of the stored program. This machine was finally built in 1952.

Historians are divided on who should be given credit for building the first electronic computer. John Atanasoff built the first prototype in November 1936, but the event was not seen as highly significant because the device was only a model. Eckert and Mauchly's claims were invalided by an American court, partly because of their knowledge of Atanasoff's prior work. Eckert's reaction to Atanasoff's claim was 'he lies like a rug'.

5.6 BIRTH OF THE MODERN-DAY COMPUTER

The adoption of the stored program concept heralded the birth of the modern-day computer. The principle of holding the program electronically in the computer was important because plug boards and programs on tape limited the flexibility of computing machines. Von Neumann is recognized as the originator of the stored program concept.

The British had been working with the Americans on computer projects for a number of years, in particular with a brilliant mathematician named Alan Turing. During the Second World War a number of electronic machines were constructed to decipher German army codes. The project was code named 'Colossus' and was kept highly secret for many years after the war. In 1948, a team at Cambridge University led by M. V. Wilkes built the first electronic digital computer with a stored program.

In the early 1950s computers were large, slow, expensive, and very unreliable devices with little commercial value. Over the next 40 years very few changes were made to the architecture of the machines, but improvements to the physical hardware and software resulted in unbelievable advances in their performance.

5.7 MEMORY ADVANCES

The advances that fuelled the computer revolution most of all were those in the area of *memory technology*. With the acceptance of the stored program concept came the recognition that large quantities of instructions and data would have to be held electronically in the main storage area of the central processor. Valve technology had been improved by computer pioneers, in particular Presper Eckert, but high quality valves were still expensive and relatively unreliable. To store 2000 characters in memory, over 15 000 valves were required, and the failure of even one during processing would cause an entire operation to abort.

The first memory technology to replace the valve was the *delay line*. The device worked on the basis that a shock wave was set up in one end of a bath of mercury. The wave was detected at the other end of the bath and converted into an electric current which was used to repeat the shock wave. The shock wave took some time to travel the length of the tank and this delay permitted a stream of pulses, representing characters of data, to be stored. The size of delay lines varied but was normally in the region of 120 characters. This same principle was used with cathode ray tubes (William's electrostatic tubes) and nickel wire. The delay lines were much more reliable and less bulky than valves, but they had one major disadvantage: access to data was slow because each character was continuously circulating in the delay line and could only be read on passing the enquiry station.

Another popular storage innovation was the *magnetic drum*. The drum allowed machines to have larger and cheaper memories, but it was still serial and therefore relatively slow.

The breakthrough came in 1954 with the arrival of *core storage*. This technology consisted of thousands of tiny iron rings threaded on thin wires. Each ring represented a piece of data which depended on whether it was magnetized in a clockwise or anticlockwise direction. Core storage made large, high-speed, reliable computer memories a reality and was still being used in the early 1970s.

The best, however, was still to come. In 1948 three physicists at the Bell research laboratories built the first *transistor* for which they were awarded the Nobel Prize. The transistor is a switching device made of semiconductive material (normally silicon) that permits current to flow in one direction but not in the other. The transistor was a direct replacement for the valve: it was faster, more reliable, and much cheaper. By the early 1960s, most computers used this new technology. As a result machines were much smaller, used less electricity, and generated less heat. The transistor was still quite expensive to produce, though, and had to be manually wired to the circuit-boards.

At this time the Americans were spending huge sums of money on putting a man on the moon, and one of their main priorities was to miniaturize the electronics involved. This research led to the development of *planar technology* where a number of transistors were placed on a single slice of silicon material. This device was called an *integrated circuit* or 'IC' but is more commonly known as the *computer chip*. The race was on to pack more and more transistors onto a single chip. This gave rise to *Moore's law* which states that the number of components that can be held on a chip will double every year. By 1989 a chip with over four million components had been built and the trend towards more components shows little sign of abating.

The final step in the saga of the silicon chip began in the early 1970s with the realization that the logical circuitry of the machine could also be etched into the silicon — a computer on a chip. Early research in this area was not directed at the computer industry but was concerned with building a *microprocessor* for universal device control. Almost all commercial, household and personal appliances such as typewriters, washing machines, motor vehicles, tape recorders and even watches contained mechanical or electromechanical controls that were both expensive to manufacture and difficult to maintain. Microprocessors costing a few dollars could be programmed to control these devices to a level of sophistication previously unknown. With the addition of a power supply, keyboard, screen, and a few other bits and pieces, the microprocessor became a microcomputer. The year 1977 saw the arrival of the Apple, Tandy, and Commodore, and in 1981 came the more powerful IBM PC range which grew in magnitude again with the announcement of the PS2 in 1987.

To fully appreciate the impact that large scale integration has had on the computer industry, one has only to examine the changes in machine price/performance over the period. The transistorized IBM 360 Model 30, released in 1965, was 45 times faster than the IBM Model 650, built in 1953 and containing drum memory. The 370 Model 135, dating from 1971 and using integrated circuits, was five times faster again, and the IBM 4341 with large scale integration, released in 1979, was a further five times faster. The price of processing a single instruction was reduced a thousandfold over the same period. It is often said that if car manufacturers had made similar advances over the same period, a Rolls Royce would cost R25 today and consume one litre of petrol for every 5000 km travelled.

5.8 PERIPHERAL DEVICES

While the central processing unit was growing in speed and capacity, the *peripheral devices* needed to input, output, and store the relevant data were also advancing.

5.8.1 Input devices

Most data were initially captured onto punched cards or paper tape, prior to input into the computer. Paper is bulky and not reusable. Later devices, however, used magnetic tape and discs.

The growing demand for immediate access to totally up-to-date information led to the use of on-line terminals. In this system data were communicated directly into the central processing unit from the terminal which could be located at the point where business is conducted. The computer was thus able to assist in validating the data. Unfortunately this process was still labour intensive and error prone.

The next step was to design input devices that could see and read in the same way that we do. Now *optical character readers* can read handwritten documents, words can be digitized and looked-up in a dictionary, and pictures can be matched to a library of stored images.

5.8.2 Storage devices

Punched cards and paper tape were the secondary storage media of the early machines but were not suitable for large volumes of data. Magnetic tape drives, very similar in concept to the tape recorder, were introduced in the early 1950s and they soon became the most important storage device.

One major problem with tapes is that data are stored *serially* and therefore a particular item of data can only be accessed by reading through the file from the beginning. This problem encouraged research into direct access devices and led to the development of the *magnetic disk*. The disk resembled a number of gramophone records stacked on top of one another and read/write heads moved in between the platters to access every surface.

The first disk storage system was the RAMAC developed by IBM in 1956, with five million characters of storage spread over 50 disks and a data-access time of less than a second. IBM's current offering, the model 3380, is physically smaller than the RAMAC yet can hold 1500 times more data and access it 50 times faster. Indeed, one 3380 can hold more data than all the RAMACs produced in their five years of manufacture.

The next major milestone in disk technology came in 1971 with the introduction of the flexible or floppy disk to provide cheap random access in small computer systems. 1974 saw the adoption of *Winchester disk technology* where smaller, lighter read-write heads rode closer to the disk surface in a sealed environment. This development led to the proliferation of hard disks in mini- and microcomputers as the sealed unit is not affected by dust and dirt in the air.

Other developments included huge mass-storage devices that could hold terabytes (billions of characters) of information, ROM chips for read-only access, and magnetic bubble memory for non-volatile solid state storage. The technology which is most likely to make an impression over the next five years is *optical storage* using the same technology as the compact disk. Optical devices are currently being developed to write as well as read in much the same way as current magnetic disk technology.

5.8.3 Output devices

Printers were the major output device of the 1950s and 1960s. The most famous computer printer ever developed was almost certainly the IBM 1403, announced in 1960. The device used a circular chain of characters rotating at high speed in front of the paper and, when the required character passed by, a hammer would be activated to push it forward. The 1403 generated high quality printout at speeds of up to 2000 lines a minute and many of these machines are still in use.

Today the computer screen is an essential output device because much work involves making enquiries into the current status of the computer's data. Cathode ray tubes were used in the early 1950s as operator consoles but their major role began with the advent of on-line real-time systems.

Modern output devices include microfilming equipment, laser printers, colour printers and plotters, high resolution screens, flat screens, and a large number of special devices such as speech synthesizers and robot arms.

5.9 MODES OF OPERATION

Early computer systems operated in *batch mode.* This meant that business transactions were recorded on paper documents, copies of which were sent to the computer department for punching onto card or magnetic tape. The process was both labour intensive and susceptible to error. Once the data had been verified for errors, they were read into the computer and processed. Normally reports containing details such as the status of customer accounts and levels of stock were only produced at the end of each month.

Many applications, such as payrolls, were highly suited to this cyclical approach, but others required the constant review of up-to-date information. The first major system to encompass the on-line real-time approach was SABRE, developed for American Airlines in 1962. No fewer than 1200 terminals were located at travel agencies throughout the United States and linked to a central computer through the existing telephone network. Prior to SABRE, flights were booked by phone. Manual flight records kept at the central location were often incorrect or out of date and a number of seats were normally left vacant in case of problems. Now everything relating to the proposed flight could be interrogated and the flight could be booked in a matter of minutes.

Real-time applications using data communications networks have largely taken over from the traditional batch approach. Data communications networks not only permit remote access to information: they also enable the data to be captured from source. The transaction, moreover, can be conducted on a terminal linked to the computer, such as a cash register or an automatic teller machine, so that computer input can be generated as a by-product of the business transaction. To assist with the capture of data, a number of sophisticated input devices have been developed, such as document-readers and bar-code readers. Devices to accept voice and visual input are currently available but neither have made a major impact.

5.10 OPERATING SYSTEMS

Early commercial computers consisted of hardware and applications software. This meant that each program written to perform a business function, such as printing payroll cheques, also had to manage all the necessary housekeeping functions such as where to position data in memory, operator communication, storage locations on disk and tape, and error procedures in case a peripheral malfunctioned. This overhead was expensive but was common to most programs.

It led to the development of *systems software programs* dedicated to running the machine. As computers have advanced, so this software has become more sophisticated. The control programs for the IBM 650 comprised 5000 instructions. Ten years later the IBM 360 was launched with an operating system of several million instructions that took 5000 man-years to develop.

With the increase in processing speed, commercial computers were bogged down by the slow speed of their input devices. It was common for the central processing unit (CPU) to be waiting more often than working. One of the major attributes of the IBM 360 software was that it enabled the machine to process a number of programs at the same time, switching from one to the next according to the availability of input/output data. This concept was termed *multi-programming.*

Another factor limiting computer performance was that, although each program being executed had to reside in memory, only a small part of the program was being processed at any one time. This led to a development known as *virtual storage* where only the active parts of a program were held in the CPU and the balance was stored on disk.

5.11 THE PROGRAMMING PROCESS

Computers were designed to perform a limited number of primitive operations such as moving data around the CPU and performing basic arithmetic. A computer program is simply a set of instructions, each one containing the operation code together with addresses of the data to be processed. These instructions are known as *machine language* and are very 'unfriendly' and tedious to code as they describe each simple step that the machine must perform.

This problem led to the development of *assembly languages* where the operation codes were represented by more meaningful mnemonics and the data were given symbolic addresses. The assembly code would have to be translated into machine code using a program specially designed for that purpose. While 'assembler' was almost as difficult to code as machine language, it demonstrated the value of translation programs.

The late 1950s saw the arrival of what were called the *high level languages*. This term was derived from the fact that the programmer could use an instruction to describe a process such as 'print' or 'read' and the translator would convert this into the many machine language instructions required. High level languages also allow the programmer to express the problem in familiar terms. FORTRAN was designed to address scientific problems and is very similar to algebra in its notation. COBOL was written in a kind of abbreviated English and was more suitable for commercial problems. The value of both languages was that they were developed by groups that were independent of any particular manufacturer. They were standardized and could be transferred from one machine to another with minimal changes. By 1960, COBOL had become the main commercial programming language.

The 1980s saw the widespread use of *fourth generation languages*, often termed *non-procedural languages*. In an attempt to improve programmer productivity, more work was switched to the computer. All the programmer was required to do was to describe what was needed. How the process would be performed could be worked out by a sophisticated translation program.

The programming process has changed little over the past 30 years whereas hardware technology has taken huge strides forward. In 1955 the computer department budget was split approximately 80 : 20 between hardware and software expenditure. By 1985 this ratio had been reversed and it was obvious that programming productivity was becoming a bottleneck in commercial computer installations. Some organizations have found the latest languages to be many times more productive than the now outdated COBOL, but claims vary widely.

5.12 SYSTEMS DEVELOPMENT

The systems development process was initially very haphazard and personal styles were prevalent, resulting in poor quality applications and maintenance nightmares.

The first steps to improve the process were made in the programming phase. Simple concepts of program structure were proposed by Dykstra, a Dutch mathematician, in the 1950s.

Attention then shifted to program design as large systems were difficult to build and maintain. In 1964 Larry Constantine proposed a modular approach to systems design, where large problems were broken down into simple manageable pieces.

Today the emphasis in systems development has switched to the *front-end analysis* process. Research has shown that successful systems require the accurate definition of the user's needs. Techniques such as *data flow diagrams* have been developed for this purpose. With a more disciplined and formal approach to systems development, the process of software manufacture is slowly changing from an art to a science.

Unfortunately, while structured techniques helped to enhance the quality of computer systems they did little to improve productivity. With the rapid acceptance of computers in the 1970s, most organizations have been unable to meet the demand for new applications. This backlog, together with the arrival of cost-effective microcomputers, has resulted in a large number of end-users writing their own systems. Some projections estimate that by the turn of the century, 75% of in-house software will be developed by end-users.

More recently, *information systems* (IS) departments have looked to the computer to assist in developing systems by automating life-cycles. *Computer assisted software engineering* (CASE) environments permit analysts, designers and programmers to generate diagrams, documentation and even program code, and so improve their efficiency and effectiveness.

5.13 COMPUTER APPLICATIONS

Probably the clearest evidence of the computer revolution is displayed in the change in commercial applications over the last 30 years.

Initially, computers handled major record-keeping functions with their high volumes of transactions. For years managers had recognized that their data files contained valuable business information, but manual extraction was too slow and labour-intensive to make this worthwhile. Using the raw power of the computer, *management information systems* (MIS) prospered.

The most important change in computer-usage came with the development of on-line networks. The machine has become an essential part of the way we do business: banking ATMs process most client withdrawals and deposits; point of sale devices in supermarkets ring up prices, and stockbrokers sell shares on advice from their computer.

Computer systems have changed from centralized batch environments to decentralized on-line systems but, in the main, their boundaries are those of the business entity.

Over the past few years the concept of *electronic data interchange* has become important in a number of vertical markets, where an industry undertakes to communicate business transactions electronically through a service provider rather than through traditional paper documentation. While this concept is still in its infancy it offers enormous improvements in cost and efficiency to those organizations that can make it work.

5.14 CONCLUSION

Today the computer, with its ever-increasing cost/performance advantages over human processors, is being used almost everywhere: architects and engineers design, secretaries generate correspondence, typesetters set pages, supervisors schedule workloads, doctors minister to patients, teachers educate, farmers cultivate, lawyers express opinions — all with the help of computers.

But this may only be the beginning: the pace of change in computer technology and communications continues to accelerate.

On the hardware side, the machine architecture designed by Babbage is finally collapsing. With the four megabit chip a reality, engineers are looking at parallel processing technology to take us into the twenty-first century.

On the software side, traditional machine languages are giving way to artificially intelligent programs. These use a base of knowledge and an inference program to deduce answers in much the same way as humans do. Unfortunately we understand very little about how the human brain functions and can only simulate the process. Many scientists believe that, when we can emulate human thinking, the superior speeds of computer hardware will enable us to build super-brains.

Christopher Evans in his book *The Mighty Micro* submits that current computers have the intellectual level of tapeworms, but there is nothing preventing them from becoming as intelligent or even more intelligent than their creators. The only thing that is certain is that the computer revolution has only just begun.

5.14.1 Computer generations

The development of computers since the early 1950s is often classified into five stages or generations. The first four were designated by a major change in memory technology, while the Japanese coined the fifth generation to herald their ambitious project to develop a new computing architecture of parallel processors with artificial intelligence-based software.

Below is a table illustrating the major characteristics of machines in each computer generation. Concepts not covered in this chapter will be discussed later in this module.

FIGURE 5.1. The five computer generations.

Generation	Characteristics	Technology
First generation 1950–1958	CPU circuitry	Valves
	Main storage	Drum/delay lines
	Secondary storage	Tape
	Input	Card/paper tape
	Output	Printers
	Software	Machine oriented
	Applications	Batch accounting
	Languages	Machine

Generation	Characteristics	Technology
First generation 1950–1958	CPU circuitry	Valves
	Main storage	Drum/delay lines
	Secondary storage	Tape
	Input	Card/paper tape
	Output	Printers
	Software	Machine oriented
	Applications	Batch accounting
	Languages	Machine
Second generation 1958–1964	CPU circuitry	Transistors
	Main storage	Magnetic core
	Secondary storage	Tape/disk
	Input	Card/magnetic tape
	Output	Printers
	Software	Software packages
	Applications	Batch accounting
	Languages	Machine/assembler
Third generation 1964–1975	CPU circuitry	Integrated circuits (IC)
	Main storage	Core ICs
	Secondary storage	Disk/ROM/tape
	Input	Key to disk/on-line terminal
	Output	Printers/terminals/ graphics
	Software	Operating systems
	Applications	On-line/integrated
	Languages	Cobol/Fortran/Assembler
Fourth generation 1975–today	CPU circuitry	Large scale integration (LSI)
	Main storage	Very LSI (VLSI)
	Secondary storage	Disk/ROM/tape/optical
	Input	Terminal/special purpose
	Output	Printers/terminals/ graphics
	Software	DBMS/TP monitors
	Applications	On-line/integrated/PCs
	Languages	COBOL/4GLs
Fifth generation Next	CPU circuitry	Ultra LSI (ULSI)
	Main storage	Ultra LSI (ULSI)
	Secondary storage	Disk/optical/ULSI
	Input	Application terminals
	Output	Application terminals
	Software	Knowledge-based
	Applications	National
	Languages	4GLs/LISP/PROLOG
Sixth generation Possibilities	CPU circuitry	Organic
	Main storage	Organic
	Secondary storage	ULSI
	Input	Voice/vision
	Output	Voice/robotics
	Software	Computer-generated
	Applications	International
	Languages	Natural

REVIEW QUESTIONS

1. Who is acknowledged as having 'invented':
   a) the computer;
   b) the electronic computer;
   c) the stored program concept?
2. Who developed the first device to handle large volumes of data?
3. What contributions did the following people make to the development of the modern day computer?
   a) Blaise Pascal
   b) Joseph Jacquard
   c) George Boole
   d) George Stibitz
   e) Howard Aiken
   f) Eckert and Mauchly
4. How do we differentiate between the different generations of computers?
5. Give a brief description of the following terms:
   a) plug board;
   b) delay line;
   c) core storage.
6. What, in your opinion, are the three major technical advances that have fuelled the computer revolution?
7. What do we mean by structured analysis, design and programming?
8. What are the major differences between the various generations of programming languages?
9. What do we mean by the term *artificial intelligence*?
10. What did Apple, Tandy and Commodore do in the late 1970s?

SELECTED REFERENCES AND RECOMMENDED READING

Augarten, S. 1984. *Bit by Bit—An Illustrated History of Computers.* New York: Ticknor and Fields.
Blohm, H., Beer, S. and Suzuki, D. 1986. *Pebbles to Computers.* Toronto: Oxford University Press.
Capron, H. L. 1990. *Computers — Tools for an Information Age.* Second edition. Redwood City, California: Benjamin/Cummings.
Evans, C. 1982. *The Mighty Micro.* London: Victor Gollancz.

CHAPTER 6 Hardware

6.1 THE COMPUTER: AN ELECTRONIC PROCESSOR

The basic concept of how a computer functions is very easy to understand. A computer works in the same way as a mechanical processor, a manual processor, or any other processor. It is probably easiest to draw a comparison between a computer processor and the manual processor that it has largely replaced — the accounts clerk.

FIGURE 6.1. Components of a manual information processing system.

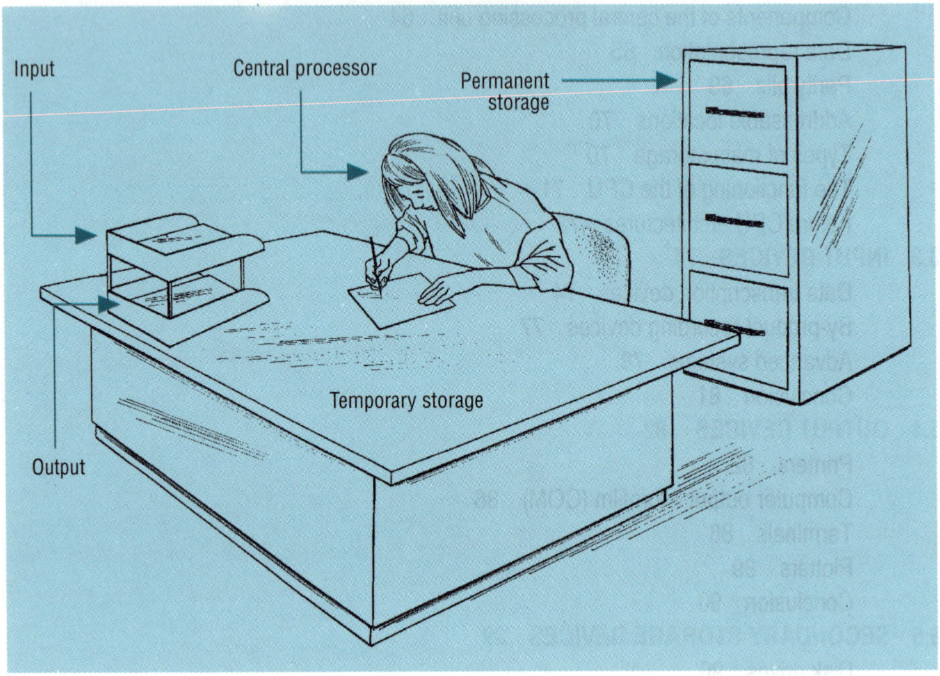

A clerk in a manual accounting environment receives data concerning the day-to-day running of the business. This is represented by the 'in' tray in Figure 6.1. The clerk represents the central processor and has the abilities required to transform the input data into information stored away in his or her memory. Once this process is complete, the information is dispatched out of the system through the output function represented by the 'out' tray in Figure 6.1. The clerk will require certain permanent data about such things as customers, stock items or employees, and these would be kept in separate files in the A4 filing cabinet shown in the picture.

Finally, every clerk has a work area which is represented in the diagram by a desk top. This area allows the clerk to keep any data concerning the job being worked on close at hand while the job is done.

A computer works in exactly the same way (see Figure 6.2). The data are fed into the computer through the *input function*, which could be a computer terminal in an airline office, an automatic teller in the high street, or a cash till in a supermarket. The intelligence in a computer system is represented by a box or boxes known as the *central processing unit* (CPU). Once a computer has processed the data, it shows the results

FIGURE 6.2. Components of a computerized information processing system.

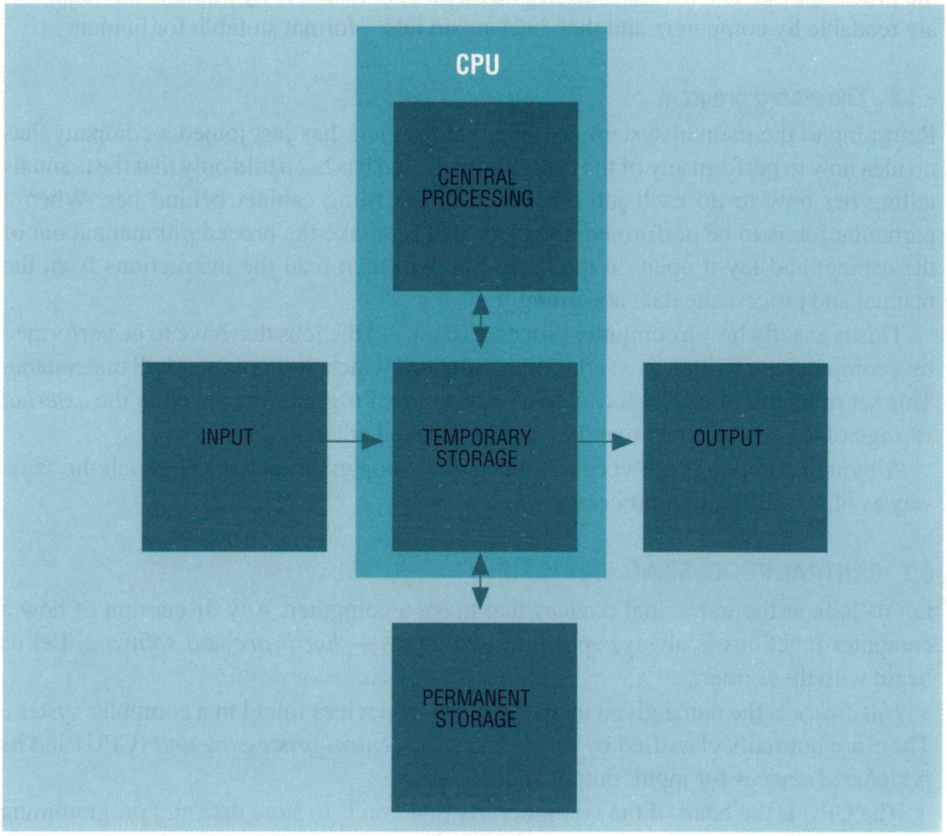

through the output function represented by such devices as printers, plotters and display screens. As in a manual system, computers have permanent storage devices where data can be stored until needed, the more common devices being computer disks and tapes.

Finally the computer has its own 'desk top': a large temporary storage area forming part of the CPU function. This holds current data during processing.

To complete the picture it is necessary to discuss two further issues: *data representation* and *the stored program*.

6.1.1 Data representation

In order to read one must be familiar with the 26-letter alphabet and the decimal numbering system. In a manual processing system, data and information will be represented by these letters and numbers. The clerk or processor will be able to read data directly from an input document or report. The input and output functions merely involve the presentation of data to — and information from — the clerk or processor.

Digital computers, however, do not represent information as different characters or codes. Instead they represent it as groups of *switches* which are either on or off. The input and output functions therefore represent not only the transfer of data to and from the processor but also the translation of data that are readable by humans into data that are readable by computers and then back again into a format suitable for humans.

6.1.2 The stored program

Returning to the manual system, assume that the clerk has just joined a company, has no idea how to perform any of the tasks required, and has been told only that the manuals telling her how to do each job are stored in the filing cabinet behind her. When a particular job is to be performed, the clerk will first take the procedural manual out of the cabinet and lay it open on the desk. She will then read the instructions from the manual and process the data accordingly.

This is exactly how a computer processes data. All the jobs that have to be performed by a computer are written as a series of instructions which the computer will understand. This set of instructions is referred to as a *program*. Programs are saved in the *external storage* of the computer so that they can be recalled when required.

Although computers are very advanced and complex, they work in much the same way as other information processors.

6.2 CENTRAL PROCESSING UNIT (CPU)

Let us look at the individual devices that make a computer. Any discussion of how a computer functions is always split into two topics — *hardware* and *software*. Let us begin with the former.

Hardware is the name given to all the physical devices found in a computer system. These are normally classified by function, ie. the *central processing unit* (CPU) and its *peripheral devices* for input, output and storage.

The CPU is the heart of the computer. Its function is to store data and programming instructions, to control the sequence of operations being performed by the computer, to give commands to all parts of the system, and to carry out the necessary processing required by the program instructions. This section describes the various components of the CPU, discusses how data and instructions are represented in the machine, and finally follows the CPU through a set of instructions to explain how it functions.

6.2.1 Components of the central processing unit

The CPU consists of three functional areas (see Figure 6.3 opposite):

- main storage
- control unit
- arithmetic logic unit.

Main storage

The function of main storage (also referred to as *main memory*, *primary storage* or *internal storage*) is to provide temporary storage for instructions and data during the execution of a program. Often one will hear people saying things like 'that machine is 640K', or 'that is a 4MB computer'. This refers to the number of characters that can be held in main storage. The 'K' (kilobyte) is 1024 characters, so 640K indicates that the

FIGURE 6.3. Diagram of the central processing unit.

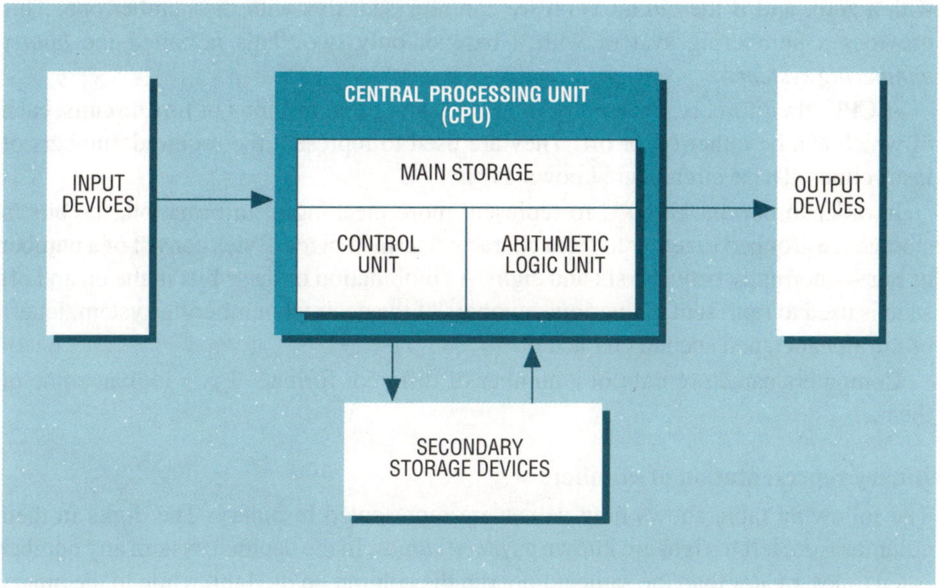

main storage can hold 655 360 characters. As storage areas get larger, so we need more terms to describe them. Thus a megabyte (MB) represents one million characters, a gigabyte (GB) represents one thousand million (one billion) characters, and a terabyte (TB) is one trillion characters.

Control unit

The control unit directs and controls the various functions of the CPU. It controls all input and output devices, the movement of data into and out of storage, and the routing of information between main storage and the arithmetic logic unit.

Arithmetic logic unit (ALU)

The ALU has two main functions. It performs the arithmetic required by the program — ie. it adds, subtracts, multiplies and divides, and it performs certain logical operations, for example the comparison of two numbers to determine which is the greater.

6.2.2 Data representation

The CPU performs the processing function of the computer system. The data are brought into the CPU, stored temporarily, processed through calculation and logic, and the results are then output. The question is 'how are the data and instructions represented electronically inside the CPU?'

The numbering system that we use today is called the *decimal numbering system* and it has a base of 10. This is due to the fact that before the use of electrical and mechanical devices, human beings used ten fingers to count. Computer systems do not have fingers to count on, but they do have circuits. In the same way as a light can be either on or off, so electrical circuits have two absolute states. If the circuit is off we can represent this with a zero, and if the circuit is on we can represent this with the number one. This provides a numbering system with a base of only two. This is called the *binary numbering system*.

A CPU, therefore, is made up of thousands and often millions of tiny circuits, each of which can be either on or off. They are used to represent the required numbers or instructions. These circuits are known as *bits*.

In order to permit the CPU to represent more meaningful information, the bits in storage are grouped together to form characters termed *bytes*. Bytes consist of a number of bits — normally between six and eight. A combination of these bits in the on and off state is used to represent the various numbers of the decimal numbering system, letters of the alphabet, and special characters.

Computers can store data in a number of different formats. Let's look at some of them.

Binary representation of numbers

The following table shows how values are represented in binary. The digits in their columns from left to right are known as *place values*. In the decimal system any number is ten times greater than the same number in the column on its right, while in the binary system it is only two times greater. Obviously we need many more digits to represent binary numbers. Reading from the table, a decimal 12 is the same as 1100 in binary.

FIGURE 6.4. Representing numbers 0 to 15 in binary and decimal.

	Decimal		Binary			
Place value	10	1	8	4	2	1
	0	0	0	0	0	0
	0	1	0	0	0	1
	0	2	0	0	1	0
	0	3	0	0	1	1
	0	4	0	1	0	0
	0	5	0	1	0	1
	0	6	0	1	1	0
	0	7	0	1	1	1
	0	8	1	0	0	0
	0	9	1	0	0	1
	1	0	1	0	1	0
	1	1	1	0	1	1
	1	2	1	1	0	0
	1	3	1	1	0	1
	1	4	1	1	1	0
	1	5	1	1	1	1

To extend this concept, the number 59213 would need to be spread over 16 bits (2 bytes) and would look like this in binary format:

FIGURE 6.5. The number 59213 in binary.

BYTE 2	BYTE 1
11100111	01001101

The computer does all its arithmetic in binary format. The following table shows you the value of each bit position for the number 59213.

FIGURE 6.6. The values of bit positions for the number 59213.

Bit position	Bit representation	Bit on or off	Value of on bits
1	1	1	1
2	2	0	0
3	4	1	4
4	8	1	8
5	16	0	0
6	32	0	0
7	64	1	64
8	128	0	0
9	256	1	256
10	512	1	512
11	1 024	1	1 024
12	2 048	0	0
13	4 096	0	0
14	8 192	1	8 192
15	16 384	1	16 384
16	32 768	1	32 768
	Total of all on bits =		59 213

Character format

While binary representation is efficient for computation and storage, data moving in and out of the computer are normally held in character format where each byte contains a single character. There are 256 possible combinations of bit settings in an 8 bit byte, more than enough to represent all the numbers from 0 to 9, upper and lower case alphabetic characters, and special characters such as /, . * & " ? !.

Unlike binary representation, there is no mathematical basis behind the setting of bits. As long as each character has a unique representation of bit settings, the computer can make the necessary translation from a human-readable format to machine-readable format and back again.

There are two major coding conventions used by most computers, the *extended binary-coded decimal interchange code* (EBCDIC, an 8 bit code used in IBM mainframes) and the *American standard code for information interchange* (ASCII, a 7 bit code used mostly in mini- and microcomputers). Examples of the various character representations are shown in the example below:

FIGURE 6.7. Character representations in EBCDIC and ASCII.

Character	EBCDIC	ASCII
A	11000001	1000001
B	11000010	1000010
C	11000011	1000011
D	11000100	1000100
E	11000101	1000101
F	11000110	1000110
G	11000111	1000111
H	11001000	1001000
I	11001001	1001001
J	11010001	1001010
K	11010010	1001011
L	11010011	1001100
M	11010100	1001101
N	11010101	1001110
O	11010110	1001111
P	11010111	1010000

Character	EBCDIC	ASCII
Q	11011000	1010001
R	11011001	1010010
S	11100010	1010011
T	11100011	1010100
U	11100100	1010101
V	11100101	1010110
W	11100110	1010111
X	11100111	1011000
Y	11101000	1011001
Z	11101001	1011010
0	11110000	0110000
1	11110001	0110001
2	11110010	0110010
3	11110011	0110011
4	11110100	0110100
5	11110101	0110101
6	11110110	0110110
7	11110111	0110111
8	11111000	0111000
9	11111001	0111001

Although the eight bits could easily hold values greater than nine, the convention is that only one character will be contained in each byte. This format is often termed *binary coded decimal*. All data moving into or out of the computer are in this format and need to be converted to binary prior to arithmetic computation.

Packed format

Because the character format wastes storage space, a popular way of storing numeric data is to pack two numeric digits into each byte (four bits each). This should be clear from Figure 6.8 below. The four bits on the far right are usually reserved for the sign which indicates whether the number is positive or negative.

FIGURE 6.8. Packed format.

8 9	9 7	2 8	9 +
10001001	10010111	00101000	01011100

One major problem facing computer programmers is that streams of 1s and 0s are very difficult to read. A shorthand quickly emerged. This involved using *octal* (base 8) and *hexadecimal* (base 16). Figure 6.9 compares the different systems:

FIGURE 6.9. Decimal, binary, octal and hexadecimal notation.

Decimal	Binary	Octal	Hex
0	0000	0	0
1	0001	1	1
2	0010	2	2
3	0011	3	3
4	0100	4	4
5	0101	5	5
6	0110	6	6
7	0111	7	7
8	1000	10	8
9	1001	11	9
10	010	12	A
11	1011	13	B
12	1100	14	C
13	1101	15	D
14	1110	16	E
15	1111	17	F
16	10000	20	10

We have discussed various ways in which data can be stored in the computer, including binary, character, and packed formats. There are also others. Each representation has advantages and disadvantages in terms of processing and space efficiency.

It is important to understand that the settings of a particular byte would mean one thing in binary format and something entirely different in character or packed format. The machine must therefore be aware of the format of the data that it is processing in order to understand the contents of the individual bytes.

6.2.3 Parity bits

During processing, millions of characters of data are being moved, modified and manipulated within the CPU. There is an obvious danger that one of the bits within a character might lose its status of 'on' or 'off' and therefore represent a different number or letter of the alphabet. The validity of each character can be ensured by adding an extra bit to the character called a *parity bit*.

Computer manufacturers have used both odd and even parity systems in their computers. With an odd parity system the total number of *on* bits in a single character must add up to an odd number. If this is not the case the parity bit is set 'on' to make the number odd. Even number parity systems work in exactly the same way, except the number is made even instead of odd. These systems ensure that if one bit loses its 'on' or 'off' status the CPU will be able to detect the error.

6.2.4 Addressable locations

The main storage of the CPU comprises many thousands or millions of bits combined to form characters. In the movement of data and instructions within the main storage there is a real danger that the CPU will not know where everything has been stored. To obviate this problem each group of eight bits (which, it will be remembered, may be considered as an entity known as a *byte*) can be addressed individually by the control unit. Whenever data are stored within the CPU, the address is stored for later reference. Some machines work with groups of characters known as *words* — usually two characters (16 bits) or four (32 bits) in parallel. This improves the speed of processing.

6.2.5 Types of main storage

Earlier on we mentioned the use of circuits within the CPU to represent the bits which make up each byte of data. The earliest commercial computers used *vacuum tube* technology to represent these bits but the system was both slow and bulky and the vacuum tubes generated a great deal of heat. They were also very unreliable.

The next major approach to storage technology was known as *fixed magnetic storage*, commonly referred to as *core storage*. This consisted of small doughnut-shaped metal rings that could be magnetized in one of two directions.

In the late 1950s, transistors replaced vacuum tubes in the electronic circuitry of the control unit and ALU. This technology was itself replaced by the *integrated circuit* (IC) where all the elements of an electronic circuit were etched onto a silicon wafer, often referred to as a *microchip*.

These circuits were miniaturized further with the advent of VLSI (*very large scale integration*) and ULSI (*ultra large scale integration*) and they very soon replaced core storage as the major primary storage technology.

The advance of the microchip is generally accepted as the major force behind the computer revolution. Microcircuit technology offers many advantages over core storage. Chips are smaller, faster, and cheaper. Chips that are smaller than a thumbnail can contain hundreds of thousands of bits of storage. They are, however, *volatile* in nature: this means that a loss or interruption of power will result in the loss of the information stored in the chip.

A glossary of CPU terms

We have been using a number of computer terms to describe the size, speed and performance of the CPU. Here is a glossary of most of the common terminology.

FIGURE 6.10. CPU terms.

Memory sizes	Kilobyte Megabyte Gigabyte Terabyte	2^{10} (1024 bytes) 2^{20} (1 million bytes) 2^{30} (1 billion bytes) 2^{40} (1 trillion bytes)
Memory divisions	Bit Nibble Byte Half word Word	A single switch 4 bits (½ a byte) 8 bits 2 bytes 4 bytes
Memory speeds	Millisecond Microsecond Nanosecond Picosecond	1 thousandth of a second 1 millionth of a second 1 billionth of a second 1 trillionth of a second
Processing speed	Megahertz MIPS	Millions of cycles/sec instr./sec

Speed of processing

Just how fast can a computer process data? This depends on many factors such as the processing speed of the machine, the time taken to access and return data to their storage location, the volume of data, and the complexity of processing. What we can say is that the CPU is very fast. Most modern mainframes can perform some functions in speeds that are measured in nanoseconds (billionths of a second).

To appreciate how fast a nanosecond is, if we compare one nanosecond to one second the ratio would be the same as:

- one mile is to 2000 return trips to the moon, or
- one minute is to 1900 years.

6.2.6 The functioning of the CPU

Let us now follow the CPU through a few steps or instructions in a program in order to see how it functions. When the CPU control unit has been instructed to run a program, it starts by loading the program into main storage. The control unit decides where to store the program and each instruction is stored in the sequence in which it will be executed.

When the program has been loaded into main storage, the control unit will process each instruction using an approach consisting of two stages: the *instruction stage* and the *execution stage*.

Instruction stage

This stage involves three functions:

- loading the instruction into a control register;
- decoding the instruction to determine what it must do;
- setting up the electronic circuitry to perform the task.

Execution stage

At this stage, the instruction that was set up in the previous stage is performed. A number of different types of instructions could be executed including those that:

- fetch data from main storage and load them into registers in the ALU;
- manipulate data via the ALU;
- return the results from the ALU to a predefined area in main storage;
- read or write data from main storage to input/output devices.

Figures 6.11.1 – 6.11.3 illustrate how a CPU might add the contents of storage locations 7 and 8 together and put the result in storage location 9. When the computer performs the program it begins by loading the program instructions and the values to be added in main memory. The control unit then processes each instruction in sequence until the last one is completed.

You can see from this short example that a program is just a number of instructions issued to the CPU, and that the control unit is responsible for decoding each instruction and requesting that the various elements of the computer perform their function in the correct sequence.

One would think from this example that writing a program to add 500 numbers would be a very tedious process. However by adding an instruction to read new values from the keyboard or storage device, and another to branch back and repeat the same instructions again, this small program will add numbers until no more data are available.

6.2.7 Future CPU architectures

The CPU design of today's computer is often termed the *Von Neumann architecture*. Von Neumann was an American scientist who had a strong influence on the development of the CPU design as discussed earlier in this module.

Today, however, his model is often termed the *Von Neumann bottleneck* due to the limited processing capability of what is effectively a serial operation. Modern central processing units only handle one instruction at a time and, while there are hardware and software techniques to maximize the CPU's processing power, it is highly inadequate for handling some of our modern day applications. Conventional CPUs are more than adequate for work in business environments where they spend more time moving numbers around than they do processing data. Applications in the field of artificial intelligence and scientific simulation, however, require immense processing power for which these CPUs are totally inadequate.

RISC technology

One new development which has already resulted in a new generation of very powerful mini- and microcomputers is RISC or *reduced instruction set computer* technology. Every computer has what is termed an *instruction set* which is a group of basic commands that can be interpreted by the control unit and performed. Recently, computer scientists have realized that many of these commands are used very infrequently and can be performed by a combination of other even more basic instructions. This reduction in the number of operations that can be performed by the machine may have limitations

Fig 6.11.3

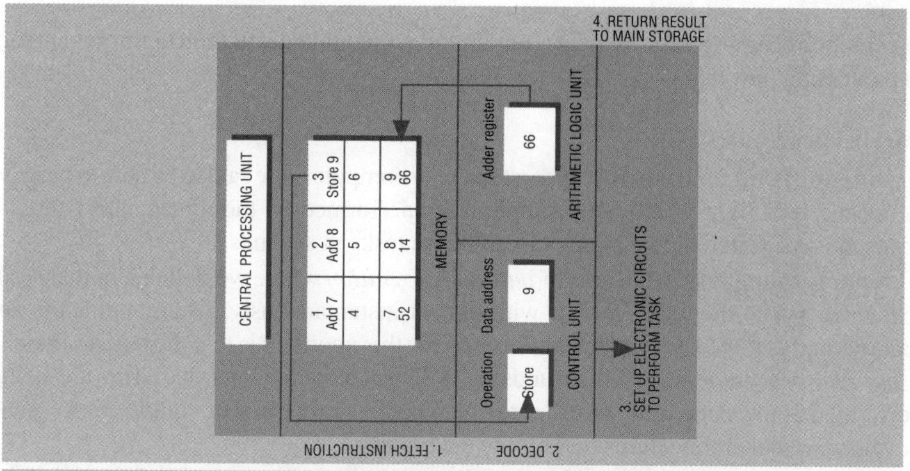

Fig 6.11.2

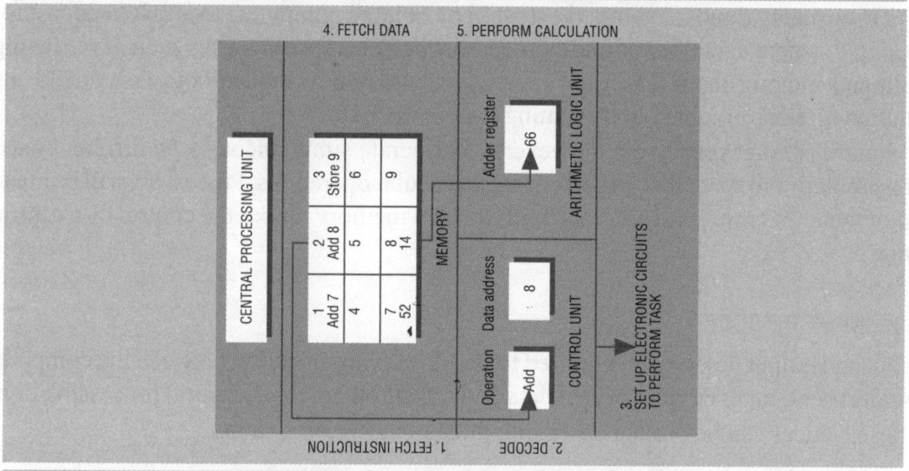

Fig 6.11.1

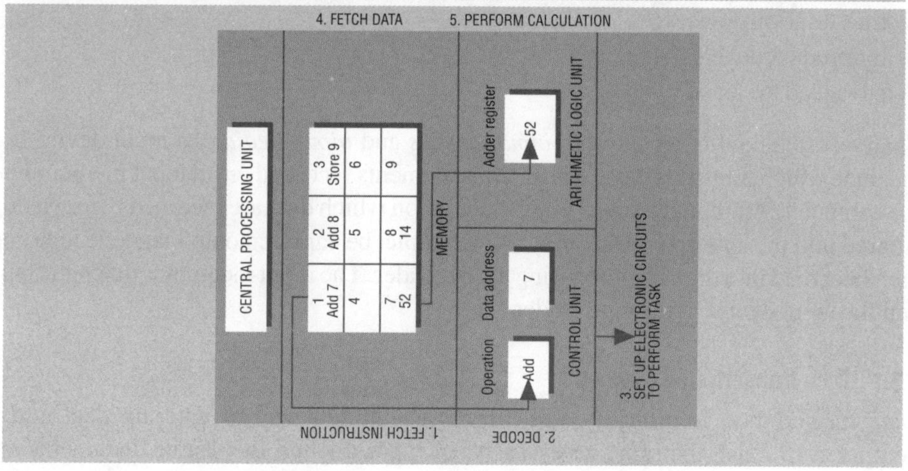

FIGURE 6.11.1. Add contents of memory address 7 to accumulator.

FIGURE 6.11.2. Add contents of memory address 8 to accumulator.

FIGURE 6.11.3. Store accumulated answer in memory address 9.

in certain processing environments, but on the whole it leads to radical improvements in processing power.

Parallel processors

It is often difficult for laymen to understand why computers are said to be able to process at the speed of light when many simple tasks performed by these machines can take hours or days. Often humans can perform these tasks in seconds.

A prime example is in the area of *pattern recognition* where we find that humans can recognize a face they are familiar with almost instantaneously, while computers are painstakingly slow. The fundamental reason for this anomaly is that the human brain is a *parallel processor*: many thousands or millions of processing activities are being performed at the same time. In order to enhance the real power of computers we must develop parallel architectures that mimic the brain.

This is being done to a limited extent in most large computers today. It happens, for example, where a number of microprocessors perform specific tasks such as retrieving data and moving them down the processing pipeline to reduce both delays and the amount of work involved in presenting data to the CPU.

Future parallel processors, however, will operate simultaneously on different parts of a problem and specialize in performing particular operations. Processors will be made up of many microprocessors, each with its own memory, under the control of a central unit.

6.3 INPUT DEVICES

Input and output devices are required to provide communication between the computer and its users. Input devices accept data and transfer them to the central processing unit. These devices can be broken down into three main classifications:

- transcription devices;
- by-product devices;
- advanced systems.

There is often confusion between *input devices* and *input media*. An input device is a machine which transmits data or program statements recorded on an input medium into the computer. An input medium is the material on which data are recorded before being entered into the computer. Data may, for example, be captured onto magnetic tape and then later read into the computer using a tape reader. The input medium is magnetic tape and the input device is the tape reader.

6.3.1 Data transcription devices

Data transcription is probably still the most common way of entering data into a computer. In much the same way as a typist types a letter, the source documents are handed to a punch operator who keys in the data on a key entry device. The operator obviously works at a pace that is much slower than that at which the computer can work and therefore, in the past, the data were unlikely to be transmitted direct to the computer.

FIGURE 6.12. Input devices.

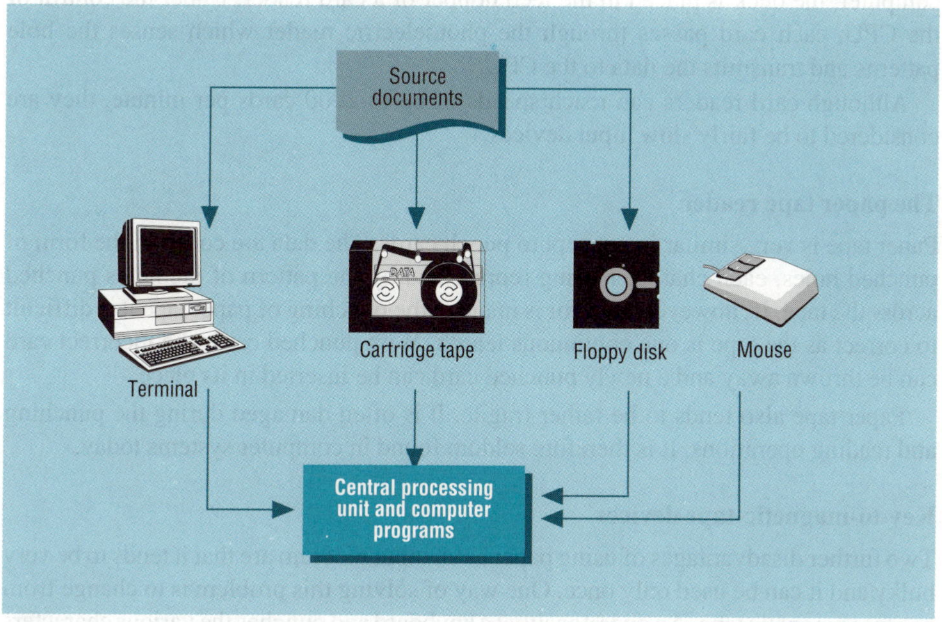

Instead information was captured in computer-readable form on a medium such as card or tape which could be entered into the computer at a convenient time.

Today, because computers are cheaper and sophisticated enough to be involved in other processing while the operator is busy keying in the data, the concept of *direct entry* has evolved. Here data are not captured onto an intermediate medium but are transferred directly to the computer itself.

One major advantage of direct entry is that the computer can assist the operator by validating the data as they arrive and indicating possible errors at the time of capture. Where the data are captured prior to input, the CPU cannot assist in identifying errors and another method of input verification must be used. This may involve the operator having to enter the data twice. On the first pass the data will be captured onto the input medium, and on the second pass the device will be required to check that the information has been correctly captured. Such a process is known as *verification* and is obviously very time-consuming. For more on data entry, read the chapter on modes of processing.

The card reader

The card reader was one of the earliest and most popular computer input devices. While it can still be seen in some mainframe installations today, it is gradually being phased out.

The punch operator keys in the data using a keyboard that is very similar to that of a typewriter. With every key depression the punch machine makes little holes in the card to represent the character concerned. The keystrokes are then repeated on another machine which verifies the data. When the data on these cards are required by the computer, the deck is placed in the feed hopper of a card reader. Under the control of the CPU, each card passes through the photoelectric reader which senses the hole patterns and transmits the data to the CPU.

Although card readers can reach speeds of up to 2000 cards per minute, they are considered to be fairly slow input devices.

The paper tape reader

Paper tape is very similar in concept to punch cards. The data are coded in the form of punched holes, each character being represented by the pattern of the holes punched across the tape. If, however, an error is made in the punching of paper tape it is difficult to correct as the tape is one continuous length. With punched cards the incorrect card can be thrown away and a newly punched card can be inserted in its place.

Paper tape also tends to be rather fragile. It is often damaged during the punching and reading operations. It is therefore seldom found in computer systems today.

Key-to-magnetic-tape devices

Two further disadvantages of using paper as an input medium are that it tends to be very bulky and it can be used only once. One way of solving this problem is to change from paper to magnetic tape. An operator sits at a keyboard and punches the various characters of data onto the magnetic tape in much the same way as is done with paper tape or punched cards.

One of the major advantages of using magnetic tape to input data into a computer is that the information can be read extremely quickly. The transfer of data into the CPU is a function of the speed at which the tape passes over the read heads together with the density at which the data are packed onto the magnetic tape. In ideal conditions, transfer rates of up to a third of a million characters per second have been achieved. For more on magnetic tape devices, read the section on secondary storage devices.

Key-to-disk

Key-to-disk systems are among the most sophisticated of the data transcription devices. In the more basic systems a floppy disk is used. This is very similar in appearance to a 45 rpm gramophone record that is still in its cover. The data are put onto the disk and later read into the CPU from a floppy disk drive. The floppy disc is taking the place of magnetic tape.

Larger key-to-disk systems involve the use of hard disks and usually a certain amount of microprocessing logic. This means that the capture device is itself a small computer. It enables the operator to use certain error-correction functions and to store and retrieve data when required. These systems are obviously expensive and normally a number of operators are linked to a single system. When the data are to be loaded into the computer either the disk can be mounted onto a disk drive which is linked to the computer, or the disk drive may be linked to the computer itself. The hard disk will be discussed in more detail in the chapter on secondary storage.

Computer terminals

The most conventional method for capturing data into the computer is to have a terminal linked directly to the computer.

When the data are entered into the terminal, they are transferred directly into the CPU. From there they are stored on a secondary storage device or processed immediately. Not only does this do away with the need for a temporary storage medium, but the computer can use its logic to assist in the detection of errors made by the operator. For further discussion of terminals see the section on output devices.

6.3.2 By-product recording devices

Data transcription devices require that the source documents are captured by an operator as a separate exercise. By-product recording devices bypass this capture operation by generating the input media as by-products of the original transaction.

For example, if a customer were to purchase something on credit he may be provided with an invoice giving details of the transaction. A copy of the invoice could be used as a source document to be input into the computer later. However, the system may be automated to the extent that the original sale is keyed into the cash register or point-of-sale device and *while the sales clerk is generating the invoice* the machine also generates a record of the transaction for on-line transfer to the CPU or storage on some medium such as magnetic disk. The data transcription process has been eliminated.

Cash registers

A very common form of by-product recording device is the cash register. Magnetic cassette tapes are used inside the device to record the cash and credit sales that are rung up on the cash register. At the end of the day the tapes are taken to the computer and read in using a paper tape or magnetic cassette reader.

Point-of-sale devices

The point-of-sale device is merely a more sophisticated version of the cash register. A point-of-sale system usually comprises a number of terminals which are placed around a store with a small computer controlling them.

As each transaction is entered at a terminal, a record of the stock items and credit details is automatically entered on the microcomputer. At the end of the day these transaction details are then read into the main computer for processing.

Because the point-of-sale terminals are linked to a computer, the system can be given enormous sophistication. For instance, if the store management wishes to verify a customer's credit standing prior to making a sale, the computer can look up the credit status of each customer and can provide the sales clerk with the necessary warning when a customer of poor standing attempts to make a purchase. Details such as stolen credit card numbers can be entered into the system and will enable it to check when a customer attempts to make a fraudulent purchase.

Most large shops in South Africa have installed, or are planning to install, point-of-sale equipment on the shop floor. The major reason for this, apart from increased credit control, is that it enables the company to obtain up-to-date information on what has been purchased and this allows management to make rapid decisions in terms of stock recording and sales trends.

6.3.3 Advanced systems

We have discussed two of the methods of entering data into a computer. The first required a separate capturing exercise while the second incorporated this exercise into the creation of the original source transaction. Advanced systems attempt to automate the input process still further by the use of special-purpose hardware devices.

Optical character recognition (OCR)

Optical readers use photoelectric cells to measure the amount of reflected light from a particular set of characters, and they transfer the details to the computer. Early devices could only recognize certain characters printed in special type fonts (see Figure 6.13) and were susceptible to error if the characters were not perfectly formed.

FIGURE 6.13. OCR fonts.

OCR A Alphanumeric

0123456789

ABCDEFGHIJKLMNOPQRSTUVWXYZ

{}%?&"*+$,.-/'=|;:■

Optical readers are now capable of identifying hand-printed numbers and typed letters in various fonts. Reading speeds also vary from less than 100 characters per second to over 2000 characters per second.

The potential advantages of optical character recognition are reduced cost, increased speed, and a reduced chance of error because transcription to a different medium is avoided. The removal of the transcription operation can also result in greater efficiency for the data processing operation as a whole.

Early attempts at using OCR readers to input large quantities of data in mainframe environments were, in most cases, unsuccessful. This was mainly due to the expense of the equipment and high error-rates in reading the data.

Optical mark recognition (OMR) is very similar to OCR, except that the readers detect marks or lines called *bar codes* rather than characters (see Figure 6.14). Just about every article you can purchase today has a square on the label which contains a number of black horizontal lines. This is the bar code.

The theory behind the use of the code is that all articles will have a special number and this is represented by a particular bar code. As the customer checks his or her purchases out, the bar-code scanner will detect the code and transmit it to the computer. The computer will then check the price it has been told and charge the customer the appropriate amount.

FIGURE 6.14. A bar code.

This code follows the European Article Numbering System [EAN].
This is a 13 digit bar code where the digits represent the following:

First 3 digits	= Country code
Next 4 digits	= Company code
Next 5 digits	= Product code
Last digit	= Check digit

6 001306 000910

Apart from eliminating the need to price-mark every article, the system should also eliminate incorrect or fraudulent ringing-up by the till operator. It can also speed up the check-out process considerably. One major problem the bar code has created is that customers often do not like purchasing goods when the price is not shown on the article. Prices are therefore normally also displayed on the supermarket shelf.

Magnetic ink character recognition (MICR)

If you look at a bank cheque you will find a number of rather formalized characters printed across the bottom (see Figure 6.15).

These are the details of your bank account number. The characters are written in magnetic ink and can be read by a magnetic ink character reader. The reader works by first magnetizing the characters and then passing them under a read head so that the details can be identified.

MICR technology was developed for the banking industry. Without this process cheques would be cleared between banks at a much slower pace than is presently the case. However, MICR has not been applied to any degree outside this industry, mainly because of the development of the optical reading process which requires less cumbersome and less costly preparation and equipment.

Voice recognition devices

While the early developers of this type of equipment were hopeful that it would allow people to carry on conversations with their computer, this hope has not yet been realized. Voice input devices are very limited, recognizing only an elementary vocabulary of simple commands.

With voice recognition the computer must try to identify individual words and must also understand the meaning of groups of words. Unfortunately very few people use exactly the same words to express the same request.

Voice recognition will become important in the future for workers who need to enter data into the computer whilst using both hands, and also for individuals with physical disabilities. However, the devices are currently too expensive and unreliable for general use.

FIGURE 6.15. Magnetic ink character recognition.

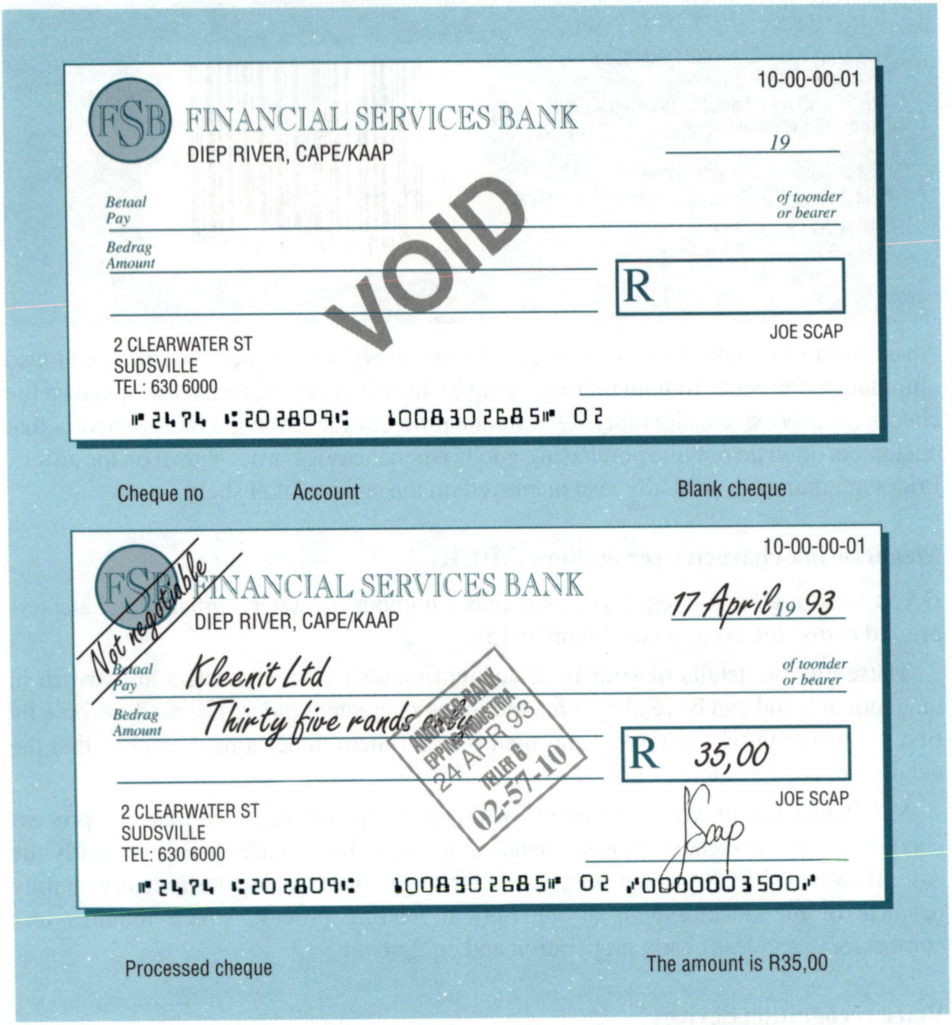

Touch-tone devices

In many cases people want to communicate with a computer from a remote area. An example of this would be customers wishing to enquire about the status of their bank accounts from home. Here the more modern touch-tone telephones can be used to enter the data which are then transferred down the telephone line to the computer.

The electronic mouse

The standard computer keyboard has been, and still is, the easiest way to enter numbers and letters into the computer. However, when the user wants to draw pictures using the computer, or to point to one of a series of options, a mouse is often a more practical alternative. The device looks like a small mouse which is moved around on the surface of the desk beside the computer. A pointer on the screen moves according to the movement of the mouse, giving the user the ability to point and draw on the screen. The mouse is commonly used for graphics and desktop publishing applications. It is a supplement to the keyboard rather than a replacement.

Touch-screens

One would think that having the ability to touch the screen, rather than moving a pointer with a mouse, would be the ideal way of communicating graphic input to the computer. Touch-screens have been available for a number of years but have not gained great popularity, mainly because of the additional cost and the fact that the finger is rather large relative to the size of the screen, with the result that the user can only point to an approximate position.

Light pens

Prior to the advent of the electronic mouse and touch screen, in applications where it was desirable for the user to point to things on the screen rather than using the keyboard, a device called the light pen was often used. By pressing the pen against the screen the user could select from various options displayed on the screen.

The joy stick

Like the mouse, the joy stick is an input device that is used to move the cursor on the screen. It looks like a small gear shift and is used almost entirely for computer games.

Graphics tablets

In the *computer aided drafting* and *computer aided design* fields, architects and engineers are computerizing their drawings. Once the original diagram is captured by the computer it can be manipulated and modified very easily to provide an updated drawing. One way of capturing the raw information is to place the diagram on a graphics tablet which is sensitive to touch or sound or some other form of stimulation. The outline of the diagram is then traced using a special pointer. The coordinates of the drawing are digitized by the computer and stored away for later reference.

6.3.4 Conclusion

As computers move from an era of mainframes processing large quantities of accounting information to an era when computers of all sizes are being used in a multiplicity of applications, so the variety of input devices is growing at a corresponding rate. The computer user no longer has to go to great lengths to put his data in the format required by the computer.

Ultimately there is no doubt that computers will be able to understand what we say, read our correspondence and documentation, and even watch our every movement. Their ability to input data from their environment will match our own. Whether this will be a desirable state of affairs only time will tell.

The following table summarizes the major features of input devices described in this section.

FIGURE 6.16. Input devices — summary of major features.

Paper tape	Inexpensive, difficult to use, obsolete
Punched cards	Staple for many years; seldom used
Key to tape	Batch input; limited editing
Key to disk	As key to tape, with sophisticated editing
Terminal	On-line editing, immediate feedback, capture data at source
OCR	High-speed document processing, bar coding
MICR	High-speed document processing capital intensive equipment
Voice	Emerging technology; increasingly important
Touch screen	User friendly, low data volumes
Electronic mouse	Good for graphics/desk-top publishing

6.4 OUTPUT DEVICES

Input devices are used to enter data or programs into the computer by converting the characters from a form readable by humans to a form readable by machines (binary format). The purpose of an output device is to reverse this conversion process and to generate the results of the computer's processing activities in a form which is again readable by humans.

The more popular output devices include:

- printers;
- microfilm;
- terminals;
- plotters.

Not all computer output needs to be readable by humans. If there is a need to transmit data from one computer to another, this may be done by merely outputting the data on, for example, magnetic tape, and mounting the tape as input on the other machine.

6.4.1 Printers

The printer is probably still the most used output device and it generates a permanent paper copy of the information (often referred to as *hard copy*). Printers come in many sizes, from the smallest daisy-wheel printer, not unlike a typewriter in quality and performance, to large laser printers with speeds of 20 000 lines per minute.

Printers are normally classified as:

- impact printers;
- non-impact printers.

FIGURE 6.17. Output devices.

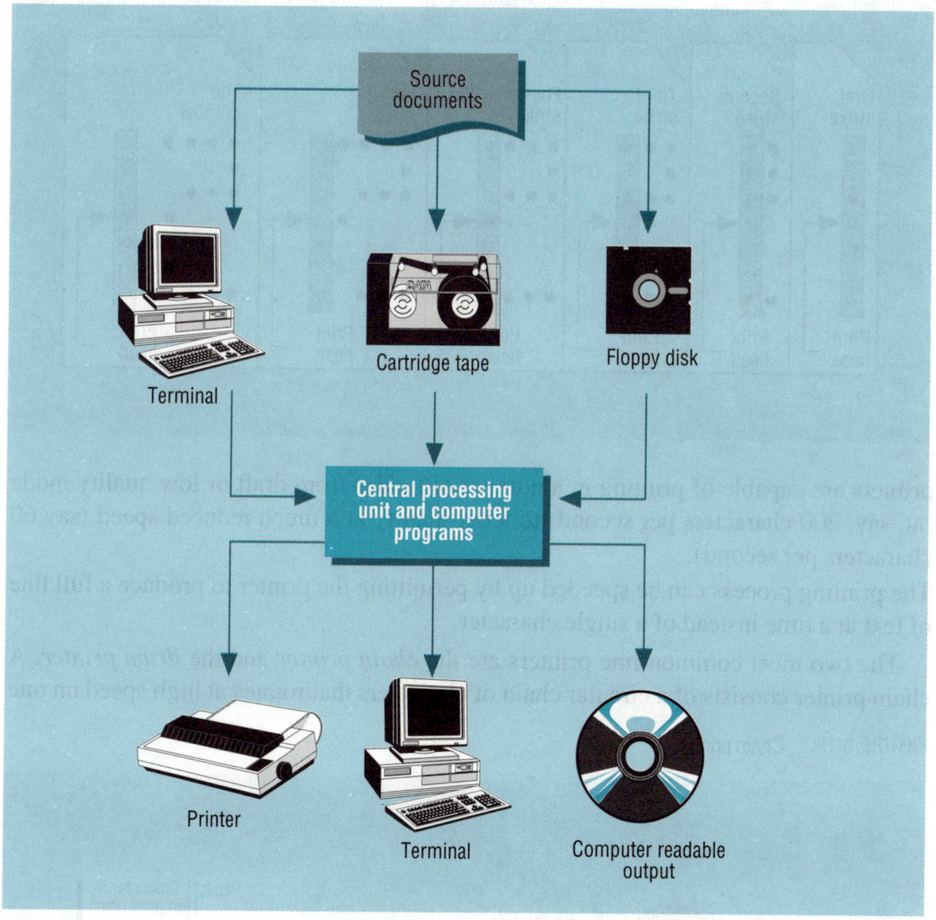

Impact printers

The impact printer generates its characters through a mechanism which physically strikes the paper (much the same as a typewriter). The smallest and slowest of these are the golf ball and daisy-wheel printers. With these devices, each character is generated separately as the head travels across the page from left to right. This type of printing is called *character printing* and the characters are generated one at a time in the sequence in which they appear.

Today, most character printers are matrix printers generating each character by printing a series of small dots on the paper (see Figure 6.18).

Initially, matrix printers did not generate characters of a high quality and organizations used daisy-wheel printers for external correspondence. Today, matrix

FIGURE 6.18. How the matrix printer works.

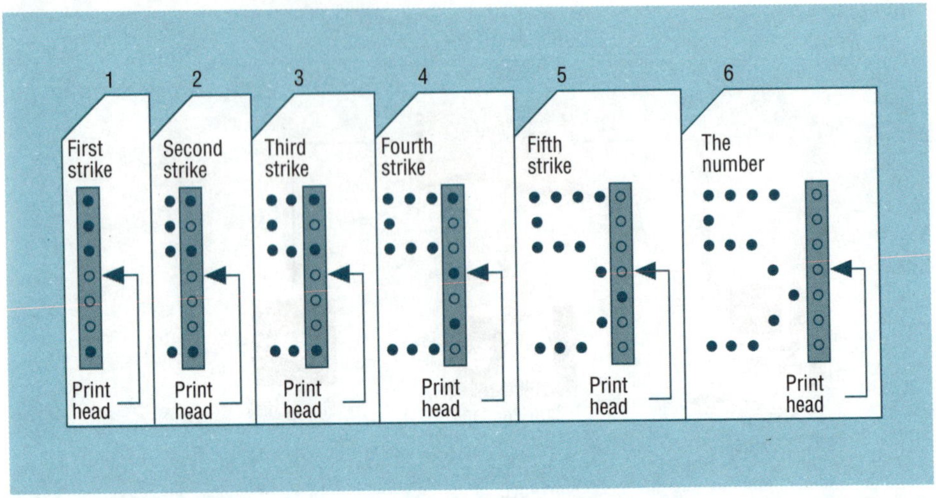

printers are capable of printing in a number of modes from draft or low quality mode (at, say, 200 characters per second) to letter quality at a much reduced speed (say 60 characters per second).

The printing process can be speeded up by permitting the printer to produce a full line of text at a time instead of a single character.

The two most common line printers are the *chain printer* and the *drum printer*. A chain printer consists of a circular chain of characters that rotates at high speed on one

FIGURE 6.19. Chain printer.

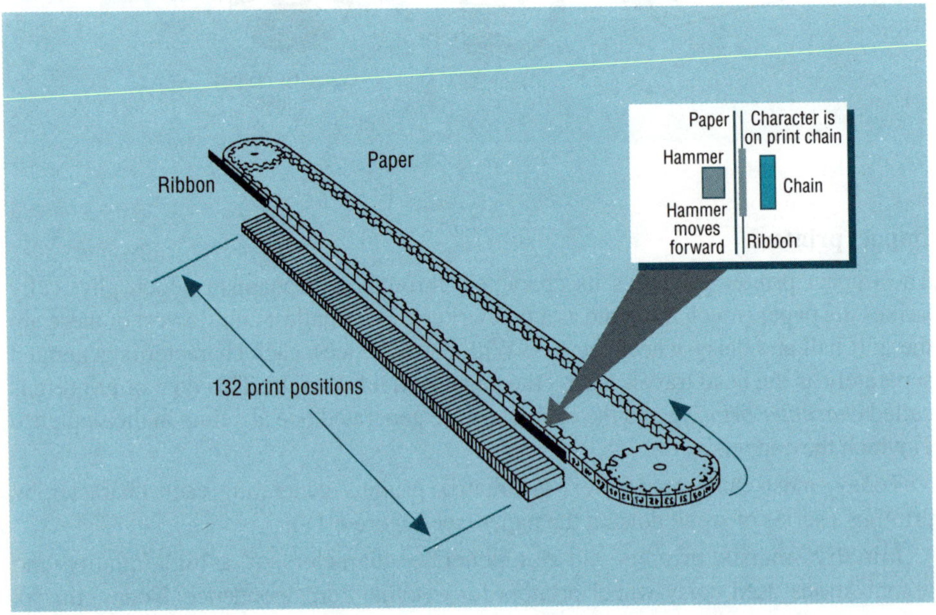

side of the paper. There is a hammer or striker for each print position on the other side of the paper and, as the appropriate character passes, the hammer comes out and strikes it. An entire line is printed after one revolution or less of the chain.

The drum printer consists of raised characters placed in circles around a drum. As with the chain printer, the drum rotates, and after one complete revolution of the drum a complete line is printed.

Impact printers can be extremely fast and some of them are capable of printing 2000 lines per minute.

Non-impact printers

While impact printers physically strike the paper, non-impact printers do not. The reason why non-impact printers are becoming more and more popular is that impact printers have a large number of moving parts and are noisy and prone to mechanical failure.

Non-impact printers can work by spraying the paper with ink, using magnets, using electrical charges, or using heat.

The *ink-jet* printer uses a nozzle and sprays ink onto the paper to form the appropriate characters (see Figure 6.20). As with the matrix printer, these characters consist of dots. In order to obtain the correct character the ink is controlled by a number of vertical and horizontal magnetic deflectors. Colour printouts can be generated using a mixture of the three primary colours.

FIGURE 6.20. How the inkjet printer works.

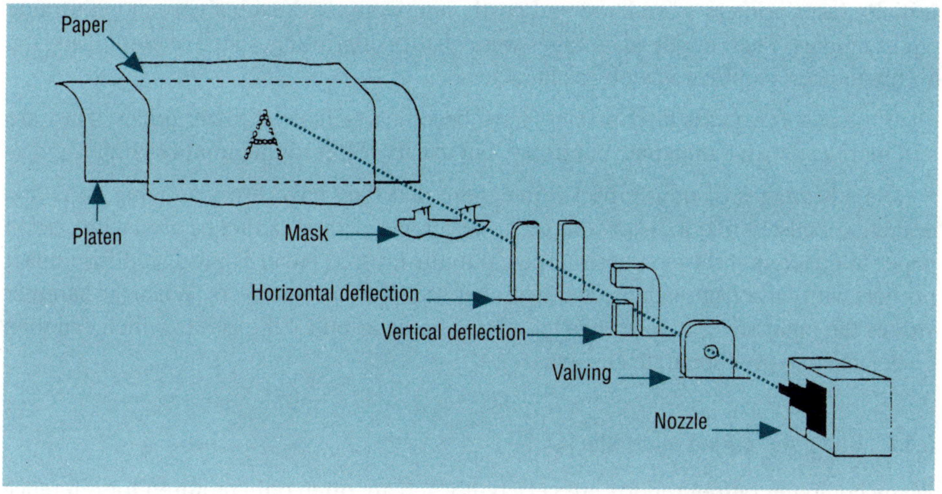

Thermal printers use paper that is sensitive to heat. The print head consists of wires similar to those of the matrix printer. These may be heated individually. The wires, when placed near the heat-sensitized paper, cause a character to be burned onto the paper.

The *laser printer* places images on a rotating drum by means of a laser beam. The drum picks up a toner powder on the laser-exposed areas and this powder is then pressed

FIGURE 6.21. How a laser printer works.

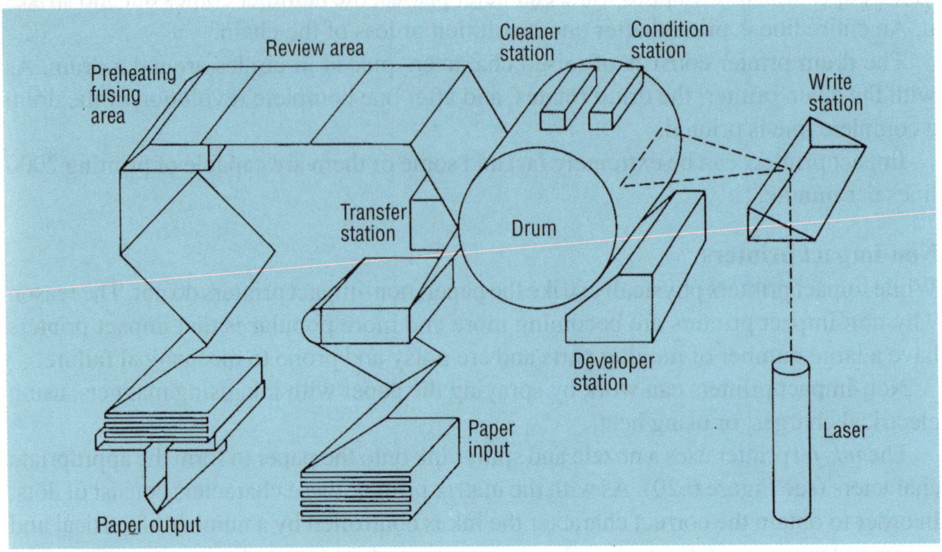

and fused into the paper to form the characters. This process is almost identical to that used by modern photocopy machines (see Figure 6.21).

Initially laser printers were large and costly and were used exclusively in mainframe environments. Their major advantages were quality of printing, speed of output, and the ability to print graphics as well as characters.

Over the past few years laser printers have become available at lower prices. They are still more expensive than matrix printers but usually offer higher quality output.

The advantages of non-impact printers are that they have fewer moving parts and operate silently. A major disadvantage, however, is that they cannot be used with carbon paper to generate multiple copies. Special multi-layered paper is produced for impact printers with carbon or reacting chemicals between the various layers. When the hammer strikes the outer sheet it generates the same character on all the layers which can then be detached to give separate copies.

6.4.2 Computer output microfilm (COM)

Many computer output reports are very bulky and are often only required for reference purposes (in law or historical research, for example). In the past these reports were photographed onto microfilm and the original reports were destroyed in order to save storage space. This was a costly process as the original report had to be produced prior to filming. COM permits the machine-readable output to be transferred directly onto microfilm (see Figure 6.22).

The microfilm can be created in large rolls (not unlike a 16 mm film) or on postcard-size sheets called *microfiche*. COM output for commercial purposes usually

FIGURE 6.22. Computer output microfilm process.

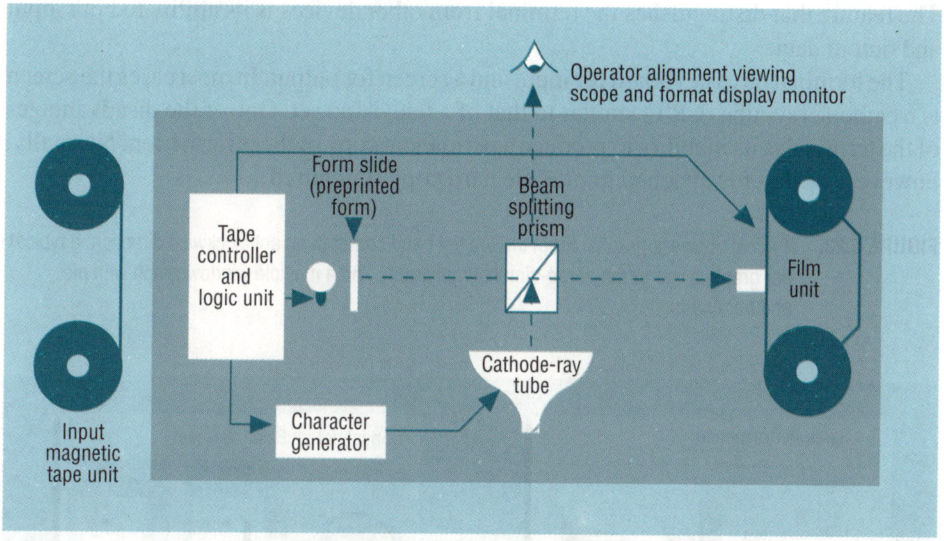

magnifies pages by a factor of 48. This permits a maximum of 288 computer pages to be filmed on one microfiche.

The early COM devices worked in much the same way as cameras in that the film had to be developed after processing. The equipment was expensive and so few computer installations had their own COM equipment. Filming was normally done at computer bureaux. Installations that required microfilm output transferred magnetic tapes of the required reports to these bureaux.

COM processors using laser technology and heat-sensitive film have reduced equipment costs and have also by-passed the need to develop the film after processing.

There are many advantages in using COM rather than paper output:

- less storage space is required;
- if documents are to be sent by mail, microfilm can substantially reduce the postage costs;
- where the report is very large it is usually quicker to retrieve data from microfilm than from paper documents;
- multiple copies can be made of the film. These are both robust and cheap. While a computer report on microfilm costs approximately the same as a computer report on paper, it is much cheaper to use microfiche if a large number of copies of the report are to be generated.

COM cannot be read with the naked eye and so one of the major disadvantages is that special reading equipment must be purchased and must be at hand when information is required. The microfilm reader works in very much the same way as a slide projector in that it enlarges the image onto a screen.

6.4.3 Terminals

The feature that distinguishes the terminal from other devices is its ability to both input and output data.

The terminal has a keyboard for input and a screen for output. In most cases the screen is a cathode ray tube (CRT) similar to that of a television set. One of the disadvantages of the terminal is its inability to produce a permanent copy of the information. Normally, however, a printer is attached to provide hard copy if required.

FIGURE 6.23. Typical business graphs. From the top left hand corner in an anticlockwise direction: a typical bar graph, a line graph, three-dimensional graph, and a multiple window graph with pie and bar charts.

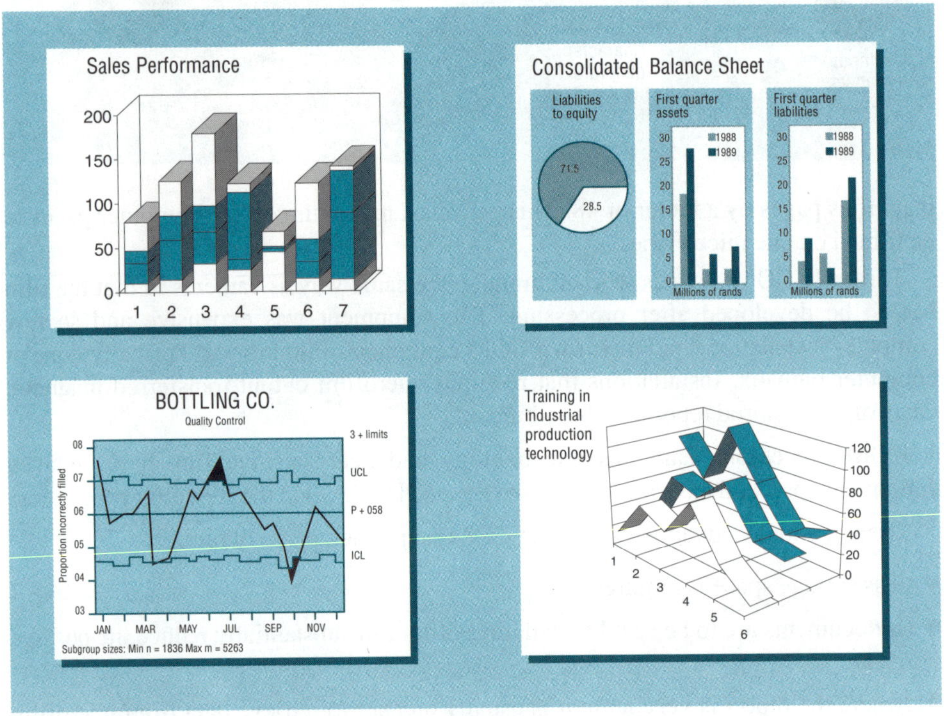

Terminals can be equipped with microprocessors and buffer storage areas. These additions expand the capability of the terminal. It is often possible to program and store data in the terminal prior to transmission to the computer. Terminals with no intelligence are referred to as *dumb* terminals, while those with special features are called *intelligent* or *smart* terminals.

Many terminals today are special application devices such as *automatic teller machines* (ATMs) and *point-of-sale devices* (POSs). They are designed to perform specific tasks and make transactions more efficient and easier for consumers.

6.4.4 Plotters

The plotter is an output device that produces drawings and graphical displays of data (see Figure 6.23). It is normally a flat bed or drum with paper stretched over it. The graphs and drawings are put on the paper by electromechanical or electronic means. Electromechanical devices have an arm containing a pen which moves over the paper, while the electronic plotter generates images using a beam and these are then transferred to paper.

Plotters have many uses. They produce engineering drawings and graphical displays such as trend charts, bar charts, pie charts, maps, and even works of art.

Generating output from a plotter tends to be expensive and time consuming.

For these reasons the visual display unit is a more popular way of generating graphic displays. Terminals with colour screens and the ability to generate graphic pictures are being used increasingly in business.

6.4.5 Conclusion

One of the more recent computer buzz words to capture the imagination of the computer industry is *multimedia.* Whereas in the past most communication between man and computer was addressed through the use of text on the screen or on paper, multimedia includes the use of sound, graphics, still photographs and video. The ultimate goal of multimedia is to make the user interface more stimulating and therefore more informative. Chapter 12 covers the user interface in more detail.

The following table highlights the major features of output devices covered in this section.

FIGURE 6.24. Output devices — summary of major features.

Printed reports	Permanent output; Large range of price and quality.
COM	Minimal storage requirements; robust and cheap; sophisticated referencing methods.
Terminals	Temporary output; interactive on-line enquiry.
Plotters	Presentation colour graphics.

6.5 SECONDARY STORAGE DEVICES

At the beginning of this chapter we discussed some functions of a computer — input, processing, and output. Much of the information entered into a computer, however, is required to be stored permanently (see Figure 6.25). For example, if a new employee joins a company, his payroll details (such as his employee number, name and address, salary and number of dependents) are entered into the computer. These data will assist the computer in compiling the monthly payroll.

Data are never stored permanently in the CPU. The reason for this is that the CPU's main storage capacity tends to be quite small, relatively expensive, and *volatile* (temporary). What is required is a storage device that can hold vast amounts of

FIGURE 6.25. Secondary storage devices.

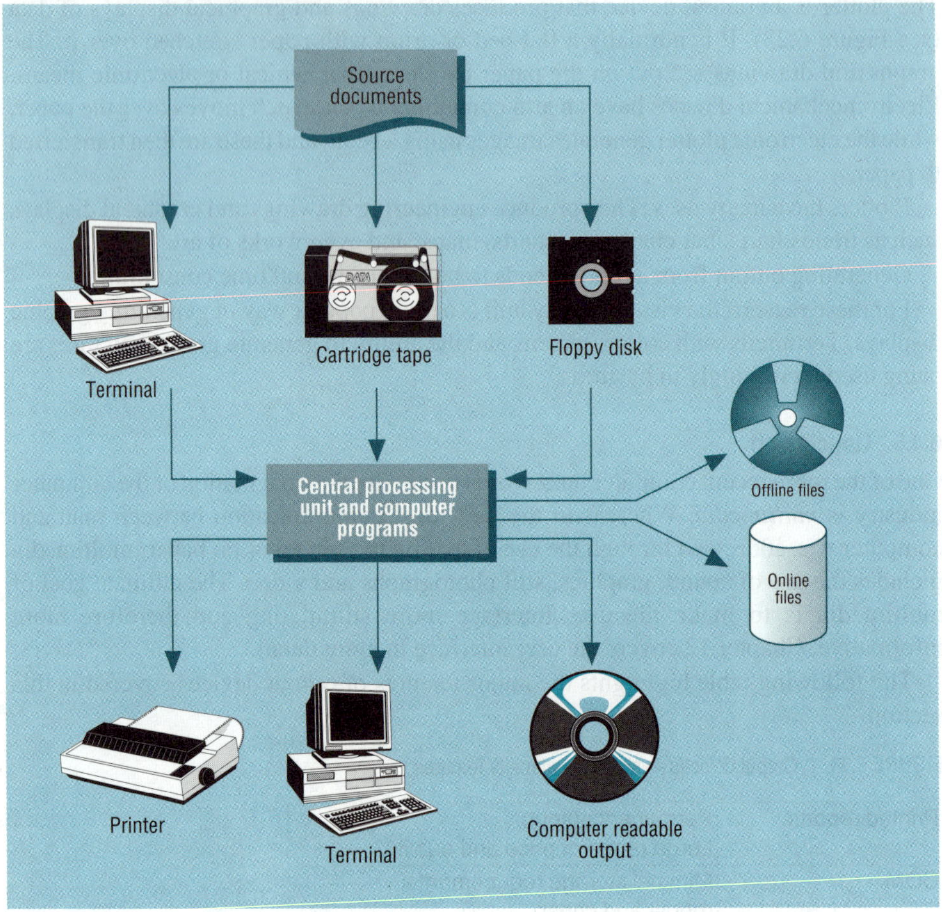

information cheaply and in such a way that it will not be destroyed in the event of a power failure.

The most common secondary storage devices are electromechanical. They include devices such as hard disk drives, floppy disks drives, and magnetic tape drives. There are also a number of non-mechanical storage devices and these will be discussed at the end of the chapter.

6.5.1 Disk drives

Although disk drives vary in size and capacity, they all function in a similar way. A disk consists of one or more circular platters similar to gramophone records. When mounted on a disk drive it rotates at high speed. As it rotates, read/write heads move onto the disk and access data on its surface (see Figure 6.26).

The surface of the disk is divided into a number of concentric circles called *tracks*. Although the size of the tracks decreases as one moves to the centre of the disk, each

FIGURE 6.26. Magnetic disk.

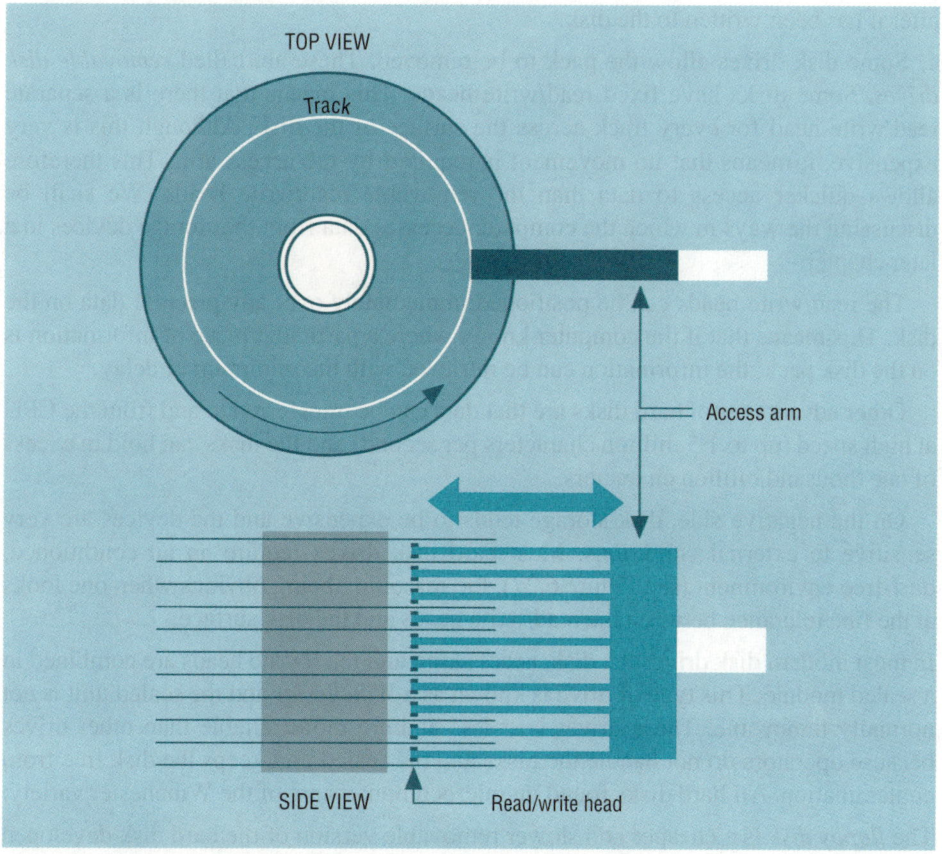

track can hold the same number of characters. The disk surface is covered with magnetic material and each character is represented by a series of magnetized spots along the track.

For the purposes of this description, assume that the disk pack has ten separate platters. The top surface of the top platter and the bottom surface of the bottom platter are not used, so there are, in fact, 18 magnetized surfaces on this single disk. The disk drive has an *access arm* with a read/write head for every magnetized surface, so there will be 18 read/write heads on this disk drive.

When the disk is spinning on the disk drive, the access arm moves into the disk and positions itself at the track where the data are to be written or read. The arm is positioned so that data can be obtained from any of the 18 tracks.

It is more efficient to store data on the same track on different surfaces rather than on a single surface across a number of tracks because this means the access arm is not required to move. The same track going across all the disk surfaces is known as a *cylinder*.

Data are written to a disk using the same procedures as those used in the reading process. To check for accuracy, some disk devices automatically read each piece of data after it has been written to the disk.

Some disk drives allow the pack to be removed. These are called *removable disk drives.* Some disks have fixed read/write heads. This means that there is a separate read/write head for every track across the surface of the disk. Although this is very expensive, it means that no movement is required by the access arm. This therefore allows quicker access to data than the removable read/write heads. We shall be discussing the ways in which the computer accesses data from the storage devices in a later chapter.

The read/write heads can be positioned immediately over any piece of data on the disk. This means that if the computer knows where a particular piece of information is on the disk pack, the information can be retrieved with the minimum of delay.

Other advantages of hard disks are that data can be transferred to and from the CPU at high speed (up to 1.5 million characters per second) and the disks can hold in excess of one thousand million characters.

On the negative side, disk storage tends to be expensive and the devices are very sensitive to external conditions. Most hard disk drives require an air-conditioned, dust-free environment (see Figure 6.27), the reasoning being obvious when one looks at the fine tolerance between the read/write heads and the disk surface.

In most modern disk drives the disk, access arm, and read/write heads are combined in a sealed module. This type of drive is known as a *Winchester* and the sealed unit is not normally removable. These drives cost less and are more reliable than other drives because operators do not handle the disks and the sealed unit keeps the disk free from contamination. All hard disks found on microcomputers are of the Winchester variety.

The *floppy disk* is a cheaper and slower removable version of the hard disk developed for microcomputers. It is gradually being superseded by the 3.5 inch inflexible disk known as the *stiffy* which is more robust and can store more information.

FIGURE 6.27. Comparative size of magnetic disk contaminants.

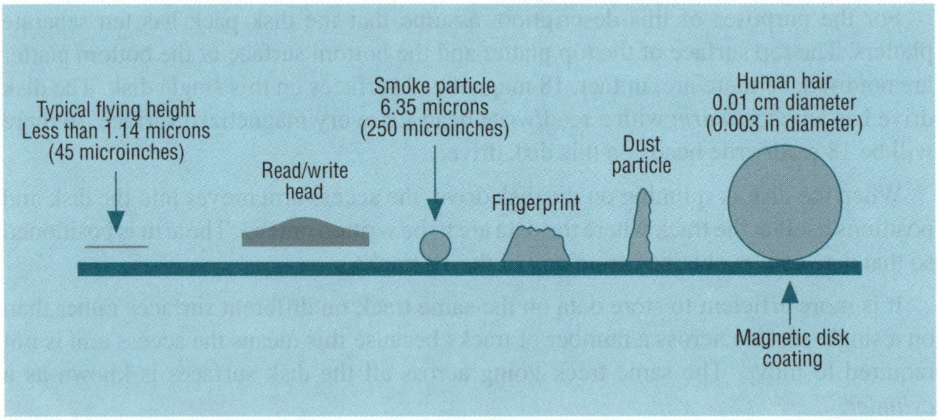

6.5.2 Magnetic tape devices

We have discussed magnetic tapes in the earlier section on input devices. While the disk has overtaken magnetic tape as the most popular method of storing data in a computer, tape is still used extensively — in particular for keeping archive copies of important files.

The data are coded so that each character is recorded as a series of tiny magnetic spots across the seven or nine tracks. Thousands of characters can be recorded in a single centimetre of tape (see Figure 6.28). As with a tape recorder, the tape can be overwritten and hundreds of passes are possible.

To indicate where the beginning of the tape is for recording purposes, an aluminium strip called a *load point marker* is stuck to the tape after the first 6 metres or so (these 6 metres being used for threading). Similarly, the physical end of the tape is marked by another aluminium strip called the *end-of-reel marker*.

The data are read into the computer from the magnetic tape using a device called a *tape drive*. The tape drive holds the magnetic tape reel and also a second reel for taking up the read tape. The tape passes under a read/write head and the data are picked up and transferred to the CPU.

Modern tape units tend to use cassettes as they are less bulky to handle and are sealed against dust.

The main advantage of using magnetic tape storage is that it is cheap, the tapes are easily transportable from one computer to another, a small magnetic tape reel can store many millions of characters of information, and the transfer of data from magnetic tape to the CPU is extremely fast. These advantages often make the tape medium more

FIGURE 6.28. Magnetic tape.

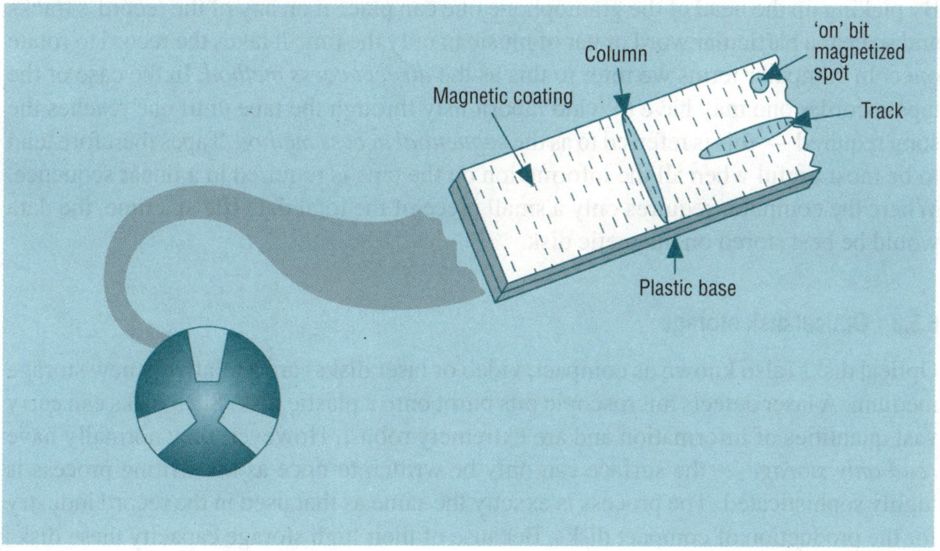

FIGURE 6.29. Sequential and direct access.

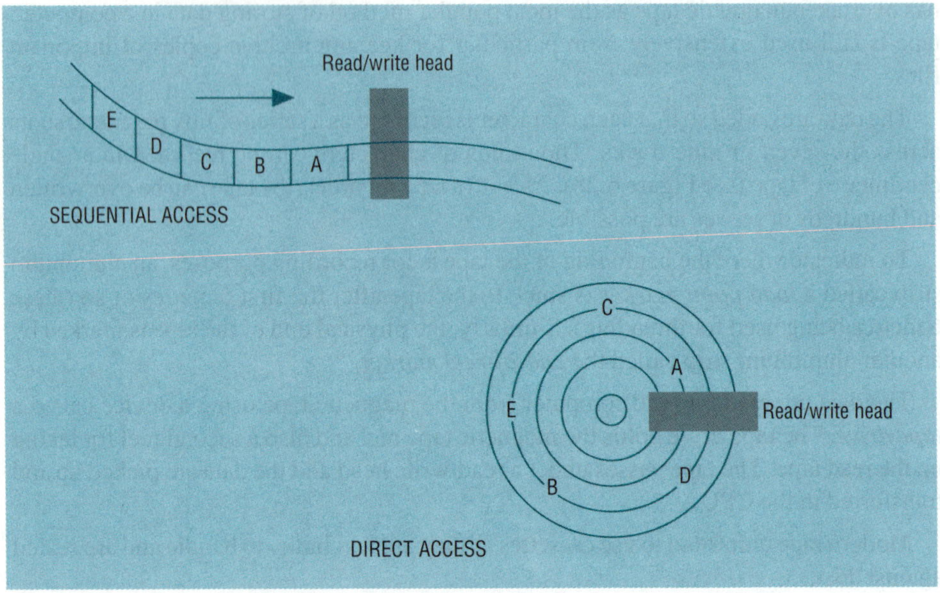

suitable than the disk pack, which tends to be quite expensive and too fragile to transport safely.

One major disadvantage of the tape, however, is that it is not efficient for accessing data in any way other than in a strictly sequential order. The difference can be seen when one compares a gramophone to a normal home tape recorder (see Figure 6.29).

By picking up the head of the gramophone one can place it on any of the record's tracks and so hear a particular word or bar of music in only the time it takes the record to rotate once. In computer terms we refer to this as the *direct access method*. In the case of the tape recorder one may have to wind laboriously through the tape until one reaches the song required — this is referred to as the *sequential access method*. Tapes therefore tend to be most useful when all the information on the tape is required in a linear sequence. Where the computer requires only a small piece of the total data file at a time, the data would be best stored on magnetic disk.

6.5.3 Optical disk storage

Optical disks (also known as compact, video or laser disks) are a relatively new storage medium. A laser detects microscopic pits burnt onto a plastic disk. Such disks can carry vast quantities of information and are extremely robust. However, they normally have *read only storage* — the surface can only be written to once as the writing process is highly sophisticated. The process is exactly the same as that used in the record industry for the production of compact disks. Because of their high storage capacity these disks are ideally suited for storing images and are currently used almost entirely in education and the entertainment industry.

6.5.4 Fixed magnetic devices

The computer industry is continually searching for better storage devices. The important factors to be considered are the speed of access to the data, the size of the device, and the cost (both to purchase and to maintain the device). Fixed magnetic devices have great advantages in speed over their moving magnetic counterparts. They are, however, more expensive in terms of their storage per character.

Magnetic core storage, dealt with in the discussion of the CPU, can be used as fixed magnetic storage. Unlike other CPU storage systems, the characters are not lost when there is a power failure. Core storage is, however, expensive to manufacture and takes up a lot of space.

Bubble memory provides another option for storing computer data. Tiny magnetic spots are created in a thin garnet wafer and are manipulated electronically to store and move data in digital form. The major advantage of this is that it is one of the few non-volatile solid state technologies.

6.5.5 Microcircuit storage

In our discussion of the CPU we examined memory technology that involved the creation of circuits on silicon chips (semiconductors). The main reason why this memory would be unsuitable for secondary storage is that it is volatile. It is possible, however, to use a burning device to permanently set the switches on silicon chips and so prevent the contents of storage being lost in a power failure. This special-purpose memory is known as *read only memory* (ROM).

The disadvantage of ROM is that while it can be read, it cannot be rewritten. It is, however, ideal for storing special programs which are not changed and which are required frequently by the CPU.

Further developments are PROM (programmable read only memory), whose content can be changed by special procedures but not by the use of standard programming processes, and EPROM (erasable programmable read only memory), which allows the switches to be reset back to zero and then programmed again.

In situations where the access to data must be almost instantaneous, the secondary storage device can be a bank of memory chips often referred to as a *cache memory*. At the start of the day the data are loaded into the cache store where they can be accessed quickly by the computer. Cache stores are really just an extension of the main memory.

6.5.6 Hierarchy of secondary storage

We have discussed a number of storage technologies in the last few chapters including random access memory (RAM) which is semiconductor storage normally found in the main storage of the CPU, ROM and fast cache storage, magnetic bubble memory, disk, tape, and optical disk storage. No one type of storage technology is supreme — each has unique advantages and disadvantages.

One normally finds a hierarchy of storage technology within a large organization with semiconductor storage offering fast random access to data when it is required while, further down the hierarchy, fixed disk technology will offer access to large volumes of data at an acceptable response time and cost. Finally, at the furthest end of the hierarchy we find magnetic tape and optical disk technologies that provide vast storage facilities at very low cost, but require a fairly lengthy delay before the data can be accessed. This type of storage is ideal for backup and archival purposes where data must be retained but are seldom required.

6.5.7 Conclusion

Over the past decade there has been a strong trend towards direct access storage, and in particular magnetic disk, as computer users require a particular item of data with the minimum of delay. Magnetic tape, once the common form of data storage, has now been relegated to taking backup copies of computer files for security and historical purposes.

The new challenge for hardware manufacturers in the 1990s is to develop storage devices capable of handling the huge files required for multimedia applications. For example, approximately 200 typed pages could fit on a double density 5.25 inch floppy disk with a capacity of 360 kilobytes. A single screen frame of animated colour video would use over one megabyte of storage. Given that the image is refreshed at a rate of 25 frames per second, a minute of video would require over a gigobyte of storage which is beyond the capacity of all but the largest magnetic and optical disks.

The following table summarizes the major features of storage devices covered in this section.

FIGURE 6.30. Secondary storage devices — summary of major features.

Magnetic disk	Fast, direct access for on-line storage. Expensive and sensitive to environment.
Magnetic tape	Sequential access only. Off-line storage, high capacity. Used for back-up/archives.
Optical disk	Very high capacity, mostly read only. Sophisticated indexing techniques.
5.25" floppy disk	Inexpensive; removable; ideal for microcomputers; vulnerable to loss of data.
3.5" stiffy disk	As per floppy disk but more robust.
Tape streamer	Used for backing up hard disks.
Bubble memory	Non-volatile electronic storage; future uncertain.
ROM	Fast access; limited capacity; expensive. Read only.

PROM	Write Once, Read Many times (WORM) version of the ROM chip.
EPROM	Same as ROM except that contents can be erased and rewritten.
RAM	Very fast access read-and-write storage; volatile and expensive.

REVIEW QUESTIONS

1. Draw a diagram depicting the major components of an electronic digital computer.
2. Briefly describe how a CPU functions.
3. How would you code the number 9 in binary, octal, and hexadecimal?
4. Why are some numeric values stored in packed format?
5. What is a *parity bit* and what purpose does it serve?
6. Input devices can be classified into three major groupings. Identify these classifications and give examples of devices in each category.
7. What peripheral devices would you expect to find attached to:
   a) a mainframe computer;
   b) a stand-alone microcomputer?
8. Name four different types of printer and identify the major strengths and weaknesses of each type.
9. What is the main advantage of using magnetic disk storage rather than magnetic tape? Give reasons why magnetic tape storage is used at all.
10. Give reasons why we don't use the same storage technology for secondary storage as we do for main storage in the CPU.

SELECTED REFERENCES AND RECOMMENDED READING

McKeown, P. G. 1986. *Living with Computers.* Orlando, Florida: Harcourt Brace Jovanovich.

O'Brien, J. A. 1991. *Introduction to Information Systems in Business Management.* Sixth edition. Boston: Irwin.

CHAPTER 7 Computer classification

7.1 INTRODUCTION

So far we have dealt with computers as if they were a single common group of machines. In fact, they come in a great many shapes and sizes. There are a number of special-purpose machines, including analog computers (used for applications such as process control) and scientific machines used by organizations such as the military and weather-forecasting bureaux.

On the commercial side computers have been classified into three groups. These are the *mainframe*, the *minicomputer* and the *microcomputer*. This chapter describes the origins of each and then takes a closer look at the microcomputer.

7.2 MAINFRAME COMPUTERS

The larger classes of commercial computers fall into the *mainframe* category. The name 'mainframe' originates from the fact that the central processing unit is normally housed in its own box separate from the peripheral devices. Owing to their size, all computers prior to about 1965 could be classified as mainframe machines.

7.3 MINICOMPUTERS

As a result of changes in machine architecture in the early 1960s it became possible to build a range of smaller commercially viable computers. These became known as *minicomputers* and the first machine was marketed by the Digital Equipment Corporation (DEC) in 1965.

The arrival of the minicomputer was a major breakthrough. It meant that computing power was available to many organizations that were previously unable to afford the giant mainframes.

7.4 MICROCOMPUTERS

With the advent of *large-scale integration* (LSI) and *very large-scale integration* (VLSI) came the very powerful microprocessor chip. Early silicon chips (around 1970) were used for calculators, watches, and even washing machines and motor carburettors. The computer industry quickly saw the potential of these processors and, by adding memory, a keyboard, a monitor, and disk drives, it created the microcomputer (see Figure 7.1). The definition of a microcomputer could, therefore, be a 'computer built around a single microprocessor chip'.

Microcomputer architecture is different from that of the minicomputer and the mainframe. The central feature of any microcomputer is the *bus* (see Figure 7.2) which is merely the channel through which data and control information pass to travel from one part of the machine to another.

The design of a microcomputer is *modular* (it consists of self-contained units). It is often referred to as *open architecture* because it allows the machine to adapt to the needs of its user. Each computer is sold with a main circuit card, referred to as the *mother board*, incorporating a microprocessor and containing enough main memory (made up of RAM chips) to support the required processing (see Figures 7.3 and 7.4).

FIGURE 7.1. Components of a microcomputer.

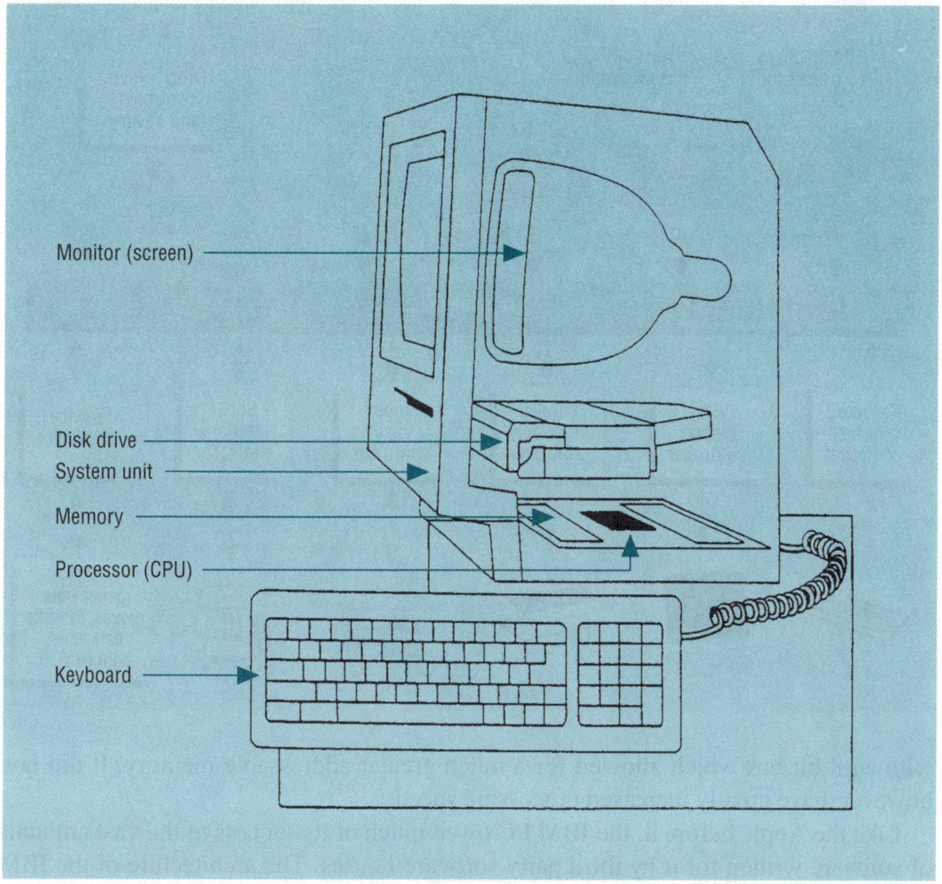

A commercial machine is likely to have, at the very least, a keyboard, printer, video display and floppy disk drives for off-line storage. These devices come in many different shapes and sizes and so the required interface card is plugged into the systems bus to connect the device to the computer.

As the density of circuits on the microprocessor chips increases, so the chips become more powerful. There are currently three major levels of microprocessors, the 8-, 16-, and 32-bit chips. The first microprocessor chips to be widely used were the 8-bit chips. These processed data and instructions one character at a time. Two disadvantages of this design were that processing a character at a time was quite slow and the limited size of the address registers restricted main memory to a maximum of 64 000 characters. The 8-bit machine was highly successful between the years 1977 and 1981, the most popular machines being the Apple II, the Radio Shack TRS 80, and the Commodore Pet.

In October 1981, IBM entered the microcomputing arena with the announcement of its PC range. The microprocessor chip used in the PC was the Intel 8088, a 16-bit chip

FIGURE 7.2. Microcomputer architecture.

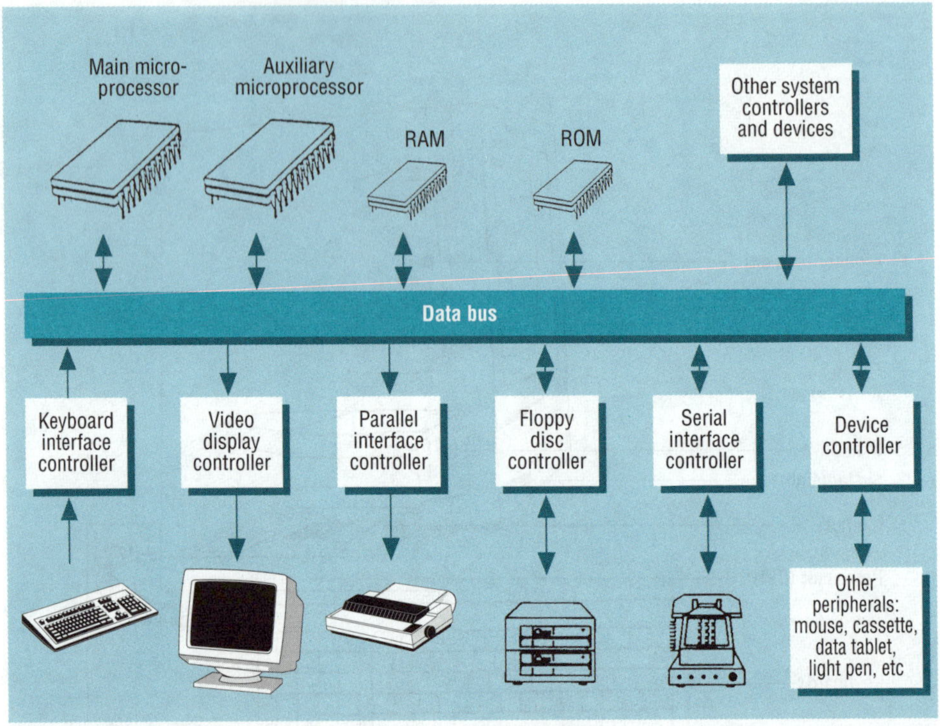

with an 8-bit bus which allowed for a much greater addressable memory. It did not, however, have greatly increased processing speed.

Like the Apple before it, the IBM PC owed much of its success to the vast amounts of software written for it by third party software-houses. The architecture of the IBM machine quickly became the industry standard with most of the main competitors either dropping out of the race or building clones of the IBM machine.

The introduction of the Intel 80286 chip in the IBM AT range saw the arrival of a true 16-bit architecture with vastly superior processing speed. The 32-bit versions (80386 and 80486 chip) have superseded the 80286 range, offering increased power to the user.

The latest IBM offering is their PS range. This range includes machines at four major levels ranging from a slightly enhanced PC to a true 32-bit processor. New options include 3.5 inch disk drives, enhanced graphics facilities, and new operating software.

FIGURE 7.3. Performance characteristics of personal computers.

Model	Processor	Max memory	Speed (MHZ)	Bus Size
PC	8088	512K	4.77	8 bit
XT	8086	1 MByte	8	16 bit
AT	80286	16 MBytes	12/16	16 bit
PS/2 50	80386	4 GBytes	25/40	32 bit

FIGURE 7.4. The microcomputer mother board.

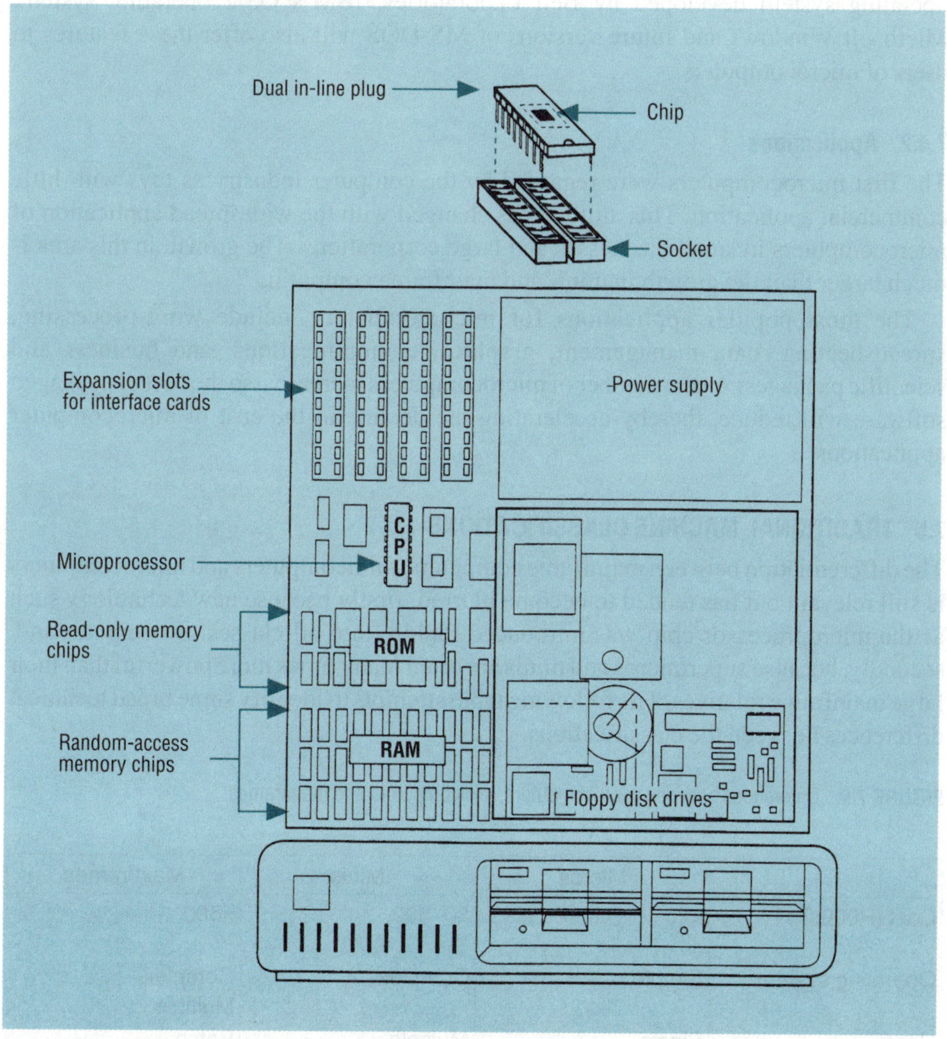

7.4.1 Microcomputer software

Early microcomputers either had no operating system or they had one that was customized for them. In the late 1970s a standard operating system for the 8-bit micro was developed and was called CP/M (control program for microcomputers).

With the introduction of the PC, IBM commissioned a software house called Microsoft to develop an operating system for their machines. This operating system, known as MS-DOS (Microsoft disk operating system) became the industry standard and almost all microcomputers use it (albeit in slightly different forms).

With a microcomputer, the operating system supports a single user in a single task environment. With the increased power of microprocessors, users are looking for operating systems with multi-user/tasking facilities. This is available under the UNIX operating system developed by Bell Laboratories. IBM's OS/2 operating system, Microsoft Windows and future versions of MS-DOS will also offer these features to users of microcomputers.

7.4.2 Applications

The first microcomputers were regarded by the computer industry as toys with little commercial application. This attitude has changed with the widespread application of microcomputers in small businesses and large corporations. The growth in this area is much larger than the growth in mini- and mainframe computing.

The most popular applications for microcomputers include word-processing, spreadsheeting, data management, graphics, communications, and business and scientific packages. As the number of microcomputers increases, so the cost of packaged software will reduce, thereby accelerating the decline in the cost of microcomputer applications.

7.5 TRADITIONAL MACHINE CLASSIFICATIONS

The differentiation between mainframe computers, minicomputers and microcomputers is still relevant but has tended to become blurred, firstly because new technology such as the microprocessor chip was introduced rapidly into all classes of computer and, secondly, because supermicros and minis are often many times more powerful than their large mainframe relatives. The following table attempts to identify some broad technical differences between the classifications.

FIGURE 7.5. Differences between microcomputers, minicomputers and mainframes.

	Micros	Minis	Mainframes
Cost (R000s)	<20	20–500	>500
Operating system	Simple	Complex	Complex
Users	Single On-line	Multiple On-line	Multiple Batch On-line
Languages	Basic dBASE LOTUS	Specials RPG	COBOL and 4GLs
Secondary storage	Diskette	Disk	Disk Tape
Memory size	<4MB	1MB–4MB	>4MB
Environment	Normal Office	Air cond.	Air cond. Power supply

Any categorization based on technical attributes is unlikely to be relevant for many years in an industry changing as fast as the computer industry. There are, however, massive differences in the ways that organizations use small machines and large ones. Large computer installations normally have a computer department to support them, including management staff and an army of data processing professionals. When the computer hardware has cost a company only R25 000 to purchase, however, it is unlikely that the company will pay large sums to have tailor-made software programs developed, special accommodation facilities constructed, or dedicated personnel assigned to it.

It is therefore much more realistic to classify computers in terms of *personal computers*, *small business systems*, and *large business systems*. The table below gives some idea of the differences between these three categories.

FIGURE 7.6. Differences between personal computers, small business systems, and large business systems.

	P/C	SBC	LBC
In-house support	None	Limited	Extensive
IS management	None	Part-time	Full-time
Software	Packages	Packages	In-house
Controls	None	Informal	Formal
Users	Large business Personal Remote users	Large business Small business	Large business
Hardware	Micro	Various	Various

Some of the security and control problems that are inherent in the smaller business systems will be discussed in a later module.

While the classifications of mini-, micro-, and mainframe computers reflected technical differences between various types of computer, and were at one time very relevant, new technology made these differences less and less apparent. It is now more appropriate to regard all hardware as being of the same family and to look at computers more in terms of their environment than in terms of their hardware characteristics.

REVIEW QUESTIONS

1. What is meant by open architecture and what type of computer is normally built to this design?
2. Identify four different types of microcomputer, explaining how each differs from the others.
3. What advantages would a personal computer have over an on-line terminal when linked to a computer network?

REFERENCE AND RECOMMENDED READING

Capron, H. L. 1992. *Essentials of Computing*. Redwood, California: Benjamin/Cummings.

CHAPTER 8 Data communications

8.1 INTRODUCTION

It is not difficult to imagine the advantages of being able to access a computer from the site of your business transactions rather than just from the site of the computer. For example, before the advent of data communications it was very difficult to check a customer's credit position prior to a transaction taking place. In banks and shops the staff had to rely on old balances from previous computer reports or outdated lists of people who were over their credit allowance. In many cases transactions were permitted to go through without any checks at all.

Today's on-line, interactive systems have changed all this. Now remote users can enter new data and interrogate the latest information with almost no delay and with no restriction on their distance from the central computer installation.

Data communication has widened the scope of commercial computing to the extent that it will soon be in every shop, office and home. It is therefore important that the student has some understanding of the hardware, software, and design considerations which go into the development of a data communications network.

8.2 BASIC COMPONENTS OF A DATA COMMUNICATIONS SYSTEM

There are six main components that make up a data communications (Datacom) system (see Figure 8.1):

- the central processing unit;
- input/output storage;
- communications channels;
- communications control devices;
- terminal devices;
- software.

8.2.1 Central processing unit

Every computer system has a CPU at its heart. This raises the issue of whether the CPU is different in any way when it is driving a data communications network. There are, in fact, a number of unique considerations to be taken into account.

The first is that most on-line systems work on the basis that the remote user should be able to access the system at any time for a varied number of applications. This means that the CPU must have some portion of its processing capacity available at all times to process incoming requests. Unlike batch systems, requests to on-line systems are difficult to schedule and the number of transactions per hour varies considerably throughout the day, making it impossible to allocate a set amount of processing power to the remote users. It is very important that the number of transactions should never be so great that the CPU is unable to handle them. This means that CPUs tend to be very large when they support large on-line networks.

Often an on-line network becomes so important in the performance of a person's day-to-day routine that he is unable to do his job without it (eg. in the case of an airline reservation system). Where a computer system is of such strategic importance there are

FIGURE 8.1. Components of a data communications system.

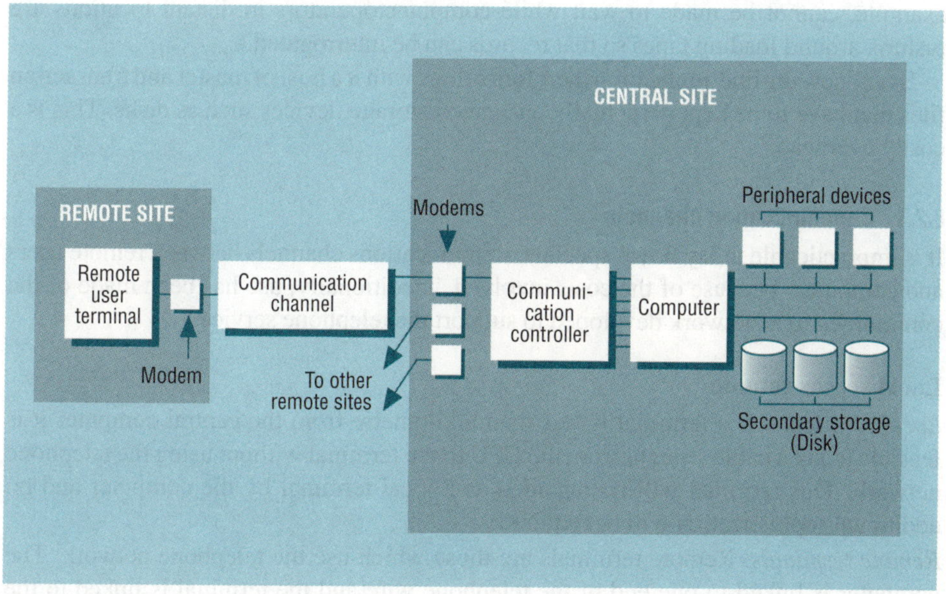

usually two CPUs so that if one malfunctions, the other can continue to support the on-line network.

A large amount of housekeeping must be carried out by the computer while it is driving an on-line network. This can place a large burden on the CPU. Often specialized hardware is added to the configuration in order to perform the housekeeping. These additional tasks will, therefore, be discussed in the section dealing with communication control devices.

So far we have thought of computers in terms of one CPU surrounded by a cluster of peripheral devices. In early on-line networks this concept did not change and the early terminals were merely remote input/output devices. With the advent of silicon chips and the microprocessor, however, remote terminals were able to do some of the work themselves and so reduce the load on the host computer.

This trend has continued so that it is quite common to find micro-, mini-, and even mainframe computers all interacting together in a single data communications network. This concept of dispersed computer processing power is called *distributed processing*.

8.2.2 Input/output storage

In batch systems the input data was processed every day, week or month, depending on the volume of transactions and the requirement for up-to-date information. In the time between these processing runs the data were not required by the computer and were stored on magnetic tape (off-line) in order to free the more expensive on-line storage (normally disk).

In a data communications environment the systems designer has no such option. All applications which could be used by one of the remote operators must have the data that will be required immediately accessible to the CPU. Customers queuing in a bank, for example, cannot be made to wait while computer operators in distant locations are rushing around loading tapes so that records can be interrogated.

Every new on-line application therefore brings with it a host of master and transaction files that have to be kept perpetually on-line on storage devices such as disks. This is a costly overhead.

8.2.3 Communication channels

It is impracticable to lay down special communications channels between remote users and computers because of the costs involved. Traditionally, use has been made of the communications network developed to support the telephone service.

Local versus remote

Local terminals. If a terminal is less than a kilometre from the central computer it is feasible to lay a cable straight from the CPU to the terminal without using the telephone network. This terminal will be regarded as a local terminal by the computer and no additional sophistication will be required.

Remote terminals. Remote terminals are those which use the telephone network. The computer is linked to one end of the telephone wire and the terminal is linked to the other. There are a number of technical issues to be resolved when considering the introduction of a data communications link and we shall look at some of the more important ones.

Communication links

There are several kinds of communication link, each having its own unique features (see Figure 8.2).

The main types of communication link are:

- *Coaxial cable.* This cable consists of a copper core enclosed within a metallic sheath to prevent electrical interference. Coaxial cable is normally used for short-distance transmissions within a building or office environment.
- *Telephone cable.* Standard voice-grade telephone lines are still the most common carriers of data communications, although they are mainly used for local connections from an office to the nearest telephone exchange. The line is normally made up of a pair of insulated copper wires wrapped around each other (commonly referred to as a *twisted pair*).
- *Microwave channels.* Over the past few years microwaves have taken over from land-lines for long-distance transmissions as they are more cost-effective. Data are transferred between microwave towers in line of sight of each other in the form of high-frequency radio waves.
- *Satellite transmission.* Communications satellites are fast becoming the most promising data communications carriers. The larger versions launched into space by the American space-shuttle will serve as relay stations for communications from any two points on the globe. Latest estimates suggest that the satellites will substantially

FIGURE 8.2. A network displaying a variety of communications links.

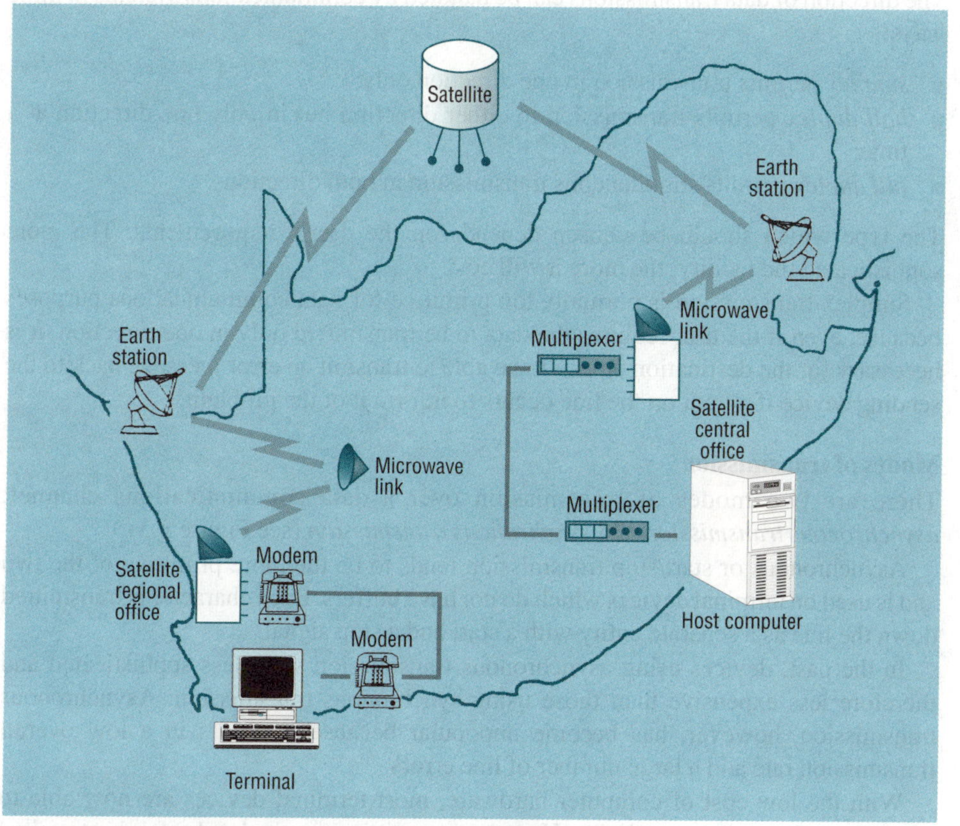

reduce the time and cost of communications compared with the current ground networks. Data are transmitted as low frequency radio waves to the satellite which has a stationary orbit. The signals are then relayed to the receiving station. At present the cost of this method of transmission is high.

- *Fibre optics.* One major problem in data transmission is that it is difficult to transmit more than a certain number of characters per second over current voice-grade telephone lines. There are, however, a number of experimental channels made from *fibre optic cables.* Lasers transmit the information thousands of times faster than other transmitters and with very few errors. The data are transmitted in digital format and so it is not necessary to translate them to analog and then back to digital (this translation process will be discussed later in the section dealing with communication control devices). This increased transmission capacity has made many communications-carriers consider the development of digital networks in which even voice transmission will be digitized. However, the massive investment that has already been made in voice-quality lines will probably not permit a rapid change-over to digital networks.

Transmission direction

The direction of data transmissions can be handled by communications systems in three ways:

- *simplex* permits transmission in one direction only;
- *half duplex* permits transmission in either direction but in only one direction at a time;
- *full duplex* permits simultaneous transmission in both directions.

The type which should be chosen depends on the user's requirements. The more sophisticated the facility, the more it will cost.

Simplex transmission is normally too primitive for data communications purposes because, even if the user requires the data to be transmitted only in one direction, it is necessary for the destination device to be able to transmit an error message back to the sending device if a fault on the line occurs to inform it of the problem.

Modes of transmission

There are two modes of transmission over a data communications channel: *asynchronous transmission* and *synchronous transmission* (see Figure 8.3).

Asynchronous or start/stop transmission tends to be the more primitive of the two and is used on terminal devices which do not have buffers. Each character is transmitted down the line as a separate entity with a start and a stop signal.

In the past, devices using asynchronous transmission were less sophisticated and therefore less expensive than those using synchronous transmission. Asynchronous transmission, however, has become unpopular because it results in a low overall transmission rate and a large number of line errors.

With the low cost of computer hardware, most terminal devices are now able to support synchronous transmission. Here the transmitting terminal and receiving terminal are synchronized and characters are sent along the line in a continuous stream or block. There is, therefore, no pause between characters and no start or stop bits. This provides more efficient line-utilization.

Line usage

There are three major categories of line usage:

- dial-up;
- leased;
- SAPONET.

In many circumstances the remote terminals are not required to be connected to the host computer for more than a few minutes a day and it would be an expensive overhead to have a continuous link between the two nodes. In these cases a *dial-up line* is suitable. Here the terminal operator merely picks up a telephone, dials a number which links into the host computer, and places the handset into a box called an *acoustic coupler*. The acoustic coupler is linked to the terminal and this enables the data transmission to take place.

FIGURE 8.3. Asynchronous and synchronous data transmission.

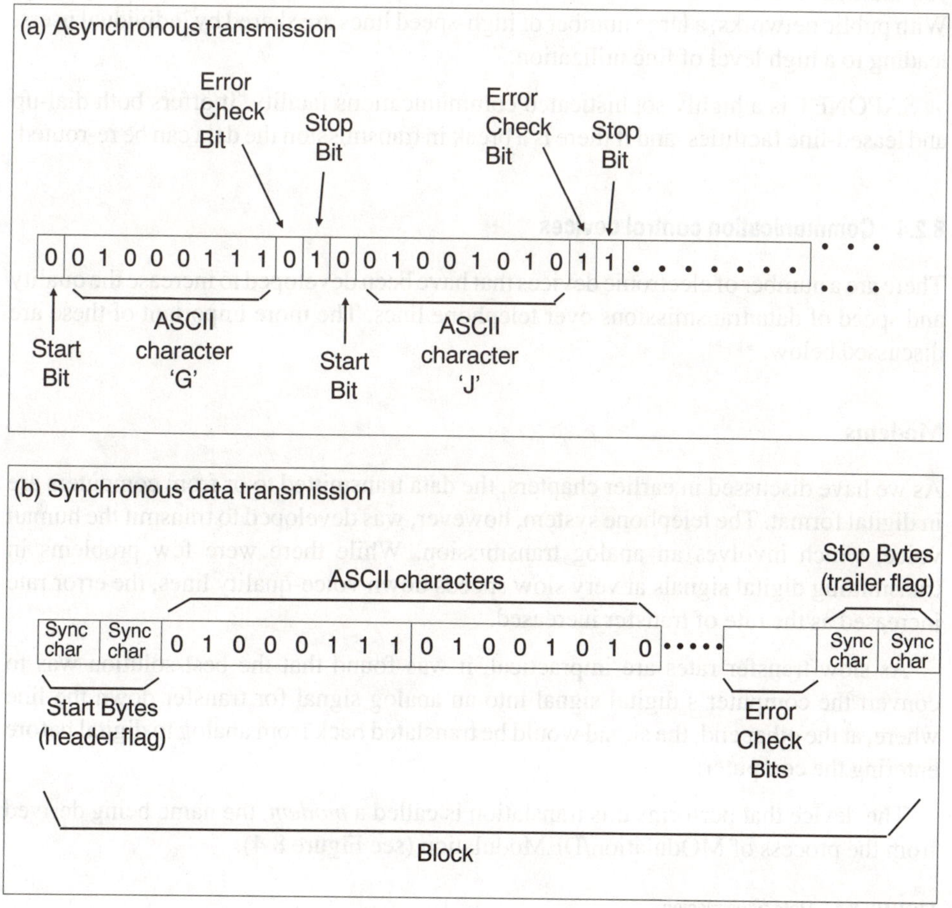

When the connection is no longer required, the handset can be returned to the telephone. The user is charged in the same way as if a normal telephone call had been made. These lines are often referred to as *switched lines* because the transmission must pass through the telephone switching service.

An alternative is the *leased, or dedicated, line*. Here the terminal and the host computer are permanently connected. The main advantage of having a permanent line is that the telephone department will try to ensure that the line is relatively clear so that there is less chance of interference and, therefore, of errors in data transmission. In addition there is a standard monthly charge for the line which can work out cheaper than the cost of normal telephone calls.

In most developed countries there are one or more *public data communications networks* or *public carriers*. In South Africa this facility is marketed by TELKOM and is called SAPONET.

With dial-up and leased lines, organizations are responsible for their own data communications and take the risk that the telephone lines may not function adequately. With public networks, a large number of high-speed lines are shared by individual users, leading to a high level of line utilization.

SAPONET is a highly sophisticated communications facility. It offers both dial-up and leased-line facilities, and if there is a break in transmission the data can be re-routed.

8.2.4 Communication control devices

There are a number of electronic devices that have been developed to increase the quality and speed of data transmissions over telephone lines. The more important of these are discussed below.

Modems

As we have discussed in earlier chapters, the data transmitted to or from computers are in digital format. The telephone system, however, was developed to transmit the human voice, which involves an analog transmission. While there were few problems in transmitting digital signals at very slow speeds down voice-quality lines, the error rate increased as the rate of transfer increased.

As slow transfer rates are impractical, it was found that the best solution was to convert the computer's digital signal into an analog signal for transfer down the line where, at the other end, the signal would be translated back from analog to digital before entering the computer.

The device that performs this translation is called a *modem*, the name being derived from the process of MOdulation/DEModulation (see Figure 8.4).

FIGURE 8.4. Data transmission.

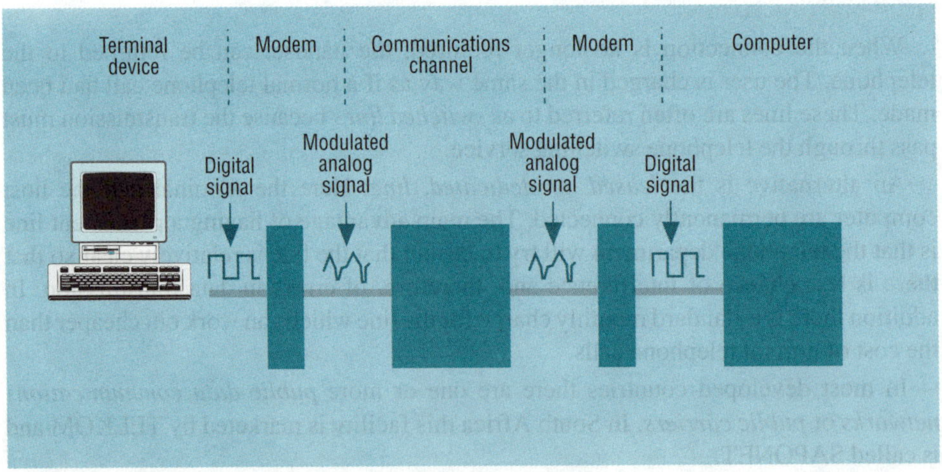

Multiplexors

One of the major problems in communications is how to get maximum usage out of the transmission line. While each terminal should have access to a line when it is needed, it would be expensive, especially with long-distance lines, to have a separate channel for each terminal.

The multiplexor (Mux) accepts a number of lines in at a remote location and compresses all the transmissions down a single line. At the other end, another multiplexor will reverse this process.

There are a number of methods of multiplexing. The two most common are:

- *time division* — increasing the rate of the transmission down the single line to the sum of the speeds of the individual input lines (see Figure 8.5);
- *frequency division* — each input line is allocated a frequency band and the various signals are transmitted simultaneously at different frequencies (see Figure 8.6).

Concentrators

The concentrator is similar to a multiplexor but is more sophisticated. Terminal operators do not always keep a constant flow of data passing through the line: a concentrator is able to detect a lack of activity and pass any spare transmission time to terminals that require it. Both the multiplexor and the concentrator are available in varying levels of sophistication and in many cases they have their own error detection and correction facilities.

Communications controller

This is a specialized minicomputer or microcomputer which controls the data communications network, performing a number of specific functions that the CPU is unable to perform. While these devices can carry out a number of functions, they are mainly used for the detection of errors on the lines and for contacting remote terminals to determine if they are in a position to send or receive messages.

Front-end processors

Even with the assistance of a communications controller, a computer often loses up to 30% of its processing capacity by performing the housekeeping functions necessary to support an on-line network.

The alternative is to place a smaller computer between the controller and the host mainframe and to put it in charge of all data communications activity, thereby freeing the host computer for other tasks. Some of the duties that the front-end processor can perform are: controlling access to the network, assigning priority to incoming and outgoing messages, and logging all data communications activities.

8.2.5 Terminal devices

Many different devices can be linked to a computer. These include the standard CRT, special-purpose terminals such as point-of-sale and banking terminals, and even other micro-, mini- and mainframe computers. Additional computers may create a hierarchy

FIGURE 8.5. Time division multiplexing.

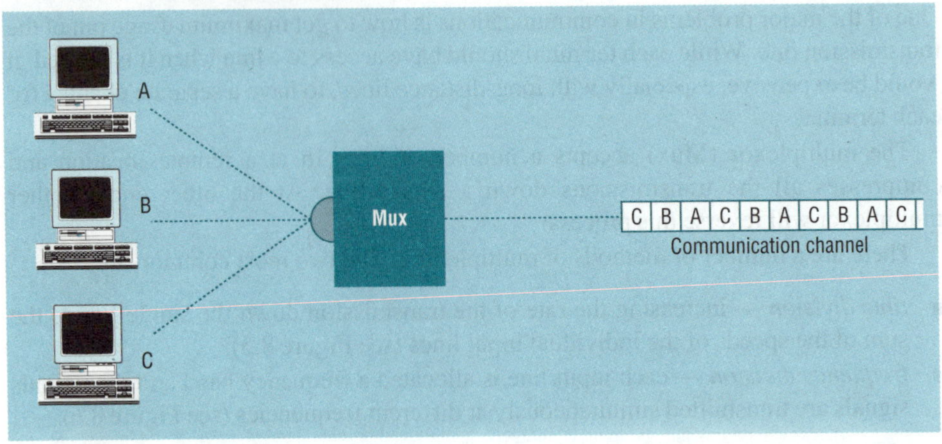

FIGURE 8.6. Frequency division multiplexing.

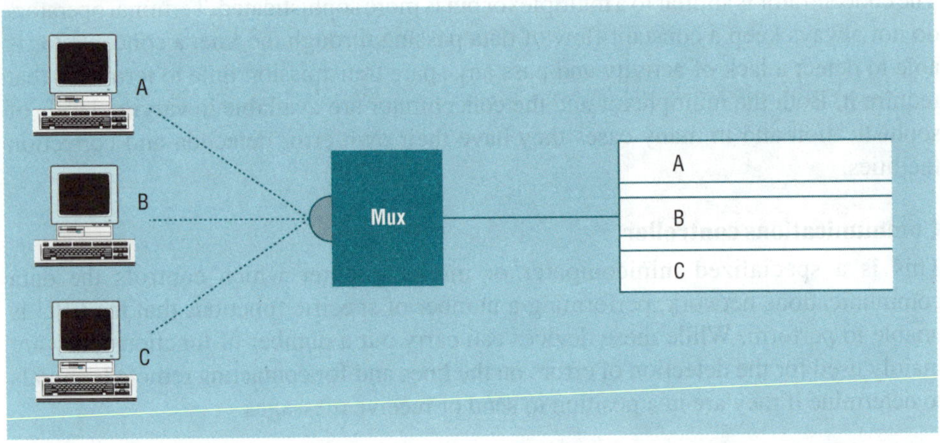

— microcomputers which are connected to the host mainframe, for example, may themselves have remote terminals.

8.2.6 Software

Apart from the normal software required in any computer, the host machine will also require a control program to oversee its data communications activities. This program (called the *teleprocessing monitor* or *TP monitor*) is involved in activities such as connecting and disconnecting communications links, forming queues, routing messages in the network, and logging statistics concerning errors and general communications activities. Its more mundane duties, such as error detection and correction, will depend on the level of sophistication of its communication control devices.

These specialized software programs will reside in the main memory of the CPU and will therefore represent a substantial overhead in terms of both CPU storage and processing cycles.

8.3 PROTOCOLS

Data communication protocols can be defined as *the rules for the exchange of data between devices on a network.*

When a terminal wishes to transmit a message in a network it needs to know if the network is already busy. It must also know whether the message has been received after it has been transmitted (see Figure 8.7).

The rules concerning how data should be transmitted in a network depend on many factors such as the speed, direction and mode of transmission, and the network's size and configuration. There are a number of standard protocols which have been developed

FIGURE 8.7. A typical data exchange using the BISYNC protocol.

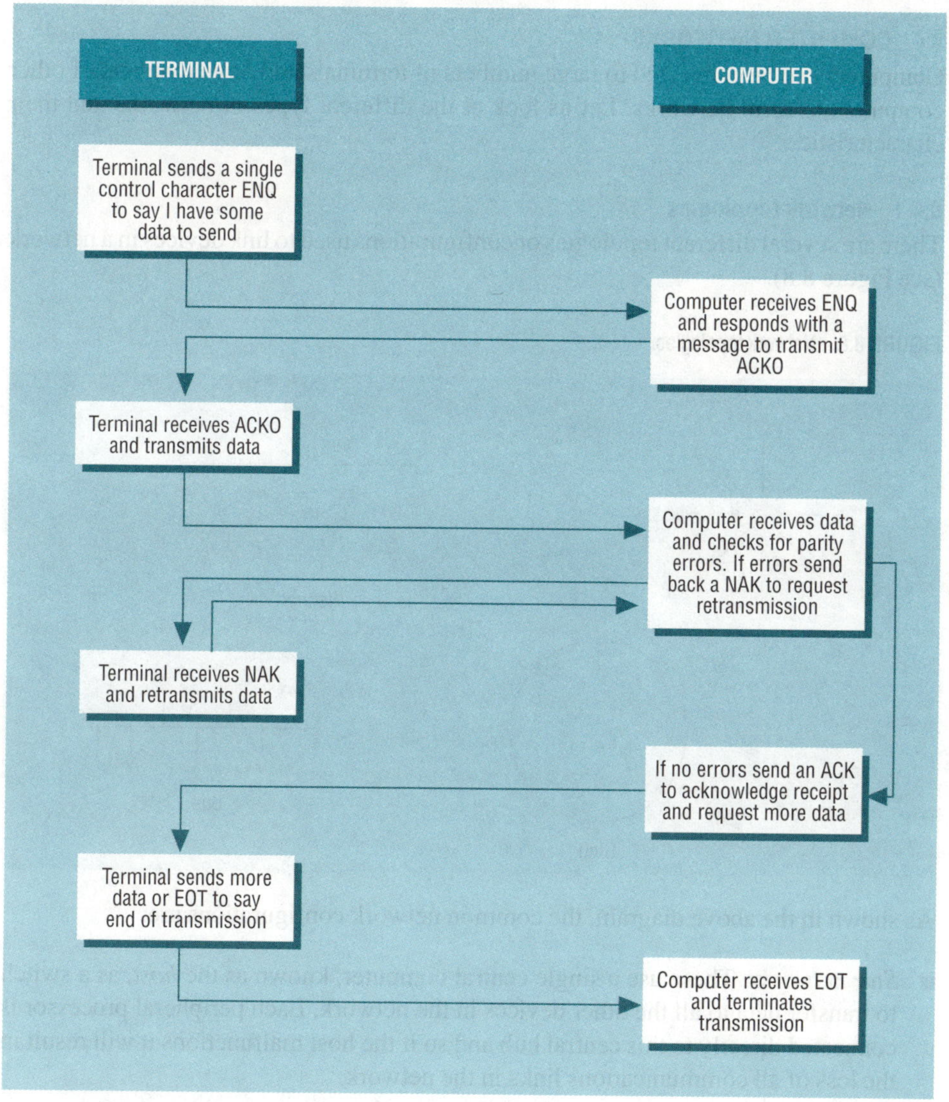

to control network communications. As the world's computers and computer networks gradually come together into one huge communications network, so the need for standard rules of communication increases.

In the past certain companies with a large share of the market set their own communications standards in order to lock users into their particular equipment. Today, however, many of the standards organizations are strong enough — and have enough government backing — to enforce their own standards. In the communications area the International Standards Organization (ISO) has defined a set of communications protocols called the *open systems inter-connection* (OSI) model. This model has gained wide acceptance in the computer and telecommunications industries and new protocols and equipment are being designed and built to comply with its specifications.

8.4 COMPUTER NETWORKS

Computers can be connected to large numbers of terminals and large numbers of other computers to form networks. Let us look at the different types of networks and their characteristics.

8.4.1 Network topologies

There are several different topologies or configurations used to link devices in a network (see Figure 8.8).

FIGURE 8.8. Network topologies.

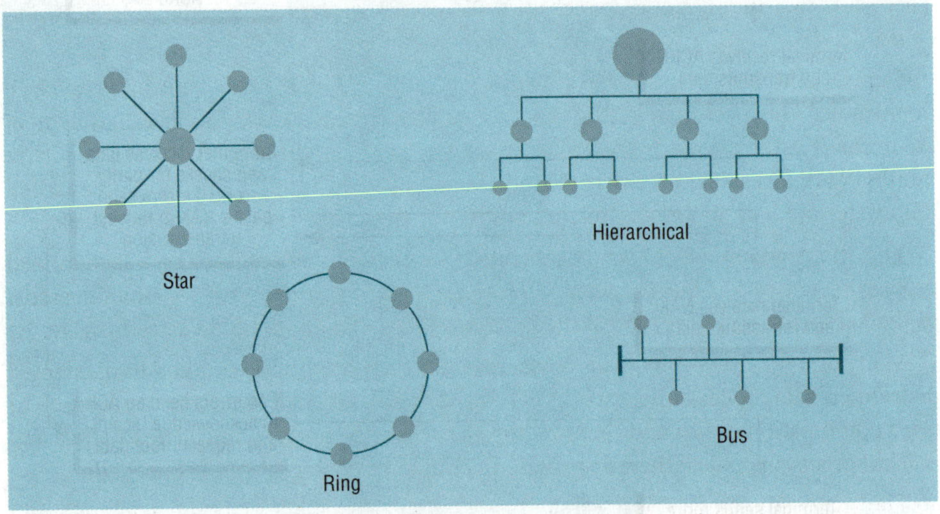

As shown in the above diagram, the common network configurations are:

- *Star networks*. These use a single central computer, known as the *host*, as a switch to transfer data to all the other devices in the network. Each peripheral processor is connected directly to this central hub and so if the host malfunctions it will result in the loss of all communications links in the network.

- *Hierarchical networks.* Like the star network, there is a main (host) computer that controls the communication links to a number of secondary devices. Many of these devices, however, may well be computers themselves, communicating with devices at a lower level in the hierarchy. This structure is commonly referred to as *distributed data processing*: processing is done at a local level and results are summarized and transmitted up the hierarchy.
- *Ring networks.* Each device, whether it be a computer or peripheral device, is connected to a circular communications channel. No single device controls the network and all the devices are normally a similar size and work at a similar speed.
- *Bus networks.* These are very similar to the ring configuration except that the channel is a single line with transmissions passing up and down it rather than a ring with all transmissions being made in the same direction.

8.5 WIDE AREA NETWORKS (WANs)

Wide area networks normally connect computers and terminals over a large geographical area using the communications hardware and software discussed earlier in this chapter. Networks in large organizations are used to support such applications as electronic funds transfers, point of sale systems, home shopping, and airline booking systems.

8.5.1 Centralized versus distributed data processing

There are two major philosophies that dictate the design of a wide area network: *centralized data processing* and *distributed processing*.

Centralized networks are controlled by a single computer, normally a large mainframe. This performs all the processing. The terminals and peripheral equipment are normally dumb devices that transmit data to and from the central processor. Where intelligent devices such as microcomputers are attached to such a network, they often require terminal emulation software in order for them to appear as dumb terminals.

The main advantage to an organization in the implementation of a centralized processing network is that the control of the major computing facility — including most of the hardware, software, and skilled personnel — is likely to be easier to manage.

Many organizations, however, have taken the alternative approach and implemented distributed data processing networks. These normally follow a hierarchical approach or use a combination of star and ring topologies to place computers both at head office and at local processing sites, thereby providing computer power where it is needed.

The main advantage of distributed processing is that the data are gathered, and information is generated, close to the location of business. Only summary information necessary for senior management control is passed up the network hierarchy. Users become more responsible and more aware of the role of the computer in their business. At the same time the cost of transmitting vast quantities of data over many miles of communication lines is vastly reduced. Finally, various parts of the hierarchy can operate in isolation and so the network becomes less reliant on a single controlling machine.

8.5.2 Line configuration

Wide area networks can use a number of configurations to link devices on a network.

- *Point-to-point.* In this configuration a line is dedicated to linking the computer to each individual device. Point-to-point is normally used for dial-up or switch lines.
- *Multi-drop.* Where an organization has a number of remote terminals that are required to be on-line to the computer at all times during the working day, the point-to-point configuration method would be very expensive. An alternative approach would be to link a number of devices on a single line (with or without the use of a multiplexor) and have transmissions dropped off at the required devices.

The multi-drop technique reduces the costs of the line but it requires some sort of control to ensure that terminals do not try to utilize the line at the same time. The two multi-drop protocols which are commonly used are *polling* and *contention.* In the polling approach, the host computer polls the various terminals to ask them whether they would like to transmit, and holds the line open for them if they have some data to send. With the contention approach, terminals transmit data if the line is not in use but must wait while other transmissions are being made.

8.5.3 Public networks

Many organizations need to communicate with large numbers of users spread over a wide area. In many instances the users must be linked to the network during working hours but the *volume* of traffic is too low to justify dedicated lines. One example here might be where a lecturer at the University of Cape Town would like to be able to communicate with other academics nationally and internationally using electronic mail.

One solution to this problem is to use a *public network* — a basic communications service offered to organizations and businesses. The communications infrastructure required to offer this service is usually government-owned or operated by public companies. In South Africa TELKOM is the common carrier, linking up with specialized carriers in areas such as satellite transmission. In many instances the basic service on a public network is enhanced with additional services to the user and becomes known as a *value added network* (VAN). In South Africa there are a number of public networks, the most important being SAPONET, DIGINET and BELTEL.

SAPONET is a public network operated by TELKOM. The two main services offered are SAPONET-C, providing a discrete communications path between two or more users, and SAPONET-P which provides packet-switching facilities. With the X.25, or *packet switching protocol*, users transmit the data from their computer or terminal via the standard telephone system to a switching centre where it is encapsulated in 128-character pieces and transmitted to the required address. As its name implies, this protocol reduces every transmission to a series of little packets. Users can remain connected to the local switch but they are only charged for the number of packages transmitted. In this way users receive a service with the convenience of a leased line at a cost which is close to that of a dial-up facility.

DIGINET, the South African digital data network, began service in 1986 and uses a combination of optical fibre cable, digital microwave, and coaxial cable for major inter-city routes. The network allows users to transmit data in digital form rather than using conventional analog transmission. The major advantages of this network are cost (modems are not required), a reduction in transmission errors (DIGINET error rate is said to be 1% of conventional analog transmission), and a higher transmission rate.

BELTEL is the local videotex system offered by TELKOM. This value added network is an electronic communications system that offers users access to a host of computer services and data bases. Network users are able to access BELTEL by connecting their personal computer to the telephone jack using an interface card and modem. They can then use the services on offer such as news (international affairs, sport and weather), commercial banking, home shopping, and hotel and travel bookings. Service providers can lease pages from the BELTEL database to advertise their products. They can also link their mainframe to the network using a *gateway* to provide a more sophisticated service.

8.6 LOCAL AREA NETWORKS (LANs)

LANS are used to connect a number of devices within a limited geographical area, such as an office block or factory. While there are certain advantages in being able to communicate between offices in a particular department, the major justification for LANS is for users to share common peripheral devices, computer software, and data.

8.6.1 Network configurations

The topology of a local area network, like that of a wide area network, can vary considerably.

- *Star networks.* Like the WAN, the LAN can be controlled by a single processor or host machine. This device, when it is used in a LAN, is known as the *server* and it normally controls the secondary storage and output devices. While the network will be made up of many computers capable of processing in a stand-alone mode, they will rely on the server for network communication.
- *Token ring.* One popular LAN configuration proposed by IBM is the token ring approach. The network has a ring topology and devices communicate by passing their message to the LAN from where it is transmitted to the required address. To ensure that transmissions do not collide and that data are not lost, an electronic token is passed around the network and picked up by any device wishing to transmit. The token is held during the period of transmission and then released back into the network for further use. Devices can only transmit while they hold the token.
- *Carrier sense multiple-access with collision detection* (CSMA/CD). This protocol was made popular by Ethernet and operates on bus and ring topologies. The system works on the basis that all devices on the network must listen for any sign of traffic prior to transmission. If two devices transmit at exactly the same time, and as a result the communications collide and are lost, the sending node will not receive an acknowledgement that the data have arrived and will therefore transmit again. This protocol is simple and inexpensive but is inefficient when there is a large amount of traffic on the network.

REVIEW QUESTIONS

1. Explain what modems are used for.
2. Differentiate between simplex, half duplex, and full duplex transmission.
3. What is a multiplexor and how does it work?
4. Explain the difference between point-to-point and multi-drop communication lines.
5. How does the star network topology differ from that of ring networks?
6. What is a protocol and why are standards important?
7. Explain why synchronous transmission is normally faster than asynchronous transmission.
8. What is a LAN and why is it different from a WAN?
9. What are the major differences between centralized and distributed data processing facilities?
10. What is a TP monitor and what are its major functions?

SELECTED REFERENCES AND RECOMMENDED READING

Schultheis, R. and Sumner, M. 1989. *Management information Systems — The Manager's View.* Homewood: Irwin

O'Brien, J. A. 1991. *Introduction to Information Systems in Business Management.* Sixth edition. Homewood: Irwin

CHAPTER 9 Software technology

9.1 INTRODUCTION

In the previous chapter we discussed the hardware which makes up a computer system. Computer hardware is not very different from any other complex piece of machinery. The power of the computer lies in its ability to follow a sequence of instructions provided to it in the form of a computer program. Such a program is referred to as *computer software*. Software is generally classified into two categories: *systems software* and *application software*. Before we look more closely at this distinction we need to know a little more about computer programs and how they have developed.

9.2 THE STORED PROGRAM CONCEPT

Very early computers did not use programs as we understand them today. The instructions to perform a particular task were *hard-wired* into the machine: they were built into the circuitry, and when the computer was required to perform a different task the appropriate changes had to be made to the electrical circuits. This made the computer very inflexible: in a commercial environment it would be required to do a large number of different tasks on a regular basis.

The concept of the stored program was developed by John von Neumann. His proposal was that computer programs should be stored electronically in the memory of the processor. By loading different sets of instructions, the computer should be able to do different tasks with no alteration to its hardware. The concept of software being separate from the hardware was a fundamental breakthrough.

9.3 MACHINE LANGUAGE

The computer was designed to carry out a limited number of basic operations. It could, for example, be instructed to read data into its memory, perform arithmetic on those data, make logical deductions about certain conditions, and output the results of its computations. One could therefore program a computer to perform any task by simply breaking the task down into its basic operations and then instructing the computer to perform those operations in the correct sequence. Each instruction starts with an *operation code* which tells the computer which activity it must perform, followed by an *operand* or *parameter code* giving more detail where necessary. The following machine language instructions add two numbers together.

OPERATION CODE	OPERAND	
1010	11010	load number into store
1011	11001	add second number to store
1100	11011	save result

When program instructions are written at the level that the computer can understand, they are known as *machine language instructions*. It would seem that to write a computer program, one merely has to learn the fundamental activities that a particular machine can perform and write a set of machine language instructions to do the task required. However, this is not as easy as it seems.

Machine language has a number of serious drawbacks:

- Machine language differs between computers, so programs and programming skills are not easily transported between machines.
- There are a large number of basic activities involved in even the easiest procedure such as adding two numbers together, as can be seen from the example above.
- Finally, the format of machine language is very 'unfriendly'. Both the operation codes and the following operands are reflected as binary numbers and, consequently, it is almost impossible to identify what a program will do without very careful evaluation of the code.

9.4 MACRO

The development of the MACRO was the first in a long line of techniques developed to make the job of the programmer easier and more efficient. The MACRO was simply a set of machine instructions to perform a standard task. It enabled the programmer to handle groups of instructions and so perform the programming task more quickly.

9.5 ASSEMBLER LANGUAGE

One of the major reasons why machine language was so difficult to use was because all instructions were expressed as numbers in their binary form. ASSEMBLER language is very similar to machine language in structure, but the operation codes and operands are represented in a more usable form. The previous example is rewritten in ASSEMBLER language to illustrate the difference:

OPERATION CODE	OPERAND	
LD	GROSS	load gross into store
AD	TOTAL	add total to gross
ST	NEWTOT	store result in newtot

Obviously the computer cannot understand ASSEMBLER language and so a special translation program which accepts ASSEMBLER language instructions and converts them into machine language had to be developed. This is also known as an ASSEMBLER.

9.6 HIGH LEVEL LANGUAGES

Writing programs in assembler language was still a very laborious operation, but the first major step in the evolution of programming language had been taken: the recognition that computers did not have to be programmed in machine language, and that statements could be translated into machine language prior to execution. The programmer no longer had to be concerned with each simple machine operation. As long as the programmer could define all the activities required to perform a certain task, the translating program could break this down into individual machine operations.

The late 1950s and early 1960s brought a flood of what were termed *high level languages* onto the market. The two languages that gained the widest recognition were:

- FORTRAN (FORmula TRANslator), a program with a notation very similar to algebra, designed to solve scientific problems;
- COBOL (COmmon Business Oriented Language), a language for business applications which uses sentences that are very similar to English.

These languages heralded a major breakthrough in the programming process because they were easier to learn and use than the earlier assembler and machine languages. Programs written in these languages could be used on many different computers simply by taking the high level language code and translating it to the required machine code. Translators for high level languages were known as *compilers*.

The change from ASSEMBLER to COBOL and FORTRAN did have one disadvantage. The high level languages tended to generate many machine language instructions, some of which were only necessary under certain circumstances. High level language programs tended, therefore, to operate more slowly than their predecessors. In an environment where hardware was expensive and programming skills were not, it was often more efficient to write programs in assembler than, for instance, in COBOL.

Today this is seldom the case as programming skills are costly, the cost of hardware is continuing to decline, and compiler translation has become more effective.

There are many high level languages in use today, each with its specific advantages and disadvantages. We shall now look at the more important of these languages.

9.6.1 COBOL (COmmon Business Oriented Language)

COBOL is the most popular business programming language. In 1957 the American Department of Defence, together with other computer users and manufacturers, formed a group called the CODASYL (Conference of Data Systems Languages) Committee. It aimed to develop a programming language which was well-suited to solving business problems and which could be used on any computer. By the early 1960s the use of COBOL was widespread, mainly due to the fact that the American government would only purchase computers that could be programmed in COBOL.

The following COBOL code is taken from a payroll program and illustrates how the language would handle a salary calculation:

```
IF HOURS-WORKED GREATER THAN 42

MULTIPLY HOURLY-WAGE BY 42 GIVING BASIC-PAY
  SUBTRACT 42 FROM HOURS-WORKED GIVING OVERTIME-HOURS
  MULTIPLY HOURLY-WAGE BY 1.5 GIVING OVERTIME-RATE
  MULTIPLY OVERTIME-HOURS BY OVERTIME-RATE
     GIVING OVERTIME-PAY
  ADD BASIC-PAY, OVERTIME PAY GIVING PAYROLL
ELSE
   MULTIPLY HOURLY-WAGE BY HOURS-WORKED GIVING PAYROLL.
```

9.6.2 FORTRAN (FORmula TRANslator)

FORTRAN was developed at much the same time as COBOL. FORTRAN is primarily used by engineers, scientists and mathematicians. The language handles calculations in a format that is very similar to algebra and has many built-in arithmetical functions. Unlike COBOL, FORTRAN does not handle large volumes of data efficiently and is therefore not suitable for commercial applications. Below is an illustration of the same payroll problem written in FORTRAN code:

```
20 IF (HOURS.GT.42) GO TO 30
   PAYROLL=FLOAT(HOURS)*WAGE
   GO TO 40
30 PAYROLL=(42*WAGE)+(FLOAT(HOURS-42)*(1.5*WAGE))
```

9.6.3 PL/1 (Programming Language 1)

PL/1 was developed by IBM as a general purpose high level language. It incorporates the strengths of both COBOL and the FORTRAN languages, and is therefore suitable for both commercial and scientific applications. However, the language was never supported by other computer manufacturers and did not threaten the popularity of COBOL and FORTRAN. PL/1 had a major disadvantage in that its increased sophistication led to the program compiler being very large; program development could only be undertaken on very large mainframe computers. The same payroll problem as before would be:

```
IF HOURS > 42 THEN
  PAYROLL= 42*WAGE+(1.5*WAGE*(HOURS-42))
ELSE
  PAYROLL=HOURS*WAGE
```

9.6.4 BASIC (Beginners' All-Purpose Symbolic Instruction Code)

BASIC was developed as a teaching language at Dartmouth College in the United States. It is very similar in construction to simple FORTRAN. People with little or no programming experience can learn to program in BASIC in days while it takes weeks and months to master other high level languages.

An advantage of BASIC is that it can be *interpreted* rather than *compiled*. When languages are compiled, the computer passes the high level programming language (known as the *source code*) to the compiler for translation into machine language code (known as *object code*). Once the translation process is complete, the object code can be executed by the computer. During the development of a new computer system this process is repeated again and again as the programmer identifies and corrects problems, often referred to as *bugs* in his program.

The BASIC language interpreter solves this problem by combining the translation and execution processes. The computer submits the BASIC source code to the translator, known as the *interpreter*, and each statement is translated into machine language and executed immediately. This means that a programmer can be testing his code seconds after having changed it.

One disadvantage of interpreters is that once the program is working well and is in daily use, the source code is translated every time the job is run. This does not occur with compiler languages. Many versions of the BASIC language can be used with both interpreters and compilers, the former for program development, and the latter to generate a final machine language version.

The BASIC language is simple but powerful and it has been found to be ideal for the growing microcomputer market. Many computer manufacturers have taken the original version of BASIC developed at Dartmouth College and added additional features to handle the requirements of commercial systems. Unfortunately the upgrading of BASIC from a teaching language to a commercial language happened without the setting of common standards: BASIC languages became very different.

With the development of the IBM PC and the MS-DOS operating system, many new microcomputers use MS-BASIC as developed by the Microsoft Corporation. This version may well become the industry standard. The same payroll code as before looks like this in BASIC:

```
20  IF HOURS > 42 THEN 50
30  PAYROLL=HOURS*WAGE
40  GOTO 60
50  PAYROLL=42*WAGE+(1.5*WAGE)*(HOURS-42)
```

9.6.5 PASCAL

PASCAL was developed in Switzerland in the late 1960s and is named after the French mathematician, Blaise Pascal. The language seems to be ideal for program development in that it is powerful and easy to learn, it can be used on small and large computers alike, and it is well structured to eliminate problems which originate from poor programming techniques. Unfortunately there are also many different versions of PASCAL. Its main disadvantage is probably that it has only recently gained widespread commercial approval. Universities have for many years been pushing the PASCAL language, but commercial translators were not available on the market until fairly recently. Today PASCAL is in a strong position to threaten the supremacy of COBOL and BASIC in the commercial environment, but computer departments are now looking, instead, at a new generation of programming tools currently being developed. These are known as *very high level languages* or *fourth generation languages*.

The payroll calculation from above, shown in PASCAL, would look like this:

```
IF HOURS > 42
  THEN BEGIN
        PAYROLL=(42*WAGE)+((HOURS-42)*(1.5*WAGE))
  END

  ELSE BEGIN
        PAYROLL=HOURS*WAGE
  END
```

9.7 VERY HIGH LEVEL LANGUAGES

Over the past few years a number of new programming languages have been developed. Attempts have been made to categorize these languages with terms such as 'natural languages', 'non-procedural languages', 'fourth generation languages', 'user-oriented languages' and 'very high level languages' (VHLL). All of these are attempting to achieve a single goal: to simplify the programming process by the use of complex language translation programs, often termed *intelligent compilers*.

In the past, programmers had to be aware of how the machine language instructions that they would ultimately generate would process the data to provide information. Nowadays, programmers need to know very little about the way the computer works: they only need to describe their problem to the machine.

The intelligent compiler's job is to take the problem, as defined by the programmer, and generate the machine language code necessary for the computer to perform the various tasks. As these compilers become more sophisticated, so programming languages can become more problem-oriented. By looking at the names given to the new groups of languages one can gain insight into modern programming trends.

9.7.1 Natural languages

Languages grouped under the term 'natural languages' are attempting to move away from the semantics of the computer and towards the semantics of human speech. Rather than BASIC language statements such as

```
10  OPEN 'PAYROLL.DAT' FOR INPUT AS #1
20  WHILE NOT EOF(1)
30  INPUT #1,BR,NAM$,SAL
40  IF BR=03 AND SAL>OSAL THEN ONAM$=NAM$, OSAL = SAL
50  WEND
60  PRINT ONAM$;'GETS THE MOST MONEY'
70  CLOSE 1
80  END
```

it would be better if the code would read:

```
WHO GETS THE MOST MONEY IN JOHANNESBURG BRANCH?
```

Few real advances have been made in this area because the spoken word is very imprecise (there are many ways of saying the same thing).

9.7.2 Non-procedural languages

Historically, instructions in programs have had to be sequenced in the order in which they were to be performed. With non-procedural languages it is important for the programmer to tell the computer what must be done, but there is less emphasis on how this should be achieved. Intelligent compilers will be able to determine how the job will be performed and in what sequence the activities need to be addressed.

9.7.3 Fourth generation languages (4GLs)

This term has caused some confusion in the computer industry because it has never been clearly defined what a fourth generation language is.

James Martin, a prominent American computer consultant, author and educationalist, has been quoted as saying that a fourth generation language is one that provides at least ten times more productivity than the COBOL programming language. It is non-procedural and operates in an interactive and integrated programming environment. Such tools as the on-line editor (which assists program entry and update), the data base (to handle the complexities of data storage and retrieval), and the data dictionary (to store data about data) are combined to provide the programmer with a more sophisticated and efficient programming environment.

9.7.4 User-oriented languages

User-oriented languages are those designed specifically for non-programmers. Because the user is unlikely to be very knowledgeable about program syntax and the way the computer works, these programs use developments in the area of natural and non-procedural languages in order to achieve their goals.

9.7.5 Very high level languages (VHLL)

The term 'very high level languages' really encompasses all the developments that have been discussed above. The assembler language is known as a low level language because it is structurally very similar to machine language. As translation programs became more sophisticated, so the programming languages became more problem-related and computer-independent. COBOL was known as a high level language and was developed more than 25 years ago. The advent of new programming languages with intelligent compilers represents a further step in this evolutionary process. With the term 'high level languages' already reserved, the next obvious step was 'very high level languages'.

9.8 FUTURE DIRECTIONS

Over the last 20 years great strides have been made in improving the efficiency of computer hardware. The enormous reduction in hardware costs relative to software costs has been mentioned earlier. It is unfortunate that, while computer technology has been moving ahead at great speed, the software production process has hardly improved since the late 1950s. With the increased use of computers in today's society, the lack of qualified programmers and their poor level of productivity has created a bottleneck — hence the sudden interest in better programming languages.

The problem is being tackled on two fronts. The first approach is to increase the productivity of the professional programmer. Over the past decade much was done in an attempt to improve the quality and quantity of programmer output with techniques such as structured programming, interactive programming environments, and automated programming aids. These improvements had little effect on overall programming productivity (claims of increased productivity were seldom greater than 25%). With the new generation of programming languages, claims have been made that productivity can be increased by as much as 25 times and that man-years of work can be compressed to man-weeks.

The problem is also being tackled on a second front with the idea of software being developed by non-programmers. Usually the person wishing to use the computer does not have the necessary expertise to write the program code. The result is that the end-user must clearly communicate his needs to the computer professional, who may have little experience of the user's particular part of the business. The computer professional may well attempt to design a solution and then pass it on to a second computer professional for programming on the computer. This process has obvious limitations, but has been necessary because of the high level of technical expertise required to program a computer. With today's user-oriented languages, there is a move towards end-user programming.

Obviously, many of the operational systems in an organization are much too complex to be designed and written by 'amateur programmers'. Programs to simply analyse and report on data previously captured in the system, however, are ideal for the end-user to program.

Today, most very high level languages are being used by competent professional computer programmers to improve their productivity. In the future we will see more and more end-users solving their own problems with user-oriented languages.

The ultimate goal is often termed the *man-machine interface*: in the future, computers should be able to take any end-user request and translate it into the necessary machine instructions required for it to perform the task. Gradually professional programmers will be required only for highly sophisticated programming tasks. Their role will increasingly be to support the end-user rather than to generate the program for him.

9.9 SYSTEM SOFTWARE

Having discussed the concept of the computer program we can now look at the two major software classifications: *system programs* and *applications programs*. System software consists of computer programs which control and support the computer system and its data processing activities. These programs can be broken down into three separate groups (see Figure 9.1):

The groups are as follows:

- *systems management programs* — these include the most important systems software programs that manage and control processing, data handling, and data communications;
- *systems support programs* — these include the service programs which perform general purpose tasks such as maintaining program libraries, and backing up and sorting data, the security software which ensures that only authorized individuals have access to the system, and also monitor programs which oversee the performance of the machine and record the use of the machine's resources by the users;
- *systems development programs* — to assist in the building and maintenance of new applications. This category includes translating programs that convert programmer

code into machine language, and a multiplicity of application development software programs used to assist and automate the development process.

FIGURE 9.1. Classification of system software.

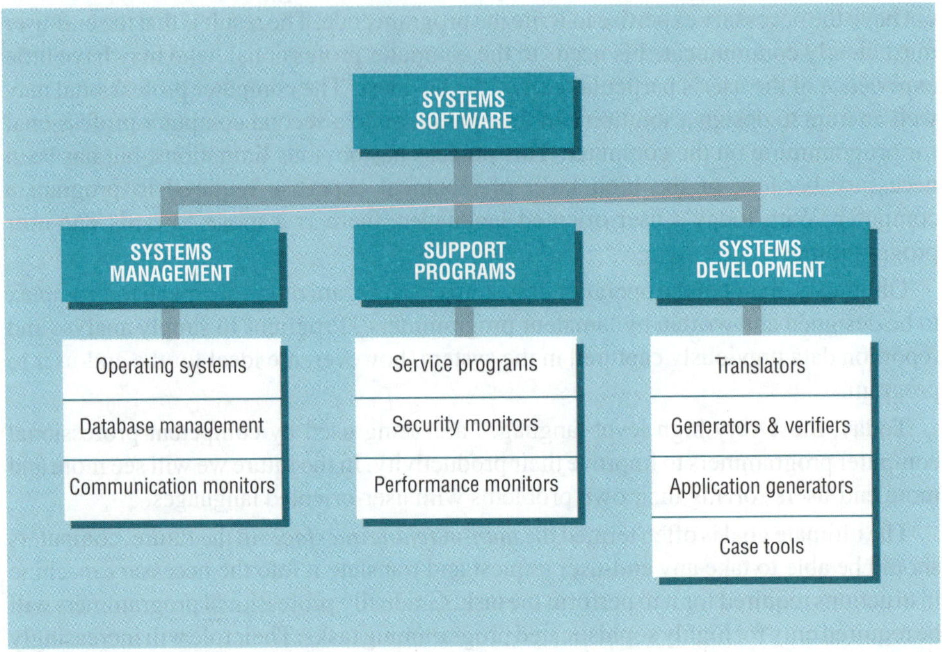

9.10 SYSTEMS MANAGEMENT PROGRAMS

9.10.1 Operating systems

The operating system consists of a number of programs which have taken over many of the functions previously performed by human operators. Part of the operating system remains permanently in the main storage during computer processing and is often referred to as the *executive* or *supervisor*.

These programs are responsible for running all the other business programs (application programs) and for many other housekeeping tasks. Some of the functions of the operating system are:

- scheduling and loading of jobs to provide for continuous processing;
- control over selection and operation of input/output devices and file handling;
- provision for error-correction routines;
- recording details of processing for control and analysis;
- communicating with the computer operator via the console typewriter;
- spooling, multiprogramming and virtual storage.

Spooling

Spooling (abbreviated from *simultaneous peripheral operations on-line*) is a technique used to improve the performance of a computer.

Normally input and output devices are extremely slow compared to the central processing unit. There is therefore a likelihood that the central processor will spend much of its time waiting for data to arrive from slow input devices or for pages of output to be printed before it can continue processing subsequent transactions. This phenomenon is referred to as being *I/O bound*: it means that the input/output devices are a bottleneck reducing the workflow through the machine. Computers can also be CPU bound where the processor is busy and the peripheral devices are idle.

Spooling is a process by which all input required for data processing is read into the computer and stored on special input areas on fast-storage devices such as disks. When the program that requires the data is started, it can receive the data much more quickly from the disk and is therefore able to execute it in a shorter time. In addition, the output generated from the program is written to disk to save time, and this output is later transferred to the printer as a separate exercise.

Multiprogramming

Multiprogramming also attempts to improve the efficiency of the computer. Each program working in the machine can be broken down into input, processing, and output. The processing performed by the CPU is done at great speed while input and output functions are generally much slower. Even in a spooled environment, where the CPU transfers data to and from disks rather than slow input/output peripherals, there is still a great deal of idle time for the CPU while these functions are being performed.

Computers which are capable of multiprogramming have the ability to hold more than one business program in their main store at a time, and when the program currently being processed is waiting for input or output, the CPU works on another program until such time as the first program is ready to begin processing again.

CPUs are so fast in comparison to their peripherals, and business programs in general require so much data transfer, that large modern mainframe computers can often effectively process 15 different programs at one time. It is important to note that while the programs are all residing in the CPU, the computer is not processing them simultaneously. Where a computer is capable of processing two programs simultaneously, it is referred to as a multiprocessor and is effectively a dual CPU machine.

Virtual storage

The computer loads programs into the main store in order to process them. Prior to the introduction of virtual storage, a whole program had to be loaded and thus the number of programs that could be processed simultaneously depended on the amount of main storage available. This situation was inefficient as only a small part of each program is ever active in the machine at any point in time, the remainder being inactive but occupying valuable main storage space.

Virtual storage is a technique by which the main store is broken down into small areas referred to as *pages*, normally about 4000 characters in size. Where a page of programming instructions has not been used for a certain length of time, the computer writes these instructions out to disk and uses the memory that has been released for instructions which are required by some other program.

Pages of instructions are swapped in and out of the CPU as they are required. Virtual storage thus has the effect of utilizing the computer's main storage very efficiently by allowing more programs to be processed at the same time. In a virtual storage machine the main memory is referred to as *real memory* and the space on disk where the inactive pages of the programs are stored is referred to as *virtual storage*.

9.10.2 Database management systems

Information is frequently a corporate resource that can be utilized by many different people. For this reason it is often necessary to pool data in such a way that they may be accessed by many people. One obvious concern with this approach is that, if the data resource is not carefully managed, unauthorized changes could be made. Moreover, where data are shared among users, we may well find that they do not all require a particular piece of information in the same form. Finally, we have the complex task of building and maintaining relationships within the database. It is important to be able to link customer data to the transactions made by a particular customer; equally it should be possible to link stock item records to records of sales of the same items.

All these highly important yet complex tasks are performed by a specialized software program called a *database management system* (DBMS). This program normally works in conjunction with a *data dictionary* — a program that retains data about data — in order to assist in handling the database. For more information on database management systems, read the appropriate section in the chapter on files and access methods.

9.10.3 Data communications monitors

While much data communications technology is hardware-based, all networks require a specific communications monitor to manage and control them. Its tasks would include logging users in and out of the network, handling new requests and passing them onto the relevant application for processing, detecting and correcting transmission errors, and assigning priorities to the various users. Like the operating system and database management system, the *teleprocessing monitor* (TP monitor) remains resident in the main memory of the computer while on-line applications are being run.

9.11 SYSTEMS SUPPORT PROGRAMS

9.11.1 Service programs

There are certain day-to-day activities that all computer systems perform. These common activities require a set of computer programs. Rather than a programmer coding a set of instructions each time these functions are required, a set of programs known as *utility* or *service* programs are available for general use. The functions of such programs might include:

- creating and maintaining program libraries;
- sorting and merging data files;
- copying files for back-up;

- printing the contents of files;
- testing and debugging aids.

9.11.2 Security monitors

In today's world of hackers, viruses and electronic espionage, computer security has become a hot topic. In the past, installations were protected with locked doors and access control points. Today's on-line networks make this kind of security irrelevant because anyone with a telephone could theoretically have access to any network linked to it in any part of the world.

While individual applications can have their own access security built in, requiring user identification and individual passwords, these procedures are seldom adequate against professional hackers and employees with inside information. Most large installations are turning to sophisticated software packages that provide a secure environment for all applications regardless of their level of confidentiality. Products like IBM's RACF (resource access control facility) limit the user's access to information and system resources, taking into account the ownership of data and the user's need to know. The RACF also monitors user activity and reports on security violations.

9.11.3 Systems performance monitors

Mainframe computers handling several tasks at one time, using data management facilities and on-line terminals, make it almost impossible for managers of the facility to monitor the machine's performance and tune it for maximum efficiency. *Performance monitors* record the use of the CPU and its peripheral devices and enable operations managers to identify processing bottlenecks.

It is important to identify which jobs have been run by the computer and how they used the machine's resources. Job accounting packages are normally run on mainframe computers to produce a file of transactions containing job statistics. These can be used for management and costing purposes.

9.12 SYSTEMS DEVELOPMENT PROGRAMS

A number of highly sophisticated programs have appeared over the last ten to fifteen years to aid the development of new commercial applications. We will cover many of these in more detail later in the module on systems development.

9.12.1 Translating programs

The use of translating programs has already been discussed in the section on stored programs.

When the CPU executes a program, the instructions must be in machine language. There are, however, a number of disadvantages in having the programmer write his programs in machine language. The code is very cumbersome and difficult to learn and each computer has its own unique language which could be converted into machine language by translation programs (see Figure 9.2).

FIGURE 9.2. Language translation process.

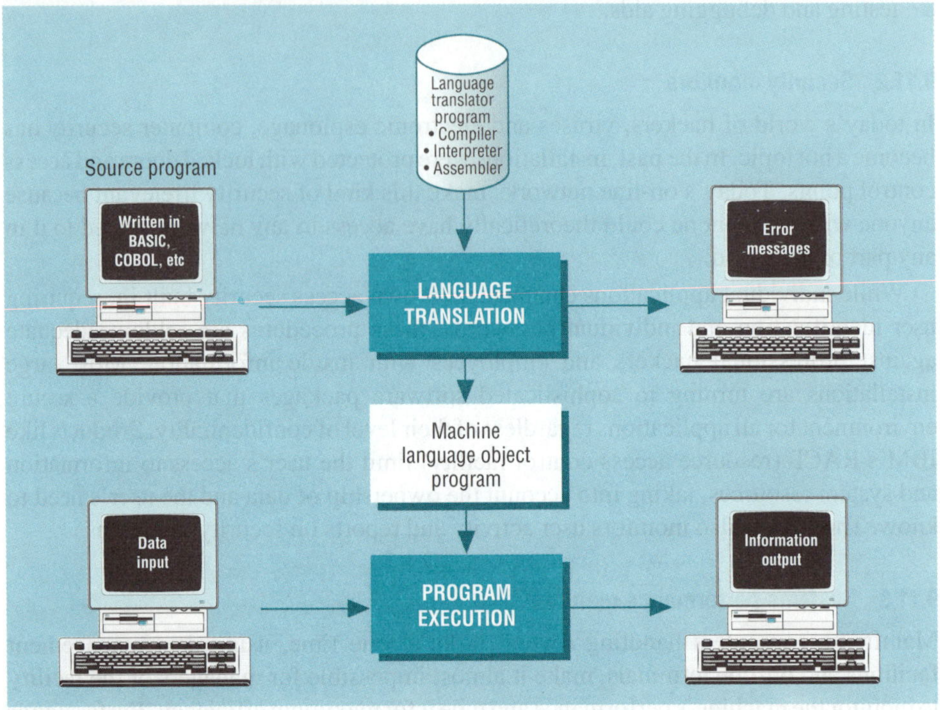

There are three basic types of translation program:

- *assemblers* — translation programs that convert assembler language into machine language programs;
- *compilers* — programs that translate high level language programs into machine language programs;
- *interpreters* — high level language translators that convert each of the source program's instructions into equivalent machine language instructions and execute them before translating the next instruction from the source program.

9.12.2 Generators and verifiers

Some of the early products assisted the programmer by testing program codes for possible logical errors and by drawing program flow charts from the code for documentation purposes.

Later, code generators were developed that allowed programmers to specify the program in a structured form not unlike written English before having the final program code created through a code generator.

9.12.3 Application generators

In the early 1980s *application generators* were developed that allowed the IS profession (and even, in some cases, the end-users of systems) to define problems for the computer in terms of inputs, outputs and processing requirements. These packages then generated the necessary program code. While this development created excitement in the computer industry, most commercial applications were too large and complex to be developed in this way.

9.12.4 CASE tools

Perhaps the most exciting software development in this area is the introduction of CASE tools (computer assisted software engineering). Very little has been done in the past to automate the work of the IS department. There was great potential for using software to help programmers and analysts to chart problems, maintain data dictionaries, generate and verify codes, and build prototypes of systems. CASE tools attempt to fill this gap. They are in their infancy but have already been found to be viable in the development of large, sophisticated computer applications.

9.13 APPLICATION SOFTWARE

Application software refers to programs written to solve the user's business application needs. Application software includes, for example, programs to process company payrolls, accounts receivable, general ledger, and stock/inventory control.

Traditionally, most application programming was done by an organization's own staff. This had the advantage of providing the company with programs which were tailored to meet its exact needs.

Unfortunately substantial costs, missed deadlines and personnel crises associated with in-house software development caused many organizations to make greater use of application software packages. These perform most standard business system functions such as payroll, warehousing and distribution, general ledger, and creditor control. The packages tend to be generalized according to industry groupings or functions. Most can be modified to fit the needs of particular organizations more closely.

9.14 APPLICATION SOFTWARE CLASSIFICATIONS

Most large businesses today rely on computers to administer their major business applications. Twenty years ago computers existed only in the larger organizations and their role was limited to scientific and accounting problems. Today they can be found in even the smallest one-man enterprise and their applications are extremely wide.

9.14.1 Classification by application functions

Possibly the easiest way to classify application software is to group it into three major functional areas: *general purpose*, *business* and *other* (see Figure 9.3).

General purpose applications

These are programs that can perform standard routines for users in many areas of an organization. This classification covers word-processing packages, spreadsheet programs, presentation graphics packages, and data management systems.

FIGURE 9.3. Classification of applications software by function.

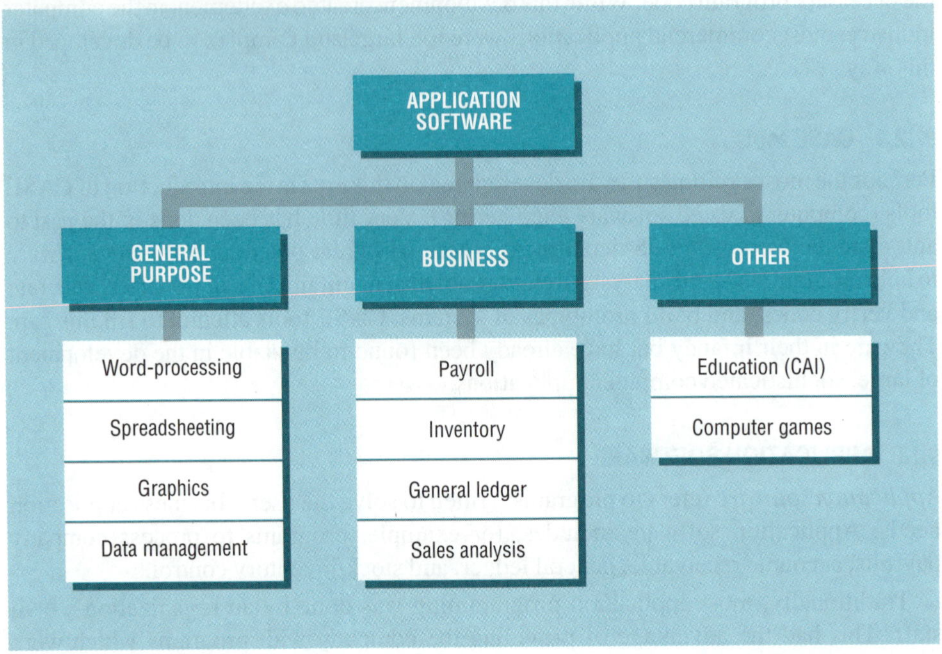

Business applications

This classification usually includes the majority of application software programs in a business. It comprises all applications that automate business processes such as payroll, stock, marketing, sales, production, general ledger and many others. Where the business has a technical orientation (such as in a building company or a chemical refinery) these applications may well have a scientific bias — for example to work out the stress requirements of a concrete beam or the best mix of raw materials to produce a particular chemical.

Other applications

This classification is a catch-all and includes a multiplicity of other applications which do not fit neatly into the previous two categories. Here we would include categories such as computer-aided instruction and computer games.

9.14.2 Classification by organizational hierarchy

The previous classification grouped applications by their particular business function. One can, however, also base the classification of applications on the type of support role they provide to the organization. One can look at the organization as a management pyramid with operational systems forming the base of the pyramid and three levels of management above this (see Figure 9.4).

FIGURE 9.4. Classification of applications software by organizational support level.

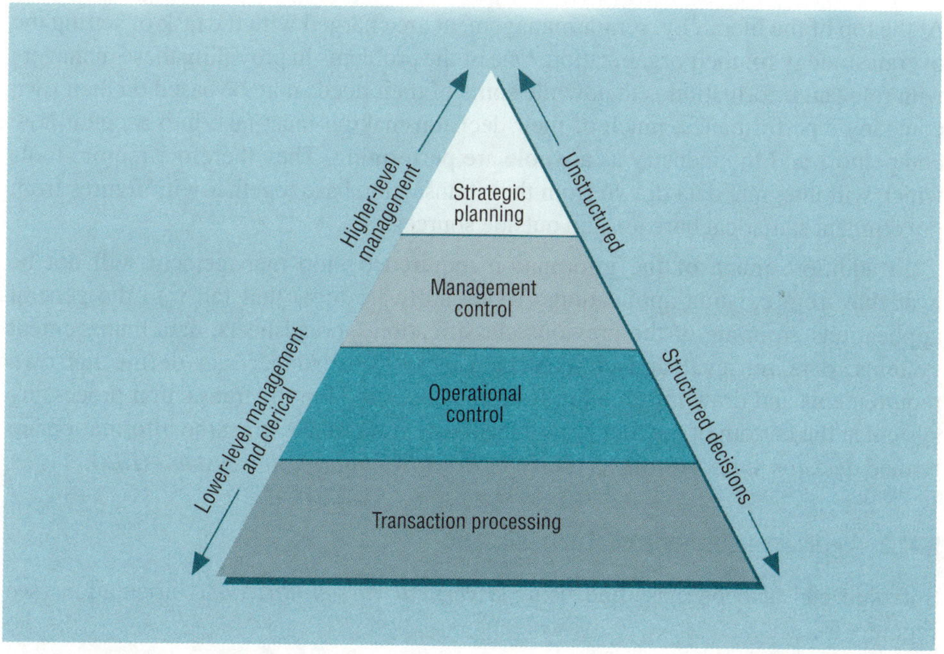

Transaction processing

At the lowest level we have the transaction processing systems that perform the day-to-day processing activities of the organization. These would include the generation of employee cheques in a payroll system, the generation of statements in a debtor system, and the production of a purchase order in a creditor system.

Operational control

This level includes all processing that will assist management in controlling the transaction processing systems below. It is important to note that every commercial application is likely to generate both transaction processing output and operating control reports.

Management control

At this level, top managers are making strategic decisions based on overall company policy. The information systems can assist by providing the manager with information about the level of business activity in the organization. He may want to know whether the organization is reaching the targets that were set at the beginning of the business cycle, or he might want to know about the performance of the company in various geographical areas. While much of this information could be drawn from standard reports generated by the organization's business applications, the manager may also obtain selective reports that are only generated on request.

Strategic planning

At the top of the hierarchy, senior management are charged with the task of setting the overall strategy for their organization. One of the problems in providing these managers with relevant information is that, while some of their needs may be based on their own company's performance, much of their decision-making must take into account how competitors and the industry as a whole are performing. They therefore require tools which will integrate data drawn from their transaction base together with figures from government statistical bureaux and outside sources.

In addition, much of the information required by top management will not be available from existing applications. Using software tools that fall into the general applications grouping of the previous classification (spreadsheets, data management systems, data retrieval and enquiry packages) the manager can define his own requirements and draw information from the data stored in the transaction processing system at the bottom of the hierarchy. The tools required to extract the information are termed *decision support systems* (DSS) or *executive information systems (EIS)*.

9.14.3 Vertical versus horizontal classification

Software can also be classified using a *vertical versus horizontal* orientation (see Figure 9.5).

Software can be seen as a general purpose application to perform a particular function within an organization. For example a debtors' package will enable a company to maintain a record of items sold to customers on credit and will generate the necessary statements, accept payment, and perform all the other activities required to manage the application. A small organization wishing to acquire a debtors' package may well evaluate a number of popular debtors' packages being sold by the local software vendors.

In many cases, however, the type of business that an organization functions in would require it to have a debtors package which is non-standard in that it requires particular features unique to that particular type of business. Where there are enough people in a particular industry to justify the development of special industry-specific software applications, *vertical market applications* are set up. These packages do not normally address a single function in the organization but generally cover all the applications required by a particular industry, together with links that allow data to pass from one application to the next. This is known in the industry as *systems integration.*

Horizontal applications include such systems as invoicing, debtors, creditors, general ledger and payroll (in the accounting and finance fields), personnel, training, word-processing (in administration), credit control, sales analysis and market research (in marketing) and inventory, quality control and materials control (in manufacturing).

If we were to look at the vertical market we would find all of these applications would form part of one or more of the particular systems which have been developed for a specific industry or manufacturing process. Common vertical market packages include construction packages, hotel and restaurant packages, manufacturing or MRP systems,

FIGURE 9.5. Classification of applications software by market orientation.

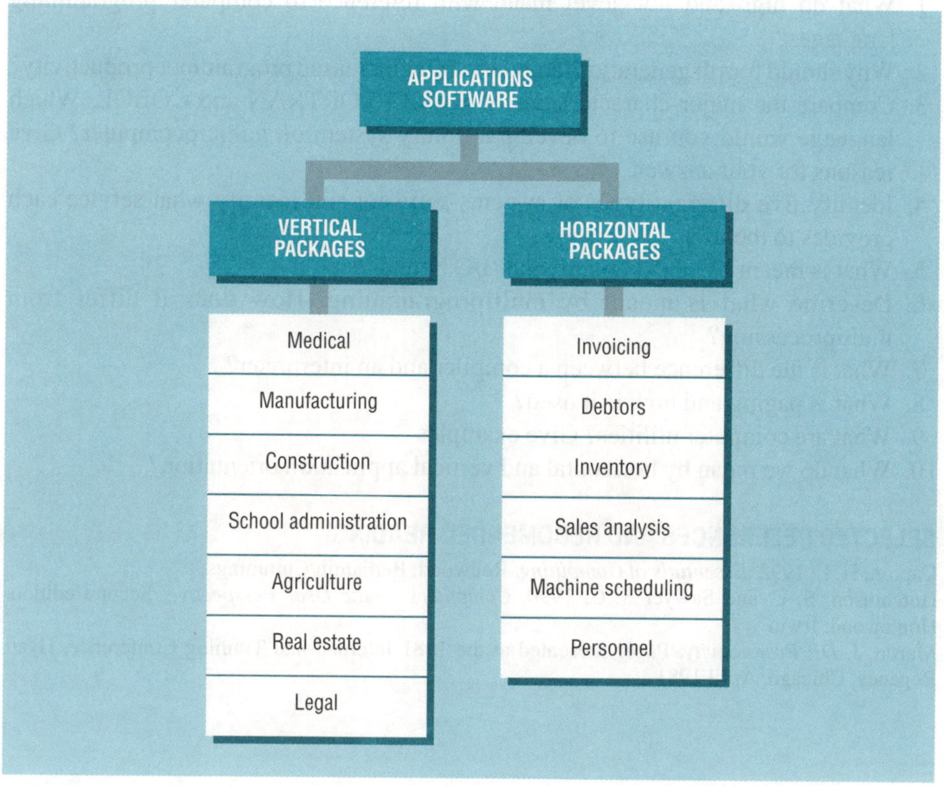

real estate packages, legal packages, medical and dental packages, airline reservation packages, and systems used in agriculture.

9.14.4 Conclusion

It is important to understand that application packages can be seen from three different perspectives:

- they can be seen in terms of the actual business function that they perform;
- they can be seen as providing support for the four levels of management within the organizational hierarchy. It is important to appreciate that while some applications support a particular level in the hierarchy, in many instances a single application may provide functional support across all four levels in the hierarchy;
- finally, there is the issue of vertical and horizontal application orientation. Here again it is important to note that this classification has been derived from the specific requirements of unique sectors of business and industry. Manufacturing systems support the manufacturing process but they would include many of the business functions found in most companies (such as purchasing and inventory control).

REVIEW QUESTIONS

1. What do high and low level mean with reference to computer programming languages?
2. Why should fourth generation languages offer increased programmer productivity?
3. Compare the major characteristics of BASIC, FORTRAN and COBOL. Which language would you use to develop a library system on a microcomputer? Give reasons for your answer.
4. Identify five different types of systems software and identify what service each provides to the user.
5. What is meant by 'CPU bound' and 'I/O bound'?
6. Describe what is meant by multiprogramming. How does it differ from multiprocessing?
7. What is the difference between a compiler and an interpreter?
8. What is paging and how is it used?
9. What are computer utilities? Give examples.
10. What do we mean by horizontal and vertical application orientation?

SELECTED REFERENCES AND RECOMENDED READING

Capron, H. L. 1992. *Essentials of Computing.* Redwood: Benjamin/Cummings.

Hutchinson, S. E. and Sawyer S. C. 1990. *Computers — the User Perspective.* Second edition. Homewood: Irwin

Martin, J. *DP Productivity.* Paper presented at the 1981 International Training Conference, Hyatt Regency, Chicago. April 1981.

CHAPTER 10 Files and access methods

10.1 INTRODUCTION

Files are an essential part of the information system because they contain the working data which will be used to make a variety of decisions within the organization. In a manual data processing system the files are typically kept in filing cabinets and are arranged logically either in numerical or alphabetical order. Computer systems also use files, although the data are recorded not on paper but on a storage medium such as magnetic tape or disk. This chapter explains the concept of computer files and describes the various ways in which they can be organized in order to provide the best possible access to data.

10.2 DATA STRUCTURE

Consider a drawer in a filing cabinet containing all the sales invoices for the current week. The drawer represents a file of the company's weekly sales, made up of a set of logically related transactions or records. Each invoice represents a record containing all the information relating to a particular sale.

The invoice itself can be broken down into several parts called *fields*. For example, 'customer name' is a field, 'customer number' is a field, 'item shipped' and 'extended price' are also fields. When all of the fields necessary to describe this particular sale are put together they become a *record*.

Each field in the record is made up of a number of characters. The length of the field is determined by the size of the data it contains. For example, the 'customer number' field might be five characters long in order to hold a five-digit 'customer code' while the 'customer name' field might be 30 characters in length.

To summarize:

- a field is a collection of characters;
- a record is a collection of logically related fields;
- a file is a collection of logically related records.

10.3 TYPES OF FILES

10.3.1 Master files

These are files of a fairly permanent nature such as a 'customer master file', 'employee master file' and 'stock master file'. These master files normally contain both data of a static nature, such as customer names and addresses, and data which will change on a monthly or weekly basis, such as 'current month's purchases' on the customer master file, or 'current month's overtime hours' on the employee master file.

10.3.2 Transaction files

These files are compiled from the various monthly transactions captured from original source documents. The 'sales' file is created from the invoices received over a particular period. It is used to update the master file and to generate detailed reports on a periodic basis. Once the processing cycle has been completed, a new transaction file made up of the latest batch of transactions will be created and the old file will be discarded.

10.3.3 Table files

These are reasonably permanent. They are used for reference purposes when it is more efficient to maintain data in a reference table rather than storing the information on the particular master file records. Examples of this type of file are price list files, rates of pay files, and PAYE tax table files.

10.4 ACCESS TO FILES

Once a file has been created there must obviously be a means of identifying and accessing each particular record within the file. This is done by giving each record a unique key; the record will be recognized and identified by that particular key.

Examples of key fields are:

- customer number in a customer master file record;
- stock code number in a stock record;
- employee number in a payroll record.

This key field can also be used to sequence the file so that the records can be arranged in much the same way as they may be arranged in a manual data processing system.

10.5 PROCESSING ACTIVITIES

There are several different ways of accessing records in files in order to process them. There are three major processing activities: *file enquiry*, *master file maintenance*, and *file updating*.

10.5.1 File enquiry

When access is made to a particular record simply to ascertain what is in the record, this is referred to as a *file enquiry*. Note that it does not involve any alteration to the record itself.

10.5.2 Master file maintenance

From time to time new records must be added to files, old records may need to be deleted, and existing records on files may need to be changed. In a customer master file, for example, new customers are continually being added, customers who are no longer purchasing from the organization must be deleted, and changes to customers' addresses, credit ratings, and other personal details need to be kept up to date. These particular activities come under the heading of *maintaining the files*.

10.5.3 File updating

Updating is the process by which data from the transactions files are used to update the current position on the master files. For example, customer invoice information can be used to update the customer's current balance fields on the customer master file. Note that the old data on the record are replaced by the new data.

10.6 RECORD LENGTH

Files can be made up either of records which are all the same length (*fixed-length records*) or records of differing lengths (*variable-length records*). Every record in a fixed-length file will consist of the same fixed number of fields and characters and will never vary in size. However, in variable-length files there may either be more fields in one record than in another or the fields will themselves vary in size. Variable-length records obviously offer more flexibility to the systems designer, but they are also more difficult to program.

10.7 FILE LABELS

There are two types of file labels, *internal* and *external*. External file labels are merely the physical labels which are written on the outer casing of a file, such as the magnetic tape reel, in order to assist the librarian and operators to identify the file.

Internal file labels are magnetic records written on the file itself. There is one label called a *header label* at the beginning of the file, and another called the *trailer label*, at the end.

The header label is used to identify the file and normally contains the file name, the date when the file was created, and perhaps the date when the file will no longer be required — often referred to as the *purge date*. Most computers have the ability to check the header label before the file is processed in order to ensure that the correct file has been mounted.

The trailer label normally has an indicator to identify the end of file and a count of the number of records in it for control purposes.

10.8 BLOCKING OF RECORDS

When records are written to tape or disk they are separated by a gap known as the *inter-record gap* (IRG). These gaps often take up more space on the storage medium than the data themselves. They also slow down processing in the case of magnetic tape because the tape is stopped and then started again between each inter-record gap. One method of solving this problem is to group the records together in sets of two or more and send them out to the storage medium as a group. Such a group of records is known as a *block* and the storage device receives it as though it were a single record and writes it out as such. This cuts down on the number of inter-record gaps used and improves the space utilization on the tape.

Blocking illustrates an important difference between logical and physical records. A number of logical records can be stored as one physical record.

10.9 FILE ORGANIZATION

10.9.1 Sequential

The simplest type of file is known as the *sequential file*. Here all the records are arranged in ascending or descending sequence according to a record key. In a telephone directory, for example, the alphabetical arrangement of last names is the primary key for the organization of entries (records). Other keys might be a customer number, a stock item code, or an employee number.

Sequential files are most commonly associated with magnetic tape, but they can be supported by most other storage devices too. Much sequential file processing involves the sorting of data. In a sequential file update procedure, for example, transactions are first sorted into the same order as the master file. Then the first record from each file will be read. If there are no transactions for the master record, it will be written onto a new master file. If there is a transaction, it will be processed against the master record and the modified record will be written onto the new file. Transaction and master records will be read as needed.

One major problem with sequential files is that individual records can be retrieved only by searching the file in sequence from the beginning until the correct record is located. In extreme cases the computer may have to read the entire file. Sequential files may be placed on relatively low-cost storage media such as magnetic tape, and the capacity of such media is virtually unlimited. However, entire files must be read and recreated to process any updates, even if only a few records are to be changed.

10.9.2 Random access

To overcome some of the problems of sequential file organization and to provide more rapid retrieval, *random access files* are used. With this access method it is not necessary to search through an entire file in order to read, add, modify or delete a particular record.

Each record is accessed independently of all other records and access times are therefore very fast. Random (direct) access files are normally stored on magnetic disk. Records are accessed by referring to the physical address of the record on the disk.

To assign a record to a specific address, an arithmetical formula (called an *algorithm*) is typically applied to a field in the record. As a result of this address conversion process, data will not normally be sorted in sequence on the disk. In addition, gaps may appear between records, resulting in the inefficient use of the disk storage devices.

It is also difficult to determine which areas of storage are available for use for new records. It is common to find, on writing a record to a disk, that a record has already been written to a particular address. Programming for such a system is often complex and while direct access files provide faster access to individual records, they tend to be more difficult to manage.

10.9.3 Indexed sequential access

With the *indexed sequential access* method (ISAM), records can either be read sequentially or directly. To read a file directly, ISAM uses indexes to tell the hardware where to find a specific record.

Consider what you would do if you wanted to find a book in a library. You would first search the library index until you found the name of the book you wanted. A reference number would then direct you to a specific rack and from there you would search sequentially until you found the correct title.

ISAM works very much the same way. The machine first goes to a master index which tells it where on a disk it will find a record; it then goes to that area and, having found the approximate place where the record is, it reads sequentially until it finds it.

As the index itself can be very large, it can be structured in hierarchical form to improve access speed (see Figure 10.1). It is important to remember that the indexed sequential access method can be used only on devices that have direct access capability — ie. disks or diskettes.

FIGURE 10.1. Searching an indexed sequential file.

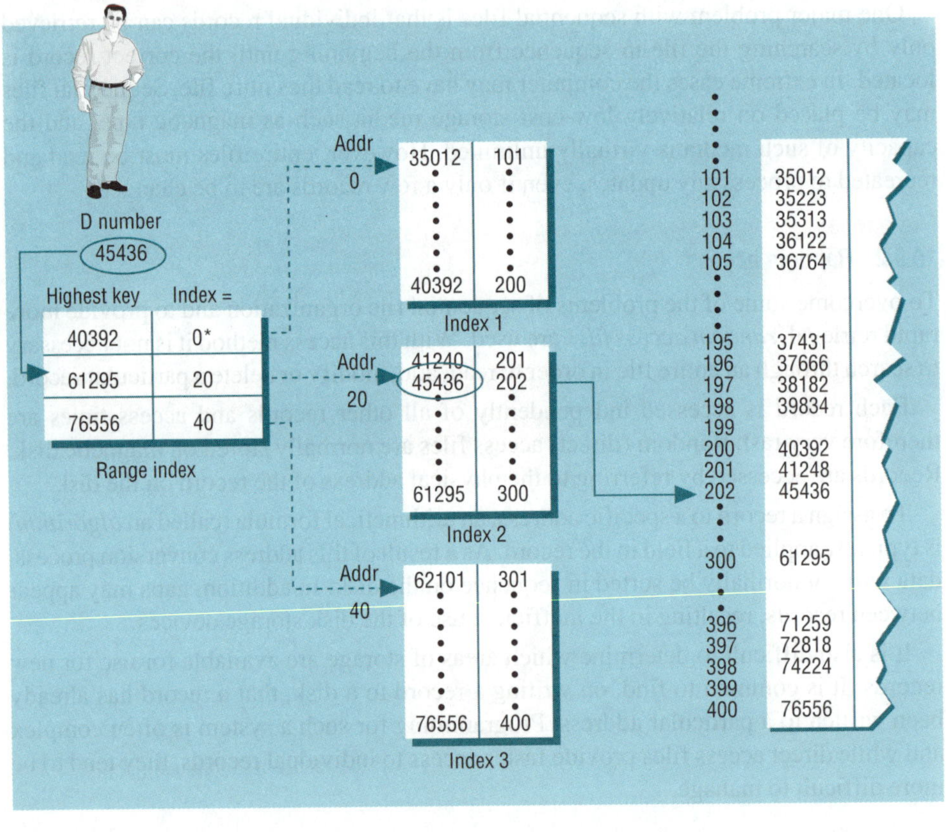

10.9.4 Comparison of the access methods

The following table highlights the major differences between the three *file organization* methods:

FIGURE 10.2. Major differences between the access methods.

	Sequential	Indexed sequential	Random
Storage device	Tape/disk	Disk	Disk
Sequential access	Fast	Fast	N/A
Direct access	N/A	Medium fast	Fast
Space usage	Good	Fair	Poor
Programming	Simple	Fair to complex	Fair to complex
Update	New file	In place	In place
Failure condition	Restart program	Recover file from backup Restart program	Recover file from backup Restart program
Common usage	Batch systems High hit rates	Require sequential and direct access	Realtime systems High speed/direct access

10.10 DATABASE SYSTEMS

Most organizations have data requirements that are so complex that traditional file organization is inadequate. This section explains what *databases* are and how they work. It then looks at the terminology used to describe the various database concepts, and discusses the advantages and disadvantages of this new technology.

10.10.1 What is a database?

Traditionally, as each new computer system was developed, so files were designed containing the required data fields. Each application was responsible for validating and maintaining its data. This build-up of independent applications was soon found to have inherent weaknesses. These weaknesses included the following:

- Some data were common to more than one application but had to be input and validated separately for each system. This resulted in more work for clerical staff and the computer, increased use of secondary storage, and a greater danger of errors.
- File descriptions were locked into each program and so a change to a particular file involved changing all the programs that used it.
- In many instances, management information reports could not be obtained from the computer because the information crossed application boundaries. The idea that data *belongs* to a particular application is really an oversimplification as the records of an organization have many interrelationships. If, for example, a customer purchases an article on credit, the debtors' system should be accessed for credit details and the updating of balances, the stock system should be accessed to adjust the inventory levels, the wages system must be accessed to increase the salesman's commission, and the sales statistics system must be accessed to adjust the monthly sales figures.

One solution to these problems is to integrate the various files into a common pool of data, known as a *database*, which can be accessed by many different applications. Database systems are designed so that many applications operate on the same physical data yet the *logical database* (the way the database is viewed by an application program) will probably be unique for every program. A database system can greatly reduce the

FIGURE 10.3. Traditional file system.

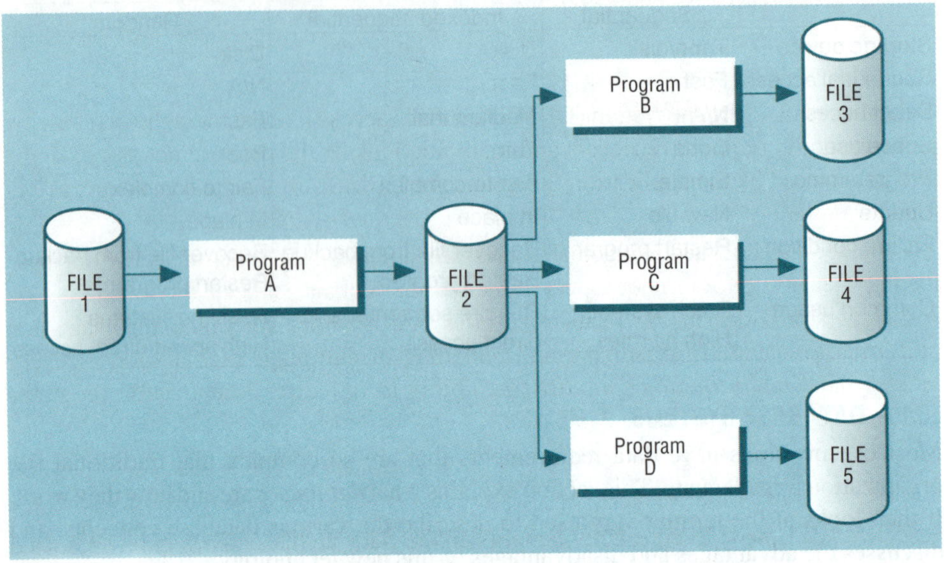

FIGURE 10.4. Database management system.

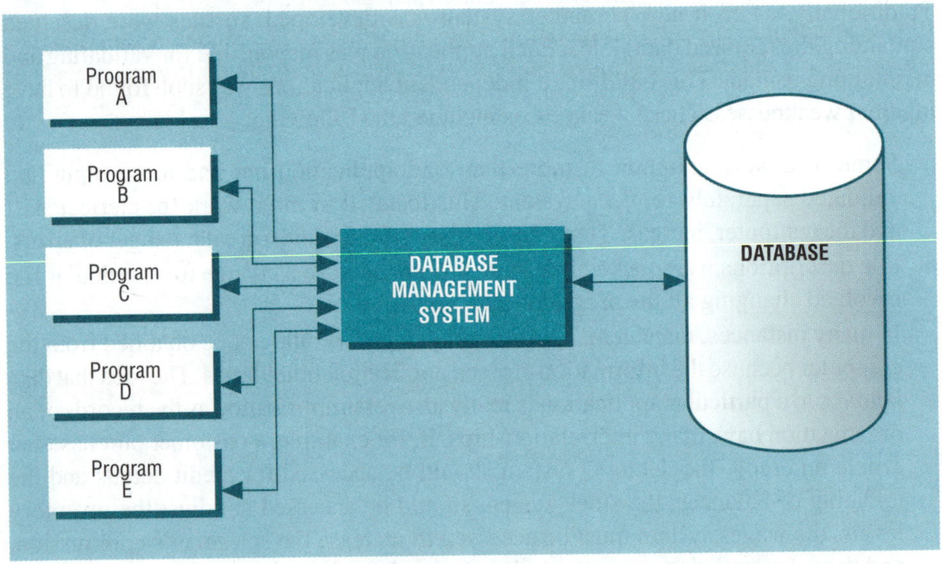

amount of redundant data stored yet it can also efficiently support many application programs.

To make programs independent of the structure and format of data in the central pool, no application program is allowed to access the pool directly. Instead a software package called the *database management system* intercepts all data requests from programs.

The difference between traditional file systems and database management systems is illustrated in Figures 10.3 and 10.4.

10.10.2 Database management systems

A database management system (DBMS) controls access to the data in the database by performing the required retrievals and manipulations. If the data are not stored in the format required by the applications program, the DBMS software makes the necessary transformation.

Data linking and accessing techniques are not the only functions of a database management system. A major aspect of the DBMS package is the quality of supporting software it provides in the form of utilities and modules for obtaining usage and performance statistics, organizing and reloading or dumping, back-up and recovery security, and *multi-thread capability* (the ability to run several application programs concurrently against the same database).

10.10.3 Database architecture

A DBMS can provide enormous benefits if the data in the database are organized properly. Most DBMSs require descriptions of three entirely different views of the data.

Outlined below is a general architecture for a database system. One can think of a database in terms of three general levels called *schemas* (see Figure 10.5):

Physical schema. The internal model, or physical schema, is a model of how the data are stored in a database. It defines the type of records stored, the index fields, and the

FIGURE 10.5. Three views of a database.

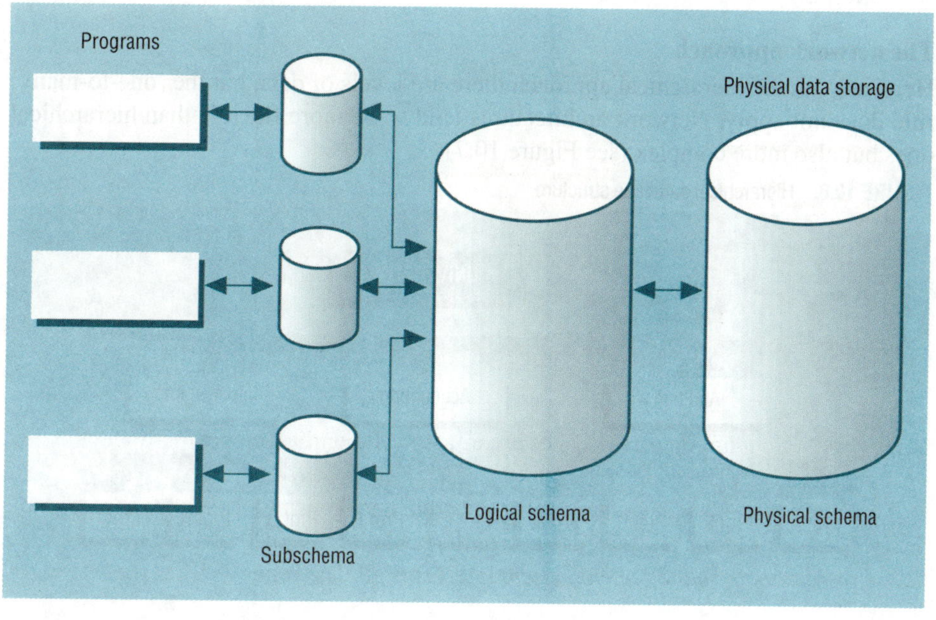

physical sequence of data in the database. In designing this model, the designer takes account of such things as access time and the number of records to be stored.

Subschema. The external model or subschema is a view of the data as a particular user sees them. The user is only concerned with a part of the total database and his view therefore does not correspond to the physical arrangement of the data.

Logical schema. The data model or logical schema provides a view of the real structure of the data, which is probably quite different from the way in which it is physically stored. The logical schema consists of information about all the data stored in the database with no reference to storage or access methods.

10.10.4 Database structures

One of the critical differences between traditional and database file organization is that the latter is more concerned with how organizations might want to use the data. This involves taking into account the many often complex interrelationships between the records in the database. Three basic data models have been developed to provide these relationships: the *hierarchical approach*, the *network approach*, and the *relational approach*.

The hierarchical approach

In this model data are represented by a structure that is similar to the root system of a tree, with data arranged in levels. The elements further down the system are subordinate to the ones above, like the hierarchy of employees in an organization. Finding a record usually requires you to start at the top of the hierarchy and work downwards to the required data. One important rule is that while each level can have a number of subordinates, these subordinates can only point to one superior. This is termed a *one-to-many relationship* (see Figure 10.6).

The network approach

Here, as with the hierarchical approach there are levels of data, but the 'one-to-many' rule does not apply. Network architectures tend to be more flexible than hierarchical ones but also more complex (see Figure 10.7).

FIGURE 10.6. Hierarchical database structure.

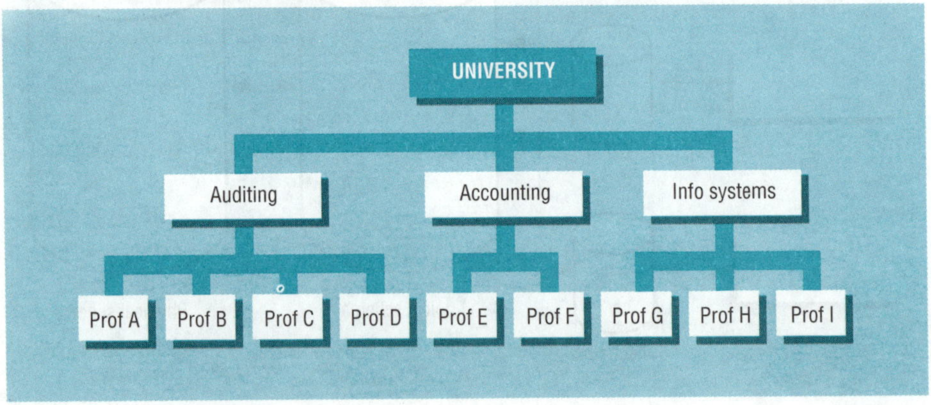

FIGURE 10.7. Network database structure.

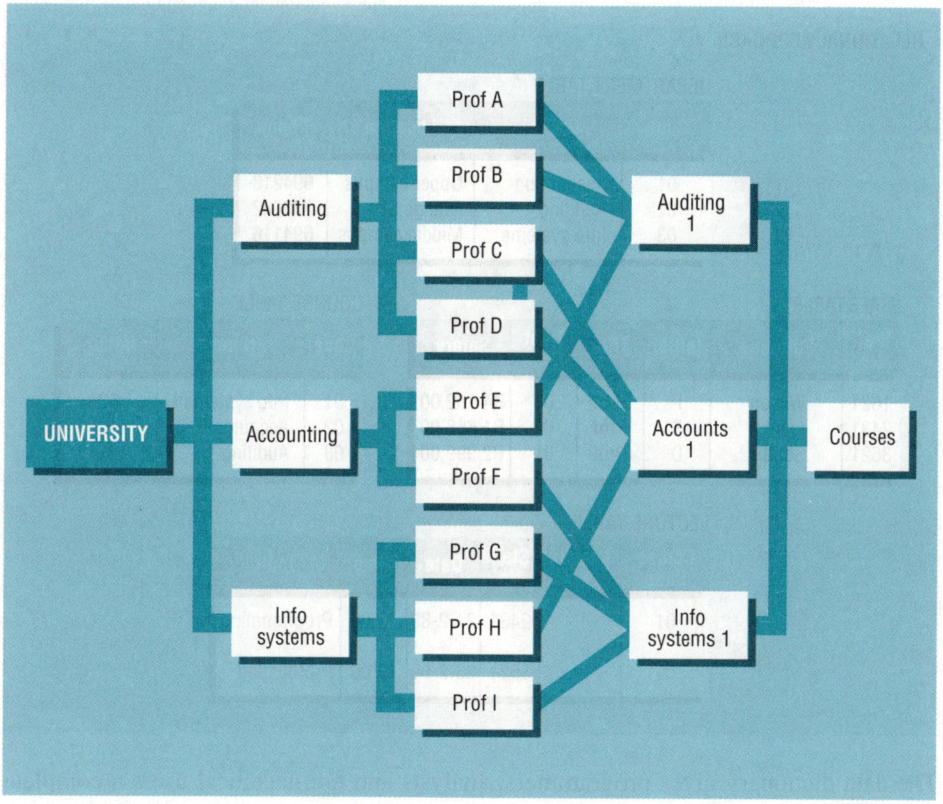

The relational approach

This model was first advanced by Dr E. F. Codd of IBM in 1970. It is based on the mathematics of sets. The concept of a relational database is essentially a very simple one. Information is represented in tables known as *relations*. These contain only one key, and all the data elements are dependent on that key. The relational approach encourages a flexible view of the data with no preconceived structure. This results in a high degree of data independence. Changes to the data therefore cause little or no disruption to the system as a whole (see Figure 10.8).

10.10.5 The data dictionary

A data dictionary is a software system for managing and controlling data definitions. In essence it holds data about data. It contains descriptions of a company's data, information about its technical characteristics and about the interrelationships between items of data. It also includes information about where the data are used, systems and procedures, and a full cross-reference facility.

A data dictionary is particularly useful for controlling the amount of redundant data items. It can also generate source language data descriptions, thereby eliminating transcription errors.

FIGURE 10.8. Relational database structure.

RELATIONAL APPROACH

DEPARTMENT TABLE

Code	Name	Location	Phone
01	Accounting	Upper campus	694213
02	Auditing	Orange St.	243642
03	Info systems	Middle campus	694116

STAFF TABLE

Staff No	Surname	Initial	Title	Dept Code	Salary
1621	Wilson	P	Prof	03	R4 162,00
2431	Frank	S	Prof	01	R1 666,00
3621	Smith	D	Prof	01	R2 999,00

COURSE TABLE

Code	Name	Venue
01	Info systems I	6B
02	Accounts I	4C
03	Auditing 1	2a

LECTURE TABLE

Course Code	Lecture No	Staff No	Date	Time	Topic
01	1	2431	21-2-89	12:00	Programming
01	2	3621	23-2-89	12:00	Prototyping

The data dictionary gives programmers, analysts and non-technical users a complete reference-system for all the available data, and so it is of prime importance that it be accurately maintained. This task is the responsibility of the *database administrator*.

10.10.6 Advantages and disadvantages of database technology

To summarize, the major advantages of the database approach are:

- it controls data duplication — files can be integrated so that data are stored only once;
- data independence — the programs and the database can be altered independently since the data organization and access techniques are not built into the programs;
- it provides a corporate view of the data — management reports can cross application boundaries;
- data protection — the privacy and integrity of data can be centrally controlled.

In theory the database concept provides a solution to many thorny data problems, but in practice there are costs involved. These are:

- processing overheads — the DBMS is a large program which will take a significant percentage of the computer's main storage and reduce processing speed. DBMSs are complex programs and each database needs to be tuned to reach optimal processing performance;

- software costs — DBMS software for mainframe systems can easily run into millions of rands;
- people costs — the database should be designed and controlled by competent personnel. As the responsibility for data is no longer vested in the individual applications, the *database administrator* (DBA) provides this function. The DBA decides what data should be in the database and how they should be held. The DBA sets authorization-checks for users of the database and validation procedures for updating it. He also defines strategies for backing up and recovering, enforces standards for documentation, and organizes the database to interface efficiently with all related systems.

10.10.7 A practical example

Not all databases operate in exactly the same fashion but the following example is typical of a request for a particular record on a database management system (see Figure 10.9).

1. The program requests a record from the database management system.
2. The database management system finds the subschema used by that particular program.
3. The database management system obtains a schema and examines the physical database description required.
4. The DBMS issues an instruction to the computer operating system requesting that it read the required records.
5. The operating system transfers the required records into the systems buffer.
6. The database management system assembles the logical records required by the program from the physical data in the systems buffers.

FIGURE 10.9. How a data management system works.

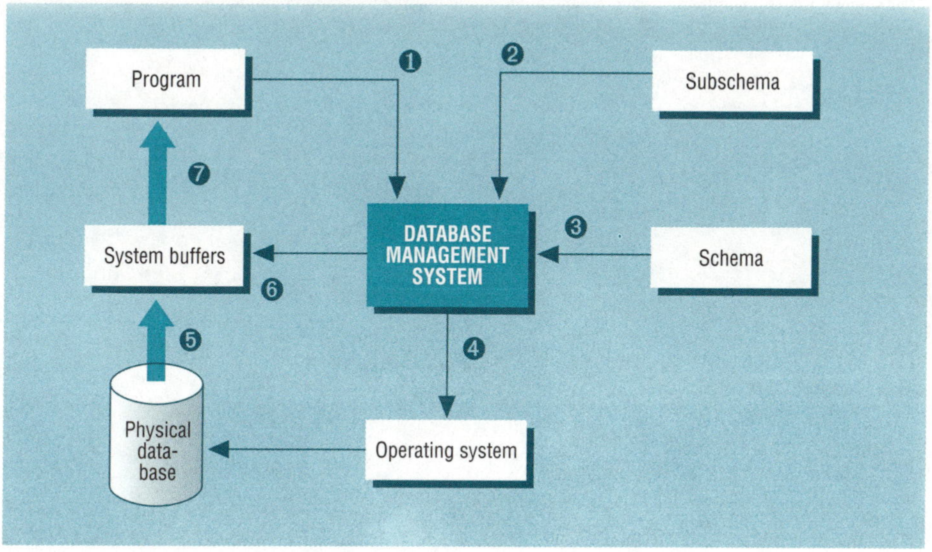

7. The DBMS transfers the data from the systems buffers to the work area of the particular program in the CPU.

This example emphasizes two major aspects of database implementation.

The first is that the logical record requested by the application program can be very different from the physical record residing on the storage device. The interdependence of the program and data is fundamental to the database concept.

The second issue is that while the database concept might be relatively straightforward in theory, its implementation involves a number of highly sophisticated software programs requiring extensive support from both computer and data processing personnel.

REVIEW QUESTIONS

1. Define the following terms: character, field, record, file and database.
2. Describe the function of blocking.
3. What is a record key and what function does it perform?
4. What are the advantages and disadvantages of sequential file organizations?
5. How are sequential, indexed sequential, and random access files organized?
6. What is a database?
7. Explain how database systems can benefit users.
8. What do we mean by a database physical schema, a logical schema, and a subschema?
9. Explain how a relational database organizes data.
10. What are the following: a DBMS, a DD and a DBA?

SELECTED REFERENCES AND RECOMENDED READING

Capron, H. L. 1987. Tools for an Information Age. Menlo Park, California: Benjamin/Cummings.

Hutchinson, S. E. and Sawyer, S. C. 1990. *Computers — The User Perspective.* Second edition. Homewood: Irwin.

CHAPTER 11 Modes of processing

11.1 INTRODUCTION

There are a number of different ways that a computer can be used to process data. Business transactions normally occur at random intervals during the reporting cycle. In many computer applications there is no need to enquire about or report on these transactions until the end of the reporting period. In other applications, however, there may be a real need to look at the status of a particular record — be it a customer master record or a stock master record — at any time. If this information is to be completely up-to-date, the master record must be updated whenever a transaction occurs. Systems that provide immediate access to up-to-date information tend to be more costly and sophisticated in their development and use of computer resources. It is therefore important to identify the reporting requirements of each application prior to making a decision on which mode of processing to use.

Before we look at batch or on-line processing it is important to understand a little more about the processing cycle. To do this we will take the simple example of a company payroll system.

Let us assume that the employees of a company are paid a salary cheque at the end of each month. For administrative and government purposes the company is required to retain information about PAYE and other deductions, and to generate management and control reports.

We would start by capturing all the data about the employees — their names, addresses, salaries and deductions. These would be permanent data which would seldom change and which would form part of the payroll master file. Keeping this information up-to-date on the master is known as *master file maintenance*.

It may be necessary to capture certain information monthly to help calculate the final salary totals. Most payroll systems accept time sheets detailing the hours employees worked in each month. The process of capturing these transactions and checking them for errors is referred to as *transaction validation*.

Paying the employees would involve selecting the master record for each employee, accessing his corresponding time sheet record, calculating his payroll details, printing his cheque, adding his details to the necessary management and control reports and, finally, *updating* his master record with his year's accumulated PAYE and deductions.

All systems normally follow this process, regardless of whether they are batch or on-line.

11.2 BATCH PROCESSING

In a batch processing system, data are accumulated in batches over a period of time before being processed. There is, therefore, a time delay between the origination of the transaction and the subsequent receipt of information or output by the user.

Batch processing is ideal for systems such as payrolls. Most changes or updates in a payroll system, such as increases in salaries and changes in special employee allowances, occur on a monthly basis. There is seldom a need to know the status of an employee's overtime or a change in his marital status or other personal details during the month. It is therefore quite reasonable to make all changes to the payroll master file, and all transactions such as overtime hours, at the month-end when the files can be updated and the necessary output produced. If more up-to-date reports are required, then it would be possible to change the batch processing cycle from monthly to weekly or even daily. Reports and enquiries would never be more than a week or a day out of date.

11.2.1 Master file maintenance

The first step in the processing cycle is to update the master file with any changes for the processing period. In the payroll example there might be a number of new employees, employees who have retired or been fired, and changes in employee addresses and marital status. These changes to the master file must be coded and run through a program which will check them for errors and then make the necessary changes to the master file (see Figure 11.1).

If employees are granted increases and their basic salary fields are updated, controls must be in place to ensure that errors are detected and corrected. The best control in this area is the *run to run control* where a manual record is kept of the generation number of the master file and a count of the number of master file records with totals of all important quantitative fields.

Perhaps the latest payroll master file is generation 18, with 365 employee records and a salary total of R1 110 050. When the next master file maintenance update run is made, the data controller should calculate the impact of additions, deletions, and changes to the master file. When the master file maintenance program is complete, the control report for generation 19 should be reconciled against the manual log.

These controls ensure that no unauthorized changes have been made to the master file at any time in the processing cycle. Once the master file is up-to-date, we are in a position to process the monthly transactions against it.

FIGURE 11.1. Master file maintenance in batch mode.

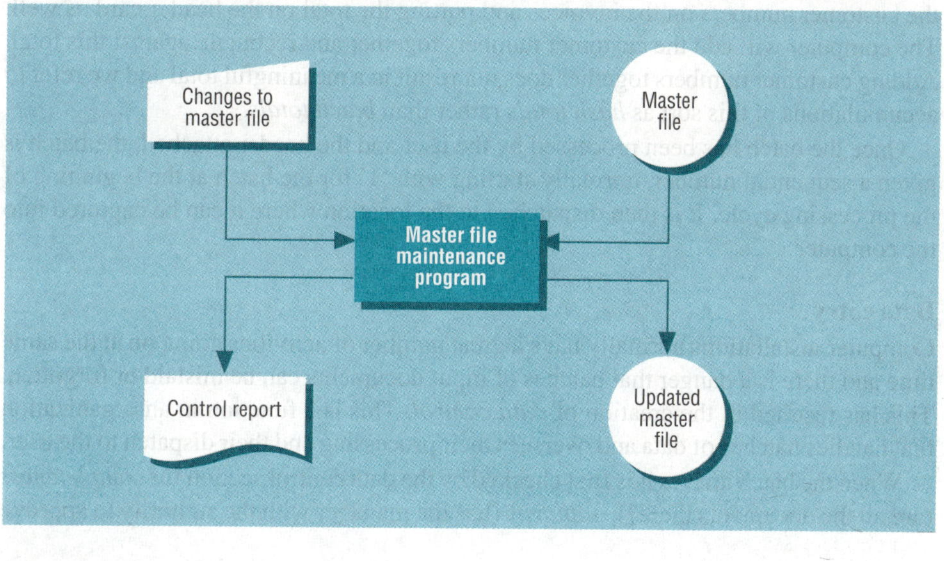

11.2.2 Transaction validation

We shall now go through the steps in the batch processing cycle in order to illustrate exactly how it functions. Figure 11.2 should be helpful here.

Batching of transactions

At the source of the transaction the details are captured onto a pre-printed form, normally termed the *source document*. This might be an invoice, an order form, or an employee time sheet, depending on the type of application.

Single documents could easily be mislaid being transported to the processing centre and so the batch system gets its name from the technique of holding back the documents until there are a sufficient number of documents, or until a particular period of time has elapsed. At this point the documents are group together to form a batch. The documents in the batch are counted and the total is encoded on a sheet attached to the front of the batch. This sheet is referred to as a *batch header*.

While this transaction total will help to ensure that all the documents are entered into the system, there is no guarantee that the data on those documents will be correctly entered. The documents may be copies of invoices and the total value for each invoice must be correctly entered into the computer. One precaution that assists in identifying errors is that of adding up the total value on each invoice in the batch and putting this total onto the header card as well. This number is referred to as a *batch total*.

When transactions are entered into the computer at some future date, the machine will begin by counting the number of transactions and the total invoice value for that batch. It will reconcile these totals against the transaction count and batch total entered from the header card. Any discrepancies will highlight a possible data entry error or an error in the compilation of the batch. This can be identified and corrected.

One other problem could be that the customer number on a particular transaction might be incorrectly entered into the computer so that the wrong customer is debited with the invoice amount. In batch systems we can resolve this problem by adding up all the customer numbers on the invoices and putting the total on the header card as well. The computer will add the customer numbers together and reconcile against this total. Adding customer numbers together does not result in a meaningful total and we refer to accumulations of this sort as *hash totals* rather than *batch totals*.

Once the batch has been processed by the user and the header attached, the batch is given a sequential number, normally starting with '1' for the batch at the beginning of the processing cycle. It is then dispatched to the location where it can be captured into the computer.

Data entry

Computer installations normally have a great number of activities going on at the same time and there is a danger that batches of input documents can be mislaid or forgotten. This has resulted in the creation of *data control*. This is a function in an organization that handles batches of data and oversees their processing and their dispatch to the user.

When the batch arrives it is first checked by the data control section for *completeness* (are all the documents there?), *authority* (has the manager with the authority to approve

FIGURE 11.2. Transaction validation in batch mode.

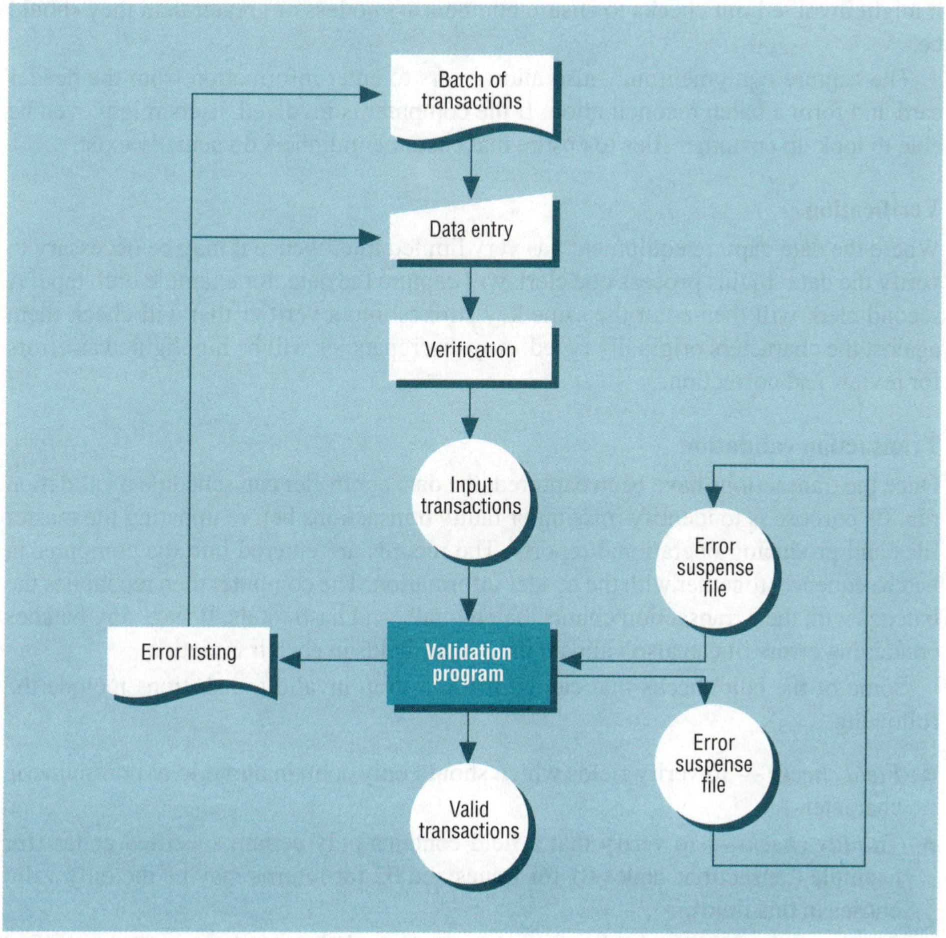

these transactions signed the relevant documentation?) and *accuracy* (a cursory check to see that the documents have been filled in correctly). The batch can then be accepted for processing and its details are entered into the batch log book. This serves as a record of when the batch was received as well as its current status in the processing cycle.

The data controller will next schedule the batches for data capture. Certain batches are processed on a daily basis and must be handled as a matter of urgency while others often are only required at month end.

In the data capture section the various transactions in each batch are encoded onto magnetic tape, floppy disk, hard disk, or even directly into the computer. The purpose of this process is to convert the data into a computer readable form.

Basic edit checks

The data capture equipment may have some limited intelligence of its own which can help to check the data as they are entered. Checking might include simple edit checks where the machine is told to expect numeric or alpha-numeric data in certain fields, or it might involve limit checks to ensure numbers are no less or greater than they should be.

The capture equipment may also allow users to enter information from the header card and form a batch reconciliation. If the computer is involved, users might even be able to look up customer files to ensure that customer numbers do actually exist.

Verification

Where the data capture equipment has very limited intelligence it may be necessary to verify the data. In this process one clerk will capture the data, for example onto tape. A second clerk will then enter the same key strokes into a verifier that will check them against the characters originally typed. Any discrepancies will be highlighted as errors for review and correction.

Transaction validation

Once the transactions have been captured, the data controller can schedule a validation run. Its purpose is to identify missing or faulty transactions before updating the master files and producing operational reports. The records are entered into the computer in batch sequence, together with the header information. The computer then reconciles the batches with their transaction counts, batch totals, and hash totals. It flags any batches containing errors. It can also validate individual fields in each transaction.

Some of the edit checks that can be made to trap invalid transactions include the following:

- *Field checks* — to verify fields which should only contain numeric or non-numeric characters.
- *Validity checks* — to verify that a field contains only certain specified codes (for example transactions codes 01 for issues and 02 for returns may be the only valid entries in this field).
- *Limit or reasonability checks* — a value cannot be below or above certain specified limits.
- *Sign checks* — used where a number can only be positive or negative.
- *Sequence checks* — where the next number should always be larger than the previous one and, in some cases, where a missing number might indicate a lost transaction.
- *Check digits* — where the number is self-validating. This works by putting the numeric field through a standard calculation to derive an answer which is normally a single or double digit figure. This figure is then attached to the original code to form a self-validating number. When the number is entered into an input device, the original portion can then be put through the same calculation. The check digit derived should match the check digit portion of the number entered. This technique is obviously not fool-proof as two different numbers could generate the same check digit. However the most common error in data capture is the transposition error, where two numbers are swapped around (an entry clerk might type 32 instead of 23). Check digit calculations are specially designed to identify this kind of error.

- *Completeness checks* — where the computer checks that fields that must be entered have not been left blank.
- *Table look-up* — where the computer checks that a particular code does exist in the system. This is used to verify codes such as stock numbers, employee numbers, and customer numbers. It compares the data with the appropriate master file to determine whether all the codes exist.

Where the computer identifies transactions that are in error in a batch, the whole batch is flagged. Normally many batches are processed at one time and the validation program will generate the following:

- a file of transactions from all the valid batches;
- a listing of the valid batches and their transactions. This will be kept as an audit trail in order to verify later that a particular transaction was processed;
- a report of all invalid batches with errors highlighted;
- an error suspense file.

The error suspense file

Batches are often fed into the computer from a single file on a floppy disk or tape. Half of the batches may have been invalid and half may have been correct.

To ensure that no transactions are mislaid or incorrectly entered, each batch must be retained until it is correct. However, it is difficult to separate the valid batches from the invalid batches on the input tape and very inefficient to repeat the capture process. The technique most commonly used in batch systems is to have the validation program write all the transactions of an invalid batch to a suspense file.

The data controller will check the error report and will code the necessary corrections. The error may have originated in the data capture. As the data control department still has the source documents, this is easy to identify. If a source document appears to be in error — for example, if a customer number is invalid — the data controller will contact the user or return the document to the user area for the problem to be resolved.

When the next batch validation run is made on the computer, corrections will be made to invalid batches in the previous run. These will be merged with the relevant batch of transactions on the suspense file and be pushed through the entire validation process again. A logbook is maintained by the data controller to record when each batch is received by the operations department, and to record the status of the batch in terms of whether it has been captured, validated and accepted by the system. The user normally marks the last batch sent at the end of the time period as final to indicate that this is the last batch for a particular processing cycle.

Timing is vitally important in a batch system. The company will do business with its clients on a daily basis. At some point a decision must be taken that a certain transaction will be the last transaction for that particular week or month. All transactions from then on will go into the next processing cycle.

A large organization might have hundreds of outlets scattered over a large geographical area. Deadlines play an important role in the system as delays from one or two branches can cause problems such as late delivery of statements to customers or a delay in paying employees.

11.2.3 Update program

Once all the transactions for a particular processing period have been validated and corrected, they can all be brought together to implement the master file update (see Figure 11.3). The master file will be in a particular sequence and it is often necessary to sort the valid transactions into the same order prior to the update.

FIGURE 11.3. Update program.

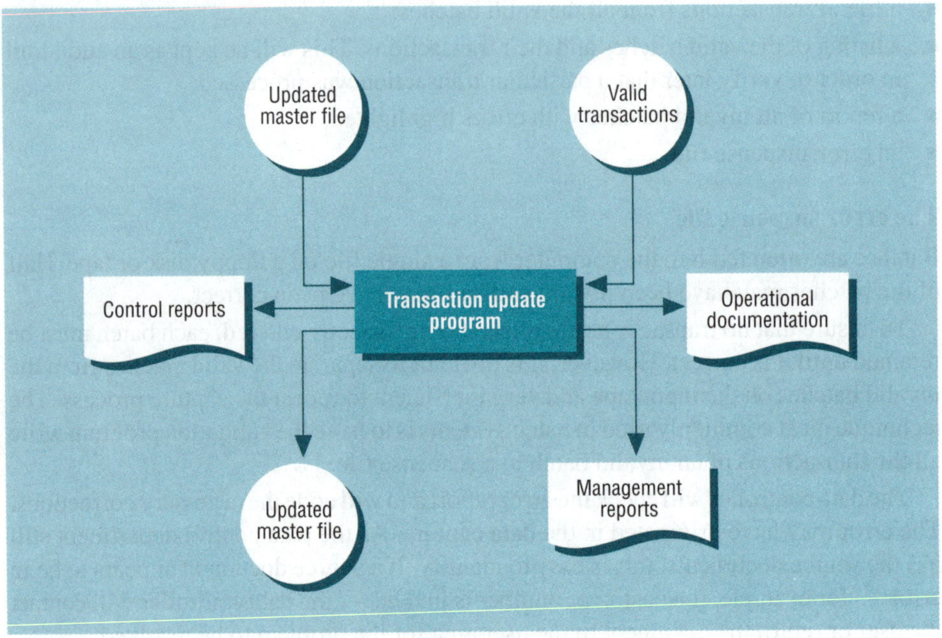

The update process would normally involve:

- reading a record from the master file;
- reading all the transactions for the master record (for example all sales transactions for a particular customer);
- processing the transactions together with prior totals on the master record to arrive at the current position;
- writing the updated record back to the master file;
- generating any operational documentation that is required such as customer statements or salary cheques;
- generating any management reports that are required;
- generating control reports to reconcile prior master file balances and transaction activity against the new master file.

Data control reconciliation

The data control function is responsible for reconciling control totals to ensure that all transactions have been processed correctly, that output is distributed to specified staff, and that the source documentation is labelled and archived.

User reconciliation

The user will receive the final control report and can perform his own reconciliation to ensure that all transactions for the month were correctly entered into the system.

11.2.4 Summary

Batch processing has many disadvantages. It is labour intensive and susceptible to error, and the data are never completely up-to-date. On the plus side, the programs are normally relatively simple and the computer equipment need not be expensive. Processing can also be scheduled for non-peak hours.

11.3 ON-LINE ENTRY MODE

In many cases transactions originate at locations which are a great distance from the central computer. The transportation of these transactions to the central processing area, and the dispatch of the output reports back to the remote offices, can often take many days.

One way of speeding up the processing cycle is to capture the transactions at the remote locations and transmit them through a data communications line to the central computer. If the remote offices are also provided with a printer, the output can also be dispatched quickly by the same communications link.

There are two modes of on-line entry. With the first there is a data capture device such as a floppy disk encoder at the remote location. Transactions are captured onto floppy disk to be transmitted later in a single batch down the communications line. Alternatively, a computer terminal can be linked by a communications line directly to the computer and transactions can be transmitted down the line as they occur.

In both the above instances the transactions are not used to update the relevant master files when they are received by the central computer. Instead, they are stored in a secondary storage device until such time as a batch processing update run is scheduled.

11.4 ON-LINE UPDATE MODE (REAL-TIME)

Many situations require transactions to be processed and the relevant files updated immediately. Future enquiries and decisions must be based on the current situation and not on the last-reported information. For example, when money is drawn from an ATM the account holder's record must immediately reflect the new balance. Processing systems of this type are referred to as on-line update systems and are commonly said to be working in *real-time*.

In the on-line update mode each transaction becomes a batch which is processed on demand. The input, validation, updating and output processes must be performed for each transaction as and when it occurs (see Figure 11.4).

FIGURE 11.4. On-line real-time system.

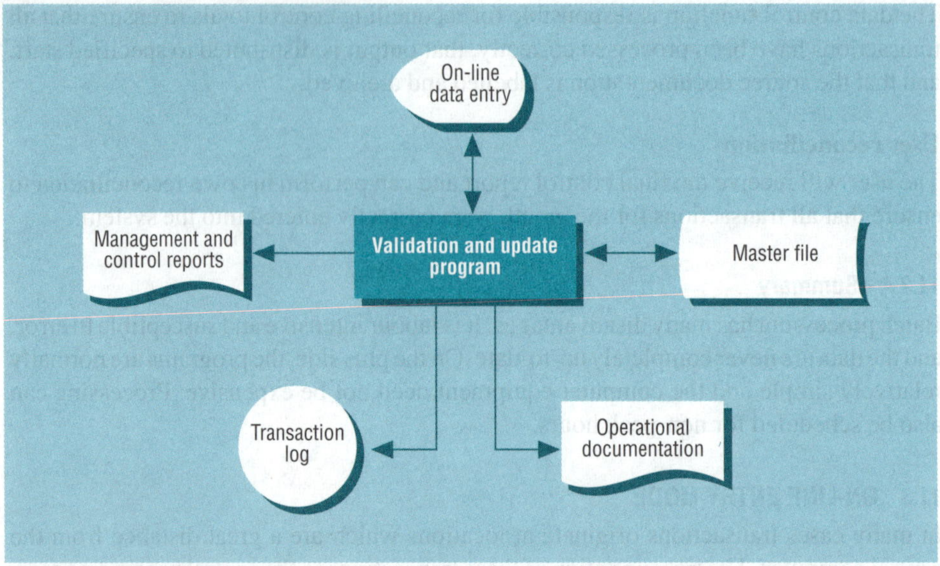

Airline booking systems are normally on-line update systems. Records of the availability of seats on all planes are kept on a central computer. The computer is linked via terminals to a worldwide system of travel agents. Each agent can gain access to the flight records and make a reservation on a particular flight. The reservation is recorded immediately so that the next enquiry for that flight finds that the seat in question has been reserved.

The on-line real-time environment has obvious advantages over the batch approach:

- the computer can assist in the data entry process and can highlight errors while the transaction is generated;
- information from the system is always up-to-date;
- the system is not cumbersome and labour intensive.

A number of features of real-time systems make them both costly and difficult to maintain. The costs will vary with the service that the system provides. The better the service (ie. the shorter the response time), the more costly it becomes in terms of hardware and software. We now look at some of the factors which lead to these high costs.

11.4.1 Response time

As the enquiry and update processes now form part of the transaction's origination, it is important that the computer be able to respond quickly to the terminal operator's requests. Furthermore, the computer must be able to handle peak periods (such as lunch times) when customers are likely to be arranging travel bookings.

11.4.2 Reliability

As the terminal operator requires information from the computer in order to conduct each transaction, it is important that the machine does not malfunction. Long or regular periods of computer down time can seriously impair the running of the business. It is therefore quite common to see strategic elements of computer hardware duplicated so that if, say, one CPU fails, a stand-by machine can be brought into use.

11.4.3 Storage requirements

In an on-line update system all the records and files that will be required by the on-line terminal operators must be able to be accessed with great speed. The data must therefore reside on direct access storage devices so that each individual query can immediately access the required master record.

11.4.4 Software

Special systems software programs are also required to handle the operational requirements of an on-line network with many simultaneous users accessing the system. Such programs are known as *teleprocessing monitors*.

11.4.5 Controls

As each transaction is entered into the computer individually there is a danger that users will not be alerted if a power failure prevents a document from being entered or causes the document to be lost. Even in a power failure, controls over transaction values and document counts must still be maintained. The most common method of control in on-line systems is for the computer to retain control totals for each user and enforce a reconciliation when processing for the day is complete.

11.5 TIME-SHARING

Time-sharing is the apparently simultaneous use of a computer by a number of users. There are many businesses that require a computer at random intervals but cannot afford or justify the purchase of their own machine. One answer might be to send the data to a service bureau for processing. This may not be convenient, however, especially if the user wishes to work interactively with the machine.

Time-sharing systems are used by people such as engineers who make large and complex calculations (such as the stress coefficient on a high-rise building). Each calculation is conditioned by the previous analysis. Users of time-sharing systems normally require the use of a powerful and sophisticated machine at infrequent intervals and at a location convenient to them.

One answer is to have a remote terminal installed at the user's premises. This is linked to a time-share computer system. In this way, through the use of a simple computer terminal and telecommunications link, the user can have the power of a large mainframe computer at his disposal. The large time-sharing system can often have as many as 200 people using the system at the same time. The success of the network depends on the computer being able to process all the user requests with little apparent delay so that each user is therefore under the impression that he has his own dedicated system.

REVIEW QUESTIONS

1. Explain how batch processing differs from real-time processing.
2. What is a hash total?
3. What do the following edit checks do:
   range check
   validity check
   check digit
   completeness check
   table look-up?
4. What is meant by master file maintenance?
5. What is the purpose of a suspense file?
6. What are the duties of a data controller?
7. What is meant by 'run to run controls'?
8. How do we ensure that no transactions are lost in
   (a) a batch environment and in
   (b) an on-line real-time environment?
9. Explain the concept of time sharing.
10. What are the three major steps in the data processing cycle?

SELECTED REFERENCES AND RECOMMENDED READING

Leitch, R. A. and Roscoe Davis, K. 1992. *Accounting Information Systems — Theory and Practice.* Second edition. New Jersey: Prentice-Hall.

CHAPTER 12 The user interface

12.1 INTRODUCTION

We have seen the hardware and software components of the computer system and some of the ways in which processing can be performed. How these are experienced by the users of a system is of vital importance. A system with a good *user interface* is likely to be used readily and perceived as successful — one with a poor interface will be regarded as unsuccessful, regardless of its technical brilliance.

If users don't like the system, or find it difficult to use, they will not use it.

The standardization of interfaces is also of vital importance. Consider the poor user who has to interact with a financial planning system, a budget system, a personnel system, and a production planning system. If each of these has its own unique way of presenting screens, processing choices, and using function keys, the user will find it very difficult to switch between systems. The same key on one system may mean 'save what I have done' while on another it means 'discard this screen'!

The effort and cost involved in training also rise in direct proportion to the number of different interfaces which users encounter.

In this chapter we will be dealing with the development of user interfaces, the types of interfaces now in common use, emerging standards, and some future trends.

12.2 EVOLUTION OF THE USER INTERFACE

Early machines such as the huge ENIAC were designed for a very limited range of tasks and had limited computing power. The program as a separate entity was not well understood. If users wanted the machine to perform a different calculation they had to physically rewire parts of the circuitry! This was very tedious and expensive, and required very high levels of skill.

The machines which followed were only slightly better than this. Many of these had huge 'plug panels' or banks of switches to turn on and off various options and paths built into the machine's processing logic. These consoles were much beloved by the makers of early science fiction movies. Most data input was achieved with switches or punched media (cards and paper tape). Again, the programmers and operators required a great deal of skill to interact with these computers, and end-users interacted with them only through these skilled professionals.

Rapid progress began with the advent of video display terminals. These enabled data to be captured through a keyboard and screen, with the information being written to tape or disk for later processing. Consoles were added to computers, allowing operators to interact with them using typed commands instead of switches or punched cards. The provision of terminals allowed users to retrieve information and display it at their own location without the need for printouts. On-line systems were developed which allowed transactions to be entered immediately into the computer.

Most of the early on-line systems used character mode terminals capable of displaying only numbers and upper case letters. What actually appeared on the screen, what format it took, and how attributes such as function keys were used were left up to individual systems analysts and programmers. Most systems intended for expert users (eg. programmers, operators, statisticians, scientists etc.) made use of a command-driven interface, where the user would type commands using a very strict syntax. Systems for less expert users (eg. commercial transaction processing and enquiry systems) tended to use a combination of menu screens and 'fill in the blank' formatted displays to guide the operator through predefined functions and sequences. Some graphics workstations became available, but these were restricted by cost to specialist applications such as astronomical image-viewing.

Two key developments changed the situation radically. The first was the advent of personal computers with relatively cheap graphics capabilities, and the second was the development of the *graphical user interface* (GUI) at the Xerox Palo Alto Research Center (PARC).

Cheap personal computers made graphics accessible to the masses and to a very wide body of applications developers. At first, they were used to display results of calculations (in the form of graphs or graphical models), to play games, and to draw rudimentary geometric shapes. Gradually, however, the power of graphics was harnessed to provide a new way of dealing with the computer.

Researchers at PARC developed the STAR workstation. The idea was that the screen behaves like a 'virtual' desktop. An area on the screen with a border, known as a *window*, represents the surface of the desktop. Displayed in the window are small pictures or icons representing objects. These could be drawers (representing storage), folders (representing the related parts of a project) or individual sheets of paper (perhaps representing a word processing document or spreadsheet), and maybe a rubbish bin (allowing the user to discard objects). The user would work with the objects using familiar concepts. He might, for example, open a folder to access the documents inside it, drop things into drawers to put them away, and place documents in the rubbish bin to discard them. This interaction is normally accomplished using a pointing device — most commonly a mouse.

The Xerox work was a research project, but its concepts were applied commercially in the Apple Lisa and Macintosh personal computers. Commodore users had a similar interface in GEM on the C64, and later Intuition on the Amiga. The IBM PC world was much slower in adopting the graphical approach, but the idiom was widely copied and now underlies several products including Microsoft Windows and IBM's Presentation Manager. The mid-range systems world (mainly Unix) has seen similar interfaces emerge on workstations such as the Sun and Hewlett Packard. Predominant amongst these is X-Windows.

Let's explore the different types of interface now in common use.

12.3 COMMAND-BASED INTERFACE

Operating systems such as DOS or Unix are typical of the character/command-based interface. These are intended for expert users. They are good for directing the computer to do what the user wants, but the commands and options must be used in particular sequences. Typical activities might include creating and copying files, browsing through directories on the screen, displaying the contents of a file, running a utility program, editing a program source file, compiling a program, executing it to test it, and so on.

Fig 12.1 illustrates a sample session in DOS where the user displays all files on the disk in the A drive and then copies some of the files to the disk in the B drive.

FIGURE 12.1. Command-based interface.

```
A: \>dir  /w

Volume in drive A has no label
Directory of  A:\
COMMAND COM  IPX        COM  NET3       COM  AUTOEXEC BAT  CONFIG SYS
CED     COM  BOOK       WK1  IS3LOTUS   WK1  DATABASE PRN  DATA   WK1
CELL    WK1  DATABASE   BAK  DATABASE   DOC  NORMAL   GLY  DAYS   WK1
IS1APPL BAK  IS1APPL    DOC  IS1_TUTS   WK1  CCODES   WK1  NAMES  WK1
NORMAL  STY
        21 File(s)    124928 bytes free

A: \>copy *.com b:
COMMAND.COM
IPX.COM
NET3.COM
CED.COM
        4 File(s) copied

A:\>
```

12.4 MENU-DRIVEN INTERFACE

Less expert users, such as sales clerks in a store, would normally need to interact with the computer in a predefined and controlled way. This is often accomplished with menus and gaps to be filled in on screen. The menu structure is normally hierarchical and displays the choices that the user must make — eg. to process sales or print sales reports. The user chooses from the available functions, but the system imposes discipline in terms of what the user sees and what the user is allowed access to. The predefined formatted screens provide guidance and information that enable the user to complete a given task, such as a sale or return. Such systems are typically fairly easy to use, but relatively inflexible — the user can only accomplish what the analyst and developers have anticipated.

Figure 12.2 is an example of a menu system and the demand report that can be requested.

FIGURE 12.2. Menu-driven user interface.

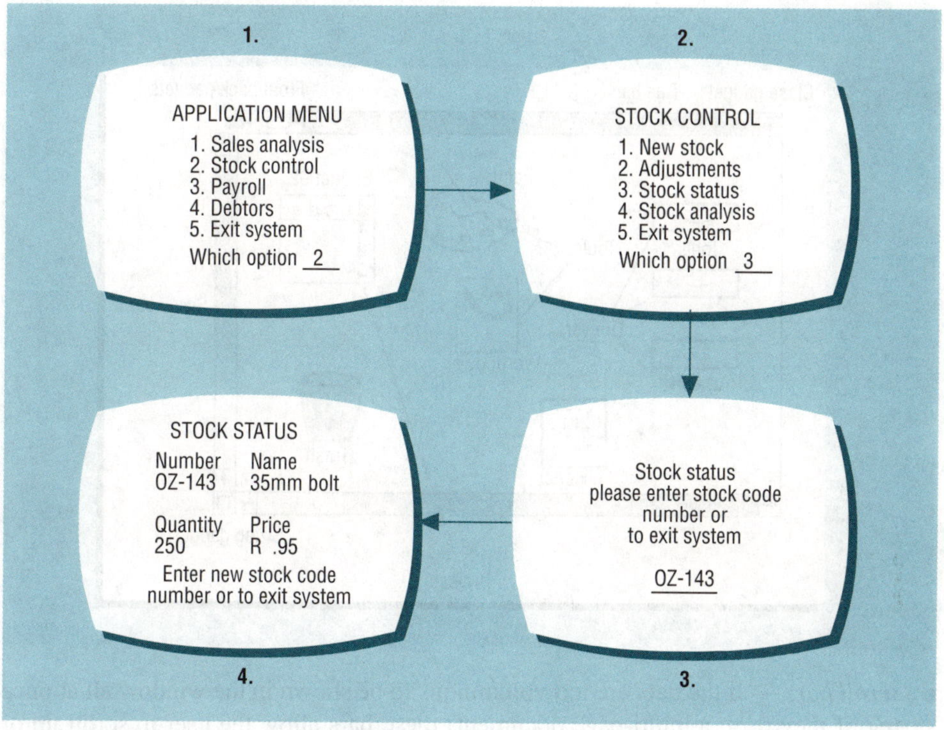

12.5 GRAPHICAL USER INTERFACE

Developers have now built *graphical user interfaces* (GUIs — pronounced 'gooeys') which allow the user to interact with a variety of packages in a consistent way. These use concepts from the PARC research and the graphics power of personal computers. GUIs have major benefits in terms of training and error avoidance, and they enable users to exploit the full power of software packages since users are able to explore the facilities available in packages more easily.

We shall now look at some key features of a GUI environment.

12.5.1 Windows

These are bordered areas on the display (see Figure 12.3). They normally deal with a particular function — there might be a window containing spreadsheet data, and another containing a graph derived from the data in the spreadsheet. Windows can normally overlap, like sheets of paper on a desk. They can be moved in front of, or behind, one another as required. They also usually provide several gadgets which allow the user to manipulate and customize them:

- *close button* — this allows the user to close the window when it is no longer required;
- *pane buttons* — these allow the window to be brought to the front or sent to the back;

FIGURE 12.3. Windows user interface.

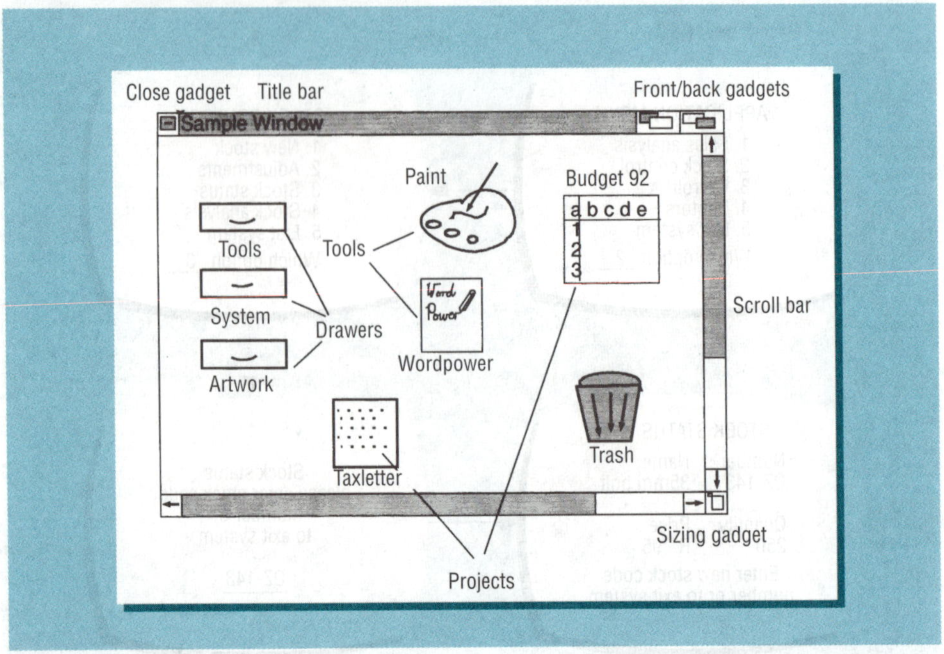

- *scroll bars* — if the data are too voluminous to be shown in the window all at once (eg. if they form a multi-page document) these bars allow the user to scroll up or down and left or right to see hidden portions of the document;
- *page buttons* — these may allow documents to move forward or backward a page at a time;
- *size handle* — this is normally in the bottom right-hand corner. Pointing and dragging with a mouse will usually allow the user to alter the size of the window;
- *title bar* — this is the top border of the window and normally provides identification and status information. It may also allow the user to drag the window to a new position on the screen.

12.5.2 Icons

These are the little pictures representing objects within a window. Typical icons include:

- *drawers* — these represent storage areas. Opening them by selecting them with the mouse and clicking will normally result in the opening of a new window which shows the objects stored in the drawer;
- *tools* — these represent programs and applications providing processing and functionality. Examples include spreadsheets, graphics programs, word processors, communications packages, databases etc. When a tool is selected, this will normally take the user into the application. The user can then begin using its own screens and facilities;

- *projects* — these represent the related files for a particular job a user was performing. An example would be a particular spreadsheet and the related graphics produced from it. The project will normally know which tool produced it. Selecting the project will normally result in the tool being loaded, with the project data immediately loaded and available;
- *trash can* — this represents a rubbish bin and works just like a real one. Users drop things that they no longer want into it. It is possible to retrieve things from the trash can as long as no-one has 'emptied the trash' which would delete the information permanently.

12.5.3 Pull-down menus

Many windows will have a wide range of functions available which are not necessarily displayed as icons. Someone who is working in a word processor will not really want a large number of pictures in the middle of the text, so additional functions are typically provided by pull-down menus, accessed with another mouse option (eg. by holding down the right button, or clicking on the title bar). Major menu options are normally listed across the top of the screen. As the pointer passes over each major function, the sub-functions which relate to it are displayed in a drop down list. Moving a highlighted bar over the required choice and selecting it with the mouse will normally activate the choice in question.

A typical pull-down menu display is shown in Figure 12.4.

FIGURE 12.4. Pull-down menu display.

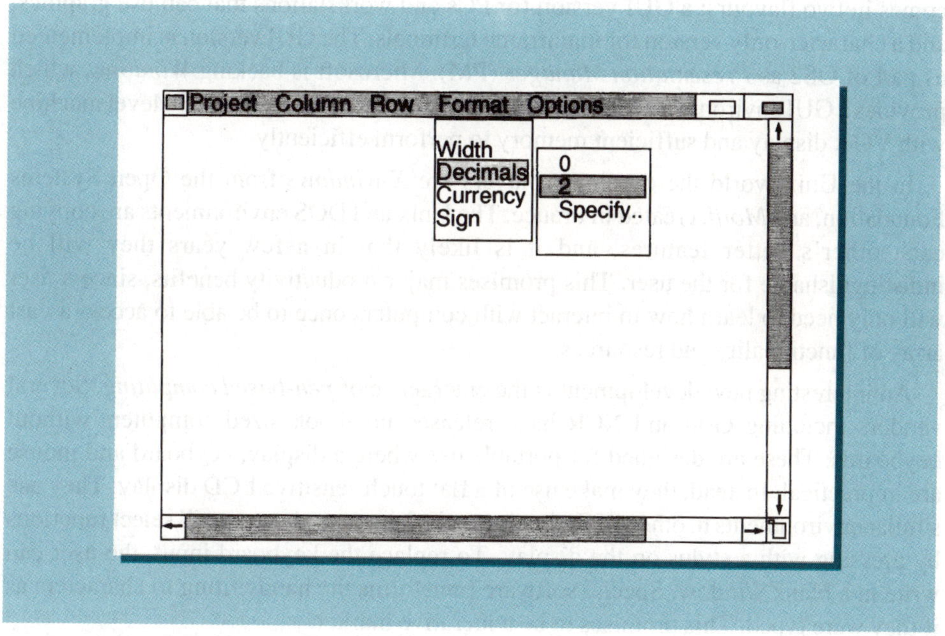

12.5.4 Clipboard

This works just like a normal clipboard. You can 'cut' or 'copy' information from a window to the clipboard, which is a temporary storage area, and then copy it into the same window later, or into another window. This second window could even belong to another application. This would, for example, allow the user to transfer a set of figures from a spreadsheet into a word processor document without retyping. Another example would be to transfer a symbol from a graphics package into a document.

12.6 FUTURE TRENDS IN USER INTERFACES

Standardization of the interface is extremely important. Increasingly sophisticated applications mean that there are many functions and options to choose from. Users are interacting with many more products. People need packages that offer a common 'look and feel'. If they can provide common file formats for easy data exchange, and ways to cut and paste between packages, so much the better.

The user should always be able to interact with his system in a consistent way, irrespective of differences in the underlying software. This would drastically reduce the learning curve for a user. Very little learning would be required to assimilate a new package which operates in the same environment and with the same idiom.

Software vendors are looking for the next big market. They are trying to provide the 'desktop' GUI environment to the millions of existing computer users, and they are opening up new markets through its extreme ease of use and consistency. As a result, IBM and Microsoft are battling for supremacy of their own 'standards'. IBM has created *common user access* (CUA) as part of its *systems application architecture* (SAA). This comes in two flavours: a GUI version for PCs and workstations that can use graphics, and a character-only version for mainframe terminals. The GUI version is implemented as part of OS2 as *Presentation Manager* (PM). Microsoft is backing *Windows*, which provides a GUI environment for PCs. PM and Windows both require a 286 level machine with VGA display and sufficient memory to perform efficiently.

In the Unix world the dominant players are *X-windows* from the Open Systems Foundation, and *Motif*, created in France. The Unix and DOS environments are copying each other's better features, and it is likely that in a few years they will be indistinguishable for the user. This promises major productivity benefits, since a user will only need to learn how to interact with computers once to be able to access a vast array of functionality and resources.

An interesting new development is the emergence of *pen-based computing*. Several vendors including Grid and NCR have released notebook sized computers without keyboards. These are designed for portable use where a display, keyboard and mouse are impractical. Instead, they make use of a flat touch sensitive LCD display. They use similar environments to other GUIs, but instead of a mouse, the user will select functions by pressing with a stylus on the display. To replace the keyboard input, the user can write in a blank window. Special software transforms the handwriting to characters as if they were typed. This promises to be a lucrative market.

REVIEW QUESTIONS

1. What do we mean by the acronym GUI and why is it important?
2. Compare the DOS user interface with WINDOWS giving the advantages and disadvantages of each.
3. What GUI environments are currently available to commercial users?

SELECTED REFERENCES AND RECOMMENDED READING

Capron, H. L. 1992. *Essentials of Computing*. Redwood, California: Benjamin/Cummings.

MODULE 2 KEY POINT SUMMARY

The important issues highlighted in this module are as follows:

- While the origins of computing date back many hundreds of years the first electronic computer was used commercially in the early 1950s.
- *Computer hardware* is made up of the central processing unit (CPU) and its peripheral devices used for input, output and storage.
- *The central processing unit* is the 'brain' of the computer, controlling the interpretation and execution of instructions. It contains:
  - main storage, where the program instructions, data and temporary working are held during processing;
  - control unit, which directs and controls the CPU and its external devices;
  - arithmetic logic unit, used to perform mathematical calculations and logical comparisons.
- *Input devices* are required to transcribe data into a form usable by the computer. They can be classified into three broad areas:
  - Data transcription devices: the data is keyed in and stored on some temporary medium (such as punch cards, magnetic tape or disk) or transferred directly to the computer.
  - By-product devices, where the operator's primary task is not to capture the data (e.g. a check-out clerk in a supermarket) but the device used is able to capture the necessary input as a by-product of the original operation.
  - Advanced systems, such as optical scanners and voice recognition devices, which attempt to automate the input process totally.
- *Output devices* reverse the 'translation' process by converting characters from binary form (their representation inside the machine) into a form which is readable by humans.
- Important output devices include:
  - printers classified into impact and non-impact, and line and character versions
  - computer output microfilm (COM), where information can be captured onto microfilm without having to generate a printed hard copy
  - terminals for temporary displays
  - plotters to produce drawings and graphical representations.
- *Secondary storage devices* such as magnetic disks and tapes are used to store data within the computer system for processing at some future date.
- For historical reasons people have tended to categorize computers into three main types — the mainframe, mini and microcomputer. As new technology has been absorbed into the computer industry, these groupings are no longer so well defined. Today it is more practical to view computers in terms of their role in the business environment — as personal 'work stations' or small and large business machines — rather than in terms of their hardware characteristics. Forty years have seen phenomenal advances in computer performance and yet the best may still be to come.

- Following the philosophy of making the computer more accessible, there is a tendency towards providing users with remote input and output devices linked together via telecommunications networks. The main components of such systems are the communications channels (normally those used for telephone communications) and special-purpose control devices (designed to increase the quality and volume of data transmission).
- Having discussed all the major categories of computer hardware, we now turn to the other major element of any computer system — the software. The power of computers lies in their ability to follow a sequence of instructions (software), termed a *computer program.*
- There are two main classifications of software:
  - Systems software: general programs which were written to support the computer system (often referred to as housekeeping programs). These include the operating system which does many of the tasks previously performed by the human operator, general-purpose utility programs for tasks such as copying and sorting data, and translation programs for converting instructions written for the computer into the language which the machine can understand, ie. machine language.
  - Application software encompasses all the programs which have been written or purchased to solve the business needs of the organization. Examples of these would be programs to process the company's payroll, debtors and stock.
- Programs can be written in the language of the computer, but this tends to be both difficult and time-consuming. Today there are a number of special higher-level languages that are written specifically to solve problems in the commercial, scientific, and educational fields. The programmer writes the instructions in the language of his choice and the computer then translates them into machine language prior to execution.
- As with a manual system, computers must have an organized method of data storage to ensure that the necessary data can be accessed when required. The facts of the business are filed in a method very similar in concept to a manual filing system and there are three main ways of organizing the data:
  - Sequentially: reading through the data from the beginning and selecting the records required.
  - Randomly: going directly to a particular piece of information.
  - Indexed sequentially: having the ability to access data sequentially or directly.
- Computer systems are being used in more and more areas of each business and creating files for each application has tended to fragment the organization's data. One solution is to integrate all the files into a common pool of data, known as a database, which can be accessed by many different applications.
  - A specialized software program called a data base management system (DBMS), which looks after the data. Because the complex relationships between the various data items make it difficult to access and update the data, the DBMS takes over this role and the application programs merely have to request the necessary data from the DBMS.

- An individual or group of people called the data base administrator (DBA) who is responsible for specifying the contents, relationships and structure of the data base.
- To assist the DBA, there is a system software program called a data dictionary (DD). The DD is really just another data base in which all the 'data about the data' are kept.

- There are a number of different modes of computer processing:
  - Batch mode: where input to the system is accumulated and processed periodically.
  - On-line entry mode, which is essentially the same as batch except data are transmitted from remote locations via data communication links.
  - On-line update: often referred to as realtime processing where each transaction is entered and processed as it occurs so that the computer can always reflect the current situation.
- The acceptance of new computer systems is to a large part dependent on its ease of use. Over the last ten years the interface has evolved from complex and cryptic command-based systems to the graphical interface where the screen can be made to simulate the user's working environment.

COMPUTER HISTORY

1. Abacus
2. Napier's Bones
3. Hollerith's Tabulator and Sorter
4. Pascal's Adding Machine
5. Integrated Circuit
6. Valve Memory
7. Core Storage
8. Babbage's Difference Engine

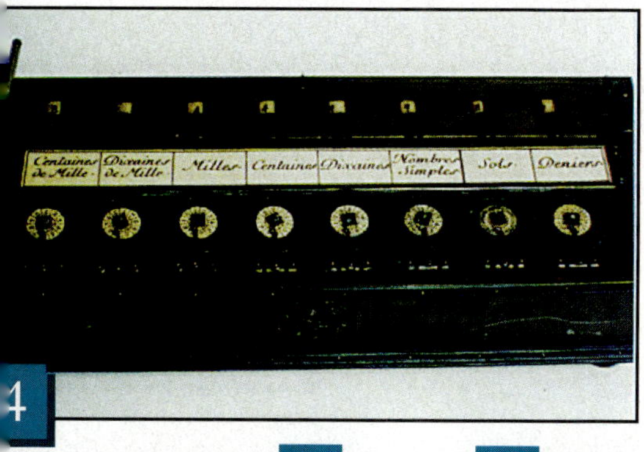

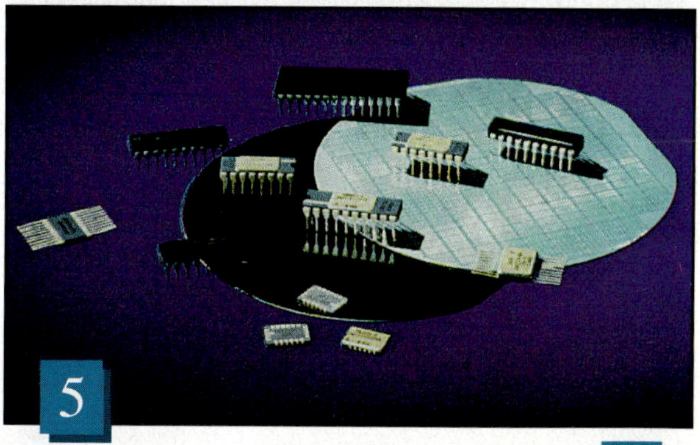

Input Devices

1. Keyboard
2. Flat Bed OCR Scanner
3. Pen Based Computer
4. Touch Sensitive Screen
5. Point of Sale Terminal
6. Bar Code Scanner
7. Mouse
8. Digitizer Tabler

I

2

3

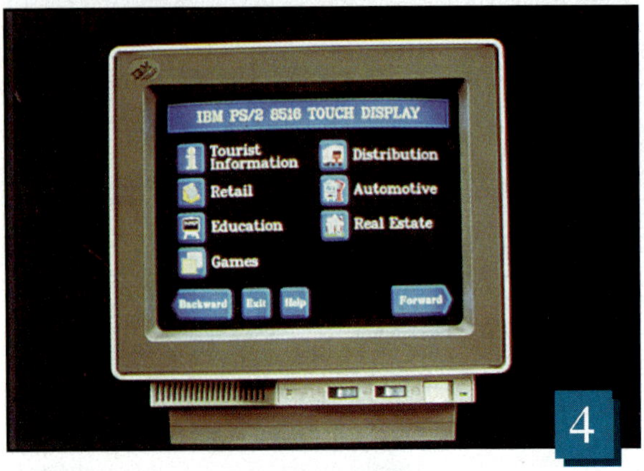

4

5

6

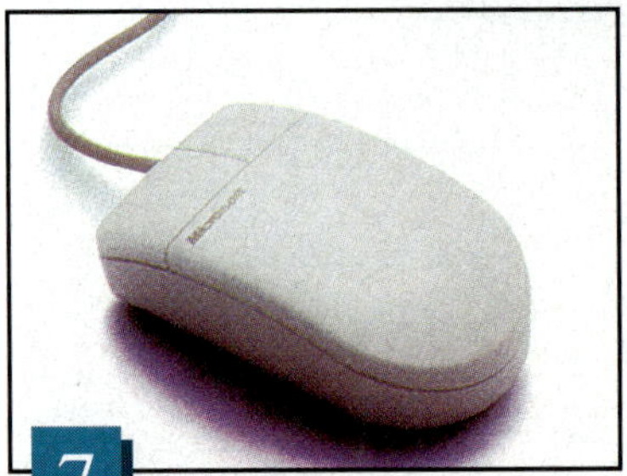

7

8

Output Devices

1. Microfiche
2. Colour Graphics Screen
3. Plotter
4. Microfiche Reader
5. Matrix Printer
6. Colour Printer
7. High Performance Laser Printer

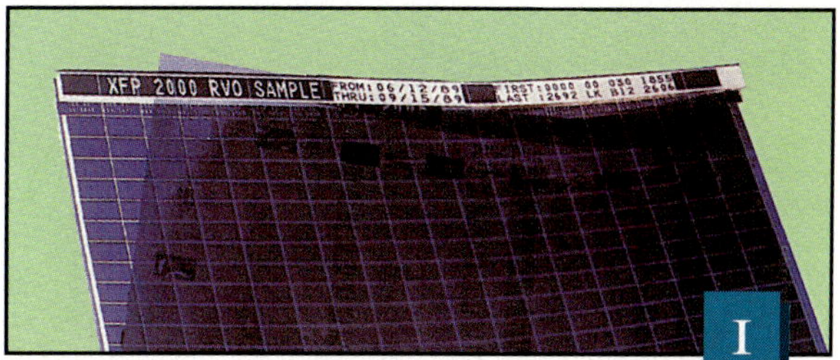

1

2

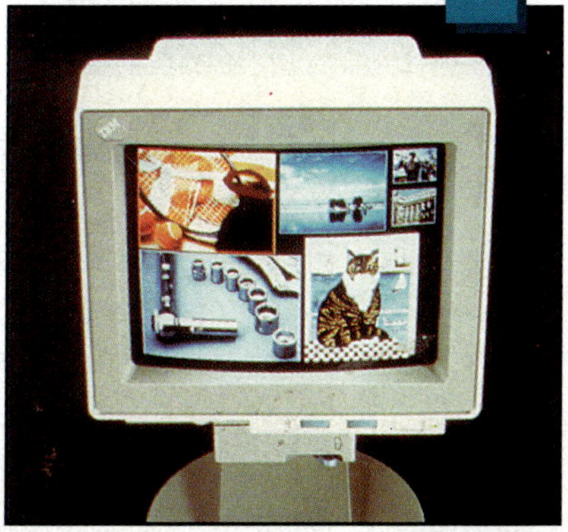

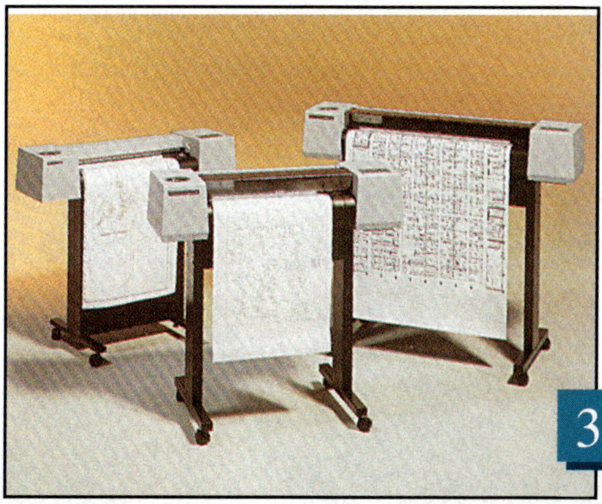

3

5

6

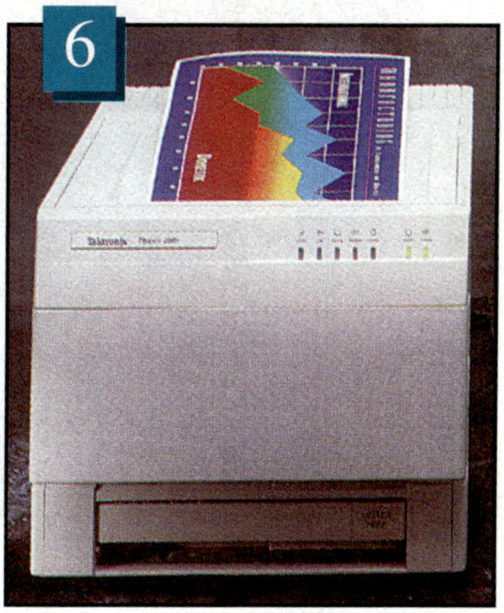

7

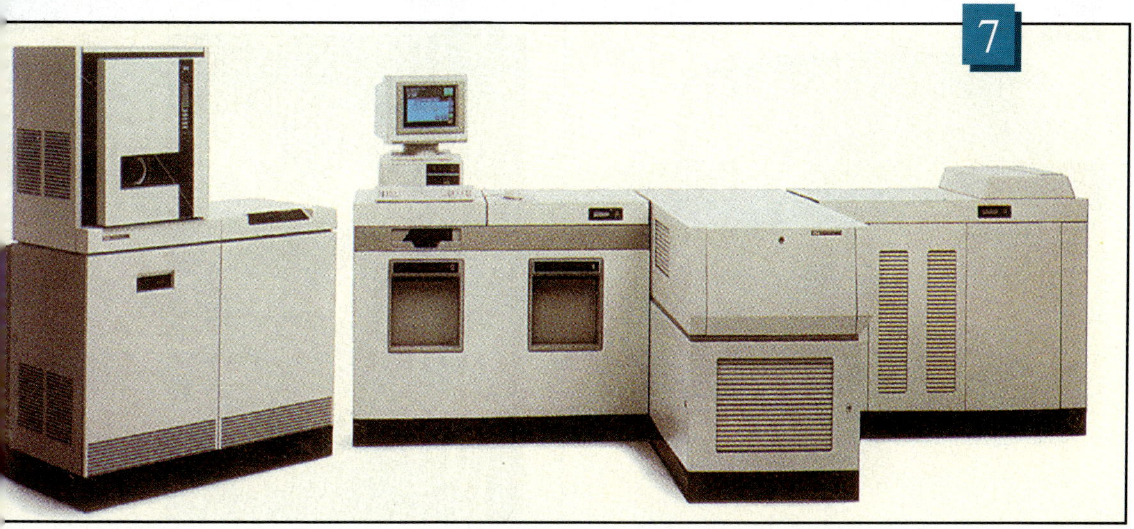

Storage Devices

1. Internal View of Mainframe Disk Drive
2. Internal View of PC Hard Disk Drive
3. $3^1/_2$ inch Floppy Disk (Stiffy)
4. Optical Disk
5. Magnetic Tape and Cassette
6. Magnetic Tape Drives
7. External View of Robotic Arm System (This mass storage device gives automated fast access to over 5,000 cassette tapes).
8. Internal View of Robot Arm in Cartridge System

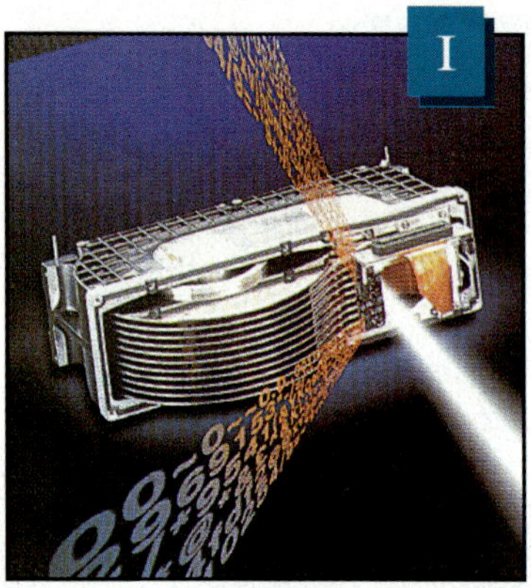

1

2

3

4

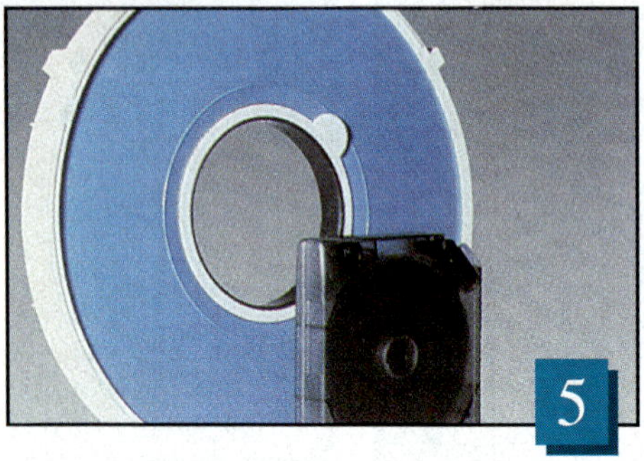

5

6

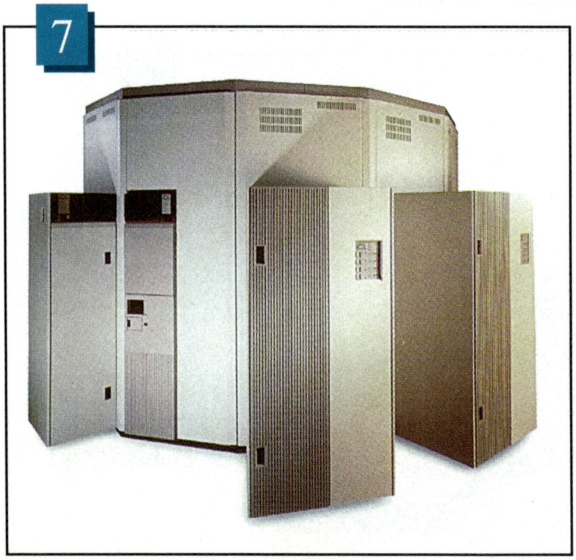

7

8

PERSONAL COMPUTERS

- Desk Top PC
- Notebook PC
- Handheld PC
- Palmtop PC
- Device Interface Card
- Internal view of PC showing interface card on mother board

1

2

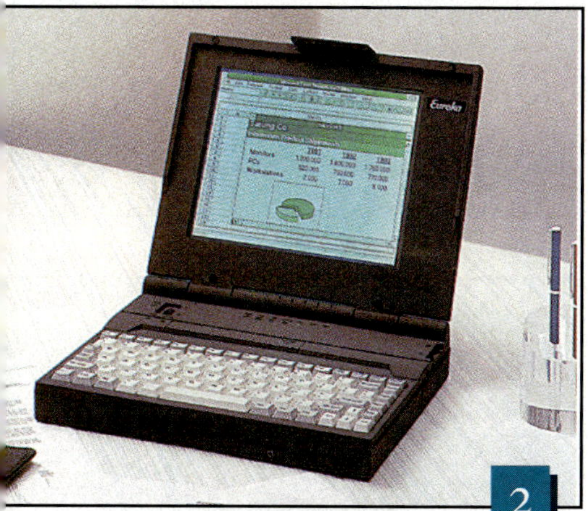

3

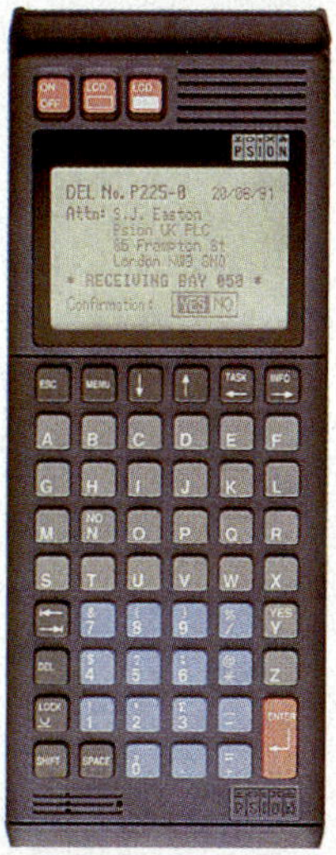

4

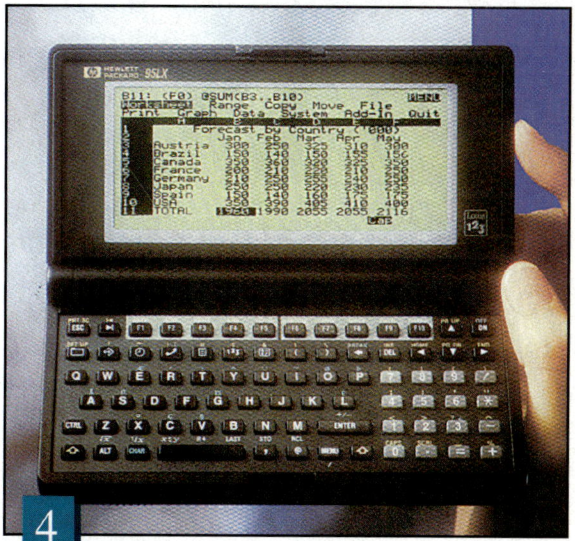

5

6

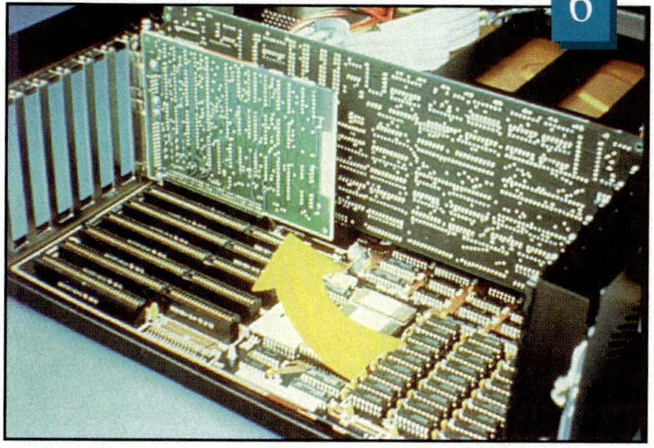

Data Communications

1. Optic Fibre (This single strand can carry up to 3,000 simultaneous telephone conversations)
2. Cables and Connectors
3. Modem
4. Communication Controllers
5. Satellite Dish
6. Microwave Tower

1

2

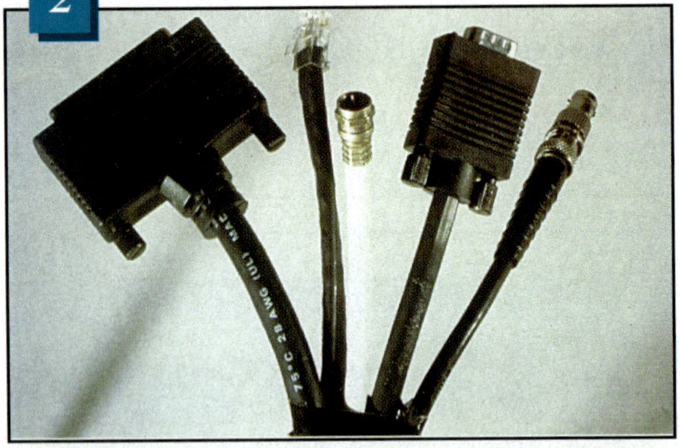

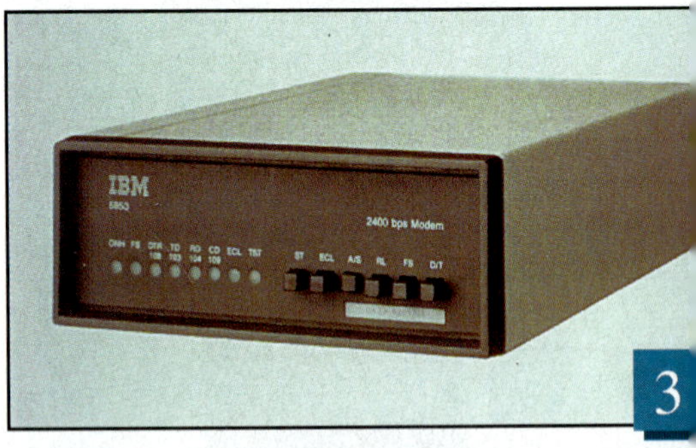

3

4

6

5

GRAPHIC USER INTERFACE (GUI)

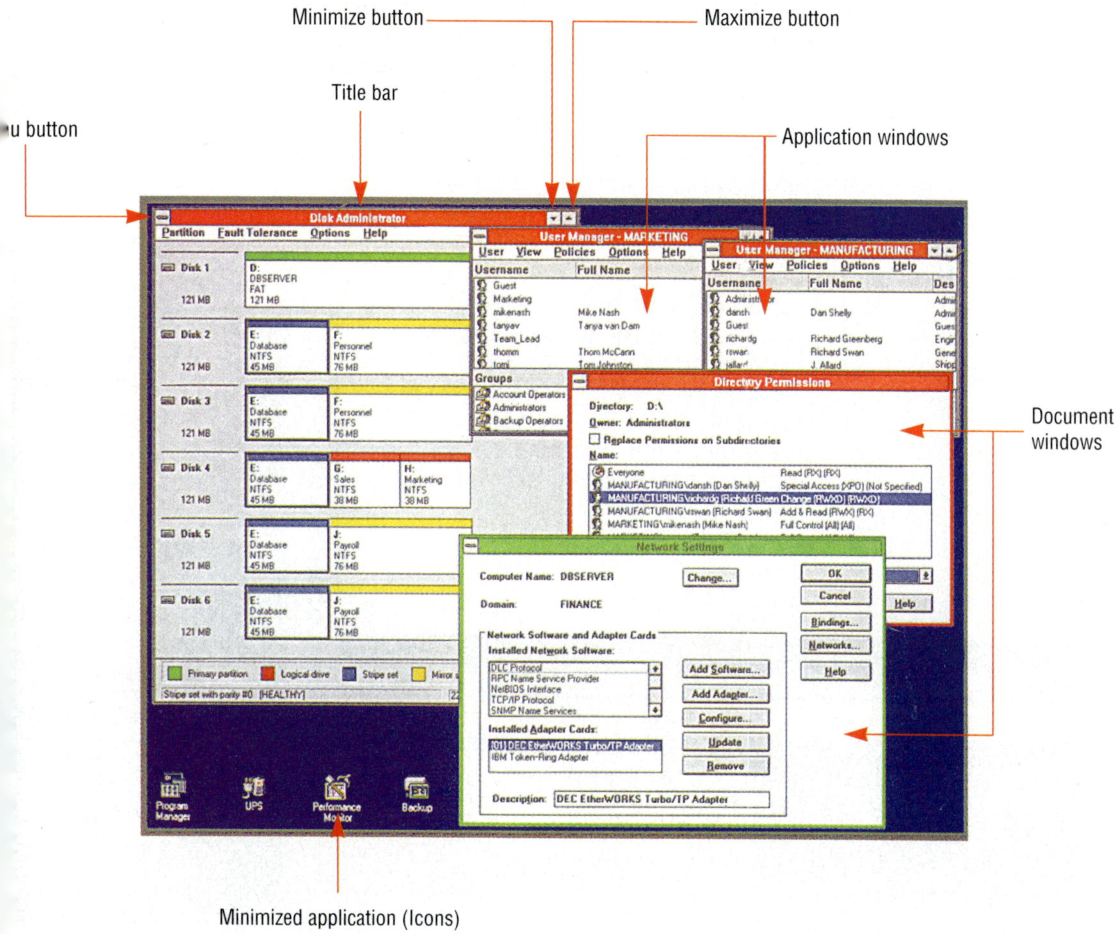

the past, computer operating environments were ›mmand-based and difficult for novice users. With ɛ widespread use of computers, more friendly ways ' communicating with the machine had to be ›veloped. One technique is to use pictures and aphics to make the screen mirror the way the end ›er works. One such GUI is Windows from icrosoft. This operating environment simulates the er's desk top, allowing the user to select applications d computer resources by pointing to the appropriate cture (icon) with a mouse. Two additional vantages of GUI environments are that they provide common 'look and feel' to their applications (how u instruct the computer to perform tasks will be the me whether you are using a spreadsheet, word ocessor or graphics package), and data can easily be ansferred from one application to another.

hile workers prefer to work at one task at a time, ɛre are always interruptions from clients or fellow ›rkers needing information. Where applications are computerized, this often requires the user to close down the application or document currently active, in order to access the information required. While typing a letter, a secretary may be asked to print out the latest budget figures from a spreadsheet file. This second task may then be interrupted by a phone call to set up a staff meeting, requiring access to the computer-based electronic calendar. Using Windows, the user can open multiple applications (or windows) on the screen (or desk top) and switch from one task to another as required.

Each application window has its own title bar, menu button (click on this with the mouse to activate the command menu), 'maximize' button (to increase the window size), and 'minimize' button to reduce the application to an icon at the bottom of the screen. In addition, a number of document windows can be opened within each application, allowing the user to work with a number of separate word-processing documents at the same time.

The term 'multimedia' describes the use of sound, graphics and animation, as well as text-based data, in an application. The technology required to digitize sound and vision into data files has been available for many years, the major barrier to its commercial use being the huge volumes of secondary storage required to hold this data. With the development of file compression algorithms and the commercial application of optical storage (CD-ROM), multimedia applications are now commonplace. The picture below with adjoining text is taken from Encarta, a multimedia encyclopedia developed by Microsoft and available on a single CD-ROM.

More than 25,000 articles and 17,000 multimedia elements help you learn about every subject from *aardvark* to *zygote.* Encarta includes the complete text of the 29-volume 1992 *Funk & Wagnalls New Encyclopedia*, plus more than 1,000 new articles, created exclusively for Encarta, that cover history, modern culture, and computers.

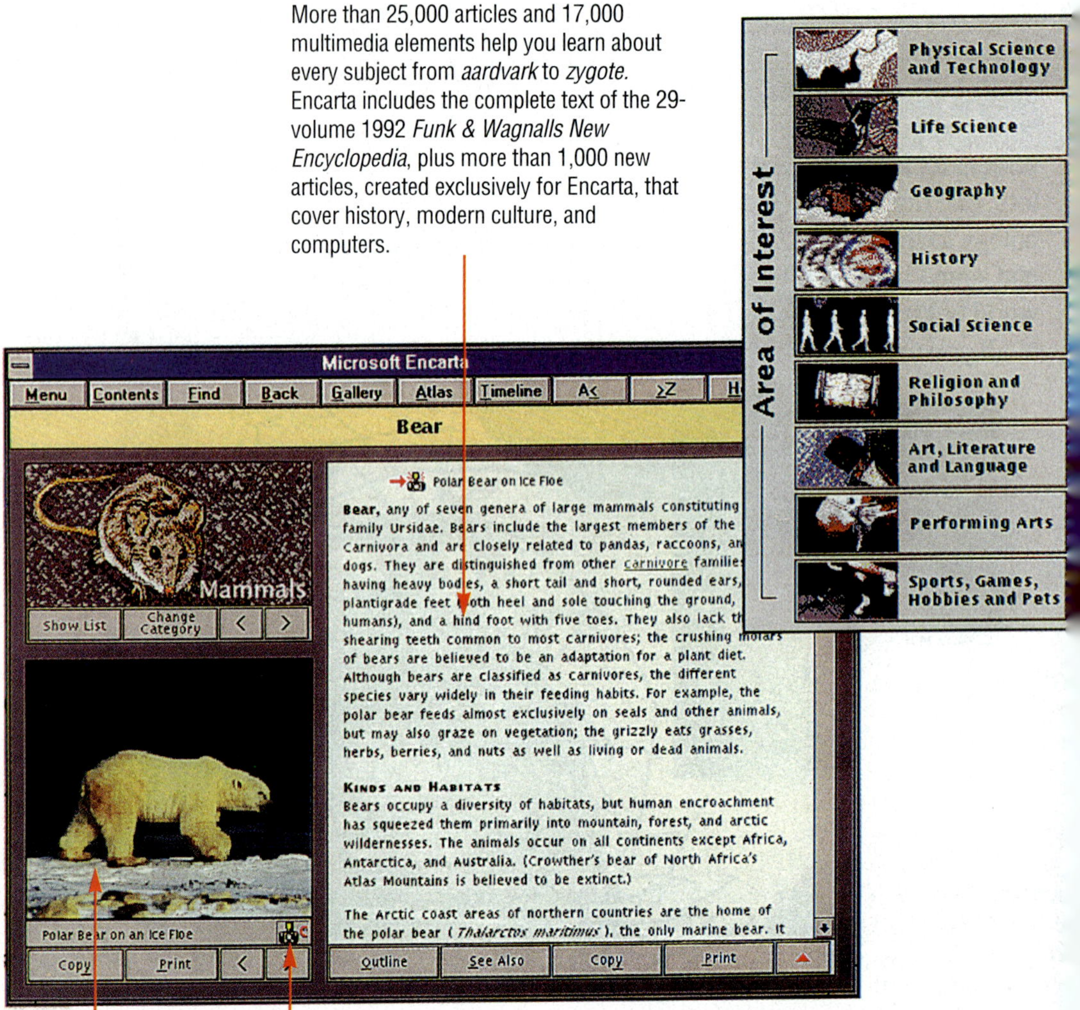

Thousands of images show you more than words can say. Learn with the help of high-quality colour photographs and illustrations exclusively prepared for the computer screen.

Thousands of sounds make a feast for your ears. Listen to 350 jazz, classical, and world music segments, hundreds of bird and animal sounds, over 100 readings by authors, samples of more than 45 languages, nearly 5,000 word pronunciations, and more.

MODULE

3 Information systems development

OBJECTIVES

This module is concerned with the development of information systems. It describes the development process from inception through to final implementation. Each of the following stages are described in detail:

- The formulation of an information systems strategy and the development of the systems plan
- Defining use requirements using such techniques as entity-relationship modelling and data flow diagrams
- Performing a preliminary systems design. This section focuses on using the joint development method, involving both users and systems personnel
- The detailed design of a system, paying particular attention to man-machine dialogue
- The implementation of a system
- Managing the information systems development project

This module examines the development process primarily from the perspective of a user. It describes the process of developing sound systems that satisfy the needs of the user community. There is thus very little emphasis on technical processes such as programming aspects or module design. On completion of this module the student should therefore have an understanding of user issues in systems development.

CHAPTER 13 An introduction to systems development

13.1 WHAT ARE BUSINESS INFORMATION SYSTEMS?

In one of the earliest works on general systems theory, Bertalanffy describes systems as 'sets of elements standing in interaction'.[1] What this means is that a system consists of a number of components (elements) that have a defined relationship. It is this relationship which binds them so that the system may operate.

This definition may sound so vague as to be useless, but in fact it describes any system perfectly. The purpose of the circulation system, for instance, is to circulate blood around the body. This is achieved by the interaction of the various components such as the heart, the arteries and veins, and the kidneys. A motor vehicle consists of an engine, transmission, suspension, and a passenger support mechanism, each of which interact to transport the driver and passengers.

In subsequent definitions people have added that the elements interact to achieve a defined goal. This has now achieved fairly universal acceptance.

A *business system* can be defined as 'sets of procedures that assist people to manage and control the operations of an organization'. These procedures are defined in such a way that specific relationships are established between the various components of the system. These components may be people within the organization, the market, the computer, filing cabinets, and so on.

Within an organization there may be many different *types* of systems. For instance, there are physical systems such as those for moving products from storage to dispatch trucks. There may be simple little systems for making and distributing coffee to employees. There may be security systems for screening people entering and leaving the building.

One type of system that has recently become prevalent in most organizations is the *information system*. If one builds on the definition that was developed earlier, then an information system (IS) is *a structured set of procedures for processing, storing and distributing information, designed in such a way as to best serve the goals of the organization.*

Notice that the above definition does not include the word 'computer'. In almost all cases information systems do, in practice, include the use of a computer these days, but computer technology is not a prerequisite for a business information system. For example, a secretary who writes details of customer complaints on little cards and summarizes them every month for the boss, has an information system.

13.2 THE PROPERTIES OF A BUSINESS INFORMATION SYSTEM

If one examines business information systems, certain common properties can be found. Most of these have their roots in systems theory and are therefore applicable to all systems (not just information systems).

13.2.1 Elements of a system

All systems consist of *elements* or activities. These elements may themselves conform to the definition of a system — in other words there may be a system within a system. In this case they would be referred to as *subsystems*. Suppose, for example, an organization makes and sells sewing-machines. One system of that organization would be the manufacturing system. But within that system there is a group of activities concerned with scheduling. This group is then referred to as the production scheduling subsystem of the manufacturing system. Subsystems may themselves consist of sub-subsystems, and so on.

All elements in a system or subsystem are related. Some are related by physical space (they share the same premises), others are related by transactions. Yet others may be related by time (a system may depend on output from another subsystem).

13.2.2 Boundaries

All systems can be delimited by a boundary which represents the extent of influence of that system. The influence of a business information system may extend beyond the limits of the organization; for instance, it may influence its suppliers or its customers.

One of the prime functions of the system analyst is to *specify* the boundaries of a system. This is done in order to set a limit on the extent of the system to be developed.

The importance of this process may be illustrated by considering what might happen if boundary-setting were not done. Suppose an analyst is requested to analyse an accounts receivable system. This interacts with a stock system so that would probably also be analysed. Stock needs to be purchased, so the analyst would then turn his or her attention to the purchasing system, and so on. Twenty years later a total organizational information system would be specified (which would be totally out of date).

The interaction of systems with other systems or subsystems is known as *coupling*. A tightly coupled system would depend strongly on another system or sub-system. Loosely coupled systems would only have a slight influence on the activities of each other.

13.2.3 Growth

Systems seldom remain static. From the time that they are conceived, their functions change or expand as the organization changes or expands. All systems move from initiation, to development, to maintenance, and finally to decay. This process is termed the *systems life cycle*. There are two ways of viewing this life cycle. One is to regard continual development and maintenance as a repetitive cycle. The other is to regard maintenance as part of development so that the system just keeps on growing; it seldom reaches maturity.

13.2.4 Control mechanisms

All systems tend towards disorder and fragmentation. If left to their own devices, they would eventually disintegrate. The fact that they don't disintegrate is due to mechanisms that control their activities. These controls can either be *continuous* or *discrete*. Continuous control is applied continuously while a system is in operation. For example, the brain monitors the function of the heart and tells it to either speed up or slow down depending on the oxygen requirements of the body. Discrete control, on the other hand, is applied only when a system breaks a rule. An example might be when a boy is punished after he throws a cricket ball through a window. He is not monitored constantly by a parent every time he throws the ball!

13.2.5 Feedback

The purpose of feedback is to correct any differences between the current operation of a system and a desired level, or to highlight areas of inefficiency. Many systems operate at an inefficient level simply because there is no method of measuring or reporting certain inefficiencies. Measuring performance implies that there is a *standard* against which one can compare. In practice this standard is achieved by objectives which are established by both the user and the analyst before the system is developed.

13.2.6 Structure

Some systems have clearly defined elements; the functions to be performed within these systems are specified to the minutest degree. There is very little exercising of discretion by the people involved in the system. In other systems, however, there is very little structure — the participants almost make up the rules as they go along. Structure is a function of the *level* of the people using the system: the higher up in the organization they are, the less the structure (as a general rule). Thus systems that are used by clerks and first line managers are normally highly structured. Systems used by senior managers (such as planning systems) have less structure. Figure 13.1 illustrates this concept.

FIGURE 13.1. The nature of systems in an organization.

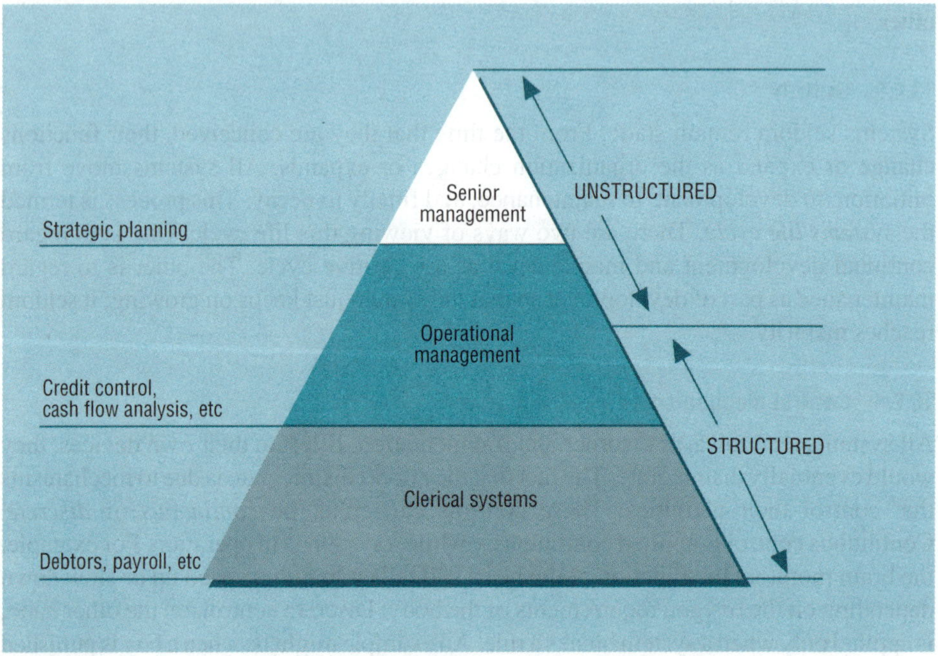

Almost all business systems follow a standard format. There is a subsystem to handle the maintenance of standing data (data that do not change frequently), there is a subsystem to process transactions, one to produce reports, and finally one to handle periodic processing. Let us take an example of an accounts receivable (AR) system to demonstrate what is meant by this. The AR system would consist of the four components described above. The function in each component would be:

Standing data maintenance

Adding new debtors.

Changing existing debtor information (such as names, addresses etc).

Deleting existing debtors.

Transaction processing

Capturing and posting invoices, receipts, journals etc.

Reporting.

Printing aged analyses, statements, overdue letters, debtors ledger, etc.

Periodic processing.

Transferring the data at year-end to a history file.

Deleting dormant accounts.

Producing mailing lists.

13.3 CATEGORIZING BUSINESS INFORMATION SYSTEMS

There are many different types of systems in operation in business today. If a systems analyst wishes to describe a system to a fellow analyst it is therefore helpful to have a standard method with which he can describe that system. There are a number of ways in which systems are described today.

13.3.1 Commercial or scientific

This dichotomy refers to the orientation of the system — whether it be commercial or scientific. The former normally refers to the business processes that are used in the day-to-day running of the business, for example the processing of accounts, the scheduling of activities or the planning of future events. Scientific systems are those that assist in the design of products or services, such as pipe flow analysis or stress analysis.

13.3.2 Scope of usage

Systems vary greatly in their scope of usage as defined by the number of people involved in the system and the boundaries of that system. Thus there are *individual* systems, used and controlled by only one person. There are also *departmental* systems used by individual departments (marketing or salaries, for instance). *Divisional* systems extend across multiple departments. An example is a name and address system used by accounting, marketing and sales. *Organizational* systems, as their name suggests, are used by the whole organization, while *inter-organizational* systems are used by a number of companies. An example of the latter in South Africa is the Computicket reservation system.

13.3.3 Processing characteristics

Systems may also be described according to their processing characteristics. Many business systems are driven by transactions (for instance invoices, credit notes, remittance advices). These are referred to as *transaction processing systems* (TPSs). They are concerned with the storage and processing of large volumes of transactions. Typically there are very few computations to perform, so the load on the processor is low. *Decision support systems* (DSSs), on the other hand, have a high computation overhead and a low requirement for storage. An example of a DSS is a linear program to calculate the optimum blend of products to be mixed into chicken feed. The 'optimum' is defined in terms of nourishment and cost. This system would have no transactions — the cost and nourishment data would be fed in as parameters.

With the above breakdown, one can fairly accurately define the scope, type and capabilities of a business information system. For instance, a 'departmental transaction processing system for wages' indicates an administrative support system for processing wages. A 'scientific, individual decision support system for scheduling the delivery of crude oil in a pipeline' describes a system used by an engineer using scientific algorithms to optimize the pumping of crude oil.

13.4 SYSTEMS FOR COMPETITIVE ADVANTAGE

In the 1970s and early 1980s a large amount of research was performed into the way that firms compete and, more specifically, into the way that information and information systems contribute to the competitive process. This resulted in a large number of papers being published concerning the potential contribution of the computer and the management implications of using the computer to enhance the competitive capability of the organization.[2]

Essentially, the computer can be used in one of five ways. The first is to *establish links with the suppliers* of products to the organization and to bind them to the organization. The second is to *establish links with the buyers* of the organization's products, thus stopping them from using competitors. The third is to *stop people from switching* from the organization's products to a competitor's products by raising the cost of switching. The fourth is *creating barriers to prevent potential competitors from entering into the organization's market*. The final method is by *creating new products or services* that effectively keep competitors guessing, making those competitors follow rather than allowing them to take the lead.

These competitive forces are shown pictorially in Figure 13.2.

Almost any system can be enhanced to improve a firm's competitive capability *if the analyst and user are aware of the potential contribution of information and information systems in the competitive arena.* For example, an order entry system can simply be a means of capturing, verifying and storing customer orders. It can also be a means of enhancing a firm's competitive capability by locking in customers. Consider the instance of a pesticide/fungicide distributor in the Western Cape. This company has developed a system whereby its major clients are given personal computers and appropriate software. This allows them to check which products are appropriate for the particular

FIGURE 13.2. The competitive forces model.

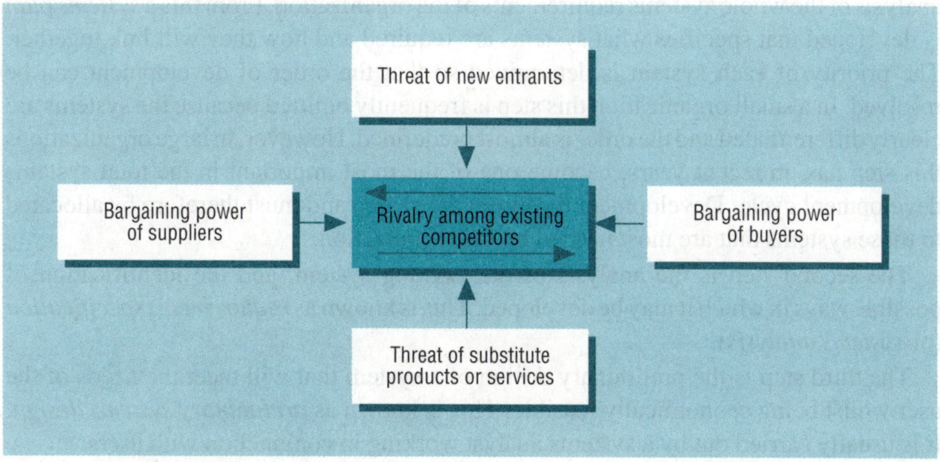

crop they are growing and the availability, price, and discounts pertaining to such products. By merely entering the appropriate code they can make an order and issue delivery instructions. The order procedure is simple, accurate, and informative. More importantly, the customer is hardly likely to use another supplier whose systems are clumsy and where orders take weeks rather than hours to execute. Information technology has effectively locked a customer into the organization.

This aspect of competitive support has opened a new door for information systems. Information technology can now become fully integrated into all aspects of organizational activities and play a positive, aggressive role, rather than being merely a support tool. The other side of this coin is that systems become more complex and they must therefore be planned and developed more carefully. Errors in development take on a new dimension, being costly in terms of lost opportunities.

13.5 THE SYSTEMS DEVELOPMENT LIFE-CYCLE

When businesses first commence operation, all their systems are usually manual and they are improved later through trial and error. As the firm grows, so does the volume of transactions, until bottlenecks appear and the flow of information is interrupted. The ability of manual systems to respond to requests for information in the required time-frame is impaired. At that point management has to decide whether to improve the manual systems or to automate them. If the latter route is chosen then the procedures for producing the information have to be redefined to allow conversion from a manual method to a computerized method. New rules have to be designed to take advantage of the computer's capabilities. Inevitably, because of the computer's ability to sort and summarize data quickly, information flows will change and the quality of information will improve. The process of redefining these flows, formulating the new procedures, and developing them to make use of the computer, is known as *systems development*. Depending on the size of the system, the process may take from a few weeks to many man-years (as in the case of an airline reservation system).

The development of a system involves five discrete steps. The first is a strategic analysis of the whole systems requirements of the organization. From this a *systems plan* is developed that specifies what systems are required and how they will link together. The priority of each system is determined so that the order of development can be resolved. In a small organization this step is frequently omitted because the systems are clearly differentiated and the order is almost predefined. However, in large organizations this step has, in recent years, become one of the most important in the total systems development cycle. Development resources are scarce and must therefore be allocated to those systems that are most needed by the organization.

The second step is the analysis of the existing system, and the identification of possible ways in which it may be developed. This is known as *requirements specification* (or *systems analysis*).

The third step is the preliminary design of a system that will meet the needs of the user whilst being economically feasible. This is known as *preliminary systems design*. It is usually carried out by a systems analyst working in conjunction with users.

From there the systems development cycle moves to the fourth stage, known as *detailed systems design*. Here the full details of the system are specified. Program specifications are developed. Potential errors are identified and appropriate procedures are developed to counteract those errors.

The last step is *systems implementation*. This is where the programs are written and tested. The system is then converted from its existing form into a form that can be used on the computer, and the user operates the system with live data.

Each of the phases has a number of components. These are shown diagrammatically in Figure 13.3.

There are a number of points to note:

- The diagram shows the life-cycle as a linear set of processes with each process starting when the previous one is complete. This is seldom the case in practice. There is often iteration between the analysis and design processes. As users see more and more of the system, especially during the testing phases, so they may change their minds. This may entail a return to the preliminary design phase, or even to the requirements specification phase. An objective of systems development is to reduce the iteration as much as possible. It will seldom, if ever, be eliminated.
- The less a user sees of a system prior to implementation, the more he or she is likely to resist it. For this reason it is necessary to involve the user in as many of the life-cycle stages as possible, and the earlier the better. Many organizations will even make significant users part of a strategic planning team.
- There are always difficulties in communicating technical specifications to non-technical people. Analysts and designers are used to working in computer terms whereas users are versed in the business aspects. The complex systems development cycle is necessary to overcome this communication gap and to avoid expensive specification or design errors.
- Changes to the system become more expensive as the development process progresses. Consider the building of a house. To change the house during conception

FIGURE 13.3. The systems development cycle.

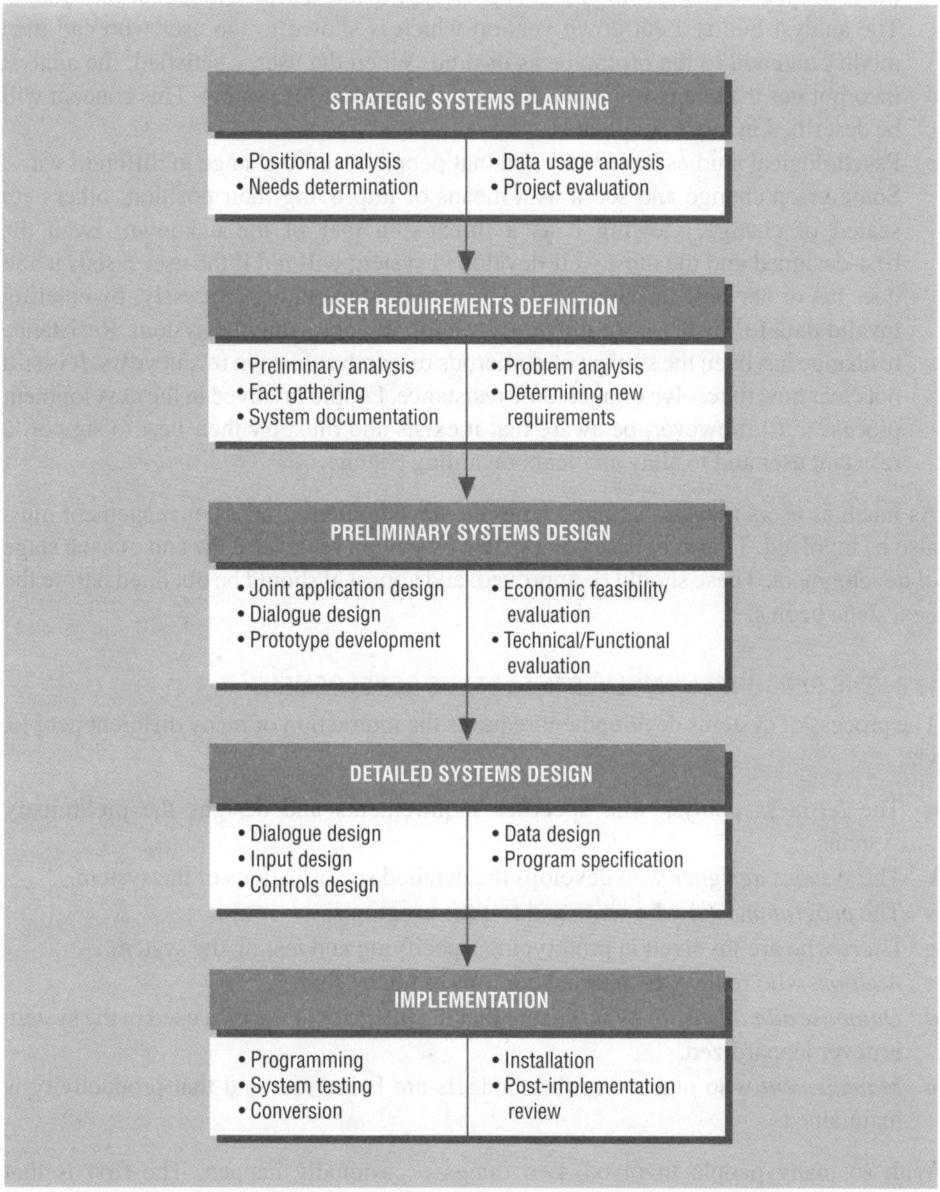

is relatively easy; an eraser rubs out some lines and a pencil puts in some new ones. To change the house during construction is a bit more difficult. A builder has to break down the walls and the bricklayer and plasterer has to rebuild. This analogy applies to systems development generally. The more users see of a system, the more changes they are likely to require, but the further down the development path the system is, the more expensive a change becomes. This is another reason why it is important for a user to see the system in its early stages of development. This reasoning has led to the concept of *system prototyping*. A prototype is like a scaled model of the system. The analyst builds a cut-down version which is shown to the user who can then modify and add to the prototype as desired. When the user is satisfied, the analyst incorporates the changes into the full-scale version of the system. This concept will be described in more detail later.

- Psychological studies have indicated that people react to change in different ways. Some grasp change and see it as a means of improving their position; others are scared of change, viewing it as a threat — a fear of the unknown. Even the best-designed and the most well-developed system will fail if the user resists it and does his or her best to sabotage it. This can be done either expressly, by entering invalid data for instance, or implicitly, simply by not using the system. Resistance to change has been the subject of numerous research studies in recent years. It is still not clear how to resolve or overcome resistance. People involved in the development process must, however, be aware that it exists and must try their best to support a resistant user and to allay any fears regarding change.

As much as users need to be involved in the development process, management must also be involved. This may be accomplished by having reviews at the end of each stage of development. These should be approved, and approval should be obtained before the next stage begins.

13.6 THE PERSONNEL INVOLVED IN SYSTEMS DEVELOPMENT

The process of systems development requires the interaction of many different people, viz:

- The *business analyst* who specifies requirements and designs the preliminary systems.
- The *systems designer* who develops the detailed specifications of the system.
- The *programmer(s)* who write and test the programs.
- *Users* who are involved in prototyping, specifying and testing the system.
- *Auditors* who review the internal controls of the system.
- *Database administrators* who ensure that the integrity of the data used in the system is never jeopardized.
- *Management* who make sure that budgets are being met and that productivity is maintained.

With so many people involved, two things occasionally happen. The first is that information is sometimes incorrectly communicated. To prevent this, all decisions and proposed actions should be properly documented during the systems development process. This is a function of *project management* (which is discussed more fully in a later chapter). Secondly, friction occurs between the various parties. This is particularly likely to occur if the development period extends to many months (or even years), or if deadlines are missed. This can be avoided by appointing an appropriately trained project manager whose job is to manage the people involved in the development process.

Finally, in any organization of reasonable size there will typically be many users vying for scarce systems development resources. It is therefore important to have a body of senior personnel overseeing the projects to ensure that potential conflicts are resolved. This body is usually called a *computer steering committee* (CSC).

13.7 THE COMPUTER STEERING COMMITTEE AND SYSTEMS DEVELOPMENT

The realization of the computer's full potential in helping management to achieve its business objectives is greatly assisted by significant management involvement in information systems. One of the most important reasons for involving management is that accomplishment of the goals in the 'business plan' will largely depend upon making information available to management for planning and control. It is necessary that top management from the various functional areas of the company participate in the planning and controlling of the IS function in order to ensure that the goals and objectives set are responsive to the company's requirements. This participation is generally formalized through the computer steering committee. The responsibility for directing the day-to-day activities of information systems still resides with IS management, but the CSC will direct them in setting their goals and objectives and it will be the responsibility of information systems to report to the CSC on their progress and problems.

People who might sit on a CSC are:

- the IS manager;
- managers who will be users;
- the external auditor;
- a senior executive;
- either the MD or his appointed representative.

The CSC should never be allowed to become too large. Big committees are not effective at making decisions. Ideally the committee should consist of between four and six people.

Some of the responsibilities of the steering committee are:

1. to define corporate objectives for systems projects;
2. to evaluate proposed (conceptual) systems projects and to make selections from alternatives;
3. to establish priorities among systems projects which have been investigated and approved;
4. to monitor the progress of projects currently being performed;
5. to evaluate the effectiveness of IS operations on a continuing basis; and
6. to establish communication channels between the IS department, the users, and senior management.

The extent to which these tasks would fall within the responsibility of the committee must be defined in order to avoid overlaps with those of IS line management. This delimitation differs from company to company.

Setting goals and objectives for systems projects is a difficult task. They should not be too general, nor should they be confused with system characteristics (eg. interactive versus batch processing). As an example, the following might be included in the basic objectives of information systems:

- To develop systems and equipment capabilities which will maximize the service levels provided to customers.
- To utilize only proven hardware and software in the implementation of systems.
- To assure the most cost-effective use of computing resources through systematic evaluation of current and proposed systems.

These objectives are put in writing to provide the basis for determining the desirability of proposed projects. Evaluation of the potential of proposed projects in relation to the objectives will then permit the committee to function fairly and effectively.

The committee meets regularly to review progress on current projects, in order to ensure that deadlines are being met and that anticipated benefits are being achieved. This review usually takes place at least monthly and each project team submits a formal progress report in a standard format in advance of the review meeting.

The committee continuously evaluates the status and effectiveness of the company's IS operations. To do this, it needs to know how equipment capacity is being utilized and what service levels are being attained, preferably for comparison against predefined budget estimates or standards.

A reporting system is used as the vehicle for the communication of performance. Relevant information about the projects is sent to the user departments and the IS division.

13.8 CONCLUSION

The systems development cycle focuses on *rigour*. The objective is to get the design right the first time. Thus the emphasis is on a *top-down* approach to development. This entails starting with a broad picture of the total system, and then narrowing it down until a detailed understanding is obtained of every aspect. One proceeds, as it were, from the abstract to the detailed. Logical models are developed of the application functions, working in abstract, before proceeding to physical models of actual system procedure.

This chapter has provided an overview of the development process and introduced some of the terms that will be used. The following chapters describe, in more depth, the development cycle outlined in section 13.5. The techniques used in analysis and design will be described in detail.

REVIEW QUESTIONS

1. Describe, using Bertalanffy's definition of a system, the solar system, a farm, a student project, and the nervous system.
2. Give two examples of different types of systems that one could expect to find in a university.
3. Why is it that when one uses the term 'information system' one almost automatically thinks in terms of a computer?
4. Why is it that the boundaries of a system are so important yet so difficult to specify?

5. What phase in the systems life-cycle would you think the planet earth is in? Give your reasons.
6. Why is it that standards are so important in determining feedback?
7. Describe the subsystems that one would specify for a system to handle the ordering of food for a university cafeteria.
8. Section 13.5 describes a systems development life-cycle (SDLC) and discusses iteration. Draw a diagram of the SDLC and show how iteration occurs between the various steps.
9. Who would make a better systems analyst, an adaptor or an innovator? Who would make a better leader in a large organization?
10. Is a computer steering committee not just an excuse for bad management since the functions performed by a CSC could surely be performed by a *good* IS manager?
11. Are all organizations capable of using Porter's model as a basis for determining the level of competition? Justify your answer.

REFERENCE

1. Bertalanffy L. 1956. General systems theory. *General Systems*, **1** (3).
2. McFarlan, F.W. 1984. 'Information Technology changes the way you compete.' *Harvard Business Review*. **62** (3) 98–103.

CHAPTER 14 Information systems planning and strategy

14.1 INTRODUCTION

In the early years of business computing, systems generally had a single function and did not interact with other systems. The majority of systems were for transaction processing in the administrative arena, and were concerned with the cost-reducing applications. As the use of information technology grew in business, however, so the complexity and size of the *applications portfolio* increased.

What exactly is meant by this term 'portfolio'? Many organizations with computers have a number of systems that have already been computerized and a number that are waiting to be developed. All of these together are termed the applications portfolio. The systems awaiting development comprise the *development portfolio* while those that have already been computerized are called the *installed portfolio*.

The simplest environment in which to plan is one characterized by:

- a single product that does not change;
- a homogeneous market;
- a short planning time-scale;
- a stable organizational and marketing environment.

By contrast, a complex planning environment is one:

- that is continually changing;
- where the products have a long lead time;
- where there is such competition for resources that political bargaining determines the allocation;
- where there are complex decision criteria.

Planning for IS development falls into the second category and is generally a complex, risky task. There are many factors contributing to that complexity, and these are discussed below.

14.2 FACTORS INFLUENCING THE COMPLEXITY OF IS PLANNING

14.2.1 The hardware technology

Since its introduction in the early 1950s, business computing technology has developed extensively. Developments have taken place in hardware, in software techniques, and in uncovering new areas for the use of information technology. Although there have been many developments in hardware (such as increasing the power of processors and the capacity of storage devices), perhaps the two most significant from a business viewpoint have been the development of data communication facilities and the development of the microcomputer.

Data communications facilities

In the initial stages of business computing, systems were developed for a single application area and at a single site. The computer contributed to a centralized processing environment. In those days it was relatively straightforward to justify and plan for information systems since the costs and benefits were easily identified, and there was not a multiplicity of users. The possibility of creating decentralized or distributed systems became a reality with the introduction of data communications. The number of users with access to the computer increased, as did the complexity of the systems. This served to increase the time needed to develop the systems. It also brought more users into contact with the computer, as well as creating more opportunities for its use. From a planning viewpoint, the analysis of the contribution of a system to the organization became more complex and the number of systems in the applications portfolio increased.

The microcomputer

Few developments have had such a dramatic impact on business practice as the microcomputer. Its introduction to business in the late 1970s brought about a complete change in the possible methods of processing data and producing information. In addition, its competitive pricing changed the fundamental cost ratios of information systems.

Prior to the introduction of the micro, systems development was performed in a centralized IS department, and there was a technological aura around computers which disturbed users. The micro, however, improved the level of user knowledge and understanding dramatically, and enabled users to apply information systems technology to a completely new set of tasks. One of the most important of these is *distributed computing*.

While it can be argued that the microcomputer has simplified systems in some cases, in corporate integrated systems the distribution of data and control introduces new dimensions of complexity. More importantly, however, the micro has contributed significantly to the *applications backlog* (discussed below). The IS planner must now be concerned with a wider spectrum of users, and a with larger number of systems competing for development.

14.2.2 The application areas

The use of computers has grown in four evolutionary phases. The first phase involved assisting routine clerical tasks. The processing of data occurred in a linear fashion (data and instructions were fed into the machine and the answers are returned with no iteration). The second phase was the use of common databases. The third was what has been termed a *cybernetic decision-making* phase, where there is iteration between the decision-maker and the computer system. In this phase the data are confined within the boundaries of the organization. The fourth phase was where those boundaries were expanded to include econometric and competitive data.

The computer embraces all aspects of corporate or organizational activity where information is used. The following application areas, in particular, are being addressed more and more vigorously:

- decision support systems;[1]
- office automation, including text and information processing, electronic message switching, facsimile transmission (faxing), electronic filing, and digital exchanges;
- expert systems;
- systems for competitive advantage.[4]

14.2.3 The demand for IS resources

With the spread of computing power throughout the organization, and as an increasing number of users come into contact with the computer, so more and more IS applications are proposed. Since development resources are limited, IS divisions have, for a long time, been unable to implement systems as fast as they are being proposed. The result is that an applications backlog starts developing. Even as early as 1980 a research project performed by IBM identified that 290 out of 300 of their large customers had a backlog of 20 or more applications. More recent research efforts indicate that, despite the advent of tools such as fourth generation languages, the backlog in almost all organizations has extended even further.

James Martin[4] suggests that when the real backlog extends to years (as in the case of most installations), users do not even bother requesting the development of applications that they need. There is thus an *invisible backlog* that is considered to be almost as long as the real queue.

This backlog means that users are reluctant to propose systems because they think that there is no chance of development. They are then driven to considering the purchase of microcomputers, or the use of outside facilities. Both options result in the development of fragmented systems that may not integrate well into the corporate IS structure. Alternatively, the user may become vociferous in his demands for development resources, thus placing great pressure on the planning team.

14.2.4 The planning horizon

The planning horizon of companies depends on many factors, such as the nature of the company, the industry in which it operates, and the management culture. It may vary from one year to 20 years or more. The norm would appear to be three to five years.

A system may take as long as two years to develop and may have an operational life of 15–20 years during which time it will require extensive modification and enhancement. Add to this the two or three years that it is in the queue awaiting development and IS management is being asked to plan the implementation of systems that will still be affecting the organization in 20–25 years' time!

14.2.5 The scarcity of IS resources and end-user computing

An analysis by the National Computing Centre in the United Kingdom describes a 'world-wide skill crisis' in computing.[7] The descriptions of the effect of this shortage on the IS function range from 'the major constraint for users today' to 'the shortage has reached critical proportions'.

The effect of this shortage, coupled with the introduction of the microcomputer, has led to the concept of end-user computing — users performing their own system development. This, in turn, has created a new set of demands for computing resources throughout most organizations. In fact, it is estimated that end-user computing will account for almost 90% of all computer use by the turn of the century. In discussing this issue, Canning describes two concerns of IS management, viz. *uncontrolled proliferation* of those resources, and *justifying the cost* of the facilities. Both warrant further discussion.

Whereas before the advent of end-user computing, IS planners needed to consider the allocation of hardware resources at one site only, now they are forced to consider multiple locations with a wide diversity of applications. The problem becomes more acute where there are trade-off situations, such as expanding a mainframe computer (with benefits for many) versus additional micros for single departments, or, even worse, single users.

Planning for the introduction and acquisition of such resources requires a high level of communication between users and planners. Where the microcomputers are purchased from user budgets there is a temptation to purchase them in isolation and to ignore such factors as standardization, public access, and information security, all of which are the domain of the planning team.

So, as can be seen from the above, there are many factors that complicate the process. Many IS managers, when faced with this, give up in despair. It is because of this complexity, however, that organizations *must* plan.

14.3 THE ORGANIZATIONAL INFLUENCE ON IS STRATEGIC PLANNING

In 1983, McFarlan and McKenney published a seminal series of papers[6] in which they proposed the concept of a *strategic grid* whereby the role of IS and the function of IS planning would vary according to the nature of the organization and the strategic significance of information technology. They suggest that there are four categories of IS role: strategic, turnaround, factory, and support. These can be shown in the form of a grid (as in Figure 14.1) where the two axes represent the strategic impact of the installed portfolio and the strategic impact of the development portfolio.
The categories are as follows:

- *Strategic.* This describes the situation where companies are critically dependent on the IS activity. Both the installed systems and those systems awaiting development are considered strategic to the success of the organization. Companies in this category are typically banks, insurance companies, and electronic service suppliers.
- *Turnaround.* Companies in this category can be severely impacted by poor IS performance, but they are not as critically dependent as those in the strategic sector. The strategic value of installed systems is low, while that of proposed systems is high. A manufacturer embarking on the development of an integrated manufacturing information system, for instance, would fall into this sector.
- *Factory.* Companies in this category may be significant users of information technology but they are not dependent on its performance. They are, in effect, the opposite of the 'turnaround' category, in that the strategic value of installed systems is high, but that of proposed systems is low. An example of this category is a retailer who has just implemented an integrated point-of-sale, funds-transfer and purchase-order management system.
- *Support.* In this category IS is not a major factor in the organization, and has little strategic significance. Information technology is typically used purely for

administrative support. Organizations with well-established, unchanging information requirements — such as municipalities — fall into this category.

FIGURE 14.1. McFarlan's strategic grid.

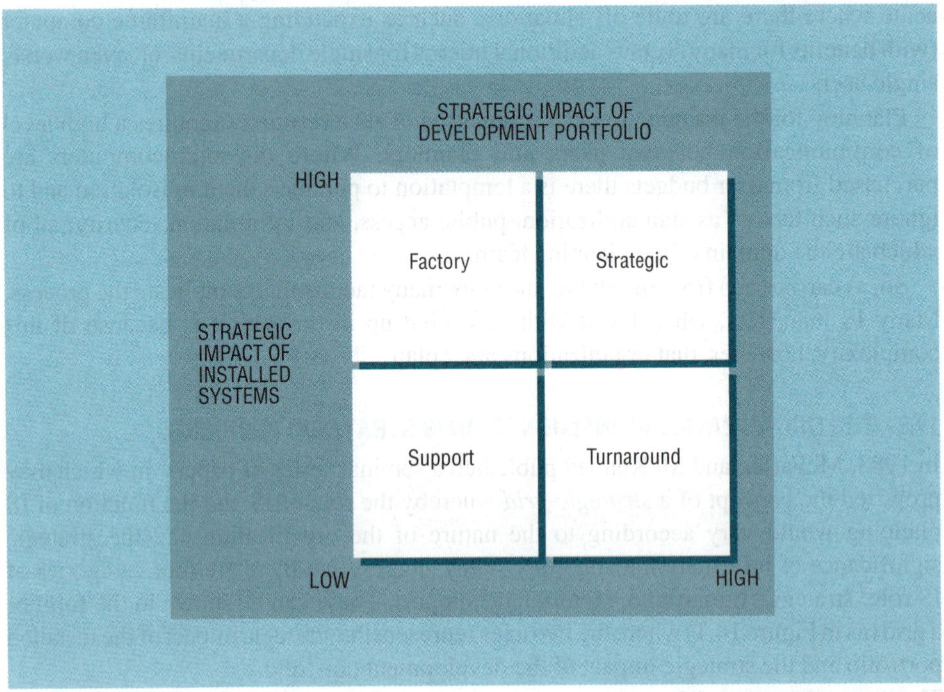

The nature of IS planning, and the link between IS and the corporate plan, will (and should) vary significantly in each of the above four categories. In the 'strategic' sector, companies will be aggressive users of IS. The IS planners and IS management will be constantly searching for new ways to use information technology in the organization. Indeed, in some organizations, such as banks and publishers, the plans for the use of IT and the development of information systems could set the framework for other activities in the organization, and, as such, might pre-define those other activities. In these organizations the ranking of information systems would play a critical role in the total IS planning function. At the other end of the extreme, the 'support' category would consist of passive users who merely follow other companies in the use of IT. One would not expect IS planning to be a significant factor in these organizations.

The conclusion to be drawn is that it is not possible to derive a standard approach to planning that would apply to all businesses.

Plans for the future use of the technology must be laid in a dynamic environment. It is difficult enough to derive a plan based on known technologies, yet organizations have to plan according to their *expectations* of future hardware and software developments because of the long planning time-frame.

14.4 THE THREE IS PLANNING TIME-FRAMES

IS planning has essentially three time-frames. In the long-term there is *strategic planning*. IS managers need to be concerned with the implementation of systems in ten or even twenty years. To do this they need to have a strategy for developing systems and for making the optimum use of computing technology within their organizations.

In the medium-term they must know what hardware is to be installed and which specific applications need to be developed. This requires what is referred to as *tactical planning*. In the short-term IS managers need to set expenditure budgets and to deploy their resources in detail. This requires *operational planning*.

14.4.1 Strategic planning

At this level the IS manager is concerned with answering a number of fundamental questions:

- What will my organization be doing in five or ten years' time?
- What technological opportunities are there in that time-frame, and what systems need to be developed or enhanced?
- Can those opportunities be implemented cost-effectively?

To answer the first question, the IS manager must have an understanding and knowledge of the business's long-term plan. This is why people talk of the IS plan being a subset of the organization's strategic plan. No planning is possible at a strategic level without a detailed understanding of the IS department's role within the organization. This is referred to as *positional analysis*. A prominent researcher and practitioner in the IS field, Richard Nolan, postulated that all IS organizations move through six stages of development in terms of management control.[8] These are shown diagrammatically in Figure 14.2.

The six stages are as follows:

- The first stage is termed *initiation*. The organization experiments with the technology. People are trying to come to terms with the technology and to understand its possible uses. It is characterized by a high learning curve.
- The second stage is *contagion*. As more and more uses are found for the technology, so it spreads throughout the organization. The budget for computing increases dramatically.
- In the third stage — *control* — there is a reaction to the rapidly increasing budgets and there are moves to implement controls such as charge-out systems and stricter project management techniques.
- Stage four, called *integration*, signifies a move towards integrating the systems that have been installed and an attempt to rationalize networks.
- The fifth stage is where organizations move towards *data administration*. Whereas in the past they have been concerned with systems, they now become concerned with data as a corporate resource, ensuring that each item of information stored in the computer is accurate and is not duplicated anywhere, and that all information relevant to decision-making in the organization is held in storage.

FIGURE 14.2. Six stages of data processing growth.[8]

GROWTH PROCESSES

Applications portfolio	Functional reduction applications	Proliferation	Upgrade documentation restructuring of existing applications	Retrofitting existing applications using database technology	Organization integration of applications	Application integration 'mirroring' information systems
DP organization	Specialization for technological learning	User-oriented programmers	Middle management	Establish computer utility and user account teams	Data administration	Data resource management
DP planning and control	Lax	More lax	Formalized planning and control	Tailored planning and control systems	Shared data and common systems	Data resource strategic planning
User awareness	'Hands off'	Superficially enthusiastic	Arbitrarily held accountable	Accountability learning	Effectively accountable	Acceptance of joint user and data processing accountability
Level of DP expenditures	Stage 1 Initiation	Stage II Contact	Stage III Control	Stage IV Integration	Stage V Data administration	Stage VI Maturity

- The final stage — *maturity* — is where the organization is completely computerized and is managing its data in a controlled manner. Nolan does not in fact think that any organizations have, as yet, reached this stage.

Nolan has identified a number of characteristics that management should look for to assist them in identifying which stage they are in. In Figure 14.2 those characteristics are labelled down the left hand side — 'applications portfolio', 'DP organization', etc. Once they have plotted their position, management can look forward on the chart to determine what is *likely* to happen next. It should be noted that this chart is not totally prescriptive: some organizations may enter the model at stage two or even three and jump straight to stage five. However, most organizations will enter at stage one or two and progress to stage five.

Strategic planning in the information systems area has essentially three aspects: identifying the systems to be developed (this is known as the *systems plan*), planning how to manage and control those systems and the data used by them, and planning for the use of technology. Technology planning encompasses:

- the application architecture;
- the network architecture;
- the hardware and software to be installed;
- the integration of the above;

- the skills needed for the above;
- security requirements;
- education requirements;
- service level requirements by the business.

14.4.2 Tactical planning

At this level the planners are more concerned with the foreseeable future and the plans become more concrete. They are concerned with which specific applications need to be developed and in which sequence. They will schedule those applications and make sure that the necessary skills are available. Specific plans will be drawn up for the installation of hardware and software.

14.4.3 Operational planning

This is the lowest planning level. Budgets for each item of expenditure are prepared. Each member of the IS division is allocated to a specific task for a period (usually one or two years). If items of hardware or software have been ordered in this period, the actual delivery dates are scheduled and the plans include details of how they will be installed with the minimum of disruption. Application development schedules will be drawn up for all projects to be developed in this period.

14.5 DEVELOPING THE INFORMATION SYSTEMS PLAN

Let us return to the systems development cycle. In Chapter 13 we mentioned that the first step in the development process is to formulate the *systems plan*. This typically involves several stages.

14.5.1 Examine the business's activities

This involves breaking the overall organizational function into its component activities. Each of these is then divided further into its sub-activities. The relationships that exist between each are then ascertained. Later this will show the system linkages. To give an example, a manufacturing organization would be broken down into the following: acquisition of raw materials, stores, production scheduling, production, product delivery, billing. Each of these is further subdivided — for example, billing might be subdivided into invoicing and accounts receivable; production would be split into scheduling, production control, and so on. This approach is often termed *functional decomposition*. Where applicable, each of the above would then be divided further into *business entities* until a complete understanding of the organizational activities, and how they link together, is reached.

14.5.2 Determine the needs of the business

While the first step (functional decomposition) aims at defining what currently happens in the organization, the analyst must also attempt to determine what *should* happen. To do this there are essentially two approaches as outlined below:

FIGURE 14.3. A process diagram.

Subject data bases	**Employee**					**Manufacturing**							**Marketing**			**Customer**				**Materials**						**Financial**	**Planning**	
DATA ENTITIES	Department	Employee	Benefits	Payroll	Training	Product	Product strucuture	Mfg. process	Work centre	Plant	Process type	Equip. type	Competitor	Sector	Region	Salesperson	Customer	Order	Agent	Finished goods inventory	Warehouse	Vendor	Raw materials	Raw materials inventory	Purchase order		Strategic	Annual
Application systems																												
FINANCIAL																												
Purchasing							A															U	U	U	U			
Accounts payable																						A	A			U		
General ledger						U	A	A												A	A					U		
Cost accounting																				A				A		U		
MANUFACTURING																							U		A	U		
Production scheduling							U	U																				
Plant process control								U	U		U	U																
Inventory control						A														U	U							
ADMINISTRATION																												
Personnel planning	U	U	A	A	A																							
Payroll/Personnel	A	U	U	U																								
Training	A	A			U																							
MARKETING																												
Sales analysis						A							A		U	U	A	A	A									
Profitability reporting		A				A																				A		
Order entry						A								A	A	U	U	U	U	A	A							
DECISION SUPPORT																										A		
Strategic planning										A			A	A												A	U	A
Budgeting																										A	A	U

A Access only
U Update

- *Strategic analysis*. The business is examined in terms of its competitive strategy, and the analyst searches for better methods of, for instance, serving its customers or for obtaining products from its suppliers. This approach is based on the works of Michael Porter.[2]
- *Critical success factors*. This method was developed by John Rockart of the Massachusetts Institute of Technology. The analyst interviews senior management to determine those factors that are critical to the long-term success of the organization (called CSFs). These are then examined to determine the appropriate information requirements and to determine how systems can be developed to provide that information.

With the information that is obtained with these two techniques, the decomposition chart is modified, to be ready for the next step.

14.5.3 Determine the data usage

The data that are used by each business entity are then defined.

These are termed *data classes*. From these a *process/data diagram* is developed as shown in Figure 14.3. This shows which user is the owner of each data class, who is allowed to access that class, and who is allowed to modify it. The data classes are then grouped according to logical dependencies (for example, all customer data are grouped together, all product data are in another group, and so on). From the above it is then possible to determine the systems that are required to process the data.

14.5.4 Evaluate the systems projects

The next stage is to evaluate the systems and to determine both the best way to develop them and the order in which they should be developed. The development effort for each system is estimated and resource requirements (people, capital and computer time) are determined. The priority sequence is a function of three factors. The first is *technological requirements* (system B might require data generated by system A, so system A would be developed first). The second is *economic requirements* (the budget for a system might be so large as to require its deferral until funds are available). Finally there is *organizational need* (the organization might not be able to function without a particular system).

After synthesizing all the above, the systems plan is documented. Its contents are then circulated to all senior people in the organization, and comments and criticisms are called for. These are then analyzed and incorporated or rejected, and the final systems plan is documented.

14.6 CONCLUSION

A point to note is that strategic planning is not a 'once-off' exercise. It is a continuous activity, with a lot of effort, both formal and informal, structured and unstructured, going into the development and revision of the plan.

Strategic planning of the IS function is critical. Canning,[1] reported a high correlation between a lack of planning and IS failure. He concluded that the only way for companies to make a success of IS is to select 'the most appropriate general structure for your future information system needs'. This is not an easy task. There are many factors to consider, and there is ample evidence of the need for an appropriate methodology to guide the planners through this 'IS planning maze'.

REVIEW QUESTIONS

1. Why is it that two organizations in the same industry, both of which installed a computer exactly twenty years ago, now have completely different development and installed portfolios?
2. Data communications has been described as the single most important factor affecting business information systems in the last twenty years. What do you think will be the most important factor in the next twenty?
3. How has the managerial decision-making environment changed since the Second World War?
4. The introduction of the microcomputer led to the term 'personal computing'. What effect has personal computing had on the applications backlog?
5. What is the status of the skills backlog in South Africa? How do you think this will change in the next decade?
6. Describe your academic institution in terms of McFarlan's strategic grid. Do academic and research computing fall into the same block on the grid?
7. Take two large, well-known institutions and attempt to fit them into Nolan's stage model. Justify your answer.
8. Is it likely that organizations will ever reach the maturity stage? Justify your answer.
9. How long do you think it takes to develop a strategic plan for a billion rand organization? What are the factors that might influence your answer?

SELECTED REFERENCES AND RECOMMENDED READING

1. Canning, R. Planning your future information systems. *Analyzer*, **21** (1).
2. Harmon, P. King D. 1985. The engineers behind expert systems. *Computerworld*, March 18.
3. Keen, P. G.W., Morton, M.S. 1978. *Decision Support Systems: An Organizational Perspective.* Reading Massachusetts: Addison-Wesley Publishing Co.
4. Martin, J. 1984. *The Information Systems Manifesto*. Savant Research Studies. ? England.
5. McFarlan, F. W. 1984. Information technology changes the way you compete. *Harvard Business Review*, **62** (3).
6. McFarlan, F. W. and McKenney J. L. 1983. *Corporate Information Systems Management: The Issues Facing Senior Executives.* Richard D. Irwin .
7. National Computing Centre. NCC Bulletin No 2.
8. Nolan, R. L. 1982. *Managing the Data Resource Function. Second edition.* New York: West Publishing Company.
9. Parsons, G. 1983. Information technology: a new competitive weapon. *Sloan Management Review* **25** (1).

CHAPTER 15 Defining user requirements

15.1 INTRODUCTION

This stage of the systems development cycle focuses on an individual system. It is concerned with what the system does, and what it is supposed to do. The analyst, or team of analysts, gathers facts about the system, determines problems, identifies processing bottlenecks, and ascertains shortcomings.

This user requirement definition stage has four phases to it. These are:

- The *preliminary analysis* which determines the extent of the work involved and defines the scope and objectives of the analysis effort.
- The *review of the existing system* which is concerned with gathering facts from the user.
- *Documenting the system.* This involves using specific diagramming techniques which assist in ensuring that all aspects of the system are covered and that they are correctly specified.
- *Defining the problem areas.* Any problems in the existing system are identified and their causes are isolated.

15.2 THE PRELIMINARY ANALYSIS

In the past, systems were designed in a piecemeal fashion in response to requests by users. Today, as a result of an improved understanding of the IS function, it is more common to develop systems according to a pre-defined *information systems plan.* IS management prioritizes systems and creates a project team to develop each system. The first task of such a project team is to undertake a preliminary analysis. This involves determining the exact extent of the system, identifying the reasons for requiring a new system, identifying the objectives of the system with the user, and determining an initial estimate of the effort involved in developing the system.

Determining the extent of the system involves defining the *boundaries.* The analyst and the user attempt to determine what the system *includes* and what it *excludes.* This is a function of the user's budget and the feasibility of automating the processes or activities of the system.

The second activity involves identifying why the system is required. This is undertaken in order to provide more explicit background information about the system and the rationale for redevelopment. There are typically a number of reasons: it may be in the firm's strategic interest to develop a system; there may be processing bottlenecks; the firm's activities may have changed, or there may be a new idea concerning the use of technology.

The user then specifies the *objectives* of the system. These are expressed in business terms, for example, to reduce the outstanding debt by 25%, or to reduce the stock holding by R3 million. The analyst will also define technological objectives — these might involve, for instance, processing a specific number of transactions in a certain period of time.

The final activity is to establish an initial estimate of the projected development time. This will obviously be refined as the project is more accurately specified. At this stage it provides management with an estimate of the amount of effort involved.

Note that these objectives and estimates later become the means of determining the subsequent success or failure of the system.

This preliminary systems analysis is really what it says — preliminary. The outputs are vague, the estimates are fuzzy, but it is a starting point. It provides the analyst, the user, and management with an understanding of the effort involved, and it is the basis for making the first decision — whether or not to proceed with development. Assuming that the decision *is* to proceed, the process then moves to the second step: that of gaining an understanding of the mechanics of the present system.

15.3 GATHERING FACTS CONCERNING THE EXISTING SYSTEM

The analyst must now assimilate *all* the facts concerning the existing system. Omissions at this stage can have serious consequences later, so the emphasis is on thoroughness, on attention to detail, on letting nothing pass by, on uncovering exceptions.

There are a number of methods of extracting information. Probably the most important is interviewing, although others — questionnaires, observation, and document gathering — have their place, depending on the system's environment.

15.3.1 Interviewing

An interview is a systematic process. It is planned in detail, rehearsed, and carefully documented afterwards. It is very important that the analyst acquires the skill of interviewing. A sloppy interview will result in a loss of information, or a distortion of detail. Successful interviewing involves four phases:

- planning and preparing the interview;
- scheduling the interview;
- conducting the interview;
- documenting and following up any discrepancies.

Planning and preparing the interview

Before interviewing the user, the analyst must ensure that he or she has a thorough understanding of the business and how the user fits into the organizational structure. A visit to the user's department will familiarize the analyst with the physical environment, and a review of procedure manuals will also give some understanding of the existing system. The purpose of this is to gain as much understanding as possible *before* the interview. This will avoid wasting time unnecessarily — confirming facts is quicker than gathering them in the first place.

The analyst must next prepare a structure for the interview, listing all the topics and areas that should be covered. Questions should be written out where necessary, especially if the sequence is important, or if the user is known to be difficult. If time is of the essence it may be necessary to write out all the questions and send them to the user beforehand. Before attempting to contact the user for the first time it is often useful to ensure that management announces to all concerned parties that interviewing is to take place. This will help break down any resistance barriers.

Scheduling the interview

When selecting people to interview, a normal practice is to start with the head of the department and then to work downwards. At the lower levels it is usual to start at the beginning of a business process and then to follow that process through to its logical end.

When contacting users the analyst should always state the purpose of the interview and its estimated duration. In most cases the interview will take place at the user's office at a time that is convenient to him or her. If it is known, however, that the user is frequently interrupted by telephone calls then an attempt should be made to schedule the interview at a neutral and convenient location.

Conducting the interview

Effective interviews are always started with care. The analyst will introduce himself or herself, stating the purpose of the interview and its objectives. Time limits will be specified and agreed so that the user knows how much is expected.

The objective of an interview is to extract information from the interviewee. This is achieved by making him or her *talk*. One of the best ways of achieving this is to ask open-ended questions — ones that require a descriptive response. A series of closed, yes/no type questions should be avoided — they do not encourage spontaneous answers, the ones that so often contain hidden and unexpected details. The user should be set at ease. The analyst must always be a good listener.

One of the difficult problems is that of note-taking, or documenting the interview. If the user is asked to stop every few minutes while the analyst takes copious notes then the flow of information will be disrupted and the user may lose interest. Notes should be cryptic, mere reminders which can be filled in after the interview. Recorders can be used, but the user must be asked whether they are acceptable. They are generally not to be recommended as many people become 'microphone shy'.

The analyst must not be afraid to repeat complex details. 'Excuse me, Mr So-and-so, may I repeat this to make sure that I have it right?' is a good tactic. It makes the user feel that the details are important and, by implication, that he or she is important.

Closing the interview is often as important as the opening. Key details are summarized and, more importantly, the door is left open for returning for further information or for clarification.

Documenting and following up any discrepancies

Immediately after the interview the analyst should sit down and document the information that has been gathered. After even an hour or two details could be forgotten or confused, so *this should be done as soon as possible after completing the interview.* Many good analysts will ask the user for a convenient office for half an hour. Once again, this attaches a measure of importance to the process. This will impress the user.

Queries, or areas where the analyst is unsure of the details, should be followed-up as quickly as possible. If a follow-up interview is necessary then this should be planned and prepared just as meticulously as the first.

Interviewing is a key analytical skill. The process must be thorough. The whole systems specification effort, and by implication the new system itself, rests on this task.

15.3.2 Questionnaires

Questionnaires are not considered to be as effective as interviews. The information obtained is too highly structured and impressions and feelings are harder to detect in questionnaire responses. However, the questionnaire may be of considerable use if, for example, an analyst is attempting to gain an overall impression of user satisfaction with an existing system. It might ask users to list problems they have experienced. These will then provide good input for the first series of interviews.

Where a questionnaire is to be used, the analyst should obtain the help of somebody with experience in questionnaire design. There is a considerable difference between a well-designed questionnaire and a poorly-designed one, not the least of which will be in the integrity and reliability of the information obtained.

15.3.3 Observation

This is often the best method for obtaining information about a system, or for verifying details provided during an interview. A person who is trained in systems can often spot bottlenecks or problems where none were thought to exist.

Observation requires *patience* and *attention to detail* if it is to be carried out effectively. It is, however, expensive — the analyst needs to devote a considerable amount of time if the observation process is to be successful.

15.4 DOCUMENT GATHERING

When studying the existing system the analyst must gather together all the latest documents relating to that system. The documents concerned are:

- *Source documents*. Examples are customer orders and requests for work.
- *Input forms*. These may be used where data are transcribed from a source document onto a computer capture document.
- *Reports*. There are many different kinds of report. For instance there may be forms that are prepared for transmission to another department — a picking list to draw stock, for example. There may be exception reports, and there may be detailed reports.
- *System documentation*. This includes all rules and procedures for processing the data.

It is important for the analyst not only to obtain copies of documents, but also to find out:

- who prepares them;
- who checks them;
- who uses them;
- how frequently they are produced;
- how long they are.

Note that these documents will form a very important input into the design process, so it is important that care is taken in collecting and documenting *all* documents.

15.5 DOCUMENTING THE EXISTING SYSTEM

Documenting the existing system serves two purposes. It provides a means of communicating information about the existing system to the development team, but, more importantly, it also enables details to be verified with the users. The emphasis is always on *correctness.*

The larger a system is, the more important it is to have a standard method of documenting information and procedures. Specific tools assist in communicating an understanding of the system. These are the *entity-relationship diagram* and the *data-flow diagram.*

These two techniques are important because all information systems are concerned with the accumulation, storage and presentation of information. The more effectively data can be captured and processed, the better the system will be. The analyst and the user must therefore fully understand the flow of data, and the relationships in the system that bind it all together. The entity-flow diagram and the data-flow diagram assist the analyst to understand the data better and to communicate that understanding to the user. In addition, they help the analyst by providing a means of decomposing problems to an understandable level.

15.5.1 The entity-relationship diagram (ERD)

This technique was first devised by Peter Chen in the late 1970s. It was initially used as a tool to design the data in databases, but now its use has spread to systems analysis. Essentially, it depicts the entities that exist in a system and the relationships that exist between those entities. An entity is defined as *an object containing related data and about which data are to be stored in a system*. Examples are: a supplier, a product, a library book, a customer, a course, and so on.

There are strict rules for depicting ERDs. Entities are shown as rectangular boxes. Lines between the boxes depict the relationships. Each end of the line indicates the degree of the relationship. If only one of the entities may exist at any one time it is shown as an inverted equal sign. If many of the entities may exist, the entity is depicted by the tail end of an arrow. Figure 15.1 gives an example. Assume that we wish to show that students study for a degree and that they may only ever study for one degree. The degree entity may exist only once and so it has the inverted equals sign. Many students may study for that degree so the student entity has the arrow tail-end sign.

From this one could deduce that there are three classes of relationship that may exist:

- one-to-one;
- one-to-many;
- many-to-many.

FIGURE 15.1. An example of a entity-relationship diagram.

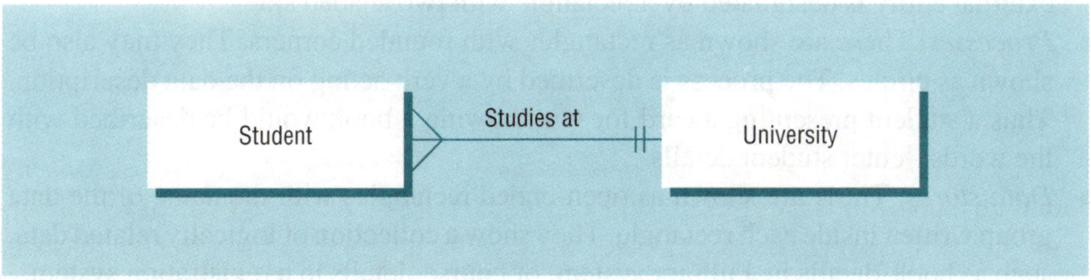

In addition, the ERD gives narrative information about the relationship. For instance, if we wish to show the relationship between a customer, an order, and a product, we would do so as in Figure 15.2

FIGURE 15.2. The relationship between a customer, an order, and a product.

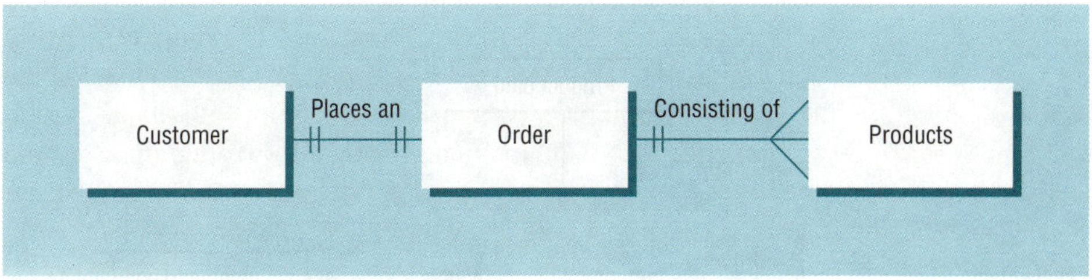

15.5.2 The data-flow diagram (DFD)

This is far more detailed than the ERD. As its name suggests, it shows how each element of the data is modified or stored as it flows through the system. There are specific symbols used in DFDs. These are symbols for: external entities, process boxes, data stores, and data-flows (see Figure 15.3).

FIGURE 15.3. Data-flow diagram symbols.

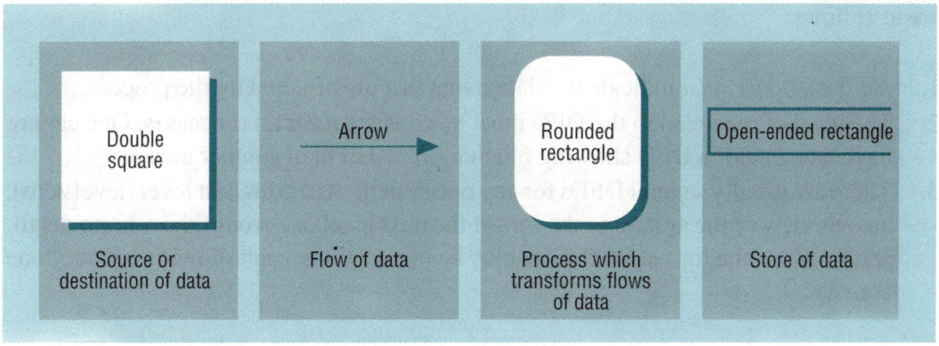

These symbols have the following meanings:

- *External entities.* These are sources and destinations of data that exist beyond the boundaries of the system. An example in a stock system would be the supplier of the stock item. In library system it would be the student with a registration card. The external entity is designated by a rectangle with two shaded sides.

- *Processes*. These are shown as rectangles with rounded corners. They may also be shown as circles. The process is described by a verb acting on the data description. Thus a student presenting a card for withdrawing a book would be described with the words: 'enter student details'.
- *Data stores*. These are shown as open-ended rectangles with the name of the data group written inside each rectangle. They show a collection of logically related data, such as book-details in a library system, or course-details in a registration system.
- *Data-flows*. These are depicted by an arrow that connects a data store, or an external entity, to a process. The data items that are affected by the process are written above or below the arrow. The arrow indicates the direction of the data-flow.

FIGURE 15.4. Example of a data-flow diagram.

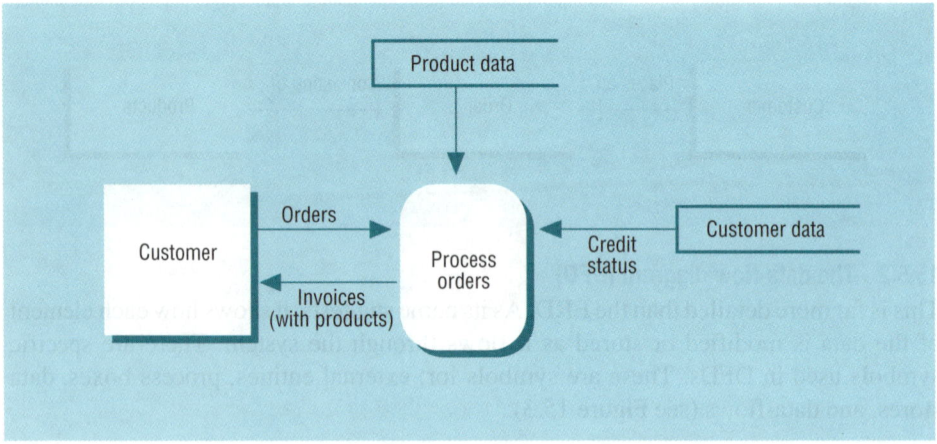

As can be seen in the diagram, there are specific rules for documenting the flows. These are as follows:

1. All data-flows *must* indicate the data items that are affected by the process.
2. The level of the detail in the DFD must be consistent for all processes. One cannot have one area of a DFD showing much more detail than another area.
3. There are usually several DFDs for any one system. At the highest level (level zero), an overview of the system is shown. At the next level one would show more detail, and so on. At the lowest level there may be many DFDs, each showing a part of one activity.

15.5.3 The system description and the system hierarchy chart

Although we have described the ERD and DFD in some detail there are two other techniques that are used in documenting systems. These are no less important. The first is the *system description*. This takes a narrative form and describes the system, normally from the user's point of view. It states the inputs, processes, and outputs, and the level of control required in the system.

The second is the *system hierarchy chart*. This takes the functions of the system and organizes them in a hierarchical fashion. It assists the user and the analyst in ensuring that the description of the system is complete. An example is shown in Figure 15.5.

FIGURE 15.5. A systems hierarchy chart.

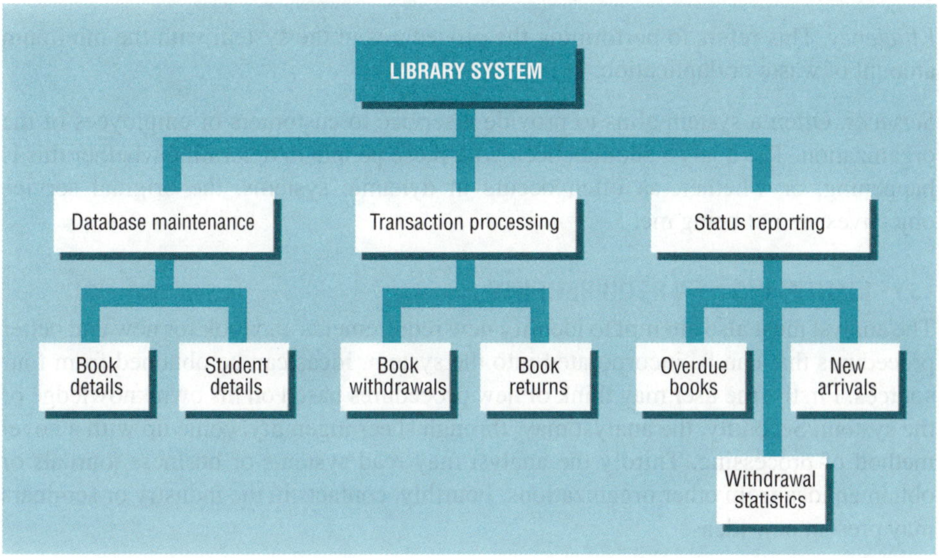

15.6 DEFINING THE PROBLEM AREAS

The next step in the preliminary analysis is to examine the documentation and identify all the problems in the existing system. James Wetherbe refers to a mnemonic, 'PIECES', in classifying the possible problems. This stands for:

- Performance
- Information
- Economy
- Control
- Efficiency
- Services

Performance. This refers to the ability of the existing system to respond to the user requirements within a satisfactory time-frame. Bottlenecks are frequently created which disrupt response times, causing delays. These may result from a duplication of processes, from a resource being incapable of processing transactions quickly enough, or from the fact that the path which a data item has to travel is too lengthy.

Information. This may not be presented in the best possible manner for use, or within the correct time-frame.

Economy. Economy is an aspect that is frequently disregarded by analysts. It refers to the cost of producing information versus the benefit to be derived. With old systems, the user is often getting what he needs, but the cost of producing it is far in excess of the benefit the user is deriving.

Control. All systems tend towards disorder, and the correct form and amount of control is necessary to ensure that they do not disintegrate. It is the responsibility of the analyst to check the level of control being applied and to determine if this is adequate.

Efficiency. This refers to performing the procedures in the system with the minimum amount of waste or duplication.

Services. Often a system aims to provide a service to customers or employees of the organization. The analyst should check with these people to determine whether this is happening, or whether, as often occurs in dynamic systems, the original service objectives are not being met.

15.7 IDENTIFYING NEW REQUIREMENTS

The analyst must also attempt to identify new requirements and look for new and better procedures that can be incorporated into the system. Ideas can be obtained from four sources. Firstly, the user may think of new procedures based on his own knowledge of the system. Secondly, the analyst may, through sheer ingenuity, come up with a novel method of processing. Thirdly the analyst may read systems or business journals or obtain an idea from other organizations. Fourthly, contacts in the industry or seminars may present new ideas.

15.8 PROTOTYPING

One of the problems frequently faced during requirements specification is that an analyst may suggest features to a user that cannot easily be visualized by that user. To assist this visualization process, a prototype is often developed. This is a scaled-down model of a system.

Prototypes can vary enormously in their complexity and levels of detail. Depending on the tools that are available, the prototyping process may take hours, days, or even weeks. If a sophisticated environment is available, with high level languages, screen design facilities, data dictionaries, and so on, analysts will be able to prototype at high speed, allowing for swift interaction between the user and the development team.

Prototyping has become a necessary part of the development process. It allows the user to see the system before the requirements specification is finalized. Parts of the prototype may even be created by the user. This attempts to ensure that the analyst does not specify the system using false assumptions or give the user something that is not needed or that is incorrect.

15.9 CONCLUSION

The analyst now has all the facts concerning the system. He or she will have a thorough understanding of the procedures involved and the data that drive, or are driven by, those procedures. The final action in this analysis phase is to verify the details by reviewing the documentation with the user. Where users are required to pay for systems development, the documentation will be signed as being correct. This forces a thorough examination to ensure correctness.

At the end of this phase of the systems development cycle a *user requirements definition* is produced which details all that was found. It includes all the diagrams that were discussed earlier plus a narrative describing the system. The user must be aware of, and understand, all the contents of this document. Proceeding to the next stage depends on the user agreeing to the contents of the user requirement definition.

REVIEW QUESTIONS

1. If preliminary analysis is so vague, why is it worth doing?
2. You have an interview with a prospective employer for your first job. Plan the interview.
3. How would you decide after the interview whether it was successful or not (assuming the employer will only let you know the outcome of the application in a week's time)?
4. You interviewed a rather obnoxious user whose parting words were: 'That was a total waste of time. I hope I'm not going to be bothered by you again!' You now need to clarify an important area of the system and he is the only person who can help you. What would you do and what approach would you use?
5. Describe three instances where an analyst would use questionnaires.
6. Draw an entity-relationship diagram of:
   - a library withdrawal/return system;
   - a cinema;
   - a restaurant.
7. Select a simple system that you are a part of (a residence system, or the library, or a system in a family business, for example) and describe the flow of data through that system using the DFD method.
8. What problems were there in the registration system used at your institution?

SELECTED REFERENCES AND RECOMMENDED READING

Wetherbe, J.C. 1984. *Systems Analysis and Design: Traditional, Structured and Advanced Techniques.* New York: West Publishing Co.

CHAPTER 16 Preliminary systems design

16.1 THE PRELIMINARY SYSTEMS DESIGN (PSD) PROCESS

Analysis, described in the previous chapter, is an information-gathering process. The objective is to understand the existing system and the needs and requirements of the user. The purpose of preliminary systems design is to take the output from the user requirements definition stage and build a *conceptual model* of the new system. In other words, analysts and users, as a team, design a blueprint of a system that will satisfy the requirements both of the user and of other sectors of the organization that may fall under the sphere of influence of the system.

There are many design objectives for the development team to work towards. The system must meet the user's demands to process work and produce the required output, it must keep within an IS resource budget, it must meet the security requirements of the auditors, and it must meet management's need for control.

These objectives may be attained by following certain procedures. The first is building a conceptual solution of the system. The essential features of the system *from a user's viewpoint* are defined during this process. Thus, the way the system interacts with the user, the input and output dialogue, the requirements for access to the data, and the security levels, are all identified. The authority for changing data, and the responsibility for correcting mistakes, are assigned at this point.

During the PSD, alternative processing methods are examined and the most cost-effective are selected. The optimum methods for producing information are also selected. The basis on which the user communicates with the system — known as the *user/machine dialogue* or simply *dialogue* — is decided.

Building and logically testing a solution to a system is an exacting process that requires the input of a large number of people. Designers, managers, users, auditors, and technical software experts should all participate. Obtaining input and agreement from so many people can be a lengthy, tiresome process, and it is for that reason that a technique known as *joint application design* — or JAD — was introduced. It should be noted that JAD is a technique. It is not a stage in the development cycle.

16.2 JOINT APPLICATION DESIGN

The term *joint application design* is used to describe the process whereby all parties involved with a system meet and, in a very short period of time, build a system to satisfy the business's needs. JAD can also be, and often is, used to replace or supplement the interviewing process that was discussed in the previous chapter. JAD is a very thorough process designed to reduce the time taken to design the system from weeks and months to two to four days.

There are many ways of organizing JAD sessions with users and analysts, but it is usual to have three sessions. The first is a *pre-workshop session*. This establishes the scope and objectives of the design effort — it prepares the people who will be involved, and it lays down the logistics of the workshops. The second is the *construction workshop*. A solution is constructed here by all participants working through consensus. Finally, there is the *post-workshop session* which is used for validating the solution and approving the final design.

16.2.1 The participants

A JAD session has six groups of participants. These are:

- *Users.* All those who will use the system, or be responsible for it, are present. They may not all be there at the same time but, where their contribution is deemed appropriate, they sit in on the proceedings.
- The *information system analyst* who was involved in the analysis process and who may also be responsible for the design of the system.
- *Technical advisers* who assist the analyst with technical considerations relating to the new system. Examples of these advisers are: database administrators, data communications specialists, and operations personnel.
- *Scribes* who document the proceedings of the JAD session. Full documentation should be available within a week of the completion of the session.
- A *session leader* who conducts the proceedings according to session procedures.
- A *senior management representative.* He or she would start the JAD session and participate in its conclusion. This role involves facilitating, and ensuring that the correct level of importance is attached to the session.

16.2.2 The session

This is usually held away from the workplace so that there will be no disturbances. Technical support consists of video and slide equipment and a microcomputer for developing the user dialogue. Typically, space is available for between 15 and 20 people.

IBM's guide gives the following agenda for a proposed JAD session:

- *Planning.* Who initiates the work to be performed by the system?
- *Receiving.* Where, when and how is the work received?
- *Acknowledgment.* How is the work reported and uniquely identified?
- *Monitoring and assigning.* Who performs the work and in what sequence?
- *Processing.* How is the work processed and who monitors its progress?
- *Recording.* How does the system record when the work is processed and who does it notify?
- *Sending.* Where is the work distributed to and who is notified?
- *Evaluating.* How is the success or failure of the system determined and what follow-up procedures are necessary?

The existing system will have been reviewed prior to the JAD session, so the session is only concerned with the *new* system. The effort is directed towards building a satisfactory conceptual solution to the users' problems. User/machine dialogues are established. Where necessary a prototype of the new system is developed or, if one was used in requirements specification, it is enhanced.

16.3 USER/MACHINE DIALOGUE

All systems involve communication between the user and the computer, and vice versa. The user enters transactions into the system and gives commands concerning the processing of data. The system, in turn, has to produce information to be used by the user (errors and exceptions, the status of the system, processing details, and so on). This flow of information is termed *the dialogue*. There are two types, the *input dialogue*, where the user enters data and parameters into the system, and the *output dialogue*, where the system produces information to be acted upon by the user.

16.3.1 Input dialogue

There are many different forms of input dialogue that one can use. These are:

- *Question and answer*. The computer asks questions serially and, as the user responds, the next question is displayed on the screen. This form of dialogue is most useful when inexperienced users are operating the terminal since there is prompting for every answer — little initiative is required.
- *Form filling*. A complete screen is displayed to the user with all the questions that need answers. The user works through the screen, keying in the answers required. An advantage of this method is that the screen can be designed to simulate an input document, thus facilitating the data capture procedure.
- *Menu selection*. This is probably the most common form of dialogue. The user is presented with a menu containing a variety of options. The one required is then selected by keying in the appropriate choice.
- *Windows*. Systems frequently consist of many sections, each of which has options that are listed in the form of a menu. The movement through these menus can frequently become confusing. To assist a user moving from one menu to another, those menus are shown on the screen in the form of 'windows'. This assists the user in *navigating* through the system, or moving from one section to another.
- *Mnemonics*. This approach is used only in high-speed on-line systems such as that used by the South African Airways. The user, usually a highly-trained expert operator, keys in codes which are recognizable only to himself and the computer. This form of dialogue cuts down on transmission time between the terminal and the computer.
- *Graphics*. The principle of using graphics is that one displays information in pictures and graphs rather than in tabular form.

16.3.2 Output dialogue

In designing the output dialogue there are a number of factors that the design team has to bear in mind. These are:

1. *How the output will be used*. If it is an operational report (such as for credit control) then a very detailed output should be produced. If the information is required by management then summary reports should be produced. The output should always be easy to use.
2. *The cost of producing the information*. While terminals are ideal for certain types of output, they may be much more expensive than hard copy and therefore may not justify the cost.

3. *The volume of information that needs to be produced.* It is no use producing a 200-page report for the managing director, or producing a 100-page sales analysis daily, neither of which could be used to improve the performance of the organization.
4. *The frequency with which reports will need to be produced.* Certain output has fixed requirements (eg. statements), while others may be determined by the designer.

16.3.3 The level of dialogue

There are a number of factors that determine the level of dialogue — ie. whether to use simple methods such as question and answer and windows, or faster input methods such as mnemonics. These factors are: the expertise of the user, the hardware available, and the frequency with which the system is to be used.

- *The user's expertise.* If this is very low then the system should be designed in such a way as to prompt the operator continuously and to provide assistance throughout the input stages. If the operator is an expert then excessive prompting should not be used as this slows down the input operation. One frequently finds a mix of skills in a system: some users are highly skilled whilst others are new and inexperienced and are required to operate the system with very little prior training. Where this occurs the system will have to have two modes of entry, *idiot* and *expert mode.*
- *The hardware available.* Certain types of hardware (such as microcomputers) lend themselves to a very 'user-friendly' environment. For instance, error conditions can be highlighted in colour, or a noise can be made when an error occurs. Other devices, such as hand-held terminals, do not have such sophisticated capabilities and therefore limit the design features.
- *The frequency of use.* The more an operator uses a system, the more expert he or she will become. A person who uses it less than once a month will never be an expert and will probably always require comprehensive computer assistance.

16.4 THE FEASIBILITY OF THE NEW SYSTEM

During the JAD session, users and analysts will select the most feasible solution. Feasibility is defined in terms of *economics* and *functionality.*

Economic feasibility is determined by performing a cost-benefit analysis. This involves assessing the benefits of a particular solution and offsetting these against the cost of that solution.

All *costs* associated with the new system are detailed in the feasibility study report, and an indication of the accuracy of the costs is given. Examples of cost items that are highlighted are:

- increases in the number of staff and therefore salaries;
- computer hardware;
- computer software;
- stationery costs;
- office equipment, such as tables and filing cabinets;

- the cost of any special electrical equipment required.

Benefits normally fall into two categories — *tangible* and *intangible*. The former are those that can be easily quantified, such as saving money. The latter are not easily quantified and require a subjective assessment on the part of the analyst or user, or both. Examples of this category are: improvement in management decision-making, and improved staff morale.

A table is constructed as shown in Figure 16.1. The costs are subtracted from the benefits for each year of the life of the system. The net figure is then discounted and a percentage return for each solution is calculated. If the return is positive then the project is feasible; if not, then it will probably be rejected (there may, however, be cases where management decides to proceed with a system even if the return is negative).

FIGURE 16.1. Table for assessing costs and benefits.

		Cost benefit analysis — OA Corporation			
Costs	**Year 1**	**Year 2**	**Year 3**	**Year 4**	**Year 5**
Systems development	45 000				
Operations		6 000	6 400	7 000	7 800
Maintenance		13 000	14 000	14 000	16 000
TOTAL COSTS	45 000	19 000	20 400	21 000	32 800
Tangible benefits					
Staff savings		12 000	15 000	18 000	21 000
Machine displacement		4 000	4 400	4 800	5 300
Intangible benefits					
Improved customer service		20 000	22 000	24 000	27 000
TOTAL BENEFITS		36 000	41 400	46 800	52 300
NET BENEFITS	(45 000)	17 000	21 000	25 800	28 500
NET PRESENT VALUE AT 15%	18 919				
RETURN ON INVESTMENT	33%				

The second step in this feasibility activity is to check for *functional feasibility*. This is achieved by ensuring that all the functions requested by the user are incorporated in the design. Frequently a prototype is used to assist in this validation process.

The third step is to check for *technical feasibility*. The objective here is to ensure that the hardware is capable of performing the tasks required of it and that the software can support the specified activities of the system.

16.5 DOCUMENTING THE SELECTED SOLUTION

The final stage in the preliminary systems design phase is the production of the *system proposal*. This contains details of virtually everything that has been performed in the analysis and design phases — the details of the existing system, the problems and needs of the users, the alternative solutions and details of their costs and benefits, and finally the proposed solution. In particular, the potential *impact* of the system on other departments in the organization is documented, together with the system's expansion capabilities.

Impact can be measured in terms of the workload involved in either preparing input data or in examining documentation. An example of this might be a marketing information system which requires salesmen to fill in detailed forms concerning visits to clients. The report should highlight this so that the sales manager can determine how much time his salesmen are going to spend filling in these forms (instead of selling).

In determining whether to pursue a project, management must be aware of how the system can *expand* to cater for future requirements. The JAD team should know how well the hardware or software can cater for increased volumes or additional reporting requirements within the organization. In performing the cost-benefit analysis, the JAD team should place figures against likely upgrades to the equipment that is being recommended.

As an example, consider a situation where an invoicing and debtors system is being specified. It is determined that the requirements for on-line storage are 60 million characters and the equipment that is being proposed caters for 100 million. The team should then specify in the report what the cost of an additional 20 million characters would be, so that management can budget for increased expenditure should the need arise.

The system document — or proposal — is then sent to the computer steering committee which evaluates it and either decides to proceed with the proposed system, to delay it, or to withhold authorization (reasons for the latter decision might be insufficient funds, or too great an impact on the organization in terms of workload, etc).

If the CSC approves the project, it then moves into the *detailed systems design* phase.

REVIEW QUESTIONS

1. Explain the difference between a *conceptual model*, a *physical model* and a *logical model* of a system.
2. What are the advantages of a JAD approach to systems design over a more unstructured way of involving the user? Would it be much quicker not to involve the user at all in systems design?
3. Why is dialogue so important in systems design?
4. List the different forms of input dialogue and specify the advantages and disadvantages of each approach.
5. Airline reservation systems require a very high level of skill on the part of the operator before commencing use of the system. Would it not have been better systems design to have introduced two levels of dialogue so as to allow less skilled people to operate the system too, thus allowing them to become productive sooner?
6. What are the advantages and disadvantages of developing a prototype of an information system?

7. What tools are needed for successful prototyping?
8. What techniques can one use to place reasonably accurate figures against intangible benefits in a cost-benefit analysis? What role can management play in this process?
9. Is it possible to make allowance for risk in a cost-benefit analysis? If so, how? If not, why not?
10. Who would provide the expertise necessary to determine the future expansion requirements and capabilities of a system?

SELECTED REFERENCES AND RECOMMENDED READING

1. Porter, M. 1980. *Competitive Strategy: Techniques for Analysing Industries and Competitors.* New York: Free Press.
2. Wetherbe, J. C. 1984. *Systems Analysis and Design: Traditional, Structured and Advanced Concepts and Techniques*. New York: West Publishing Co.

CHAPTER 17 Detailed systems design

17.1 INTRODUCTION

The *preliminary systems design* (PSD) gives a broad picture of the design of the system at a high level. The *detailed systems design* now specifies *exactly* what the system is to do. The programmers and database designers work from the PSD specifications. It is important, therefore, that those specifications are complete and accurate.

Designers have to anticipate problems that may occur and they select appropriate actions to safeguard against such problems. Controls must be designed so that the user can be sure the system works correctly. This is an exacting phase and one that needs considerable attention to detail.

17.2 DETAILED DIALOGUE DESIGN

At this stage the designer takes the specification from the JAD session and finalizes the dialogue to be used in the system. This involves specifying in detail the navigation paths through the system, the output to be produced by the system, and the methods for getting data into the system.

The appropriate output medium is selected and the details of exactly what is to be produced are specified. Layouts are standardized and specified so that programmers can produce the necessary program code. All possible error conditions are determined.

Let us first examine the detailed output design. There are two main types of output which the designer has to specify: *hard copy* (or printed output) and *terminals*.

17.2.1 Hard copy

Hard copy is probably the most common form of computer output but, owing to the spiralling cost of paper, it can also be the most expensive. There are two types of hard copy: pre-printed stationery and plain paper.

Pre-printed stationery

As it is expensive to pre-print computer stationery, this is normally used only where the organization is endeavouring to project its image to outsiders (to the customers of the company, for example). Typical examples where pre-printed stationary would be used are:

- invoices;
- credit notes;
- statements;
- cheques.

An example of pre-printed paper is shown in Figure 17.1.

Plain paper

This is commonly referred to as eye-line and comes in two standard depths, 200 mm and 280 mm. It is much cheaper than pre-printed paper, but the designer has to worry about such factors as column titles and the spacing on the report to ensure that it is both readable and usable.

FIGURE 17.1. Example of a pre-printed form.

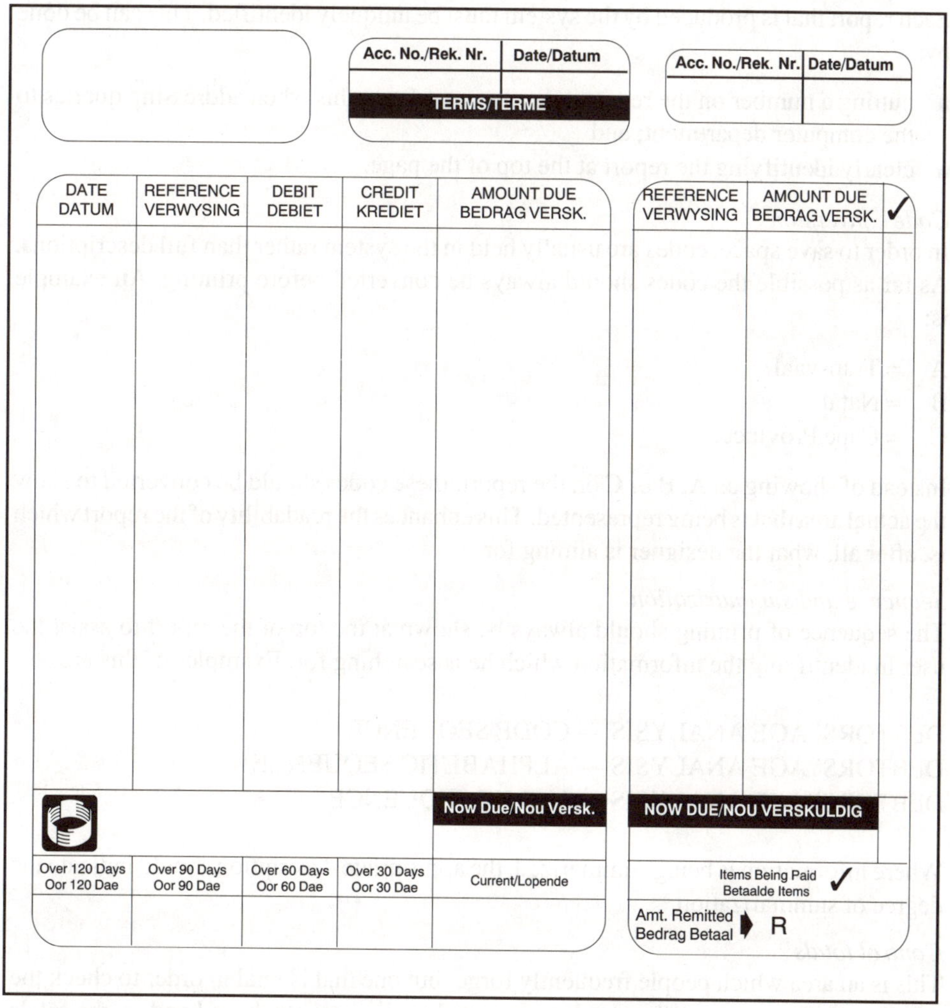

Acc. No./Rek. Nr.	Date/Datum
TERMS/TERME	

Acc. No./Rek. Nr.	Date/Datum

DATE DATUM	REFERENCE VERWYSING	DEBIT DEBIET	CREDIT KREDIET	AMOUNT DUE BEDRAG VERSK.
				Now Due/Nou Versk.
Over 120 Days Oor 120 Dae	Over 90 Days Oor 90 Dae	Over 60 Days Oor 60 Dae	Over 30 Days Oor 30 Dae	Current/Lopende

REFERENCE VERWYSING	AMOUNT DUE BEDRAG VERSK.	✓
NOW DUE/NOU VERSKULDIG		
Items Being Paid Betaalde Items		✓
Amt. Remitted Bedrag Betaal	R	

Carbon copies

With hard copy output one can normally produce carbon copies of any report. The copies should be limited to those users who really need the report. With both pre-printed and eye-line stationery there are two types of copying paper that can be used: one is OTC (one-time carbon), the other is NCR (no carbon required). In general terms NCR is a cleaner method of producing multiple copies, but it is more expensive than OTC and does not photocopy as well.

Hard copy design considerations

When specifying hard copy reports there are a number of design considerations to bear in mind. These are: identification, code conversion, sequence, summarization, and control totalling.

Identification

Each report that is produced by the system must be uniquely identified. This can be done by:

- putting a number on the report — users can refer to this when addressing queries to the computer department; and
- clearly identifying the report at the top of the page.

Code conversion

In order to save space, codes are usually held in the system rather than full descriptions. As far as possible the codes should always be converted before printing. An example is:

A = Transvaal
B = Natal
C = Cape Province.

Instead of showing an A, B or C on the report, these codes should be converted to show the actual area that is being represented. This enhances the readability of the report which is, after all, what the designer is aiming for.

Sequence and summarization

The sequence of printing should always be shown at the top of the report to assist the user in identifying the information which he is searching for. Examples of this are:

DEBTORS' AGE ANALYSIS — CODE SEQUENCE
DEBTORS' AGE ANALYSIS — ALPHABETIC SEQUENCE
DEBTORS' AGE ANALYSIS — VALUE SEQUENCE

Where information is being summarized, the appropriate description should indicate the degree of summarization.

Control totals

This is an area which people frequently forget but one that is vital in order to check the validity of the system. Where values are produced — eg. stock on hand — the totals should be shown at the end of the report. If there are no value columns being printed, for example, in a debtor's name and address listing, one should still indicate, at the bottom of the report, how many debtors are on the report.

Exception reporting

The designer always endeavours to show the user only the information which is relevant. One would not give a managing director a 100-page report, as there is no chance of that much detail being read or absorbed. It is frequently advisable to consider *exception reporting*, especially when designing reports for management.

In a debtors system, for example, the debtors clerk who is in charge of credit control needs a full listing of all debtor credit limits and current balances so that, if a telephone call is received from a customer, the information can be easily retrieved. A credit control manager, however, would be interested only in those debtors who are over their credit limit. A second report, therefore, would be produced with just the exceptional cases on it.

Turn-around documents
Frequently a report will be sent to a user who will make corrections and subsequently send the report back for capture into a further system. The designer should anticipate this and endeavour to ensure that the fields that are being captured are in the same sequence as those presented on the report. This will greatly speed up the capture process.

Using layout charts
When designing reports for plain stationery, a printer layout chart is used as shown in Figure 17.2. This form is merely for the assistance of the designer, to ensure that the report is spaced out correctly. A few notes are important:

- The standard width for most business printers is 132 positions. However, some printers are only 80 columns wide. The designer must ensure that the capacity of the printer on which the report is to be printed is known before designing the report.
- When filling in numeric characters in a report, the maximum width of the field must be indicated. This is done using 9s (as in Figure 17.2).
- When filling in alphabetic/numeric fields the maximum width of a field is indicated with Xs.
- All control totals should be indicated as well as the report headings, the page numbering and the date of production.

17.2.2 Terminals

There are many types of terminals on the market today: VDUs, microcomputers, typewriters, telex machines, plotters, FAX machines, voice activated machines, music makers, and so on. Many of these are now finding their way into the business arena in some surprising applications. The majority of terminals today are VDUs and microcomputers which have the ability either to work on their own or to send and receive data from a central computer.

Response times
An important consideration in designing screens is that *the more information that is transmitted between terminal and computer, the slower the response will be.* By 'information' we mean not only the answers that the user keys in but all questions and prompts that appear on the screen. In applications where time is very important, the analyst will, during preliminary systems design, have calculated the response times based on the volume of data that is expected to be transmitted, and will have projected the number of terminals required to handle the volume of transactions. These will be confirmed by the designer who will endeavour to ensure that the system operates within the response time limits set by the analyst.

Error and failure considerations
Probably one of the most important considerations when designing terminal dialogue is to ensure that all errors are taken into account. The simplest form of error is where a

FIGURE 17.2. An example of a printer layout chart.

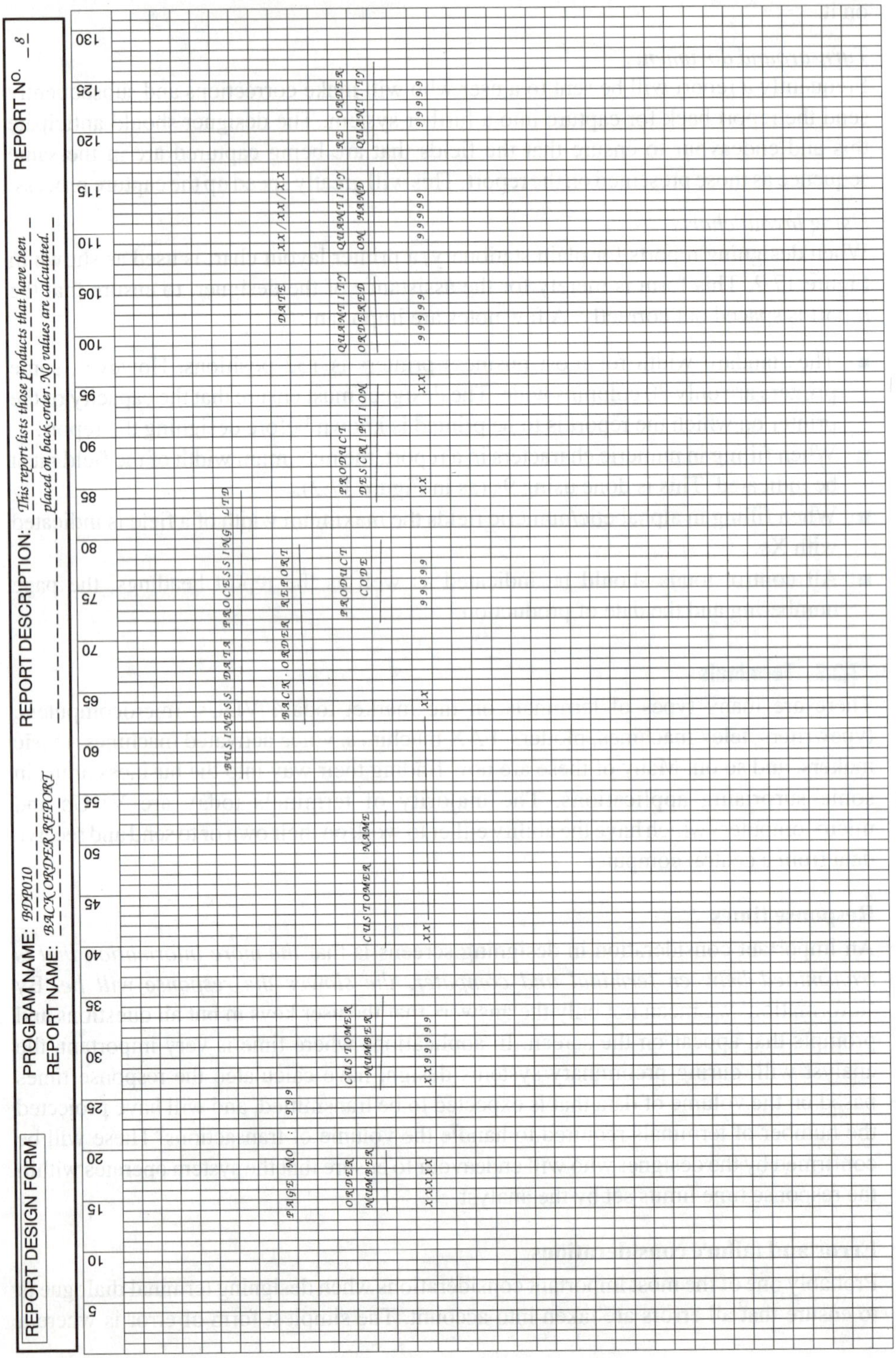

user keys in the wrong code; a more complex one is where a program, through incorrect logic, updates a database incorrectly. The computer should trap all the different kinds of errors and display appropriate messages back to the user.

Failure conditions — when the computer loses power, for example — are more difficult to circumvent. It is important, however, to have restart facilities available so that the user can determine accurately what has been processed, what was in the course of being processed at the time of the failure, and what has not been processed.

Security considerations

Security is becoming increasingly important, simply because there are so many terminals in use in business and the knowledge of users is increasing. This means that the opportunities for people to abuse the system are increasing. Designers must cater for this by building in safeguards such as passwords and terminal recognition by the computer in an effort to circumvent the problem. More details of this will be given in the module on 'control and security'.

Screen design techniques

When designing screens, the designer makes use of a screen layout chart. This, like the printer layout chart, is for the assistance of the programmer. The same rules apply, with the exception that the maximum size of the screen is normally 24 rows by 80 columns. There are, however, smaller and bigger screens and one must therefore know beforehand what hardware will be utilized. An example of a screen layout chart is shown in Figure 17.3.

One of the easiest ways to draw the attention of the user to important questions or error conditions is to highlight (by colouring, underlining, or flashing) the information that the user *must* see. A problem is that such highlighting can become an annoyance and may distract the user. Care must therefore be exercised in its use. Highlighting is available on most terminals today. It is controlled by the program driving the screen.

The designer of a system should balance cost against the functions that are provided for the user. It is possible to provide users with many facilities, but these will obviously cost a lot in terms of time in the programming, development, and testing phases of the system. Knowing what to put in and what to leave out is a function of experience as no specific guidelines are available.

17.2.3 A note on microfilm/microfiche

Microfilm and/or microfiche is generally used either where large reports are to be frequently accessed by users or where copies of reports are required to be stored for a period of time. These are a very efficient form of storage and retrieval, although optical disks are starting to making the use of microfilm and microfiche redundant.

17.3 INPUT DESIGN

There are seven concerns which the analyst will have when designing the input to the system. These are:

1. What input is needed for the system?

FIGURE 17.3. Screen layout chart.

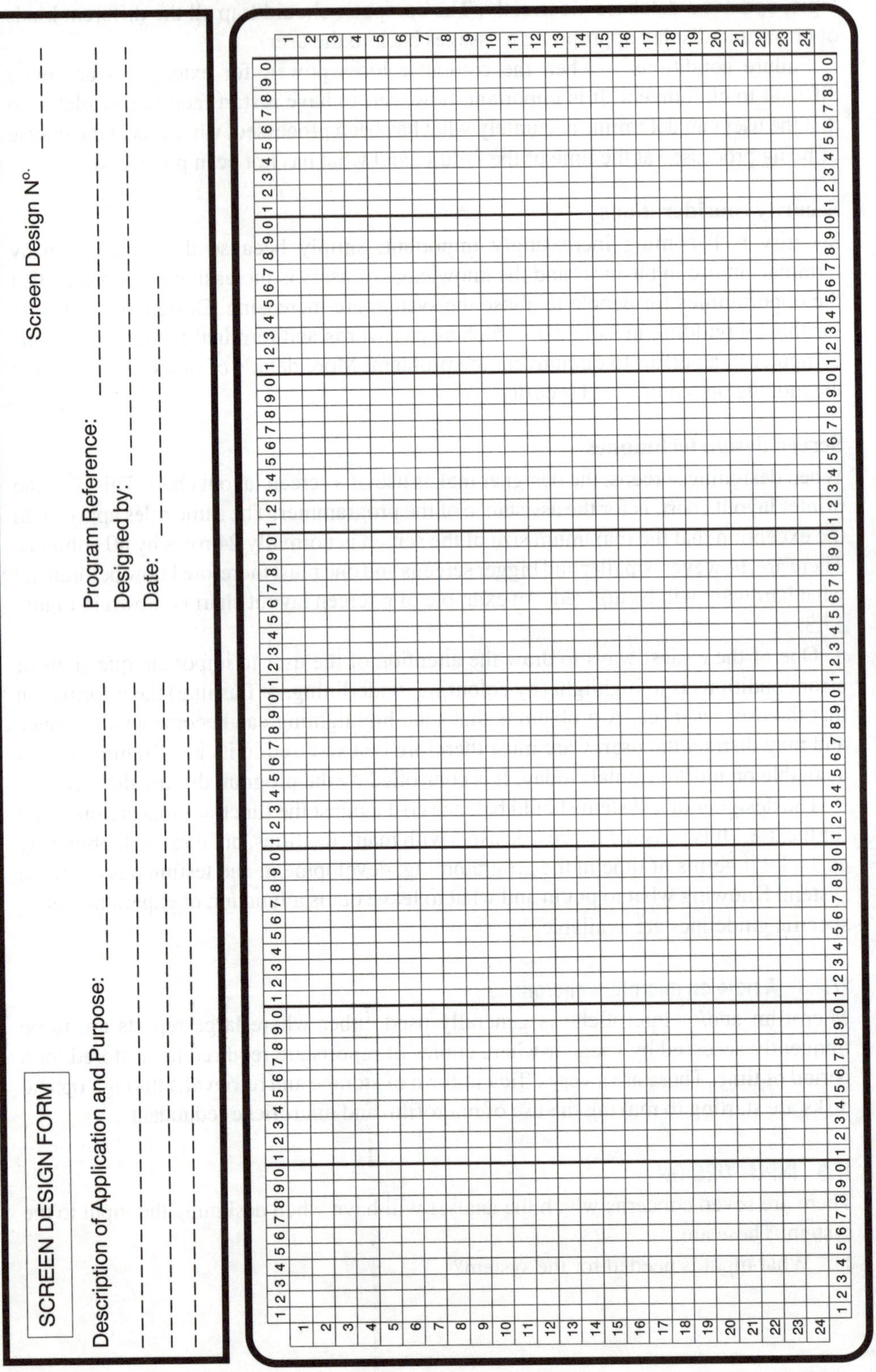

2. Where do the data originate?
3. What should the form of the source documents be?
4. What medium should be used for capturing the input into the system?
5. What device should be used?
6. What provisions should be made for an audit trail and for verifying the input?
7. Should the process of preparing and capturing the input be centralized or decentralized?

Many of these questions will have been answered during the JAD session, but the answers should be confirmed during detailed design.

What input is needed?

The input for any system is determined by the output. The designer should, by analysing the output, construct a data dictionary and then determine what information is already in the system, and what additional input is required from the users to either set up or update the databases.

Data origination

The designer should now determine which user department will generate the source document. Wherever possible, the transcription of data from one form to another should be avoided — data should be captured as close to the source as possible.

Format of the source document

In modern systems, the source document is usually the working form used by the user department. It might, for example, be an invoice or an order. The designer determines what information should be coded onto the source document (for example, customer name or product code) and defines how the user will insert the appropriate codes. Care should always be taken that data are captured into the system in the same sequence as the data appearing on the source document.

Format of the input record

The designer must determine whether the fields are to be of fixed or variable length and decide the maximum field sizes which have to be captured into the system.

The use of codes reduces the amount of input required but may increase the time required to prepare the document, as a user may need to look up the code prior to inserting it on the document.

Well-designed input documents can help to reduce errors considerably, thereby increasing the productivity of the operators who capture the data.

The input medium

Where possible an attempt is made to utilize equipment that already exists in the installation.

The provision of audit trails

One of the most common errors made in systems design is to omit an adequate audit trail either for the users or for internal or external auditors. The user must be able to check the total volume and value of all source documents and ensure that these agree with the output to ensure completeness of processing.

Centralization versus decentralization of data capture

The designer should confirm where the data should be captured, and decide on the mode of transmission, using batch or on-line mode.

The following are the stages that take place in the *batch* capture of data:

- *Original recording* — where data are recorded onto source documents.
- *Transmission* — where the source documents are sent through to the data capture department.
- *Transcription* — where the source documents are captured onto a data capture medium (eg. diskette or tape).
- *Verification.* This can be achieved either programmatically or using data capture hardware.
- *Input.* The data are entered into the system.
- *Sorting.* The data capture records are sorted into a specific sequence.
- *Control.* Audit trails are printed on a report by the computer to allow the user to balance the input.

The following is the sequence of events that takes place for *on-line* data capture:

- *Original recording* — where the source documents are prepared by the user department.
- *Capture* — where the documents are entered into the computer through a terminal.
- *Verification* — this is normally performed during capture.
- *Transmission* — the input is sent electronically to the computer to be processed. The input records will go directly to the machine.
- *Control* — reports will be produced which will be sent back to the user for verification of input.

There are fewer steps in on-line capture but, because the process is interactive, the *total* time for the capture of a large volume of transactions will be slower than in batch capture.

17.3.1 Input form design

Having analysed the requirements for an input form, the next stage is to design the form itself. (See Figure 17.4 for a copy of an input form.)

The following points should be borne in mind when designing an input form:

- *Identification.* All forms should be clearly identified by a title. Where it is important to keep a check of the number of forms issued, they should be numbered in sequence.
- *Readability and use.* All forms have to be easy to use and easy to fill in. They must be as simple and legible as possible. Ample space must be provided for the insertion of data. A user should never be required to squeeze desired information into the available space.

- *Physical factors.* If the form is required to be sent to many departments for signing or transcription, the paper should be thicker than normal to allow for handling.
- *Instructions.* It is often desirable to help the user to fill in the form by placing instructions on the form itself.
- *Multiple copies.* Where multiple copies of a form are required, the analyst should decide which method of carbonization should be used — either OTC (one-time carbon), or NCR (no carbon required). Whichever method is used, the analyst should ensure that the operator can easily obtain the required number of copies. (If six copies are required the user should not have to put too much pressure on the paper to make the sixth copy legible.)
- *Use of check-off boxes.* Where options are available it is often advisable to provide those options in separate boxes and merely require the user to tick the appropriate one.

FIGURE 17.4. Example of an input form.

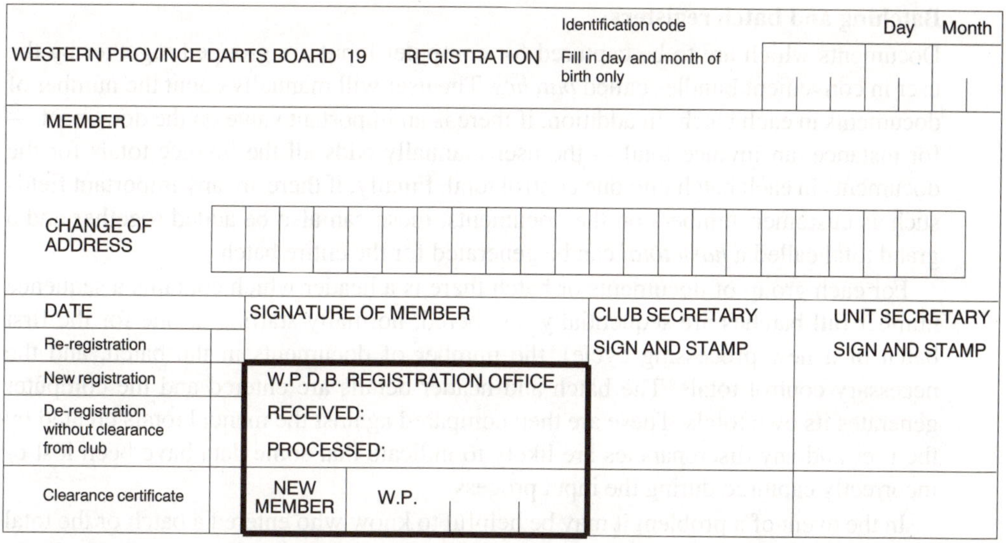
WESTERN PROVINCE DARTS BOARD 19 REGISTRATION

Identification code

Fill in day and month of birth only

Day

Month

MEMBER

CHANGE OF ADDRESS

DATE

Re-registration

New registration

De-registration without clearance from club

Clearance certificate

SIGNATURE OF MEMBER

W.P.D.B. REGISTRATION OFFICE

RECEIVED:

PROCESSED:

NEW MEMBER

W.P.

CLUB SECRETARY SIGN AND STAMP

UNIT SECRETARY SIGN AND STAMP

This section has described the more important rules to be followed when designing output and input forms. This is certainly the most critical stage of the development process, since the forms are the media through which the user communicates with the computer and vice versa. If the design of the input and output forms does not cater for control of the data and information then the designer's efforts will be wasted.

17.4 CONTROLS DESIGN

The person designing a system must ensure that there are sufficient controls to *maintain the integrity* of the system. This does not necessarily mean protection against fraud (although this is obviously an important aspect), but it is more concerned with assisting the users in balancing the system, thereby ensuring the completeness and accuracy of processing.

A business system typically consists of four subsystems: one to set up the information in the databases, one to process input, one for the output, and the final subsystem for periodic processing. Each of the above components must have adequate controls to ensure that the databases and processes are correct. The following section will describe a framework that can be applied to almost any application. There might be minor differences from system to system, but the principles remain the same. Note that there is a substantial overlap between manual and computerized controls. This is inevitable since, ultimately, *people* will provide the highest level of control.

17.4.1 Control techniques

Before getting down to the details of the controls design, there are a few principles that need to be explained. These relate to batching and batch registers, error procedures and control reports.

Batching and batch registers

Documents which are to be captured for computer input are grouped together by the user in convenient bundles called *batches*. The user will manually count the number of documents in each batch. In addition, if there is an important value on the document — for instance, an invoice total — the user manually adds all the invoice totals for the documents in each batch into one control total. Finally, if there are any important fields such as customer numbers on the documents, these can also be added together and a grand total called a *hash total* can be generated for the entire batch.

For each group of documents or batch there is a header which contains a sequence number (all batches are sequentially numbered, normally starting at one for the first batch of a new processing cycle), the number of documents in the batch, and the necessary control totals. The batch and header details are entered and the computer generates its own totals. These are then compared against the manual totals created by the user and any discrepancies are likely to indicate that some data have been lost or incorrectly captured during the input process.

In the event of a problem it may be helpful to know who entered a batch or the total value of a batch. This may be achieved by using a batch register. An example is shown in Figure 17.5.

FIGURE 17.5. Accounts receivable batch register.

BATCH REGISTER — ACCOUNTS RECEIVABLE

Date	Batch No.	Type	Value	Number	Entered by
01/03/93	2020	Receipts	1015.62	14	Paula
03/03/93	104	Invoices	33 119.68	35	Jenny
04/03/93	2021	Receipts	9100.00	8	James
04/03/93	2022	Receipts	11 215.00	11	Paula

The batch register serves as a valuable balancing aid since by adding, for example, all the receipt batches for the month, the total can then be checked against the total value of receipts printed for the month on the debtor statements. The two totals should agree. If they do not, then there has been a serious hiccup in the system.

17.4.2 Error procedures

A common problem in early batch systems was that errors would be rejected by a validation program and would then get 'lost' in the correction cycle. This was because the controls over those errors were inadequate. A method that is commonly used to prevent this is that of 'suspense files'. Errors are written to a suspense file at the same time as they are printed on a report. The user, on receipt of the report, corrects the errors and resubmits them. The computer then matches the resubmissions to the suspense file. On a successful match the record is dropped from the suspense file. If the computer cannot find a match, the correction is not allowed into the system. The advantage of this approach is that, by examining the suspense file, one can determine, at any time, which errors have not yet been corrected by the user. All errors are therefore adequately tracked and controlled. Figure 17.6 diagrammatically explains this procedure.

Another method is to control errors at the batch level. If an error is found in a batch, that batch is tagged as being incorrect and the details are stored in a batch control file. At any time the user can interrogate the batch control file to determine which batches are still invalid.

17.4.3 Control reports

These are also used as aids in checking the totals maintained in the system. Every time values or the number of records are changed in the system, a report should be printed. This should be done on completion of the task and should summarize the activities that have taken place. A control report is also used as a run-to-run control by printing brought-forward and carried-forward balances. Details of the use of control reports will be discussed later in this chapter.

Having highlighted these principles, we can now proceed to discuss details of controlling applications.

17.4.4 Standing data controls

Figure 17.7 describes the process involved in controlling the maintenance of standing data. In all business systems, source documents are used as a basis for changing the standing data. They may be informal documents, such as a letter from a customer advising of a change of address, or formal documents such as the 'change of master file details' used in government departments. These should be grouped together to form a batch (which may contain any convenient number of documents) the details of which should be entered in the batch register. The batches are then captured into the computer using the update programs. Errors are rejected and are sent back to the user for correction. A new batch is made up and the process is restarted.

FIGURE 17.6. The use of error suspense files.

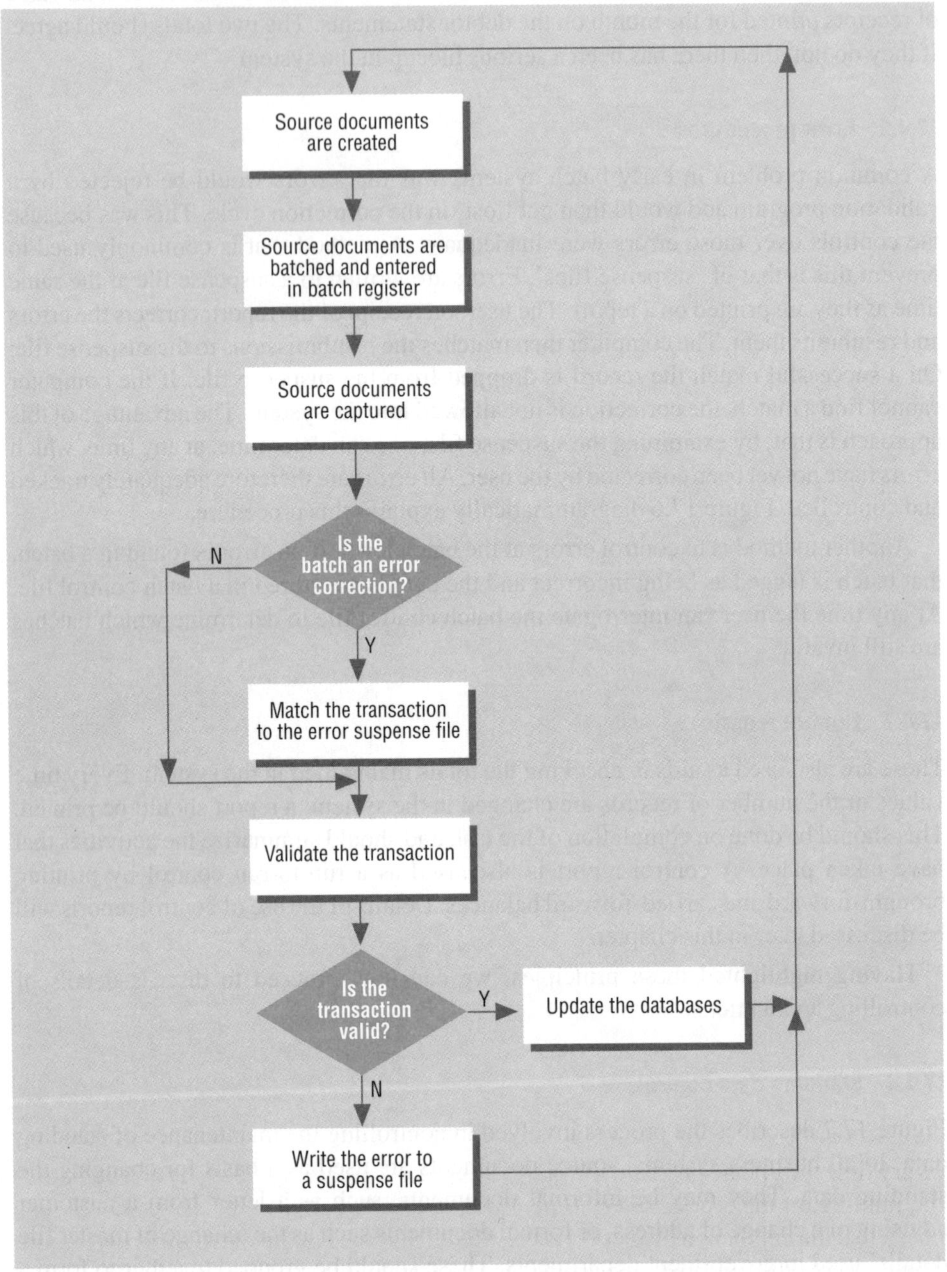

The update program should produce an update control report at the end of *every* run. An example of such a report is shown in Figure 17.8. Notice that there is a run number printed on the top right hand side of the report. The computer has an internal counter.

FIGURE 17.7. Overview of the database maintenance function.

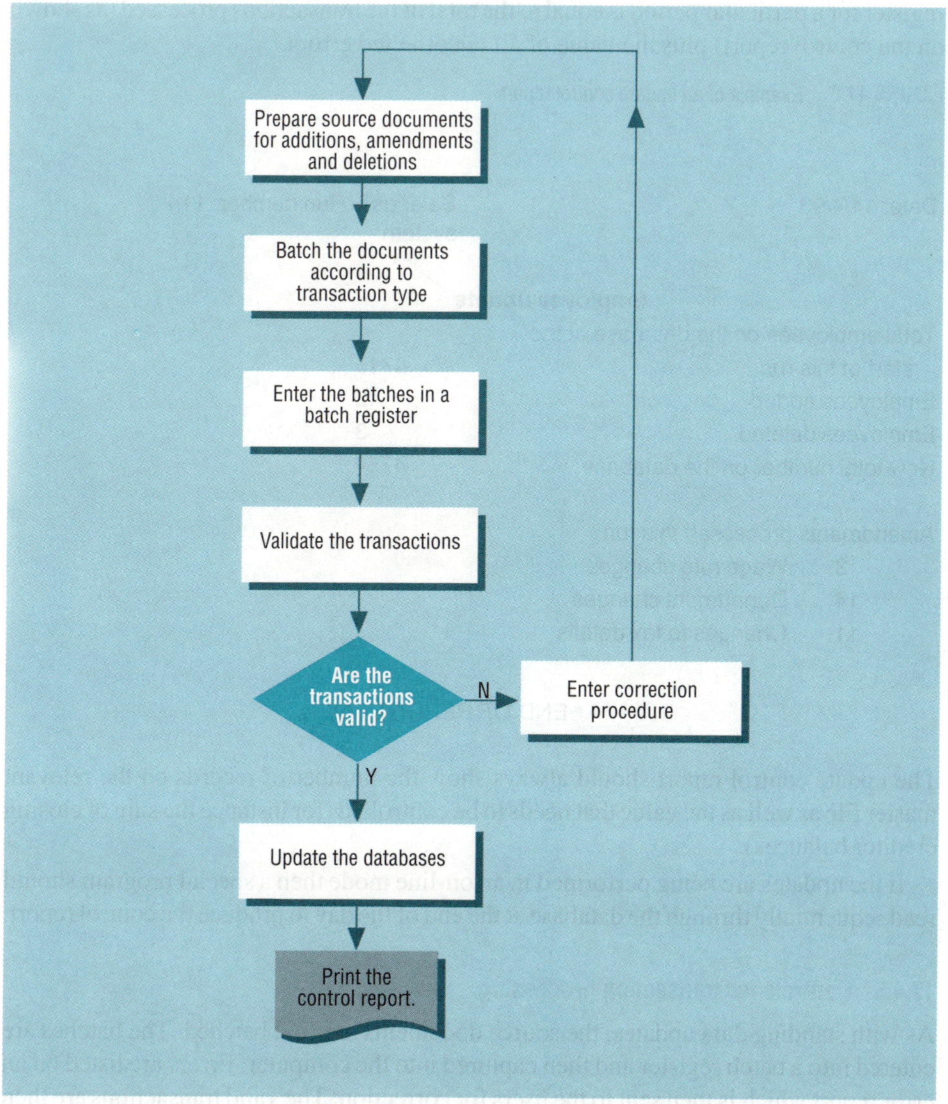

Every time the update program is run the computer increases its count by one and prints the number on the report. Every time a user receives a control report he should then check that the number on that report is one higher than the number on the previous report. This is one of the fundamental aspects of application control — ensuring completeness of processing.

Notice, too, that there is a brought-forward and a carried-forward balance on the report. The brought-forward balance of the current report should be the same as the carried-forward balance on the previous one.

Yet a further control would be to ensure that the total of all the batches in the batch register for a particular period is equal to the total of the transactions processed (as shown on the control report) plus the value of all uncorrected errors.

FIGURE 17.8. Example of an update control report.

Date: 14/4/93	Salaries system	Run number: 114

Employee update

Total employees on the database at the start of this run	4715
Employees added	42
Employees deleted	3
New total number on the database	4754

Amendments processed this run:

3	Wage rate changes
14	Department changes
11	Changes to tax details

*** END OF REPORT ***

The update control report should always show the number of records on the relevant master file as well as the value that needs to be controlled (for instance the sum of closing creditor balances).

If the updates are being performed in an on-line mode then a special program should read sequentially through the database at the end of the day to produce the control report.

17.4.5 Controls for transaction processing

As with standing data updates, the source documents are first batched. The batches are entered into a batch register and then captured into the computer. Errors are listed on an error report which is then sent to the users for correction. The valid transactions are then updated into the databases, and a control report is produced.

The purpose of the validation program is to reject any incorrect data, thereby ensuring that only valid transactions are allowed into the update section of the system. The validation program would therefore be run *before* the update program. The kind of checking carried out by this program has been dealt with already in Chapter 11.

17.4.6 Controls for reporting

Figure 17.9 shows the procedures to be followed for the production of reports. The important point to remember is that the operational reports should always have the

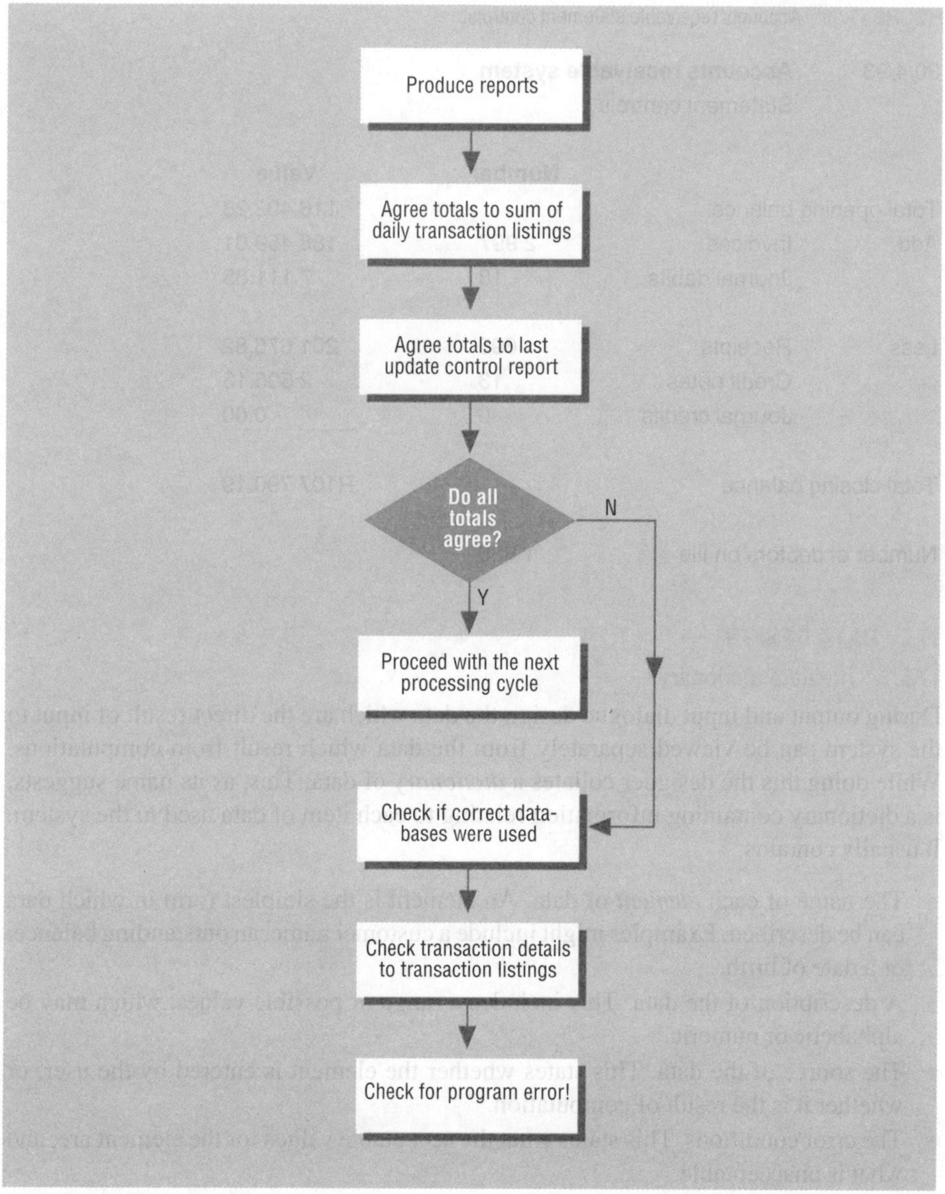

FIGURE 17.9. Control procedures — reports.

necessary totals to ensure that all information has been processed. Figure 17.10 shows an example of the controls at the end of an accounts receivable statement run. The transactions total can be balanced with the update control report, as can the total debtor balances.

FIGURE 17.10. Accounts receivable statement controls.

30/4/93 **Accounts receivable system**
Statement controls

		Number	Value
Total opening balance			116 402.28
Add	Invoices	2 997	188 459.01
	Journal debits	18	7 111.85
Less	Receipts	698	201 676.82
	Credit notes	13	2 506.13
	Journal credits	0	0.00
Total closing balance			R107 790.19
Number of debtors on file		1 880	

17.5 DATA DESIGN

17.5.1 The data dictionary

During output and input dialogue design the data which are the direct result of input to the system can be viewed separately from the data which result from computations. While doing this the designer collates a *dictionary* of data. This, as its name suggests, is a dictionary containing information relating to each item of data used in the system. It usually contains:

- The name of each *element* of data. An element is the simplest form in which data can be described. Examples might include a customer name, an outstanding balance, or a date of birth.
- A description of the data. This includes a range of possible values, which may be alphabetic or numeric.
- The source of the data. This states whether the element is entered by the user, or whether it is the result of computation.
- The error conditions. This states what the acceptable values for the element are, and what is unacceptable.

At the time of drawing up the data dictionary the designer notes all exceptions to the rules and writes them into the data dictionary.

On completion of the dictionary the designer commences *data modelling*. The purpose of this is to group the data elements together to create database structures. This must be done so that there is optimal use of storage and so that the data can be retrieved according to the needs of the user. If data are successfully modelled, the databases should need little restructuring as the system is modified or enhanced after installation. One of the main difficulties in the data modelling stage is ensuring that the resulting databases will easily integrate into future systems. The designer needs to pay attention to flexibility and has to look ahead to foresee future system structures.

The main technique used in data modelling is the *entity relationship technique* (ERT) discussed in the PSD phase.

Building an entity model

All entities in the ERD are extracted and the data items that uniquely identify each entity are listed. For example, assume one wishes to develop a database for recording student details. First an entity table consisting of all data items to be stored on the system is constructed.

The next stage is to list the data elements that apply to each entity and to build entity/key tables. An example for student details is given in Figure 17.11.

FIGURE 17.11. An entity/key table for student details.

STUDENT DETAILS
Student name
Student address
Next of kin
Degree
Course code
Course name
Faculty
Mark obtained
Residence code
Residence name

FIGURE 17.12. Student data elements in first normal form.

STUDENT DETAILS
Student number
Student name
Student address
Next of kin
Degree
Residence code
Residence name

STUDENT – COURSE
Student number
Course number
Course name
Faculty
Mark obtained

FIGURE 17.13. Student data elements in second normal form.

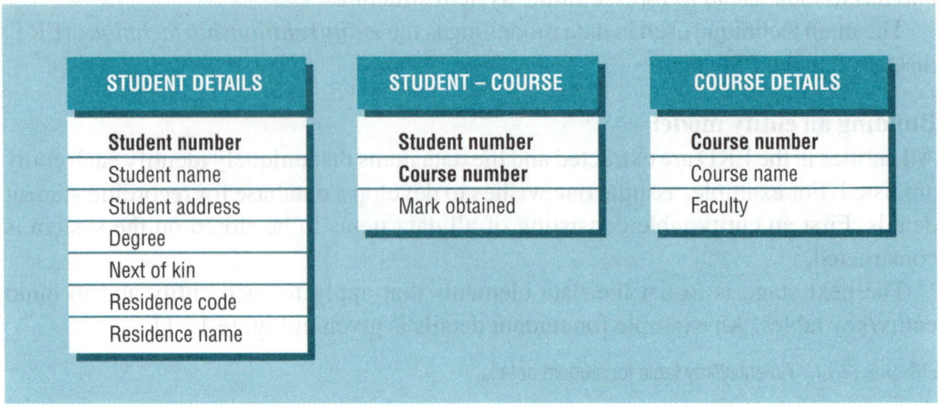

FIGURE 17.14.

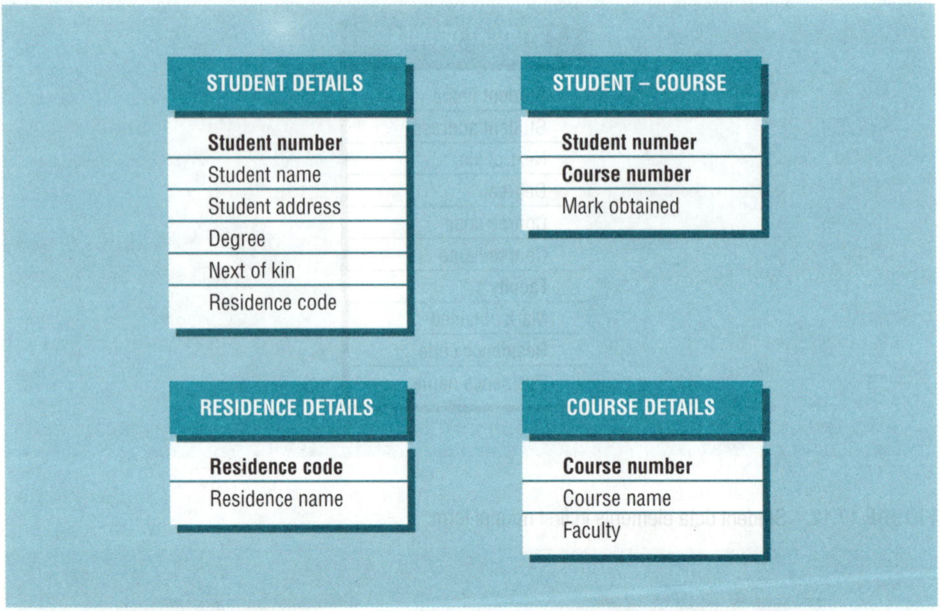

The entity/key tables are now ready to be *normalized.* Normalization means grouping the elements in such a way that they can be extracted and displayed in the most efficient and flexible manner. It usually proceeds through three stages.

Stage 1 — Remove all repeating groups, thus forming fixed-length groups of data. The data are now in *first normal form*.

In the example, the student course details are identified as a repeating group (a student may take many courses). These are removed to form a new table as in Figure 17.12.

Stage 2 — Remove any elements that do not depend on the full unique identifier (also known as the *key*). The keys are in bold type in Figures 17.12 to 17.14. The data are now in *second normal form*. In the example, the course name is dependent on the course number but not the student number, so the course details are removed to a separate table as in Figure 17.13.

Stage 3 — Remove any attributes that are dependent on other attributes. The data are now in *third normal form*. In Figure 17.14 the residence number and name have been placed in a separate table and only the residence number remains in the student table. By this stage all many-to-many relationships will have been removed.

It is possible to proceed as far as a *fifth normal form*. However, this procedure is rare as it is only used in extremely high-volume systems.

The normalized data structures now define the databases which can be constructed. It is usual for the designer to simulate the processing of data by ensuring that questions posed by the user can be answered quickly and easily by the system.

17.6 PROCESS DESIGN

The designer now divides the system into subsystems, and then divides each subsystem into logical functions or processes, each of which will become a program. He aims for certain design objectives:

- The system and programs have to be easy to maintain and modify.
- The integrity of the data must be ensured, so rigorous validation programs must be set up.
- The system should be easy to work with and easy to understand.

Breaking systems into small, logical programs that perform specific procedures usually results in those systems being easy to understand, easy to work with, and easy to maintain.

The designer then specifies each program in the system. In particular, the following are specified:

- *A statement of function.* This is normally in narrative form and describes the functions of the program. It should also state how the program fits into the system.
- *The input and/or output dialogue.* The dialogue that was determined in the detailed design phase is now specified. The layouts relevant to each program are grouped together.
- *Processing details.* This gives details of all functions and computations that are to be performed by the program *in exact terms*. There should be no room for the programmer to misconstrue details or to make assumptions.
- *Controls.* Where controls are being used (eg. number of records on an input file) details must be given of how to process them.
- *Exceptions.* This is the most difficult part of the specification. All deviations from the main line of processing must be declared. Examples of typical exceptions are: authority overrides, discounts (settlements or cash), special processing exceptions, and status checking.
- *Security/recovery.* Where the program has to have special security procedures (eg. password control), these are specified. Likewise, if recovery procedures are

required, details of how to recover, and from where, are furnished. If long reports are to be printed then details of how to restart from a specific page number are given.

The specifications provide the input for writing the programs. They have to be detailed and accurate or errors will be introduced at the programming stage. Careful walk-throughs with the design team, together with reviews by the project leader and the user, will help to ensure the correctness of the specifications.

At this stage the design of the system is complete and construction is about to commence. The user should have been involved in the whole design process through the JAD sessions and should sign-off the detailed design. If this has occurred there should be no surprises on implementation of the system, thus avoiding unnecessary maintenance. The objective of *good* systems design is, after all, to get it right the first time.

REVIEW QUESTIONS

1. Why is dialogue design performed in preliminary systems design and again in detailed systems design? Is this not unnecessary repetition?
2. How would you decide whether to use hard copy or screen displays in output design?
3. Design a report listing student names, numbers and marks in descending order by subject, for use by external examiners. The report must show the number of students who passed and failed and the average mark.
4. Give an example of where a turnaround document could be used.
5. What is the difference between error recovery and disaster recovery?
6. What is the purpose of an audit trail and why are audit trails important in an information system?
7. 'Most information systems use screens to capture transactions directly from source documents, so input forms are usually unnecessary.' True or false? Justify your answer.
8. What is the principle behind batching?
9. How could errors be controlled if one did not use a suspense file?
10. What is a run-to-run control and how is it used in verifying the correctness of a system?
11. What is data modelling and what are its objectives?
12. The following data have been extracted from the system details for a medical aid system. Normalize the data to third normal form.
    Member number
    Member name
    Member address
    Member sex
    Spouse number
    Spouse name
    Spouse age
    Dependant number

Dependant name
Dependant sex
Dependant age
Member past disease code } — repeated per disease
Member past disease name } — repeated per disease
Spouse/dependant past disease code} — repeated per disease
Spouse/dependant past disease name } — repeated per disease
Member's income
Member's age
Member's monthly contribution

CHAPTER 18 Systems implementation

18.1 PROGRAMMING AND PROGRAM TESTING

Having completed the specifications, the designer hands them to the programmer, who writes the instructions to perform the job. It is normal for a number of programmers (from three to 12) to be involved in a system. Communication problems and false assumptions can therefore frequently arise if the specifications are not complete. The larger the programming team, the more accurate the specifications have to be.

When coding is complete the programmer performs a 'desk-check'. This involves simulating the movement of data through the program before running it on the computer. This is done to attempt to eliminate as many problems as possible without wasting valuable computer resources.

The program is then entered into the computer through an input device — usually a terminal. The next step is to compile the program. In this process a compiler will read the source program, check the syntax and convert the 'English-like' statements into machine language. If there are errors in the source program the compiler will list the errors and the programmer will check and correct these before recompiling the program.

Once the program is error-free, the programmer then enters test data to determine whether it is working correctly or not. The test data should resemble live transactions as closely as possible. If they do not, the programmer will not be performing realistic tests.

Specific areas that the programmer tests are:

- The program must be proven to be able to process the data within a reasonable time-frame.
- Where the program is writing out data, it must be able to handle overflow situations.
- It should not be possible to terminate the program abnormally through logic errors.
- If a program is running and the power fails it should be possible to restart with a minimum of delay.
- The programmer should ensure that the test data can correctly process every exception that has been specified.
- Program-to-program control. Assume a situation where one program (A) writes out a file that is read by another program (B). When the programmer is testing program B he or she should, as part of program testing, ensure that the file from program A can be read and processed correctly. Frequently, in practice, program B is completed before program A. To save time the programmer then creates an input file and tests the program. In so doing, data are created according to the way the program has been written — which may well differ from the way program A writes out the file. This can result either from incorrect specifications or from incorrectly written programs.

Assuming that all testing has been satisfactorily completed, the system is now ready to move into the final phase — testing and acceptance by the user, and implementation. The success of the system will to a large extent depend on how well the system has been specified and tested. If this has been done poorly, the subsequent maintenance load and the total cost of the system will be far higher than the initial budget would have allowed for.

18.2 SYSTEM TESTING

This stage ensures that all the programs in the system work together and perform the functions that were laid down in the system specifications. The analyst or project manager now draws up test data which will be used to simulate the live situation as closely as possible. Special attention is given to the handling of incorrect data and the processing of exceptions. If the program specifications have been well conceived and the programs correctly written, then the data should be correctly processed. In almost all situations, however, minor (but in some cases major) corrections are required to rectify discrepancies.

Once the analyst is satisfied that the system is working, the user will test the system using system data. This is done for two reasons:

- As an education tool. During this phase the user will be learning to use the system — how to balance the input, how to request reports, etc.
- As an acceptance test. Once the user has completed the tests he or she is saying 'I have tested the system and found it to be working satisfactorily. I am now ready to take responsibility for it.'

Again, at this stage, errors that are detected in the programs will be corrected and retested. If the analyst has not performed the system tests adequately and the user finds a large number of errors, this may destroy the user's faith in the system. It is therefore important for the analyst to test thoroughly prior to handover to the users.

The system has now been written and tested and is ready for the final phases — conversion and implementation.

18.3 SYSTEM CONVERSION

Conversion is the process of changing from one method of processing to another, eg. from one computer system to another, or from a manual system to a computer system. In both cases the data have to be captured so that the new system can be set up.

18.3.1 Converting from an existing system

One of the major problems of converting from an existing system is that the data will not be in a format which is compatible with the new one. To overcome this problem the analyst designs a separate subsystem to convert the data in the existing system to a format — and a medium (such as magnetic tape) — which will be compatible with the new system. Special programs are written for this purpose as well as to read the databases and load them on the new system. The data will frequently have to be reformatted in order to cater for the requirements of the new system; care must be taken that nothing is lost during this process.

18.3.2 Converting from an existing manual system

In this instance a large volume of data may have to be captured in a short period of time. From the time that the data are captured to the time that the system actually runs live, the data must be maintained and kept up to date even though the programs may not necessarily be updating them. Special procedures have to be laid down to ensure that this process is carried out properly. Frequently, outside sources (such as data capture bureaux) are used to cater for this heavy demand during the conversion process.

18.3.3 Data balancing

Where data are transferred from one system to another, or from a manual system to computer, it is obviously important to ensure that the new databases are accurate and complete. The point of reference taken is usually the old database or file, but it is often found to contain errors. This problem may be overcome by substantiating the values in the old file prior to conversion (if stock is being computerized, for instance, a stock count would be performed to validate the existing records). The values in the new database are then compared with the old to establish their correctness. In an extremely large file it is often not considered appropriate to check every item — random checks will attempt to determine the accuracy of the data, while control totals will be used to verify the completeness of the data. The selection of random samples would normally either be done on a rand value basis, or by selecting every *n*th block or record. The analyst tries to ensure that the conversion programs are specified to produce control totals that will enable the user, or the internal or external auditor, to balance the values *easily*.

18.3.4 Procedural testing

If the analyst has performed his job well there will probably be new procedures for the user to perform. The reason for this is that a computerized system will take advantage of a completely new set of facilities that were not available in a manual system.

The capture and processing of data, and the ability of the computer to produce reports in many different forms, will contribute to many changes in the user's functions. Although the good analyst will model these changes and attempt to ensure that there are no inconsistencies, they still need to be tested in a 'live' situation.

This testing of the new procedures may take place either before the new system goes live, or, as is more often the case, after the new system is implemented. The problem with the latter approach is that it is difficult to make changes to the system if some of the procedures are found to be unworkable. It is therefore usually recommended that the system is simulated prior to implementation, and that any errors are corrected immediately.

18.3.5 Critical areas during conversion

The following factors have to be borne in mind prior to and during the conversion process:

1. Special one-time programs may have to be written to cater for conversion. This can be an expensive process and should be kept to a minimum.
2. Special procedures have to be set up to balance the data that have been captured to ensure both accuracy and completeness.

3. The timing of the conversion process may be critical. It may have to be scheduled for weekends or carried out during the night.
4. Frequently data are lost during the conversion process because of inadequate security. The person in charge of the process should ensure that data are checked at strategic points such as after all major database updates.
5. Adequate audit trails and control totals have to be built into the conversion programs to assist the user in balancing the new data.

18.4 INSTALLING THE SYSTEM

Implementation is the most critical phase of the whole systems development process. The user must follow certain procedures before running live in order to ensure that the new system is correct. There are five methods by which this may be achieved:

- parallel runs;
- pilot site;
- modular (staged or phased);
- direct implementation;
- simulation.

18.4.1 Parallel runs

The user runs the new system and the old side by side for an agreed period of time. This should be long enough to ensure that all processing cycles are adequately completed and checked (in a debtors system, for example, the parallel runs would need to last for at least one month to ensure that the month-end procedures are adequately covered).

Parallel running imposes heavy burdens on the user to check the two systems for the period of time that the parallel run is taking place. This can be quite onerous and frequently outsiders are brought in to assist. It is, however, the most common method employed as it ensures that the new computer procedure is performing at least as well as the existing manual one.

18.4.2 Pilot sites

This method is frequently chosen where an organization is installing a system at several branches. One branch will be chosen which is representative of all the others and the system will be installed at that site for an agreed period of time. There is then a direct cutover from the old system to the new and the users are assigned the task of running and checking out the new system. The major disadvantage (compared with the parallel run approach) is that if a major fault is found in the new system the users have to convert back to the manual system until the new one is corrected.

18.4.3 Modular

The modular (or staged, or phased) approach is chosen where an application can be split up into sub-systems, each of which can be installed independently. Thus, for instance, a system may be slipped into various sections so that the recording sub-system is implemented first, followed by an automatic re-ordering sub-system, followed by a management reporting sub-system. The advantage of this approach is that the impact of failure is comparatively small. Each unit can be installed and run live for a time, until the user is satisfied with it.

18.4.4 Direct implementation

This method is employed only where the system to be installed is of relatively minor significance to the organization. What happens is that at a specified time the old system is discarded and the new one is brought in. Any errors are corrected at the time that they occur. The user does not have any means of going back to the old system.

18.4.5 Simulation

This is frequently employed where no manual system exists. The user simulates all the input data as though they were intended for the live system and computes the result manually, based on assumptions about what is going to happen; these are then checked with the computer results. This can be an expensive method but it may be the only way in which a system can be verified.

18.5 POST-IMPLEMENTATION REVIEW

The user is now ready to run the system. It should be noted that if systems development takes place without involving the user then the system has a high failure potential because of user resistance. The user should be involved from start to finish — specifying requirements, checking the output design, drawing up test specifications, etc. Through this involvement he or she will both identify with the system and will appreciate all the ramifications of producing the final output.

The final phase in the system development cycle is the *post-implementation review.* It normally takes place three to six months after the installation of the system. The purposes of the review are:

1. To determine whether the objectives specified in the preliminary analysis (see Chapter 15, 15.2) have been met and, if not, why not.
2. To ensure that the users are using the system correctly and that the reports are fulfilling their purpose.
3. To satisfy oneself that the system is maintainable and flexible.
4. To highlight shortfalls in the development process so that any mistakes can be rectified in future systems.

18.6 MAINTENANCE AND FOLLOW-UP

After installation the system moves into the maintenance phase. Here amendments and enhancements are made throughout its life. Very few systems are static. The average life of a system is ten to fifteen years, depending on the quality of the original development process. Poor development standards can be very costly while good standards and techniques can be a boon to both the users and the organization.

The installation of a system does not represent the end of the cycle. Over time the user will request changes. These may be a result of:

- Changing circumstances in the business. As the organization develops, so the transactions increase and the requirements of the users change. The system will therefore require modifications to mirror those changes.
- The user might request additional information which will help perform the system tasks better.
- The system requirements may initially have been incorrectly specified. As the system is used, so these requirements will be corrected.

18.6.1 The distribution of work

The workload in the system development cycle is shown in Figure 18.1. If the system has been well written (according to the user's requirements and using modular techniques) the maintenance load would follow line A. If it has been badly written, however, the system would require a heavier maintenance load represented by line B. It is therefore necessary to design a system which is responsive to change and to attempt to anticipate future requirements during the analysis and design stages. This is not an easy task but the experienced analyst and designer will pay particular attention to the aspects of output and data design.

Output design is probably the most *volatile* (ie. changeable) area. As the user becomes familiar with what is being received, so he or she will request additional reports or change existing ones.

Data design is the most difficult aspect to modify, although the use of database management systems reduces the maintenance load. Changes in computation methods or in output are relatively easy to accommodate, but requests to store additional items of data can be time-consuming as the whole system may require retesting. This is partly

FIGURE 18.1. The workload distribution during systems development.

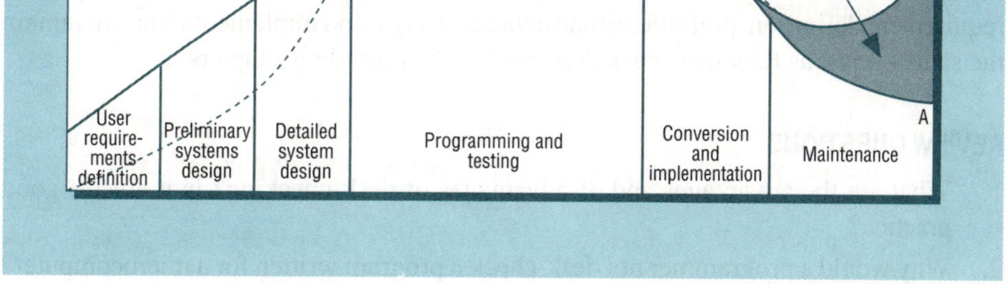

why data analysis and data modelling are so important, particularly in large organizations.

The correction of errors and implementation of enhancements occurs over the lifespan of a system. Indeed, a large number of installations will devote 70 – 80% of their total analyst and programmer work-force to these functions. Although this work is essential, it can stifle an IS department's ability to respond to requests by users for new and profitable systems. Large benefits will accrue by paying careful attention to analysis, by designing and implementing systems that are highly responsive to user requests, and by using established project management techniques.

18.7 A NOTE ON DOCUMENTATION

During the entire systems development process, from planning right through to the post-implementation review, various documents and diagrams will have been produced — by the user, the developers, or by both working together. These have to be rigorously assembled and filed because they make up the *system documentation*. The initial requirements specifications, the JAD session output, the detailed design specifications, are all part of the system documentation. They describe what the system does and how it does it. If correctly filed and maintained, there is no need to have a specific documentation phase in the systems development cycle — it can be an automatic output from each stage.

18.8 CONCLUSION

The systems development cycle is an arduous process that is constantly undergoing refinement as information systems personnel, academics and consultants strive for better methods of producing more rigorous systems. New techniques are developed which, after much testing, become accepted by the IS community and become incorporated in the systems development cycle. An example of this is CASE — Computer Assisted Software Engineering.

CASE is a term used to describe the automation of the systems development process. Many tools are available to assist development staff, and more are becoming available. Diagramming programs are available to produce data-flow diagrams and entity-relationship models. Data dictionary software is available, as is rapid prototyping software. Analysis and design workbenches — software specifically intended to assist analysts and designers — are on the market. More and more of this software will, no doubt, become available to make the process more efficient. But the principles of requirement definition, preliminary and detailed design, and implementation will remain the same — just as they have been described in the preceding chapters.

REVIEW QUESTIONS

1. What are the advantages and disadvantages of desk-checking? Is it always good practice?
2. Why would a programmer not desk-check a program written for a microcomputer?

3. What is the difference between a syntax error and a logic error? Which is usually cheaper to correct?
4. What is the difference between system testing and user testing?
5. What are the objectives of user testing?
6. A department store with twelve branches throughout the country is currently system testing a new merchandising system. What method should it use for converting from the existing manual to the computer system? Justify your answer.
7. Who should be present at a post-implementation review?
8. What would you, as a potential chairman of a post-implementation review, place on the agenda?
9. It has been said that up to 80 % of systems staff are currently devoted to the maintenance of information systems. Why is that figure so high? Is it likely to change in the future, and if so in what direction?

CHAPTER 19 Project management

19.1 INTRODUCTION

All through the description of the systems development cycle we have stressed the importance of project management. We conclude this module with a more detailed description of this function. We first discuss IS projects and the problems with managing them; then we split project management into two activities: *project planning*, and *project control*. The chapter concludes with a section on status reporting.

19.2 THE DEFINITION OF AN IS PROJECT

A project is a unique job or group of interrelated activities with a specified objective. It should be completed according to defined constraints such as budgets, duration, and both user and technical specifications.

Examples of projects in the information systems environment could include any of the following:

- the implementation of computer hardware;
- the acquisition of a package;
- the development of a tailor-made system using in-house resources;
- the enhancement of a system.

19.3 WHAT IS IS PROJECT MANAGEMENT?

Project management involves the planning and controlling of projects such as those suggested above. *Project planning* involves, first of all, defining the work to be done (or breaking the overall task into activities). Secondly, planning involves setting time limits for each of those activities. Thirdly, it involves identifying the resources required to complete the work.

Project control involves monitoring the progress of the project against the plan. Actual schedules and costs are compared to the plan on a regular basis and, if there is a discrepancy, corrective action is taken.

The main objective of project management is to achieve optimal use of resources during the project life-cycle. Those resources may include manpower, machinery, money, materials, and information.

19.4 PROJECT PLANNING

Effective project planning does not happen by chance; there are two elements that are necessary. These are:

- *Project organization.* This is essentially the starting point of the project. An appropriate manager must be assigned, the team must be selected, and the project charter must be specified (this includes the scope of the project and the budgets).
- *Work breakdown.* This involves splitting the system into units that are small enough to be controlled in an effective manner.

19.4.1 The project organization

The project manager is the key person in project implementation as he or she has to direct and motivate the project team so that the goals of the project (set by top management) are fulfilled. He or she must have certain characteristics in order to create the correct project environment for successful system installation. The ideal characteristics include the following:

- *Honesty and integrity*. These qualities create an atmosphere of trust and respect within the project team. He or she should be wary of making promises (to increase motivation) that cannot be fulfilled.
- *Technical competence*. The project manager should be technically aware of the global implications of the project. Ideally, the project manager should not be the technical specialist on the project as this will lead to conflict with the project team members, who may feel that the manager is trying to do their job. Sufficient technical knowledge is, however, necessary in order to appreciate the project team's problems.
- *Business management competence*. The project manager must have thorough knowledge and experience of the principles of management. Good communication skills are necessary to pass on project information and decisions to top management and the project team.
- *Awareness*. The project manager must constantly be aware of, and alert to, possible problems and conflict areas during implementation.
- *Goal orientation*. The project manager should constantly direct the project team towards the goals of the project.
- *He or she must be a 'people person'*. This means relating to the personal problems of the project team. Furthermore, an 'open-door' policy (so that the team may feel free to approach the project manager with any problem) is also recommended. If this policy is not maintained the project manager may only be in a position to identify the problem when remedial action is too late.
- *Decision-making ability*. The project manager must be able to make quick decisions on pertinent information so that the project implementation is not delayed. There should be a bias for *action* and not *reaction*.
- *Business awareness*. A thorough knowledge of the company's system is also desirable so that the project manager can evaluate the system without being misled by company politics.

How does top management go about electing the project manager? Each candidate should be evaluated against the aforementioned characteristics. It is important that he or she is chosen by top management so that the project team and the users recognize top management's commitment and respect for the project manager.

The major responsibilities of the project manager cover the following areas:

- successfully implementing the system with the available resources whilst complying with the allocated budget and time constraints, and producing the required level of performance;
- assisting in the fulfilment or achievement of the prescribed benefits;

- making decisions on project problem areas;
- promoting communication between top management, the user, and the project team in order to attain successful installation;
- negotiating with top management for all resources required for the project;
- resolving conflict between the users and the project team before it becomes destructive;
- reporting on progress to top management in clear and unambiguous terms;
- planning and controlling the project in order to optimize the use of resources in the company's interest and in line with project objectives;
- personnel management, which covers the motivation of the project team and providing training and education so that they can do their job efficiently.

Figure 19.1 summarizes the project manager's responsibilities.

FIGURE 19.1. Project manager responsibilities.

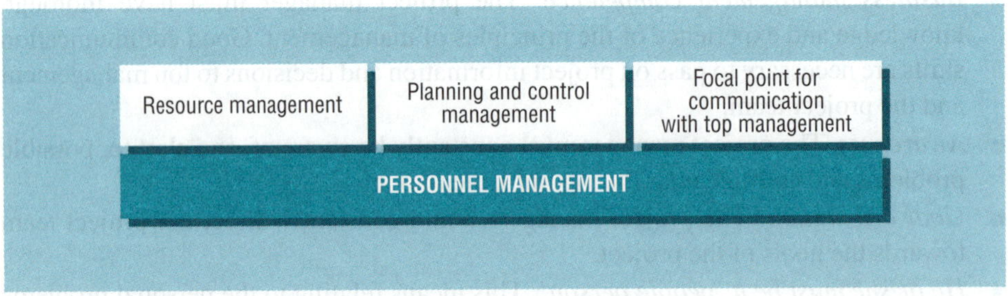

The project manager can only fulfil the objectives of the project if there is a committed and dedicated project team. The members of the team are responsible for obtaining results that fulfil the objectives and goals set by the project manager and top management. They must also provide meaningful information that enables the project manager to report progress on system implementation and success.

The *steering committee* is the key controlling body that monitors project progress. This committee forms an effective communication platform so that top management, user management, and information systems management can work together towards successful system implementation.

The *project charter* should be comprehensively and unambiguously stated by the steering committee. It should cover the following key aspects:

- the goals and objectives of the project;
- the expected results (eg. reports, programs) with a clearly specified schedule;
- the lines of communication (protocol);
- the decision-making bodies and frequency of report-back to these bodies by the project manager;
- the standards and methodologies that should be used when implementing the system;
- the project budget.

19.4.2 Work breakdown

The first function of the project manager is to break the project into activities that can be individually scheduled and developed. This can best be done by making sections that can be proved to be working individually, yet which, when fitted together, will also work as a whole. This implies that the interfaces between the various sections must be clearly defined. Effective project management depends upon an effective work breakdown which also maintains product integrity (ie. fulfils the user's requirements). A poor breakdown can result in problems such as cost overruns, schedule slippages, and poor documentation (to mention but a few).

Work breakdown is made up of the following elements:

- The *identification element*. This answers the questions 'what does the system consist of?' and 'if the system is broken down, will the subsystems still maintain the integrity of the total system?'
- The *control element*. This answers the question 'how do I control changes to the subsystems?'
- The *auditing element*. This answers the question 'does the system I am building satisfy the stated needs?'

From what has been said, it should be obvious that one of the most important aspects of project management is *change control*. This function must ensure that all changes to the system are recorded and distributed to the relevant team members. In this manner budget overruns, schedule slippages and specification deviations can be traced throughout the implementation process.

Let us take an example of a project manager developing a library system. He would first estimate the time needed to determine user requirements. This would then be broken down into, say, three units: interviewing the acquisitions section, interviewing the loans section, and visiting other libraries. This is the work breakdown activity. Dates would then be set against each activity and dependencies determined (those activities that *must* precede others). Finally, a complete plan would be drawn up detailing all the individual activities, each with its own budget.

To summarize, the project manager starts with the project charter given to him by the steering committee. From his knowledge of systems development the total development effort is then broken down into activities which can later be tracked. Budgets are then set against each of these activities.

19.5 PROJECT CONTROL

The poor use and lack of awareness of project control techniques has led to the late implementation and overspending of many projects. Project control starts with the allocation of work to individuals who assume responsibility and accountability. The project manager must then track progress on each of the work units and report on it both upwards to his managers, and downwards to the team members. There are a number of methods of tracking and reporting, two of which are discussed below *Gantt charts* and *network analysis*.

19.5.1 Gantt charts (bar charts)

This is a conventional method for controlling a project (see Figure 19.2). The activities that make up the complete project are identified and their associated durations are depicted by lines (bars).

FIGURE 19.2. Typical systems development chart.

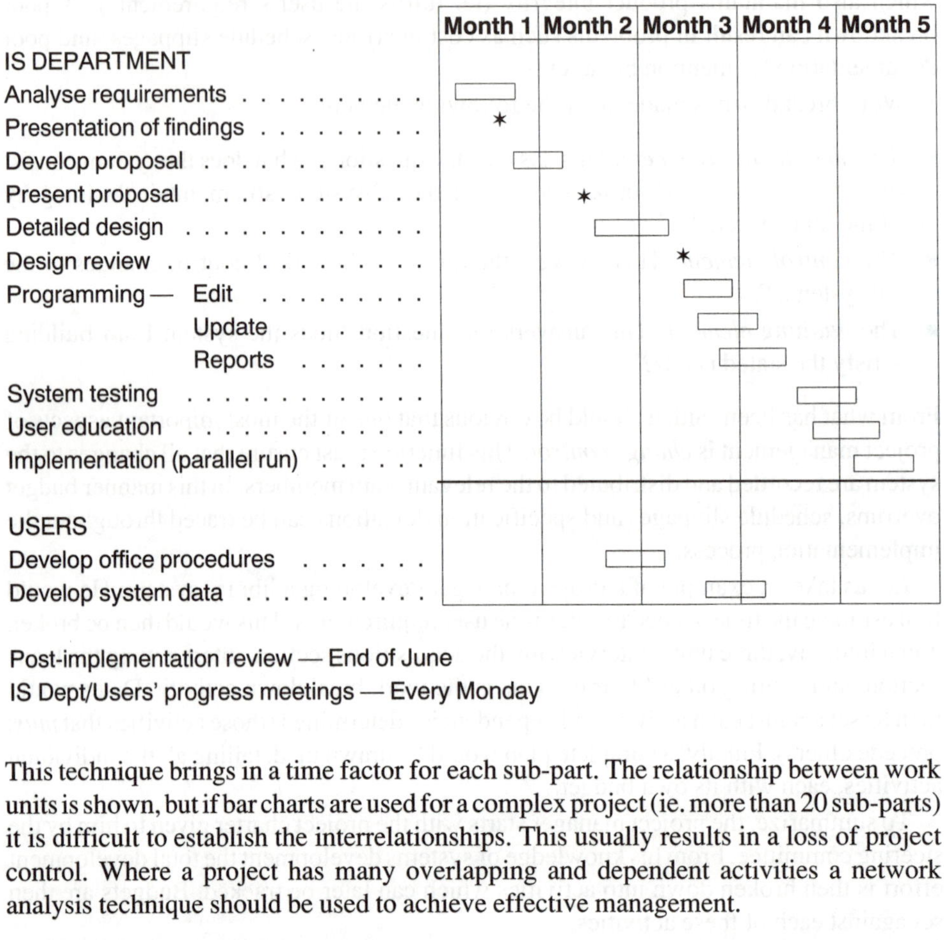

This technique brings in a time factor for each sub-part. The relationship between work units is shown, but if bar charts are used for a complex project (ie. more than 20 sub-parts) it is difficult to establish the interrelationships. This usually results in a loss of project control. Where a project has many overlapping and dependent activities a network analysis technique should be used to achieve effective management.

19.5.2 Network analysis

Network analysis, unlike Gantt charts, models the interdependencies of the activities that make up the project. The activities are represented as a network of nodes and arrows (see Figure 19.3). Network analysis provides a substantial amount of useful information which enables the attainment of effective project management. This information might include:

- the interrelationship of project elements;
- the start and end dates and duration of each element;

FIGURE 19.3. Critical path network.

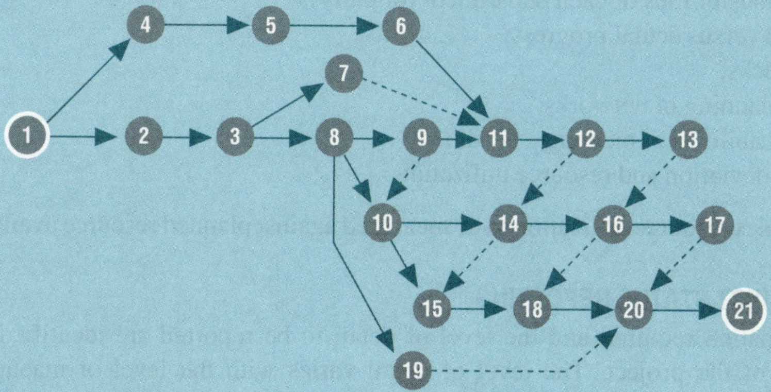

Activities	Nodes		Time		
	Start	End	A*	M*	B*
Systems analysis	1	2	2	3	4
Order equipment	1	4	8	10	15
System design	2	3	3	4	4
Order debtors stationery	3	7	5	6	10
Program debtors stationery	3	8	5	6	10
Program debtors	4	5	1	1	1
Commission equipment install equipment	5	6	1	1	1
Training on hardware	6	11	1	1	1
Dummy (wait for stationery)	7	11	0	0	0
Test	8	9	1.5	2	4
Programs stock	8	10	2	3	5
Order Invoice stationery	8	19	5	6	10
Dummy (testing)	9	10	0	0	0
Document operations	9	11	1	1	1
Test stock	10	14	1	2	3
Program invoicing	10	15	2	2	3
Train debtors	11	12	1	1	1
Install debtors	12	13	1	1	2
Dummy (training)	12	14	0	0	0
Dummy (one-month installation)	13	16	4	0,4	4
Dummy (testing)	14	15	0	0	0
Train stock	14	16	0.1	0.1	0.1
Text invoicing	15	18	0.5	1	1.5
Install stock	16	17	1	1	1
Dummy (training)	16	18	0	0	0
Dummy (one-month installation)	17	20	4	4	4
Train invoicing	18	19	0.5	0.5	1
Dummy (wait for stationery)	19	20	0	0	0
Install invoicing	20	21	0.5	0.5	1

***A** = Best time
B = Worst time
M = Most likely time

- the feasibility (cost and resource utilization) of the project implementation;
- alternative implementation strategies;
- the responsibilities of each department (or party);
- planned versus actual progress;
- bottlenecks;
- the re-planning of networks;
- the probabilities of meeting a deadline;
- project deviation and resource utilization.

It also enables resource utilization to be measured against planned resource availability.

19.6 PROJECT STATUS REPORTING

The information required and the level of detail to be reported are identified at the beginning of the project. The level of detail varies with the level of management reporting (ie. the project team will report to the project manager at activity level, whereas the project manager will consolidate the activities to form tasks and will report at task level to top management). Let us, for example, look at the contents of the project manager's report to top management. The project status report usually highlights the following:

- the progress of the system (planned versus actual);
- the project network (at task level);
- budgeted versus actual expenditure for the system to date;
- projected expenditure to completion;
- forecasted completion cost versus budgeted completion cost.

Further information needs to be presented on the report to ascertain progress in identified problem areas (ie. to identify whether corrective action has been, or has to be, taken).

The following information is an example of what could be reported for each *task*:

- The previous month's objectives and the progress identified against them. The following month's objectives are also identified.
- The previous month's problem areas and the corrective action taken. The present month's problems, with indications for recommended solutions.

With the aforementioned information on a project status report, top management will be able to clearly see the progress of the project. A professional, trusting relationship is built up. Top management's commitment to, and involvement in, the project is greatly improved. Consequently, the chances of success are greatly enhanced.

19.7 WHY DO IS PROJECTS FAIL?

Project management is a multi-disciplinary skill requiring experience in the fields of finance, personnel, and operations management. It is not often that one finds an IS person with a blend of all three skills. In addition, IS projects typically involve people from many different areas in an organization (this is particularly true if the project is an all-embracing one such as the implementation of a manufacturing system). These people have different skills and different backgrounds, making communication extremely difficult.

There are numerous reasons why projects do not meet either financial targets or time limits. The following list highlights the main ones:

- The project plans may be over-optimistic.
- Plans may be based on inadequate information, resulting in cost and/or schedule overruns.
- The project management and planning process may not be formalized.
- Project objectives may not be clearly defined and visible to all concerned.
- The project manager is sometimes not a full-time member of the team. This may also be a problem with other key members of the team such as senior system analysts.
- The users are sometimes not involved in the planning and hence are not committed to the project schedules.
- The team may become demotivated during long projects.
- There may be poor change control procedures. Unnecessary changes can be very demotivating for the project team, especially if the plans are not modified according to the new requirements.
- The project manager may not be sufficiently educated and trained.
- The most senior systems analyst sometimes becomes a project manager, even if he or she has little flair for management.
- Standard methodologies may be ignored or bypassed due to time constraints or ignorance.

The above list contains many different problems. Any one of them could cause a project to fail miserably.

In conclusion, the essence of effective project management is effective planning and controlling of the available resources. If you fail to plan, you are going to fail.

19.8 CONCLUSION

Chapters 13 to 19 have dealt fairly fully with the systems development cycle. Many techniques used in the activities of systems analysis and systems design were described, most of which would be used even in small projects.

We have deliberately not been exhaustive in our discussions of areas such as data modelling and data-flow diagramming. Whole books have been dedicated to each of these techniques, so we could not deal with them adequately in a few chapters. We believe, though, that we have given enough detail for the student to gain sufficient understanding of the building blocks needed to develop systems. It is necessary to understand not only each of those blocks but how they interact.

Many books talk of *structured techniques*. Systems development used to be a very linear, physical process. There was very little emphasis on data-flow, on data design, on user requirements, on user dialogue. To counter this, the techniques described earlier were developed — techniques such as data-flow diagramming, functional decomposition, entity-relationship modelling, data modelling, and programmer teams.

These used to be referred to as 'structured techniques'. They have now become so heavily used in the development cycle that the term 'structured' is, we believe, fast becoming obsolete and they should merely be referred to as 'development techniques'.

REVIEW QUESTIONS

1. Should maintenance of an information system be regarded as an IS project?
2. How does IS project management differ from, say, construction project management?
3. Why is change management considered such an important aspect of a project manager's responsibilities?
4. A large part of a project manager's time is spent communicating with people. Who are those people and what is typically communicated?
5. Select any project (for instance, making a table) and construct a work breakdown structure for it.
6. Now construct a Gantt chart for the same project.
7. How frequently should the status of a large (45 man months) project be reported? How would that frequency change with a small project?

MODULE 3 KEY POINT SUMMARY

- The success of a system depends on numerous factors, but probably the most important is the ability of the user to communicate his or her requirements to the analyst in precise, concrete statements.
- Although certain organizations tend to overplay the committee function, the one committee that is vital is the computer steering committee. It performs a very necessary monitoring and planning function for information systems.
- The better the design (both of the system and of programs) the easier the system will be to maintain and therefore the less the total cost of the system will be.
- An error will cost far more if detected during the implementation stage rather than during analysis. The analyst and users must check the design very thoroughly prior to handing over the specifications to the programmer.
- The input to the system, and the output from it, are the interfaces between the user and the computer. Emphasis should be placed on usability and control.
- The emphasis in file design should be on simulating the requests of the user by asking: 'what information will he need?' and 'in what sequence will he require it?'
- Testing is performed by the programmer, the systems analyst, and the user. All of these phases are important, but the analyst should endeavour to hand over as 'clean' a system as possible to the user for testing. If it is full of errors the user could well become disenchanted before it even goes live.
- The users should be able to operate the system without constantly requesting the assistance of the developers. The only way to ensure this is by involving them in all development phases.
- All IS projects should be defined with key dates and objectives assigned to each date. A project that only has one milestone — the final handover — is almost certainly doomed to failure.
- Where possible, choose a project leader with managerial skills rather than a technical expert.
- Project management should always be a formal procedure. If not, the method of reporting progress on a project will be haphazard and management will not be able to take the steps necessary to ensure timely completion.

MODULE

4 Information systems management

OBJECTIVES

This module explores the problems associated with the management of IS resources in a commercial organization. It examines the relationship between information systems and other departments and the criteria for selecting, acquiring and installing computer equipment. It also analyses the ongoing managerial problems associated with information systems.

The following chapters will:

- Describe a typical organizational structure for an in-house IS department, and discuss alternative structures.
- Explain the major functions of various staff members in the IS operation.
- Outline the advantages and disadvantages of IS charge-out systems and explain how such a system may operate.
- Describe the criteria for evaluating vendors of computer equipment.
- List the steps to be followed in acquiring and implementing new IS technology.
- Describe the external sources of expertise available to IS or user managers.
- Explain how packages can be used and the advantages they offer over tailor-made solutions.
- Discuss the trend towards end user development of new applications and the need to provide adequate support and control.

CHAPTER 20 Managing the IS function

20.1 INTRODUCTION

Information systems assist divisions such as finance, accounting, marketing, and production to process data and produce much-needed information. In the majority of cases the computer is not a revenue-producing item — its contribution is measured in terms of improvements to clerical or managerial efficiency. Since many departments require IS resources, it is the function of the IS manager to resolve potential conflicts in the demands placed on IS resources and to provide a level of service that will satisfy the vastly different requirements.

IS is a highly technical area in a very dynamic field. Every day there are new announcements concerning processors, communications technology, peripherals, software, and so on. Users often feel threatened by all this change and can be afraid of a close involvement with the IS department. The IS manager therefore has a responsibility to attempt to bridge this gap through the introduction of systems that are visible and effective and by providing education at all levels in the organization.

In the past IS had a highly technical emphasis rather than a managerial emphasis. IS managers have therefore often been appointed on the basis of technical rather than managerial skills. In addition this has led to staff dissatisfaction and high turnover in a large number of IS departments. IS is a young industry and there is a lack of standards for measuring the performance of analysts and programmers — IS managers have therefore had to rely on intuitive or subjective methods of appointing and promoting staff, often with disastrous results.

All the above indicate that the information system manager's (ISM) job is not an easy one. It requires personnel management skills as well as a broad knowledge of technical, legal, and marketing principles.

The functions of the IS manager can be divided into *establishment* functions and *continuous* functions. The establishment functions can be subdivided as follows:

- establishing the position and structure of the IS department;
- setting standards for the department;
- creating an administrative support structure; and
- selecting equipment.

The most important continuous functions are:

- recruiting and motivating staff;
- securing and controlling the data and resources; and
- planning and scheduling resources.

Many of these topics will be covered in this chapter. The rest will be dealt with in the remainder of this module.

20.2 POSITION OF IS WITHIN THE ORGANIZATION

In the early 1950s and '60s the majority of systems were financially oriented (towards debtors, creditors or general ledger, for instance). As a result, responsibility for the information systems function was given to a senior financial officer in the organization

— the financial director or the company secretary, for instance. In many smaller organizations IS reported to the accountant. Figure 20.1 illustrates the traditional structure:

FIGURE 20.1. IS in the organization — traditional structure.

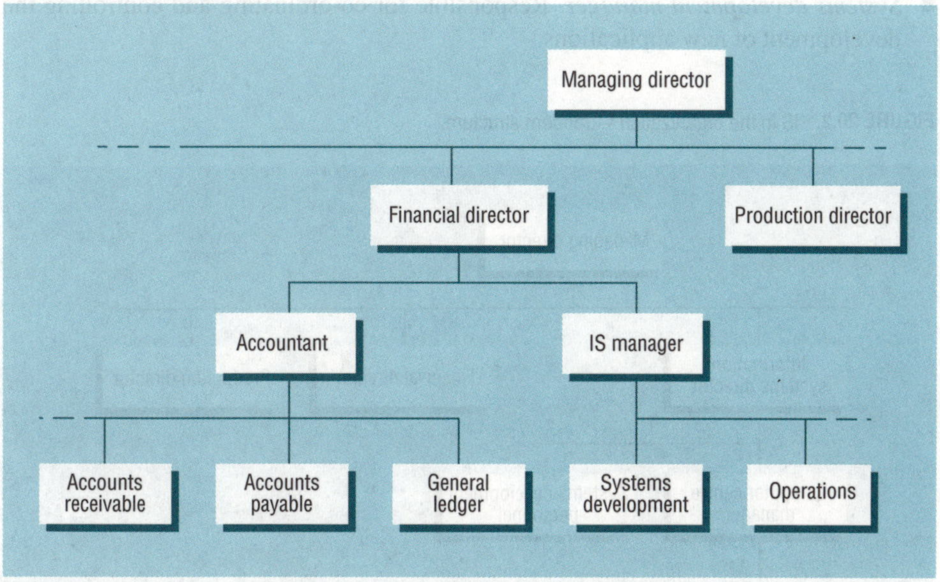

Today, information is seen as a corporate resource and more and more systems are being installed in the non-accounting divisions. A large number of production control and logistical systems, for instance, are being implemented and the financial director is no longer seen as the obvious person to be responsible for computing. The modern trend, therefore, is for information systems to report to an IS executive who is a member of the board of directors, and whose sole function is the control of information systems (see Figure 20.2). This removes the potential for conflict which frequently arose under the traditional approach. Information systems have therefore become more of a corporate function.

20.3 STRUCTURE OF THE IS DEPARTMENT

One of the functions of the IS manager is to set up an organization structure that:

- caters for the advancement aspirations of his personnel;
- maximizes staff productivity;
- instills control by allowing for effective supervision.

The structure of the IS department also depends on its size. Task specialization and middle management positions are most common in large mainframe installations. The organization chart in Figure 20.3 depicts a typical large IS department.

The IS management staff are as follows:

- *IS manager*. Oversees the IS function including data processing, data communications, and office automation. Main responsibilities are long-term planning and management control of IS.
- *Systems development manager*. Responsible for co-ordinating and controlling the development of new applications.

FIGURE 20.2. IS in the organization — modern structure.

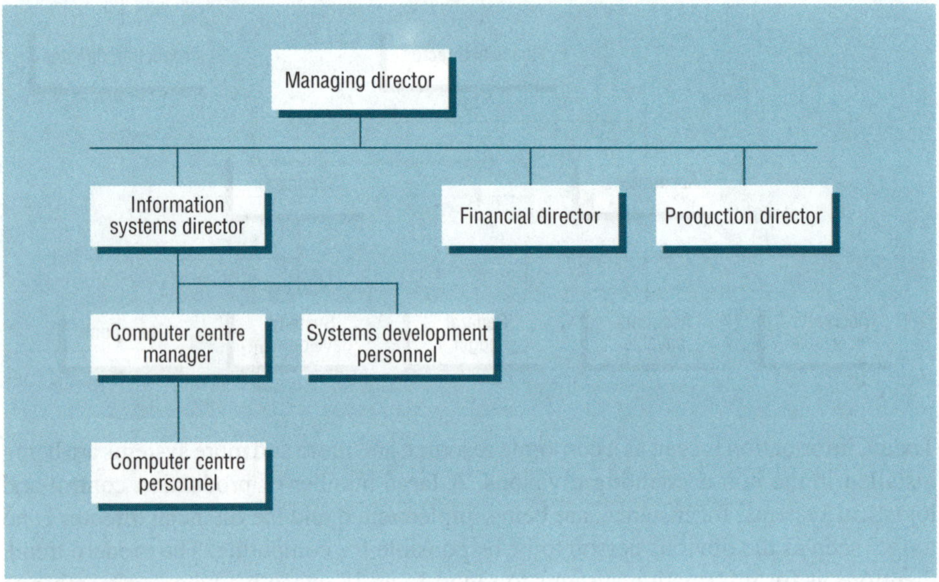

FIGURE 20.3. Organization chart for a large IS department.

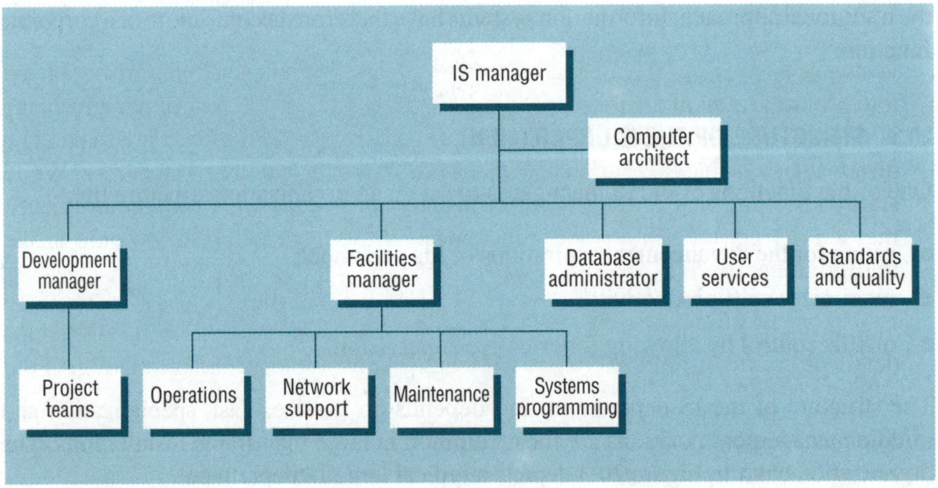

Figure 20.4 illustrates the typical *traditional structure* with programming and analysis as separate pools of skills, each reporting to different managers. The advantage of this approach is that it leads to the optimum usage of development resources — programmers and analysts can be switched from system to system as the need arises. A disadvantage is that it is difficult to establish a long-term, meaningful career path for personnel, especially programmers. A further disadvantage is that the personnel involved in projects do not identify strongly with the projects on which they are working.

FIGURE 20.4. Development staff — traditional structure.

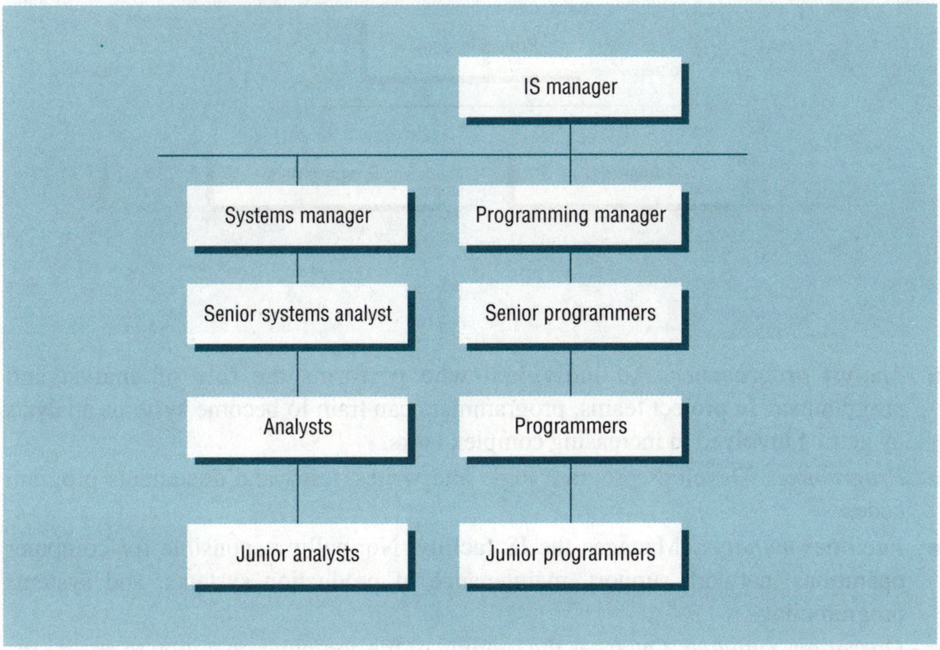

Using the *project-oriented structure*, however, development personnel are organized into project groups along the lines of the structure in Figure 20.5. A major advantage is that the personnel identify with the projects in which they are involved. The disadvantage is that this approach can lead to an inefficient use of resources. While staff do become very proficient in the business areas associated with their projects, they do not get the same overall awareness of the business as they would in the traditional approach.

- *Systems analyst.* Gathers and analyses data to determine user requirements. Develops detailed systems specifications and oversees the development and installation of the system.
- *Systems designer.* Normally a role performed by the systems analyst. Takes the broad conceptual solution and develops the detailed specification.

FIGURE 20.5. Development staff — project-oriented approach.

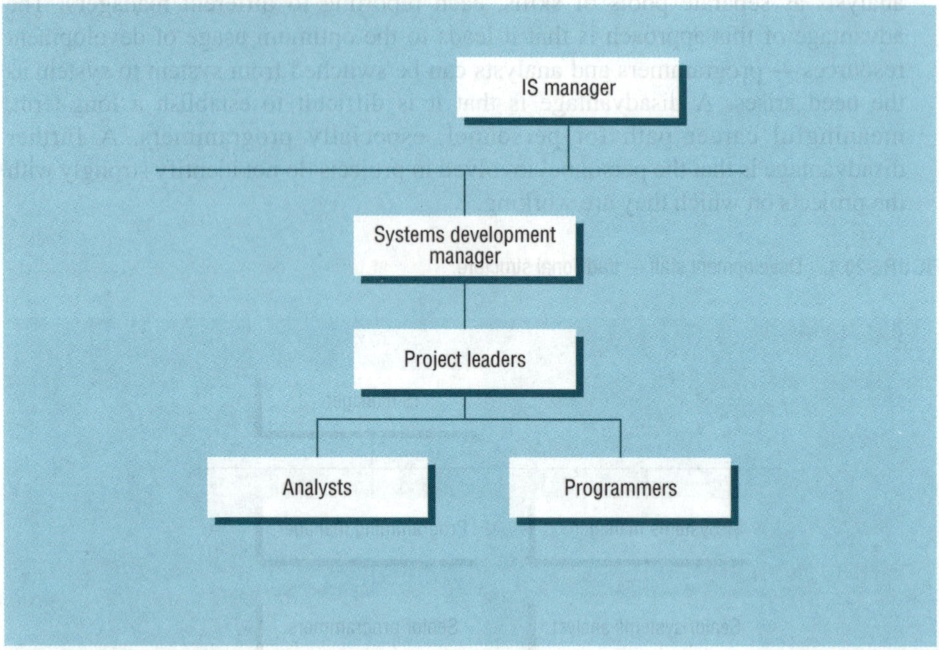

- *Analyst programmer.* An individual who performs the role of analyst and programmer. In project teams, programmers can train to become systems analysts by getting involved in increasing complex tasks.
- *Programmer.* Develops program logic and writes, tests, and documents program codes.
- *Facilities manager.* Manages the IS facility. Normally responsible for computer operations, network support, maintenance of production systems, and systems programming.
- *Operations manager.* Oversees the running of the computer operation to ensure the required level of service is provided to the users.
- *Data control.* A clerical function controlling the security and integrity of user data processed by the various applications.
- *Data capturers.* Key entry personnel responsible for capturing user data onto machine-readable media. With the growth of on-line systems this function has almost entirely disappeared.
- *Scheduling.* A clerical function which involves scheduling the mix of production jobs to achieve optimal machine utilization and service levels for users.
- *Operators.* Monitor and control computer operations from the central computer console. Their task includes initiating scheduled jobs, mounting disks and tapes where required, and loading special stationery on the printer.
- *Maintenance.* Programmers and program analysts who are responsible for the modification and enhancement of existing programs.

- *Systems programmers.* Technical programmers responsible for installing and maintaining the systems software (operating system, teleprocessing monitor, and DBMS).
- *Network support.* Individuals responsible for the design, installation and maintenance of computer networks. Their task includes the specification and selection of communication hardware, software, and control equipment.
- *Database administration.* Designs and maintains the corporate databases. Enforces database standards, controls, and integrity.
- *Information centre manager.* Oversees the information centre and plans the supply of computer services to end-users. Provides assistance and training to end-users who are developing their own applications.
- *Standards and quality assurance.* As the name suggests, this group is responsible for defining, setting, and maintaining standards and procedures.

20.4 FURTHER FUNCTIONS OF THE IS MANAGER

- *Setting standards for the installation.* It is the responsibility of the IS manager to decide on the standards required in the installation and then to ensure that they are established and enforced.
- *Setting up an administrative support structure.* The IS manager must have the appropriate secretarial and clerical resources to handle normal departmental administration. This would typically consist of secretaries, typists, librarians, clerks, etc.
- *Staff motivation.* The IS manager's job is to recruit and develop the managers immediately beneath him (who will then do the same for their own staff members). This level comprises such people as the systems development manager, the computer centre manager, and the software support manager. One of the biggest problems facing the IS manager is the retention of staff. There is a severe shortage of skilled IS personnel, and industry averages indicate that there is a very high turnover of information systems staff. It is therefore up to the IS manager to provide a stimulating and rewarding environment so as to retain existing employees and to provide an attractive environment for new staff.
- *Security of the IS department.* One of the most important functions of IS managers is to ensure that adequate security and control procedures exist to protect the resources that they administer. It is important to note that the IS manager's job as regards control and security is to institute and administer the policies that are laid down by senior corporate management.
- *Information systems planning and strategy.* In small and medium sized installations, all planning activities are normally handled by the ISM. In large businesses a separate function would be responsible for drawing up the long- medium- and short-term plans. These would then be very thoroughly reviewed by the ISM.

20.5 EVOLVING IS MANAGEMENT ACTIVITIES

A number of management and control procedures have been developed to assist in the handling of problem areas. These are known as *change control*, *problem management* and *service management*.

20.5.1 Change control

In every organization there is a constant stream of requests for changes to operational systems. There is a danger that time will be wasted on irrelevant changes which provide the organization with little real benefit. Changes must also be controlled to ensure that untested enhancements are not released into the production environment. Change control involves the formalization of the change request, an evaluation of its impact, procedures to ensure that testing is divorced from production, formal updating of documentation, and the controlled release of the final version into the operational environment.

20.5.2 Problem management

In the past, IS departments tended to manage by crisis. Problem management is a technique whereby one is able to identify problems before they occur in order to take the necessary action. It is based on measurement and monitoring procedures that enable management to understand its environment and to quickly identify deviations from the norm. In the past, many organizations found that they had insufficient capacity to drive their critical applications and were forced to make unsatisfactory interim arrangements during the lead time necessary to upgrade their machinery. Careful monitoring of machine utilization will warn management of impending capacity problems so that appropriate measures can be taken.

20.5.3 Service management

Historically, operations management was responsible for providing computing resources on the basis that the computer was available for use if required. However, now with large numbers of users vying for scarce machine resources, and the need to provide fast and reliable service to on-line users, the concept of service management has evolved. Here IS management undertakes to provide a level of service to the user. This will include an undertaking as to the availability of computer resources, response and turnaround times, and a minimal level of downtime.

REVIEW QUESTIONS

1. How does the job of the IS manager differ from other service-oriented managers in the organization (such as the personnel manager)?
2. How does an IS manager stay up-to-date in the technology field?
3. If, today, an IS division is processing only accounting systems, should IS continue to report to the senior accounting person?
4. Are there any structures other than the traditional and the project-oriented ones that could be used for the IS division?

5. Describe in detail how an IS manager would go about establishing standards for a medium-sized installation.
6. What strategies could an IS manager employ to avoid losing staff? Be specific in your answer.
7. How would the job of an IS manager differ between large and small IS departments?

SELECTED REFERENCES AND RECOMMENDED READING

McNurlin, B.C., and Sprague, R.H. 1989. *Information Systems Management in Practice*. Second edition. Englewood Cliffs: Prentice-Hall.

CHAPTER 21 Acquisition of computer technology

21.1 INTRODUCTION

There are a number of major problems which every business encounters when acquiring new computer technology. The first is to specify computer requirements accurately enough for potential suppliers to respond. The second is to find suppliers who may be able to offer solutions. These problems are often exacerbated by the fact that the user is not computer-literate while the supplier knows very little about the business. The two must therefore find some common ground.

In this chapter the term *computer technology* refers to any combination of computer hardware, applications and systems software, and any peripheral or accessory equipment used in their installation.

21.2 COMPUTER SELECTION

Computer selection is not an easy process and there are a large number of horror stories concerning the wrong machines being purchased and supplier promises not being met. It is important to recognize that the responsibility for machine selection lies with the organization (which often has little IS expertise). A formal, structured approach to selection, incorporating the following steps, will go a long way to ensuring that the best machine is chosen:

- STEP 1: Draw up the requests for proposal (RFP).
- STEP 2: Send the RFP to those suppliers who will be able to respond.
- STEP 3: Evaluate the responses and select a short-list.
- STEP 4: Evaluate short-listed suppliers.
- STEP 5: Select the most favoured supplier.

21.2.1 Step 1: Draw up the requests for proposal (RFP)

The request for proposal (RFP) describes the nature of the business and the nature of the systems that will be running on the computer equipment. It also indicates to the supplier how systems problems are to be addressed. The RFP is based on an earlier study of the user's requirements. The more detailed this document is, the better the responses will be from the suppliers. There are two possible approaches to take: one can either document the systems and leave it up to the supplier to select the equipment which is correct for the job, or one can specify in detail to the supplier what he should be tendering (eg. one may merely say 'give us the equipment necessary to process 10 000 debtors per month' or, alternatively, 'provide us with a two megabyte computer with 500 megabytes of disk storage and six printers'). A typical content list of the request for proposal would be as in Figure 21.1.

21.2.2 Step 2: Contact suppliers

At this stage a list is drawn up of all those suppliers who could offer suitable equipment for the job. The names of these suppliers can be obtained from business contacts, from general references, or from a consultant. Copies of the RFP are then sent to each supplier, requesting them to respond by a specific date.

FIGURE 21.1. Request for proposal — table of contents.

REQUEST FOR PROPOSAL — INVITATION TO TENDER

TABLE OF CONTENTS

SECTION 1	THE INVITATION
SECTION 2	CONDITIONS OF TENDER
	— Return Date
	— Acceptance and Rejection
SECTION 3	INTRODUCTION
SECTION 4	GENERAL SYSTEMS APPROACH
SECTION 5	THE SYSTEM(S) TO BE COMPUTERISED
SECTION 6	APPLICATION SOFTWARE
	— Packaged
	— Tailor-made
SECTION 7	HARDWARE REQUIRED
SECTION 8	THE TENDER
	— Hardware Specification
	— Delivery Dates
	—Testing
	— Costs
	— Back-up
	— References
APPENDIX i	ANALYSIS OF VOLUMES
APPENDIX II	MASTER FILES
APPENDIX III	MANUALLY CAPTURED INPUT
APPENDIX IV	PRINT VOLUMES

21.2.3 Step 3: Select a short list

The responses to the tender are evaluated. Responses that are obviously unsatisfactory are weeded out, and the three or four that are considered most suitable are selected. Examples of criteria for eliminating suppliers are:

- price not competitive;
- support inadequate;
- lack of adequate hardware;
- lack of adequate software.

21.2.4 Step 4: Evaluate short-listed suppliers

At this stage, each of the short-listed suppliers' offerings is verified by attending demonstrations and evaluating hardware and software. Existing installations may be visited to learn more of each supplier's strengths and weaknesses. The contracts of each of these short-listed suppliers may also be reviewed at this stage.

It is now possible to judge all the short-listed suppliers. To do this, an evaluation form may be drawn up and completed as in Figure 21.2. This will assist in making the final decision.

FIGURE 21.2. Sample supplier evaluation form.

Factor	Supplier "A"	Supplier "B"	Supplier "C"	Supplier "D"
PRICE				
EXPANSION CAPABILITY				
HARDWARE RELIABILITY				
THROUGHPUT CAPABILITY				
BACK-UP				
DELIVERY SCHEDULE				
SUPPLIER STABILITY				
TECHNICAL SUPPORT				
SYSTEM SUPPORT				
TRAINING				
MANUALS — READABILITY				
SYSTEM SOFTWARE				
PROGRAM DEVELOPMENT AIDS				
NUMBER OF OTHER USERS				
AVAILABLE PERIPHERALS				
TOTAL				

Rank each factor on a scale of 1 – 10, where: 1 = Standard not acceptable, 10 = Excellent

Note that this is not a definitive solution. The major purpose of the form is to force one to think about the good and bad qualities of each supplier and to note these. The supplier with the highest score may, in fact, not be chosen but it is a good decision support tool forcing one to think objectively about each supplier.

One may want to perform a more quantitative analysis of the available packages in order to negate 'gut feelings' or value judgement. Some techniques which are commonly used to evaluate hardware or software include:

- *Simple scoring* — as displayed in Figure 21.2. Although this method is better than 'gut feelings', it in no way attempts to measure the relative importance of computing attributes.
- *Weighted scoring* — with this technique we allocate a weighting to attributes, indicating their importance (important = 5 and unimportant = 1). Scores are then multiplied by the weightings to give a weighted total. This process ensures that important attributes have more impact in the final purchase decision.
- *Emphasis scoring* — certain attributes can be defined as mandatory or assigned a minimum value which must be attained. This ensures that all essential attributes are present in the product.

21.2.5 Step 5: Make a final selection

This is the most difficult step because, inevitably, there will be two or three suppliers who are offering very similar equipment at a very similar price. At this stage one resorts to more subjective evaluation and selects, for instance, on the basis of rapport with the salesman.

It should be noted that merely following the above steps will not guarantee a successful installation. It will, however, make one aware of problems and limitations which might otherwise have been missed. To this extent, the chances of selecting the correct equipment will improve significantly.

21.3 FINANCING

The financing of a computer configuration should be treated in the same way as the purchase of any other medium- to long-term asset. Despite the decreasing costs of hardware, the purchase of a micro-, mini- or mainframe computer still represents a large capital investment for most companies, and the same criteria should be applied by management as would be applied to the purchase of land and buildings or plant and equipment.

There are a number of options available for acquiring computer hardware and software. The alternatives are:

- outright purchase from a manufacturer or retailer;
- rental of the equipment;
- purchase of the computer under a suspensive sale agreement;
- acquiring the use of the computer under a lease agreement.

21.3.1 Outright purchase from manufacturer

When equipment is purchased with full payment, ownership of the equipment passes to the purchaser. As the cost of a computer is going to be a significant investment for most companies, it is important to understand and evaluate the methods of raising funds. Although there are many methods available to a company, it must be noted that it is generally accepted that one should fund medium- to long-term assets with medium- to long-term debt. This statement is made on the assumption that the acquirer of the asset performs a full analysis, taking into account the interest rates, the cost of capital, opportunity costs, and so on.

The most obvious method of paying for a lump sum purchase is to use cash reserves. This is the cheapest form of finance available but it is generally not considered financially prudent to liquidate revenue-producing assets to finance a non-revenue-producing asset such as a computer. Generally, cash reserves are used to finance working capital (ie. funds required for day-to-day transactions) and surplus funds are reinvested in revenue-producing investments. Unfortunately, not many companies are in the position where they are able to pay cash for the purchase. However, micro- and small business computers, because of their low price-tags, are usually funded in this manner.

21.3.2 Leasing

This is basically an agreement between a finance company and the computer-user. The finance company purchases a computer selected by the user and then rents it to him for a fee which represents the cost of the equipment plus interest. The period of a lease varies according to the user's requirements but is normally between two and five years.

In this type of agreement the finance company has no real interest in the equipment except that it does help secure the loan. The finance company is therefore really interested only in obtaining payment of the amount due.

Should the user wish to cancel the agreement, this can be done but it means that all outstanding amounts have to be paid. An allowance against future interest will be granted, thereby reducing the total amount due. The full cash purchase price will have to be paid as well as interest to the date of cancellation.

Ownership always remains with the finance company, even after all lease payments have been made. Owing to the taxation implications of leases, the end-of-lease procedures must be considered. At the end of the lease the leasing company will have recovered all their costs and profit and therefore will either lease the equipment again at a nominal rate, or sell the equipment. The proceeds of the sale will be returned to the user who must reflect them as income for taxation purposes. The full lease payments are allowed as a deduction from taxable income, and the cost of the equipment is not reflected as an asset in the balance sheet.

21.3.3 Suspensive sale agreements

This is effectively the same as a lease, except that ownership automatically passes to the user on payment of the last instalment. In practice, ownership is normally assumed from the beginning of the contract. Rates of interest and repayment terms are the same as for leases.

The main difference between this and a lease agreement is the tax implication which allows the equipment, purchased on suspensive sales, to be reflected as an asset in the balance sheet. The full cost price plus interest is usually depreciated over a three-to-four year period. The monthly repayments are not deductible from taxable income.

Further tax implications of leases and suspensive sales are discussed later.

21.3.4 Rental from the manufacturer

The final possibility is to rent the equipment from the manufacturer. Only the larger suppliers offer this facility. The major advantage of renting is that a company can upgrade the equipment without a financial penalty. The rental term is normally one, two, or five years, although the cost of rental is so much higher than leasing that if long-term financing is being considered then a lease or suspensive sale will generally be more favourable. Under a rental agreement, the supplier is normally responsible for the maintenance of the hardware.

The more important aspects of the methods of acquisition are summarized as follows:

Advantages of renting

- No initial capital outlay.
- Payments are even and predictable.
- No long-term commitment liability.
- Overcomes risk of obsolescence.
- Rent payment is tax deductible.
- Maintenance included — ensures close relationship between user and supplier.
- Advantage of dealing with reputable vendor.
- User can rent from several suppliers.
- Quick, cheap installation for first-time user.

Disadvantages of renting

- Most expensive form of finance.
- If prime shift agreement exists, ineffective scheduling and operating could prove costly.
- Close link with supplier limits freedom and independence.

Advantages of purchasing

- Cheap form of financing.
- Normal advantages of ownership with respect to independence and usage.
- Wear and tear is tax deductible.
- Possibility of additional tax benefits.
- Status/public prestige of owning a computer.
- Increase in assets reflected on balance sheet.
- Possible recovery of initial outlay if equipment sold.

Disadvantages of purchasing

- Highest initial outlay.
- Highest overall risk.
- Separate maintenance agreement — lack of close contact with vendor.
- Restricted applications if system cannot meet new requirements.
- Impedes cash flow by tying up capital.
- May prevent investment in more profitable projects.
- As machine ages there may be difficulty in obtaining new peripheral equipment and the people to run or upgrade the system.

Advantages of leasing

- Additional tax benefits usually passed on by lessor.
- Cheaper than rental.
- Minimizes and regulates cash flow.
- Allows user a free choice of equipment at relatively low risk.
- May be able to sublease in the event of early cancellation.

- Cancellation is often free from penalty.
- More flexible than purchase.
- Maintenance usually included.
- No initial capital outlay.
- Lease may be extended at reduced lease premiums.
- Lease payment is tax deductible.

Disadvantages of leasing

- Financial penalties if lease terminated early in some cases.
- Lessee has to rely on maintenance by third party (vendor).
- Poor flexibility for upgrading — only purchase and HP are worse.
- More expensive than purchase.
- Ownership remains with lessor — not reflected on balance sheet.

21.2.5 Factors influencing the decision

Taxation

Before 1985, when computers were used wholly or mainly in a process of manufacture, the special taxation investment and initial allowances of 30 % and 25 % respectively were allowed to be deducted from taxable income. However, now the only deductions allowed are the full rental or lease repayments, or, when ownership is with the user, a depreciation write-off over three to four years of the full cost of the equipment.

Other financial considerations

When buying capital equipment, its effect on cash flow must always be considered, as well as its effect on the balance sheet. Borrowings can drastically change a balance sheet (and its associated ratios), resulting in a reduction in the company's borrowing power.

The cost of money must also be determined and evaluated in order to determine the cheapest form of finance for the company.

21.4 CONTRACT NEGOTIATION

Negotiating a contract is usually the final stage in the equipment acquisition process and is the final bargaining point between supplier and purchaser. It is indeed unfortunate that this is the case since purchasers would be in a far stronger position if they were to negotiate the contract terms whilst evaluating the short-listed suppliers. The selection process would be lengthened but since the purchaser would be in a far stronger position to negotiate terms the additional time would be more than offset by the advantages.

A contract should not be viewed as the final arbiter in the case of dispute between purchaser and supplier — it is an opportunity for both parties to specify what each expects the other to do, and to specify what it is that is being purchased and sold. If the stage is reached where there is a dispute and a contract is needed to reconcile differences then things will already have gone too far, and only a court will settle the matter.

21.5 COMPUTER CONTRACT CLAUSES

What clauses would one then expect to find in a computer contract? The following list, while not comprehensive, covers the more common and important clauses.

21.5.1 Specification of hardware and software

This will specify in detail all the hardware that is being sold by the supplier, and should include any equipment that the supplier may have indicated he would provide free. If software is being purchased from the same source, then it is important that the original software specification should be appended to the contract. The hardware supplier should specify, in the contract, that the hardware will satisfy the processing requirements of those specifications. In this way the purchaser is being covered in the eventuality of the supplier having underestimated his equipment, or — even worse — where the supplier knowingly under-specified in order to win the contract.

21.5.2 Price of equipment

The contract should specify the price of all hardware and software that is to be purchased and the dates on which the hardware and software will be installed. Where progress payments or retentions are being exercised, these should be specified together with the dates when the payments are to be made. This is quite normal, particularly where a contract is covering payment for tailor-made software.

21.5.3 Delivery

The estimated delivery dates of the equipment are included in the contract. Suppliers will frequently not allow themselves to be bound to a date but, where possible, outside limits should be specified.

The contract should also state whose responsibility it is to deliver the equipment to the customer's site, and who is to pay for delivery from the supplier to the customer's premises.

21.5.4 Acceptance of the equipment

This is probably one of the most difficult clauses to specify in a contract, but an effort should be made to specify how the customer is going to satisfy himself that the equipment is adequate to perform the job, and therefore to accept that the equipment and the software have been delivered in good condition. A good target to aim for, but one which is seldom allowed by the supplier, is to specify that the system should run parallel successfully for one month before payment is made. Suppliers are aware that implementation can take a long time and they are therefore reluctant to accept the condition. An alternative is to specify that a retention of 20 % or 25 % is held, pending live running.

21.5.5 Changes to the specification

This applies particularly to a software contract where changes could (and most probably would) be made to the specification during the course of development. The contract should specify the cost of the changes and whether they will affect the contract or not. Frequently changes can be made to a system which do not affect the time taken to develop the system. However, other changes can drastically affect the time and these should obviously be paid for by the customer.

21.5.6 Warranties/guarantees

If the supplier has verbally, or in writing, stated that his equipment can perform certain functions and the selection of a supplier is dependent on its capability of performing those functions, then these must in all cases be written into the contract. This applies particularly to the operating system or the system software which is supplied with the equipment.

21.5.7 Training

Where training is to be provided by the supplier the contract should state the method of training, the price, the duration, and where the training is to take place. It should also state how many people are to be trained.

21.5.8 Trade-in or buy-back clauses

This covers the situation where the purchaser of the equipment wishes to trade-in his computer for another with more facilities. The contract should then state the terms under which the supplier will trade-in the equipment and what value will be received. Normally this is computed at the rate of 25 % per annum, but it can vary with each supplier. If a computer is being rented then the buy-back clause is not applicable.

21.5.9 Confidentiality

This specifies that any information which the supplier may have obtained during the equipment selection and acquisition procedure will be confidential.

21.5.10 Limitation of liability

This will state the limitation of liability in case of a damages dispute by either party. It is exceedingly difficult to assess the financial handicap resulting from non-performance, but any sums that are specified in the contract should be reasonable.

21.5.11 Arbitration

This is the procedure that is to be adopted if either of the parties disagree on the interpretation of any of the clauses. Arbitration is usually quicker and cheaper than taking the dispute to court, but agreement as to the use of an arbitrator must be made in advance. Essentially this clause will specify who the arbitrator should be and who should pay the fees. In most contracts the chairman of either the Computer Society or the Law Society is specified.

21.6 GENERAL CONTRACT CONTENTS

In order to ensure that the contract covers all communications between the purchaser and supplier, it is good practice to append all documents to the contract. Examples of these documents are:

- request for proposal from the purchaser;
- response by the supplier;
- any advertisements and brochures used by the supplier;
- specifications and manual from the supplier;
- any memoranda covering conversations between the purchaser and supplier.

There are other clauses which can be specified in the contract but these depend on the type of services or the particular equipment being purchased. Examples are:

- maintenance agreements;
- sale of system to third party;
- duration of the agreement;
- protection against patent and copyright;
- penalties for delay and default.

The following checklist shows all important issues which may or may not be covered in the contract. It is offered as a guide to ensure that either the purchaser or the supplier does not leave any of them out in error.

21.6.1 Computer contract checklist

I. Basic contract outline

- Hardware configuration
- System performance
- Acceptance test
- Inclusion of software manuals
- Compatibility guarantees
- Software configuration
- Reliability performance
- Inclusion of hardware manuals
- Inclusion of proposal
- Field modification guarantees

II. Cost and terms of payment

- Term of agreement
- Non-payment (non-completion)
- Applicable taxes
- Charges and method of charging
  - Overtime usage
  - Transportation
  - Services
  - Maintenance/off-hour maintenance
  - Insurance
- Method of payment
- Non-payment (acceptance test)
- Pass-through of tax credit

III. Delivery

- Specific delivery dates
- Delays in delivery
- Early delivery option
- Advance of delivery

- Irreparable delays
- Site-planning responsibility
- Installation responsibility

IV. Rights of use

- Unrestricted use and function
- Postponement
- Component substitution
- Manufacturer interface
- Upgrading of hardware and software
- Unrestricted location
- Component cancellation
- Charges and attachment
- Communications interface

V. Other vendor services

- Support and assistance
  - Total number of years
  - Calibre of staff by category of support
  - Schedule
- Education and training
  - Available curriculum
  - Guarantee of continuation
  - Rights to future courses
  - Available allotment
  - Syllabi and materials
  - Rights to teach internally
- Machine time
  - Amount
  - Schedule
  - Location
- Documentation
  - Availability
  - Reproduction rights
  - Guarantee of continuation
  - Future materials

VI. Supplies required by the system

- Required supplies
- Acceptable vendors
- Acceptable specifications
- Availability guarantee

VII. Reliability and maintenance

- Parameters to be used
- Back-up availability
- Replacement
- Spare parts
- Access needs
- Continued availability
- Guarantees
- Disaster availability
- On-site maintenance
- Response time
- Space and facilities

VIII. User options

- Purchase option
- Purchase price in time
- Rental credit
- Trade-in values

- Title passage
- Availability of expansion units
- Options to upgrade
- Alternative source

IX. Price protection

- Prior to delivery
- Expansion units
- Supplies
- During term
- Maintenance
- Services

X. Damages or penalties

- Breach prior to delivery
- Liquidation damages
- User costs
- Upgrade-downgrade penalties
- Breach after delivery
- Maximum damages
- Breach of consent

XI. Miscellaneous clauses

- Compliance with all laws
- Force majeure
- Disclosure
- Liability
- Title
- Sole agreement
- Contract assignment
- Consent to breach
- Jurisdiction
- Cross-guarantees
- Conformance to standards
- Survival beyond completion
- Insurance responsibility
- Patent infringement
- Business termination
- Amendments in writing
- Favoured nations
- Authority
- Arbitration
- Vendor and user company standard policies

21.7 IMPLEMENTATION CONSIDERATIONS

This section examines some of the matters to be considered when installing equipment for the first time. It is split into three sections: the first covers general installation criteria for the siting of computer hardware; the second section pays special attention to mainframe considerations, and the third deals with mini- or microcomputers.

21.7.1 General siting considerations

If a computer is being installed for the first time, then its location within the building should be carefully considered. The factors that affect its location include:

- data flow;
- security;
- manufacturer's requirements;
- general business considerations.

Data flow

The computer department must be situated in a position where input and reports can be channelled efficiently to and from the user departments.

Security

It must be possible to prevent unauthorized persons from gaining access to the computer and its immediate environs. There must also be adequate precautions to prevent possible damage to the equipment and programs through fire, flooding, and other natural disasters. It is worth noting that tapes and floppy disks can be damaged at much lower temperatures than stored paper, so normal fire-resistant cabinets will not offer adequate protection.

Manufacturer's requirements

Consideration must be given to scheduling the delivery of the equipment and ensuring that it is physically possible to negotiate flights of stairs, narrow corridors, etc. The weight of the equipment and the amount of floor space required, as well as the operating clearances, must be established.

Other aspects are:

- the provision of a clean power supply with an emergency back-up where necessary;
- the temperature, humidity, and clean-air tolerances of the equipment;
- the installation of false flooring to protect the cables and air conditioning ducts.

General business consideration

Obviously provision must be made for the supply of office furniture and telephones, etc. The selected location should be in an area where any future expansion can be catered for.

21.7.2 A computer room layout

A typical IS mainframe complex consists of the following sections:

- the main computer room;
- the library;
- stationery store;
- special accommodation;
- data preparation section and data control section;
- office accommodation;
- room for ancillary paper-handling equipment.

The main computer room

The central processor and certain peripherals, such as disk drives, tape units, operator consoles, and printers, are housed in this room. The room will usually be subject to stringent temperature and humidity control. It will normally have a raised floor to cover the air-conditioning ducts and the multitude of power cables that are usually present.

Library

In large computer installations it may be necessary to allow for a separate section within the computer room where disk packs, tapes, etc. are stored in an organized way — this is normally referred to as a *library*.

Stationery store

To reduce the fire hazard, the continuous stationery used by the computer for printing should preferably be stored in a separate location. As boxes of paper can be heavy, the store should be within easy reach of the printers.

Special accommodation

If a really large installation is planned, it might be necessary to allow for such areas as an air-conditioning room to house the main air-conditioning equipment and back-up power generators.

Data preparation section and data control section

All input to be keyed into the system, and all output from the system, will be received, prepared for input, controlled, balanced, and dispatched from this section. It may consist of subsections operating autonomously, depending on the size of the installation.

Office accommodation

Sufficient office accommodation must be set aside for:

- the IS manager and other managers or supervisors;
- the operators;
- systems analysts and programmers.

Room for ancillary paper-handling equipment

Multi-part continuous stationery must be separated and burst to make it into a usable format. The usual equipment to do this includes:

- *Guillotines.* Sophisticated guillotines can be found that can do various operations simultaneously, such as decollating, trimming, and cutting paper.
- *Decollators.* These separate the various copies, remove the carbon, and trim-off sprocket holes.
- *Bursters.* These separate the continuous stationery into individual pages.
- *Folding machines.* These fold invoices, etc. and insert them into envelopes.
- *Shredders.* These shred old and unwanted reports.

Large numbers of installations are handling hundreds of thousands of pages of continuous computer paper every month. Combinations of the above equipment will usually be found in these installations. Even if a company is handling only small volumes, a *burster* or *guillotine* will save valuable time. It is preferable to keep this function in a room separate from the main computer area.

21.7.3 Mini- or microcomputer layouts

Although the requirements for mini- or microcomputers are not as stringent as for mainframes, it is important to consider the physical aspects that are required and to ensure that they are adequately planned for and installed prior to commissioning the new equipment.

Office space

All too frequently mini- or microcomputers are placed in a general office with no thought of control or access to the equipment. Where possible, the computers should always be situated in a separate office.

Lighting

The person who is involved in capturing data will be sitting in front of a screen for up to seven or eight hours a day. It is therefore important that an attempt is made to make the environment as conducive to work as possible by eliminating glare from the screen. A soft neon-type light is preferable to a harsh spotlight. Note that this is also applicable to operators at terminals in mainframe environments.

Work space

Adequate work space should be provided for documents and for the filing of completed work. This is frequently overlooked.

Power

One of the most common causes for complaint after the installation of a mini- or microcomputer is that power is not evenly supplied. The following points should always be checked and possibly rectified prior to the installation of a computer:

- *Direct power*. Clean power should be supplied by running a line directly from the main power supply to the computer. After doing this, a power monitor should be rented to check that the fluctuations on the line are not going to severely disrupt the computer once it is installed.
- *Battery back-up system*. A large number of microcomputers are now being sold with a battery back-up system. Even if they are not marketed by the supplier, it is possible to purchase one independently and to add it to the machine.
- *Static*. In extremely dry climates, a very large amount of static electricity can be transmitted through carpeting. If carpets are installed in the office where the computer is to be located, they should be treated with a suitable material to remove static electricity. Alternatively, the carpets should be removed and a linoleum-type flooring installed.
- *Air conditioning*. Air conditioning is required for some of the bigger machines, particularly where fixed disks are being used. However, on the smaller microcomputers, air conditioning is generally not required, although it does make the operator's life a lot more bearable as some of the machines produce a large amount of heat.

21.8 CONCLUSION

Careful planning of accommodation is required regardless of the size of the computer. Even if a microcomputer is being installed, a lack of forethought can have disastrous results. Although machines have changed considerably in the last two decades in that air conditioning is no longer mandatory for the smaller computers, there are still a large number of factors to be considered.

REVIEW QUESTIONS

1. How would the five steps outlined in the section on computer selection differ when selecting a large mainframe or a microcomputer?
2. What are the relative advantages and disadvantages of specifying a technical RFP versus an application-based RFP?
3. Could one consider approaching the Computer Society of South Africa for a list of suppliers of computer hardware?
4. Assume that you were about to attend a demonstration of computer hardware to be given by a hardware supplier. List which aspects of the hardware and the supplier you would specifically look out for.
5. Assume that you have purchased a computer for cash and after three months find out that it is not processing all your data in the time available. It is, however, performing as specified in the manuals. What recourse have you against the supplier and what options do you have available?
6. Why, if it so costly to take people to court, is contract negotiation considered so important? Is this applicable for all sizes of computer?
7. You are about to purchase a computer to control sophisticated equipment on your factory floor. It will not perform any accounting-oriented systems — it is merely for process control. How would you specify the acceptance criteria in the contract? Would your criteria change for, say, a reservation system for a travel agent?
8. You are about to purchase a computer system from a friend. As part of the acquisition procedure you gave him a full specification of your accounting systems that were drawn up by a consultant. He (the supplier) was asked to provide a system that would satisfy the specification requirements. After implementation you find out that he used your specification as the basis for selling a system to a competitor. What would you do?

CHAPTER 22 The charge-out of computer costs

22.1 THE NEED FOR A CHARGE-OUT SYSTEM

The computer is increasingly being seen as an information repository. Its purpose is to provide the organization with information at a reasonable cost. To achieve this, the IS division must use its resources (hardware, software, and people) as efficiently as possible. Without a method for measuring and recording the utilization of equipment and for allocating that usage to the various systems that are processed, management will have no means of deciding whether usage is optimal. The reasons for having a charge-out system are:

- If costs are not allocated to departments utilizing the facility, there is little incentive to measure the use of IS department resources.
- Without a charge-out system there is a tendency for users to make demands on IS resources without determining the effectiveness or profitability of their requests. The result is that the resources will always tend to be fully utilized. Management will therefore have no guide as to when additional resources are really needed.
- There is no method of quantitatively assessing the effectiveness of the computer division. Without a charge-out system, management will have to rely on subjective factors such as user satisfaction.

22.2 CHARGE-OUT MODELS

The concept of using a charge-out system to control the use of the IS resource was suggested in the early 1970s. The work of such people as Dearden and Nolan[1] did much to improve the understanding of the use of a charge-out mechanism in the IS environment. In the initial stages it was seen as a means of controlling the costs of data processing, but organizations soon used it to control priorities amongst users (*resource allocation*). The basis of the procedure is that systems are developed according to the user's ability to pay for those systems. The acquisition of IS resources is then determined by the length of the queue and the value of systems waiting in that queue.

McFarlan and McKenney[3] propose three basic methods of charging for IS resources. These are:

- the *allocated cost centre*;
- the *profit centre*;
- the *investment centre*.

They also describe a fourth method — *the unallocated cost centre*. This is the extreme case where IS is considered a free resource. No costs are charged other than on a memorandum basis.

22.2.1 The allocated cost centre

Costs are charged to the users in such a way that there is full recovery of all IS costs. There are currently many methods for determining IS costs. The most comprehensive set of guidelines is that drawn up by the Institute of Cost and Management Accountants[2], who suggest three methods of charging, viz. a *broad apportionment*, *actual cost*, and a *user tariff*.

- *Broad apportionment.* Costs are allocated to users on a broad basis such as estimated use or departmental salaries.
- *Actual cost.* This is the recommended procedure. The actual costs incurred for hardware or people are charged. Estimates, based on past experience, are used as a basis for quoting development costs to potential users.
- *User tariff.* In this method a charge is levied to the user based, not on actual cost, but on a user-specified tariff such as the number of documents submitted, or lines on a report.

22.2.2 The profit centre

This form of charge-out assumes that the IS department is an autonomous body and will make a profit on its services. In the pure form, users are free to contract outside the organization if a lower quote is obtained. In practice, however, this is implicitly disallowed. Note that the method of charging is the same as in the allocated cost centre approach except that a profit margin is added onto the costs charged by the IS division.

22.2.3 The investment centre

The IS department is effectively removed from the organization and becomes a separate operating concern, perhaps as a subsidiary of the main holding company. It is then measured on the basis of residual income, or 'a profit centre where a carrying charge for net assets employed is subtracted from the profit figure for both budget and actual performance.'

22.2.4 Rationale

The underlying rationale in each of the above cases is that the management of the IS division will allocate resources according to the normal business principles of attempting to maximize profits or minimize costs. Although it would appear that the charge-out model is only relevant to the management control of IS operations, it has frequently been proposed as a means of allocating priorities and resources, ie. a planning tool.

22.3 BENEFITS OF A CHARGE-OUT SYSTEM

Provided that the charge-out system is drawn up to accurately reflect the real costs of data processing within the organization, benefits should accrue to IS, the user department, and to management. The following are the more important benefits of its implementation:

- it aids the control of IS costs;
- it aids the evaluation of the operating efficiency of the IS installation;
- it provides a measure of profitability for each IS cost centre and for the entire IS department in cases where services are charged to a user or customer;
- it provides project leaders with realistic cost rates to be used when estimating the cost of a proposed project;
- it permits a comparison of the actual costs of processing a system against budgeted costs that were estimated prior to the development of that system.

22.4 METHODS OF CHARGING FOR COMPUTER COSTS

If the actual cost method (outlined above) is used, costs can be charged out in many different ways but there is one overriding consideration: *whichever method is chosen, it must be simple to calculate and understand*. Some of the alternatives are outlined below.

22.4.1 Transaction charge rate

With this method the user is charged per transaction for the number of transactions that are processed by the system. This method is simple to use but can lead to an under- (or over-) recovery of costs by the IS department. It is also not totally realistic because with any job there is always a set-up overhead which should be recovered.

22.4.2 Minimum charge plus transaction rate

This is the same as the transaction charge rate, but includes a job set-up charge.

22.4.3 Resource charge

This is a charge to the user for each resource that is used by a system, such as:

- CPU memory;
- disks;
- tapes;
- terminals;
- printers.

This method is simple to use in a batch environment, since the running of programs can be scheduled and accurately measured. In a multiprogramming environment, however, it is far more difficult to measure usage. Operating systems in large mainframes often have measuring facilities to calculate the resource usage by transaction type or program.

22.4.4 Fixed charge

Frequently users and IS will meet at the start of a financial year to decide on a charge for IS services for that year. This will be based on the budgeted cost of the IS department and the estimated usage breakdown by each user. This is a very simple method to use and is generally most favoured by users.

22.5 DEVELOPING A CHARGE-OUT SYSTEM

The needs of individual companies vary tremendously, but by following a few basic rules any company should be able to design an effective system.

A few rules are listed below:

22.5.1 Step 1: Assess the overall status of IS services within the company

Sophisticated controls cannot be implemented in a department that is not 'ready' — ie. where the controls hinder its operation, or where its staff cannot see the relevance of such controls. The controls over the IS department cannot, and should not, be more advanced than those for any other department within the company.

22.5.2 Step 2: Evaluate the accounting system

Accounting systems are the basis for management control. It therefore follows that a sound accounting system should be in place before attempting to develop a charge-out system. Such a system must accurately record all IS costs, thus providing the platform for establishing and measuring IS recoveries.

22.5.3 Step 3: Assess the current charge-out approach

The system should communicate to managers the consequences of their decisions to use the IS services. It should also motivate users to employ resources more efficiently. A charge-out system's usefulness can be measured using four criteria:

- understandability;
- controllability;
- accountability;
- cost.

A sophisticated system would include a detailed bill being sent directly to low-level users as well as to high-level managers.

The proposed system should, wherever possible, match what is in use elsewhere in the organization. Thus, if personnel and marketing, for instance, use a profit centre approach, so should IS.

22.5.4 Step 4: Determine what to charge

Before allocation to cost centres, costs are accumulated into eight specific major cost-accounting classifications which lend themselves to identification of the type of cost incurred in order to satisfy regulatory and economic decision-making requirements. The following descriptions pertain to individual accounts within this structure:

Salaries and related employment expenses

- Gross remuneration
  Management
  Non-management
- Benefit costs (pension, medical, etc.)
- Training
- Acquisition expenses

Occupancy and related space expenses

- Rent (probably on allocation)
- Utilities — electricity, water, etc.
- Cleaning and services
- Repairs and maintenance
- Insurance and other costs

Equipment expenses

- Computer hardware
  Rental, lease charges or depreciation
  Maintenance
- Other equipment
  Rental, lease charges or depreciation
  Maintenance

Communication and related transmission expenses

- Terminal hardware
- Data transmission hardware
- Maintenance equipment
- Data communication line costs

Supplies

- Magnetic tape
- Disk packs
- Stationery
- Packaging material (output media distribution)

Other operating expenses

- Subscriptions, manuals, etc.
- Office stationery and supplies
- Telephone (excluding data transmission)
- Postage
- Printing

Allocated expenses

- Share of central overhead

Unallocated expenses

- Costs incurred by information systems which cannot be allocated, eg. experimental or development costs and hardware and software conversions.

22.5.5 Step 5: Develop objectives and strategy

The objectives should be stated clearly, stressing user accountability. Objectives could include the following:

- assisting managers and project leaders to assess the cost-benefit of a system during a feasibility study;
- establishing a standardized basis for charging user departments for the use of IS resources;

- making managers responsible for, and aware of, the actual cost of IS services provided to them;
- motivating managers to make decisions about the use of services on the basis of the costs of providing those services.

22.5.6 Step 6: Educate IS and user personnel

IS personnel will view a charge-out strategy as an unnecessary control and may attempt to sabotage the system by entering inaccurate data. Users often see it as 'paper money' and do not take it seriously. It is important that both IS personnel and users are educated about the reason for, and benefits of, its implementation.

22.5.7 Step 7: Implementation and review

Management control and charge-out strategy should be ratified, implemented, and reviewed by a high-level steering committee. This is important since the systems recommended could have far-reaching effects.

22.6 CONCLUSION

Charge-out systems are seldom recommended for a young IS department (less than one or two years old). They are only installed when information systems have become established and when the users can see the benefits of computerization. If implementation is followed carefully then information systems, users, and senior management should all benefit.

REVIEW QUESTIONS

1. Bearing in mind that there is a substantial cost in setting up and running a charge-out system, is such a system justifiable in terms of cost?
2. What are the costs associated with setting up and maintaining a charge-out system?
3. What are the advantages and disadvantages of an investment centre approach against a profit centre approach?
4. To the best of your knowledge, are there any companies in South Africa using the investment centre approach?
5. How would you go about drawing up a user tariff for a debtors system? Give examples and figures as part of your answer.
6. How would you go about establishing a charge for using a printer in a mainframe installation? Make up figures to illustrate your answer.
7. Assume that you have just been appointed IS manager in an established company that is about to acquire a large computer system. The rest of the company uses charge-out systems to recover costs. Would you try to implement a charge-out mechanism? Justify your answer.
8. You are the accountant and you are responsible for computing in a medium-sized business that has only microcomputers. You are concerned that some of the computers are not at all justified from a financial viewpoint. What would you do?

SELECTED REFERENCES AND RECOMMENDED READING

1. Dearden, J., Nolan, R. L. 1973. How to Control the Computer Resource. *Harvard Business Review* (November-December).
2. Institute of Cost and Management Accountants, *Management Accounting Guidelines —No. 4 Charging for Computer Services.*
3. McFarlan, F. W., McKenney J. L. 1983. *Corporate Information Systems Management: The Issues Facing Senior Executives.* Homewood, Illinois: Richard D. Irwin

CHAPTER 23 External sources of computer skills

23.1 INTRODUCTION

There are a number of ways that the IS department can call on resources outside the organization to improve the effectiveness and efficiency of the computing service to their users. Firstly a business does not have to purchase its own computer. There are specialized organizations, known as service bureaux, that will process a company's work for it.

The systems development process has recently become more costly than hardware in terms of the IS budget. There is widespread recognition of the inability of IS personnel to generate reliable systems which meet the needs of the user cheaply and in a reasonable time frame. IS departments are recognizing that while some of their systems are so unique that the software must be 'tailored' in-house, there are massive advantages in using generalized pre-written software packages.

This chapter also deals with the topic of external computer expertise — software houses and consultants. Organizations with their own computers and even, in many cases, with fully-fledged IS departments often require the assistance of outside IS professionals for a variety of reasons. Some of the advantages and disadvantages of using outsiders will be discussed in the final part of this chapter.

23.2 SERVICE BUREAUX

The service bureau can be defined as a commercial organization with its own computer facilities which offers a range of computing services for hire.

While service bureaux offer the traditional IS facilities such as data capture and batch processing, they have, in the past few years, widened the range of services they offer (this will be discussed in more depth later in the chapter). When looking at the service bureau as a possible alternative to an in-house computer services department, there are three major issues to consider:

- what the advantages are of using a service bureau;
- whether the service bureau industry is threatened by the advent of small business computers;
- any special considerations that should be taken into account when using a service bureau.

23.2.1 Why use service bureaux?

Lack of IS skills

One of the major reasons for using a service bureau is that an organization wants to computerize a system but there are no IS skills within the organization. It is quite common for first-time users to contemplate the use of a service bureau in order to familiarize themselves with computerized systems prior to purchasing a machine of their own.

Costs

It is difficult to generalize and say that in-house computing is either cheaper or more expensive than processing through a service bureau. It is, however, likely that the initial capital investment in machines and staff training will be greater when setting up your own IS department than in using a service bureau. Service bureaux tend to charge according to usage and, therefore, if an organization is very small and has few transactions, it is quite likely that it could get its work done more cheaply at a bureau than in-house. Many organizations start this way and, as their volumes increase, so their service bureau charges grow. This increase would have been less rapid on an in-house machine as the cost of the hardware (which includes spare capacity for growth) is fixed.

Seasonal processing

There are a number of organizations that have high volumes of transactions at seasonal or irregular times of the year. For instance, the Cape Matriculation Board has all student results on computer but most of its work is done only twice a year. If an organization does not have other significant applications, resources tend to be underutilized for the balance of the period and it is often more profitable to use a service bureau than to carry the fixed overheads of an in-house IS department for the entire period.

Systems overloads

It is fair to say that more and more applications are being found for computers, and most organizations are experiencing enormous growth in their IS facilities. As in-house facilities become overloaded, so newer and more powerful equipment is purchased. In many cases management is slow to recognize the predicament and, because of long lead times in the purchase and installation of new equipment, they may find that they do not have sufficient processing power to handle their organization's immediate needs. One solution to this problem is to allow a bureau to process non-critical applications rather than delaying them until new equipment has arrived.

Specialist services

There are a number of computer applications which are difficult to justify in-house because of their requirements for special hardware or software expertise. A typical example is the production of computer output microfilm (COM). COM processors are designed to produce large quantities of microfilm. However, many organizations want certain of their records on film but do not have the volumes to justify the purchase of their own equipment. The obvious solution is to share the facilities with many other users by means of a service bureau facility.

Non-involvement policy

Finally, there are many organizations which, through bad experiences in the past or a fear of the unknown, are unwilling to get involved in information systems but, at the same time, recognize the importance of maintaining a competitive edge. While, on paper, it would appear that large organizations with great volumes of data could easily justify the installation of an in-house computer, this non-involvement policy has two advantages. First, there are a large number of in-house IS departments that, through bad management, planning and control, are highly inefficient and put the entire organization at risk. Secondly, bureau organizations owe their existence to their expertise and their ability to control the costs of information systems.

23.2.2 Bureau survival

In the past, most bureau business came from medium-to-small organizations that could not justify the costs of an in-house IS department. Now with the advent of the microcomputer, computerization is within reach of even the one-man business. It is therefore logical to assume that this trend directly threatens the existence of service bureaux. In considering whether service bureaux will survive the microcomputer boom, there are a number of factors to take into account.

First, the service bureaux have recognized the inherent dangers of the microcomputer and have, in many cases, diversified the services they offer. Apart from standard batch processing, software development, and data capture facilities, they now offer their services as computer consultants, personnel consultants, and even as computer hardware vendors. Many bureaux have realized that a number of their clients are contemplating the purchase of an in-house machine and feel they are well placed, because of their intimate knowledge of the client's business applications, to sell an in-house solution.

The second point to consider is that many users of service bureaux are not there simply because of the size of their organization. Other factors which we have also discussed, such as specialist services, seasonal processing, and the desire to stay uninvolved, are all valid reasons for using a bureau.

Service bureaux owe their profitability to their efficient usage of hardware and people. While hardware costs are becoming less and less important, the efficient utilization of skilled IS professionals has become the most important criterion in running an IS shop, and this factor may continue to give service bureaux a competitive advantage over in-house installations.

The above factors seem to indicate that the service bureau still has a place in our IS community. However, over the past few years there has been an obvious move away from batch-type processing into the area of interactive systems where users are able to interrogate up-to-date data files via their own terminals. Service bureaux recognize this evolutionary change and most of the progressive organizations are offering on-line services to their clients. This new processing environment is much more complex to develop and operate than the old batch systems and, instead of obtaining the maximum utilization from their equipment, they will be forced to provide most of their processing power during office hours. In addition, there are the problems of remote equipment and communication costs to overcome.

23.2.3 Special considerations when using a bureau

Selection

When selecting a service bureau, considerations such as the costs of the service and the facilities offered should be taken into account. Charges may vary considerably according to the bureau's level of expertise in a particular application and the possibilities of using generalized software for a company's systems. One factor, however, that must be paramount is the reputation of the service bureau. It is important that you determine how long the organization has been in business, its financial strength (and therefore its ability to survive during hard economic times) and the size and satisfaction of its users. This can be determined only by requesting the names of all the bureau users and randomly selecting a number of organizations to interview.

Operational considerations

When using a bureau there are a number of fundamental procedures which must be introduced to ensure that the partnership has some chance of success. First, a liaison officer must be set up within your organization and he must communicate with a prearranged contact person at the bureau. If no formal communication channels are provided there will undoubtedly be chaos as users individually phone through to the bureau when arranging processing or enquiring on the status of work.

Contracts

As with all business arrangements, it is important to confirm and document all decisions made on the type and cost of service to be provided. While a contract is obviously a good idea, it should not be seen as a document to be taken out and dusted off prior to going to court, because by then one will be incurring legal costs and the IS schedule will be suffering. The contract is a confirmation that all the important parts of the arrangement have been well thought-out and formally agreed to prior to the agreement being concluded.

Controls

There are a number of important controls in the area of ongoing processing such as *run* authorization forms, stationery registers, and security considerations: these will be discussed in detail in Module 5. One control which can be stressed, however, is that of reviewing the service bureau charges.

Most service bureau charging systems are transaction-based and are, in many cases, computer-generated. There is always a good possibility that unscheduled reruns of programs due to faults such as power failures, hardware failures, and even operator errors, will be charged to the client. The only way to detect these charges is to insist on a detailed account and to match this back to a manual processing log which must be maintained in your own organization.

23.3 PACKAGES

Packaged software can be defined as pre-written programs that perform a defined function. In the early 1980s the use of generalized packages was minimal, except in the systems software area (operating systems, translators, and utilities). Today, however, few organizations contemplate developing a new system without looking at pre-written software. The main reason for this change in emphasis is the cost of software development.

23.3.1 Software trends

We have seen that while the ratio of hardware to software costs for an IS department in 1970 was 80 : 20, this ratio has now been fully reversed. Unfortunately, these figures are made even more unpalatable by the fact that there is a serious shortage of IS personnel just at a time when there is a rapid increase in the use of computers — and therefore in the need for new software.

There are three possible solutions to the software dilemma:

- an increase in programmer productivity through the introduction of better development tools;
- the use of non-programming people to develop systems using special user-friendly languages;
- the introduction of pre-written packaged software.

23.3.2 Increases in programmer productivity

The first solution, increases in programmer productivity, has made little impact since the early 1980s. Research has tended to indicate that the use of new tools and techniques has never increased the programmer's productivity by more than 25 %. Very recently, however, the introduction of fourth generation languages has in some cases shown productivity increases of up to 40 times over the conventional commercial programming languages. While their use is currently not widespread enough for one to assess the likely impact of these languages, it is obvious that their introduction will have a major impact on the systems development backlog.

23.3.3 End-user programming

While the first solution to the software dilemma was the evolution of better systems development tools, the second advocates that the user should no longer rely on the assistance of a specialized third party to develop his computer systems but should undertake the work himself.

With the increased sophistication of computer software and a greater level of computer literacy within the business community, the concept of the man-machine interface is fast becoming a reality. Today there are software packages such as applications generators which permit the user simply to detail the inputs and outputs of a particular program and have the software package generate the necessary file structures and program code required to process the data. Fourth generation languages are also 'friendly' enough to be used by non-IS personnel.

It would be incorrect to suggest that programmers will soon become redundant because most of this software is in its infancy and can only deal with the very simplest of applications systems.

The marriage of man and machine, however, has as its ultimate goal the ability of the person with the problem to communicate that problem directly to the computer.

23.3.4 Packages

The final solution is for the organization requiring software to purchase a packaged system — a pre-written set of computer programs. Software written for multiple users will go a long way towards alleviating the systems development backlog.

There are a number of reasons for using a package in preference to developing one's own in-house system.

- *Immediate availability*. Packages are pre-written and so there is no lead time from the decision to acquire the software to the actual program implementation.
- *Demonstrability*. The system can be demonstrated to the user before any costs are incurred. With conventional systems development the user cannot see the working system until the programs have been written. The user therefore cannot ensure that the output is really what he needs. Changing the system at this point tends to be very costly.
- *Lower cost*. Although it is not always the case, most packages are written in anticipation of sales to multiple users and therefore the costs of systems development (and a fair profit to the developer) can be written off over all the expected sales. It is therefore likely that such packages will be substantially cheaper than the cost of developing systems in-house. The cost is also known, while in most systems development projects the costs tend to escalate over the development period.
- *Greater reliability*. Packages tend to be very reliable because all the errors which were originally in the system have been discovered and fixed at the first few sites. (This advantage does not apply if one is the first user of a new package!)
- *Better documentation*. Writing documentation has never been a popular pastime in computer departments, and programmers, analysts, operators, and users suffer from a lack of an adequate written description of systems. Packages are usually well documented. The systems documentation is one way of communicating how a package works to a prospective purchaser, and is therefore a valuable part of the marketing effort.
- *Better user training*. Training courses are often inadequate for several reasons. Many organizations do not realize the strategic importance of training the user and underemphasize it. Staff are unlikely to be trained or even well-experienced in user education, and the effort put into planning courses is likely to be influenced by the number of times the course will be run. With packaged software, the vendor is likely to stress user training as this aspect is likely to have the most impact on whether the installation is successful or not. Furthermore, the people doing the training would have both the skills and the experience to do it effectively.
- *Ongoing support*. Most reputable packages are sold with an ongoing support option. This means that, for a small annual charge, the purchaser has the continued support of the vendor should any programming problems arise, as well as access to any improvements or enhancements to the package in the future.
- *Low risk*. A large number of systems development projects have never been completed due to problems such as excessive costs, loss of key development staff,

and time overruns. A package is a finished article and therefore carries a lower risk of failure.

23.3.5 Disadvantages of packages

The disadvantages of using packages include:

- *Unsuitability.* The package does not always meet the organization's requirements. This problem will be expanded on in the following section on package selection.
- *Processing inefficiency.* Because of its general nature the package is inefficient in its use of storage and its speed of processing. (With the decrease in the costs of hardware this disadvantage is becoming less significant.)
- *Incompatibility.* The system may be difficult to use because it does not have the same report layouts, data names, and general terminology as the in-house procedures. It is possible that the package will not be compatible with other computer systems within the organization.
- *Non-South African packages.* Many packages are developed overseas and are therefore non-standard (in terms of local terminology, method of processing, and format). This really only applies to accounting packages and to those where government regulations are involved.
- *Modifications.* One danger of a package is that the purchaser may modify it in order to meet his particular requirements. While modifications seem the obvious solution in order to tailor a package to a particular organization, there are some major problems inherent in this approach. If one looks at the advantages of packages, one sees that changes will affect just about every one of those advantages. For instance, the package will no longer be immediately available, will need to be retested, and will not be as reliable. It will probably be more expensive and may well not have the changes reflected in the standard documentation or in the user training. Another major problem is that when the system is enhanced, any changes will have to be included in the enhancement. This may mean that the additional cost of amending the system will be encountered every time the programs are upgraded. Finally, there is a greater danger that knowledge of the particular idiosyncrasies of modified software is lost as programmers in the vendor organization come and go.

23.3.6 Package selection

When selecting a package there are a number of criteria that should be investigated before making a final decision:

- *Choosing a reputable vendor.* When one purchases a software package one is often given only the machine language version. This means that one is unable to make amendments to programs, and will be unable to fix problems when they occur. It is therefore vitally important that the software vendor should be capable of offering a high level of support for the package throughout its useful life. The vendor organization's financial backing and reputation in the marketplace are therefore of major importance.

- *Considering the functions and output of packages.* Obviously one can only use a package if it matches the needs of one's organization. Careful analysis of the package by IS and user personnel is necessary. This can be done by reading the documentation available and by attending demonstrations of the working system.
- *Documentation, training and education.* These aspects have been discussed already and it goes without saying that prior to the purchase of a package, one should determine the quality and quantity of these.
- *General.* Other points to consider when purchasing a package are whether it will be enhanced on a regular basis or whether it has any particular machine or operating system requirements, and whether there are any packages which are unique to one's own particular industry (such as the construction and medical packages).

23.3.7 Forced fit versus choice of fit

In the late 1980s a number of pressures led many of South Africa's largest organizations to accept mainframe packages.

These pressures included the inability of IS departments to build and maintain complex applications to meet the user's requirements and the emergence of sophisticated mainframe packages to address vertical markets such as insurance, banking, and manufacturing.

One major problem encountered in the acquisition of mainframe applications is that no one package is likely to mirror the organization's current systems, yet modifications to the package would be dangerous for all the reasons given above.

Many large organizations have taken a conscious decision to change the business rather than change the package. While at first this may appear to conflict with all that we have learnt about meeting the user's requirements, it actually carries enormous benefits.

If one is able to alter one's business to fit the package, the software development and maintenance problems are minimized. The critical question is whether users can and will adapt to a new method of doing business.

Organizations that are prepared to adapt their business to the demands of software packages need to approach the software selection process slightly differently using what is termed the *choice of fit approach*[1]. In the past we determined the user's requirements and then selected software to meet those requirements. This approach is known as *forced fit* in that the user's requirements do not take account of the functions in available packages and differences must be forced on the package (as package customization) or on the users (as changes to the way they do business). The choice of fit approach demands that developers study available packages before developing the user's requirements, and so limit those requirements to functionality available in the software. This approach tends to provide a closer fit between package and user requirements.

23.3.8 The role of packages

There is little doubt that we are in an era in which packages are becoming more and more acceptable to the IS community. While systems software and utility packages have been marketed for some time, most organizations are now looking at applications packages. Growth in demand will lead to an increase in the number and quality of programs on offer. Today the package is predominantly a small machine option where systems tend to be simpler and IS budgets smaller. In the near future, however, most software may well be delivered 'off the shelf' and the tailor-made system may become as rare as the tailor-made suit.

23.4 CONSULTANTS AND SOFTWARE HOUSES

In the previous two sections we discussed the concept of service bureaux and externally developed software (packages). In this section on external sources, we look at the use of people external to the organization who can assist in the IS function.

This expertise falls into two broad categories: the *computer consultant* and the *software house*.

23.4.1 Computer consultants

A computer consultant is an individual who hires out his IS skills to assist an organization, normally in an advisory capacity. This service may include one or more of the following:

- the feasibility study;
- selection of hardware, software, and computer personnel;
- hardware location and environmental requirements;
- cost-benefit analyses;
- preparation of the job specification for tender purposes;
- designing of systems and programs after conducting a requirements analysis.

There are a number of reasons why a computer consultant may be approached. The main reasons are:

- there is no in-house expertise in information systems (a situation common among very small installations);
- specialist expertise is required in a certain area such as machine acquisition where a knowledge of the available equipment on the market is important;
- the organization requires an unbiased opinion, eg. the evaluation of key IS personnel.

23.4.2 Types of consultants

There are three general categories of computer consultants.

- *Manufacturing representatives.* The larger computer manufacturing firms have well-trained teams of analysts who offer advice and assistance to existing and potential new clients. While these individuals are often very up to date on their own particular equipment, they tend to push their own product. One major advantage of using manufacturers' representatives is that they often do not charge for their services.

- *Independent consultants.* These individuals have no connection with any specific computer manufacturer and therefore tend to be unbiased in their choice of hardware and software. However, because they are making a living by offering their skills, they are more expensive than manufacturers' representatives. While their obvious selling point is independence, there is a danger that past experience and personal preference may bias them towards a particular computer solution.
- *Accounting and auditing profession.* Most large auditing firms now have a management services group containing some computer expertise. The main advantage of using one's firm of auditors to assist in the computerization of one's organization is that they should have an intimate knowledge of the organization and its systems, reducing the time required for investigation. Another advantage is that the auditor will have no connections with any particular manufacturing organization. Unfortunately the smaller accounting practices tend to have limited experience in the computer field and in many cases are unable to offer their client sound advice in this area.

23.4.3 Use of consultants

There are a number of rules which all organizations should follow when using consultants.

Firstly, they should determine whether in-house resources should be spent on training personnel in a special knowledge area, or whether it would pay to use an outside consultant.

Secondly, they should select the consulting firm carefully. The selected firm should specialize in one's particular problem area and have references to back up its expertise.

Thirdly, they should not let the consultant become embedded in the organization. He would love to become part of the organization's permanent payroll, so it is necessary to set project goals and a specific timetable for reaching those goals.

Finally, when using consultants, organizations should not neglect their own employees. It is very demotivating for staff to be given all the mundane programming work while outsiders grapple with the latest technology.

23.4.4 Software houses

Where an organization does not, for some reason, want to write a particular software application in-house, but at the same time cannot find a suitable software package on the open market, it can employ a third party organization called a *software house* to develop the programs. While a number of software houses have diversified, and now offer services such as consultancy, their role is in the development of tailor-made software.

When contemplating the use of a software house there are a number of special managerial considerations to be taken into account:

- There is the problem of the existing software base within the organization. A new system written externally may well be difficult to interface with existing programs.

- The second consideration is the reputation of the software house. There are a large number of moonlighting programmers and one-man practices in the software business and there are obvious risks in employing organizations such as these to perform systems development functions.
- Prior to selecting a software house, an organization should possess a résumé of the software house's previous clients in order to evaluate its past performance. One should also attempt to assess its size, financial backing, and experience in order to evaluate whether it is likely to be in business at least for the next few years.
- Businesses should always insist on a detailed contract with the software house. This is not necessarily to provide legal leverage in the case of a dispute but rather to force both parties to the contract to formalize their arrangements and to put them in writing.
- It is important not to forget the financial aspects of the contract. Software houses can normally be paid by lump sum, or on a time-and-materials basis. There is a distinct risk with the time-and-materials contract that there is no real incentive for the software house to get the job done as quickly as possible.

23.4.5 The future of software houses

The software house fulfills an important function in that it is the main source of tailor-made software for the small machine environment. These organizations can provide stimulating employment for many highly-skilled and motivated information systems professionals who find the formality and bureaucracy of large in-house computer departments too restricting.

However, the money that can be earned in software development has also encouraged inexperienced IS people into the software area with negative results. As time goes on, the IS industry will mature, and with this will come the necessary controls on public practice.

REVIEW QUESTIONS

1. What is a computer service bureau and why did this industry flourish in the 1960s and '70s?
2. The development of the minicomputer and then the microcomputer were expected to kill the service bureau industry as small companies were able to afford their own in-house facility. While growth in the service bureau has slowed, it is still an important and profitable industry. Why?
3. What are the advantages of packaged software over in-house development?
4. Modifying a package to meet the requirements of a particular organization would appear to make good business sense. What are the disadvantages of this approach?
5. What do we mean by the 'forced fit' and 'choice of fit' approaches to selecting a software package?
6. When should an organization hire the services of a computer consultant?
7. What are the dangers inherent in using outside consultants?

8. While software houses are an important segment of the computer services industry, users of their services should be aware of the potential for problems in a number of areas. Discuss.

SELECTED REFERENCES AND RECOMMENDED READING

1. Baker, W. J. 1989. *Purchasing Applications Software: Choosing the Right Package.* Auerbach Information Management Series.

CHAPTER 24 End-user computing

24.1 INTRODUCTION

End-user computing is one of the major growth areas in the industry today. The microcomputer has emerged as an essential tool for people in business. End-users are shunning the traditional approach to computing in ever increasing numbers by becoming computer literate and solving their problems themselves instead of going through the information systems department. Let us start by investigating the reasons behind this trend.

24.2 THE END-USER COMPUTER REVOLUTION

24.2.1 Applications backlog

The main reason for the end-user computing (EUC) revolution has been identified as the *applications backlog* — a term used by James Martin, a prominent American computer consultant. This term describes the inability of information systems departments in large organizations to keep abreast of the massive demand for new computer applications. On one hand the opportunities for using the computer in new areas of the business are growing at an astounding rate, while on the other hand the computer department has a growing load of existing applications to maintain. The result is that the IS department can only respond to the most critical requests from end-users and, even there, projects may be scheduled for two to three years in the future.

24.2.2 Computer literacy

A second trend which has fuelled the EUC revolution is the increase in computer literacy among computer users. Computer studies are taught at schools; most university courses include a computer awareness programme, and microprocessors have invaded many areas of everyday life, from the motor-car console to the automatic teller machine (ATM) in the high street, from the programmable telephone to the word processor. Many still feel threatened by this invasion, but many others seize the opportunity to use the power of the computer in their everyday work.

24.2.3 Packaged applications

A third and very important reason for the growth in end-user computing is the wealth of sophisticated and user-friendly software packages that have been developed over the past decade. Word processing software, spreadsheeting programs such as Lotus 123, user-friendly fourth generation languages such as dBase IV, and graphics packages, have all made the microprocessor a simple tool to use while enormously increasing its potential.

24.2.4 Cost benefit

One must not forget the economics of the situation. Over the past ten years microcomputers have greatly increased in power and sophistication. The cost of this equipment has consistently dropped while the price of almost everything else has increased. In the past, personal computing was a costly exercise and purchases required lengthy justification. Today a microcomputer costs much the same as an electronic typewriter and is well within the budget constraints of an office manager.

24.2.5 Office automation

The EUC revolution is helped by the current rapid introduction of *office automation* (OA) in the larger organizations. As people are taught to use microprocessors and terminals for electronic mail and word processing, so they see the potential for computing in other areas of their work environment.

24.3 EUC APPLICATIONS

With the move to end-user computing, a number of studies have been conducted. The most important of these was the Kendall survey[2], carried out by IBM in 1980. This aimed to determine which applications are ideally suited for end-user development. The conclusion was reached that approximately 50 % of each organization's computer applications could be termed *operational*, and these included all the large transaction-based systems requiring large volumes of data input and master file updating. These systems would remain within the domain of the information systems department. The other 50 % of the applications were broken up into two groupings. The first was a small group of applications (forming approximately 5 % of the total) that was used on a regular basis. For reasons of efficiency and control these systems would best be developed and maintained by the IS department. The other 45 % of the applications were identified as relatively simple programs that were generally used only once. These were mainly reporting programs. These applications were ideal for end-user development. Many end-user developed applications (UDAs), however, are fully-fledged operational systems. This can cause problems as most UDAs are poorly designed and seldom documented, and are therefore difficult to maintain.

24.4 MANAGING END-USER COMPUTING

Let us now look at the approach required to support the end-user computing community.

A centralized information systems department could be described as a closely-knit, tightly-controlled group of computer professionals — a far cry from the undisciplined and diversified band of amateur programmers found in the end-user computing area. Many IS managers fear that the trend to end-user computing will lead to chaos, while others see the trend reducing their power and stature in their organizations.

End-user computing has become a reality and the major question is how to best make the transition to this new environment. Thomas Gerrity and John Rockart[1] discuss three possible approaches which they term the *monopolistic approach*, the *laissez faire approach* and the *managed free economy*.

24.4.1 Monopolistic approach

The monopolistic approach is characterized by the information systems department retaining firm control over all end-user activity. Here all access to computer tools is provided through the mainframe terminals so that activities can be monitored and controlled. Users are educated and supported by IS personnel, and the purchase of stand-alone personal computers is difficult to justify. The major reasoning behind this approach is that IS must retain firm control of the end-user computing environment in order to ensure the quality of the systems developed. The philosophy is that trained users supported by professional programmers will provide good program code, adequate documentation, and adequate systems controls and security. In addition, good programs will run efficiently on computers.

The reasons for the failure of this management style is that it does not address the real problems in the computer environment. The applications backlog, for example, is unlikely to be addressed by this limited approach. Hardware efficiency is almost irrelevant at today's cost of processing power, and the rigid documentation standards maintained by the IS department are not so important where it comes to the simple, one-off management information reports generated by end-users. In a nutshell, end-users can do it quicker and cheaper than this formalized IS dominated approach will permit.

24.4.2 Laissez faire approach

The laissez faire approach is the opposite to the monopolistic approach. The end-user is permitted to do exactly as he pleases. This is based on the belief that end-user computing cannot be planned for or controlled, and therefore cannot be managed. The result is that the information systems department maintains control over the operational systems and end-users are free to do what they like within the constraints of their own budgets.

This approach has as many problems as the first in that there is no overall plan or philosophy to the implementation of computing in the various divisions of the organization. In many cases applications will not be cost-effective and the same system will be developed in different areas of the organization at the same time. Because of the lack of training and support from the IS department the users may make poor decisions as to the type of hardware and software they require for their applications, and this will lead to compatibility problems in the future. This fragmented approach can only lead to chaos in the long run.

24.4.3 Managed free economy

The final approach proposed by Gerrity and Rockart is that of the managed free economy. This is based on a sounder philosophy. This approach recognizes that the IS department should try to guide the end-user rather than control him. Ultimately the end-user is responsible for all decisions and applications developed in his particular area, but the IS department provides training, support, and guidance on critical decisions such as hardware and software purchases. The end-user is free to make the final decision but is made aware that the IS department will only provide support for a select group of software tools and the purchase of equipment which is not on the list recommended by IS may result in incompatibility with other networks and devices in the organization. This approach permits the organization to plan the direction of end-user computing and its role in the overall computer strategy of the business. End-user managers will almost certainly follow the suggestions that they are given.

24.5 THE INFORMATION CENTRE

A function that arose in the 1980s, as a result of the emergence of end-user computing, was termed the *information centre* (IC). With end-user computing, users are given terminals and access to a corporate database through an ultra high level or fourth generation language. Data are then extracted or manipulated by users according to their specific requirements. End-users need support both in assessing their business requirements and in the use of the tools to extract and manipulate data. This is the function of the information centre which consists of experienced IS personnel who have an understanding of business analysis and of high level languages.

The IC may or may not be attached to an organizational division but the task of the IC staff is to provide education and support to all users. A small number of IS staff can handle a large number of users, and in this way the total support requirement of the IS division is reduced. The rest of the systems development staff can then concentrate on the development and maintenance of new applications.

REVIEW QUESTIONS

1. What were the driving forces behind the end-user computing revolution?
2. What were the important conclusions reached in Kendall's study on programming productivity?
3. What are the monopolistic, laissez faire, and managed free economy approaches to end user computing? Give situations where each approach would be considered the most appropiate to use.
4. What is an information centre and what purpose does it serve?

SELECTED REFERENCES AND RECOMMENDED READING

1. Gerrity, T., Rockart J. 1986. End-user computing: are you a laggard? *Sloan Management Review* (Summer) Vol. 27, pp. 25-34.
2. Kendall, R. C. *Management Perceptions on Programs, Programming and Productivity*. IBM Corporation: White Plains, New York.

MODULE 4 KEY POINT SUMMARY

- The IS department is a complex one, consisting of expensive equipment and highly skilled (and highly paid) employees. Ensuring that both work optimally requires a sound knowledge of management principles.
- The success of an installation depends on the hardware and software that are to process the applications for the business. The selection of both should proceed along a formal, well-defined path. A haphazard, subjective decision could well spell disaster for the organization.
- The implementation considerations vary according to the size of the machine. A mainframe, for instance, will have totally different needs from a microcomputer.
- The organization does not have to rely on in-house expertise for systems acquisition or development. It may use packages, or may rely on the skills of outsiders by using consultants or software houses.
- Charging for computer costs is a powerful medium for controlling usage by organizational departments. A method that is too complex, however, may well defeat the objective. The IS manager should consult with users during the development and implementation of such a system.
- Personal computers were initially seen as toys. As these machines became more powerful and employees more computer literate, end-users have begun to build and run their own computer applications. While this revolution has many positive aspects, management must ensure that it takes place in a controlled and integrated environment.

MODULE 5 Computer controls and security

OBJECTIVES

In this module we provide an overview of control and security techniques within the IS facility. The principles of internal control in computerized environments are no different from those in manual systems. However, the use of computers normally results in changes to individual responsibilities and processing activities which may well affect the level of internal control.

At the end of this module you should be able to:

- Identify the unique areas of concern in computerized systems.
- Translate these concerns into clearly defined objectives of internal control.
- Describe the various techniques which can be instituted to ensure that the above objectives are met.

CHAPTER 25 Introduction to controls

25.1 INTRODUCTION

In most organizations today, heavy reliance is placed on computer systems to provide accurate and easily accessible information. It is not an exaggeration to suggest that many organizations would cease to function if they were denied their computer systems. It is, therefore, extremely important to ensure that computer systems are operating effectively and that they are properly secured. In general terms, the control and security requirements of an IS operation can be summarized as follows:

- To ensure that data is accurately processed and that errors occurring can be detected and corrected.
- To provide for recovery and continued operation in the event of a malfunction occurring.
- To ensure the privacy and security of confidential information.
- To ensure that IS operations are effective — ie. that good value is being obtained for the money being spent.

The above list could be termed the *overall control objectives* for any organization, regardless of whether it uses manual systems or a computer. These objectives and the essential characteristics of accounting control do not change with the method of information processing. Obviously these objectives are very broad and must be translated into particular procedures and techniques which will ensure that the control objectives are achieved. These procedures are referred to as *controls*.

Although the broad objectives of internal control within an organization do not depend on the method of information processing used, the actual procedures used to control the system may differ between manual information systems and its electronic equivalent.

The purpose of this module is to look at the particular control requirements of a computer-based information system.

25.2 WHAT IS A CONTROL?

A control can be defined as follows:

> The plan of organization and all the co-ordinate methods and procedures adopted within a business to safeguard its assets, check the accuracy and reliability of its accounting data, promote operational efficiency, and encourage adherence to prescribed managerial policies. (AICPA Handbook.)

This is a rather grand definition, but what does it really mean? In simple terms controls are procedures implemented to assist management to keep the organization in a state of balance or equilibrium. Controls can therefore be looked on as safeguards set up within the organization to assist in the following ways:

- To prevent problems from occurring.
- Where problems cannot be prevented, to detect a problem once it has occurred.

- Finally to provide the organization with the ability to take corrective action once the problem has been identified.

Often controls are seen as a by-product of the internal and external audit function, but in reality they are a function of the growth in an organization. In a one-man business or small partnership the owners are personally involved in the daily activities and the internal control procedures tend to be informal or non-existent. As the organization grows, formal internal control procedures must be implemented to ensure that employees perform in accordance with management policy.

Some of the more important controls are:

- Personnel practice
- Segregation of duties
- Job rotation
- Operational procedures manuals
- Dual control
- Forms and documentation
- Authorization
- Accounting controls
- Budgets
- Internal audit function
- Physical controls.

The internal control objectives in a computerized environment should be no different from those in a manual system. However, the use of computers often results in major changes in responsibilities and processing activities, often weakening and in some cases invalidating the manual control techniques which had been in place. Let us now identify some of the areas where one would expect the potential for loss or damage to the organization to increase because of computerization.

25.2.1 Illogical processing

Computers are not able to perceive as human beings can, and therefore problems such as the R1 000 000 electricity account often slip through when they would be detected in a manual system.

25.2.2 Repetition of errors

In a manual system errors are made at random while in a computer system the processing rules are applied consistently, often causing repetition of errors.

25.2.3 Cascading of errors

Computers often provide the capability for one-time acquisition of data through the use of integrated systems so that the original recording of data in machine-readable form serves all subsequent applications. Unfortunately an error in one part of the system may well trigger off additional errors in other application areas.

25.2.4 Incorrect data entry

The use of computerized applications introduces a new step in the recording process, the translation of manual data into computerized format. During this translation process errors can obviously occur.

25.2.5 Concentration of data

In manual systems the corporation's data are traditionally stored in separate functional areas. In a computerized environment the data are normally centralized on magnetic disk or tape increasing the risk of unauthorized access and manipulation.

25.2.6 Inability to react quickly

One of the main reasons for implementing computer systems is their ability to process data at great speed. However, computer systems are often very inflexible and their ability to react to changes in the environment (such as the introduction of general sales tax) or even to management's changing needs (such as a request for a new output report) may take longer to implement than in a manual system.

25.2.7 Inability to substantiate processing

In a manual system there is usually documentation to substantiate the processing of each transaction. In a computer system, electronic transactions leave no such lasting evidence.

25.2.8 Concentration of duties

Computer applications tend to concentrate responsibilities that had been segregated for control purposes. This often results in users of the computer system and data processing personnel having the ability to misuse the system fraudulently.

25.2.9 Unauthorized systems access

With a large centralized store of data accessed by authorized users and IS personnel it is often very difficult to limit access to sensitive programs and data. This problem is further complicated by the existence of remote terminals in the open office environment, the misuse of passwords and the general disregard for access security in the IS environment.

25.2.10 Problems inherent in the electronic automated environment

Poor operational procedures, machine malfunctions and environmental problems such as power interruptions can result in the following problems:

- Data files are overwritten or destroyed.
- The wrong version of a program or data file is used in processing.
- Data may be processed twice or not at all.
- System is incorrectly restarted after a power failure resulting in loss of transactions.

25.2.11 Poorly specified systems

The developing of computer applications brings with it a number of new control problems not present in the manual environment. These include areas such as the system not working to the user's requirements and inadequate testing of programs.

25.3 APPROACH TO CONTROLS

There are a number of approaches to the study and the evaluation of computer controls. In the auditing profession it has become fashionable to split the area into two broad categories — general controls and application controls — and this distinction will be discussed in more detail in the chapter on computer auditing.

A second method of categorizing computer controls is that put forward by the Canadian Institute of Chartered Accountants in their publication *Computer Control Guidelines*, where they break down the various controls into areas of concern. This highly structured approach assists the student in learning and understanding the various control techniques while limiting the overlap of techniques across the various areas. This module will use a combination of both methods and categorize controls into the following areas of concern:

General and application controls

- Pre-installation controls
- People controls
- Systems development controls
- Operational controls
- Processing controls
- Documentation controls

On-line controls
Service bureau controls
Small business computer controls

For each section we shall attempt to establish control objectives which should be met to ensure that there are no weaknesses in the system. Once we have decided on the direction to follow we can then identify particular tools and techniques which could be instituted to ensure that these control objectives are met.

REVIEW QUESTIONS

1. List four control and security requirements in an IS operation.
2. Controls can be looked on as safeguards set up within the organization to assist in mainly three ways. Name and discuss these three ways.
3. Poor operational procedures, machine malfunctions, and environmental problems can result in a number of problems. Name four such problems.
4. In which two broad categories can computer controls normally be classified?

CHAPTER 26 General and application controls

26.1 INTRODUCTION

General controls cover the overall IS environment within which each set of application controls will function. They relate to all applications and provide the framework within which the computer department exercises control over the development, operation and maintenance of individual applications.

The major objectives of these general controls can be stated as attempting to maximize:

- the reliability of systems
- the continuity of processing of all systems
- the security of data, programs and equipment.

The general controls we will discuss are pre-installation, people, system development and operational controls.

Application controls, on the other hand, are concerned with the functioning of each application. They are concerned with ensuring that the processing is complete and accurate and that the user can balance the output back to the original source documents.

26.2 PRE-INSTALLATION CONTROLS

This area of concern deals with the computer acquisition process. Most organizations considering computerization and probably all organizations that have computerized their systems, are aware of the many pitfalls in selecting and acquiring a new computer. Furthermore, the mature and established computer departments are continuously going through the process of enlarging and upgrading their installation.

26.2.1 Computer justification

The first obvious question is whether the acquisition of a computer is justified. Often computers are required because the existing administrative systems are unable to cope with the current workload. However, this problem is often a result of weaknesses in the current manual system and the introduction of a computer into this environment is therefore likely to do more harm than good. Furthermore, if computerization is justified, should the organization acquire its own machine or follow in the footsteps of many first-time users in engaging a service bureau? With the above problems in mind, we can formulate our first objective in the area of pre-installation controls.

Objective

An organization must acquire a computer or the services of a service bureau only after it has determined that computerization is the best information processing alternative.

Techniques

The next step is to identify what control techniques could be used to assist in meeting this initial objective. Casting our minds back to Module 4, we recall that there are two important tools which can assist in the computerization decision.

Computer steering committee (CSC)

First, it is most important that representatives of all divisions of the organization that may be affected by the decision to computerese, are involved in the decision-making process. Therefore a CSC must be formed that comprizes representatives of both management and departments which are potential users of the facility. Involving all interested parties has the twofold benefit of committing the individuals to the final recommendation and ensuring that they are all aware of the current issues involved.

Preliminary survey and feasibility study

Once the CSC has been formed, it can initiate a formal study of the existing systems and, if justified, a detailed investigation into possible solutions. In many cases a computer consultant may be called in to assist with these investigations. With the recommendations put forward in the feasibility study, management should be able to determine whether computerization is the best alternative and what form it should take.

26.2.2 Computer selection

Our second concern is that if we have determined that computerization is the best alternative, how do we select the equipment?

Objective

To ensure that management is able to acquire the most suitable equipment to perform the task.

Techniques

Formal selection procedures

We have discussed the formalization of the selection process in Module 4 and therefore merely have to follow the important steps in the selection checklist:

- Develop a checklist of potential suppliers.
- Dispatch formal requests for proposals.
- Evaluate tenders.
- Visit potential suppliers and contact current users.
- Financial and contractual negotiation.
- Final selection.

It is unlikely that any organization can claim that the computer it has acquired is the best machine for its own particular requirements. However, the many pitfalls that can befall the uninitiated first-time user of computers can be reduced considerably by a formalized approach to the selection process.

26.2.3 Computer installation

Finally, there is a distinct risk that, when a computer has been acquired, the transition from manual to computer systems will not be a smooth one.

Objective

To ensure that the new computer is installed within the planned time-frame and with the least disruption to the organization.

Techniques

Installation planning

Once the decision to acquire a new computer has been made, management should appoint a person or group responsible for developing a formal installation plan. This document must include details about activities such as the preparation of the computer site, management and user education, conversion of files, testing of equipment and the hiring and training of IS personnel. Obviously the complexity of each installation plan will differ, but the arrival of any new computer is almost invariably associated with a multitude of teething problems and only by careful rigid adherence to the plan will these problems be minimized.

26.3 PEOPLE CONTROLS

With the acquisition of a computer there is normally a radical change in the organizational structure. First, there is a high degree of concentration of processing which, in the past, had been spread out among the many user departments. Top management has no information processing expertise and therefore is unwilling to exercise effective control over the function.

26.3.1 Separation of duties

Where previously no one individual was able to handle all phases of a transaction without the intervention of some other person (the initiation of a transaction, its authorization, recording and safeguarding of assets functions were all entrusted to separate individuals as a major principle of internal control), there is a tendency today to entrust the computer with more than the single function for which it was first intended, namely that of recording the transaction.

An example of this weakness is where sophisticated stock systems are able to check stock levels and, where necessary, issue a purchase order. While there is no reason why manual intervention cannot be introduced to ensure that the correct purchases are being made, there is often an over-reliance on the computer to perform this function.

With regard to the safeguarding of assets, there is also a tendency for computers to be able to do such things as calculate employee bonuses and payroll increases based on certain criteria. The risk here is obvious: if one person is able to exercise undue control over the IS activity they may well be able to amend programs or data in such a way as to defraud the organization. This principle is known as *separation of duties* and is potentially a major control weakness in sophisticated computer systems.

Objective

To develop an organizational structure that will provide adequate control over the concentration of functions in the IS department.

Techniques

Assignment of responsibilities

In well organized business operations, responsibilities are established by defining individual job descriptions for all personnel. Similarly, individual responsibilities should be clearly defined for all IS department personnel.

Separation of functions

The first technique should be to separate the IS function from the departments which initiate or authorize transactions and control assets. The IS department should be responsible only for the recording of business activity. Where the computer assists in the identification of a new activity such as orders or the determination of salary increases, the final authority for these transactions should be vested in the user department.

IS independence

To ensure the IS department's independence it should also report to senior management rather than to a divisional manager such as the financial controller.

Separation of duties within the IS function

Within the IS department duties should be split in order to ensure that no one individual is capable of manipulating and running a particular system. The best way to achieve this is to establish teams of individuals where the functions and activities of one person are checked or authorized by another. Thus, a programmer's code would be checked by a senior analyst/programmer in the same team; an operator's work would be checked by a shift leader, and so on.

26.3.2 Management control

One criticism often aimed at IS installations is that IS professionals have little management expertise. Furthermore, top management in the organization has so little knowledge of information systems that it treats the department as a black box and is therefore unable to evaluate its contribution to the overall well-being of the company.

Objective

To ensure that management exercises effective control over the computer department.

Techniques

Computer Steering Committee (CSC)

As has been mentioned before, the computer department performs a service by processing data for the users that had previously been done manually within the user area. There is always a great danger that the tail will wag the dog and departments will not get systems that they need but rather systems that the IS department think they need. It is therefore important that top management and users should be involved in determining the overall direction of the IS function and this is achieved through a CSC.

IS management control
IS management should exercise normal controls over information processing. Examples of these are:

- The initiation of a long-range systems plan which will provide a framework for management control and a standard by which performance can be measured.
- User charge-outs which will assist the IS department in determining its efficiency and effectiveness, while providing important feedback to the users in terms of the costs of their computer usage.
- Budgets.
- Data control and quality control to ensure that no data are lost or mishandled within the IS department.
- Staff evaluation.
- Monitoring and reviewing departmental activities.
- User department control.

Finally, apart from the data control and quality control performed by the IS department, user departments should also perform independent controls which are aimed at checking the functioning of the IS department. The payroll department could, for instance, check the processing done by the IS department by using run-to-run controls and run-generation numbers, and performing tests on data totals.

26.4 SYSTEMS DEVELOPMENT CONTROLS

In Module 3 we looked at some of the problems inherent in the systems development process and described some of the techniques which can be used to overcome these problems. In this section we do not intend to review the systems development life cycle in detail but rather to formalize the control objectives within the area and summarize the techniques needed to achieve these objectives.

26.4.1 System priorities

The first objective in the systems development area must be to ensure that the right systems are chosen for development. There has been a common failing in many organizations that the priority attached to systems development projects is in direct proportion to the amount of shouting done by the project sponsor.

Objective

Applications are converted to the computer only if it will produce greater benefits than other alternatives.

Techniques

Feasibility studies
All systems must be investigated for feasibility and cost-benefit.
Long-term planning
All development should fall within the framework of a long-term IS plan.
Steering committee

All development activity should be approved by a steering committee with user and management involvement.

26.4.2 Effective systems

A major criticism of computer applications is that they are delivered late, are over budget, and do not meet the requirements of the user.

Objective
To maximize the efficiency of the development process while generating effective systems.

Techniques
Project management
Project management techniques emphasize project definition and planning at the outset and a rigid cycle of monitoring and rescheduling the work throughout the project life cycle. The benefits are not only those of money and time. There is a tendency with late projects to rush the programming and implementation stages with obvious results: poor system and user testing, inadequate user education and insufficient documentation.
User involvement
Users must be involved in all stages of the project.
Standards
Rigid standards must be developed, published, and enforced in the areas of systems design, programming, testing and implementation. This should include the setting-up of a quality control function within the IS area.

26.4.3 Program maintenance

Another concern is that maintaining existing systems becomes a major overhead to the IS department, limiting its ability to concentrate on new application areas.

Objective
Systems that have become operational must be effectively maintained.

Techniques
Flexibility
Systems are designed to be flexible in order to accommodate possible modifications and enhancements.
Change control
User requests for changes are reviewed and authorized by senior IS staff in the light of current priorities and future development plans.
Program libraries
All operational programs are stored in program libraries to prevent unauthorized amendment.
Program testing
All changes must be fully tested and checked by the user prior to becoming operational.

26.5 OPERATIONAL CONTROLS

So far in this module we have looked at an area which could be termed *initial or set-up controls*. This includes controls which can be implemented to ensure a smooth change-over to computers from manual systems, techniques which can be used to structure the IS department, and methods by which new application software can be developed. However, the greatest area of concern within an IS department is that of control over the day-to-day functioning of the department and in particular the data centre itself. The techniques used to perform this function are normally termed *operations controls*.

26.5.1 Accidental errors

The operations area is highly susceptible to errors and scheduling problems, including as it does the scheduling function, the librarian function, the control function, and the computer room itself. Large volumes of repetitive work are performed in daily, weekly and monthly cycles and, unless these processes are carefully controlled, there is a danger that errors will creep in, with obvious implications to the organization as a whole.

Prior to setting our first control objective in the operational area we must first discuss the difference between *prevention* and *detection* of errors. The old saying 'prevention is always better than cure' is as relevant to computer controls as it is to other areas such as illness or tooth decay. And in a similar fashion, while one would attempt to safeguard the health of one's charge by implementing controls which will prevent a situation from occurring, one must recognize that it would be extremely costly to create a watertight defence against these dangers. Therefore one must always have the ability to detect that something has gone wrong and have a mechanism by which it can be repaired with the minimal loss to the organization.

Objective

To prevent and detect accidental errors.

Techniques

Application controls

Application controls (also referred to as *processing controls*) are those which are specific to a particular system or application. No two systems are identical and in the same way their control requirements will also differ. While processing controls form part of operations controls, we shall discuss them as a separate issue and in this section concentrate only on the controls that are relevant to all systems.

The control group

In large computer installations (especially those operating in the batch environment) the user does not involve himself in the processing of his work but rather hands it over to the IS department for processing. This data input, now detached from its sponsor, is at great risk in the turmoil of a busy data centre. It has to go through the process of data capture, input to the computer, error correction (if applicable), and finally dispatch back to the user. With different people being responsible for the data at different times and staff changing throughout a three-shift day, there is little possibility that the data will pass through the system unscathed.

This necessitates the creation of the data control group, individuals responsible for the user's data as they travel through the IS department. This is clerical group, separate from the operations and data capture sections, and is responsible for the following:

- Checking and logging in input from the user areas.
- Arranging data capture of the input.
- Scheduling and monitoring the processing of the data by the computer.
- Checking the output from the computer and correcting errors if applicable.
- Dispatching the final output to the user.

The control group will be discussed in more detail in the section on processing control and it will suffice here to say that they are the user's representatives in the IS area, ensuring that the data are handled correctly and on time and that any user problems and requests are always channelled through this function.

Librarian function

One of the main concerns within the operations area is that of preventing the possible loss of data once they have been created. Loss can be caused by the data being overwritten on some device or no record being kept of where the data were stored. In larger organizations a separate librarian function should exist. Library controls restrict access to programs, data files, and documentation. Thes controls are provided by a librarian function which consists of a combination of people, procedures and computer software. The library function serves two major purposes:

- It limits the use of programs, data files and documentation to authenticated users with authorized requests.
- It maintains the storage media used for files.

Some computer operating systems assist in this library control process by writing the expiry date onto the labels of the data files but most systems rely heavily on the librarian to perform this function. Most installations are continually fighting to make additional data storage areas available because the cost of storage is too high to support a large excess. The cost of an error in this area could be very great if a key master file is 'scratched' and there are problems in recovering from a backup.

Operating procedures

With the multiplicity of systems being run through the computer operations area, no one individual in the data capture, data control, or operations rooms could — or for that matter should — remember all the details for each system. It is therefore important that operations procedures should be developed for each new application and documentation made available to the relevant areas.

An example of such documentation is the so-called run manual, which contains a complete description of the program. The different sections of the run manual should consist of a description of the problem definition, the system, the program, operating instructions, relevant controls, and test procedure.

Over and above the standard operating procedures for all systems, the particular requirements for each application must be spelt out clearly in the procedural manuals. It is important that these procedures should not only be documented but that regular checks should be made to ensure that they are followed. Having stressed the need for operating procedures it is also important to note that where these procedures can be built into the system, such as in the job control language, they can reduce the possibility of manual error.

One example would be where a program can call for a particular tape by number during the processing cycle rather than providing the operator with a file name and hoping that he mounts the correct version.

Scheduling

Another important function of the control group is to schedule all computer operations in advance. The computer operators will then run the jobs in the sequence in which they have been scheduled. Advance scheduling ensures that the operators can plan their processing shifts more efficiently and that the priority of work in the key punch area can be controlled. Furthermore, the user has some idea of when his output will be ready.

Job scheduling is not normally related to the sequence of the input of data from the user departments but to the priority of the various output reports, the limitations of the computer hardware (if the computer is supporting an on-line network then certain programs can only be run at night because they would adversely affect the response time of the on-line users), and finally certain jobs must be scheduled to run before others, for example, master file maintenance programs prior to an up-date on that same master file.

Error logging

Errors found in normal processing, such as incorrect transactions or the absence of a record on the master file, should be picked up and corrected in the normal error correction cycle which will be discussed in the section on processing control. However, there are many errors which are at a more general level in that they may affect a particular application but they would not be recorded in the error report. We refer here to such problems as errors in hardware where the CPU or a peripheral device is malfunctioning. In a similar fashion a particular data file may have a damaged portion and data cannot be read into the program. Another possibility is that one of the programs in the system has an error, causing the program to stop with no obvious indication in the printout that a malfunction has occurred. Finally there is also the possibility that the operator has made an error and mounted a wrong tape or entered an incorrect parameter. Management must be aware of these problems for two reasons. First, these malfunctions may cause a problem in the application that was running at the time and the user may be unaware of this problem. Therefore there must be some record of what happened in order that any systems running at the time can be checked and possible problems followed up.

Secondly, if no record is made of problems, management will be unable to evaluate the performance of the computer operations area and in particular, where a problem is occurring frequently, take some follow-up action.

The errors can be logged in two ways. First, some more sophisticated operating systems have *job accounting packages* which monitor the processing of jobs. This log will assist in identifying program and machine malfunctions. A more summarized version of the systems log is normally printed out while the program is running and this is called the *console log*. This printout is normally used by the operator to monitor the activities of the computer but it also makes a useful hard copy review of the activities of the computer over a period of time.

In many instances the computer log is inadequate in reporting the problem, either because the computer hardware has itself malfunctioned or the program has seemingly processed without error but the operator is aware of a problem. In cases such as these a manual log of errors will ensure that all problems are recorded for later review and follow-up.

Restart procedures

Finally we look at the thorny problem of what to do when a system malfunction has occurred and the programs are required to be rerun. In many cases, particularly with on-line systems, the data will be in a partially updated form and it is critical that the files are restored to a corrected status before further processing is permitted. Normally each system has its own unique restarting procedures and these must be well documented and performed by the operators in the case of a failure. It is generally accepted that files are at their most vulnerable during systems 'crashes' and the follow-up recovery procedures.

26.5.2 Fraud

The proliferation of computers in the business environment has created expanded opportunities for criminal infiltration. The second major area of operations controls involves controls which are implemented to prevent and detect the intentional manipulation of applications commonly known as computer fraud, computer abuse, or computer crime.

Some of the controls in these areas have already been covered under organizational (people) controls and operational controls which are present to detect accidental errors.

Objective

To prevent or detect the fraudulent manipulation of data.

Techniques

Systems logs

Computer-generated and manual logs may assist in this area although they can obviously be manipulated. It is nevertheless important that records of the operations of data processing equipment (each job or run, the time it required, operator actions, and other relevant data) are listed. Techniques such as numbering the pages of the console log are not foolproof but can assist in highlighting intentional abuse of the system.

Access controls

A very important area of control in the computer centre is to limit access to unauthorized personnel. In the larger installations there has been a tendency in recent years to ensure that only the operators can gain access to the computer room, the librarian to the data files and authorized personnel to other sensitive areas such as the computer stationery store.

These access controls not only limit the possibilities of fraud but are also important for the smooth running of the installation. In the past programmers had a tendency to get involved in the activities of the computer room, bringing in their own 'rush' jobs and taking their output from the printer. This interference invariably led to scheduling problems within the computer room and the danger that output reports were inadvertently removed and mislaid.

Separation of duties

The first control is that of program libraries where even the programmers are not able to access the source code of various programs without the necessary authority. The system works as follows.

All programs are kept within a particular file called a *library* and no program can be accessed without a particular *password*. When a programmer is authorized to make a change to a program, the data control section makes a copy of the program available to the programmer by copying the source code to a particular testing library. The programmer changes the program and tests it, using the test library version only.

When the updated program has been fully tested and the user is satisfied that it is working correctly, the program is copied back to the production library by the data control section. Therefore no programmer is able to access programs which he has not been given authority to amend.

A second control is that operators should be unable to write programs. In many installations it is almost impossible to deny the operator access to the source code of programs and therefore it is important that they do not have the ability to manipulate the programs.

Another useful control is for the operators to be supervised and for no single individual to be allowed to work on their own in the computer room.

Finally, there is a tendency for people to be given duties that they are familiar with — for instance, one individual may be scheduled to produce the monthly statements because he is the only one who can line up the stationery on the printer correctly. This is an obvious control weakness and the operations manager should ensure that shifts are rotated so the same person is not responsible for the same applications on a monthly basis.

26.5.3 Physical security

We have discussed the prevention and detection of errors and fraud as our two major objectives in the area of operational controls. There is, however, a third major category of controls in the operations area, that of *physical security*. Physical security encompasses all the controls to provide against destruction of records or equipment caused by a variety of physical, mechanical, or environmental events and to ensure that in the event of a minor or major catastrophe the IS operation can continue with the minimum of inconvenience.

Objective

To provide security against the destruction of records and equipment and to ensure the continuous operation of the IS function.

Techniques

Clean environment

The first physical security consideration is that the computer should be enclosed in a sterile environment so that sensitive hardware and data files cannot be affected by dust, smoke, and radical differences in temperature or humidity. The extent to which these controls are important depends on the type of installation.

With the smaller microcomputers and even minicomputers the hardware tends to be more robust. The peripherals and, in particular, the secondary storage devices are designed to work in normal office conditions. Therefore the major consideration is that the area is relatively dust free and there is no electrical interference close to the machine.

The more sophisticated mainframe computers should always be housed in special facilities for the following reasons:

- The many cables that run between the devices tend to get in the way and so false floors with the cable running underneath them are an obvious convenience.
- The temperature must be carefully controlled using air-conditioning units because the surfaces of the storage devices are prone to normal expansion and contraction and data written at one temperature may be inaccessible at another.
- The level of humidity in the air can cause static to build up in the environment, which again can cause malfunctioning in the computer. Most air-conditioning plants therefore have the added feature of being able to control the humidity levels in the computer room.
- The computer room is normally sealed to prevent dust and smoke from entering and all air drawn into the computer room is filtered. As a further precaution, activities such as smoking, eating and drinking are not allowed within this enclosed area.

Fire equipment

With the mass of electrical equipment condensed into a small area there is always a danger of fire. Most computer facilities have two levels of fire control equipment, the first to detect possible fires and the second to assist in fighting them.

Fire detection normally takes the form of smoke detectors which are placed at strategic points in the roof around the computer installation. In the event of smoke entering one of these detectors a warning siren is set off and after an appropriate interval (normally sufficient for employees to leave the computer area) the fire-fighting equipment is brought into play.

Most installations have fire extinguishers fitted into the ceiling of the computer room and when they are triggered off the room is filled with an inert gas which, it is hoped, will extinguish the flames. This process is not without its problems. First, the most effective fire-fighting gases tend to be poisonous and in the event of an explosion, or an injury to one of the operating staff, there is a possibility that someone could die, not from the flames but from suffocation in the computer room. A second problem is that certain gases actually damage the computer itself, either because they cool the working parts too quickly or in some cases leave a thin film on the working areas of the machine which can later cause malfunctions. There are, however, a number of gases available which minimize the danger to man and machine.

Other fire precautions that can be taken are to site the installation away from possible fire hazards, to install separate emergency shut-off switches to control electrical power to the computer system and air conditioning fans, to ensure that the materials used in the computer room are as fire-resistant as possible, and to keep highly inflammable materials such as computer stationery as far away from the machine room as conveniently possible.

Disaster plan

Another control concerning physical security is the concept of the disaster plan — a master strategy which can be exercised in the event of a major catastrophe in the computer room area. It is probably true to say that not many organizations have a thorough, well-tested plan which will enable them to continue processing in the event of their computer installation being destroyed by unforeseen disaster such as fire, flood or earthquake. The reason is simple. Setting up such a master plan is costly and, in order for it to have some chance of actually working, it has to encompass every possible problem that might occur and be continually updated to accommodate the day-to-day changes in the operating environment of the computer centre. If the disaster plan could not be implemented because some minor piece of operating software was not available during the recovery then the plan would have been established in vain.

The plan must have the following ingredients:

- A back-up facility compatible to the installation's hardware configuration.
- Off-site storage of all software programs (system and applications) and up-to-date copies of all strategic data files.
- Copies of all programming, systems and user documentation also to be kept off site.

So far this list is relatively straightforward but let us look at some of the problems.

- What effects on the disaster plan will be caused by the everyday changes to the operating environment and the computer applications?
- What are the database and data communications implications of having to switch to another hardware environment which may be compatible in terms of programming but may not have the same storage and communications configuration?
- What if key personnel required for the switch-over have retired, resigned, are on leave or have even been incapacitated during the crisis?

Testing entails simulating a disaster and attempting to reconstruct the information processing facility at the back-up site without recourse to hardware, software or documentation stored at the central site. This dummy run is used to pick up problems and inconsistencies in the disaster plan while training the staff in the event of such an emergency. Some organizations have been known to stage impromptu tests of the disaster plan by locking out their employees on arrival at work on a predetermined day.

Insurance

Most organizations have realized that covering themselves for the loss of the computer hardware and physical damage to the installation is inadequate. The real costs are in trying to recreate their data and the loss of company revenue during the time that their IS installation is out of action. There are specialized insurance policies for computer installations and you can insure yourself against physical loss, staff default, defections, recovery costs and loss of profits. The major problem in this area is that as the cover shifts to things intangible such as the value of information, so it becomes more difficult to calculate insurance charges and estimate the damage.

Hardware duplication

Most IS managers recognize that various items of equipment have different levels of reliability and are more-or-less strategic to the overall performance of the installation. For example, a CPU may be as reliable in terms of the number of times it fails in a single year as a disk drive. If a disk drive gives problems the operator can probably take it off-line and continue processing with a slightly reduced storage capacity until it has been repaired. However, a computer cannot function without a CPU. If it is imperative that the facility is available to the user at all times, it may be mandatory for the organization to have a back-up CPU. Other equipment which is commonly found in strategic IS installations is a back-up power supply in the event of power failure, split air-conditioning units so that if one malfunctions the other will be able to maintain a constant temperature for a limited period, and multiple printers.

26.6 APPLICATION CONTROLS

There is a processing cycle for every IS application, starting with transaction origination and passing through the data transcription process to the computer operations area and finally back to the user. The general controls that we have discussed till now will, it is hoped, ensure that the climate in which every application runs is favourable. However, some controls must be tailored to the particular application and its processing cycle. These controls have three primary objectives:

- To ensure that only authorized data are processed.
- To ensure the accuracy and completeness of the data.
- To provide an audit trail so that any queries can be adequately traced through the system.

In this section, rather than deal with the particular objectives one by one, we shall follow the processing cycle from the user to the computer and back, looking at the various control points in the system and the various techniques that can be used at these points to achieve our objectives.

26.6.1 User input controls

Input close to source

First, the user records the initial transaction. It is important that the transaction is entered into the computer as close to the source of the transaction as possible. The more steps there are between the source of the transaction and its ultimate input into the computer, the greater the chance of errors creeping into the system.

Forms design

A second technique is to ensure that the input forms or, in the case of direct input, the terminal screens are well designed for efficient error-free entry by the operator.

Batching

Where the data has to be transmitted or dispatched for remote processing the user must record the volume of transactions, so that if any input is mislaid or incorrectly captured the problem can be detected.

A common control technique used to ensure that transactions are not mislaid prior to their input into the computer is called *batching*. See Chapter 12 for a description of this technique.

26.6.2 Data control — input controls

The next point in the processing cycle is that at which the data are passed to the data control section for transcription and input into the computer. The first step in this process is to log the input into the data control section. The log book traces the progress of each batch through the IS cycle to ensure that the data are processed correctly and any queries on the status of a particular batch can be answered.

When each batch is accepted the data control clerk normally checks the input forms for an authorizing signature if this is required, and a cursory look to determine whether the forms have been filled in correctly and that the number of batches and transactions seems correct. Once the data have been accepted by the data control section they are scheduled for data capture according to the priority of the particular application and the work load of the data capture section.

When the data are dispatched to the data preparations area for capture there are a number of controls which can be implemented to assist in this area. The first is in the design of the input forms. The speed and accuracy of the data capture operator is to a large extent dependent on the design of the input document.

The second technique which can be used is verification of the input to ensure that any errors made by the data preparation clerks can be identified before the data is presented to the computer. In the less sophisticated machines verification requires that a second operator rekey the data but more recent equipment is microprocessor based. This permits the capture device to verify fields with check digits and other checks such as numeric data and valid dates. A final control in this area is to ensure that the capture devices are maintained on a regular basis.

The data are now transferred back to the data control section where the scheduler arranges for a run of that particular application.

26.6.3 Data control — application controls

All computer systems begin with a program which validates the input prior to accepting it into the system. This process involves the *error correction* cycle. Chapter 17.4 — Controls design — describes the error correction cycle in detail, and gives a description of the appropriate processing controls such as run-to-run controls, run-generation numbers and control reports. All of this should be present in the system and should be used correctly.

26.6.4 Data control — output controls

Once the computer has processed all input data and the necessary validation and update reports have been printed, the data control group is in a position to reconcile the total of the transactions to the total of the outputs. Furthermore, they must check the output reports to verify that there are no obvious problems. If there are no corrections to be made by the data control group, the output can now be distributed to the user. Formal distribution procedures should always be present and a schedule of anticipated output preparation times should be published for the benefit of the user. Considering the seeming simplicity of an exercise to distribute paper from one area to a number of others, it is surprising how often computer reports seem to vanish into thin air or are dispatched to the incorrect area.

26.6.5 User output controls

Once the computer output has been dispatched to the user, his first duty is to conduct his own input-output reconciliation. This entails ensuring that all transactions have been processed and that the correct master files were used.

Finally the documents must be stored. The period depends on the legal retention cycle of the document. Some documents are required to be kept for a period of seven years but in the main the retention cycles are not this long. However, in a period of this magnitude vast numbers of documents can be processed and it is important that the documents are clearly marked and stored where they can be easily referenced.

26.7 DOCUMENTATION CONTROLS

We have discussed the importance of documentation in the module on systems development and prior to setting any objectives and techniques to achieve them we must first review why we have documentation and some of the problems in generating it and keeping it up to date. The major reasons for documentation are:

- to provide continuity within an IS environment by serving as a narrative of the system;
- to provide communication in the systems development life cycle between analysts, designers, programmers and users;
- to serve as a basis for assessment and review of systems for internal and external auditors;
- to formalize standards and controls in order to provide a basis against which systems can be measured, and finally

- to provide a basis for education, training and reference for clerical staff who use the system.

There are, however, a number of problems in generating even the minimum documentation which is to meet the above requirements. Such problems include:

- In the face of tight implementation schedules documentation is often left until 'time becomes available' and is rushed or incomplete.
- IS personnel often find the creation of documentation boring and try to avoid it wherever possible.
- Detailed documentation obviously becomes an overhead to the organization in the sense that to be of any value it must be updated with every change in the system.
- Finally there is a tendency for users of documentation to ignore their reference manuals and either to learn by their mistakes or to ask others more proficient in the system for their assistance.

26.7.1 Enforce documentation standards

Having looked at the pros and cons of documentation, let us start by making the assumption that documentation is a necessary evil.

Objective

Adequate documentation must exist for all systems and must be prepared and reviewed according to predetermined standards.

Techniques

Documentation standards

Publish a comprehensive document about documentation, often referred to as the documentation standards manual. This must detail clearly the minimum requirements for documentation in all of the required areas — statement of requirements, systems specification, program documentation, operating and library procedures, key-punching instructions, control requirements and user procedures. The standards manual must detail how the documentation is to be generated and what areas it must cover.

Phased preparation

A second technique in this area is to recognize that documentation should not be something which is created at the end of a project. At each stage the documentation should be presented and reviewed prior to moving onto the next milestone. In order to ensure that these standards are met the organization should have formal documentation reviews and sign-offs.

Documentation updates

Finally, because of the danger of documentation becoming outdated, all changes in the system must be reflected in the documentation and these procedures reviewed to ensure that they are taking place.

26.7.2 Documentation generation

In our first objective we looked at techniques which can be used to ensure the existence and the quality of the documentation but we have done nothing to make the creation and use of this documentation more palatable. Techniques which can be used in this area include:

- dropping some of the less necessary documentation such as program specifications and documenting the programs themselves so that they can be understood by non-programmers;
- using software packages such as data dictionaries which can not only keep a record of the file structures for the programs in the system but can also create the necessary documentation about the organization's data for those who require it.

In the area of user documentation there are two possibilities. First, one can minimize the need for user documentation by developing more user-friendly systems with menu option screens to lead the user through the system and a 'help' facility if problems occur. Secondly, review of the documentation during the user training sessions will increase the user's ability to understand and access the reference material.

With the advent of word processors the update of written material is now much simpler and there is a much smaller overhead attached to keeping large reference manuals up to date.

In many organizations today there is a recognition that documentation is a task not liked or efficiently performed by IS personnel. In many cases specialized documentation clerks are assigned to project groups with the responsibility of generating the required documentation at the various stages of the project.

REVIEW QUESTIONS

1. How can management ensure that they will acquire the most suitable computer equipment for their purpose?
2. Discuss the principle known as 'separation of duties'.
3. Name six controls that IS management should exercise over information processing.
4. How can one ensure that applications are computerized only when this produces greater benefits than other alternatives?
5. Name four ways in which existing operational systems can be effectively maintained.
6. How can accidental errors be prevented?
7. Briefly discuss three ways in which fraudulent manipulation of data can be prevented or detected.
8. Define 'physical security'.
9. Processing controls have three primary objectives. Name these objectives.
10. Give five reasons why an IS department should have adequate documentation.

CHAPTER 27 Data communication controls

27.1 INTRODUCTION

Data communication controls (or on-line controls, as they are sometimes called) are those that are concerned with the integrity of data being transmitted from remote locations. Two important reasons why they differ from those in the batch environment are, first, that we use the established telecommunications network to transmit data and therefore the organization has no control over this and, secondly, most on-line systems process in real-time mode. Because of the need for up-to-date information, transactions are not held back to be updated in batch mode since each transaction goes through the full validation, correction and update cycle as it enters the system. While real-time systems offer the user the ability to access up-to-date information, there are a number of major control implications.

27.2 RELIABILITY

The first area of concern in on-line systems is that as the network now encompasses a wide geographical area with a large number of remote peripheral devices, a communications network that was designed originally for voice communications, and a great number of often unsophisticated users. It is highly unlikely that these systems can match the reliability of the batch-processing environment.

Objective

To make the system as reliable as possible.

27.3 SECURITY

The second major danger of on-line networks is the loss of security regarding the organization's information. It is more difficult to limit physical access to remote peripherals than it is to limit access to the computer area and, furthermore, even if no unauthorized individuals could access the system via the remote terminals, there is always the danger that access could be made between the terminal and the computer.

Objective

To ensure that there is sufficient security of information at all points in the network.

27.4 RECOVERY

The area which is a major concern in all computer networks is that of system recovery. If there is a hardware or software malfunction during the running of a *batch* system, the files are restored to their status prior to the beginning of the job and the necessary programs are rerun. Unfortunately on-line systems do not work this way in that they are usually started at the beginning of the working day and update the necessary files as transactions come in. Let us look at some of the problems.

A remote terminal user enters data on the screen and sends it down the line to the main computer. The computer does not acknowledge the transmission, indicating that there is a malfunction in the system. Where is the problem? Has the terminal broken down, is the data communications line malfunctioning or is there a fault in the main computer? Even more important, did the last transmission sent by the user manage to update the necessary files just prior to the malfunction; was it currently updating the files when the system came down, or did the computer come down prior to the transaction's being received? Complicate the situation further by introducing the possibility that 500 to 1000 remote users could all be working on the system at the same time, and one has some idea of the problem.

Objective

To ensure there is no loss of data in the event of a system failure and to provide alternative manual facilities during failures.

27.5 TECHNIQUES

When studying data communication controls it is easiest to discuss the control techniques according to their location — the computer room, the communications links, or the remote terminals. Let us first look at the terminals in the remote areas.

27.5.1 Terminal controls

Reliability

At the remote terminals there are two techniques which can be used to increase the reliability of the service. First, the system should have been designed and programmed in such a way that it can be easily understood and used by the remote operators. Secondly, these operators should have been given sufficient training and have access to reference documentation so that they are competent to carry out their duties.

Security of information

We can limit physical access to terminals by putting them in rooms which can be locked or by locking the terminals themselves. Access can also be limited by the use of software controls and in particular where the user has to identify himself by the use of passwords. The advantage of software access controls as opposed to hardware access controls is that they can be very flexible, having many levels of password access according to the user's information needs.

Recovery procedures

The first requirement is that the remote user is able to continue working even though the system is no longer available to him. This normally means that manual procedures must be set up and in most cases transactions that have been processed while the system was down will have to be entered once the facility has returned to normal.

When the computer service has been restored the remote user should be assisted in restarting the dialogue. It is quite likely that transmission was lost during the processing of a customer or transaction and the operator must be given some indication of what was received by the computer and what was lost and will have to be re-entered. This is normally achieved by the computer sending each remote terminal the details of the last transaction which the computer received and processed prior to the service's being interrupted. Knowing the point at which the computer malfunctioned, the user is now able to re-enter any lost transactions.

27.5.2 Communication link controls

With reference to controls on the communication link between the terminals and the computer itself there are a number of techniques which can be implemented to ensure that our three objectives are met.

Reliability

To ensure the maintenance of a reliable service, each network should be overseen by a communications technician, often termed a *network controller* or *network manager*. In every network there are a multiplicity of things that can go wrong and in many cases it is very difficult to isolate the cause of the problem. When an operator is unable to get a response from the terminal it could be because the terminal is malfunctioning, because the data communications devices such as modems and multiplexors have problems, the telephone line used for the connection may be out of order or there may be a hardware malfunction at the computer centre.

Furthermore, in a large network there are likely to be a number of concurrent problems, some of which may affect only single users while others may black out entire areas. The key is to co-ordinate the reporting of malfunctions and the tracing and correction of faults relating to the communications network within a single group called *network control*.

A second consideration which has a major bearing on the reliability of any on-line service is the quality of the telecommunication link. While in many instances users are at the mercy of Telkom with regard to the installation and repairs to data communications facilities, there are ways of increasing the reliability of a network.

One example is the difference between dial-up facilities and leased line. In areas where the line quality is poor, dial-up communications can be very troublesome because data transfer is achieved using the normal voice communication lines. One way of counteracting this problem is to lease a line from Telkom, who will attempt to ensure that a clean line is reserved for your transmissions. However, this alternative may not be particularly palatable if the volume of data transmissions does not justify the leasing of a line.

Security of information

A common technique used to prevent unauthorized access to data while it is being transmitted is to scramble the data at the remote terminal and transmit it in its garbled form only to be unscrambled when it reaches the computer or vice versa. This scrambling is called *encryption* and can be likened to the concept of secret codes that governments use when transmitting top secret messages around the world.

Recovery procedures

One technique to assist in this area is for communications channels to be duplicated or an alternative routing to be available in the event of a line malfunction. A major advantage of the South African Post Office Network (SAPONET) is that if there is a break in communications between any two major centres, data is automatically rerouted via other centres. For instance, if the Cape Town to Johannesburg link were inoperative, data could be transferred from Johannesburg to Port Elizabeth and from Port Elizabeth to Cape Town and vice versa.

27.5.3 Computer centre controls

Finally, we must look at the control techniques which can be implemented in the computer centre itself to ensure the reliability, security and recovery of on-line systems.

Reliability

One consideration is the duplication of critical hardware devices. Central processing units are highly complex pieces of equipment and may be prone to failure. Where an on-line network must remain in service at all times it may be necessary to duplicate the CPUs so that when one is inoperative the other can support the network. Of interest is the fact that while data communications devices also perform an essential function, they tend to be simple and relatively trouble free. Therefore there is often little benefit derived from their duplication.

A second major aspect of on-line system reliability is that of software testing and maintenance. On-line programs are complex and therefore difficult to maintain. Because of the problems that can occur when a program malfunctions, it is imperative that strict program testing be carried out prior to on-line programs becoming operational.

Furthermore, the operational environment is so complex in terms of multiple concurrent users, database file access methods, and teleprocessing monitor performance that no-one can really assess whether response times obtained from the machine are good or indifferent. Today there are a number of software packages which have been developed specifically to assist in the tuning of complex on-line systems.

Finally there is the danger that the computer operators have inadequate skills to handle this sophisticated environment. Techniques to alleviate this problem include the introduction of operator training courses, building more 'intelligence' into the system's software and the structuring of operator shifts into groups which include all the necessary skills.

Security of information

First, the computer can monitor all data transmission to and from remote locations, including attempts to log onto the system. Details of all transactions or only those of a sensitive nature can be reported and even analysed by the computer prior to presentation to management.

A second area where the computer can help is in its ability to limit access to programs and files. This is best achieved through the use of passwords.

Finally, in much the same way as data files are encrypted for transmission over data communications channels, sensitive files can also be scrambled prior to storage on disk and tape.

Recovery procedures

The first important ingredient when maintaining an on-line system is to ensure that all files are regularly backed up. This ensures that if there is a major problem and files are damaged or corrupted, only a limited amount of work will be required to bring them back to their current status.

Another technique is to keep a log of all transactions coming into the system which may affect the status of the files (updates) together with a copy of the files prior to the day's processing. The computer now has all the data required to recreate the current status of files in the event of a system malfunction. The only problem with recovering data in this manner is that if the time between the last back-up and the system failure is considerable, the time required to recover the system may be measured in hours rather than minutes. A quicker, though not always more successful, way of recovering from failure is for the computer to attempt to reverse the final partially completed updates from the files.

REVIEW QUESTIONS

1. Why do on-line controls differ from those in a batch processing environment?
2. Real-time systems offer the user the ability to access up-to-date information. There are, however, a number of major control applications. Name, and briefly discuss three of these implications.
3. Discuss the control techniques which can be implemented in the computer centre to ensure the reliability, security, and recovery of on-line systems.

CHAPTER 28 Service bureau controls

28.1 INTRODUCTION

In Module 4 we looked at organizations which do not have their own in-house computer and send data away to a *service bureau* for processing. We also discussed some of the advantages and disadvantages of using service bureaux. In this chapter we shall try to formalize these concerns into major control objectives and emphasize the techniques which can be implemented.

28.2 BUREAU JUSTIFICATION

The first concern is the same as if the organization were embarking on acquiring a machine in-house.

Objective

The use of a service bureau must be the best solution to our information processing problems and we must select the correct installation to do our processing.

Techniques

First we must form a steering committee made up of management, IS expertise (if there is any in-house, or alternatively a computer consultant) and aware users. This committee will look at the alternative strategies which can be taken to computerize the organization and make recommendations to top management. They must initiate a formal investigation into the computer needs of the organization and the alternative strategies to achieve these ends. If the recommendations from this feasibility study indicate that a service bureau is the best alternative the next step is to select a suitable bureau. We have discussed bureau selection previously and this investigation can be approached on much the same lines as in a formal hardware selection project.

28.3 ORGANIZATIONAL IMPLICATIONS

Once a bureau has been selected, the next concern is that there are adequate organizational controls. Obviously the user function will remain in-house and just as obviously the computer operations function will now be based at the bureau. However, the data control function is more complex because while there is a need for a user representative at the bureau to handle the incoming data and schedule the customer's work, some of the authorization for running various jobs must come from the customer organization. If this function is passed to the user there is a danger that these additional duties will conflict with our principles of the separation of duties.

Objective

To ensure that the same separation of duties exists under a service bureau environment as can be set up in-house.

Techniques

Liaison personnel

The best solution is to appoint an IS representative in the customer organization who accepts all the input from the various users, passes it to the service bureau, and authorizes the various jobs to be run at the appointed time. One major advantage of having a single representative in each organization through which all communication is passed, is that these individuals will be aware of the current status of all applications and so can become more quickly aware when a problem arises.

28.4 PROCESSING PROCEDURES

Objective

Adequate arrangements are made concerning the processing of the applications, both in-house and at the bureau.

Techniques

Allocate processing duties

Having set up adequate organizational arrangements, the next step is to formalize the processing procedures. Who does what and when in any computer system often depends on how much involvement (in terms of functions such as data capture) the client wishes to have and, secondly, on the type of system (on-line or batch). It is important at the outset of any new application to formalize these responsibilities. This can best be done by documenting all procedural details and training the representatives in their various functions.

These procedures should include the user responsibilities for batching and reconciling computer input, how and where the data are to be captured, error correction procedures, timing of validation and update runs, and file back-up and security arrangements. Systems development procedures should also be formalized and procedures to control the program design, coding and testing, together with details about authorization for program amendments and maintenance, should also be included.

28.5 SECURITY AND CONFIDENTIALITY

Objective

To ensure that adequate controls exist at the bureau to safeguard the organization's data.

Techniques

Level of risk

On the control side, the concept of sending the organization's data to another physical location which is not under the control of the organization seems to suggest there will be a loss of security and confidentiality of the organization's data. While this must be a concern to every organization using service bureaux, the risks are normally not as great as they would at first appear.

First there is always this risk within one's own organization in the IS department and the danger is now avoided. Auditors have frequently concluded that the use of service bureaux leads to improved internal control because of the arm's-length relationship that exists between the employees of the user (who are responsible for the accurate preparation of the data) and the employees of the service bureau (who are responsible for the processing of the data). Secondly, computer bureaux are very concerned that their clients' data are as secure as possible. Not only are they liable to litigation in the event of a loss of data or breach of confidentiality, but the adverse publicity that could be caused by such an incident may well be very detrimental to the entire organization's customer base.

A new problem in this area, however, exists because of the need to transport data and information between the two locations and most bureaux have a formal pick-up and return arrangement by messenger with standard log books documenting the various movements.

Third party audits

Finally, every organization (together with its auditors) would like to satisfy itself that adequate security is in force at the service bureau. This can be achieved by the auditor visiting the bureau and evaluating the controls *in situ*. This can be an expensive process and time-consuming for the bureaux as each client's representative tramps through the organization asking the same questions again and again. One alternative currently being used in the United States is the concept of a *third party audit*. Here an independent auditing firm makes a thorough investigation of the service bureau controls and publishes a detailed evaluation.

28.6 BUREAU BILLINGS

Objective

To ensure that all bureau invoices are checked for validity prior to payment.

Techniques

Invoice/processing log reconciliation

One final major concern when using a service bureau is that the charges billed to the client for services rendered are a correct reflection of the actual processing performed. Often the customer's statement is generated at least in part from a job accounting package which runs on the computer and monitors the various resources used during the charge-out period. As with most in-house computer charge-out systems, there is a danger that the client may be charged for time incorrectly because of reruns due to operator error or failures in the service bureau hardware. The client must therefore keep a manual log of all processing performed during the period and reconcile this listing with the service bureau billing in order to verify that no additional charges have been included.

REVIEW QUESTIONS

1. How can management ensure that acquiring the services of a service bureau is the best information processing alternative?
2. Is the same separation of duties necessary under a service bureau environment as can be set up in-house? Motivate your answer.
3. List the risks involved in making use of the services of a service bureau.

CHAPTER 29 Small business computer (SBC) controls

29.1 INTRODUCTION

The owners of small businesses are prone to look on computer controls as an unnecessary, time-consuming nuisance. Although most small businesses do not need elaborate financial reporting systems, they still need a functional accounting system with sound controls to provide correct, reliable information for internal decision-makers and external parties.

There are a number of unique control concepts relating specifically to the smaller computers, the micro and the minicomputers. The first is that these machines emphasize ease of use and accessibility. In doing so they often reduce the security of the system.

A second problem in the SBCs are normally found in small organizations and as a result the separation of functions may not be practical or possible.

Finally, it is unlikely that there will be any in-house programming expertise. This will provide security in terms of the unlikelihood of unauthorized program amendments. However, the lack of expertise can create operational problems, particularly when programs malfunction.

In the main, while the computer control objectives for small machines should be no different from those of their large counterparts, this smallness can lead to a number of control weaknesses and these will be discussed in the next few pages.

29.2 SBC CONTROL TECHNIQUES

Objective

To ensure that there is the same level of control and security as in the larger computer systems.

29.2.1 Console log

The first major difference between large and small machines is that the SBCs tend to have no hard copy console log. This means that there is no computer-generated summary of the machine's processing activities. Furthermore, there is unlikely to be a printer available to the CPU and therefore console information generated would have to be stored for later printing. Here we encounter a second problem as small machines often have major limitations in terms of disk space and in the microcomputers, in particular, there is unlikely to be a permanently resident floppy disk to store this systems file. If, however, the existence of a console log is regarded as essential, software would have to be developed to maintain the necessary systems file.

29.2.2 Program access

Few of the smaller systems have features which limit access to programs; furthermore, they tend to be in languages which make them easy to write and amend. The first step to counteract this obvious weakness is to remove all translating programs, such as compilers, and all source programs from the operational systems disks.

A second very effective — if sometimes costly — control is to ensure that no in-house programming is performed and that all software is either purchased as packaged systems or tendered out to software houses.

Finally, one can restrict access to programming documentation.

While it is difficult to prevent people from accessing the operational versions of the programs, they can be audited for changes by taking a computerized hash total of all the statements in the program and making spot checks to ensure that unauthorized modifications are not being made.

29.2.3 System accessibility and user friendliness

The next weakness is that small systems tend to be very accessible and easy to use. One possibility is to limit physical access to the machine and its terminals. However, most small machines do not require a controlled environment and are often found in an open-plan office. Limiting access under these circumstances is obviously more difficult and is normally achieved via the software with user passwords.

29.2.4 Hardware checks

When data are written out to disk and tape, the more sophisticated devices read them back as they are written to verify that the characters have been correctly stored. Many of the cheaper and simpler devices do not provide these checks and so there is a greater danger of data being corrupted during the processing cycle. There are a number of ways of handling this problem.

First, separate verification steps can be run where a file is matched against its copy to ensure that no data have been lost.

Secondly, hash totals can be kept of all important fields on a file and whenever it is copied the accumulation of these fields and a cross check with a control record will ensure that all the data is present on the file.

A third method is to keep adequate back-ups of all files. There is always a danger that only the last few versions of a file are kept and, while this would seem logical at first, many problems with files are detected only after a number of cycles have been completed. Often in systems where there is a short cycle such as a daily transaction run it is common for the last uncorrupted version of the file to have been overwritten prior to the error being detected. One easy way to ensure that it is always possible to go back prior to any problem is to keep a number of back-ups from the daily cycle, a few end-of-week versions and a number of month-end and even possibly year-end files. Going back a long time in the processing cycle and trying to recreate the current status is obviously a very time-consuming process. However, in many cases there is no alternative. One very expensive and time-consuming technique which can be used to 'back-up' critical master files is to dump their contents onto paper. The main advantage of this technique is to enable the organization to limp along in 'manual' mode until the necessary computer files have been recreated.

Computer files are often corrupted through hardware and software failures and weak or non-existent recovery procedures. If the checks are there and file problems can be detected when they happen there is likely to be less of a problem later.

29.2.5 Supplier support

One major criticism of the small machine environment is that the support and expertise provided by the computer suppliers is either weak or non-existent. It is therefore important to verify the reputation of the vendor organizations prior to entering into negotiations with them.

Secondly, there is no guarantee that a particular software package will include sound controls. It is therefore important to ensure that a software package to be obtained does, in fact, include controls such as:

- Comprehensible user manuals and training guides (in the area of customized software, demand comprehensive systems specifications, and with prewritten software, ensure that adequate systems documentation and user documentation are available).
- Suitable input, processing, and output controls.
- Acceptable audit trails.
- The ability to support computer security such as the preparation of backup files and recovery procedures.

Thirdly, prior to accepting both hardware and software ensure that it has been adequately tested. Finally, ensure that everything has been considered and that there are no loose ends to be tied up. One way of formalizing this process is to negotiate tight contracts for hardware, maintenance, software packages, tailor-made programs and software maintenance.

29.2.6 IS organization

The final area of weakness in the small machine environment is that there is no formal IS section and the computer is often operated by low-level clerical staff with little or no IS training. Furthermore, there is no formal IS management function and the responsibility for the installation often falls to the chief accountant. Finally the principle of separation of duties falls away as each user may be responsible for everything relating to his particular system.

A certain amount of job separation can be achieved if the programming function remains out-of-house. The use of software houses and consultants will assist in the problem of unauthorized changes to the programs and these organizations can also be used to perform periodic audits and reviews of the installation.

Ensure that the applications are as watertight as possible, in terms of both access to the systems and built-in controls which prevent invalid and unauthorized transactions from being processed.

Provide careful management supervision of the IS function and ensure that there is adequate job rotation of people from the various user areas.

REVIEW QUESTIONS

1. In small organizations the use of a SBC can lead to a number of control weaknesses. How can these weaknesses be overcome?

2. Many small business computers do not provide all the necessary hardware checks. How can this problem be overcome?

CHAPTER 30 Implementation of a control policy

30.1 INTRODUCTION

So far in this module we have looked at the importance of controls in a computer environment; we have attempted to set objectives for what each control should achieve in its particular area, and, finally, we have looked at some of the techniques that could assist in reaching these objectives. However, every organization is different, not only in terms of the computer applications in operation, but also with regard to its organizational structure, and the management style. These differences point to one obvious conclusion: no set of standard control objectives or techniques can be developed to fit the needs of organizations in general. Each company must examine its computer function, determine the particular problem areas and develop a unique control policy to fit its needs.

30.2 COST-BENEFIT EVALUATION

One consideration which must be taken into account is that every control implemented represents an overhead. To take the situation to its ludicrous extremes, an installation can have no controls, and both the staff and the computer itself would be able to perform their duties without the additional overhead imposed by the various checks. Whether the total throughput of work in this environment would be greater than in a controlled one, would be debatable as jobs may have to be rerun as a result of problems experienced. Whatever the level of productivity within this environment, there is one thing that would be relatively certain: management would not be able to place much reliance on the output from the system because most errors would remain undetected.

The reverse of this situation would be where management has attempted to implement all the possible controls available to them to such intensity that they have maximized their ability to detect and prevent errors in the system. Unfortunately in this environment both the people and the computer will be bogged down by so many control activities that the actual work performed by the company would be reduced to a trickle. So we have the two extremes, no controls or all controls, and it should be obvious to the reader that there is little justification for either situation.

The solution is to find a level of control which will ensure that your system is safe and sound, that the controls you have placed on the system are not having a choking effect on the throughput of the organization, and that the costs of the controls are not out of proportion to the loss that would be incurred if a disruption occurred.

Cerullo and Shelton, in their article *Quantitative Evaluation*, put forward a system by which the level of control can be determined by cost-benefit analysis, using the following steps:

- Determine specific areas to be controlled.
- Identify the threats to the organization.
- Rank these threats in order of likelihood of occurrence.
- Determine the expected loss from these threats.
- Determine the control techniques which can be used to minimize each threat.
- Rank the techniques in order of their effectiveness.
- Calculate the costs of each counter-measure.
- Attempt to determine the probability of failure if each technique was implemented.

- Develop a model using the optimum mix of controls and using various combinations of techniques to try to maximize the control effectiveness while minimizing the total cost of the controls.
- Test, implement, and document your findings.
- Conduct a post-implementation review of the controls to evaluate their effectiveness.

As is obvious from this checklist, attempting to justify the cost of a control policy is unlikely to be simple or, for that matter, even particularly accurate. However, going through this process will enable the organization to gain a better understanding of the various threats which face it and the consequential losses it may well have to bear.

In the same article the authors confirmed that Pareto's 80 : 20 law works just as well for control and security counter-measures as it does for many other areas in the computer environment. Here they proved that as control counter-measures were put into effect, the first 80 % effectiveness can be achieved at a total investment of 20 %. As more money is spent on control and security less benefit is derived and, in fact, an additional 80 % investment will produce only a further 20 % control effectiveness. If one is able to identify where one's particular organization is on the curve, one can appreciate the diminishing cost-effectiveness of further control investment.

30.3 THE TOTAL CONTROL POLICY

Leonard Fine, a Johannesburg computer consultant specializing in computer controls and security, has published many articles on this topic and in particular on his theory of a *total control policy*. Rather than concentrate on particular control objectives and techniques he advocates that the main problem in the area of computer controls is at management level, where the topic is given little emphasis and no long-term commitment.

In a lecture which Mr Fine gave at the University of Cape Town he put forward the following very relevant points which we should like to summarize.

Every organization must have a formal security policy which must encompass the current requirements of the business while being tailored to fit the long-term goals of the organization.

Secondly, the determination of what controls should be used must be formally evaluated by first determining the risk and then the cost of the controls which may minimize the risk.

The next point which he emphasized was that there must be a concept of total control. By this he meant that it is stupid to lock up your house, burglar-bar your windows and put in a special burglar alarm if you leave your front door open. In the same way, controls are only as strong as their weakest link and good controls in the operational and organizational areas would be nullified by poor controls in the systems development function. This he depicted with a diagram of a total security arch supported by a number of pillars, each one an area of concern. Weakness in any one of the pillars puts the entire structure at risk.

An additional concern that was put forward was that in a normal organization there is no one person who is particularly responsible for, or dedicated to, the implementation and review of controls. Furthermore, the responsibility for these functions should really form part of every management and supervisory position. He recommends that security policy should be developed and overseen by a small selected security committee with representation from management, users and information systems. This will help to ensure commitment from all areas of the organization.

His final thoughts were in the area of *commitment.* As with a crash helmet on a motorcyclist you only really know you need it when it is too late. Mr Fine pointed out that when an article in the paper discussed a recent computer fraud, every consultant in town was inundated with phone calls from concerned managers. Unfortunately this concern was limited to a short period and then the concept of a controls policy became a memo in the bottom drawer. His solution to this problem was to tackle the organization at management level and try to make them aware of the threats that are present in their environment and the level of risk that these threats represent. Only by gaining real commitment from management can a realistic and effective security policy be developed and maintained.

REVIEW QUESTIONS

1. List the control steps to be taken in a system by which the level of control can be determined by cost-benefit analysis.
2. There is little justification for the two extreme situations 'no controls' or 'all controls'. What is the solution to this?
3. You are a consultant for a medium-sized retailer. What steps would you take in trying to implement a security policy?

CHAPTER 31 Computer auditing

31.1 INTRODUCTION

Having discussed the importance of computer controls and security, it is now appropriate to look at the role of the external auditor in this new environment. This chapter begins by discussing the difference between internal and external audit and describes the common steps in the external audit process. The second section then reviews the different approaches to auditing computer systems and the main differences between manual and computer audits.

31.2 THE AUDIT PROCESS

There are two facets to the audit function:

- The external audit whereby an independent audit firm offers an opinion on the fair presentation of an organization's financial statements.
- The internal audit whereby a management representative appraises the accounting, financial and operating controls within an organization in which he is employed.

While the external audit is a legal requirement, the internal audit function permits management to keep a constant watch on the organization and so recommend appropriate action once a problem has been detected. The internal auditor is therefore a control over other controls.

The external audit process is broken down into a number of fundamental steps, regardless of whether the system to be audited is manual or computerized (see Figure 31.1).

31.3 AUDITING COMPUTER SYSTEMS

Having summarized the major steps in an external audit, we are now in a position to discuss the impact computerization will have on this process.

The main principles of auditing remain the same regardless of whether the system is computerized or not. The main difference between computer auditing and manual auditing arises because of the additional standards and procedures that apply to computer auditing. Computerization affects the audit process in five specific areas and these will be duscussed under the headings:

- Specialized audit skills.
- Changing risks.
- Impact of centralized processing.
- Controls.
- Computer assisted audit techniques.

31.3.1 Specialized audit skills

Computer systems vary in complexity and, where the auditor lacks specific skills, it is important that the necessary specialists are available to assist. However, it is just as important that all auditors have sufficient understanding of computers to plan and control the overall audit process.

FIGURE 31.1. Auditing computer systems.

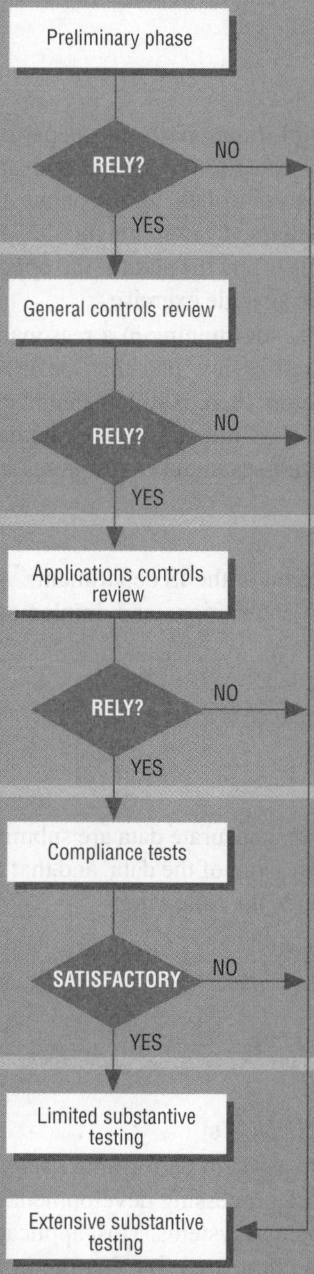

1. Preliminary Phase of the Review

This step is to understand and record the procedures and controls which comprise the accounting system. The auditor must obtain sufficient knowledge and understanding of the system to make a preliminary evaluation of the controls in place and so determine the extent of additional review required. The risk associated with the application is also assessed. The greater the impact of system error on the organization, the more extensive the controls and the substantive testing should be.

If the auditor can place some reliance on the internal records in the system it may limit the amount of subsequent work required. It is obvious that the auditor cannot rely on the internal controls in place (or it is uneconomic to do so), he will have to revert to extensive substantive testing of the system.

2. Review of General Controls

General controls can be defined as those which are concerned with the overall environment in which the organization's applications are run, and are applicable to all systems. The distinction between general and application controls is discussed in more detail in the next section.

The purpose of this step is to identify the general controls on which reliance is placed and determine how they operate. This process is normally carried out through the use of a general controls questionnaire, observation, interviews and documentation review. If the auditor finds he is unable to rely on these general controls he would abort any further evaluation of controls and begin detailed substantive testing.

3. Review of Application Controls

These are the controls specific to each accounting application covering the input, processing and output phases of the cycle. The auditor would again revert to extensive substantive texts if no reliance could be placed on these controls.

4. Design and Perform Compliance Tests

Once the internal controls of a system have been evaluated and the auditor wishes to rely on them, he will begin compliance testing. The purpose of compliance procedures is to provide reasonable assurance that internal controls on which the auditor needs or wants to rely are operating in the correct manner. From these texts the auditor may identify a weakness in the system and must consider the effect this will have on his subsequent audit procedures. If this weakness could lead to a material error appearing in the financial statements, the auditor must carry out additional tests in order to be staisfied that no material error has occurred.

5. Perform Substantive Tests

Substantive tests are concerned with verifying the substance of account balances and other information contained in the financial statements. The extent of these tests will depend on the degree of reliance that can be placed on the company's internal controls. If these have proved to be satisfactory during the controls review and compliance testing, then the extent of the stbstantive tests may be reduced.

In exceptional circumstances where the effect of a control weakness cannot be ascertained or where a material error has affected the accuracy of the financial statements, the auditor may have to qualify his audit report, in other words, state the financial statements do not fairly present the company's financial position.

31.3.2 Changing risks

Earlier in this module we discussed certain areas where computerization may increase the risk of loss or damage to the organization. The computer auditor must obviously be aware of these areas of concern.

31.3.3 Impact of centralized processing

The centralization of processing activities in the information systems department leads to a useful categorization of controls into two categories; general and application controls. In manual systems each application is controlled in a separate functional division of the organization while in a computerized environment the processing activities for each application are centralized. This offers the auditor the opportunity to review IS controls that relate to all applications in a single exercise.

Once it can be ascertained that the applications are running in a reasonably secure environment, the particular systems that required review can then be investigated. However, if the general controls cannot be relied on, there is little value in continuing with the applications review. Even if the controls within a specific application are excellent, that system is at the mercy of the weaknesses in the environment in which it is run.

General controls include the following:

- controls over the organization and administration of the IS department;
- controls over the application development, acquisition, and implementation of computer programs;
- controls over program maintenance;
- controls over the physical security of data and access to it;
- controls over program execution;
- controls over continuity of programs.

Application controls are implemented to ensure that accurate data are submitted to the computer, that no errors are made during the processing of the data, and that the output reconciles to the input. Application controls include the following:

- input controls;
- database and file controls;
- processing controls;
- output controls.

31.4 COMPUTER ASSISTED AUDIT TECHNIQUES (CAATs)

This involves using the power of the computer to assist in performing *compliance* and *substantive* testing. During the early years of data processing development, computer systems were audited in much the same way as manual systems. Most applications were written in batch mode, making it easy for the auditor to verify that the inputs to the computer systems equalled the outputs thus avoiding the necessity of auditing the computer processing function. This method was known as auditing *around* the computer or auditing *without* the computer.

This approach is no longer widely used as it assumes that any problems that occur in the processing of data will be detected by manual procedures. The transaction volumes and complexity of modern computer systems make this assumption a very dangerous one.

A second technique is called auditing *through* the computer or auditing *with* the computer and here the auditor makes use of the computer to audit itself. This technique is normally based on the existence of an audit package made up of a number of specialized programs to enable the auditor to interrogate files in the system and to follow an audit trail. A typical computer audit package would include:

- A report generator program to list information from master files and transaction files.
- Interactive enquiry programs to retrieve information from on-line systems.
- Logging programs to monitor activity in the system.
- Comparison programs to verify that versions of programs and files have not been tampered with.
- Test data generators to create data for testing applications.

There are a number of major advantages to using computer assisted audit techniques. Where there are balances and transactions on magnetic storage devices to be audited, or where there is a loss of visible evidence such as an audit trail, then access must be made to the computerized data. However the use of CAATs can also offer major advantages over manual auditing methods. The power of the computer can enable the auditor to deal with high volumes of data with great speed and accuracy and, in many cases, lower cost. Other spin-offs include the ability to get acquainted with the client's computing facilities and the ability to meet the expectations of the client in terms of up-to-date audit techniques.

CAATs can be used both in compliance and substantive testing. With compliance tests (testing computer controls) one important technique is the use of test data. By passing carefully prepared test data through an application, the auditor is able to test the input, file processing and output controls.

With substantive tests (verifying accounts, balances and other information) the techniques must be geared towards the processing of large quantities of data, and computer audit software such as enquiry programs and retrieval packages are most commonly used. These products are normally high-level languages which will enable the auditor to examine data files, retrieve data, compare data, and generate reports. Common uses of the computer audit software are:

- Accumulation of control totals on balances.
- Identification of exceptional balances/transactions.
- Sequence checks on transaction files.
- Recalculation of computer-generated totals.
- Comparison of two files to identify differences.

31.5 CONCLUSION

There is a multiplicity of computer assisted auditing techniques on the market. It is important, therefore, to realize that there is nothing unique about computer auditing. In information processing, as manual systems became computerized, people tended to draw a black box around their automated applications. This was unfortunate because with a minimum level of computer literacy most businessmen recognize that computer systems are very similar to their manual equivalent. In the same way the computer audit is regarded as a highly complex and technical exercise while in reality it is merely the manual exercise but with the computer performing all the drudgery. There is definitely a severe shortage of qualified computer auditors in South Africa and worldwide. However, it is the authors' opinion that this deficiency is not so much a reflection of the complexity of computer assisted auditing techniques but it rather results from three other peripheral problems.

The first is the lack of basic computer literacy in the accounting and auditing professions. With the introduction of more computing education and exposure at schools, universities and in the work place, this situation should improve over time.

Secondly, the computer industry is currently seeing rapid changes in technology and the auditors have found that the familiar batch system is rapidly being replaced by complex interactive database environments. Audit personnel are finding it difficult to keep pace with these advances, and with the computer revolution showing no signs of abating, this situation is unlikely to improve in the near future.

The third problem is one of compatibilities — the fact that most commercial computers today are very similar but in few cases are they compatible. There can be few professions more affected by lack of standardization in the computer industry than the auditing profession. Each client makes a separate choice as to how his particular installation will look both in hardware and software terms. The external auditor is therefore required to audit a number of computer systems, each residing on different machines with different operating systems and application programs written by different programmers, in different languages and differing levels of expertise. As if this were not enough, he is also faced with the likelihood that his computer audit software is machine-dependent and he has to use different packages on the various machines. Only when the computer industry sets and maintains a realistic level of hardware and software standardization can the audit professional hope to perform his tasks with the right level of confidence.

REVIEW QUESTIONS

1. What is the main difference between computer auditing and manual auditing?
2. Name five specific areas in which computerization will affect the audit process.
3. List six general controls and four application controls.
4. List the controls to be implemented to ensure that input data are authorized, complete, and accurate.
5. List the controls to be implemented to ensure that the output is complete and accurate.

MODULE 5 KEY POINT SUMMARY

- Internal control objectives in a computerized environment should be no different from those in manual systems. However, because of changes in responsibilities and processing activities, the technique used to achieve the same level of control must also change.
- One of the principles of internal control is the separation of duties. The use of computers tends to complicate matters by centralizing and combining functions.
- Controls in computerized systems must be designed and incorporated during the systems development cycle. Unlike their manual equivalents, computer systems can be inflexible and it is difficult to institute controls in a working system.
- Controls tend to be more important in a computerized environment because of the repetitive nature of processing. Furthermore, when problems do occur, they are more likely to be material.
- An additional concern is that computers are not able to perceive as human beings do and therefore problems might slip through which would be detected in a manual system.
- People must therefore remain the major element of control in computerized systems. The computer should merely assist by performing a selection function, channelling any possible problems to the correct personnel.

MODULE 6 Business applications

OBJECTIVES

This module gives a general introduction to the nature and structure of accounting information systems and describes each of the accounting systems that are commonly found in business. These include purchase orders and goods received; accounts payable and cash disbursements; inventory management; production management and cost accounting; marketing and sales; accounts receivable and cash receipts; personnel information and payroll; and general ledger, fixed assets, and financial reporting.

On completion of this module students should have a general understanding of the following aspects of each accounting application:

- Its nature, objectives and functions.
- The sources of data used as input for further processing, storage, and information retrieval.
- The different transactions that are processed and the way in which they are processed.
- The flow of data and information within the application and beyond.
- The structure and maintenance of the different files or record types contained within the relevant databases.
- The accounting controls to be included and maintained.
- The information requirements for the different management levels.

CHAPTER 32 The structure of accounting information systems

32.1 INTRODUCTION

Accounting may be regarded as being a service function. Its objective is to provide meaningful information to certain users. The *accounting information system* (AIS) is the system that supports the overall accounting function and makes it possible to attain this objective.

Previously, accounting systems were mainly concerned with recording and processing financial transaction data and preparing external financial statements. Today, the situation is quite different. In most organizations the accounting function is geared to support management. A large volume of information is directed specifically to helping the various management levels in planning and controlling the enterprise, in evaluating individuals and groups within the enterprise, and in solving business problems. External reporting in its various forms is still a very important function, but it entails a much smaller proportion of the total accounting effort.[4]

Although the role of the accounting practitioner has changed considerably over the years, the basic functions and objectives of accounting have not changed, nor are they likely to change. People still need to know the financial results of past business operations or the value of the organization itself. The activities of identifying, recording, processing, storing, summarizing, reporting, and interpreting financial transactions are therefore firmly established.

Accounting, however, has become more than simply recording, summarizing and reporting the financial results of an organization. It now includes various aspects of the organization itself: the delegated responsibilities, the processing methodology, the controls, and the expected outputs that make up the total system.[2]

In a business environment, a system may be regarded as an orderly method of accomplishing organizational goals. In financial management the term *system* may be used to refer to organization, procedures, decision processes, functional operations, and cost and information flows. In this sense the AIS includes the processes and procedures by which an organization's financial information is received, registered, recorded, handled, stored, reported and ultimately disposed of.[2]

32.2 OBJECTIVES OF ACCOUNTING INFORMATION

Accounting information, in the form of financial statements and other financial reports, is prepared for two separate user groups, each with different interests, needs, and points of view. One group consists of *external users.* They are concerned mainly with the financial position and performance of the business. The other group consists mainly of *internal management* and focuses primarily on organizational planning, operations, control, and decision-making. For the first group an AIS should provide financial information for general use (this is called *financial accounting*). For the second group it should provide management information aimed specifically at the various management functions (this is *management accounting*).[2]

For an accounting system to fulfil its purpose, the information in financial and other reports must be relevant, complete, and timely. These attributes are achieved by recording, processing, summarizing and reporting transactions according to certain generally accepted accounting principles. Such principles are intended to make sure that accounting statements represent the financial condition of the reporting entity fairly and that they are complete enough for users to rely on them to make decisions and to make meaningful comparisons between the financial statements of different businesses.[5]

32.2.1 Financial accounting

Generally accepted accounting principles and practices (GAAP) have evolved over the years, mainly through the co-ordinating efforts of several accounting organizations. The principles and practices set by these organizations govern the accounting process for the broad spectrum of financial transactions and specify the content and format of published financial information. To conform to the requirements of GAAP an AIS must provide transaction audit trails, guarantee the inclusion of all legitimate transactions, and provide suitable internal control procedures.

32.2.2 Management accounting

Financial information for general management purposes includes budgeting information, cost accounting information, and information derived from various management accounting models. Although such information is not governed by any set of rules, it is usually based on management's own requirements. Managers need this type of information for planning, controlling, and decision-making purposes. A particular characteristic of this kind of information is that it is oriented to the future.[2]

32.3 ACCOUNTING INFORMATION SYSTEMS IN A CHANGING ENVIRONMENT

In recent times, the development of information systems was influenced, not by changes in the basic functions of accounting, but by dramatic changes in the business environment. A modern business organization has to be flexible and responsive to social and economic changes and requirements, and one can therefore also expect changes in future business techniques and operating procedures.

Economic, social, and political changes have also altered the role of accountants. They have become financial custodians, financial advisers to owners and clients, producers and interpreters of financial indicators, certifiers of financial strength and integrity for lenders, and guarantors of financial fidelity on behalf of the investing public. In the public auditing field, qualified professional accountants increasingly have to play the role of financial and management consultants.[2]

In addition, the information systems revolution has changed the laborious manual preparation, recording, and processing of business transactions into high speed information processing systems which are very accurate. This has opened many possibilities for producing meaningful management information.

In today's business environment the accountant must assume a more positive role in the analysis and design of information systems to ensure the integrity of such systems and the information they produce. A general understanding of, and appreciation for, the use of information technology is most important for accountants as may be seen from the fact that students studying to become professional accountants are required to prove a certain degree of knowledge regarding business information systems.

Accountants, being expected to deliver accurate information about the economic life of their organizations, are finding that the technology they use presents problems of its own. In most instances they find the computers and software too complex and the processing of information too invisible. This is because accountants have allowed a whole new generation of systems to be designed by non-accountants.[5]

32.4 THE ROLE OF THE ACCOUNTANT

If accountants and auditors, as financial and managerial information specialists, are to maintain control of their discipline, they will have to move beyond competence in accounting alone. They will also have to possess and apply basic knowledge in computer science, data processing, internal and external control, and systems analysis. Only by communicating and working effectively with others in the design and installation of computer-based systems can accountants ensure that those systems meet all their needs and that they remain in control.[5]

An accountant must also have an overall understanding of all aspects of the business — especially its use of information technology (IT) — and the environment in which it operates. He or she must have the ability to be involved in the application and control of IT within the organization, and also the financial data that are processed, stored, and made available by the IT department. To be able to audit a system, an auditor must understand the functions of each application and know what controls have been built into it. The accountant is also a user of data and must therefore be aware that many of the financial data actually belong to him and that he is responsible for the accuracy, correctness, integrity, control, and manipulation of such data.

With a reasonable knowledge of the practical design and implementation of systems, the accountant will be able to advise on IT strategies that will enable the production of meaningful accounting information for management purposes.

Accountants and auditors should study and understand the following aspects of a business enterprise if they are to fulfil their roles:[3]

- business operations;
- communications;
- management decision-making;
- accounting and auditing principles;
- transaction processing;
- control;
- financial and management reporting;
- information technology;
- systems development and operation;
- databases.

32.4.1 Business operations

An AIS must relate to business operations. Many inputs are prepared by operating departments and many outputs are used to manage these operations. The accountant must therefore design and manage the AIS in harmony with the organizational structure. This emphasizes the need for a clear understanding of the organization's business.

32.4.2 Communications

Strong oral and written communication skills will enable accountants to present and motivate the results of their operations effectively. Such skills will prove to be imperative, especially when alternatives are put forward, a solution is chosen, and a choice has to be defended.

32.4.3 Management decision-making

The accountant must know which decision models are appropriate for certain analyses, and the reports he produces must reflect this knowledge. The information necessary for a particular decision must be tailored to the type of decision under consideration. It must also recognize the personal management styles and preferences of decision-makers.

32.4.4 Accounting and auditing principles

An accountant will need to follow proper accounting principles, practices and procedures when designing and operating the accounting system. He must also understand the audits to which the accounting information will be subjected.

32.4.5 Transaction processing

The transactions processed by an organization reflect and monitor its business operations. These transactions may involve operational, management information, and AIS aspects. To design and use these systems, an accountant must know which transactions have to be processed, how they are to be processed, and how each is recorded.

32.4.6 Control

Accountants must have expert knowledge of the control of business operations and information processing. A practising accountant will probably spend much of his time using such expertise. Modern, complex information systems, however, require special kinds of controls and so accountants must develop an understanding of the controls that are specific to a particular situation.

32.4.7 Financial and management reporting

The accountant must know what outputs are required, or are desirable, when designing reports that will produce the required management information. Such reports may be regular reports (eg. sales analyses) or *ad hoc* reports (to support management decisions).

32.4.8 Information technology

An accountant's ability to plan and manage business operations depends largely on his knowledge of the available technology. This includes knowledge of information systems, various types of computer hardware, databases, programming tools, decision support systems, and expert systems.

32.4.9 Systems development and operation

An accountant should participate in the development of information systems that process transactions and provide management information. As a user he may request certain functions; as an auditor he may develop controls for a new system.

32.4.10 Databases

Although accounting emphasizes the reporting of information, the full accounting cycle includes data collection and storage. An accountant should know about these aspects. This involves an adequate understanding of databases, together with an understanding of the quantity and types of data available, and methods of retrieving those data.

32.5 BASIC CHARACTERISTICS OF ACCOUNTING INFORMATION SYSTEMS

An AIS usually consists of a number of subsystems or applications. Although these subsystems are all information systems in their own right, and each one has its own specific detail and purpose, they all have basic characteristics that are generally identical. Each one of the subsystems (which work together to achieve a common goal) require *input* in the form of raw data, it has to *process* these data, and then produce an *output* to attain the system's objectives. The system automatically produces its own *feedback* by which future systems processing can be influenced. Because an AIS is specifically designed to accomplish a certain purpose, it has to operate under the aegis of predesigned *controls.* Figure 32.1 depicts a simple transaction processing model which defines the basic system characteristics into more familiar business terms.[2]

An AIS should fit into a framework called a *systems hierarchy* (see Figure 32.2) and forms a subsystem of the organization within which it operates. The AIS, however, also contains its own subsystems, eg. transaction processing and information processing systems. In addition, the AIS forms part of the operational system of the organization and will therefore also contain a number of functional applications such as purchase orders, accounts payable, and inventory. The AIS, the firm's organizational structure, and the different operations are highly interdependent (see Figure 32.3).[6]

Interdependent subsystems cannot stand alone; they usually interrelate and depend on one another for input supply. In many cases the output of one subsystem provides essential input for another one. Figure 32.4 gives an impression of the relationships between subsystems.[2]

32.6 COMPONENTS OF ACCOUNTING INFORMATION SYSTEMS

An AIS requires specific components or *elements* in order to carry out its activities. The nature of these components will tend to vary, depending on the degree of automation in

FIGURE 32.1. System characteristics expressed in business terms.

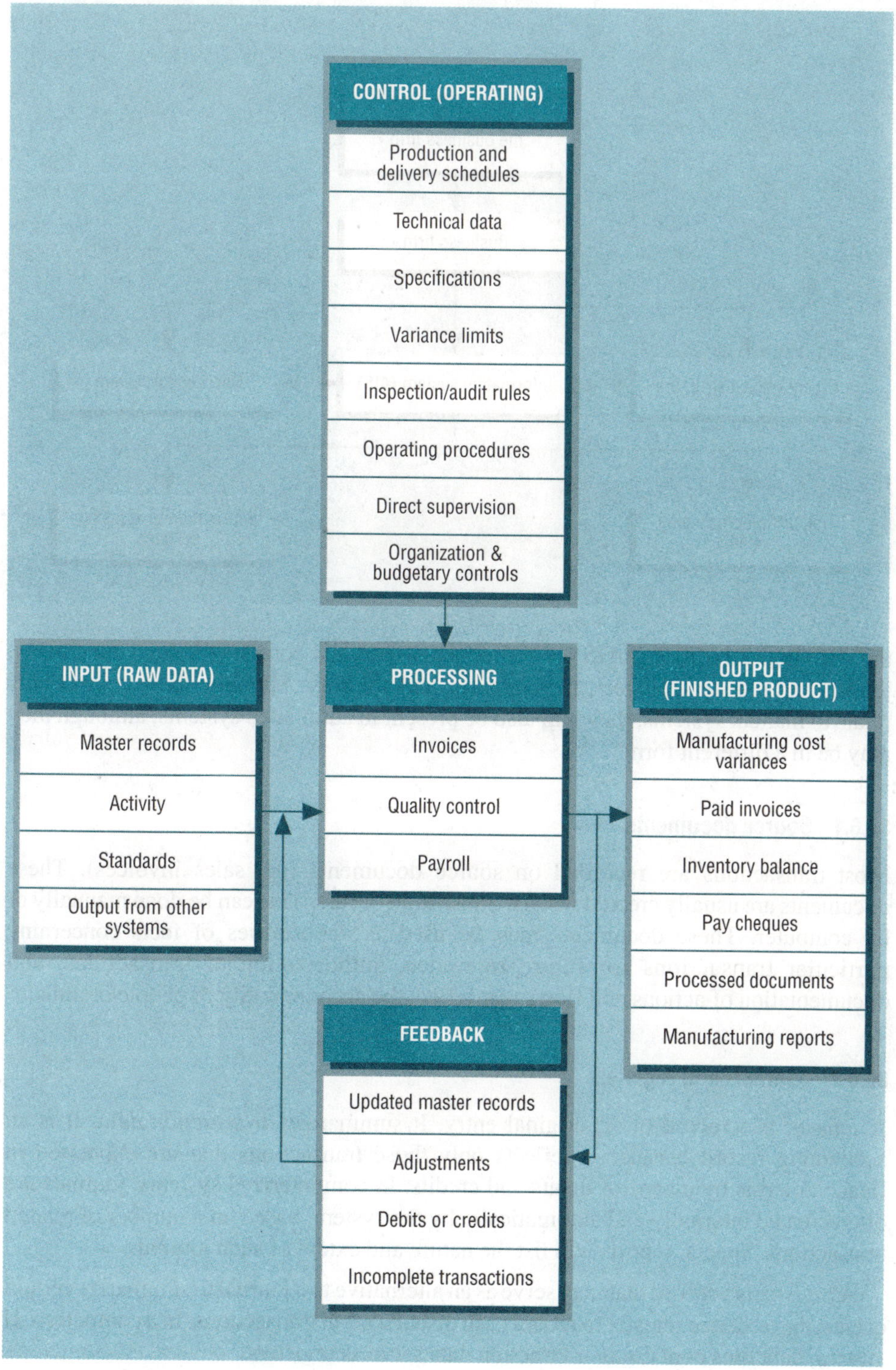

FIGURE 32.2. Hierarchy of systems.

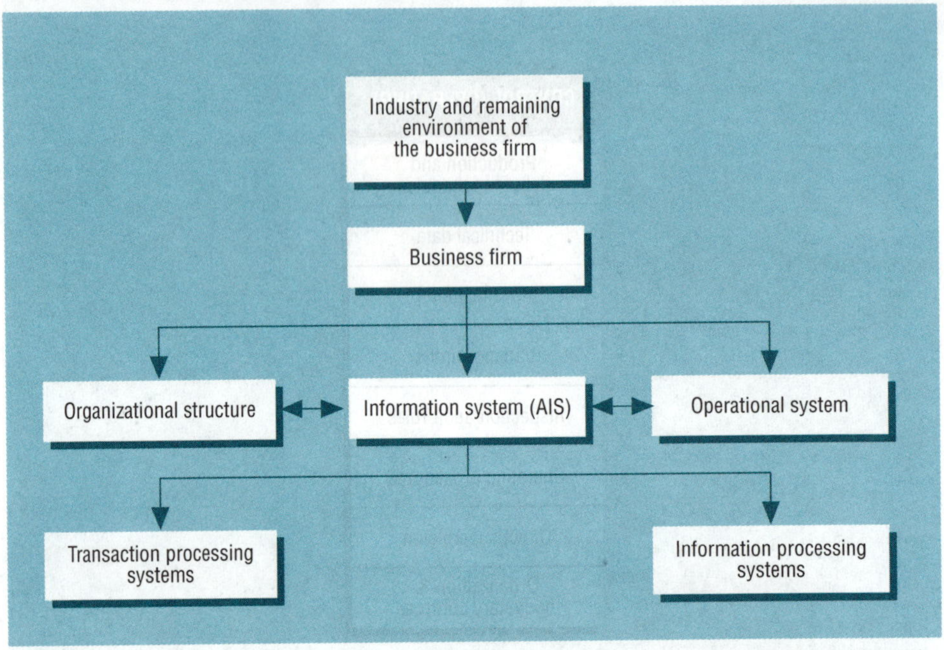

the AIS. In the traditional AIS the components generally consist of source documents, journal and registers, ledgers, files, reports, and controls. Although these components relate to manual systems, they will also be present in automated systems, although they may be in a different form.[6]

32.6.1 Source documents

Most transactions are recorded on source documents (eg. sales invoices). These documents are usually created when a transaction occurs. This can be done manually or by computer. These documents may be used as depositories of facts concerning particular transactions for future reference, authorization of transactions, and documentation of actions and flows that reflect the accountability of people or units.

32.6.2 Journals and registers

A *journal* is a record of an original entry. It summarizes *transaction data.* It is an accounting record because it reflects only those transactions that are expressed in financial terms by means of debits and credits. In computerized systems, journals are often created internally and automatically by the system, based on a number of related transactions. Special reports will list the nature and extent of such journals.

A *register* is a record that may serve as an alternative to a journal to summarize certain events; eg. a cheque register to record cash disbursement transactions. In a computerized system, data files containing transaction data serve as registers.

FIGURE 32.3. Operational system of a manufacturing firm.

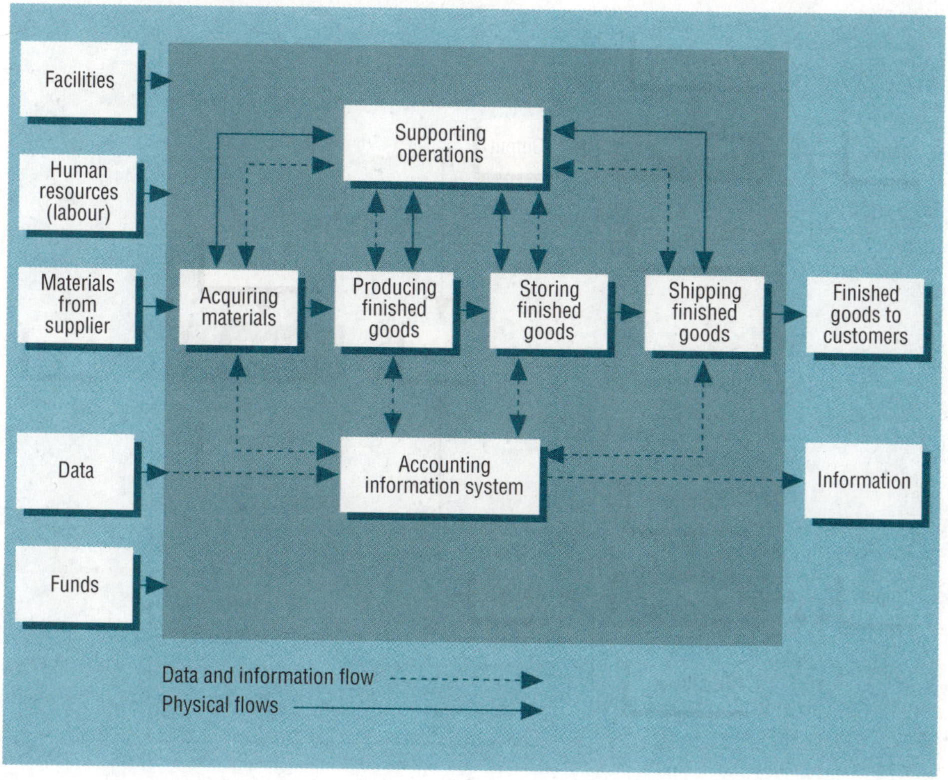

32.6.3 Ledgers

A ledger is an accounting record that summarizes the status of the accounts in financial terms. Transaction amounts that have been entered into the journals are posted to appropriate ledger accounts by way of journal entries.

A *general ledger* contains summarized financial data concerning the status of all asset, liability, income and expense accounts established by a business. A *subsidiary ledger* contains detailed records pertaining to a particular account in the general ledger (eg. debtors). An account in the general ledger that is supported or detailed by a subsidiary ledger is called a *control account.*

In computerized information systems, ledgers are usually in the form of data files with the various accounts being records in such files.

32.6.4 Files

Computerized information systems make use of data files or databases to contain the various accounts and accounting transactions that influence the status of such accounts. Four major types of files are: master files, transaction files, reference files, and history files. A *master file* contains relatively permanent records concerning an organization's

FIGURE 32.4. Relationships between subsystems.

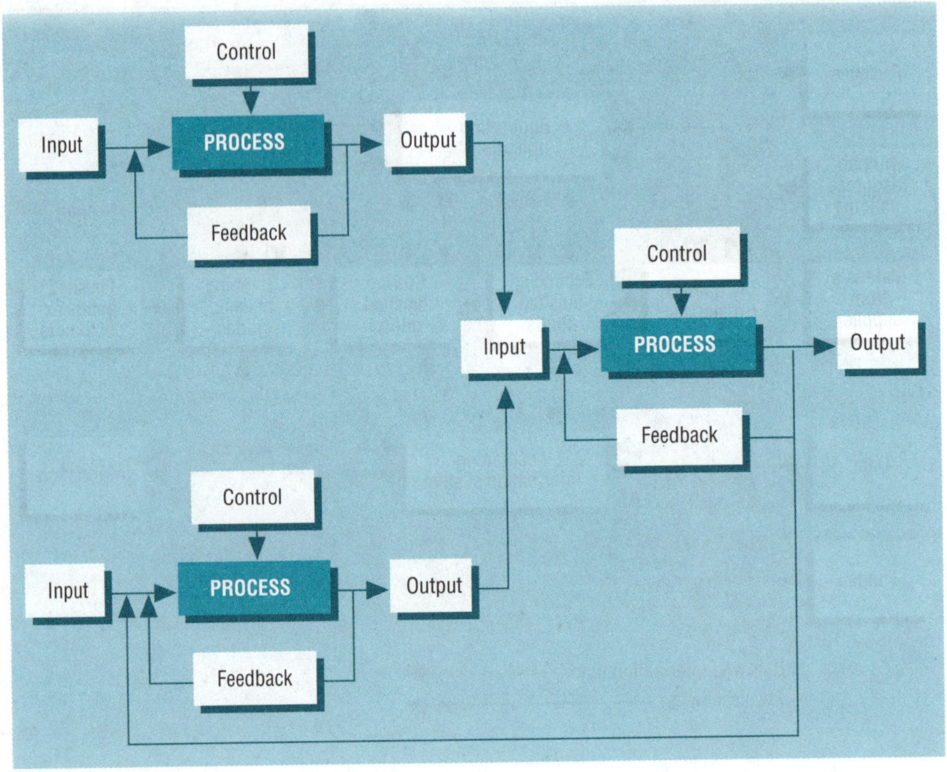

possessions and activities (eg. ledgers). A *transaction file* contains records pertaining to specific transactions (eg. a batch of sales invoices or the sales journal). A *reference file* contains data for use in performing steps during transaction processing (eg. income tax tables and price lists). A *history file* contains databases on past completed transactions (eg. sales invoices pertaining to the previous year's completed sales). A history file is an archive of past events, and also provides the means of making analyses.

32.6.5 Reports and other outputs

A variety of outputs flow from the information generation activity of the typical AIS. Among the most common are the balance sheet, income statement, and cash flow statement. However, numerous reports designed specifically for managers are also generated. Some managerial reports reflect the status of operations or resources (eg. sales summaries and inventory status reports); others are useful for managers in fulfilling their planning and control responsibilities (eg. budgets, sales forecasts, and exception reports such as cost variance analyses).

Outputs also include documents that are utilized in daily operations (eg. monthly statements), certain source documents, and outputs that are used as inputs to other steps in the accounting process.

32.6.6 Controls

Among the controls needed during the processing of transactions are a trial balance, a chart of accounts, audit trails, batch totals, and journal vouchers. A *trial balance* is a listing of all account balances in the general ledger. It provides a convenient means of verifying that the total of the debit account balances equals the total of the credit account balances. A coded *chart of accounts* is a listing of the ledger accounts and their codes. It enables transaction data to be classified and coded accurately and concisely. An *audit trail* is a set of references included on the key accounting records. It provides linkages among the various elements so that each accounting transaction can be traced from the source document to the financial outputs, and vice versa. A *batch total* enables posting errors to be detected. A *journal voucher* is a form that contains a single transaction. It provides an added measure of security because it contains a control number and includes spaces for the initials of the individuals who prepare and approve the transaction (which reflects accountability).

32.7 TRANSACTIONS WITHIN THE ACCOUNTING CYCLE

To understand the elements and activities of an AIS, one can trace the flows of basic transactions through the accounting cycle of a typical business organization. The basic transactions are identified as purchases, cash payments, sales, cash receipts, and payroll. It is important to remember that only those steps involving accounting records are discussed here. Each of these transactions, and others, will be discussed in more detail in the following chapters.[6]

32.7.1 Purchases

Source documents consist of invoices received from the suppliers of ordered merchandise, raw materials, supplies, and services. These suppliers' invoices are entered into a *purchases journal* or *invoice register,* and are then posted as credits to the individual supplier records in an *accounts payable subsidiary ledger.*

32.7.2 Cash disbursements

Copies of cheques, called *cheque vouchers,* are the source documents here. These vouchers are entered into a *cash disbursements journal* or *cheque register,* and are then posted to the individual supplier accounts in the *accounts payable subsidiary ledger.*

Cash may also be disbursed to parties other than suppliers. For instance, cash payments are made to stockholders as dividend distributions, and to banks as loan repayments. Although cheque vouchers pertaining to such payments are entered into the journal, they are not normally posted to the subsidiary ledger.

32.7.3 Sales

The flow begins with *sales invoices,* which are the source documents that contain amounts affecting ledger accounts. Data from the invoices are entered into a *sales journal* and then posted as debits to individual customer accounts in the *accounts receivable subsidiary ledger.*

32.7.4 Cash receipts

The *remittance advices* (eg. the top portions or copies of invoices) that accompany customers' cheques are the source documents. Amounts appearing on these are entered into a *cash receipts journal* and then posted as credits to the individual customer records in the *accounts receivable subsidiary ledger.*

Cash may also be received from sources other than customers. For example, cash receipts may result from loans, payments on notes receivable, and the sales of fixed assets. These miscellaneous cash amounts are entered from special documents into the *cash receipts journal* or onto *journal vouchers.* Since they do not involve payments from customers, they are not posted to the subsidiary ledger.

32.7.5 Payroll

The source documents here are *pay records* or *cheque vouchers* which are, in turn, generally based on *time cards* or *time sheets.* These documents are used in two phases: *labour distribution* and *pay-cheque processing.*

In the labour distribution phase, the pay data are entered on a register called a *labour distribution summary,* and are then posted to *expense subsidiary ledgers.* The totals from the summary are then posted to the *general ledger.*

In the payroll processing phase, the pay-cheque vouchers are entered into a *payroll register* and are then posted to the earnings records of individual employees.

32.8 A CYCLE APPROACH TO THE DEVELOPMENT OF ACCOUNTING APPLICATIONS

In the face of the difficulty, complexity, and diversity of accounting systems, a common framework called the *transaction cycle* has been established to unify the essential elements of different systems. The term *cycle* denotes something that repeats itself over and over again. In one sense, all business operations can be regarded as cycles; money is invested in the enterprise and finances various activities that, in turn, generate more money. More specifically, however, the transaction cycles are identified with broadly defined components of the accounting system.[4]

When developing a functional subsystem it is very important to carefully consider all possible demands that may be placed on it by other subsystems. This means that when designing any system, one should consider its proper perspective within the organization.

In this respect the flow of data and information is very important: eg. manufactured products constantly absorb labour, material, and overhead costs; sales are made and inventory is converted into cash; debts are incurred and liquidated; assets are acquired and creditors are paid; equity is increased or diminished through income, losses, stock transactions, and dividends. It is therefore important to view all information systems within their operating environment.

Different types of organizations exist, each categorized according to its economic purpose. These are *service organizations, merchandising undertakings* and *manufacturing concerns.*[2]

Service organizations (eg. a law firm, an accounting firm, or a television repair shop) receive income largely from the provision of specialized services and are only minimally affected by the transfer of inventory costs (materials) to the customer. The entire process of performing the service, billing the customer, and collecting money, can be viewed as a cycle of events.

Merchandising undertakings are involved mainly in two groups of activities, namely an *expenditure cycle* (the process of acquiring and holding merchandise for resale to customers) and a *revenue cycle* (the process of selling inventory to customers and receiving cash for it).

Manufacturing concerns usually introduce a third cycle of activities between the expenditure and revenue cycles, namely the *manufacturing* or *conversion cycle.* This involves the transformation of raw materials acquired in the expenditure cycle into finished products for resale in the revenue cycle.

For each of the three types of organizations mentioned, a number of supporting applications or subsystems will exist. These include *payroll, general ledger* and *property control,* and can be grouped under the *administrative cycle.*

Because a manufacturing concern contains all the transaction cycles mentioned, such an organization will be used in this module to examine each of the computerized business activities from a management perspective and an accountant's perspective. For each of the computerized business activities, its objectives, data sources, processing requirements, the flow of data and information, and management information requirements will be identified. The basic data and information flow in a manufacturing environment are shown diagrammatically in Figure 32.5.[2]

32.9 FUNCTIONAL SUBSYSTEMS BASED ON THE OPERATING CYCLE

Each one of the functional subsystems within the transaction cycles mentioned above will be geared to a different set of organizational objectives, some of which are related to each other. The ensuing chapters will examine each of these subsystems structured as follows within the operating cycle:[2]

Expenditure cycle
Purchase orders and goods received
Accounts payable and cash disbursements
Manufacturing cycle
Inventory management
Production management and cost accounting
Revenue cycle
Marketing and sales
Accounts receivable and cash receipts
Administrative cycle
Personnel information and payroll
General ledger, fixed assets, and financial reporting

FIGURE 32.5. Basic data and information flow in a manufacturing firm.

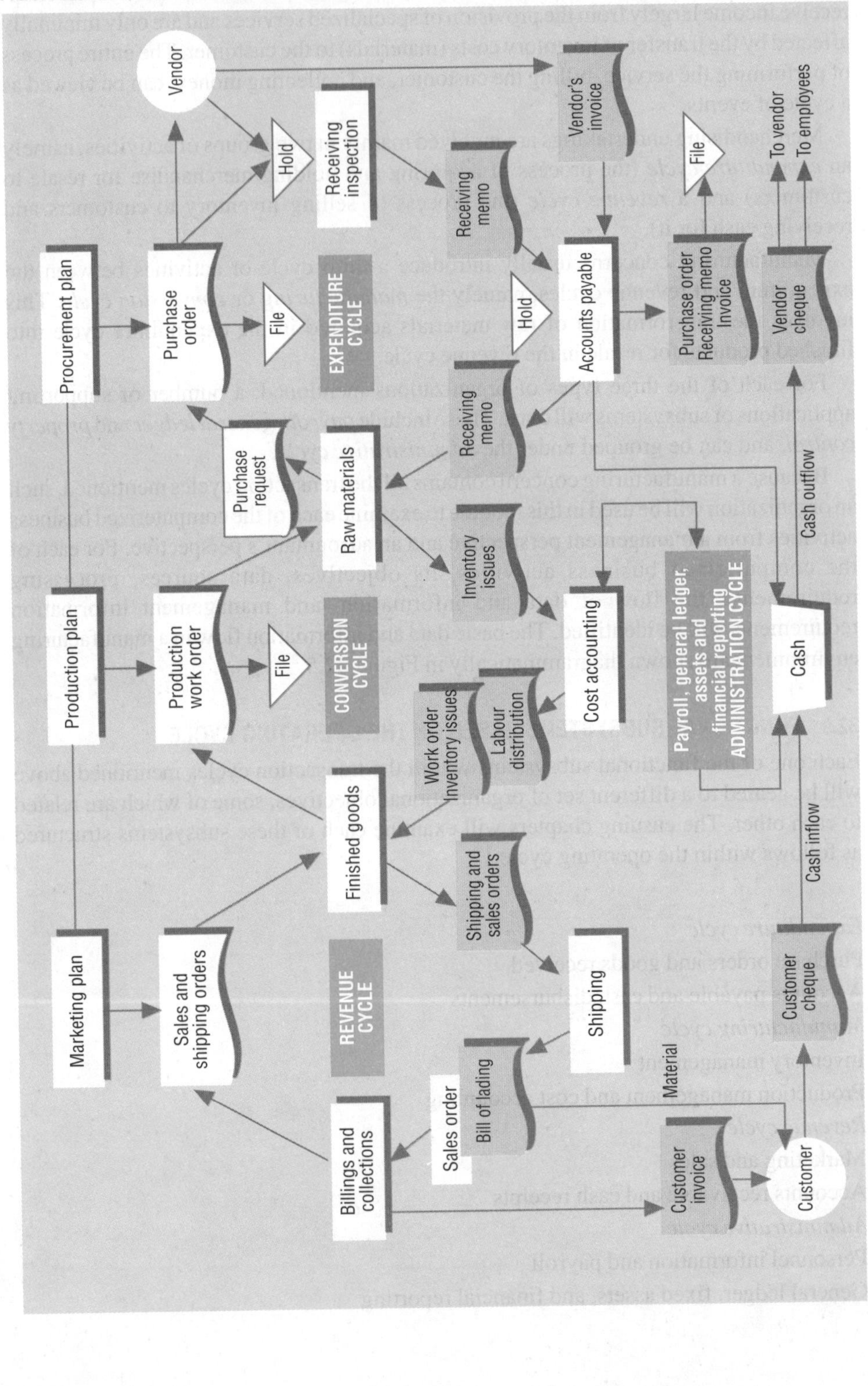

- *Purchasing* deals with the issue of purchase orders for acquiring raw materials or merchandise inventory; it may also extend to the acquisition of services from vendors.
- *Receiving* refers to the inspection and acceptance of goods delivered to the organization from outside vendors. It includes the recording of the receipt of goods, and the disposition of the goods within the enterprise.
- *Accounts payable* is concerned with the payment for goods and services acquired from outside vendors. It involves the processing of invoices received from vendors, the maintenance of records of the associated liabilities, and preparations for cash disbursements.
- *Inventory management* or *inventory control* involves accounting for raw materials, finished goods, merchandise, and supplies inventories, including the maintenance of perpetual inventory records. Inventory control includes the regulation of stock levels to ensure consistent supply and to avoid excessive inventory levels or goods being out of stock.
- *Production management* or *production control* deals with the initiation of production orders within the factory and with the tracking and control of production operations. It also includes the preparation of bills of materials, labour and machine schedules, and product routing through the factory.
- *Cost accounting* is concerned with the accumulation of product costs in a manufacturing organization. It includes the monitoring of work-in-process inventories, and may interface with a standard cost system.
- *Marketing* may be regarded as the intermediary function between production and consumption. It is a system of interrelated activities designed to develop, price, promote, and distribute goods and services to groups of customers. Marketing management also has important influences on the routine activities of production, procurement, inventory, finance, and personnel.
- *Sales order processing* is concerned with the processing of orders received from customers for goods and services. It may include the establishment of credit terms, the recording of sales tax data, and the determination of sales representatives' commissions.
- *Shipping* is the movement of products to and from warehouses as well as the preparation of the goods for shipment and the accompanying paperwork. It may also include the identification of appropriate modes of shipment, and negotiation with common carriers.
- *Accounts receivable* is concerned with the preparation of customer invoices (billing) and periodic customer statements. It includes the maintenance of records of customer indebtedness and collection activities.
- *Payroll* refers to the payment of wages, salaries, and sales commissions to employees and to the related withholding of deductions and the disposition thereof.
- *Personnel management* (closely related to the payroll system) involves the employment, education, training, welfare, and safety of personnel as well as labour relations and personnel administration. Another important function is to produce the necessary personnel information for management and decision-making purposes.

- *General ledger* provides for the traditional accumulation and processing of accounting transactions and the preparation of the trial balance. This application includes the maintenance of the various journals as well as the general ledger itself. Journal entries may be made directly into the general ledger or may be transferred from other applications such as accounts receivable. Adjusting and reversing entries may be generated internally.
- *Fixed-asset management* deals with the keeping of records relating to the valuation, custody, physical maintenance, and eventual disposal of productive assets, ie. property, plant, and equipment.
- *Financial reporting* involves the preparation of external and internal financial statements and reports, including the balance sheet, income statement, cash flow statement, and all internal reports for management purposes.

32.10 PROCESSING REQUIREMENTS

Today, most computer systems use *interactive processing:* the user enters commands and transactions through a terminal and the system responds immediately with acknowledgement of errors. Most systems described in the following chapters are based on this process; batch-oriented processes will be mentioned where applicable.

Information processing can generally be divided into two categories: *transaction oriented* and *decision oriented* processing. Transaction oriented processing aims at the operational level of the organization. Such systems are highly structured in terms of design, transaction validation, reporting, and exceptions. Decision oriented processing (also known as *decision support systems* — DSS) aims to assist in the decision-making functions of senior management. Because the information requirements vary on a daily basis, such systems are unstructured and need to be flexible and responsive to needs in the provision of information.

This module will concentrate on transaction oriented information processing as it is the most common. Its benefits are tangible and more easily quantified. Management information required at a higher level will, however, be highlighted in the chapters dealing with the different underlying subsystems.

An integrated system can utilize a database in order to process and store transactions and to retrieve information for decision-making. The data are stored in such a way that they are independent of the programs that use them. A common and controlled approach is used in adding new data and in modifying and retrieving existing data within the database.

As indicated in Figure 32.6, a management information system is the culmination of the lower levels of information processing. It possesses the capabilities of a simple data-processing system, an integrated data-processing system, and an information retrieval system. It is further characterized by additional programs that permit the user to utilize a wide variety of management algorithms for interpreting the meaning of data to support the decision-making process.

The applications within an AIS should not be thought of as stand-alone subsystems. They interact with each other and should therefore be fully integrated, sharing data and

FIGURE 32.6. Levels of data and information processing.

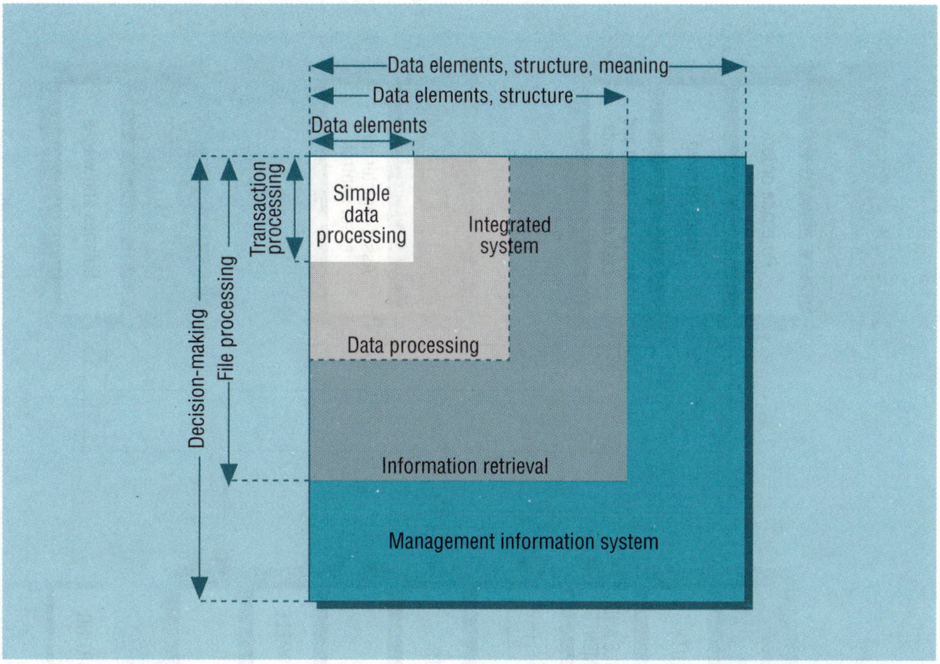

transferring data from one to the other. Figure 32.7 shows, for instance, the more important accounting relationships in a merchandising firm. Note the strong relationship between the general ledger in the centre and the other applications. The principal file in the general ledger application is the *chart of accounts* which involves the five major classifications of accounts: assets, liabilities, owner's equity, expense, and revenue. The general ledger controls most of the subsystems, draws on them for information, and produces financial reports and financial statements.[4]

32.11 SUMMARY

An AIS represents a set of resources employed by a firm to transform economic data into financial information that is useful for operating and managing its activities and reporting its achievements to all concerned. The two major functions of an AIS are to perform *transaction processing* and *information processing.* The main activities are data collection, data processing, data management, data control, and the generation of information.

An AIS deals with two specific types of information: financial information and information obtained from the collection and processing of transaction data.

In a business organization, the AIS provides information that is useful to internal management as well as to parties outside the business, eg. customers, suppliers, stockholders, employees, lenders, and government institutions. This information is produced through a series of steps known as the *data processing cycle,* which includes

FIGURE 32.7. Major accounting applications and their relationship to the general ledger.

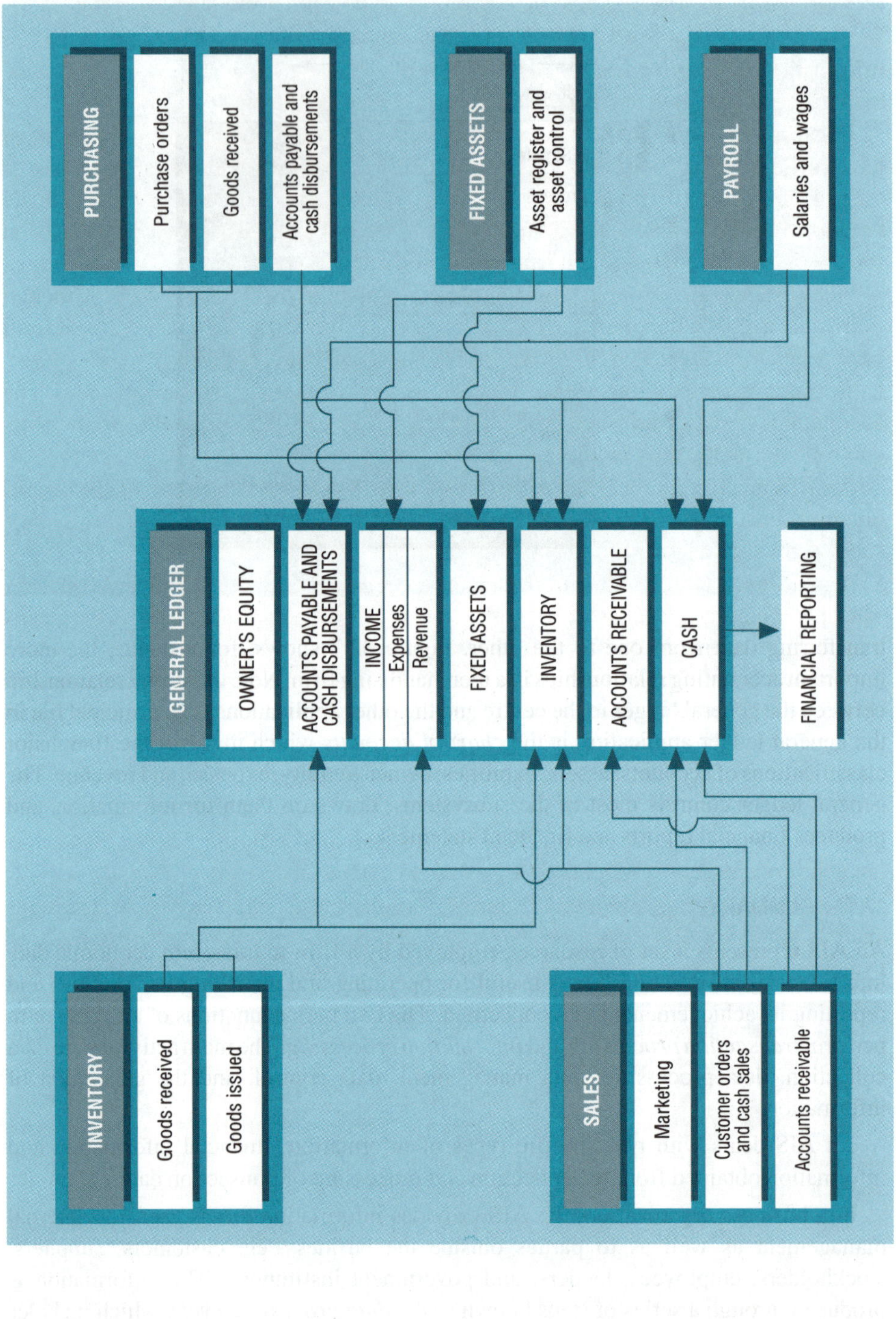

data collection, data preparation, data processing, file maintenance, and information output.

The environment in which an AIS must operate is constantly changing. Economic, social, technological, and even political changes influence the design and use of information systems. The AIS must therefore be designed in such a way as to be responsive to changing needs and technological improvements.

Because of the complex nature of today's financial environment, accountants must have sufficient knowledge of AIS. The traditional accounting functions are only part of the accounting information system, and to fully understand the role of accounting in the organization, accountants should also be able to deal with aspects such as decision processes, human relations, and data processing technology.

Accountants are involved in designing, evaluating and using AIS. Although individual accountants often perform all three roles, the degree to which they perform each depends on their areas of responsibility (eg. financial accounting).

Accounting systems must be accurate, dependable, automatic, and spontaneous. The accountant should find such systems clearly observable, definable, predictable, controllable, and readily modifiable under proper authority.[2]

An AIS must fit into a systems hierarchy. It is therefore a subsystem of the overall organizational system and the environment beyond. In turn, the AIS contains its own subsystems such as transaction and information processing systems.

An AIS must closely relate to the business operations and organizational structure. The operational system is the work system and the organizational structure is the means by which the managers co-ordinate and direct operations.

The AIS in an organization is also a subset of the *management information system* (MIS). A MIS is the set of human and capital resources within an organization that is responsible for the collection and processing of data to produce information that helps all levels of management in planning and controlling the activities of the organization.

The components of a computerized AIS include source documents, journals and registers, ledgers and files, reports and other outputs, and controls. These components are not, however, always in the same form as in manual accounting systems.

The accounting cycle of a typical business organization involves basic transactions such as purchases and cash receipts. Within the accounting cycle certain transaction cycles are established, ie. the expenditure cycle, the manufacturing cycle, the revenue cycle, and the administrative cycle. Each of these transaction cycles will deal with its related functional subsystems — eg. within the expenditure cycle, purchase orders, goods received and accounts payable will be processed.

The AIS incorporates *transaction processing* — which is directed at the operational level of the organization — and *decision support systems* to assist in the decision-making process. The various applications of an AIS are usually interrelated and the integration of the various subsystems is therefore very important.

The following chapters will deal with the applications normally found in accounting systems. In each case the following aspects will be explained:

- objectives and functions of the system;

- data sources and inputs;
- database structure;
- data flow and processing requirements;
- accounting controls;
- management information requirements.

REVIEW QUESTIONS

1. Explain the objectives and importance of accounting information in a business environment.
2. Discuss the role of the accountant with respect to the business itself and information technology.
3. Describe the basic characteristics of an AIS.
4. Name the various components of an AIS and explain how these relate to computerized accounting systems.
5. Describe the basic accounting transactions within the accounting cycle and explain the flow of these transactions through the cycle.
6. Discuss the need for a cycle approach to the development of accounting applications.
7. Describe the various transaction cycles found in a typical manufacturing concern, together with the functional subsystems found within each cycle.
8. Discuss the processing requirements for a typical AIS and explain the importance of integrating the various applications within the system.

SELECTED REFERENCES AND RECOMMENDED READING

1. Cushing, B. E. and Romney, M. B. 1990. *Accounting Information Systems —A Comprehensive Approach.* Fifth edition. Reading, Massachusetts: Addison-Wesley.
2. Davis, J. R., Alderman, C. W. and Robinson, L. A. 1990. *Accounting Information Systems —A Cycle Approach.* Third edition. New York: John Wiley and Sons.
3. Gelinas, U. J. Jr., Oram, A. E. and Wiggins, W. P. 1990. *Accounting Information Systems.* Boston: PWS-KENT.
4. Nash, J. F. 1989. *Accounting Information Systems.* Second edition. Boston: PWS-KENT.
5. Summers, E. L. 1989. *Accounting Information Systems.* Boston: Houghton Mifflin.
6. Wilkinson, J. W. 1989. *Accounting Information Systems: Essential Concepts and Applications.* New York: John Wiley and Sons.

CHAPTER 33 Purchase orders and goods received

33.1 INTRODUCTION

This chapter is the first in our presentation of the individual applications contained in the different cycles of the accounting information system (AIS). The chapters that follow are rather similar in their approach.

The *purchase order and goods received application* forms part of the *expenditure cycle.* To start business operations, raw materials, goods and services have to be ordered. When these are received, they have to be paid for and properly accounted for in an inventory.

The purchasing function forms a very important part of most businesses. The significant amounts of money involved, and the special nature of internal and external relationships, require careful consideration in order to maintain efficiency, an orderly information flow, and accounting controls.[2]

For the sake of simplicity, this chapter deals mainly with the acquisition of materials and supplies for production and operation. It further assumes that the organization is large enough to employ modern information technology (IT).

33.2 OBJECTIVES AND FUNCTIONS OF THE SYSTEM

The purchasing function involves the procurement of materials, supplies, equipment, and services at the lowest possible cost consistent with required quality standards. This is done to support the production of merchandise and products. The main goal must be the promotion of the firm's best interests through intelligent action and fair dealing that results in the acquisition of maximum value for the expenditure incurred.[2]

The functions of the system usually include the following:[3]

- identifying the need for goods or services;
- placing purchase orders;
- acceptance of goods delivered;
- validation.

33.2.1 Identifying the need for goods or services

The need for goods and services may be recognized in several ways. Inventory records may trigger a need when a certain 'quantity on hand' or 'reorder quantity' is reached; a back-order request may signal the need to place special orders; a long-term purchase contract may require orders to be placed at regular intervals; services may be required on a regular basis, or as and when required by management.

33.2.2 Purchase orders

When the need for goods or services has been identified, purchase orders have to be placed with suppliers. This function is usually carried out by a central purchasing division or department. Suitable suppliers have to be selected and specifications like unit price and quality of ordered goods have to be established. In some cases tenders or quotations for goods have to be obtained and evaluated before placing orders.

33.2.3 Goods received

When goods that have been ordered are received, counted, and inspected for damage, they should be checked to ensure that they conform to the specifications on the original purchase orders. If they do not, they should be rejected and returned to the supplier. Accepted goods have to be moved to inventory or some kind of warehouse. Services are usually accepted in writing by the recipient.

33.2.4 Validation

When invoices for delivered goods and services are received from suppliers, these have to be checked against the associated purchase orders and documents that show that the goods or services were properly ordered and received. After the amounts, discounts, and other data on the invoices have been checked, and any adjustments needed are settled with the supplier, they can be approved for payment.

33.3 DATA SOURCES AND INPUTS

The data sources (or *source documents*) used in the purchasing and receiving function are based mainly on inputs from inventory, managers, and suppliers. These include:

- purchase requisition;
- purchase order;
- receiving report;
- supplier's invoice.

Another document that is sometimes used is the *request for quotation* form which will enable a buyer to compare prices and the quality of goods from several suppliers before placing an actual purchase order.

In computerized systems, pre-formatted screens (in the same format as particular source documents) may be used to enter relevant data. Such screens can be designed to handle transactions on-line or in batches.

33.3.1 Purchase requisition

The initiation form in the expenditure cycle is the *materials* or *purchase requisition.* This form authorizes the purchasing division to place an order for goods or services. It may be generated manually, or by computer. In the latter case the user enters a request for purchasing goods or services into the computer which then processes and stores the request and prints a formal pre-numbered purchase requisition.

Key data shown on a purchase requisition include description and quantity of goods, date required, and name of user, department and cost centre. Other data may include suggested supplier, unit price, and shipping instructions.

33.3.2 Purchase order

Once a purchase requisition has been received and necessary information (like suppliers, availability, and prices) has been gathered, a pre-numbered *purchase order* can be prepared. Again, this can be done manually or by computer. In the latter case the user enters the required data into the computer which then processes and stores it and prints an official purchase order. This document must be signed by an authorized buyer and, when the supplier agrees to all the terms and conditions stated on the order, it becomes a formal contract.

The purchase order number becomes the controlling number for all activities relating to the order and the delivery of goods. This number must appear on all supplier invoices, packages, delivery notes, correspondence, etc. A typical purchase order usually has two sections: a *heading* and a *body*. The heading contains data like the supplier's name and address, shipping instructions, purchase requisition number, and other reference items. The body contains a number of line items, each pertaining to a single item of merchandise or material ordered. An item line could contain data such as item number, quantity, description, and unit price.

33.3.3 Receiving report

When materials or merchandise are received from suppliers, a pre-numbered *receiving report* is prepared by the receiving department. This document provides proof that the listed quantities of goods have in fact been delivered in acceptable condition. It contains data such as purchase order number, supplier's name and address, date received, and details of the individual items received. To document the receipt of services, a copy of the supplier's invoice may be used to acknowledge receipt and authorize payment.

33.3.4 Supplier's invoice

Some time after goods and services have been delivered, the supplying firm will issue an invoice. This is a response to the associated purchase order and a request for payment. The purchasing division of the receiving company will validate the invoice and authorize it for payment by the accounts payable division. The supplier's invoice will be discussed in more detail in the following chapter.

33.4 DATABASE STRUCTURE

The database associated with the purchasing and receiving functions interrelates with the databases for the inventory and accounts payable functions. It is therefore useful to view the database structure in a broader context, as depicted in Figure 33.1.

The database is structured as a network of interrelated records. These records can be grouped into inventory, or goods- and services-related records, and supplier-related records.[1]

The database records will consist of the following:

- master records;
- transaction records;
- reference records;
- history records (grouped together in files).[3]

FIGURE 33.1. Database structure for purchasing, receiving, and accounts payable.

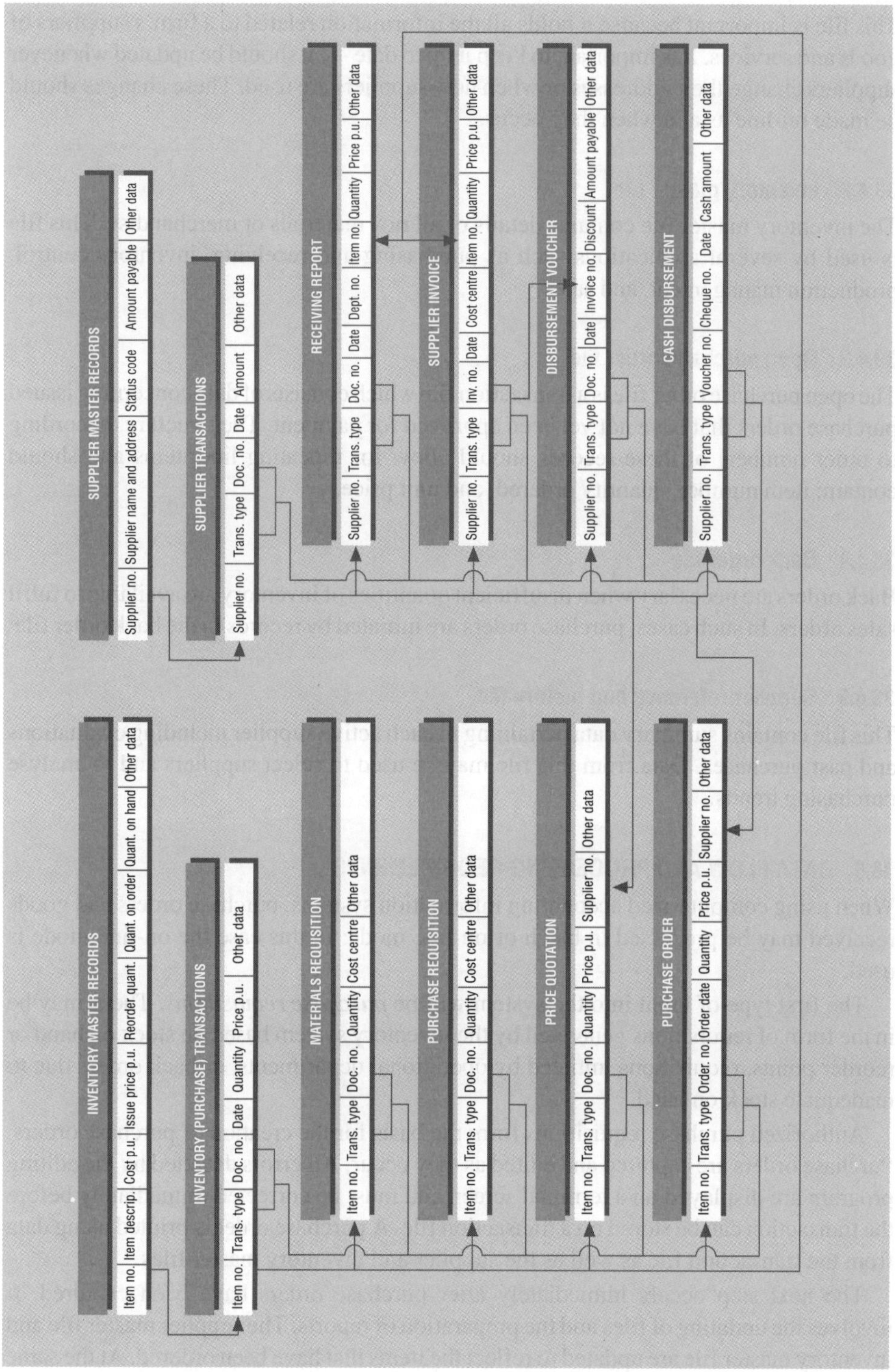

33.4.1 Supplier master file

This file is important because it holds all the information related to a firm's suppliers of goods and services. It is important to keep it up to date — it should be updated whenever suppliers change their addresses or when new suppliers are used. These changes should be made on-line as and when they occur.

33.4.2 Inventory master file

The inventory master file contains details of all raw materials or merchandise. This file is used by several applications such as purchasing and receiving, inventory control, production management, and sales.

33.4.3 Open purchase order file

The open purchase order file is a transaction file which consists of data concerning issued purchase orders that have not yet been approved for payment. The structure (according to order number) of these records should allow for repeating line items and should contain: item number, quantity ordered, and unit price.

33.4.4 Back order file

Back orders are necessary when insufficient quantities of inventory are available to fulfil sales orders. In such cases, purchase orders are initiated by records in the back order file.

33.4.5 Supplier reference and history file

This file contains summary data pertaining to each active supplier including evaluations and past purchases. Data from this file may be used to select suppliers and to analyse purchasing trends.

33.5 DATA FLOW AND PROCESSING REQUIREMENTS

When using computerized accounting information systems, purchase orders and goods received may be processed in batch or on-line mode; in this case the on-line mode is used.

The first type of input into the system will be *purchase requisitions.* These may be in the form of requisitions generated by the inventory system based on stock on hand or reorder points, requisitions initiated by operational departments, or back orders due to inadequate stock on hand.

Authorized purchase requisitions form the basis for the creation of purchase orders. Purchase orders are captured and edited as they occur. All errors detected by the editing program are displayed on a terminal screen and must be corrected immediately before the transaction can be stored on a transaction file. A purchase order is printed using data from the transaction file as well as the supplier and inventory master files.

The next step occurs immediately after purchase orders have been captured. It involves the updating of files and the preparation of reports. The supplier master file and inventory master file are updated to reflect the items that have been ordered. At the same time, the open purchase order transaction file is updated with a transaction record for each purchase order entry.

Once ordered goods are received, a receiving program checks the data against the open purchase order file. Any differences or invalid purchase order numbers will be displayed on the terminal screen. When the goods are accepted, the system will print a receiving report, update the inventory master file with the quantity received, eliminate or reduce the quantity on order, note the quantity received in the open purchase order file, and note the receipt in the supplier history file. If a back order is involved, the back order file is updated accordingly.

The output from this part of the system includes printed purchase requisitions, printed purchase orders, a listing of purchase orders placed, printed receiving reports, a listing of goods received, and a listing of back orders. Figures 33.2 and 33.3 depict system flowcharts containing the flow of data associated with the purchasing and receiving functions.[3]

33.6 ACCOUNTING CONTROLS

Internal control procedures within the purchasing and receiving functions must be designed to ensure that:[1]

- only those goods and services that are really necessary are purchased, and goods that are not needed are not purchased;
- all purchase transactions are properly authorized on the basis of established criteria;
- only those goods and services that have actually been purchased are received and accounted for;
- all valid purchase transactions are accurately recorded and processed.

Proper authorization of purchase transactions is very important because of the significant control risks associated with purchases. These risks include ordering goods or services that are not needed, ordering at unnecessary high prices, ordering from unauthorized or unreliable suppliers, and ordering poor quality products.

The use of a purchase requisition helps to overcome the first of these control risks. Budgetary control, pre-numbered requisition and purchase order forms, and the allocation of each purchase to the person who approves the requisition, will also minimize unnecessary purchases.

Formal supplier selection procedures will help to avoid the other three control risks. Criteria for selection will include low prices, reliability with respect to quality and timeliness of delivery, and integrity.

A proper set of general and application controls is necessary to minimize control risks associated with purchasing and receiving goods and services.

33.6.1 General controls

General controls include the following:[3]

FIGURE 33.2. System flowchart for purchasing.

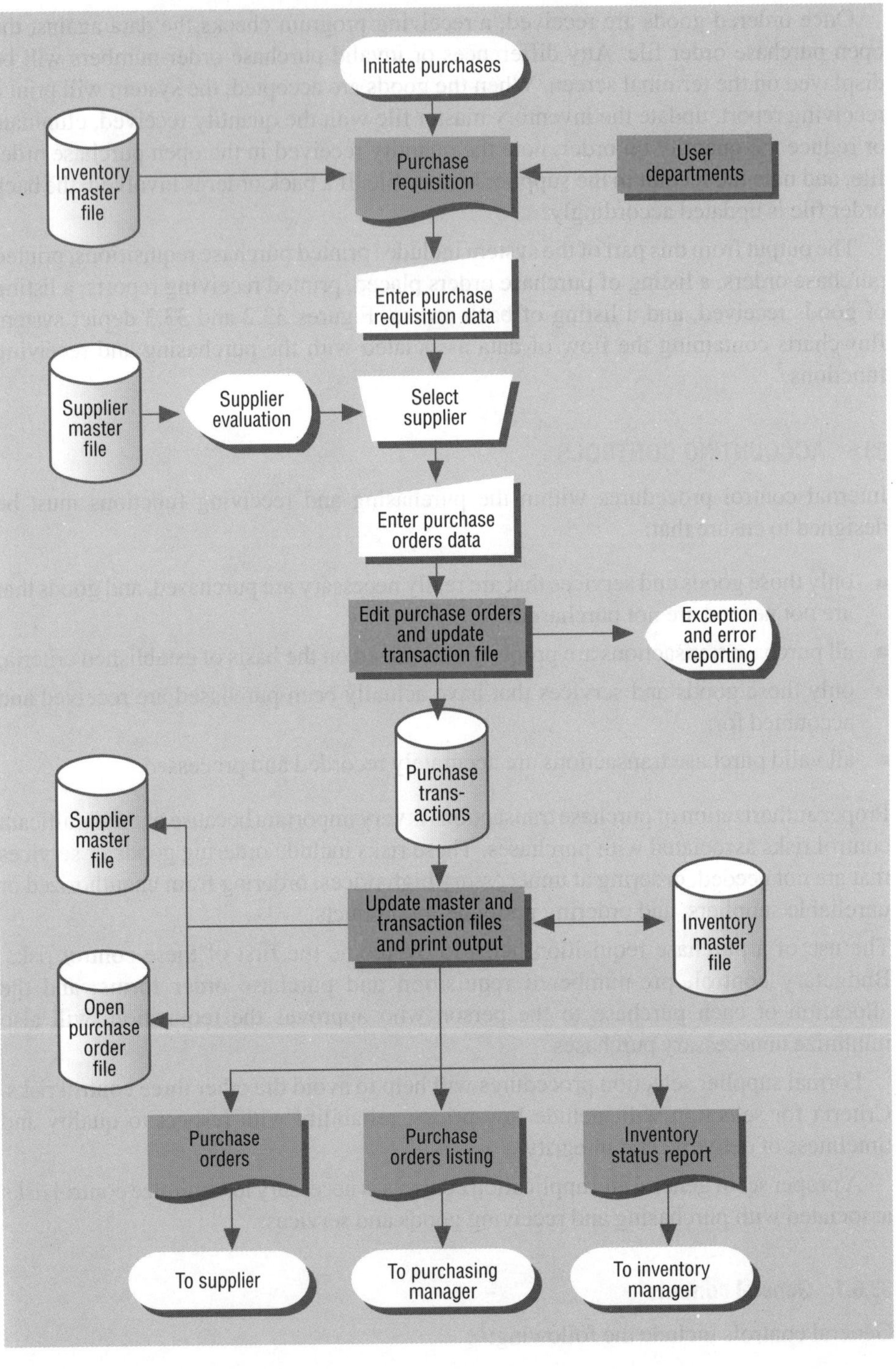

- *The separation of duties.* Units that have custodial functions (eg. receiving and inventory storage functions) should be separate from those units that keep the records (eg. purchasing, accounts payable, and inventory control functions).
- *Complete and up-to-date documentation* for controlling all processing aspects of purchasing and receiving goods and services. This will include copies of source documents, flowcharts, editing and processing programs, record layouts, and reports.
- *Security in respect of on-line systems.* This will entail the use of passwords, employing terminals with restricted functions, generating access logs, and making regular back-ups of all databases.

33.6.2 Application controls

Control points within the purchasing and receiving function include:[3]

- the determination of a need for goods or services;
- the preparation of the purchase order;
- the receipt of goods and services;
- the receipt and approval of the supplier's invoice.

The following controls are applicable to the transactions associated with the purchasing and receiving function:[3]

- well-designed and pre-numbered source documents;
- validation of data on purchase orders, receiving reports, and supplier invoices before entering them for processing;
- obtaining edit reports on entered data and correcting errors as soon as possible;
- established purchasing policies that require competitive bidding;
- verifications to ensure that all requisitioned goods are ordered, received, transferred to stores, and recorded accurately.

If the controls presented here are implemented, the purchasing and receiving function should be able to minimize the risks in its operations.

33.7 MANAGEMENT INFORMATION REQUIREMENTS

Most of the discussion in this chapter has been centred on the concepts of purchasing and receiving, and related accounting controls. Purchasing management, however, has the responsibility for the overall functioning and operation of the system. Managers should have sufficient knowledge of all operations to satisfy themselves that adequate controls are built in, and they should assume full responsibility for the accuracy and completeness of input and for the reliability of output. In addition, they must be able to convey important information concerning decision-making at the strategic level to top management.[2]

For management to be able to perform their control and decision-making functions, they need various kinds of management information. This information is usually communicated to them by way of reports: financial and non-financial reports;

FIGURE 33.3. System flowchart for receiving.

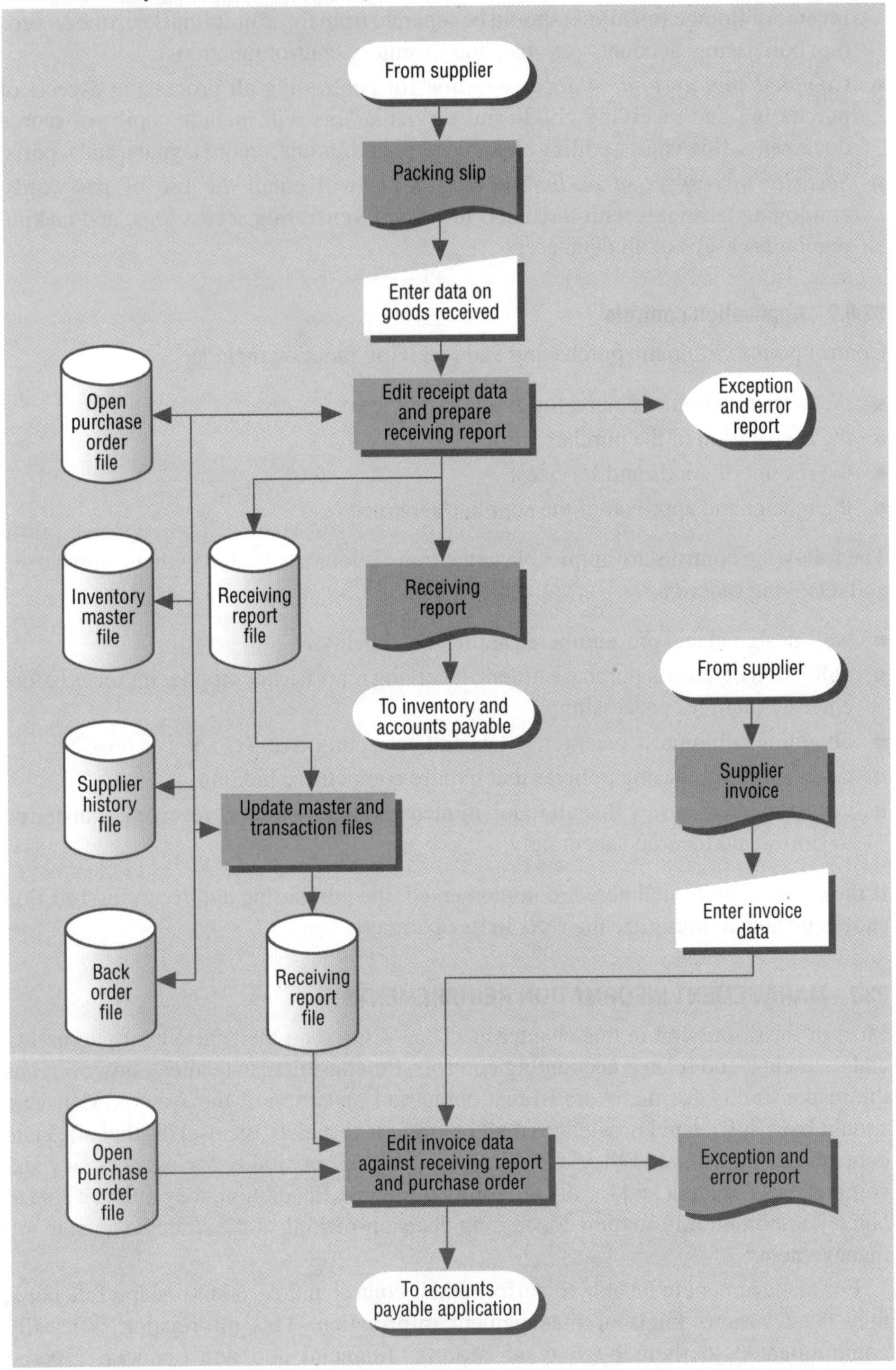

purchase-related reports; daily, weekly and monthly reports; hard copy and soft copy reports. All these reports may be classified into:

- operational listings and reports;
- exception reports;
- enquiry screens and reports;
- managerial reports.[3]

33.7.1 Operational listings and reports

These listings and reports are used for general control purposes. They are scheduled reports containing detailed and summary data of all transactions during a certain period. They help to maintain the audit trail of the system.

- *Daily purchase requisitions listing.* This is a listing containing data on all purchase requisitions received by the purchasing function.
- *Daily purchase orders listing.* This listing contains data on all purchase orders placed during the day.
- *Daily receiving reports listing.* This listing contains data on all goods received during the day.
- *Open requisition report.* This report contains data on all purchase requisitions for which purchase orders have not yet been issued.
- *Open purchase orders report.* This report shows purchases for which the related invoices have not yet been received or approved for payment.
- *Overdue deliveries report.* This report highlights those purchase transactions whose requested delivery dates have passed without the goods being received.

33.7.2 Exception reports

These reports are not necessarily regular reports, but are generated only in response to specific conditions. The system must be designed to inform management about all variances as well as abnormal and conflicting conditions, including schedule lags, price and terms variances, rejections, and cancellations.

33.7.3 Enquiry reports

The on-line purchasing and receiving system makes it possible to make enquiries interactively. Transactions can be listed and summarized in many ways and the current status of master records can be shown at any time in the form of screen displays or printed reports. Examples include:

- the status of an individual purchase order;
- recent purchase orders placed with a particular supplier;
- details of all purchase orders placed for a particular inventory item;
- the current on-hand balance for a particular inventory item;
- outstanding invoices for goods delivered by a particular supplier.

33.7.4 Managerial reports

Managerial reports are specifically designed to aid management in decision-making. They should be analytical in nature and should link up with other applications, where possible. They should not contain too much detail. They include the following:

- *Purchase analysis.* This report shows the levels of purchasing activity for each supplier, inventory item, buyer, and cost centre. It is used mainly to evaluate performance.
- *Supplier performance analysis.* This report provides a more detailed evaluation of suppliers' performance. It is used to select or reject certain suppliers based on volume, prices, compliance with delivery dates, quality of products, etc.
- *Cost of purchases analysis.* This report makes it possible to observe the various cost elements of the purchasing and receiving function. Sound purchasing management requires that all relevant costs of its function be identified, measured and expressed, for instance, in terms of purchase contracts awarded per period.

The examples discussed above illustrate how computerized accounting information systems can substantially improve the information available for those managing and operating the purchasing and receiving function. Scheduled reports can regularly provide large volumes of information for reference and audit purposes. They can also summarize this information according to various decision-relevant criteria. Exception reports can highlight specific circumstances, while enquiry reports can produce up-to-date and special purpose information on request. Managerial reports are especially designed reports containing concise information for decision-making at the highest level.[1]

33.8 SUMMARY

The purchasing and receiving function is the first application in the expenditure cycle of the AIS. Here the need for goods and services is recognized, orders are placed, goods and services are received, inspected and distributed, and supplier invoices are validated and approved.

Most of the data arise from user departments, inventory, and suppliers, and the source documents used include purchase requisitions, purchase orders, receiving reports, and supplier invoices. Pre-formatted screens are used to enter and edit data which are stored and updated afterwards in databases containing records pertaining to suppliers, inventory, and open purchase orders.

Data processing involves processing purchase transactions and updating the supplier and inventory master files.

Because a variety of control risks exist in the processing of purchase orders, certain general and application controls are applied to minimize these risks.

The most important outputs from the system are reports that provide useful management information for decision-making and controlling operations necessary to satisfy the objectives of the purchasing and receiving function of the AIS.

REVIEW QUESTIONS

1. Describe the objectives of the purchasing and receiving function of an accounting information system.
2. Describe the major functions of the purchasing and receiving system.
3. Give a brief description of the source documents involved in a system for the purchasing and receiving of goods and services.
4. Discuss the database structure and processing requirements associated with an on-line system for purchasing and receiving.
5. Describe the flow of data through an on-line system for purchasing and receiving, and indicate what interfaces with other subsystems are needed within the AIS.
6. Give an overview of the accounting controls necessary for operating a system for purchasing and receiving.
7. Explain the importance of the purchasing and receiving system in providing management information and, in this respect, describe the various reports that the system should be able to produce.

SELECTED REFERENCES AND RECOMMENDED READING

1. Cushing, B. E. and Romney, M. B. 1990. *Accounting Information Systems —A Comprehensive Approach.* Fifth edition. Reading, Massachusetts: Addison-Wesley.
2. Davis, J. R., Alderman, C. W. and Robinson, L. A. 1990. *Accounting Information Systems —A Cycle Approach.* Third edition. New York: John Wiley and Sons.
3. Wilkinson, J. W. 1989. *Accounting and Information Systems: Essential Concepts and Applications.* New York: John Wiley and Sons.

CHAPTER 34 Accounts payable and cash disbursements

34.1 INTRODUCTION

It is essential that an undertaking's obligations are handled and processed in a responsible and effective way. An *accounts payable* (or *creditors*) system is used to keep track of amounts that are owed by a firm to suppliers of goods and services (for inventory items or general office purchases), and the *cash disbursement* part of the system caters for the actual payment of amounts owed. The system also provides information for cash management purposes.

In most companies, almost all cash disbursements are effected through the accounts payable system. This includes payroll payments, petty cash funds, and tax liabilities. The accounts payable system, together with cash management, accounts receivable, and payroll, is therefore one of the most closely scrutinized systems in any organization.

Responsible handling and processing of a firm's trade obligations is very important because it directly affects the ratio of current assets to current liabilities. The process of liquidating current liabilities requires the necessary support documents for payment. This involves the functions of purchasing and receiving. Payment should never be made without proper authorization and, in most cases, payment will not be made until goods and services have been received according to the purchase agreement.[2]

34.2 OBJECTIVES AND FUNCTIONS OF THE SYSTEM

The main objective of the accounts payable and cash disbursement function is to facilitate the exchange of cash with suppliers of goods and services. This entails:

- determining that invoices are valid, authorized, and correct;
- recording and classifying expenditures promptly and accurately;
- posting obligations and cash disbursements to the appropriate suppliers' accounts and the general ledger;
- providing management with all information regarding expenditure incurred and cash outflow.[3]

Functions associated with accounts payable and cash disbursements include:[3]

- invoice vouching;
- updating and maintaining accounts payable;
- cash disbursements;
- accounting distribution.

34.2.1 Invoice vouching

This function links up with the validation function of the purchasing and receiving system. Invoices received from suppliers are checked against supporting documents to ascertain that goods and services were duly authorized, ordered, and received. The system re-calculates item amounts and totals, discounts and discount periods, as well as allocating expenditure to the appropriate expense accounts.

34.2.2 Updating and maintaining accounts payable

In most cases, goods and services are acquired on credit. This means that invoices must be posted (credited) to the applicable suppliers' accounts in the *accounts payable subsidiary ledger.*

34.2.3 Cash disbursements

Once invoices have been recorded, the particular creditors have to be paid. If suppliers allow cash discounts, amounts must be paid before the end of the discount period. The loss of cash discounts will ultimately have a detrimental effect on net current assets. Goods and services not subject to discounts should be paid before the due dates shown on the invoices.

Remittance advices are prepared which show the invoices to be paid. Cheques are then made out to pay the total amounts shown on the remittance advices. All payments are then debited to the suppliers' accounts in the *accounts payable subsidiary ledger.*

34.2.4 Accounting distribution

The accounts payable division is usually responsible for allocating invoice expenditure to the various costing and general ledger accounts. Detailed invoice data are used for costing purposes, but summarized amounts payable and cash disbursements are posted to general ledger accounts. This function constitutes the interface between the expenditure cycle and the general ledger system.

34.2.5 Other functions

The accounts payable and cash disbursement system usually also handles related functions like payroll disbursements, expense distribution, purchase returns and allowances, miscellaneous cash disbursements, and petty cash disbursements. Miscellaneous disbursements include amounts paid to acquire fixed assets, repay loans and mortgages, and make cash investments.

34.3 DATA SOURCES AND INPUTS

The accounts payable and cash disbursement system depends mainly on three independently prepared source documents, namely the *purchase order* which authorizes a transaction, the *supplier's invoice* requesting payment, and the *receiving report* which gives proof of receipt of goods or performance of services. These documents also provide the interface between the purchasing and receiving function and the accounts payable and cash disbursements function.

34.3.1 Purchase order

The purchase order is the controlling document for all activities relating to the acquisition of goods and services. This document is used to check the information on the suppliers' invoices which are sent through for payment.

34.3.2 Receiving report

This document, together with the purchase order, will confirm that goods and services shown on the supplier's invoice have, in fact, been received according to specification.

34.3.3 Supplier's invoice

The preparation of remittance advices and cash payments is triggered by approved suppliers' invoices, together with associated purchase orders and receiving reports. These also provide the basis for allocating expenditure to various cost centres and general ledger accounts.

34.3.4 Payment voucher

Payment for services rendered can also be requested by way of a pre-numbered payment voucher. In this case, invoices can be summarized and accumulated. This provides a means of grouping the vouching documents together for approval.

34.3.5 Remittance advice

The pre-numbered remittance advice is both an output and an input document. It is the result of one or more invoices to be paid to a supplier, and at the same time it is the input for the issue of a pre-numbered cheque.

34.4 DATABASE STRUCTURE

The database associated with accounts payable and cash disbursements is highly interrelated with the databases for purchasing and receiving. Figure 34.1 shows how the supplier invoice, disbursement voucher (remittance advice), and cash disbursements (cheques), relate to the supplier master file, other supplier transactions, and even the inventory master file.

The database records for accounts payable and cash disbursements consist of the following master, transaction, reference, and history records (grouped together in files):[3]

- supplier master file;
- supplier reference and history file;
- accounts payable master file;
- general ledger master file;
- supplier invoices transaction file;
- cheque transaction file.

34.4.1 Supplier master file

This file holds all information related to a firm's suppliers of goods and services. It is important to keep it up to date (eg. when suppliers change their addresses or when new suppliers are used). Changes should be made on-line as and when they occur.

34.4.2 Supplier reference and history file

This file contains summary data pertaining to each active supplier, including evaluations and past purchases. Data from this file may be used to select suppliers and to analyse purchasing trends.

34.4.3 Accounts payable master file

The accounts payable records (creditors) can be part of the *supplier master file* or they can be a separate master file containing purely accounting records linked to the supplier master file. These records store all data concerning amounts owed to suppliers and other creditors, as well as other related data.

34.4.4 General ledger master file

The various general ledger accounts each have a database record. Summary transactions are updated to the appropriate ledger accounts, eg. the *accounts payable control account* and the *cash account.* The records in the general ledger master file constitute the complete chart of accounts and show the current status of all account balances.

34.4.5 Supplier invoices transaction file

Once approved invoices have been received and updated to the *accounts payable master file,* they are stored in an invoice transaction file for future use and reference. Payment vouchers can also be stored in this file. The records in this file can cross-reference to purchase orders, receiving reports, cost centres, ledger accounts, remittance advices, and cheques.

34.4.6 Cheque transaction file

The cheque transaction file forms part of a firm's cash book. All cheque payments are stored as records in this file and correspond with the applicable invoice records that make up each payment.

34.5 DATA FLOW AND PROCESSING REQUIREMENTS

With computerized, on-line accounting information systems, it is possible to interactively enter, edit, and update supplier invoices. The flow of data is shown in Figure 34.1. The processing of accounts payable and cash disbursement transactions can be done in three steps:[3]

- validating and entering supplier invoices;
- updating accounts payable records;
- preparing cash disbursements.

34.5.1 Suppliers' invoice procedure

When supplier invoices are received, they are entered into the system, checked against the corresponding open purchase order and receiving report records, and then updated as transactions into an *invoice transaction file.* Any exceptions or errors will be shown

FIGURE 34.1. System flowchart for accounts payable and cash disbursements.

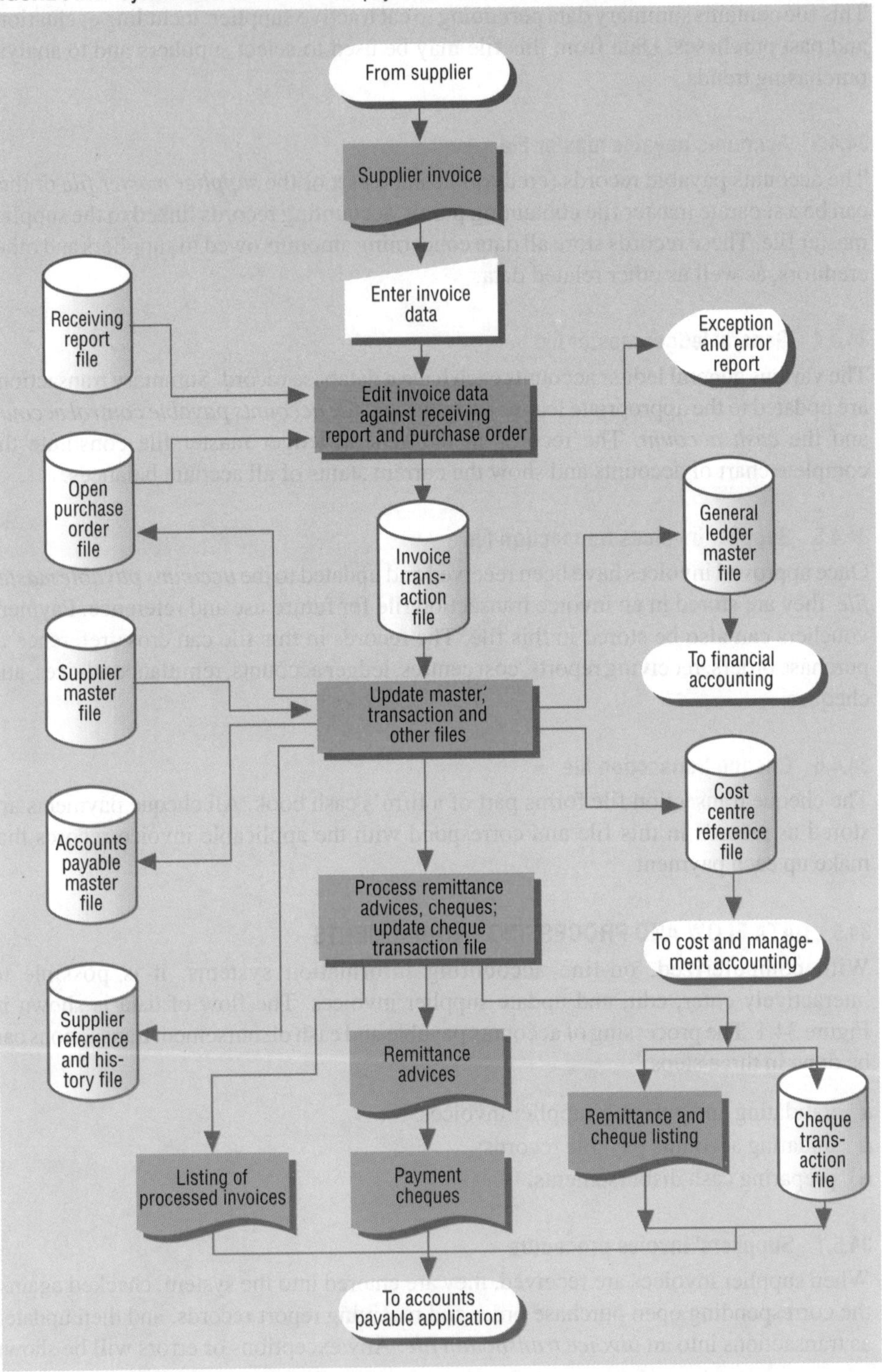

on a terminal screen or exception report. Payment vouchers are entered and edited in the same way, and they are stored in the invoice transaction file.

34.5.2 Accounts payable procedure

Accepted supplier invoices are then updated to the supplier accounts in the *accounts payable master file.* These master records will reflect the amounts payable to creditors. At the same time, the supplier reference and history file is updated with the transactions, and the applicable records in the open purchase order file are closed off.

The accounts payable application is also responsible for updating the appropriate general ledger and cost centre records. The system must automatically generate summarized and accumulated data to be updated to applicable expenditure accounts (accounting distribution) and the accounts payable control account. Where a proper cost accounting system is in operation, detailed expenditure data will be updated to various cost centres in a cost centre reference file.

34.5.3 Cash disbursements procedure

Once invoices have been updated to the *accounts payable master file* and the *invoices transaction file,* they are ready for payment. The preparation of remittance advices and cheques usually takes place in batch mode. This means that at a certain moment the system is interrogated to determine which invoices and accounts are ready for payment. The system will then produce applicable remittance advices and, for each of them, issue a payment cheque. At the same time, the cheque transaction file is updated with the payment transactions and several listings and reports are produced.

34.6 ACCOUNTING CONTROLS

Internal control procedures must be included in the design of the accounts payable and cash disbursements system to ensure that:[1]

- supplier invoices received for payment have been checked against the corresponding purchase orders and receiving reports;
- only those invoices that have been properly approved are paid;
- discounts that have been allowed are taken and payments are made before due dates;
- proper control exists over all cash outflows.

Strict internal control is necessary because this system facilitates the actual outflow of cash. It is therefore important to ensure that balances in supplier accounts are correct, amounts charged to ledger accounts and cost centres are correct, all purchase discounts are taken by paying creditors on time, invoices are paid only once, payments are made only for goods and services properly received and recorded, and cash resources are preserved.

To prevent fraud and to minimize risks, a proper set of general and application controls is built into the system.

34.6.1 General controls

The same kind of general controls would be implemented as for purchase orders and goods received (see Chapter 33). This would involve the separation of duties, complete and up-to-date documentation, and security in respect of on-line systems.

34.6.2 Application controls

Control points within the accounts payable and cash disbursement function include:[3]

- the receipt and approval of the supplier's invoice;
- the preparation of remittance advices;
- the disbursement of cash.

The following controls are applicable to the transactions associated with the accounts payable and cash disbursements function:[3]

- All suppliers' invoices must be properly matched to corresponding purchase orders and receiving reports, and all data items and computations on the invoices must be verified.
- Well-designed and pre-numbered source documents must be used.
- Data should be edited, and errors corrected, as soon as possible.
- Account balances in the accounts payable subsidiary ledger and other files must be reconciled periodically with the control accounts in the general ledger.
- Clearly established policies must exist for the valuation of accounts payable at the end of each accounting period.
- Discount periods should be monitored to ensure that all purchase discounts are taken.
- Strict control should be maintained over the signing of cheques and the authorization of bank transfers.
- Monthly reconciliation of bank accounts should be undertaken by someone who is not involved in cash disbursement activities.
- There should be periodic transaction listings, and account summaries, to provide an adequate audit trail.

34.7 MANAGEMENT INFORMATION REQUIREMENTS

The management information required from an accounts payable and cash disbursements system focuses on cash flow, payments, accounting distribution, and liabilities. Managers who are in charge of such applications should have sufficient knowledge of all operations to satisfy themselves that adequate controls are built in, and to assume full responsibility for the accuracy and completeness of input and the reliability of output. In addition, they must be able to provide top management with important information concerning decision-making at the strategic level.[2]

Management information reports may again be classified as operational listings and reports, exception reports, enquiry screens and reports, and managerial reports.[3]

34.7.1 Operational listings and reports

These listings and reports are used for general control purposes. They are scheduled reports containing detailed and summary data of all transactions during a certain period, and they help to maintain the audit trail of the system.

- *Daily invoice listing.* This listing will contain data on all invoices received and processed for payment.
- *Remittance advices and cheques.* These are the end products of the system and may be grouped under the 'operational listings and reports' heading because of their operational nature.
- *Daily payments listing.* This listing contains data on all invoices, remittance advices, and cheques associated with actual payments made.
- *Cheque listings.* These are used for bank reconciliation purposes.
- *Open amounts payable report.* This report contains data on all invoices or accounts payable that have not yet been paid.

34.7.2 Exception reports

These reports are generated only in response to specific conditions (eg. exceptions to particular rules). The system must be designed to inform management about all variances as well as abnormal and conflicting conditions, including unapproved invoices for payment, discrepancies, price variances, discount due dates missed, and maybe double payments.

34.7.3 Enquiry reports

The on-line accounts payable and cash disbursements system makes it possible to make enquiries interactively. Transactions can be listed and summarized in several ways and the current status of master records can be shown at any time. Such enquiries can be in the form of screen displays or printed reports. Examples include:

- the status of a particular invoice;
- recent payments made to a particular supplier;
- details of all invoices received from a particular supplier;
- details of invoices paid in respect of a certain cost centre;
- the outstanding amount payable to a particular supplier;
- details of a single cash disbursement.

34.7.4 Managerial reports

Managerial reports are specifically designed to aid management in decision-making. They should be analytical in nature, not contain too much detail, and should link up with other applications where possible. Managerial reports for accounts payable and cash disbursements would include the following:

- *Payment analysis.* This report analyses all payments made by type, supplier, and cost centre. It may be used for budgetary control purposes.

- *Accrued liability report.* A summary of all unpaid liabilities provides the basis for recognizing a firm's obligations to its creditors.
- *Cash discount performance report.* This report gives an overview of the extent of cash discounts taken (or not taken).
- *Cash forecasting analysis.* The system must provide adequate information to support the preparation of short-term cash flow forecasts.

34.8 SUMMARY

The accounts payable and cash disbursements system is the second application in the expenditure cycle of an AIS. Since it is concerned with the actual disbursement of cash, it must be strictly controlled. Approved invoices are received from the purchasing and receiving function. They are checked and then entered into the system. Other functions include updating the accounts payable master file, allocating expenditure, and making the actual cash disbursements.

The supplier invoice is the main data source, supported by the corresponding purchase order and receiving report. The remittance advices produced by the system also serve as inputs for the printing of cheques.

The database consists of the supplier master file, reference and history file, an invoice transaction file, the accounts payable master file, the general ledger master file, the cost centre reference file, and the cheque transaction file. Invoice transactions are updated to the supplier master file, reference and history file, the accounts payable master file, and the cost centre reference file. Thereafter remittance advices and cheques are produced and the cheque transaction file is updated accordingly.

The fact that payments and cash are involved, means that strict controls have to be applied to prevent fraud and other risks. For this reason several general and application controls are built into the system to minimize these risks.

Although remittance advices and cheques are important outputs from the system, the management information derived from them is imperative for decision-making and for controlling the accounts payable and cash disbursements function of the AIS.

REVIEW QUESTIONS

1. Describe the objectives of the accounts payable and cash disbursements function of an accounting information system.
2. Describe the major functions of the accounts payable and cash disbursements system.
3. Give a brief description of the various documents involved in a system for accounts payable and cash disbursements.
4. Explain how the data files associated with a system for accounts payable and cash disbursements are updated.
5. Describe the flow of data through an on-line system for accounts payable and cash disbursements, and indicate what interfaces with other subsystems within the AIS are needed.

6. Explain why it is necessary to have strict accounting controls within a system that deals with creditors and cash payments.
7. Give an overview of the management information needed to operate and manage an accounts payable and cash disbursement function.

SELECTED REFERENCES AND RECOMMENDED READING

1. Cushing, B. E. and Romney, M. B. 1990. *Accounting Information Systems —A Comprehensive Approach.* Fifth edition. Reading, Massachusetts: Addison-Wesley.
2. Davis, J. R., Alderman, C. W. and Robinson, L. A. 1990. *Accounting Information Systems —A Cycle Approach.* Third edition. New York: John Wiley and Sons.
3. Wilkinson, J. W. 1989. *Accounting and Information Systems: Essential Concepts and Applications.* New York: John Wiley and Sons.

CHAPTER 35 Inventory management

35.1 INTRODUCTION

The second cycle in the operations of a manufacturing firm is the *manufacturing cycle,* also called the *conversion cycle.* Here raw materials acquired during the expenditure cycle are converted into manufactured goods to be sold during the revenue cycle. The *inventory* function of such a firm receives, stores, controls, and issues materials and goods for this purpose. In a simple merchandising firm, no manufacturing cycle would exist and so the inventory management function could be classified under the expenditure cycle.

Various types of materials and goods may be controlled by the inventory function. These include raw materials, component parts, work-in-process, finished goods, and items held for resale. In this chapter we focus on items utilized in the manufacturing process and finished goods for general use and resale.

Inventory management is an area of primary concern to all business organizations involved in manufacturing goods and supplying them to the market. Flanked by the purchasing and marketing functions, the inventory management system resides at the very heart of the organization. Looking at inventory management from a systems point of view, one can consider two phases; *raw materials* and *finished goods.* Finished goods may also include goods acquired directly, like tools, office supplies, and other equipment (see Figure 35.1).

The most significant inventory products are those held for resale, materials consumed in the production of marketable finished goods, and items expended or capitalized in the manufacturing process.[2]

FIGURE 35.1. Physical flow of materials through an organization.

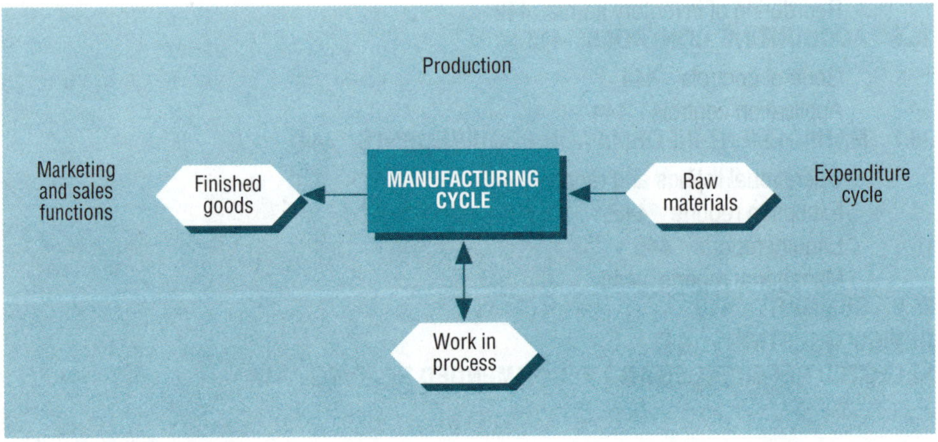

35.2 OBJECTIVES AND FUNCTIONS OF THE SYSTEM

The inventory management system is a structure of interacting people, equipment, procedures, and controls. The main objective of the inventory management system is to provide logistic support to the production and marketing functions in the most economical and practicable way. This includes the provision of timely and reliable financial information for management purposes.[2]

Particular functions within the inventory management system are:[2]

- issuing purchase requisitions;
- receiving purchased goods;
- store-keeping and controlling goods;
- issuing materials and other goods.

35.2.1 Issuing purchase requisitions

The inventory management function must provide suitable quantities of materials and goods for the normal activities of a business enterprise. The system must therefore be capable of generating purchase requisitions when:

- requests for new materials or other items are received from various internal departments;
- items needed for production or other purposes are out of stock;
- reorder points are reached.

35.2.2 Receiving purchased goods

The inventory function must receive materials and other items in accordance with the specifications stated on purchasing requisitions. It must be able to record data concerning received items as shown on the corresponding receiving reports or supplier invoices.

35.2.3 Store-keeping and controlling goods

The system must be capable of recording and processing received goods, and keeping track of them within a store-keeping environment (store or warehouse). Access to inventory assets should only be permitted when authorized by management. The recorded accountability for inventory items must be compared with the physical items on hand at reasonable intervals. Any variances must be reported instantly.

35.2.4 Issuing materials and other goods

The system must be able to handle, control, and process all issues of materials and goods in accordance with user requisitions supplied. Such user requisitions may come from the various internal departments.

35.3 DATA SOURCES AND INPUTS

A manufacturing environment usually has three major types of inventory. These are *raw materials for the production function, work-in-process,* and *finished goods for the marketing and sales functions.* The inventory management system's primary source document is the *user requisition for materials or goods.* Other source documents are purchase orders, packing slips, and supplier invoices for recording goods received.

35.3.1 User requisition

A user requisition may come from the marketing and sales department (eg. a shipping order or warehouse requisition for finished goods), the production department (eg. for raw materials to be used in the production process), or other department (eg. for office furniture or stationery). Work-in-process items are usually requisitioned to be further processed by the production department into finished goods.

35.3.2 System generated purchase requisitions

Although these purchase requisitions are produced by the system, they also constitute a form of input. They become input because of the need for the purchasing of additional goods (in the same way as user requisitions become input when inadequate quantities are available).

35.3.3 Purchase orders

When purchase requisitions have been submitted to the purchasing department, and items have been ordered, the purchase order is used to update the inventory master file with these data.

35.3.4 Packing slip

When ordered goods are received, the packing slip (delivery note) or supplier invoice serves as an input to update the actual stock on hand in the inventory master file.

35.4 DATABASE STRUCTURE

The inventory database interfaces with various other databases. Figure 33.1 shows how the inventory database relates to the purchasing and receiving databases. The database records for the inventory management system consist of the following master, transaction, and reference records (grouped together in files):

- inventory master file;
- open purchase order file;
- receiving report file;
- back order file;
- inventory issues transaction file;
- general ledger master file;
- cost centre reference file.

35.4.1 Inventory master file

The inventory master file contains details of all raw materials or merchandise. This file forms the heart of all activities dealing with raw materials and other goods pertaining to the manufacturing and sale of finished goods. It is used by several applications such as purchasing and receiving, production management, and sales.

35.4.2 Open purchase order file

The open purchase order file is a transaction file which consists of data concerning purchase orders that have not yet been approved for payment. The structure (according to order number) of these records should allow for repeating line items containing item number, quantity ordered, and unit price. For the inventory system it will contain details of all items ordered but not yet delivered or paid for.

35.4.3 Receiving report file

When materials and goods are received into inventory, detailed data are stored in the receiving report file from which receiving reports are produced.

35.4.4 Back order file

Back orders are necessary when insufficient quantities of products are available to fill sales orders. In such cases purchase orders are initiated by records in the back order file and, when these items are received into inventory, the back order file is updated accordingly.

35.4.5 Inventory issues transaction file

When inventory items are issued (which may include raw materials, finished goods for the sales department, and finished goods to go to warehouses), details of such issues are contained in the inventory issues transaction file.

35.4.6 General ledger master file

The various general ledger accounts each have a database record. Summary transactions are updated to the appropriate ledger accounts — eg. the inventory control account and various expenditure accounts. The records in this file constitute the complete chart of accounts and show the current status of all account balances.[4]

35.4.7 Cost centre reference file

It is important for a manufacturing firm to gather detailed data about the costs involved in different production processes. Cost data pertaining to inventory items (eg. raw materials) issued to such processes are therefore stored in the cost centre reference file. From there they are further processed and used for cost and management accounting purposes.

35.5 DATA FLOW AND PROCESSING REQUIREMENTS

From the system flowchart in Figure 35.2, it is clear that the data flow and processing cycle takes place in three steps, namely *ordering, purchasing and receiving inventory items*, *issuing the items*, and *producing reorder instructions when reorder points are reached.*[4]

35.5.1 Purchasing and receiving

The ordering, purchasing, and receiving of inventory items is handled by the purchasing and receiving application of which the data flow and processing requirements have already been outlined in paragraph 33.5.

35.5.2 Inventory issues

Requisitions for the issuing of inventory items may come from the production department (for raw materials and other goods), marketing and sales department (for finished goods required by way of shipping orders), warehouses (where finished goods are distributed), and even other departments like the financial department (for goods like stationery and office furniture). Requisition data are entered into the system and processed to update the *inventory master file* (with items issued), the *back orders file* (where issues originate from orders that could not be filled), and the *inventory issues transaction file* (which will hold detailed data about all items issued). At the same time, the *inventory control account* in the general ledger file is updated and, where expenditure is involved, so are the applicable expense accounts. Where costing systems are in operation, the *cost centre reference file* is updated for future reference.

35.5.3 Reordering of inventory items

The inventory master file is periodically interrogated to determine whether reorder situations have arisen. Processing to determine reorder points, out-of-stock situations, and economic order quantities, will eventually produce the necessary reorder reports which serve as input to the purchasing and receiving application.

35.6 ACCOUNTING CONTROLS

Because of the various organizational interfaces of the inventory management system, internal control procedures must ensure that:[3]

- sufficient levels of inventory are maintained to maximize operational efficiency;
- the cost of carrying inventory is minimized;
- system operations are efficient;
- resource security is maintained.

Inventory management's custodial function requires strict control over items received, physical stock on hand, and items issued for use or sale. The financial investment involved is usually rather high. The occurrence of inferior items, too many items, or too few items, may result in financial losses.

Possible risks associated with inventory include theft, destruction, losses during movement, incorrect accounting, and discrepancies between physical inventory and book inventory. To prevent fraud and minimize risks, a proper set of general and application controls is necessary.[2]

FIGURE 35.2 System flowchart for inventory management.

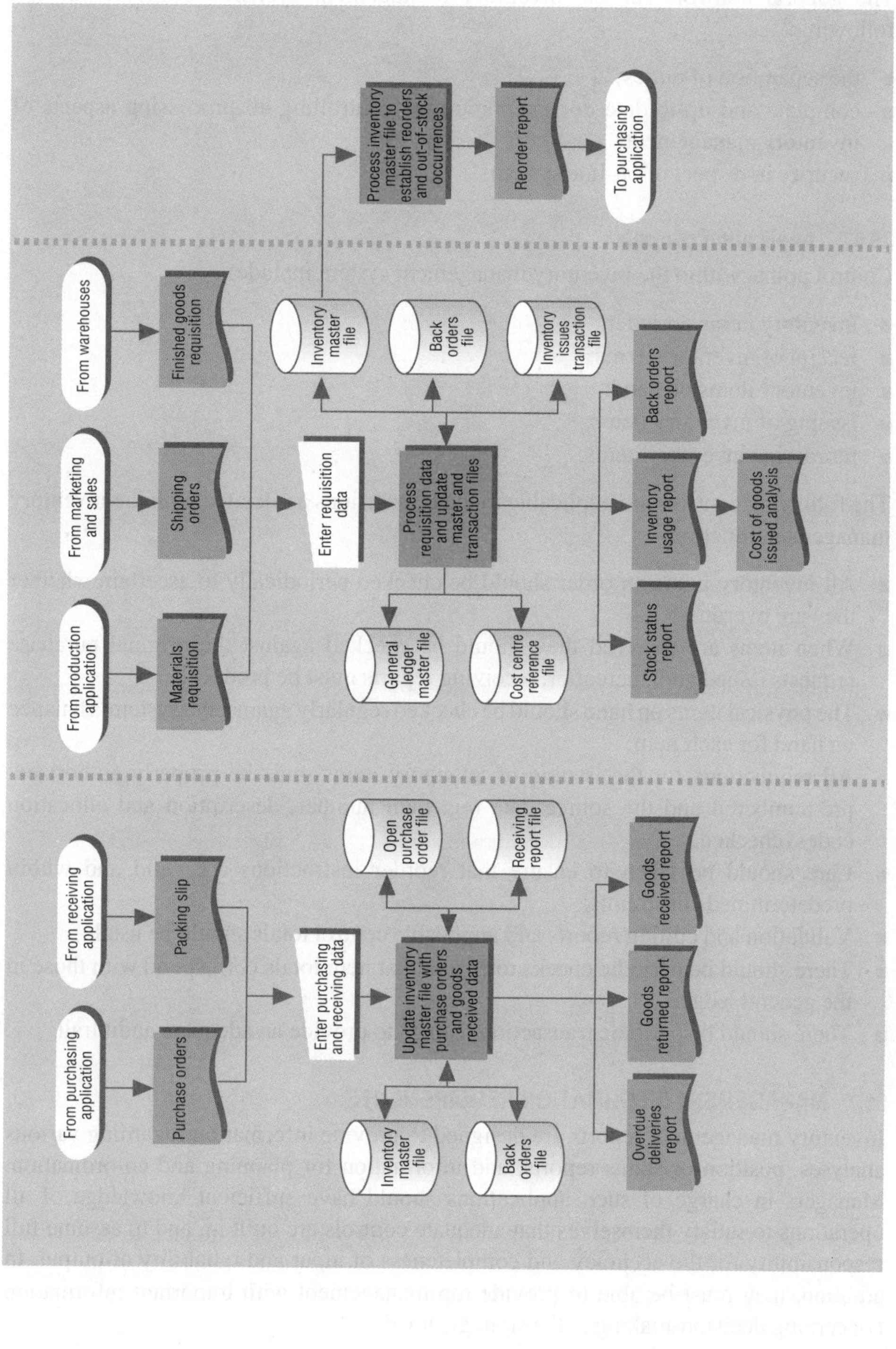

35.6.1 General controls

The general controls for the inventory management system would include the following:[4]

- the separation of duties;
- complete and up-to-date documentation for controlling all processing aspects of inventory management;
- security in respect of on-line systems.

35.6.2 Application controls

Control points within the inventory management system include:

- inventory items on order;
- receipt of inventory items;
- inventory items on hand;
- issuing of inventory items;
- reordering inventory items.

The following controls are applicable to the transactions associated with the inventory management function:[2]

- All inventory items on order should be checked periodically to ascertain whether they are overdue.
- When items are received they should be checked against the original purchase requests issued and, thereafter, receiving reports must be produced.
- The physical items on hand should be checked regularly against the system's balance on hand for each item.
- All requisitions for the issuing of inventory items must be properly authorized, pre-numbered and the source data (eg. item number, description and allocation codes) checked.
- Care should be taken to ensure that reorder instructions are valid and within predetermined constraints.
- Validation and editing reports and applicable control totals should be used.
- There should be periodic checks to ensure that item totals correspond with those in the general ledger.
- There should be periodic transaction listings to provide an adequate audit trail.

35.7 MANAGEMENT INFORMATION REQUIREMENTS

Inventory management reports are designed to provide information regarding various analyses, position or status reports, and information for planning and co-ordination. Managers in charge of such applications should have sufficient knowledge of all operations to satisfy themselves that adequate controls are built in, and to assume full responsibility for the accuracy and completeness of input and reliability of output. In addition, they must be able to provide top management with important information concerning decision-making at the strategic level.[2]

For management to be able to perform its control and decision-making functions, it needs various kinds of management information. This information is usually communicated by way of reports. These reports may again be classified as operational listings and reports, exception reports, enquiry screens and reports, and managerial reports.[4]

35.7.1 Operational listings and reports

These listings and reports are used for general control purposes. They are scheduled reports containing detailed and summary data of all transactions during a certain period. They help to maintain the audit trail of the system.

- *Daily listing with purchasing requests.* This listing contains data on all purchase requests sent through to the purchasing department.
- *Daily listing of all items ordered.* This listing contains data on all items actually ordered by the purchasing department.
- *Daily listing of all inventory items received.* This listing contains data on all items received due to purchase orders.
- *Daily listing of goods returned.* This listing shows the items which were not according to specification and which were returned to the suppliers.
- *Daily listing of requests for inventory items.* This listing contains data on all materials requisitions, shipping orders, and finished goods requisitions received.
- *Daily listing of all inventory items issued.* This listing contains full data on all materials and finished goods issued by way of materials requisitions, shipping orders, and finished goods requisitions.
- *Stock status report.* This report shows the status (eg. balance on hand and value) of all individual inventory items and their totals. These are used extensively by various departments for production control and planning purposes.
- *Reorder report.* This report is used for reordering inventory items based on reorder points and economic order quantities.
- *Back orders report.* This report shows which items have been issued due to back orders.

35.7.2 Exception reports

These reports are generated only in response to specific conditions. The system must be designed to inform management about all variances as well as abnormal and conflicting conditions, including slow-moving stock, discrepancies, and large price variances.[2]

35.7.3 Enquiry reports

The on-line inventory management system makes it possible to make enquiries interactively. Transactions can be listed and summarized in any way, and the current status of master records can be shown at any time. Enquiries can be in the form of screen displays or printed reports. Examples include:

- current status of a particular inventory item;

- status of a purchase request;
- details of receipts to date for a particular item;
- details of receipts to date for a particular supplier;
- issues to date with respect to a particular item;
- issues to date with respect to a particular cost centre.

35.7.4 Managerial reports

Managerial reports for the inventory management system would include the following:

- *Usage report.* This report contains statistics on individual inventory items requisitioned for production or other use (month or year to date).
- *Cost of goods issued report.* This report gives an analysis of the cost of goods issued to each of the cost centres involved.
- *Inventory performance report.* This report gives an analysis of the performance of this function over a period of time. Information will include turnover, average stock on hand compared to user requirements, safety stock, reorder points in relation to economic order quantities, and average value of stock on hand over a certain period.
- *Availability analysis.* This gives an analysis of the type and quantities of items available to be used by various departments for production planning, marketing, and cost estimates.

35.8 SUMMARY

The inventory management system is the first application in the manufacturing cycle of an AIS because no production can take place without raw materials and no sales can occur without finished goods being available in stock. The system interfaces with a wide spectrum of other applications and therefore strict control has to be exercised. When inventory items are received they have to be checked against supporting documents and then properly recorded and controlled, both physically and administratively.

From a business point of view, the inventory system's major function is the issuing of inventory items in the form of raw materials and finished goods to the production department or marketing and sales department. The availability of inventory items of acceptable quality, in the correct quantity, and at the correct time, is crucial to the operation of the business.

Materials requisitions, shipping orders, and finished goods requisitions are the main data sources for the issuing of stock. Reorder reports are important products from the system and form the basis for placing new purchasing requests.

The database consists of the inventory master file, receiving report file, inventory issues transaction file, and general ledger master file. Supporting files are the open purchase order file, back orders file, and cost centre reference file. Inventory receipts are updated to the master files, receiving report file, and open purchase order file. Inventory issues are updated to the master files, issues transaction file, and the cost centre reference file.

Because physical inventory items constitute an important asset to the business, strict controls have to be applied to prevent theft and other risks. For this reason, several controls are built into the system.

The management information derived from the system is imperative for decision-making and controlling the operational functions of the business.

REVIEW QUESTIONS

1. Describe the objectives of the inventory management function of an accounting information system.
2. Describe the major functions of the inventory management system.
3. Discuss the importance of the inventory management system for the normal operations of a manufacturing concern.
4. Give a brief description of the various documents involved in a system for the management of inventory.
5. Explain how the various files associated with the inventory management system support its operations.
6. Describe the flow of data through an on-line system for inventory management and indicate what interfaces with other subsystems are needed within the AIS.
7. Describe the accounting controls required within an inventory management system.
8. Give an overview of the management information produced by the inventory management system and highlight its importance to management in general.

SELECTED REFERENCES AND RECOMMENDED READING

1. Cushing, B. E. and Romney, M. B. 1990. *Accounting Information Systems —A Comprehensive Approach.* Fifth edition. Reading, Massachusetts: Addison-Wesley.
2. Davis, J. R., Alderman, C. W. and Robinson, L. A. 1990. *Accounting Information Systems —A Cycle Approach.* Third edition. New York: John Wiley and Sons.
3. Gelinas, U. J. Jr., Oram, A. E. and Wiggins, W. P. 1990. *Accounting Information Systems.* Boston: PWS-KENT.
4. Wilkinson, J. W. 1989. *Accounting and Information Systems: Essential Concepts and Applications.* New York: John Wiley and Sons.

CHAPTER 36 Production management and cost accounting

36.1 INTRODUCTION

The *production* (or *conversion*) part of the manufacturing cycle can be regarded as a recurring set of business activities and related data processing operations. The production management function includes planning the production process (eg. determining what is to be produced, how, and when), controlling the operations necessary to convert raw materials into finished products, and monitoring the efficiency and quality of these operations. The production management function is closely related to the purchasing, receiving, and inventory management functions.[1]

Data processing operations related to these activities include:

- preparing production orders;
- requisitioning raw materials for production;
- recording production activity;
- maintaining records regarding work-in-process.

This chapter deals with the production management function and the data processing operations that support it. It emphasizes the importance of the AIS in carrying out the data processing operations and in providing information to support production management. The chapter also deals with cost accounting within the production process. This facilitates the measurement of cost flows against predetermined cost standards, and the reporting of any deviations from them.[2]

An important computer-assisted component of the production process that will be discussed is *manufacturing resource planning,* known as MRP-II (to distinguish it from the original *materials requirements planning*).

36.2 OBJECTIVES AND FUNCTIONS OF THE SYSTEM

The main objective of production management and cost accounting is to facilitate the conversion of raw materials into products or finished goods. This involves ensuring that adequate raw materials are available, that orders are completed cost efficiently and in time, that finished goods are shipped on schedule, and that the required production costs are accumulated and reported.[6]

The specific functions related to these objectives include:

- entering and processing customer orders;
- planning the production process to fulfil those orders;
- controlling the production process;
- determining the costs of production orders.[6]

36.2.1 Production orders

When production orders are received, they are entered into the system and processed to initiate the production of the required products.

36.2.2 Planning the production process

The first step is to determine the specifications to which the products are to be manufactured. This is usually performed by an engineering design function. The second step is the actual production planning. The quantities of products to be manufactured are determined here along with the production schedule and the resources to be used. This function involves the *master production schedule*, the *materials requirements plan,* and the *capacity requirements plan* of MRP-II.

36.2.3 Controlling the production process

The production process is responsible for transforming the system's inputs (raw materials) into desired outputs (finished goods) in an effective and efficient manner. This involves the supply and movement of materials, the application of labour, and the use of machinery and equipment in an orderly way. The system monitors the status of production orders as they move through the production process and provides information with respect to resources used, work-in-process, and finished goods. This function is associated with the third part of MRP-II, namely *manufacturing control.*

36.2.4 Cost accounting

The cost accounting function has to be supported extensively by the AIS. Here standard costs are determined and recorded, actual production costs are calculated, variances are computed, and the overall costs of finished products are reported.[3]

36.3 MANUFACTURING RESOURCE PLANNING (MRP-II)

Manufacturing resource planning is a management tool (a planning and control technique) which simulates the functions of production and inventory control to provide management with information to answer questions such as:

- Should a new customer order be accepted?
- Is the production plan realistic?
- Where are the capacity bottlenecks?

A MRP-II system usually consists of certain key elements:

- the master production schedule (MPS);
- materials requirements planning (MRP);
- capacity requirements planning (CRP);
- manufacturing control.

MRP-II forms part of the overall production planning and control activities of a manufacturing firm. It involves the logistics or physical aspects of converting raw materials into finished goods.

It is important to be aware of the different planning horizons of master production scheduling, material requirements planning, capacity requirements planning, and the scheduling of operations. Figure 36.1 gives a pictorial comparison of the different planning horizons.

FIGURE 36.1. A typical comparison between planning horizons.

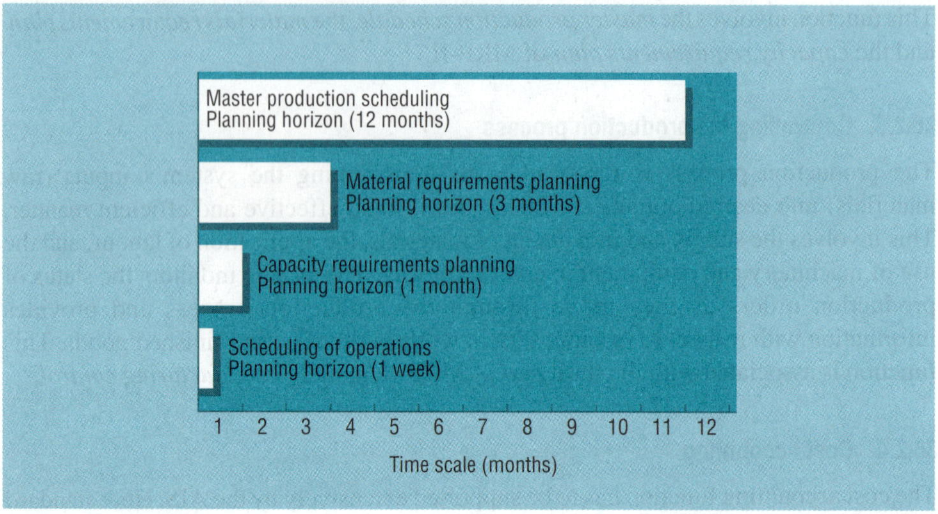

36.3.1 Functions of MRP-II

Figure 36.2 represents an overview of the planning and control systems in an MRP-II system. Planning starts with the formal definition of the *production plan,* which is a statement of management's objectives for the manufacturing plant in terms of production output rate and money. The production plan is one of the inputs to the first key element of MRP-II, namely the *master production schedule (MPS).*

Master production schedule

The production plan is converted into a product output rate per period (eg. week or month) in the form of the master production schedule. The MPS is developed through a series of interactive planning steps including resource planning, demand management, production planning, and initial capacity planning.[3]

Included in the production schedule is the product structure (outlining the materials which are used in production), routings (the work centres through which a product has to proceed — how it is made), and ordering policies (the quantity of materials or parts to be ordered).

The MPS is checked for validity against key resources (eg. available cash and available plant capacity). It should be noted that the check on key resource availability is on a global basis.

Materials requirements planning

The master production schedule is used as input to materials requirements planning (MRP) which is the second key element of MRP-II. Here the material requirements for the MPS are generated.

MRP also uses the following inputs:[3]

- bills of materials from the product structure file;
- inventory status data from the raw materials and finished goods master files;
- open order status data from the open work order file and open purchase order file.

FIGURE 36.2. The key systems of MRP-II.

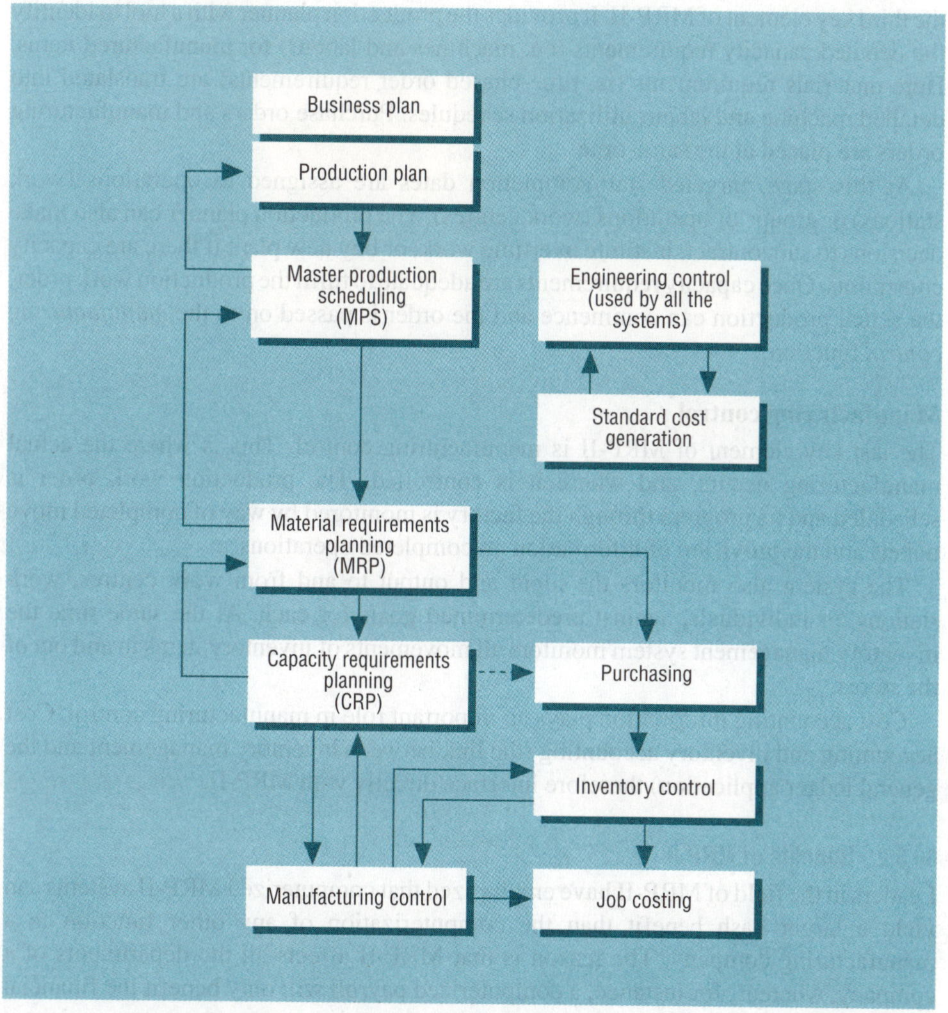

The bill of materials shows the standard raw material quantities (eg. component parts and sub-assemblies) that are necessary to produce a unit of finished goods (end products), as illustrated in Figure 36.3. By 'exploding' the bill of materials, MRP determines the standard raw materials quantities needed to produce the required number of output units shown in the MPS.[3]

The material requirements for particular products may be bought from vendors (*bought-out* items) or they may be manufactured by the company itself (*manufactured* items). The materials requirements for bought-out items are then passed on to the purchasing and receiving system and the material requirements for manufactured items are passed on to *capacity requirements planning.*

Capacity requirements planning

Materials requirements planning is followed by capacity requirements planning (CRP), the third key element of MRP-II. It provides the production planner with a tool to identify the detailed capacity requirements (eg. machines and labour) for manufactured items. Here materials requirements (ie. time-phased order requirements) are translated into detailed machine and labour utilization schedules. Purchase orders and manufacturing orders are placed at the same time.

At this stage, targeted start/completion dates are assigned to operations (work stations) or groups of operations (work centres). The production planner can also make decisions to subcontract, institute overtime work, or buy new plant if there are capacity constraints. Once capacity requirements are adequate to fulfil the production work order, the actual production can commence and the order is passed on to the *manufacturing control* function.

Manufacturing control

The last key element of MRP-II is manufacturing control. This is where the actual manufacturing occurs, and where it is controlled. The production work order is scheduled and its progress through the factory is monitored by way of completed move tickets and the provision of information on completed operations.

The system also monitors the input and output to and from work centres, work stations, or individuals, against predetermined goals for each. At the same time the inventory management system monitors all movements of inventory items in and out of the stores.

Cost accounting information plays an important role in manufacturing control. Cost accounting and inventory accounting (the link between inventory management and the general ledger application) therefore interface directly with MRP-II.

36.3.2 Benefits of MRP-II

Leaders in the field of MRP-II have emphasized that computerized MRP-II systems can yield a larger cash benefit than the computerization of any other function in a manufacturing company. The reason is that MRP-II affects all the departments of a company, whereas, for instance, a computerized payroll will only benefit the financial department.[4]

MRP-II also helps to achieve the main objectives of production and inventory management — ie. to keep inventories low, to provide a high level of customer service, and to run the plant (factory) as efficiently and effectively as possible. If one examines these objectives carefully, one will find that they are in conflict with one another. This conflict arises from the fact that to ensure customer service, products need to be in stock, which implies a high inventory level. If customer orders are falling behind schedule, one may need to work the plant overtime, which implies a less efficient manner of running the plant. MRP-II endeavours to optimize the attainment of the

FIGURE 36.3. A typical bill of materials.

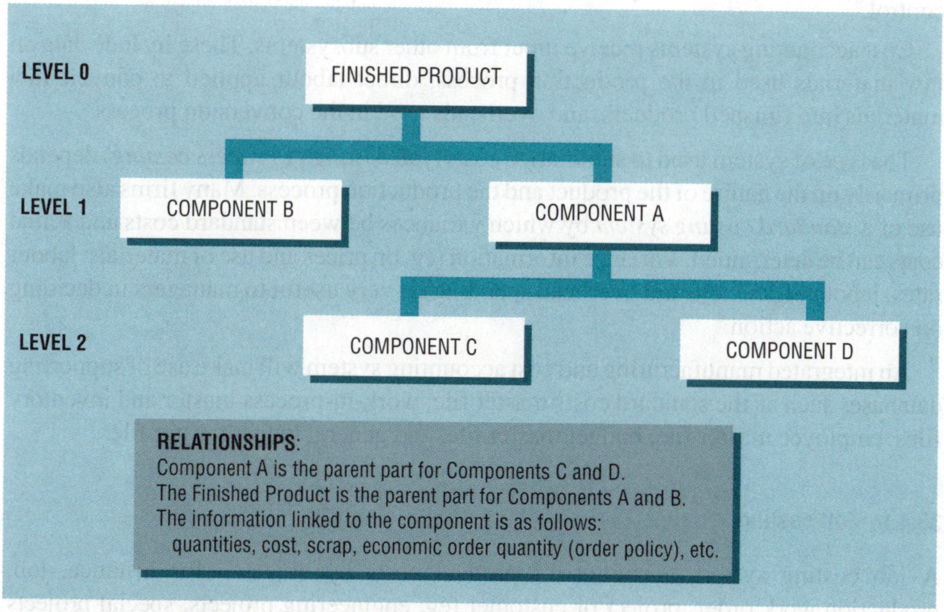

above-mentioned objectives by allowing for better communication between departments (eg. sales and inventory management).

An outflow from this is the so-called *just-in-time* (JIT) approach to the provision of materials and finished goods. It is a manufacturing method that is dedicated to producing the right items (parts, goods, etc.) at the right time, and in the right quantity.[3] This entails a strategy of purchasing, production, and inventory management which attempts to reduce in-process inventories. Factories hold inventories to a minimum at all stages of production and rely on deliveries from suppliers and other parts of the factory at the particular moment they are required in the production process.[5]

The benefits of MRP-II may be summarized as follows:

- a reduction in materials, work-in-process, and finished goods inventories;
- an improvement in customer service;
- a reduction in purchasing costs;
- a reduction in transport costs;
- a reduction in obsolescence;
- improved management information;
- accountability throughout the organization;
- improved manufacturing productivity.

36.4 COST ACCOUNTING

Cost accounting forms an important part of production management and control. Management will always be very interested in product cost per unit, regardless of the type of manufacturing. Information on unit costs is necessary to determine selling prices in order to ensure a fair return on sales. Such information is also essential for cost control.[2]

Cost accounting systems receive input from other subsystems. These include data on raw materials used in the production process, direct labour applied to convert raw materials into finished products, and overheads used in the conversion process.

The type of system used to summarize costs (*job costing* or *process costing*) depends primarily on the nature of the product and the production process. Many firms also make use of a *standard costing system* by which variances between standard costs and actual costs can be determined. Variance information (eg. on prices and use of materials, labour rates, labour efficiency, and overhead spending) is very useful to managers in deciding on corrective action.[6]

An integrated manufacturing and cost accounting system will make use of supporting databases such as the standard costs master file, work-in-process master and inventory files, employee master file, budget master file, and general ledger master file.

36.4.1 Job costing

A job costing system accounts for product costs by object — for instance, job, production work order, project or customer (eg. engineering projects, special projects by customer, and products like computers or furniture). Each product (or job) receives a unique job number to enable all related costs and operational data to be summarized. As the product moves through the production process, the work order (job number) moves with it, and all relevant costs are accumulated. The process can, however, be halted or delayed without any serious impact on other jobs. The product may be identified at various stages of completion and the value of work-in-process can be accurately determined at any time by summarizing accumulated costs incurred.[2]

36.4.2 Process costing

In some cases the production process cannot be interrupted and can therefore be regarded as *continuous.* A unit of such a product is not clearly identifiable until the entire process is completed. (This situation might apply to the manufacture of liquids such as paint or oil and substances such as wire and cement). This means that management must periodically estimate the degree of completion of work-in-process at each stage in the production process. Equivalent units are computed to arrive at a production cost per unit.[2]

36.5 DATA SOURCES AND INPUTS

Data used in the production management system come from a variety of source documents received from customers or generated by other departments. These include data obtained from sales forecasts and inventory status reports as well as various source documents used in the actual production process.[2]

36.5.1 Sales forecast

The sales forecast may be regarded as the single most important source of information for planning the allocation of resources in the production process. It is used to plan the type and quantity of products to be manufactured.

36.5.2 Stock status report

The production schedule is based on the sales forecast. It determines the quantities of various raw materials and other goods needed for manufacturing the required finished goods. This report contains data on the quantities of inventory items available for production purposes.

36.5.3 Bill of materials

A bill of materials originates from the *materials requirements plan* of MRP-II. It specifies the quantities of materials and parts to be used in a particular finished product. It provides production dispatchers with information needed to requisition all necessary materials from inventory prior to starting the production process.

36.5.4 Operations list

This list (also called a *routing sheet*) specifies the sequence of operations to be performed in converting materials and parts into a finished product. It may specify the work centres at which operations are to take place, machine requirements, and standard time allowances.[6]

36.5.5 Production work order

When an overall production plan has been developed, a schedule of manufacturing activities has been drawn up, raw materials and other goods are available, and the sequence of operations to manufacture a product has been described, the production process can be set in motion by issuing a production work order. This document is used for cost accounting purposes as well as physical flow and production control.

36.5.6 Materials requisition

This source document directs the storekeeper to issue materials, parts, or other inventory items to designated work centres or persons. It specifies the production work order number, the work centre to which materials are to be transferred, and the specific items and quantities.[1]

36.5.7 Move ticket

This document authorizes the physical movement of a production work order (work-in-process) from one work centre to the next one listed on the work order. It records the quantities of items received and contains data to help monitor progress.[6]

36.5.8 Job time ticket

Another document used to record production activity is the job time ticket. Such a document is completed by each factory worker when an assigned production operation is completed. It specifies data such as production work order number, employee number, work centre number, quantity completed, and total time consumed. These data are also used for cost accounting purposes.[1]

36.5.9 Other source documents

Other source documents used in the production process include the sales order, purchase requisition, purchase order, receiving report, and documents involved in accounts payable and cash disbursements.[6]

36.6 DATABASE STRUCTURE

The production database in a manufacturing company may be regarded as a set of closely related databases. These would include the marketing database (to be discussed in the next chapter), the purchasing database, the inventory database, the product structure file, and the production work-in-process database. The product structure file supports the production planning process, while the production work-in-process database forms the heart of the production system. The latter consists of several files, including the open production work order file, the work-in-process master file, and the production operations file.[1]

36.6.1 Product structure file

This file contains the engineering specifications for each product, including the quantities of raw materials required and the type and sequence of operations to be performed. A bill of materials and an operations list can be generated from this file.

36.6.2 Purchasing and materials inventory master files

These files contain data about quantities of raw materials and parts on order or on hand. These data are required when preparing a detailed production schedule. The *master production plan,* on the other hand, together with the bill of materials, indicates the raw materials to be ordered.

36.6.3 Open production work order file

In this file the emphasis is on the production work order. The work order number is the primary key and a record shows the description and the current status of a particular work order in the production process.

36.6.4 Work-in-process master file

This file represents the control centre of the production process. Figure 36.4 shows how the work-in-process master file relates to other files. Each work-in-process record summarizes the costs incurred for raw materials, direct labour, and overheads in respect of a particular work order. These records comprise a subsidiary ledger supporting the work-in-process inventory account in the general ledger.

FIGURE 36.4. Database structure for work-in-process.

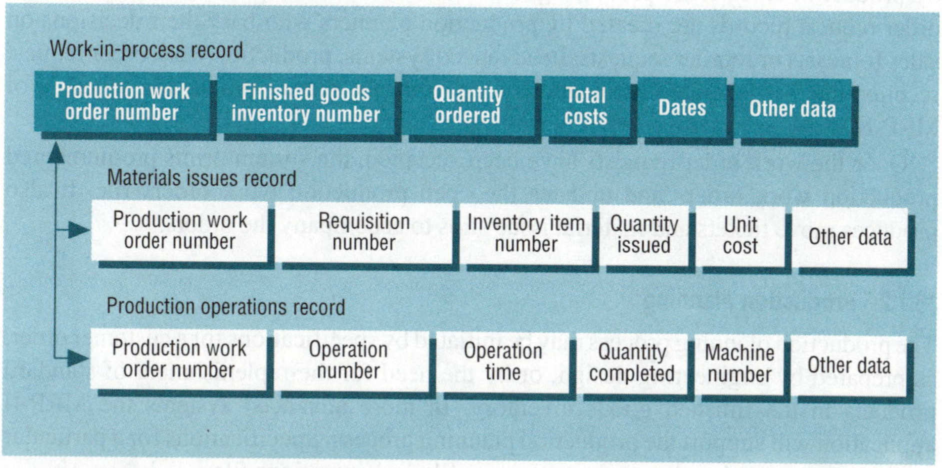

36.6.5 Production operations file

This file contains records with data regarding the production operations themselves. It is also used as a reference for scheduling and cost accounting purposes. In Figures 36.5 and 36.6 the file has been split into three separate files: the *production schedule file,* the *production operations file,* and the *standard costs file.*

36.6.6 Materials requisition file

This file contains data on all raw materials and parts issued for the production process. Although it performs an important role in production, it is actually part of the inventory management database.

36.6.7 Other files

Additional files that are frequently used in the production process are the *machine loading file,* which shows the status of each machine, and the *production history file* with data on all completed production work orders.

36.7 DATA FLOW AND PROCESSING REQUIREMENTS

The two basic activities associated with the manufacturing function are the *initiation of production orders* and the *performance of production activities.* MRP-II and cost accounting applications provide supporting functions.[1]

36.7.1 Production work orders

Initiating a production process involves creating a production work order request record containing data like finished goods inventory number, quantity to be produced, and requested completion date. After these are checked and validated, they are processed to prepare production work orders.

In the case of customer orders, order request records are usually created as a by-product of sales order processing. If, however, items are produced for inventory, order request records are created by production planners who base their decisions on sales forecasts or reorder requests. In advanced systems, production work order request records may be generated automatically, eg. from the master production schedule of MRP-II.

Once the work order requests have been accepted, the system prints pre-numbered production work orders and updates the open production work orders file. It also produces move tickets and material issue slips to accompany the orders.

36.7.2 Production planning

The production planning process may be initiated by specifications for a customer order, as prepared by engineering design, or by the need for the replenishment of standard products in the finished goods inventory. In more advanced systems the MRP-II application will support the production planning process. Specifications for a particular product are updated to the product structure file and operations file.

The system then performs several steps to initiate the actual production process; Figure 36.5 depicts the data flow associated with these steps. Firstly, the system produces bills of materials and operations lists for each product. Secondly, it produces a (revised) production schedule containing start dates and it updates the operations file. Thirdly, it produces a materials requirements report showing the materials and parts needed to fill production orders. Finally, it updates the machine loading file to assign machines to the production process.[6]

36.7.3 Production activities

Production activities are recorded in the form of detailed records as they occur. The system flowchart in Figure 36.6 shows the data flow regarding the production and completion of finished goods. A record is created for each completed production operation, containing data such as employee number, production work order number, operation number, quantity, and time spent. This record is based on the job time ticket. Machine utilization is recorded in a similar way.

As inventory items are moved from one location to another, a record is created containing data such as production work order number, material description and quantity, employee number, and departments involved (based on move tickets). Similar records will be created for transferring raw materials and completed production work.[1]

The production system performs several important steps. Firstly, it updates the *materials inventory file* to reflect the materials that are issued. Secondly, it updates the *open production work order file* and *machine loading file* to reflect completed operations. Thirdly, it updates the *work-in-process file* to reflect the amount and quantity of labour, materials, and overheads added to the process. Finally, it produces journal entries to be charged to the applicable general ledger accounts.

FIGURE 36.5. System flowchart for production planning.

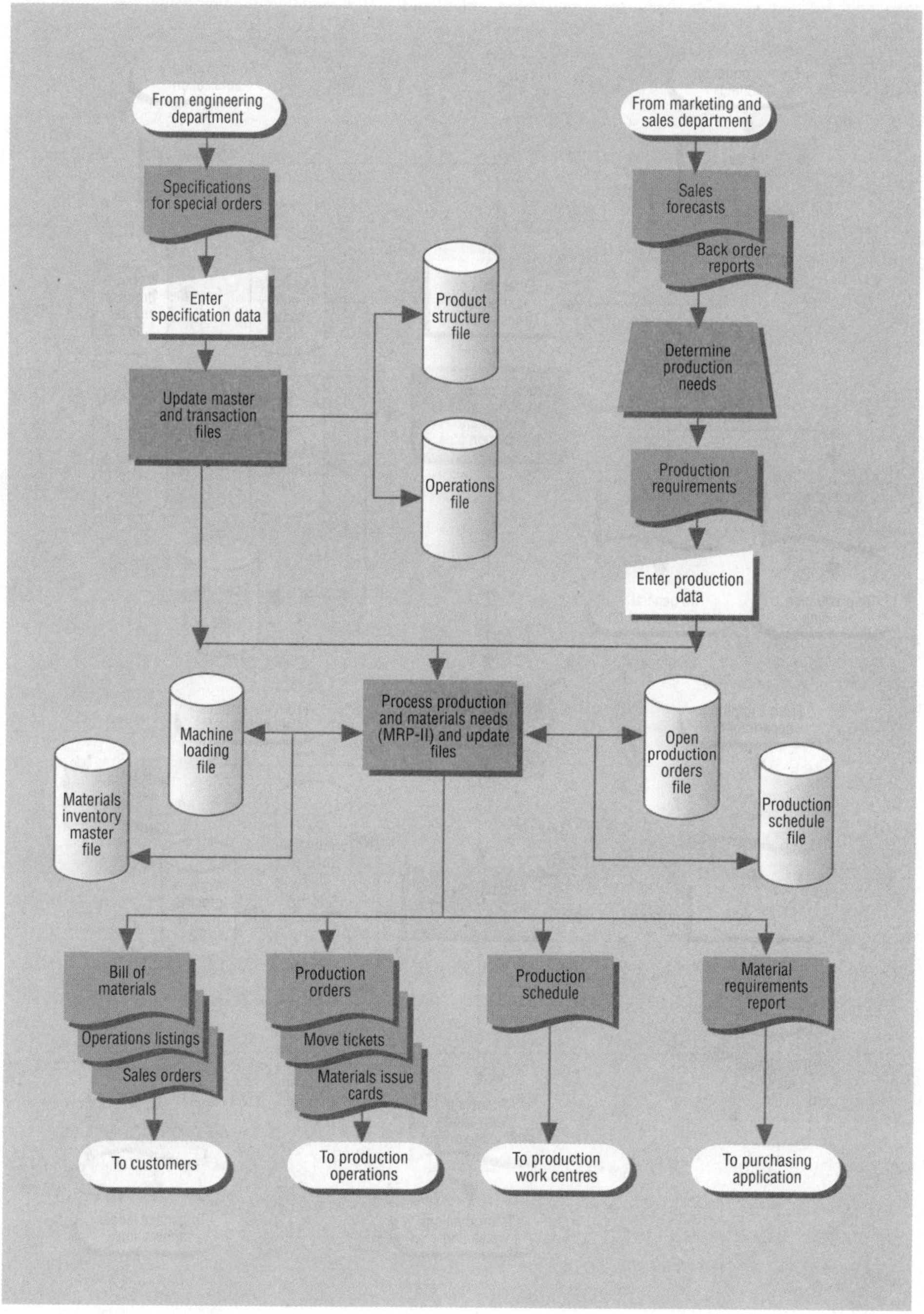

FIGURE 36.6. System flowchart for production activities.

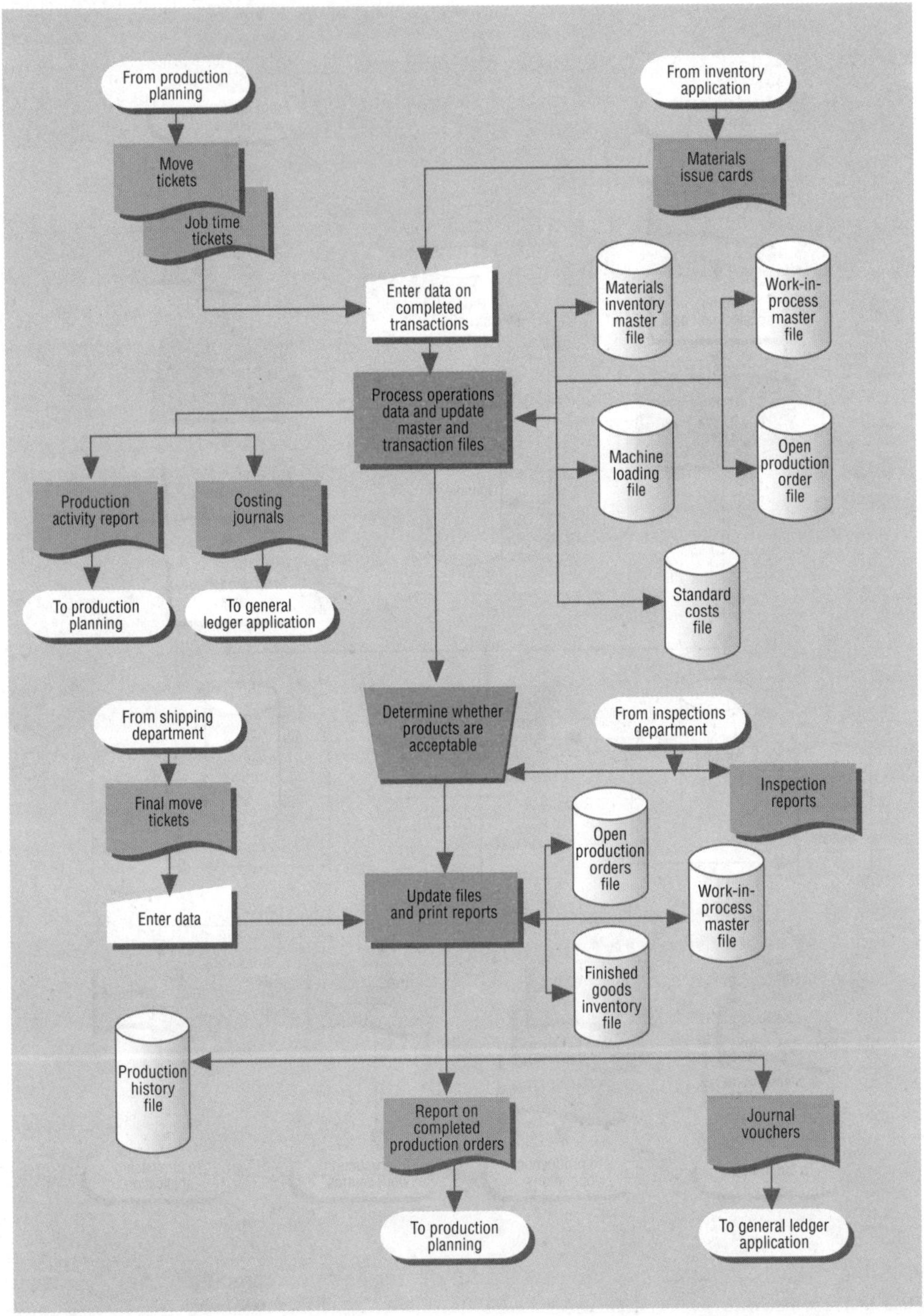

When work on a production order has been completed and finished goods have passed inspection, the results are updated to the *open production work order file,* the order is closed, and the appropriate data are then transferred to the *production history file.* The goods are transferred to the shipping department or warehouse, and data are entered by way of a final move ticket. The *work-in-process file* is then updated with final totals, and details of the new products are entered into the *finished goods inventory file.* The appropriate general ledger accounts are also updated with the transfer of incurred costs.[6]

36.7.4 Costing

Cost accounting is a very important aspect of the production process and deserves special attention. Costing should take place throughout the production process. Each cost element is based on a separate input: direct materials costs are based on materials requisitions (issue slips), direct labour costs are based on job time tickets, and overhead costs are based on predetermined recovery rates.

The costing system receives the various source documents, and processes them. When production has been completed it provides the basis for closing the work-in-process record of a job, it updates the necessary database files, and it produces cost reports such as cost summaries, variance analyses, and cost performance reports.

36.8 ACCOUNTING CONTROLS

Although production operations involve internal transactions only (no cash, no negotiations with outsiders, and only limited authority over resource costs), there is a real need for accounting controls throughout the manufacturing process. Accountants must be aware that poorly controlled productions systems have definite cost implications.[2]

It is for this reason that internal accounting controls must ensure that:[1]

- all production work is properly authorized;
- the correct operating procedures are followed;
- work-in-process inventories are properly safeguarded during the production process;
- all production activities are accurately recorded and processed;
- the correct accounting distributions take place to reflect the correct costs per unit produced;
- the right type of management information is provided at the right time to initiate corrective action, if necessary;
- accurate records of the completion status and costs of work-in-process inventories are maintained;
- all production work meets high standards of efficiency and quality.

Possible risks associated with the production of finished goods include incorrect costs charged to production work orders, inaccurate quantities of work-in-process and finished goods, production of excessive quantities of finished goods, issuing or ordering excessive or inadequate raw materials, theft or loss of raw materials and finished goods, and delays in the production of required finished goods. To minimize these risks, a proper set of general and application controls is necessary.[6]

36.8.1 General controls

General controls for the production management system would include the following:[6]

- *The separation of duties.* Units that have custodial functions should be separate from those units that keep the records.
- *Complete and up-to-date documentation* for controlling all processing aspects concerning production planning and operations must be kept.
- *Security in respect of on-line systems.*

36.8.2 Application controls

Control points within the production process include:[6]

- scheduling of the production work order;
- recording of issued materials and time-related services;
- monitoring progress throughout the production process;
- transfer of completed production work orders.

The following controls are applicable to the transactions associated with the production management function:[6]

- Authorization to issue materials and production work orders into production.
- All documents relating to the production process must be pre-numbered and well designed.
- Suitable documents (eg. move tickets) must accompany materials used for work orders through the various operations, and progress must be posted to such work orders.
- All input data must be validated by edit programs containing a wide variety of edit checks.
- Proper transfer of responsibility must take place at every step through the production process.
- Actual results regarding the use of production resources must be compared periodically with standards set for certain operations (ie. standard costing in respect of materials, labour, and overheads).
- Balances in work-in-process records must be reconciled periodically with the balance in the appropriate general ledger control account.
- Physical inventories of materials, parts, and finished goods have to be taken periodically under proper supervision, and the actual stock on hand has to be reconciled with the balances in the corresponding inventory records.

36.9 MANAGEMENT INFORMATION REQUIREMENTS

Production managers should have sufficient knowledge of all operations to satisfy themselves that adequate controls are built in, and to enable them to assume full responsibility for the accuracy and completeness of input and the reliability of output. In addition, they must be able to provide top management with important information for decision-making at the strategic level.[2]

For management to be able to perform its control and decision-making functions, it needs various kinds of management information. This information is usually communicated by way of reports which may once again be classified as operational listings and reports, exception reports, enquiry screens and reports, and managerial reports.[6]

36.9.1 Operational listings and reports

These listings and reports are used for general control purposes. They are scheduled reports containing detailed and summary data of all transactions during a certain period. Examples of these listings and reports are:

- *Production work orders.* Pre-numbered production work orders contain data to initiate the production process.
- *Move tickets and material issue slips.* These are printed to accompany the production work orders.
- *Bills of materials and operations listings.* For each product the system will print a bill of materials and operations listings which are used for production planning purposes.
- *Material requirements reports.* These reports show which materials and parts are needed to fill the production work orders.
- *Production scheduling report.* This report contains data on when and where the different production operations will take place.
- *Production work orders activity report.* This report contains data on the current status of all open production work orders.
- *Completed production work orders report.* This report shows which work orders have been completed, closed, and transferred to the history file.
- *Raw materials status report.* This report shows the current status of raw materials available for production.
- *Finished goods status report.* The current status of finished goods is shown here together with any other necessary and relevant details.
- *Production cost accounting report.* Periodic reports have to be prepared in which actual costs are compared with budgeted or standard costs (of materials, labour, and overheads) for a particular responsibility centre.

36.9.2 Exception reports

The system must be designed to inform management about all variances as well as abnormal and conflicting conditions, including the occurrence of cost variances, problems with availability of parts and raw materials, and delays in production.[2]

36.9.3 Enquiry reports

The on-line production management system and cost accounting system makes it possible to make enquiries interactively. This means that transactions can be listed and summarized in many ways and that the current status of master records can be shown at any time. Such enquiries can be in the form of screen displays or printed reports. Examples include:

- the current status of a particular production work order;
- the current status of machine loadings at a particular work centre;
- details of parts and materials used in producing a particular work order;
- details of labour costs for a particular work order;
- information on the costs, quality, or productivity performance of a particular work centre.

36.9.4 Managerial reports

Managerial reports for production management and cost accounting include the following:

- *Cost variance reports.* These reports contain information on variances between actual costs and budgeted or standard costs. This is given in summarized form per period, product, or work centre.
- *Machine utilization reports.* These reports contain information on the utilization of machines and other equipment so that management can ascertain their productivity.
- *Performance reports.* These reports contain information on the productivity and quality of the various responsibility or work centres.
- *Cost accounting analyses.* Such reports statistically analyse the various cost elements of actual production and summarize the results. (An example might be a labour efficiency analysis.)
- *Management accounting reports.* Cost data are summarized into a separate file. Regression analysis or other quantitative techniques are then used to report on, for instance, allocation bases most closely related to the different overhead categories.[1]
- *Production scheduling reports.* Decision support systems are sometimes used to simulate alternative production schedules based on information regarding current work-in-process and pending orders. These reports contain information on the results of alternatives. They are used to decide on the best way of scheduling production.
- *Forecasting reports.* Many production information systems also incorporate forecasting routines that enable management to generate important projections. Forecasting reports contain, for example, information on projected completion dates, raw materials required, and capacity and labour requirements for a specific production schedule.
- *Quality reports.* Management is particularly interested in the quality of finished products. These reports contain information on quality inspection results, eg. quality control rejections (with reasons), rework orders, accumulated costs, spoilage, scrap, and waste (with reasons).

36.10 SUMMARY

Production management systems represent the largest value flow in a manufacturing concern. Accounting information systems must therefore be able to support all the production activities and operations, and provide the necessary information to properly plan and manage them.

Proper production planning is a prerequisite for an efficient and effective production process. In many cases a computerized MRP-II management tool is used to facilitate such production planning. The key elements of master production schedule, materials requirements planning, capacity requirements planning, and manufacturing control, will ensure that the actual production operations are performed in an orderly manner.

The production process commences with a production work order. Once the planning of resources has been completed, the production process is initiated, raw materials and parts move from one work centre to another, and work-in-process is recorded and passed on to the next operation. At the same time human resources and machines are applied in the production operations and, ultimately, the required products are completed and taken into finished goods inventories. Throughout the production process all operations are costed and recorded to obtain detailed and total costs of these operations and of the units produced.

The work-in-process master file, the materials issues file, and the production operations file form the heart of the production database. Other important files used in this database are the materials inventory master file, product structure file, open production work order file, standard costs file, machine loading file, finished goods inventory file, and production history file.

Accounting controls play an important role in managing and controlling the production process. General and applications controls will prevent the loss of money due to unauthorized work performed, wrong operating procedures and repetition of operations, incorrect accounting distributions, incorrect costs charged, and poor management information for decision-making.

The system produces various kinds of valuable operating, enquiry, and management information. This is necessary for the management and control of the different production activities and in order to support the decision-making process.

REVIEW QUESTIONS

1. Describe the objectives of the production management and cost accounting function of an accounting information system.
2. Describe the major functions of the production management and cost accounting system.
3. Explain the functions and importance of a comprehensive computerized planning and control system (MRP-II) in a manufacturing concern.
4. Give a brief description of the key elements of MRP-II.
5. Discuss the importance of sound cost accounting practices in an efficient and effective production management system.

6. Give a brief description of the various documents involved in a production management system.
7. Explain the role of the work-in-process master file as a control centre in the database structure of a production management system.
8. Describe the flow of data through an on-line system for production management and cost accounting.
9. Describe the accounting controls required within a production management system and explain why such controls are necessary.
10. Give an overview of the management information produced by the production management system and highlight the importance to management of such information in general.

SELECTED REFERENCES AND RECOMMENDED READING

1. Cushing, B. E. and Romney, M. B. 1990. *Accounting Information Systems —A Comprehensive Approach.* Fifth edition. Reading, Massachusetts: Addison-Wesley.
2. Davis, J. R., Alderman, C. W. and Robinson, L. A. 1990. *Accounting Information Systems —A Cycle Approach.* Third edition. New York: John Wiley and Sons.
3. Gelinas, U. J. Jr., Oram, A. E. and Wiggins, W. P. 1990. *Accounting Information Systems.* Boston: PWS-KENT.
4. Wight, O. 1982. *MRP-II Unlocking America's Productivity Potential.* CBI.
5. Summers, E. L. 1989. *Accounting Information Systems.* Boston: Houghton Mifflin.
6. Wilkinson, J. W. 1989. *Accounting and Information Systems: Essential Concepts and Applications.* New York: John Wiley and Sons.

CHAPTER 37 Marketing and sales

37.1 INTRODUCTION

The marketing and sales function of a business organization is the first application in its *revenue cycle.* The revenue cycle exchanges products or services with customers for cash. Obtaining customer orders, executing sales transactions, and delivering products and services, are regarded as the marketing and sales function of a typical business organization.[1] Other activities such as billing customers, maintaining accounts receivable, and receiving cash payments are discussed in the next chapter under the heading of *accounts receivable and cash receipts.*

Marketing and sales may be regarded as a system of interrelated activities designed to develop, price, promote, and distribute goods and services to customers. The main purpose of these activities is to generate a flow of revenue that will absorb all related costs and expenses, provide for the replacement of diminishing capital assets, and provide an adequate return on investment.[4]

To be able to achieve the goals of the marketing function, its basic philosophy should be to learn about the customer's needs and satisfy them. The accounting information system plays an important role in providing marketing management with the information it needs. It is also important in the revenue-generating process where it is responsible for processing sales and related customer transactions.

In this chapter the close relationship between the accounting and marketing functions in a business organization will be explored. One must, however, always bear in mind that although the various business applications are described in separate chapters, they are very much interdependent in terms of both operations and information.[1]

37.2 OBJECTIVES AND FUNCTIONS OF THE SYSTEM

The main objective of the marketing and sales system is to satisfy the needs of groups of customers and, in the process, generate sufficient revenue to maximize profit. This involves obtaining adequate knowledge about the market place and recommended product prices and discounts, forecasting sales, obtaining and processing customer orders, analysing sales results and market share, and appraising product performance.[2]

The specific processing functions related to these objectives include: obtaining marketing information, producing sales forecasts, recommending prices, receiving and processing customer orders, checking the creditworthiness of customers, and arranging for delivery of products to customers.[1]

37.2.1 Obtaining marketing information

To be able to perform their duties properly, marketing executives require comprehensive, reliable, and up to date information. The AIS is an important source of such information which is available from sales order processing, cost accounting, and management accounting models based on the financial accounting system.

Other information needed from inside and outside the organization include sales forecasts, reports from customers, market research studies, market analyses, engineering specifications, and information about economic trends, technological developments, customers, and competitors.

37.2.2 Producing sales forecasts and recommending prices

Once the necessary marketing information has been obtained, marketing personnel are able to forecast sales and recommend prices. This task includes preparing marketing plans, advertising, initiating product improvements, and other activities to reach sales and profit goals.[2]

37.2.3 Receiving and processing customer orders

Although the marketing part of the system is very important to the revenue cycle, and is to a large degree interrelated with the AIS, the sales order processing application is the primary data processing component of the system.

Here sales orders are received, validated, controlled, and entered into the system. At this stage an order is processed and an invoice is produced for eventual dispatch and delivery.

37.2.4 Checking customers' creditworthiness

Where credit sales are involved, it is necessary to check the credit rating of a customer before actually supplying any goods or services. This forms part of the credit control function of the organization and is supported by the AIS.

37.2.5 Arranging for the delivery of ordered goods

Ordered goods must be physically moved to the shipping department. This often involves picking the goods from inventory or from a warehouse and moving them to a shipping dock. The goods must then be distributed to the customer, either by customers picking them up themselves, or by way of delivery vehicles, the postal service, or other common carriers. The system will be updated with these movements by way of picking lists (for movement from inventory), packing slips (for dispatch), and bills of lading (for transport).[4]

37.3 DATA SOURCES AND INPUTS

Unlike most of the other applications in the AIS, the marketing system as such is not responsible for matching or reconciling the activities of other applications. The marketing function does not, therefore, handle or process a wide variety of external or internal source documents. Its inputs largely come from information obtained for management and decision-making purposes.

The sales function, however, does make use of a number of source documents, namely the customer order, sales order, order acknowledgement, picking list, packing slip, bill of lading, and shipping notice.[4]

37.3.1 Customer order

The customer order is the customer's purchase order and therefore not a source document prepared by the AIS. It will, however, contain data necessary to produce a formal sales order for further use.

37.3.2 Sales order

The sales order is the official source document that initiates a sales transaction. It is pre-numbered to facilitate more effective control and contains the customer's order number, the price, and other relevant information. It serves as the basis for the preparation of a sales invoice.

37.3.3 Order acknowledgement

The order acknowledgement contains sales order data to acknowledge the receipt of a customer order.

37.3.4 Picking list

A picking list (rather than copies of sales orders) is often prepared to serve as authorization to supply ordered goods from inventory or warehouses. The data contained in such a list include order number, item number and description, bin location, and quantity.

37.3.5 Packing slip

A packing slip (or delivery note) is usually enclosed with goods shipped. It may contain data obtained from the sales order or picking list.

37.3.6 Bill of lading

This form is intended for carrier agents who transport the goods sold. It contains data such as goods on board the carrier, freight paid/payable, and authorization for the consignees to receive goods at destination. Copies are also supplied to the shipping department and customers.

37.3.7 Shipping notice

A shipping notice contains data about goods actually shipped to the customer and serves as proof of shipment. It is prepared by the shipping department and serves as a source document in the accounts receivable department for use in completing the sales invoice.

37.4 DATABASE STRUCTURE

The structure and content of the marketing and sales database depends entirely on the needs and expectations of individual businesses. An example of the data content and organization of such a marketing database appears in Figure 37.1. In this database, two basic types of record can be found: one contains finished goods inventory data, and the other contains customer data. The database also contains transaction records such as production work orders, sales orders, sales invoices, and shipping reports.[4]

37.4.1 Customer master file

The customer master file is used mainly when credit sales occur. Its primary key will be the customer number. Each customer will have a record containing data such as the customer's name and address, past payment performance, credit rating, trade discount allowed, and sales activity. These data are used in preparing sales invoices, shipping notices, and monthly statements, as well as in applying credit limits.

It is very important that these records are kept up to date, eg. when a customer moves to a new address, when credit is granted, or when a customer becomes inactive. Such changes should be made on-line, as they occur.

37.4.2 Finished goods inventory master file

The inventory master file is used by any firm that sells merchandise (products or finished goods). This file has already been discussed in Chapter 35 and its data could include inventory item number, description, warehouse location, unit of measure, reorder point, economic reorder quantity, unit cost, quantity on order, date of last purchase, and amount on hand.

37.4.3 Open sales order file

This transaction file contains data on sales orders that have not yet been shipped and billed. The primary key is the sales order number and the record will contain data (as repeating line items) such as product number and quantity ordered. Other data can be obtained from the applicable master files.

FIGURE 37.1. Database structure for marketing and sales.

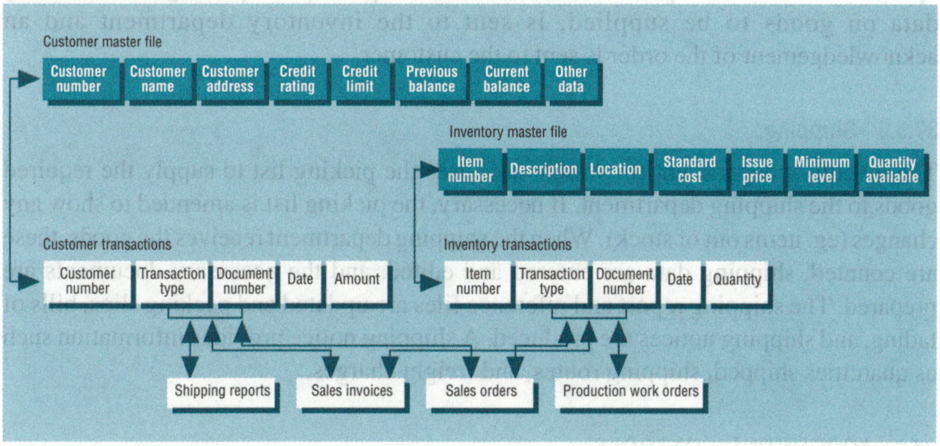

37.4.4 Open sales invoice file

The open sales invoice transaction file consists of records containing data on the individual sales invoices which remain open until payment is received from the customer or until the end of a particular period. The primary key is the sales invoice number. Other data provide details of sales transactions posted to the accounts receivable records.

37.4.5 Shipping report and reference file

The shipping report and reference transaction file (which may be two separate files) contains data such as freight rates, common carrier routes and schedules, current prices of product, and trade discounts.[4]

37.5 DATA FLOW AND PROCESSING REQUIREMENTS

Once the marketing and sales department has obtained the necessary information regarding potential customers and sales, sales staff are in a position to enter sales orders into the system. From the system flowchart in Figure 37.2 it is clear that the sales function consists of entering and processing sales orders, picking finished goods (or merchandise) from the inventory or warehouse, and shipping the goods to the respective customers.[4]

37.5.1 Sales order entry

With an on-line information system, a sales person, when communicating with a prospective buyer, can perform on-the-spot services like checking the availability of inventory, determining the status of open orders, initiating sales transactions, and confirming orders. Once a sale has been secured and the customer has submitted an order, the sales order data can be entered into the system. The system will edit the data by accessing and updating the customer master file, inventory master file, and open sales order file. In the process, credit and inventory checks are performed and, when everything has been cleared, the official sales order will be produced, updated to the open sales order file, and passed on to the accounts department. A picking list, containing data on goods to be supplied, is sent to the inventory department and an acknowledgement of the order is sent to the customer.

37.5.2 Shipping

The inventory department (or warehouse) uses the picking list to supply the required goods to the shipping department. If necessary, the picking list is amended to show any changes (eg. items out of stock). When the shipping department receives the goods, these are counted, shipping data are entered and edited, and the necessary documents are prepared. The shipping report and reference files are updated and packing slips, bills of lading, and shipping notices are produced. A shipping notice provides information such as quantities shipped, shipping routes, and freight charges.

37.6 ACCOUNTING CONTROLS

The primary objective of the marketing and sales function is to generate sales. It does not, however, play any direct role in the handling of cash or goods. Control focuses on policies and procedures regarding operations, selection of customers, control of documents, the determination of prices and sales terms, and maintaining financial relationships with customers. Where no standard accounting controls for marketing and sales exist, risks such as unauthorized acceptance of orders and violations of pricing policies should be prevented.

FIGURE 37.2. System flowchart for marketing and sales.

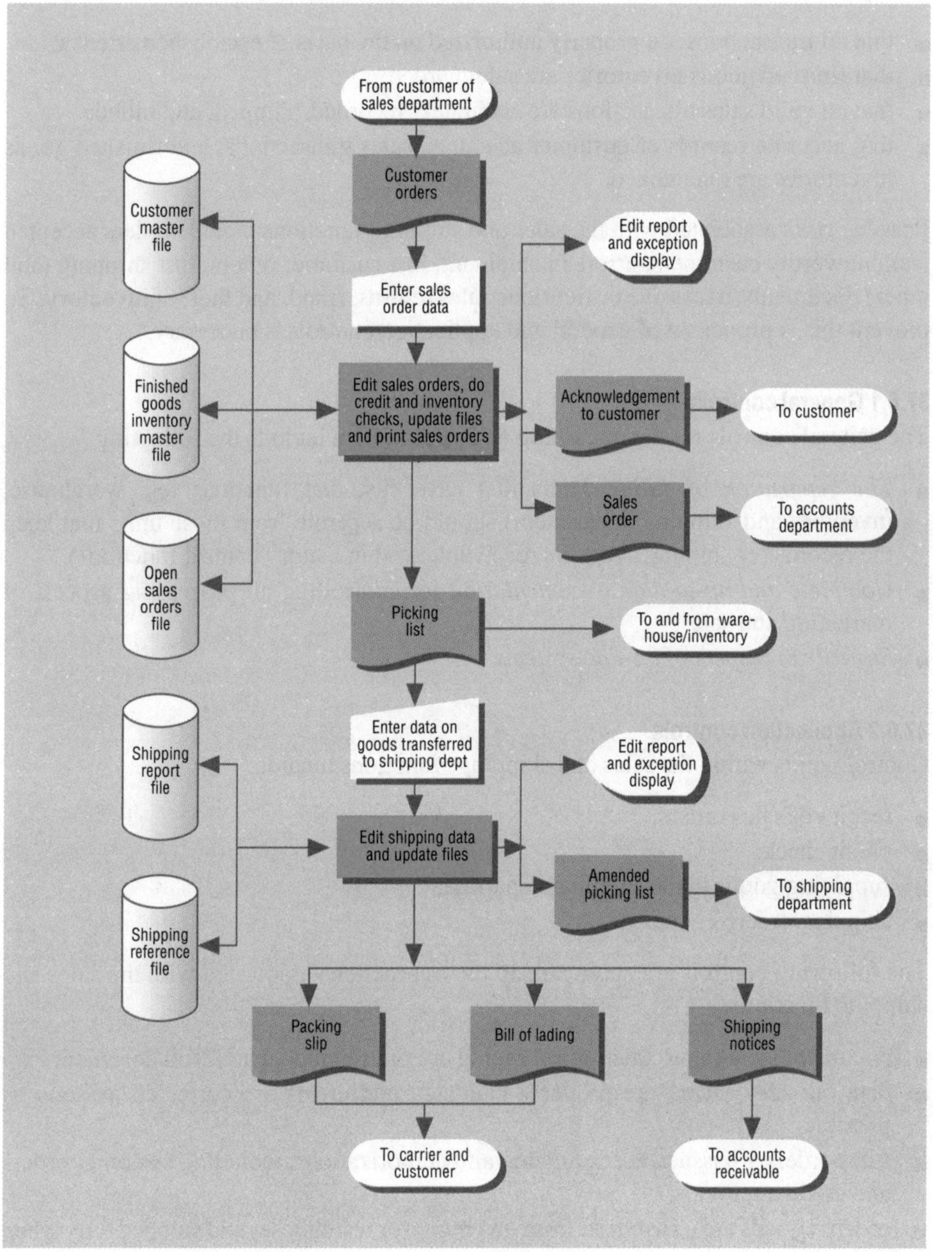

The purchasing and receiving function provides the interface between purchasing, inventory, and payment of accounts to trade creditors. The shipping function is involved in the actual exchange of goods, inventory issues, and ultimately in the creation and collection of accounts receivable. For this reason the maintenance of accounting controls is very important.[2] Internal control procedures must therefore ensure:

- that all transactions are properly authorized on the basis of established criteria;
- that finished goods inventories are safeguarded;
- that all valid sales transactions are accurately recorded, shipped, and billed;
- that accurate records of customer accounts, sales transactions, and finished goods inventories are maintained.

Possible risks associated with the sales and shipping functions include orders accepted from unworthy customers, errors in shipment, lost customer orders, lost shipping (and other) documents, excessive or fictitious sales returns, fraud, and theft of inventory. To prevent this, a proper set of general and application controls is necessary.[4]

37.6.1 General controls

The general controls for the marketing and sales system include the following:

- *The separation of duties.* Units that have custodial functions (eg. warehouse, inventory and shipping department) should be separate from those units that keep the records (eg. billing, accounts receivable, and inventory control functions).
- *Complete and up-to-date documentation* for controlling all processing aspects of marketing and sales.
- *Security in respect of on-line systems.*

37.6.2 Application controls

Control points within the sales and shippings functions include:[4]

- receipt of sales orders;
- credit check;
- supplying goods to the shipping department;
- shipping ordered goods.

The following controls are applicable to the transactions associated with the sales and shipping functions:[4]

- documents relating to sales and shipping are pre-numbered and well designed;
- data on sales orders are properly validated and errors are corrected as soon as possible;
- sales orders are issued according to valid authorizations, including customer orders and credit approvals;
- ordered goods are transferred from inventory (or warehouse) and shipped only when authorized by picking lists or stock requests;
- the correct shipping information is sent to the accounts department for billing purposes;
- sales returns, allowances, and write-offs are subject to prior approval by an appropriate manager.

37.7 MANAGEMENT INFORMATION REQUIREMENTS

Feedback information on marketing performance is the basis for continued and effective marketing management. In addition, external information about economic issues, political changes, competitor strategies, threats, and opportunities is needed. For this the marketing function must usually rely heavily on in-depth research. Apart from information on what has happened or what is happening, information is needed on what is likely to happen if a certain decision is made, how opportunities can be exploited, or how threats can be avoided, and the cost-benefit implications of alternative future actions. Marketing management usually requires internal reports containing information on product availability, operating efficiency, and customer activity.[2]

For management to be able to perform its control and decision-making functions, it needs various kinds of management information. All reports may once again be classified as operational listings and reports, exception reports, enquiry reports, and managerial reports.[4]

37.7.1 Operational listings and reports

Examples of these listings and reports are:

- *Daily listing of sales orders received and processed.* This listing contains data on all sales orders received, processed, and sent through to the shipping department.
- *Daily picking list.* This list contains data on all items to be issued from inventory or warehouse.
- *Daily shipping list.* This list contains data on all items shipped to customers.
- *Open sales orders/shipping report.* This report will contain information on all orders to be completed.
- *Status report.* This report shows the status of sales orders not yet shipped. It will show backlogs and behind schedule conditions to assist in judging the performance of carriers.

37.7.2 Exception reports

The system must be designed to inform management about all variances as well as abnormal and conflicting conditions, including late shipments, incomplete shipments, unbilled shipments, and other discrepancies.

37.7.3 Enquiry reports

The on-line marketing and sales system makes it possible to make enquiries interactively. Examples of these reports include:

- sales performance of a particular sales person;
- current status of a particular sales order or shipment;
- details of sales or profit per product, customer, or sales person;
- details of availability per product;
- details of shipments per period, product, or carrier;
- details of unbilled shipments per period;

- details of dates when certain orders are to be shipped.

37.7.4 Managerial reports

Managerial reports for the marketing and sales system would include the following:

- *Marketing performance.* This report gives a summary or analysis of the sales, profit, and marketing costs per product, period, and sales person. The information is used to detect deficiencies and opportunities which can influence planning and future actions.
- *Forecasts regarding cost/profit benefits,* which are used in decision-making about the production and marketing of particular products.
- *Sales forecasts* to establish sales quotas per sales person, product, and area.
- *Product availability reports,* which contain information about stock on hand, quantities in production, and movement.
- *Product/price analysis* to determine the profitability of products.
- *Sales analysis.* This report gives a complete analysis of sales per customer, sales person, product, or area, to establish operating efficiency.

37.8 SUMMARY

The marketing, sales and shipping functions form the first phase of the revenue cycle of an AIS. They facilitate the exchange of products or services for cash, and strict control therefore has to be exercised over the physical outflow of products.

The system interfaces with the inventory system and, together with data from the customers involved, it forms the accounting basis for the billing, accounts receivable, and general ledger applications which will be discussed later. It is also the first step in actually generating income and making a profit.

Customer orders, picking lists, and shipping notices are the main data sources for the shipment of products. These are supported and processed through the customer master file, finished goods inventory master file, open sales order file, and shipping report and reference file.

The various management and other reports facilitate proper planning, controlling and audit mechanisms which help to optimize the profit-making process.

REVIEW QUESTIONS

1. Describe the business functions which the marketing and sales application of an accounting information system must support.
2. Discuss the difference in application between the marketing, sales, and shipping parts of an AIS.
3. Give a brief description of the various documents involved in a marketing and sales system.
4. Explain the functions of each of the files associated with the marketing and sales function.
5. Describe the flow of data through an on-line marketing and sales system and indicate how this would interface with the accounts receivable and general ledger systems.

6. Describe the accounting controls required within a marketing and sales system.
7. Discuss the importance of both external and internal information for marketing purposes and describe how the sales and shipping functions can support this process.

SELECTED REFERENCES AND RECOMMENDED READING

1. Cushing, B. E. and Romney, M. B. 1990. *Accounting Information Systems —A Comprehensive Approach.* Fifth edition. Reading, Massachusetts: Addison-Wesley.
2. Davis, J. R., Alderman, C. W. and Robinson, L. A. 1990. *Accounting Information Systems —A Cycle Approach.* Third edition. New York: John Wiley and Sons.
3. Gelinas, U. J. Jr., Oram, A. E. and Wiggins, W. P. 1990. *Accounting Information Systems.* Boston: PWS-KENT.
4. Wilkinson, J. W. 1989. *Accounting and Information Systems: Essential Concepts and Applications.* New York: John Wiley and Sons.

CHAPTER 38 Accounts receivable and cash receipts

38.1 INTRODUCTION

The accounts receivable (debtors) and cash receipts system is initiated when products are marketed and sales are made to customers. Goods and services are delivered in return for payment by the customer. The accounts receivable and cash receipts system has to bill the customer, maintain customer records, and secure payment for goods sold or services rendered.[2]

Because cash is a business's most liquid asset, strict control has to be applied to maintain proper cash balances and reduce amounts outstanding by debtors. The accounts receivable part of the system is designed to keep track of all amounts owed by the customers of a business. It provides a bridge between the marketing and sales function and cash receipts.

The accounts receivable and cash receipts system is also a vital link to the general ledger application and, with its interacting structure of people, equipment, methods, and controls, it is designed to create information that will support the repetitive work routines of the credit control function, the accounts receivable function, and the cashier function. It also has to support problem solving for financial managers, and assist in the preparation of internal and external reports.[3]

38.2 OBJECTIVES AND FUNCTIONS OF THE SYSTEM

The main objective of the accounts receivable and cash receipts system is to ensure that all amounts payable by customers for goods or services received are collected in good time and, in the process, to improve the cash flow into the organization. This involves promptly and properly billing all goods sold and services delivered, determining and recording the costs involved, and managing customer accounts with accuracy and integrity.[2]

Integrity is an important characteristic of the whole process. From the initial sale through to the final settlement of the account, good customer relations remain an important goal. On the other hand, the system must provide collection capabilities that will ensure rapid cash inflow and minimize bad debts. The various functions that will meet these objectives and provide management with the necessary financial information include billing the customers, maintaining accounts receivable, receiving and depositing cash payments, and posting transactions to the general ledger.[4]

38.2.1 Preparing sales invoices (billing)

When goods have been shipped to a customer, the sales order and shipping notice serve as the basis for the preparation of a sales invoice. The billing process is not complete until the sales invoice is presented for payment. At this point the functions associated with the sale have been completed.

Two kinds of billing systems are normally used, namely *prebilling* and *postbilling* systems. In a prebilling system, invoices are prepared immediately when a customer order is accepted — ie. after inventory and credit checks have been made. In this case there is very little delay between receiving a customer's order and the shipment of goods.

In a postbilling system, invoices are prepared only after goods have been shipped and the sales order has been matched with the shipping notice.[3]

38.2.2 Maintaining accounts receivable

A separate accounts receivable (debtors) record is maintained for each customer receiving goods or services on credit. Each sales invoice is debited to its particular debtors account, and each associated cash receipt is credited to that account. The account will show an outstanding balance until all sales have been paid in full. The preparation and mailing of monthly statements is an important function of the system. This procedure has a control function, and also aids in the conversion of receivables into cash.

There are two different types of accounts receivable systems: *ordinary accounts receivable* and *revolving credit.* Within the former category there are two methods that may be employed in adjusting the balance to reflect payments and presenting information on monthly statements, namely the *balance forward method* and the *open invoice method.*

Balance forward method

The balance forward method applies a payment against the outstanding balance rather than against a specific invoice. Here all transactions at month end are cleared and the closing balance at the end of the month becomes the opening balance of the following month. This simplifies processing and makes the system easy to operate and manage. Queries, however, are not easy to sort out as the only way the history can be traced is through the actual statements which are usually filed by month. A typical statement will show:

92/10/01	Balance brought forward	1000.00
92/10/02	Invoice 1072	100.00
92/10/07	Invoice 1131	240.00
92/10/15	Receipt 665	600.50
92/10/31	Balance carried forward	740.50

With this method, outstanding balances are 'aged'. Depending on the month of the original invoice, the balance will be split and classified as 'current', 'over 30 days', 'over 60 days', etc. (depending on the requirements of the client).

Open item method

With the open item method there is no balance brought forward and all transactions are kept in the system. Each payment is matched with specific invoices and only when an invoice has been paid in full is it reported on and dropped at the end of the month. With this method, disputed invoices are more easily isolated. A typical open item statement would appear as follows:

	Transaction		*Amount owing*
92/07/16	Invoice 1072	100.00	100.00
92/08/02	Invoice 1491	206.71	306.71
92/10/08	Receipt 202	206.71	100.00
92/10/12	Invoice 2121	17.70	117.70
92/10/19	Invoice 2604	20.25	137.95
92/10/23	Receipt 479	17.70	120.25

In this example invoices 1491 and 2121 and their receipts are dropped from the system. If, however, receipt 202 had been for only R200.00, then invoice 1491 and receipt 202 would have been printed but not taken out of the transaction file.

The posting routines of this method are rather complicated. A typical problem occurs when a client sends payment for a number of transactions without specifying them, or when part-payment is made without stating the invoice(s) to which it should be allocated.

Revolving credit

Where a customer receives extended credit (eg. six months to pay), the system must cater for the outstanding balance as well as for the new instalment to be paid. Here the monthly statement must show the balance outstanding, invoices and receipts, finance charges, and deposits. The system must keep track of missed payments and should be designed to handle customers who pay more than the required minimum instalment.

38.2.3 Receiving and depositing cash payments

Cash payments from customers have to be recorded accurately, classified, and reported on immediately upon receipt. They must be listed on deposit slips and deposited into the bank account as soon as possible. The applicable accounts receivable records must be updated with the received amounts to reflect the correct balance at the end of each day. Any accounts receivable adjustments must be prepared in accordance with management's policy. Individual accounts receivable balances must be periodically substantiated, aged, evaluated, and reported on to management.[2]

38.2.4 Posting transactions to the general ledger

Summarized credit sales transactions and cash receipts transactions have to be posted to the general ledger on a regular basis. This posting function serves as the interface between the revenue cycle and the general ledger system.

38.3 DATA SOURCES AND INPUTS

A variety of source documents are necessary for the proper functioning of the accounts receivable and cash receipts system. Many of these are, however, generated by outside entities, eg. sales orders and cash receipts transactions initiated by customers. The primary source documents are the sales invoice, customer statement, remittance advice, deposit slip, and credit note.[4]

38.3.1 Sales invoice

The sales invoice, resulting directly from the customer sales order and shipping notice, serves as the main sales input to the accounts receivable function since it contains the total amount and other relevant data related to the transaction. It includes the customer's name and address, a description of items ordered, quantity, prices, shipping terms, and the total invoice amount.

38.3.2 Monthly statement

Although not strictly a source document, the monthly statement plays an important role in collecting outstanding amounts. The statement shows which invoices are payable as well as the balance owed. It also helps to control cash collections by including a remittance advice which the customer must send along with his payment. In this way the statement facilitates the recording of cash receipts and credits to accounts receivable.

38.3.3 Remittance advice

The remittance advice forms the counterpart to the sales invoice. Enclosed with the customer's payment should be a remittance advice which generally includes data such as customer name and account number, invoice number and date, and the amount payable.

38.3.4 Deposit slip

Daily deposits of cash in the bank have to be accompanied by suitable deposit slips. These slips are usually provided by the bank and include the firm's name and address, the bank's name and clearing code, the firm's bank account number, and space to list the deposits made.

38.3.5 Bad debts listing

The maintenance of accounts receivable usually includes the periodic write-off of outstanding amounts to bad debts. To facilitate this, a listing of such bad debts serves as a source document for the credit manager to initiate and authorize the write-offs. This listing will include the account number, customer name, and amount to be written off.[2]

38.3.6 Credit note

A credit note, authorized by an appropriate manager, must be prepared before any shipped goods can be accepted back or before allowances can be granted. Such a document should only be approved when clear evidence (eg. sales return notice) exists. The credit note will include data such as customer name and number, items for which credit is allowed, and the total amount credited.

38.4 DATABASE STRUCTURE

The database for accounts receivable and cash receipts consists mainly of master and transaction files that relate to customer accounting transactions. These are the customer master file, the accounts receivable master file, the general ledger master file, and transaction files such as the open sales order file, the open sales invoice file, the sales history file, and the cash receipts file.[4]

38.4.1 Customer master file

This file has already been discussed in Chapter 37. In this case its importance lies in the preparation of sales invoices and monthly statements, and credit control and collections.

38.4.2 Accounts receivable master file

The records in the accounts receivable master file relate to customers buying on credit. The primary key is the customer account number. Other data contained in this file may include customer name, current account balance, credit limit, discount code, balance at beginning of year, year-to-date sales, year-to-date payments, and data for ageing analyses.

38.4.3 Open sales order file

Together with data from the shipping notices, the open sales order file serves as input for the preparation of sales invoices. This file has been discussed in Chapter 37.

38.4.4 Open sales invoice file

The open sales invoice transaction file consists of records containing data on the individual sales invoices which remain open until payment is received from the customer, or until the end of a particular period. The primary key is the sales invoice number. Other data provide details of sales transactions posted to the accounts receivable records.

38.4.5 Sales history file

The sales history file contains data concerning sales orders and invoices in summarized form. These records are transferred to the sales history file when they are removed from the respective open files. They are retained in the history file for a certain period (eg. five years). Sales history records are used for enquiry purposes and to prepare sales forecasts and analyses.

38.4.6 Cash receipts file

The cash receipts transaction file forms the receipts part of a firm's cash-book; in the same way, the cash payments transaction file forms the payments part of the cash-book. Together with the opening balance at the beginning of the accounting period, the net result of these two files should show the actual cash balance. Records in the cash receipts file would contain data such as receipt number, date, customer name and account number, and amount paid.

38.4.7 General ledger master file

The various general ledger accounts each have a database record. Summary transactions are updated to the appropriate ledger accounts — eg. sales debited and cash receipts credited to the applicable accounts receivable control account. The records in the general ledger master file constitute the complete chart of accounts and show the current status of all account balances.

38.5 DATA FLOW AND PROCESSING REQUIREMENTS

Here the data flow and processing can be divided into three processes: *processing sales invoices* (billing), *maintaining accounts receivable,* and *cash receipts.* The first two processes are depicted in the flowchart shown in Figure 38.1 and the latter in the flowchart shown in Figure 38.2. From the flowcharts it can be seen that a combination of on-line and batch processing is used to support data entry, editing, and the control of batch totals.[4]

38.5.1 Processing sales invoices

The billing procedure starts once the shipping notices and sales orders are received by the accounting department (see Figure 38.1). Each sales order is converted into a completed invoice by using the relevant data, specifying product prices, and activating the invoice production program. After the invoices have been completed:

- they are printed;
- customers' accounts are debited;
- sales orders are closed to the *sales history file*;
- sales invoice records are added to the *sales invoice transaction file*;
- total amounts with regard to sales and accounts receivable are posted to the *general ledger accounts*;
- applicable reports are printed.

38.5.2 Maintaining accounts receivable

Any new debtors have to be allocated a unique account number and their details must be added to the appropriate database record. Any existing debtors whose static details have changed, have to be amended. The records of inoperative debtors have to be removed from the system.

The various transactions updated to the accounts receivable master file include sales invoices for customer purchases, cash receipts for payments from customers, credit notes for refunds to customers, and journals for adjusting customer balances when errors or other discrepancies occur. At the same time, the total of all outstanding balances in the accounts receivable master file must be reconciled to the balance in the accounts receivable control account in the general ledger master file.

The preparation of monthly statements is an important step in collecting outstanding debts and informing customers about products sold and the services rendered to them.

Setting credit limits and exercising credit control also form an important role in maintaining accounts receivable. In this respect, a variety of reports have to be produced which assist credit managers in collecting amounts owed in good time.

FIGURE 38.1. System flowchart for processing sales invoices.

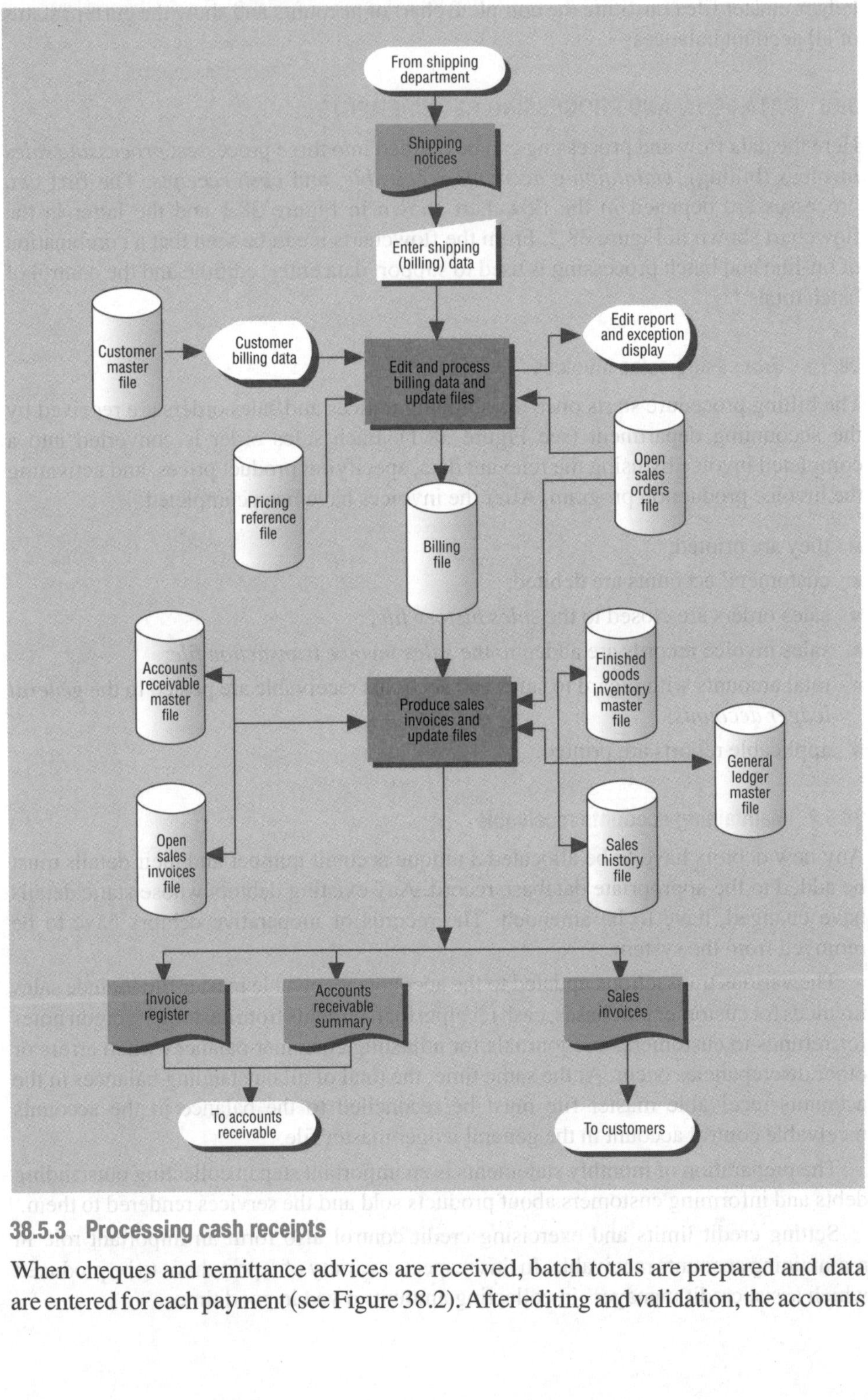

38.5.3 Processing cash receipts

When cheques and remittance advices are received, batch totals are prepared and data are entered for each payment (see Figure 38.2). After editing and validation, the accounts receivable records are credited, the affected sales invoices are marked as being paid, and the sales invoices are closed to the sales history file.

For each receipt processed, a cash receipt record is added to the cash receipts transaction file. From this file, periodic deposit slips are produced which accompany the cheques as they are delivered to the bank. At the end of the day, the totals of remittance advices (cash transactions) are compared to the totals in the cash receipts summary to verify the correctness of the processing. A summary journal entry, generated by the system and reflecting the total receipts for the day (or period), is then posted to the applicable cash account in the general ledger master file.

38.6 ACCOUNTING CONTROLS

Accounting controls in respect of accounts receivable and cash receipts are designed to facilitate the proper execution of transactions and the safe custody of a firm's liquid assets. To ensure that the preparation of sales invoices and monthly statements, maintenance of accounts receivable, and handling of cash receipts are properly executed and recorded, internal accounting controls should be designed to provide reasonable assurance that:[2]

- all shipments are billed at authorized prices and on authorized terms;
- all sales transactions are accurately billed and recorded;
- all outstanding amounts are collected from customers in good time;
- all cash receipts are properly handled and safeguarded;
- accurate records of customer accounts receivable are maintained.

Because receivables often represent a large portion of a firm's current assets, failures in the billing, accounts receivable, and cash collection processes can have a significant impact on its resources. Possible risks associated with accounts receivable and cash receipts include the misstatement of accounts receivable, fictitious credits for returns and allowances, theft of cash received, erroneous discounts and deductions, unauthorized write-offs, theft of cash by a succession of delayed postings to customer accounts, and damage or destruction of records. To prevent this a proper set of general and application controls is necessary.[4]

38.6.1 General controls

The general controls for the accounts receivable and cash receipts system would include the following:

- *The separation of duties.* Units that have custodial functions (eg. the shipping department and the cashier) should be separate from those units that keep the records (eg. billing, accounts receivable, and data processing functions). In addition, the sales order and credit control functions, whose managers authorize credit sales, adjustments, and write-offs, should be separate from other functions.
- *Complete and up-to-date documentation* for controlling all processing aspects of accounts receivable and cash receipts.
- *Security in respect of on-line systems.*

FIGURE 38.2. System flowchart for processing cash receipts.

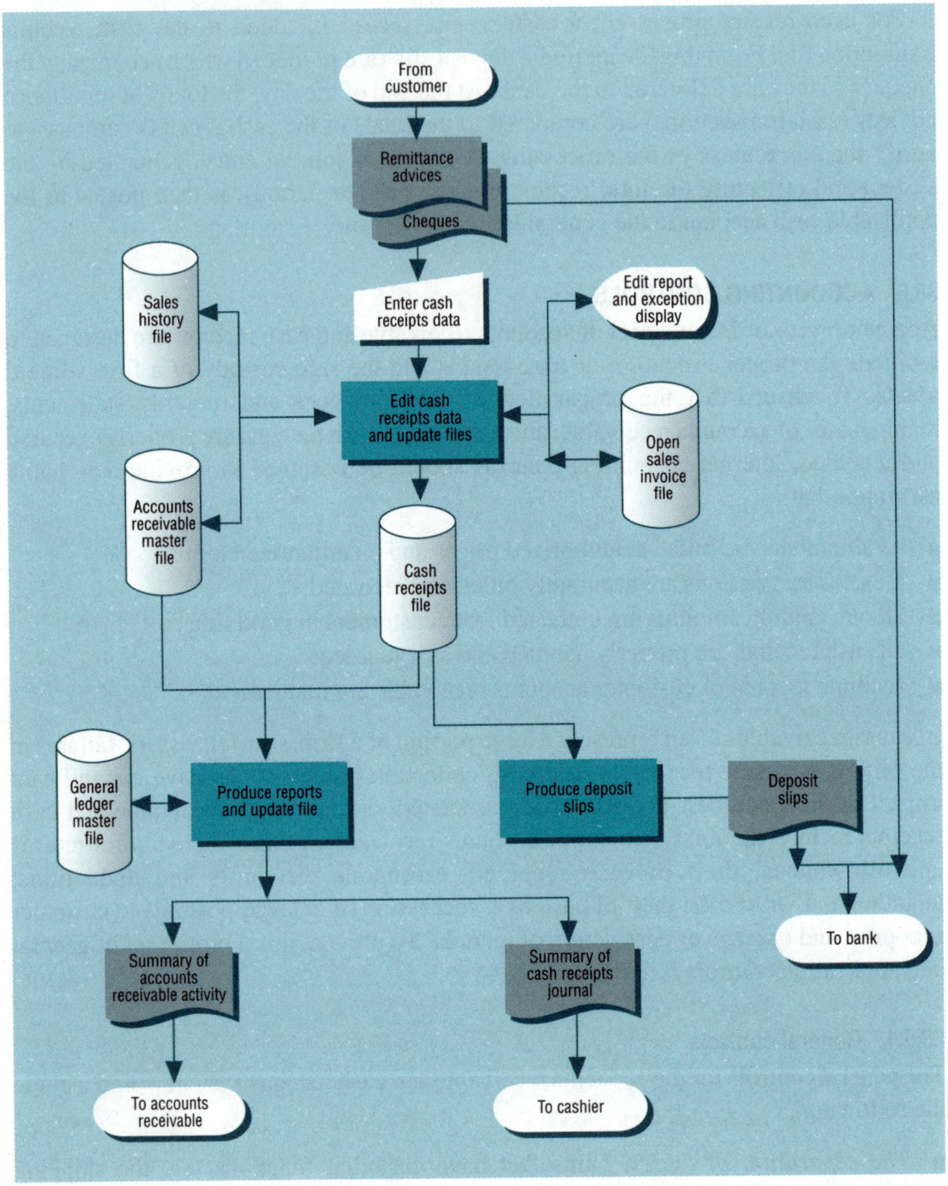

38.6.2 Application controls

Control points within the accounts receivable and cash receipt functions include:[4]

- credit checks;
- preparing sales invoices (billing);
- posting sales transactions to ledgers;

- sending out monthly statements;
- cash receipts;
- bank deposits.

The following controls are applicable to the accounts receivable and cash receipt functions:[4]

- all data items and computations on pre-numbered sales invoices are verified;
- prepared sales invoices are compared against shipping notices and open sales orders to assure that quantities ordered and billed agree with those shipped and back-ordered;
- completed sales invoices are sent to customers as soon as possible;
- all batch totals are properly computed and compared with processed totals;
- monthly statements are properly and timeously prepared and mailed to the customers concerned;
- accounts receivable are periodically reconciled with the applicable control account in the general ledger;
- all journal entries in respect of adjustments, credit notes, and write-offs are properly checked and authorized;
- all pre-numbered cash receipts are deposited with a minimum of delay;
- transaction listings and account summaries are printed periodically to provide an adequate audit trail;
- all bank accounts are reconciled monthly by someone from outside the revenue department;
- employees who handle cash are closely supervised and rotated regularly.

38.7 MANAGEMENT INFORMATION REQUIREMENTS

All reports may again be classified as operational listings and reports, exception reports, enquiry screens and reports, and managerial reports.[4]

38.7.1 Operational listings and reports

These listings and reports are used for general control purposes. They are scheduled reports containing detailed and summary data of all transactions during a certain period and they help to maintain the audit trail.[4] Examples of these listings and reports are:

- *Daily listing of sales invoices.* This listing is in effect the sales journal containing data in respect of each sales order closed off in the open sales order file and added to the open sales invoice file.
- *Daily listing of updated accounts receivable.* This listing contains data on those accounts receivable affected by sales invoices — eg. new outstanding balances and control totals.
- *Daily listings of credits passed, journals posted, and outstanding debts written off.* These listings contain data on all changes to the balances of accounts receivable other than sales invoices and cash receipts.

- *Monthly statements.* Although not really a listing or report, monthly statements do constitute a listing of debit and credit transactions per customer, providing the customers with the necessary information to pay the correct amounts owing. This information is based on data in the customer, accounts receivable, sales invoice, and cash receipts files.
- *Daily listing of cash receipts.* This listing of all cash receipts received for the day is, in effect, the cash receipts journal listing of all amounts received and updated to the accounts receivable file.
- *Accounts receivable aging schedule.* This report contains data concerning the status of the open balances of all active credit customers. It gives an analysis of overdue amounts by time periods, and flags those accounts that need to be collected. It provides operational control over collections and supports the credit manager in making decisions regarding write-offs.
- *Customer reminders.* This is a collection follow-up in the form of routine statements of unpaid balances that are automatically produced by the AIS.

38.7.2 Exception reports

The system must be designed to inform management about all variances as well as abnormal and conflicting conditions, including unbilled shipments, unsuitable credit limits, exceeded credit limits, and other discrepancies.

38.7.3 Enquiry reports

The on-line accounts receivable and cash receipts system makes it possible to make enquiries interactively. This means that transactions can be listed and summarized in many ways, and the current status of master records can be shown at any time. Such enquiries can be in the form of screen displays or printed reports. Examples include:

- current status of an account receivable, including aging information;
- details of sales per customer per period;
- details of a particular cash remittance;
- details of cash payments per customer per period;
- details of cash discounts allowed per customer;
- details of outstanding balances per area or sales person.

38.7.4 Managerial reports

Managerial reports for the accounts receivable and cash receipts system would include the following:

- *Sales analysis report.* This report provides a complete analysis of the relative effectiveness of individual sales people, sales regions, product lines, customers, and markets.
- *Collection performance report.* This report would contain information about accounts receivable turnover, average length of the collection period, and average amount outstanding.

- *Product performance report.* This report reflects results in terms of such key measures as average money value per order, profit per product, customer, or sales person, and commission earned per sales person.
- *Cash forecasts.* When historical sales data are merged with age analyses and collection performance, it is possible to produce short- and medium-range cash receipts forecasts. When recent transactions in the cash account are reflected with related historical information, such forecasts can provide information on current cash status and future cash requirements.
- *Cash discount performance report.* This report contains information concerning discounts allowed, those allowed but not taken, and those disallowed, in relation to the collection rate. It can be used to evaluate the effectiveness of cash discounts on the average collection period.

38.8 SUMMARY

The application that caters for billing, accounts receivable, and collection of amounts owing, forms the bridge between sales and the actual cash receipts. It therefore links closely with the marketing and sales application and the cash control application, and represents an important interface between the customer and the firm.[2] The system also interfaces directly with the financial accounting system represented by the general ledger (to be discussed later).

A properly designed accounts receivable and cash receipts system, which functions efficiently and effectively, will make use of source documents such as sales invoices, monthly statements, and remittance advices from customers, to ensure that data can flow smoothly within the system. These are supported by, and processed through, the customer master file, accounts receivable master file, open sales invoice file, and cash receipts file, to create and maintain appropriate accounting transactions.

Management and other reports facilitate proper planning, controlling, and audit mechanisms which help to optimize the profit-making process.

REVIEW QUESTIONS

1. Describe the objectives and functions of the accounts receivable and cash receipts application of an accounting information system.
2. Explain the difference between the 'balance forward method' and 'open item method' that may be applied in preparing monthly statements.
3. Describe the functions of each of the source documents necessary for the proper operation of an accounts receivable and cash receipts system.
4. Explain the interaction between the different data files associated with the accounts receivable and cash receipts system.
5. Describe the flow of data through an accounts receivable and cash receipts system and indicate how this would interface with the general ledger system.
6. Describe the accounting controls required within an accounts receivable and cash receipts system.

7. Discuss the importance of the various types of management reports to be produced by an accounts receivable and cash receipts system.

SELECTED REFERENCES AND RECOMMENDED READING

1. Cushing, B. E. and Romney, M. B. 1990. *Accounting Information Systems —A Comprehensive Approach.* Fifth edition. Reading, Massachusetts: Addison-Wesley.
2. Davis, J. R., Alderman, C. W. and Robinson, L. A. 1990. *Accounting Information Systems —A Cycle Approach.* Third edition. New York: John Wiley and Sons.
3. Gelinas, U. J. Jr., Oram, A. E. and Wiggins, W. P. 1990. *Accounting Information Systems.* Boston: PWS-KENT.
4. Wilkinson, J. W. 1989. *Accounting and Information Systems: Essential Concepts and Applications*. New York: John Wiley and Sons.

CHAPTER 39 Personnel information and payroll

39.1 INTRODUCTION

Since the personnel management, payroll, general ledger, fixed assets, and financial reporting functions serve all departments as well as the other processing cycles within an organization, these functions are grouped together under the *administrative cycle*.

The personnel management function is concerned with the employment, maintenance, and administration of a firm's labour force. The payroll function is closely linked to the personnel management function. It records the labour applied to the various operations, and facilitates the payment of salaries, wages, sales commissions, etc. to employees, as well as the payment of amounts deducted from employees to outside bodies.

The *general ledger* forms the basis for the financial management and reporting function and provides the formal *chart of accounts* which controls the different accounting applications of an organization. The management of fixed assets forms part of financial management in that it maintains accounting and other records relating to the organization's fixed assets — property, plant, equipment, etc. The general ledger, fixed assets, and financial reporting will be discussed in the next chapter.

In this chapter the importance of an effectively integrated personnel management and payroll system is emphasized. Although these functions are usually handled by different departments or divisions, they share a lot of employee data and should therefore be integrated to prevent problems like unnecessary duplication and inconsistency of personnel and payroll information.

This chapter describes the personnel management function and the processing operations that support it. The role of the payroll system, being one of the largest and most important applications of the accounting information system, is highlighted.[1]

39.2 OBJECTIVES AND FUNCTIONS OF THE SYSTEM

The main objective of the personnel information and payroll system is to maintain a firm's work force and, in the process, to benefit both the individual employee and the organization. This involves maintaining, promoting, and compensating personnel, and keeping and processing the necessary records that support the personnel management function.

The specific processing functions related to these objectives include:

- capturing, recording, and storing data in respect of personnel and payroll activities;
- preparing, capturing, and processing records on time worked and attendances;
- payroll processing and labour cost distribution;
- making payments to employees and outside bodies (eg. pension funds and the Receiver of Revenue).[3]

39.2.1 Capturing, recording, and storing personnel and payroll data

When a new employee has been appointed, it is necessary to capture and record all data concerning such an appointment. When changes to the position of an existing employee occur, the applicable records have to be adjusted accordingly. This must take place as soon as the changes are approved to ensure that the employee's pay cheque will reflect his current status and that the personnel information system will be up to date.

39.2.2 Preparing, capturing, and processing of time and attendance records

The work performed by employees has to be measured and recorded according to predetermined rules laid down for each activity. Employees paid hourly usually have to record the time they spend on each job using time cards. Salaried employees have to prepare attendance records for each day, and employees who receive sales commissions hand in vouchers that reflect the sales made during a particular period. These source documents are normally captured, processed into money terms, and recorded according to the batch mode of data processing.

39.2.3 Payroll processing and labour cost distribution

Payroll processing usually takes place periodically (batch processing) depending on the pay cycle (eg. monthly or weekly). The earnings and deduction records of the payroll are processed to reflect the earnings, deductions, and net pay of each employee and to produce the payslips, cheques, and associated reports necessary for payments to employees and outside bodies. At the same time the system must distribute and update the various cost centres with the amount of labour spent on each activity. These allocations are based on the time spent on various jobs or the predetermined apportionment of the costs of salaried personnel.

39.2.4 Payments to employees and outside bodies

The actual payments to employees and the transfer payments of amounts deducted from employees to outside bodies take place through the *accounts payable* application. Payments may be in the form of cheques or electronic transfers to banks or other financial institutions where the employees hold their accounts.

39.3 DATA SOURCES AND INPUTS

Any effective personnel management and payroll system requires information from a variety of sources, internal and external. The personnel information system relies particularly heavily on external information, both about the employee and about the labour market, employment agencies, etc. The accounting information system (AIS) is the major provider of internal information on personnel activities.[1]

39.3.1 Personnel take-on form

When a new employee is appointed, this form is used to create a personnel master record containing all personal information — job history, qualifications, skills, etc. It also provides the data necessary to create the payroll master record, eg. salary, department, cost centre, allowances, and deductions.

39.3.2 Personnel action form

This form is used when the status of an existing employee changes or when job performance is evaluated. It serves as input for adjusting the personnel master record and can be used to make any changes to the earnings or deduction records in the payroll database.[2]

39.3.3 Time/attendance form

For hourly paid employees, a time card or clock card is used to record the actual hours worked. It contains the name and number of the employee, date, time spent, cost centre, etc. These cards are usually completed on a daily basis and serve as input to enable the calculation and distribution of labour costs. Attendance forms or registers are normally used for salaried workers. These also serve as input for determining employees' earnings and labour costs.[4]

39.3.4 Job-time ticket

In contrast to the time card, on which the actual hours worked per day are recorded, the job-time ticket relates to a particular job or work order. The direct labour hours pertaining to a particular job are accumulated from these tickets and are used for production control and cost accounting purposes.[2]

39.3.5 Other forms

Every payroll system should have a procedure for correcting and/or adjusting payroll data and transactions. Such adjustment forms must, however, be properly authorized and adequately controlled.

When a new position is created within the organization, particulars of the post have to be recorded by way of a *job description form*. This ensures that nobody can be appointed to a position unless such a position exists and unless relevant information like qualifications or skills required, experience, salary scale, and department have been specified.

39.4 DATABASE STRUCTURE

The *personnel master file* and *payroll master file* are the two most important files in the personnel management and payroll system. The personnel master file is usually updated by the personnel department and the payroll master file is maintained by the payroll department. These two files should, however, be closely linked together (as depicted in Figure 39.1).[1]

Other files are the *job description reference file*, the *skills inventory file*, the *time-record transaction file*, and the *pay-cheque transaction file*.

39.4.1 Personnel master file

The personnel master file is probably the most important file in the system because it contains the personal data (financial and non-financial) concerning each employee (eg. name, address, qualifications or skills, work experience, salary scale, performance evaluation, and family particulars). These data are used in creating the payroll master file and also in keeping record of changes in the status of employees.[4]

39.4.2 Payroll master file

This file may take different forms. The master file itself could contain the more static data like employee number and name, department or cost centre, regular and overtime pay, and marital status. It should, however, also contain data on all earnings and deductions associated with each employee. In some cases there are separate records for all earnings and deductions; in other cases the earnings are included as part of the master file records and separate deduction records are kept in a deductions transaction file. In this case we use separate records for earnings and deductions (as shown in Figure 39.1).

Earnings data would include type of earnings (eg. normal pay, overtime pay, and various types of allowances), taxable or non-taxable indicator, recurrence indicator, pay-period amount, and year-to-date earnings. These records form the basis for the calculation of the gross earnings of each employee. The records in the payroll master file must be maintained and updated continuously by way of on-line processing.

Deductions records would include the type of deduction (eg. income tax, pension fund, and medical aid fund), reference number, rate or amount per pay period, tax-deductible indicator, and year-to-date amounts deducted. Reports for transfer payments are produced from these records.[4]

The earnings and deductions for a particular pay period are used to produce a payslip on which all earnings, deductions, and net pay of an employee are shown.

FIGURE 39.1. Database structure for personnel information and payroll.

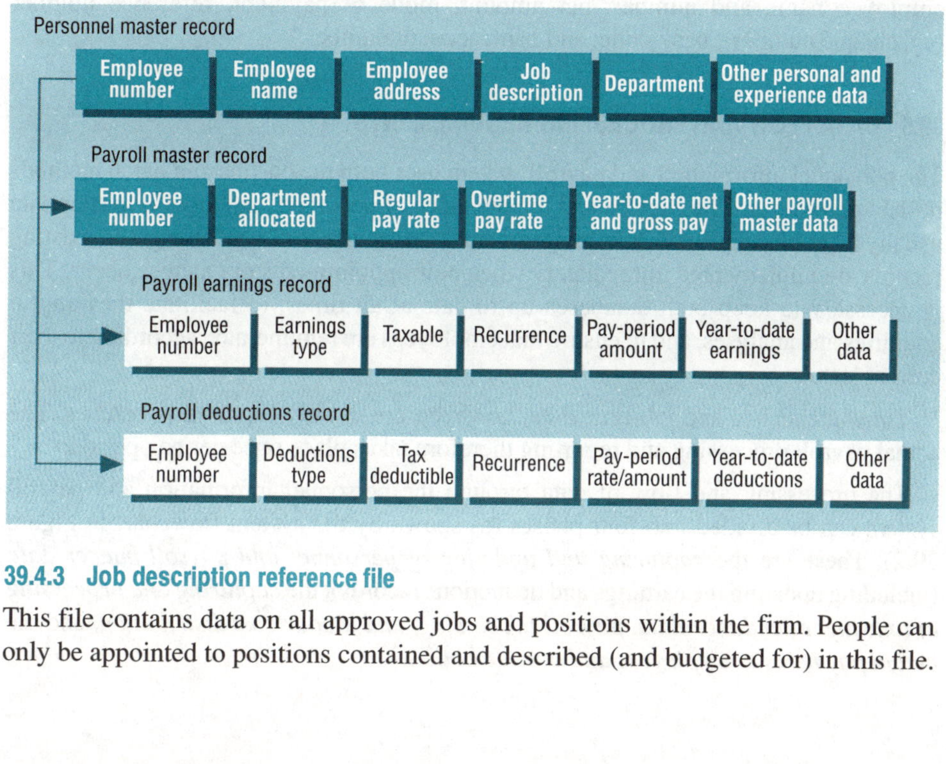

39.4.3 Job description reference file

This file contains data on all approved jobs and positions within the firm. People can only be appointed to positions contained and described (and budgeted for) in this file.

For each post, the data will include job specifications like academic qualifications or skills required, experience, salary scale, and department. Together with data from the personnel master file, this can be used to carry out labour force planning and provide statistical information on vacancies, personnel turnover, etc.[3]

39.4.4 Skills inventory file

The skills inventory file contains data on each employee's relative skills and qualifications. As they gain new qualifications or new experience through on-the-job training, this file will be updated accordingly. Such a file would enable a firm to locate qualified internal candidates when the need arises. It also aids in establishing sound salary structures.[3]

39.4.5 Time-record transaction file

This file contains data on all time/attendance forms for a particular pay period (eg. employee name and number, department or cost centre, and number of hours per activity). These data are used in processing the payroll. Sometimes job-time data (including number of labour hours spent on a job during a particular period) are also recorded in this file and used for production control and cost accounting purposes.[4]

39.4.6 Pay-cheque transaction file

This file contains data on the payments to be made to each employee. These can include employee name and number, net amount, mode of payment, reference number (eg. cheque number), bank code, and bank account number.[4]

39.5 DATA FLOW AND PROCESSING REQUIREMENTS

The personnel information and payroll system uses both the on-line and batch methods of data processing. The capture and maintenance of personnel and payroll master data usually takes place in an on-line environment — ie. new records and changes to existing records are implemented immediately when new appointments or changes occur. This is necessary to keep both databases up to date at all times, to facilitate meaningful enquiries and analyses, and to ensure that employees are remunerated according to their current status.

Time/attendance and job-time data, however, are usually captured in batches. The actual payroll processing and reporting therefore takes place once per pay period.

The processing and flow of data through the personnel information and payroll system can be divided into four phases (as shown by the system flowchart in Figure 39.2). These are the *capturing and updating of personnel and payroll master data* (including updating the earnings and deductions records), the *capturing and processing of time and attendance data, payroll processing, and labour cost distribution,* and the *actual payments to employees and outside bodies.*[4]

39.5.1 Capturing and updating personnel and payroll master data

Before new master records can be created for a new employee in the personnel master file and payroll master file, the position to which such an employee is to be appointed must reside in the job description reference file. The presence of such a job description record signifies that an approved position actually exists and is available.

The new data, or changes to the existing data, are entered by way of *personnel take-on* or *action forms.* The data are then edited and updated to the personnel and payroll master files. At the same time the skills inventory file is updated with the new skills acquired, and the necessary control reports are produced.

It also happens that the earnings and deductions records have to be updated — eg. new allowances added, or certain deductions changed or added. This is done by way of properly authorized personnel action forms. Editing and reporting of these changes has to be scrutinized by a responsible person to ensure that employees receive the correct remuneration.

The changes and updating are usually carried out using the on-line mode of data processing.

39.5.2 Capturing and processing of time and attendance data

Before any payroll processing can take place, time/attendance and/or job-time data have to be captured, edited, and updated to the time-record transaction file. The forms or tickets on which data are initially recorded are gathered in batches by the various timekeepers (or payroll clerks) and sent to the payroll department on a daily basis. Batch totals are computed for each batch before they are entered into the system. Once captured, the batches are checked, edit reports produced and, if everything is in order, the time-record transaction and payroll master files are updated with the data concerned.

39.5.3 Payroll processing and labour cost distribution

When all batches of time records during a particular pay period (eg. a month or week) have been captured, edited, and updated, and all master file changes have been made, the actual payroll processing can commence. During this processing run:

- all time records are computed into money terms;
- earnings and allowances are updated to the *current period earnings fields;*
- deductions are computed and updated to the *current period deduction fields;*
- year-to-date figures are updated;
- net earnings are computed;
- pay-cheque records are updated to the *pay-cheque transaction file* (which will be linked to the accounts payable application to actually produce the pay cheques and update the cash book).

At the same time, the total labour costs have to be distributed to the various cost centres and/or jobs. Labour cost distribution takes place through the *general ledger master file,* and job costs by way of the *cost accounting transaction file.*

FIGURE 39.2. System flowchart for personnel information and payroll.

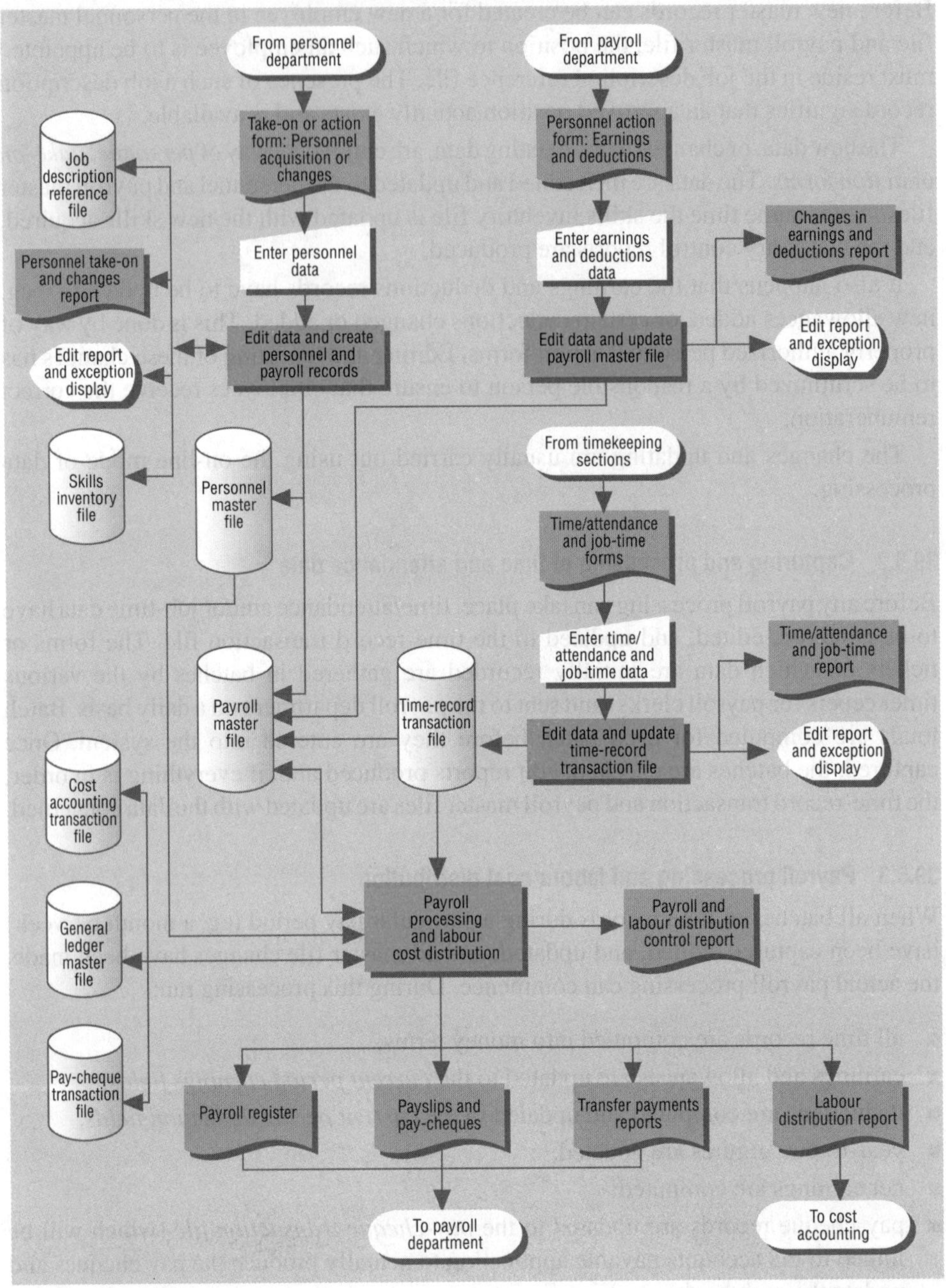

An important part of payroll processing is the production of several control reports. These include the payroll register, transfer payments reports, and labour distribution reports.

39.5.4 Pay cheques and transfer payments

The net amounts shown on the payroll master records have to be paid to the employees of a firm by way of pay cheques, bank transfers, or cash. The system, therefore, has to produce payslips for all employees, pay cheques, bank transfer statements, coin analyses, or any other means of controlling payments.

The difference between the gross pay and the net pay has to be paid to outside bodies such as the Receiver of Revenue, and pension and medical aid funds. For each of these, the necessary transaction and control reports have to be produced and transfer payments have to be arranged.

Note that the totals of employee payments and transfer payments have to tally with the total of the labour cost distribution report.

39.6 ACCOUNTING CONTROLS

Integrity and privacy are the two most important factors to keep in mind when accounting controls for the personnel information and payroll system are designed. The personal and payroll information in respect of each employee is a private matter, and proper controls must ensure that only authorized persons have access to such information. Accounting and administrative controls also have to promote integrity and prevent fraud, the latter being a common problem in payroll applications because a firm's own personnel and money are involved.[2]

Internal accounting and administrative controls must therefore ensure:[1]

- that only personnel suited for particular jobs are employed;
- that the privacy and integrity of personal and payroll information are protected;
- that accurate personnel and payroll master file records are maintained;
- that all personnel and payroll transactions are properly authorized according to predetermined criteria;
- that all payroll transactions are properly validated and then accurately recorded and processed;
- that all payments to employees and outside bodies are made on time and strictly according to the payroll output provided.

In a critical and complicated system like the personnel information and payroll system, several risks can exist. Failure of controls, or inadequate controls, may result in the employment of unqualified personnel, the improper disclosure of private information, incorrect or unauthorized payments being made to employees and other bodies, employees being unhappy when paid late or incorrectly, and fines or penalties being incurred for not meeting legal requirements.[2] To prevent such risks a proper set of general and application controls have to be introduced.[4]

39.6.1 General controls

General controls for the personnel information and payroll system would include:

- *Duties must be separated.* Units that have custodial functions (eg. the paymaster and cashier) should be separate from those units that keep the records (eg. timekeeping) and those that prepare the payroll data (eg. payroll department). In addition, the people from the personnel department who authorize and approve personnel actions should be separate from the people involved in custodial and record-keeping functions.

- *Complete and up-to-date documentation* for controlling all processing aspects of personnel information and payroll processing. This will include copies of source documents, flowcharts, editing and processing programs, record layouts, and reports.
- *Security must be maintained with respect to on-line systems.* This entails the use of passwords and the use of terminals with restricted functions when accessing confidential data, generating access logs, audit trails, and regular backups of all databases.

39.6.2 Application controls

Control points within the personnel information and payroll system include:[4]

- the take-on and changing of personnel and payroll master records;
- the establishment of each employee's pay status and changes thereto;
- the recording of time spent and attendances;
- the processing of time/attendance and payroll transactions;
- the disbursement of cash or other forms of payment.

The following application controls relate to the operation of the personnel information and payroll processing system:[4]

- the proper authorization and recording of personnel and payroll master data according to approved criteria (eg. job description references);
- all documents relating to time spent, attendances, payables, and cash disbursements should be pre-numbered, well designed and, where applicable, pre-printed with data like the employee's name, number and cost centre;
- time cards, job-time tickets, and attendance forms should be properly approved;
- hours recorded on job-time tickets should be reconciled with those shown on the corresponding attendance forms or time cards;
- proper batch control totals should be computed for all time and attendance forms before their data are entered into the system. These control totals are to be checked before any further processing can be done;
- all data on time records should be validated when prepared and entered for processing; errors detected during entry or editing have to be corrected as soon as possible;
- all edit and control reports must be checked for errors before payslips and pay cheques are printed;
- all controls relating to cash disbursements (see Chapter 34) must also apply to the payment of salaries, wages and transfers.

39.7 MANAGEMENT INFORMATION REQUIREMENTS

For management to be able to perform their control and decision-making functions, they need various kinds of management information. This information is usually communicated to them by way of reports. All reports may once again be classified as operational listings and reports, exception reports, enquiry screens and reports, and managerial reports.[4]

Payroll processing usually provides a variety of listings and reports. Some of them are for internal purposes and others are for external use, especially those for government departments.

39.7.1 Operational listings and reports

These listings and reports are used for general control purposes. They are scheduled reports containing detailed and summary data of all transactions during a certain period. They help to maintain the audit trail of the system. Examples of these listings and reports are:

- *Daily listing of personnel take-on and change activities.* This listing contains data on new personnel and payroll master records as well as on any changes made to existing master records.
- *Daily listing of changes to the payroll master file.* This listing contains data on all changes made in respect of earnings and deductions to the applicable records in the payroll master file.
- *Daily control report for time/attendance data captured.* This report contains all time, attendance, and job-time data entered into the system with control totals per batch.
- *Payroll and labour distribution control report.* This report is used for control purposes before the actual payroll register is produced. It contains summarized data on computed payroll earnings and deductions as well as on the distribution of labour costs to the various departments and cost centres.
- *Payroll register.* Together with the necessary control and summary totals, this report also contains detailed information on all earnings, deductions, gross and net pay per employee.
- *Labour distribution summary.* This report contains detailed and summarized data on all labour costs involved in a particular payroll run. It is also used for cost accounting purposes.
- *Pay-cheque listing.* This listing contains data on all payments made to employees and outside bodies.
- *Payslips and pay cheques.* These represent the actual payments made to employees. In many cases the pay cheque forms a tear-off part of the payslip.
- *Transfer payments reports.* These reports contain data on the amounts paid to outside bodies such as financial institutions, the Receiver of Revenue, pension funds, and medical aid funds.

39.7.2 Exception reports

The system must be designed to inform management about all variances as well as abnormal and conflicting conditions, including unauthorized appointments, incorrect allowances and payments, and other discrepancies.

39.7.3 Enquiry reports

The on-line personnel information and payroll system makes it possible to make enquiries interactively. This means that transactions can be listed and summarized in any way, and that the current status of master records can be shown at any time. Such enquiries can be in the form of screen displays or printed reports. Examples include:

- personnel information and status per employee;
- vacancies per job type, skill, or department;
- number and location of available skills;
- personnel turnover per department;
- current payroll information per employee;
- labour force (posts and/or employees) per department or cost centre;
- year-to-date summary of labour costs per cost centre or department;
- year-to-date or monthly details of earnings and deductions per employee;
- details or summary of overtime paid per cost centre or department.

39.7.4 Managerial reports

Managerial reports for the personnel information and payroll system would include the following:

- *Personnel strength report.* This report contains details of the personnel employed in each department (labour force) and any changes that have occurred over a given period.
- *Personnel turnover report.* This report gives an analysis of all personnel appointments, resignations, and discharges per period, cost centre, and department.
- *Personnel performance report.* This report contains details of employee performance per employee or occupational category.
- *Leave analysis.* This report gives an analysis of holiday leave, sick leave, and other leave taken over a particular period — in total and per cost centre or department.
- *Overtime analysis.* This report analyses overtime hours and amounts spent on certain jobs, cost centres, or departments.
- *Sales commission analysis.* This report gives an analysis of sales commissions paid by product, product line, or area.
- *Labour cost analysis.* This report gives a breakdown of direct labour hour costs per job, cost centre, or department.
- *Job performance report.* In this report, job costs and hours applied are analysed in comparison with standard costs and hours allowed; variances are highlighted and queried.

39.8 SUMMARY

The personnel information and payroll function manages a firm's human resources. Where organizations have incorporated their human resources planning into their strategic planning, it has helped management to understand the importance of information technology in carrying out their responsibilities. Because human resources are usually regarded as an organization's most valuable asset, the personnel information and payroll system plays an important role in maintaining this asset.[3]

The system interfaces with the production management and cost accounting system, the accounts payable system, and the general ledger system, to distribute labour costs to the applicable cost centres and jobs, and to eventually pay employees the amounts they have earned.

Source documents like personnel take-on and action forms, time/attendance forms, and job-time tickets are used to update the personnel and payroll master files as well as other files such as the skills inventory file, time-record transaction file, and the pay-cheque transaction file.

From these updated files, employees can be paid, labour costs can be distributed, and a host of management and other reports can be produced. These facilitate proper human resource planning and provide control and auditing mechanisms which help to safeguard the organization's assets and optimize the profit-making process.

REVIEW QUESTIONS

1. Describe the objectives and relating functions of the personnel information and payroll application of an accounting information system.
2. Describe the role of each of the source documents necessary for the proper operation of a personnel information and payroll system.
3. Explain why it is so important that the personnel information database and payroll database be linked closely together.
4. Explain the interaction between the different data files associated with the personnel information and payroll system.
5. Describe the flow of data through the personnel information and payroll system and indicate how it interfaces with other systems.
6. Describe the accounting and administrative controls required to ensure the privacy and integrity of personnel and payroll information within the personnel information and payroll system.
7. Outline the nature and purpose of each of the various management reports that should be produced by the personnel information and payroll system.

SELECTED REFERENCES AND RECOMMENDED READING

1. Cushing, B. E. and Romney, M. B. 1990. *Accounting Information Systems —A Comprehensive Approach.* Fifth edition. Reading, Massachusetts: Addison-Wesley.
2. Davis, J. R., Alderman, C. W. and Robinson, L. A. 1990. *Accounting Information Systems —A Cycle Approach.* Third edition. New York: John Wiley and Sons.
3. Gelinas, U. J. Jr., Oram, A. E. and Wiggins, W. P. 1990. *Accounting Information Systems.* Boston: PWS-KENT.

4. Wilkinson, J. W. 1989. *Accounting and Information Systems: Essential Concepts and Applications.* New York: John Wiley and Sons.

CHAPTER 40 General ledger, fixed assets and financial reporting

40.1 INTRODUCTION

The *general ledger, fixed assets and financial reporting application* may be regarded as the culmination of all other applications within the accounting information system. This is where the results of the other applications come together, are controlled, and are reported on in total. The overall financial results of a firm can be extracted from this application to enable financial planning to take place.

Like the other applications dealt with in this module, the general ledger application is an interacting structure of people, equipment, methods, and controls. It is designed to support both operational and informational functions, although the informational functions predominate.[3]

The general ledger constitutes a firm's *chart of accounts.* It interfaces with, and controls, all other accounting applications. It is the cornerstone of the accounting information system and the main supplier of comprehensive financial information to management.

The other applications feed summary information to the general ledger system, which in turn produces high level management reports such as income statements, balance sheets, cash flow statements, responsibility reports, performance reports, and profitability reports.

The processing interfaces within the accounting information system make it possible for the general ledger system to control and balance all accounting activities by way of a trial balance. Figure 40.1 emphasizes the importance of properly integrating the various applications within the AIS and highlights the pivotal role of the general ledger system.[4]

40.2 OBJECTIVES AND FUNCTIONS OF THE SYSTEM

The main objective of the general ledger, fixed assets and financial reporting system is the fair presentation of financial information which reflects the true operating results and financial position of an organization. This involves effective financial planning, proper organization, the use of correct procedures, the collection, recording, and control of summarized data obtained from other accounting applications, the safeguarding and recording of fixed assets, and the provision of general purpose and external financial statements and reports.[2]

The specific processing functions related to these objectives include: preparing operating budgets, prompt and accurate collection and processing of transaction data, maintaining accounting controls, recording and controlling fixed assets, and generating appropriate financial statements and reports for management and external purposes.[4]

40.2.1 Preparing operating budgets

The preparation of budgets is an important financial management function. Various kinds of budgets (eg. sales, income, and labour cost budgets) are used to control the income and expenditure of the different responsibility centres and form the basis for the preparation of responsibility reports. Another form of budget is the *standard costs budget* which is used to control production costs.

FIGURE 40.1. Processing interfaces within the accounting information system.

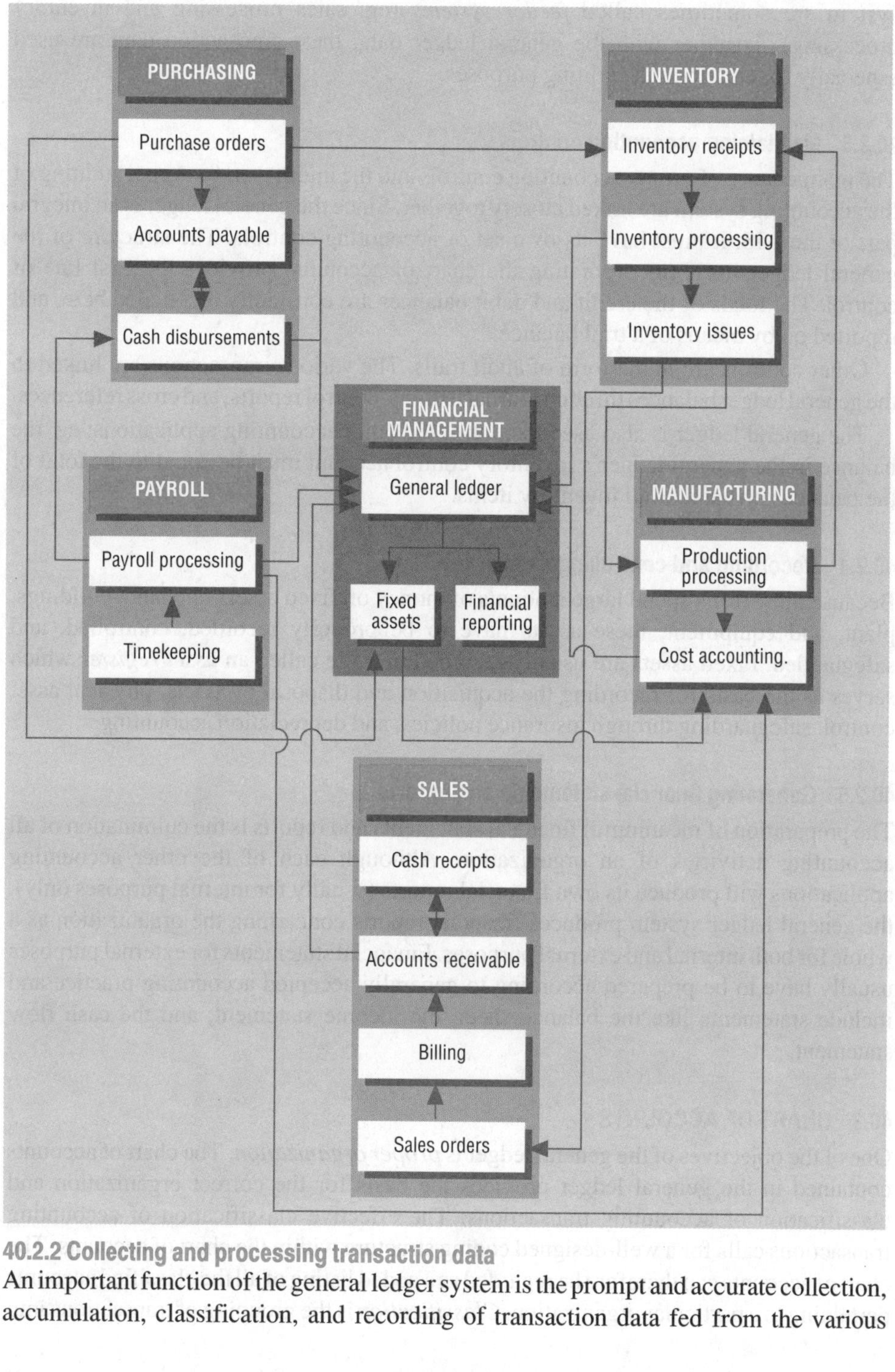

40.2.2 Collecting and processing transaction data

An important function of the general ledger system is the prompt and accurate collection, accumulation, classification, and recording of transaction data fed from the various accounting applications, and the updating of the results to the applicable ledger accounts in the *general ledger master file.* The other applications in the accounting information system are sometimes called *feeder systems* (eg. sales processing and inventory processing). Together with the general ledger data, these transaction data are used especially for enquiry and auditing purposes.

40.2.3 Maintaining accounting controls

The maintenance of proper accounting controls and the internal and external auditing of the accounting system are linked closely together. Since the general ledger is an integral part of the AIS, it must have its own set of accounting controls. The structure of the general ledger itself (incorporating the chart of accounts) provides the first line of control. The totals of the credit and debit balances are constantly reconciled here, and reported on by means of a trial balance.

Other controls are in the form of audit trails. The various transactions are linked to the general ledger balances through journal listings, control reports, and cross references.

The general ledger is also used to control the other accounting applications; eg. the balance in the general ledger's inventory control account must be equal to the total of the balances on hand of all inventory items.

40.2.4 Recording and controlling fixed assets

Because most firms spend large amounts of money on fixed assets like land, buildings, plant, and equipment, these assets have to be properly recorded, controlled, and safeguarded. Fixed assets are usually recorded in a file called an *asset register* which serves as the basis for recording the acquisition and disposal of assets, physical asset control, safeguarding through insurance policies, and depreciation accounting.[2]

40.2.5 Generating financial statements and reports

The preparation of meaningful financial statements and reports is the culmination of all accounting activities of an organization. Although each of the other accounting applications will produce its own financial reports (usually for internal purposes only), the general ledger system produces financial reports concerning the organization as a whole for both internal and external purposes. Financial statements for external purposes usually have to be prepared according to generally accepted accounting practice and include statements like the balance sheet, the income statement, and the cash flow statement.

40.3 CHART OF ACCOUNTS

One of the objectives of the general ledger is *proper organization.* The chart of accounts contained in the general ledger provides the basis for the correct organization and classification of accounting transactions. The effective classification of accounting transactions calls for a well-designed coding structure within the chart of accounts. The chart of accounts can therefore be regarded as a coded listing of all the classified accounts pertaining to a particular organization. *Classification* is the grouping of transactions into classes or categories (eg. sales transactions according to products or sales people), while *coding* is the assigning of symbols (eg. numbers and letters) according to a scheme or plan to distinguish the groups to which each item belongs and to distinguish items within a certain group from each other. Classification helps to make accounting data more meaningful to users, and coding enables data within the AIS to be used more efficiently and effectively.[4]

The chart of accounts is a very useful tool for processing accounting transactions of all types. It facilitates the recording and posting of these transactions and simplifies the preparation of financial statements and various types of regular and enquiry reports.

Although various coding schemes are available (eg. mnemonic codes, sequence codes, and block codes), it is not our intention to discuss any of them in detail. The type of coding scheme used will depend entirely on the nature and structure of the organization concerned. Most charts of accounts, however, are built around the major financial categories of assets, liabilities, equities, revenue, and expenditure, and a numeric block coding scheme is used.

Any sound coding scheme must uniquely identify an object, it must be concise and simple, it must allow for changes and expansion, and it must be standardized throughout all functions and management levels of the organization to facilitate an integrated reporting system.[4]

A coding scheme for the chart of accounts contains the general ledger account numbers which represent the primary key fields for these records. Block coding is usually applied to the major account types, for example:

Account code	*Account type*
100–199	Owners' equity
200–299	Fixed assets
300–399	Current assets
400–499	Liabilities
500–599	Operating income
600–699	Cost of goods sold
700–799	Selling expenses
800–899	Administrative expenses

In larger organizations, it is useful to incorporate subcodes for departments and responsibility centres into the chart of accounts. This will facilitate the accumulation, summarization, analysis, and reporting of accounting information according to responsibilities. Block codes for this purpose could be as follows:[1]

Code	*Department*
00	General accounts
10–19	Marketing
20–29	Production
30–39	Finance
40–49	Accounting
50–59	Personnel

Within these departments, one will find certain responsibility centres; eg. accounts payable (code 42) and payroll (code 45) within the accounting department, and purchasing and receiving (code 21) within the production department.

The balance sheet items of a simplified chart of accounts could be codified as follows:

Owners' equity (100–199)

101	Capital
105	Reserves
110–199	Other owners' equity

Fixed assets (200–299)

201	Land
205	Buildings
210	Plant and equipment
215	Allowances for depreciation
220–299	Other fixed assets

Current assets (300–399)

301	Cash
305	Accounts receivable
310	Inventory
315	Prepaid expenses
320–399	Other current assets

Liabilities (400–499)

401	Accounts payable
405	Dividends payable
410	Interest accrued
415	Deferred taxation
420–499	Other liabilities

For the income statement items of the chart of accounts, the codification could be as follows:

Operating income (500–599)

501	Sales income
505	Sales discounts
510	Sales returns and allowances
520–599	Other operating income

Cost of goods sold (600–699)

601	Direct materials
605	Direct labour

610	Indirect labour
615	Factory overheads
620–699	Other cost-related expenses

Selling expenses (700–799)

701	Advertising
705	Sales commissions
710	Telephone and postage
715	Repairs and maintenance
720–799	Other selling expenses

Administrative expenses (800–899)

801	Salaries and wages
805	Legal and consulting
810	Stationery and supplies
815	Telephone and postage
820–899	Other administrative expenses.

The coding of records (and the flexibility of such coding) is a central feature of the accounting information system. All records have a *primary key* which serves as the unique record identifier. For example, account number 20–601 (production department — direct materials) would be debited for direct materials issued by the inventory department to the production department, and account number 00–310 (general accounts — inventory control) would be credited. For a fee payable to the marketing consultant, account number 10–805 (marketing — consultant's fee) would be debited and account number 00–305 (general accounts — accounts payable) would be credited.

40.4 FIXED ASSETS

The acquisition, maintenance, and disposal of fixed assets forms an important part of the custodial functions in most organizations. Any system providing support for these functions should interface with the purchasing, accounts payable, and cash applications of the AIS. Depreciation accounting, where the cost of assets is matched with related income, must interface with a manufacturing firm's production and cost accounting applications because depreciation represents an overhead expense.[2]

The fixed asset master file (or asset register) and accounting controls associated with it will be discussed in later paragraphs. Most of the activities concerning property management centre on this file.

The risk management function often forms part of the property management function. Here potential losses that can be insured are identified, recorded, and evaluated in order to obtain and administer suitable insurance coverage. Both external and internal information is needed for this. External information includes the costs of the various types of available insurance coverage and internal information includes estimates of potential losses that would result from physical damage to assets or unavailability of assets, and other related risks. The AIS provides an important source of useful information — eg. type, location and value of all assets, payment of premiums, maintenance and funding of insurance reserves, and information about the administration of insurance claims.[1]

40.5 DATA SOURCES AND INPUTS

Because the general ledger system usually receives its source data directly from all other accounting applications, it does not need many source documents. The primary source document is the *journal voucher,* either in the form of a source document or in the form of an interface transaction prepared by the AIS.

For the fixed assets application, only a fixed asset take-on or transfer form is needed. Accounting transactions or adjustments will occur by way of journal entries.

40.5.1 Journal vouchers

The journal voucher remains the primary source of data for the general ledger system, even when the system is computerized. It specifies the general ledger accounts to be debited and credited, the amount, the reason for the transaction, and the name of the person who approved it.[2]

There are two types of journal entries. *Regular entries* (ie. recurring entries) are usually prepared automatically by the AIS to post summary data of the other accounting applications (or subsidiary files) to the general ledger. Other entries (called *adjusting* or *closing entries*) are usually entered manually, either by way of a journal source document prepared in writing, or by a form printed by the system after the necessary data have been entered. The latter must, however, also be properly authorized.

Adjusting journal entries are used to change the balances in the general ledger master file as a result of incorrect allocations or the processing of incorrect transactions. *Closing journal* entries take place at the end of the accounting period. They are used for the preparation of financial statements and for closing off certain ledger accounts.[4]

It must be noted that all types of journal entries are processed and stored in the same way.

40.5.2 Fixed assets take-on form

Formal authorization for expenditure in order to acquire fixed assets is usually given by way of a *fixed assets take-on form.* This form contains all data to be captured onto the fixed assets master file, eg. description, location, date acquired, purchase cost, and depreciation method.

40.5.3 Fixed assets transfer form

This form is a type of journal entry that is used for authorizing and transferring certain assets from one department to another. It will contain data such as asset number, description, department transferred from and to, and reasons and authorization for the transfer.

40.6 DATABASE STRUCTURE

The database for the general ledger, fixed assets and financial reporting system consists of variety of master, transaction, and history files. The most important files are the *general ledger* and *budget master files.* The general ledger transaction file and general ledger history file support the enquiry and reporting capabilities of the general ledger system. In many cases the transactions from the other accounting applications of the AIS are updated to a *general ledger subsidiary file* (eg. accounts payable) before being updated to a control account in the *general ledger master file* (as depicted in Figure 40.2). This also enhances the enquiry and auditing capabilities of the system.[1]

40.6.1 Budget master file

This file is used mainly for planning and controlling purposes. It contains data on the budgeted (planned) values of assets, liabilities, income, and expenses for the different responsibility centres of the organization. These values may be broken down on a periodic basis to provide *variable budgeting* (budgets adjusted according to expected output) in order to control the actual income and expenditure more effectively. These data, together with the results in the general ledger master file, facilitate proper responsibility reporting where variances between planned and actual figures are shown.[4]

FIGURE 40.2. Database structure for the general ledger.

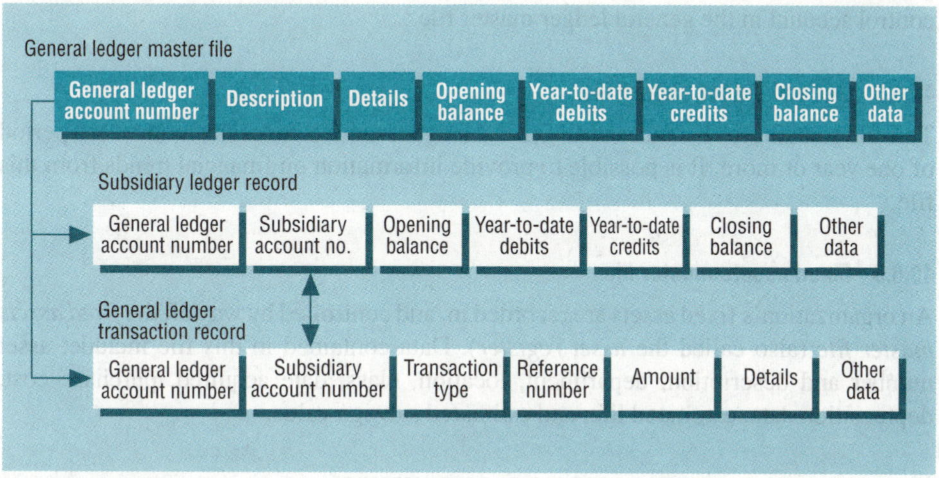

40.6.2 General ledger master file

This file's value depends largely on the design and completeness of the chart of accounts it represents. A broad range of financial reports can be produced if the classification and coding scheme is properly designed according to the organization's structure and management information needs. The file's main input comes from the transaction files created by the other accounting applications (sometimes called *feeder systems*) in the AIS. Adjusting and closing journals are the other sources of input.

The general ledger master file also provides the basis for proper auditing practices. When the master file and its supporting transactions are adequately classified, coded, and cross-referenced, it is possible to trace all transactions that make up a particular general ledger balance, or trace a particular transaction right through to its destined general ledger account.

The data contained in the general ledger master file include: account number and description, subsidiary ledger account number (if applicable), classification, opening balance, monthly debits and credits, year-to-date debits and credits, and closing balance.

40.6.3 General ledger transaction file

This file contains details of each transaction posted to the general ledger during the accounting period. It includes: voucher number, description, date, accounts debited and credited, and amount.

40.6.4 General ledger subsidiary file

In many cases the transactions for certain categories of accounts (eg. inventory and accounts receivable) are first updated to subsidiary files before being updated to the general ledger master file. The inventory master file and accounts receivable master file are therefore regarded as subsidiary files because they contain details of each of the accounts in those files. Each of the subsidiary ledgers is controlled by a subsidiary ledger control account in the general ledger master file.[1]

40.6.5 General ledger history file

This file contains the balances of all general ledger accounts for each month over a period of one year or more. It is possible to provide information on financial trends from this file.

40.6.6 Fixed assets master file

An organization's fixed assets are recorded in, and controlled by way of, the *fixed assets master file* (also called the *asset register*). Data contained in this file include: asset number and description, department, location, class, date acquired, purchase cost, depreciation data, estimated life, and estimated salvage value.

40.7 DATA FLOW AND PROCESSING REQUIREMENTS

The transaction data flowing from the different accounting applications (feeder systems), and those entered by way of journal vouchers, have to be updated to the general ledger system on a regular basis. Transactions in batches are usually updated automatically from the feeder systems and those entered through terminals are updated on-line. The processing and flow of data through the general ledger, fixed assets and financial reporting system (as depicted in Figure 40.3) are discussed under the following headings: budgeting, updating the general ledger master file, adjusting and closing entries, fixed assets, and financial reporting.[4]

FIGURE 40.3. System flowchart for general ledger, fixed assets and financial reporting.

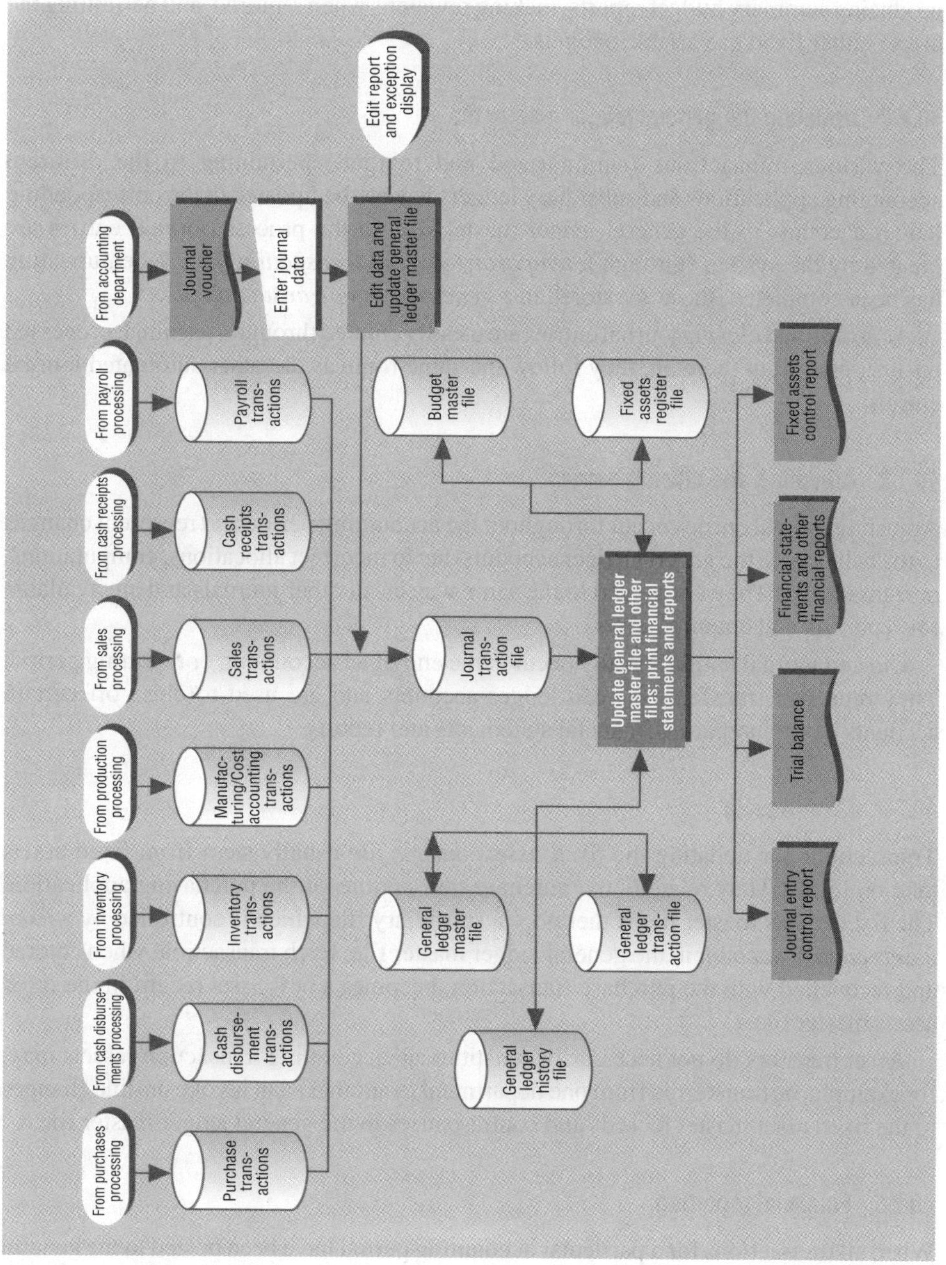

40.7.1 Budgeting

When making use of a proper budgeting system, a firm will begin by entering budgeted data onto the budget master file. This is usually done according to budget data sheets.

The budget master file is updated on-line. Provision is made to capture budget data, producing summary budget reports, making revisions when required, and permitting the use of either fixed or variable budgets.

40.7.2 Updating the general ledger master file

The various transactions (summarized and totalled) pertaining to the different accounting applications and subsidiary ledgers have to be updated to the corresponding ledger accounts in the general ledger master file. In the process, journal entries are created by the system (through a *temporary journal transaction file*). When updating has been completed, these are stored in a *general ledger transaction file.*

Adjusting and *closing* journal entries are usually entered through a terminal, processed on-line, and, from there on, they follow the same route as the other automated journal entries.

40.7.3 Adjusting and closing entries

Adjusting journal entries occur throughout the accounting period and represent changes to the balances in the general ledger accounts due to incorrect allocations, computations, or transactions. They are treated in the same way as all other journals and are available for reporting and enquiry purposes.

Closing journal entries usually occur at the end of an accounting or reporting period. They represent transfers between ledger accounts and are used to close off certain accounts before preparing financial statements and reports.

40.7.4 Fixed assets

Transactions for updating the *fixed assets master file* usually stem from fixed assets take-on forms. They relate to the purchase transactions of the purchasing application. The fixed assets master file is therefore a subsidiary file which is controlled by a *fixed assets control account* in the general ledger master file. Each transaction, when entered and reconciled with the purchase transaction, becomes a new asset record in the fixed assets master file.

Asset transfers do not necessarily constitute an accounting transaction (assets may, for example, be transferred from one department to another), but invoke on-line changes to the fixed asset master records and contra-entries in the general ledger master file.

40.7.5 Financial reporting

When all transactions for a particular accounting period have been posted to the general ledger, adjusting and closing journals have been passed, and a trial balance has been produced and checked, financial reporting can commence. The general ledger system and data from its subsystems, make it possible to produce numerous financial reports on various issues, eg. budgeting and planning reports, control reports, responsibility reports, cost allocation reports, profitability reports, and regular financial statements.

40.8 ACCOUNTING CONTROLS

The general ledger system's main function is to accurately bring together all accounting transactions produced by the other accounting applications and then produce reliable and applicable financial reports to a variety of users. At the same time it must provide adequate controls for the other applications and for the general ledger system itself.[2]

The fixed assets system, in turn, must provide the necessary controls to safeguard fixed assets and to ensure the proper recording of those assets.

The internal controls associated with the general ledger and fixed assets system must therefore ensure:[1]

- that all accounting journals and fixed asset transactions are properly authorized, recorded, and processed;
- that fixed assets are properly safeguarded;
- that any significant deviations from planned results are reported as soon as they occur;
- that the overall system is in balance at all times.

The risks associated with the general ledger and fixed assets system include:[4]

- incorrect, unposted, or unauthorized journal entries or fixed asset transactions;
- the total of all general ledger balances not being equal to zero;
- the total balances of the individual subsidiary ledger files not being equal to the balances in their respective control accounts;
- inadequate or incomplete audit trails;
- inadequate control over, or maintenance of, fixed assets.

A proper set of general and application controls has to be introduced to prevent such risks.

40.8.1 General controls

General controls to be applied in a general ledger and fixed assets system include the following:

- *The separation of duties.* Units that have custodial functions (eg. the safeguarding of fixed assets) should be separate from those units that keep the records (eg. accounting department). In addition, the function of posting journal vouchers should be separate from the functions responsible for preparing and approving these vouchers and also from the function of preparing the trial balances.
- *There should be complete and up-to-date documentation* for controlling all processing aspects of the general ledger, fixed assets and financial reporting system. This includes copies of source documents, flowcharts, editing and processing programs, record layouts, period-end schedules, and control reports.
- *Security in respect of on-line systems.* This will entail using passwords and terminals with restricted functions when accessing the general ledger file; it also involves generating access logs and audit trails, and keeping regular backups of all databases.

40.8.2 Application controls

Control points within the general ledger and fixed assets system include:

- updating automated journal entries to the general ledger master file;
- entering and updating adjusting and closing journal entries to the general ledger master file;
- regular period-end schedules and control reports;
- periodic trial balances.

The following application controls relate to the operation of the general ledger, fixed assets and financial reporting system:[4]

- journal vouchers must be pre-numbered, properly authorized, and accurately prepared;
- all allocations must be checked for accuracy and irregularities — errors must be corrected as soon as they are detected;
- the system must check that debits and credits are equal on journal entries before posting them to the general ledger;
- regular trial balances and/or exception reports have to be produced to ensure that the system is in balance;
- there must be adequate cross-referencing between accounts and transactions to ensure an adequate audit trail;
- the balances in general ledger control accounts have to be constantly checked against the total balances of each subsidiary ledger;
- suitable period-end reports have to be produced before and after the processing of closing journals to ensure that financial statements reflect the fair presentation of financial results and position.

40.9 FINANCIAL AND MANAGEMENT REPORTING

The reports generated by the general ledger, fixed assets and financial reporting system may be classified as *general ledger and fixed asset analyses, managerial reports,* and *financial statements.* These, however, also include operational listings, exception reports for control purposes, and enquiry screens and reports.[4]

40.9.1 Operational listings and reports

These listings and reports are used for general control purposes. They are scheduled reports containing detailed and summary data of transactions during a certain period and help to maintain the audit trail of the system. Examples of these listings and reports are:

- *Daily listing of journal entries.* This listing contains details and control totals of all journal entries processed and updated to the general ledger master file.
- *Daily listing of fixed asset transactions.* This listing contains details and control totals of all fixed asset transactions processed and updated to the fixed asset master file.

- *Periodic report on fixed asset location.* This listing contains details of assets by location. It serves to locate certain assets and to assist when taking physical inventories.
- *Periodic trial balance.* This control report contains the names and numbers of all general ledger accounts together with their debit or credit balances. It is used to show the current balances of each account and to ascertain that the total of all balances is equal to zero.

40.9.2 General ledger analyses

These analyses assist accountants in verifying the accuracy of postings. They include:

- a general ledger proof listing;
- a listing of changes in general ledger balances;
- an allocation of expenses to various cost centres;
- a comparison of account balances for the current period to the same period of the previous year;
- a comparison of year-to-date account balances for the current year with those of the previous year.[4]

40.9.3 Exception reports

The system must be designed to inform management about all variances from plans as well as abnormal and conflicting conditions, eg. overspent budgets, production costs exceeding standards, balances in the general ledger control accounts not being equal to the total of all balances in their corresponding subsidiary ledgers, and the system being out of balance.

40.9.4 Enquiry reports

The on-line general ledger, fixed assets and financial reporting system enables one to make enquiries interactively. This means that transactions can be listed and summarized in many ways and that the current status of master records can be shown at any time. Such enquiries can be in the form of screen displays or printed reports. Examples include:

- the current status of a general ledger account;
- the current status and location of a particular fixed asset;
- details of all transactions making up the balance in a general ledger control account (audit trail);
- details of assets purchased by a particular department during a particular period;
- a variance report regarding a responsibility centre's budgeted and actual expenses;
- details of all transactions incurred by a particular responsibility centre during a particular period;
- a cash flow report to monitor daily cash flow.

40.9.5 Financial statements

In the end, interim and annual financial statements are the most important financial reports produced by the AIS. They are the end products of the system. They are required by legislation, and have to be prepared according to generally accepted accounting practice. The annual financial statements usually consist of a *balance sheet*, *cash flow statement*, *income statement*, and *trading account*. They are used by stockholders, government departments, auditors, creditors, prospective owners, and financial analysts.

40.9.6 Managerial reports

Managerial reports are specifically designed to aid management in decision-making. They should not contain too much detail, they should be analytical by nature and link up with other applications, where possible. Managerial reports produced by the general ledger, fixed assets and financial reporting system would include the following:

- *Various analysis reports.* These reports include sales analyses, cash analyses, receivables analyses, cost analyses, and budget analyses.
- *Budget reports.* These reports provide historical information that managers need to formulate new budgets, including information on direct (controllable) and indirect (non-controllable) items.
- *Departmental performance reports.* Departmental or responsibility centre performance reports compare budgeted and actual costs per production unit, cost centre, or administrative department, and analyse any variances that may occur.
- *Management performance reports.* By aggregating cost and budget data on all departments reporting to a particular manager, the performance of such a manager can be ascertained.
- *Profitability report.* Here the income and expenses directly related to certain profit centres or products are reported. Budgeted profits are compared with actual profits, and variances are computed. This allows an objective appraisal of each profit centre or product's net contribution to total profits.

It is clear that computerized accounting information systems can substantially improve the quality of information needed by managers. Scheduled reports can regularly provide large volumes of information for reference and audit purposes. These reports can, however, also summarize this information according to various decision-relevant criteria. Exception reports highlight specific circumstances, while enquiry reports produce up-to-date and special purpose information at request. Managerial reports are specially designed reports containing concise information for decision-making at the highest level.[1]

40.10 SUMMARY

The general ledger, fixed assets and financial reporting system is the centre of all the accounting cycles within the accounting information system. It is involved in collecting, classifying, coding, processing, storing, and controlling the transaction data of the AIS. It maintains accounting controls for its own purposes as well as for the other accounting applications, and ultimately produces financial statements and reports which reflect the financial results and position of the firm.

The chart of accounts is a coded listing of classified accounts that relates to a particular organization. Sound classification and coding enables the AIS to analyse and report on the various transactions and financial results in a meaningful and effective way.

The system receives inputs from the applications in the various accounting cycles — ie. the expenditure cycle, the production cycle, the revenue cycle, and the administrative cycle. These inputs are usually in the form of automated and manually prepared journal entries which update the general ledger master file and some other files. At the end of the accounting period, closing journal entries are passed and various financial statements and reports are produced.

The risks involved with the general ledger and fixed assets system are minimized by way of proper general and application controls built into the system.

A comprehensive set of exception, enquiry, and management reporting capabilities makes it possible to provide adequate management information for planning, budgeting and control, responsibility accounting, cost accounting, and profitability accounting.

REVIEW QUESTIONS

1. Describe the objectives and relating functions of the general ledger, fixed assets and financial reporting application of an accounting information system.
2. Prepare a diagram which shows how the general ledger, fixed assets and financial reporting system interacts with the other accounting applications by way of different accounting transactions.
3. Discuss the important role of a properly classified and coded chart of accounts within the general ledger system.
4. Explain how fixed asset transactions should be processed and controlled by the AIS.
5. Explain the importance of the journal voucher within the AIS.
6. Describe the role of the budgeting system in facilitating proper financial planning and control.
7. Describe the flow of data through the general ledger, fixed assets and financial reporting system.
8. Describe the accounting controls that have to be built into the general ledger system.
9. Outline the nature and purpose of each of the financial and management reports to be produced by the general ledger, fixed assets and financial reporting system.

SELECTED REFERENCES AND RECOMMENDED READING

1. Cushing, B. E. and Romney, M. B. 1990. *Accounting Information Systems —A Comprehensive Approach.* Fifth edition. Reading, Massachusetts: Addison-Wesley.
2. Davis, J. R., Alderman, C. W. and Robinson, L. A. 1990. *Accounting Information Systems — A Cycle Approach.* Third edition. New York: John Wiley and Sons.
3. Gelinas, U. J. Jr., Oram, A. E. and Wiggins, W. P. 1990. *Accounting Information Systems.* Boston: PWS-KENT.
4. Wilkinson, J. W. 1989. *Accounting and Information Systems: Essential Concepts and Applications.* New York: John Wiley and Sons.

MODULE 6 KEY POINT SUMMARY

- An accounting information system has to be designed to conform to the organizational structure of the firm and meet the objectives of providing relevant, reliable, and timely accounting information to the managers that need it.
- Modern accounting information systems consist of a number of interrelated and integrated subsystems which all work together in attaining the common goal of providing financial information that ensures the fair presentation of a firm's financial results and position.
- The design of an accounting information system should take place according to a framework of transaction or accounting cycles. These cycles are usually the expenditure, manufacturing (if applicable), revenue, and administrative cycles.
- The purchase orders and goods received application is the first part of the expenditure cycle. To start a business, raw materials, goods, and services have to be ordered and received.
- The accounts payable and cash disbursement application rounds off the expenditure cycle. Raw materials, goods, and services that have been ordered and received have to be paid for, and this requires the control and disbursement of cash resources.
- The second accounting cycle is the manufacturing or conversion cycle. Before any manufacturing can take place, however, raw materials and other goods have to be obtained from a firm's inventory. The inventory management application therefore constitutes the first part of the manufacturing cycle.
- The production management and cost accounting application completes the manufacturing cycle. Production involves a set of recurring operations to plan and control the manufacturing of a product, and cost accounting provides the mechanisms to record and control the costs of these operations.
- Finished goods manufactured or purchased by a firm have to be marketed and sold in order to generate income and maximize profit. The marketing and sales application is therefore the first part of the revenue cycle which aims to satisfy the needs of customers and generate income.
- The accounts receivable and cash receipts application concludes the revenue cycle and ensures that all amounts payable for goods sold to customers are collected and received in good time and that a steady cash inflow is maintained.
- The administrative cycle contains applications that serve all departments and processing cycles within an organization. The personnel information and payroll application is part of it and its goal is to maintain the firm's work force and benefit both individual employees and the organization as a whole.
- The remaining application of the administrative cycle involves the general ledger, fixed assets, and financial reporting activities. Here the results of all other accounting applications are collected, summarized, controlled, and reported on. This function facilitates the fair presentation of financial information in order to reflect the true operating results and financial position of an organization.

Glossary

Accounting Information Systems (AIS). Information systems that record and report business transactions, the flow of funds through an organization, and produce financial statements. This provides information for the planning and control of business operations, as well as for legal and historical record-keeping.

Access method. Refers to the process used to locate a data item in storage or on an input medium. See also *Direct Access Method* and *Indexed Sequential Access Method.*

Access time. (1) The time interval between the instant at which a device receives a request to access data and the instant at which delivery begins. (2) The time interval between the instant at which data is requested to be stored and the instant at which storage is started.

Acoustic coupler. A modem that converts digital data into a sequence of tones that are transmitted by a conventional telephone handset to a receiving modem, which transforms the data back to digital form.

Address. A character or group of characters that identifies a register, a particular part of storage, or some other data source or destination.

Ad hoc inquiries. Unique, unscheduled, situation-specific information requests.

Algorithm. A set of well-defined rules or processes for the solution of a problem in a finite number of steps.

Alphanumeric. Pertaining to a character set that contains letters, digits, or other characters such as punctuation marks.

American Standard Code for Information Interchange (ASCII). A seven-bit standard code used for information interchange among data processing systems, communication systems and associated equipment.

Analysis. The methodical examination of information items to reveal their underlying relationships.

Application generator. A software package that supports the development of an application through an interactive terminal dialogue, where the programmer/ analyst defines screens, reports, computations, and data structures using a high-level language.

Application software. Programs that specify the information processing activities required for the completion of specific tasks of computer users. Examples are electronic spreadsheet and word processing programs or inventory or payroll programs.

Arithmetic-Logic Unit (ALU). The unit of a computing system containing the circuits that perform arithmetic and logical operations.

Array. An arrangement of data items in one or more dimensions.

Artificial intelligence. The capability of a device to perform functions that are normally associated with human intelligence, such as reasoning, learning and self-improvement.

ASCII (American Standard Code for Information Interchange). A standard code used for information interchange among data processing systems, communication systems, and associated equipment.

Assembler language. A symbolic programming language that uses symbolic operation codes and addresses. The translation of these codes into machine language is called an Assembly.

Asynchronous transmission. The sending of data down a communication line one character at a time. Each character is preceded by a 'start' signal followed by a 'stop' signal

Audit trail. The presence of media and procedures that allow a transaction to be traced through all stages of information processing, beginning with its appearance on a source document and ending with its transformation into information on a final output document.

Automated office. The combination of text and data processing.

Automated Teller Machine (ATM). A special-purpose intelligent terminal used to provide remote banking services.

Backup. Standby equipment or procedures for use in the event of failure, damage, or overloading of normally used equipment and facilities.

Bar codes. Vertical marks or bars placed on merchandise, tags or packaging that can be sensed and read by optical character-reading devices. The width and combination of vertical lines are used to represent data.

BASIC (Beginners' All-purpose Symbolic Instruction Code). An easy-to-learn procedure-orientated programming language designed for interactive use at a terminal.

Batch processing. The processing of data or the accomplishment of jobs accumulated in advance in such a manner that each accumulation thus formed is processed or accomplished in the same run. The processing of data accumulated over a period of time.

Binary number system. A basic data representation method used in computers, which is a numbering system involving the digits 0 and 1.

Binary search. A search procedure that locates the object of search by successively dividing a file or part of a file in half and searching for the object at the midpoint.

Bit. Contraction of 'binary digit'. The smallest unit of information in a binary system. A bit may either be one or zero.

Block. A string of records, a string of words or a character string formed for technical or logic reasons to be treated as an entity. A set of things such as words, characters, or digits handled as a unit.

Blocked records. Records grouped on magnetic tape or magnetic disk to reduce the number of interrecord gaps and more fully utilize the storage medium.

BPI. Bits per inch. A measure of the recording density on magnetic tape.

Bubble memory. An electronic data storage device that stores binary digits as microscopic spots (bubbles) in a thin film on garnet crystals.

Buffer. A routine or storage area used to compensate for a difference in rate of flow of data, or time or occurrence of events when transferring data from one device to another.

Bug. A mistake or malfunction.

Bus. A set of conducting paths for movement of data and instructions that interconnects the various components of the CPU. It may take the form of a cable containing the many wires or of microscopic conducting lines on a microcomputer chip.

Business Information System (BIS). Information systems within a business organization that support one of the traditional functions of business such as marketing, finance, or production. Business information systems can be either operations or management information systems.

Byte. A collection of bits, usually eight, representing a numeric, alphabetic or special character.

Cache memory. A high-speed temporary storage area in the CPU for storing parts of a program or data during processing.

Cathode Ray Tube (CRT). A device similar to a TV used to display alphanumeric characters and/or graphic information from a computer.

CD-ROM. An optical disk technology for microcomputers featuring compact disks with a storage capacity of over 500 megabytes.

Central Processing Unit (CPU). The computer unit that performs the execution of instructions.

Chain printer. An impact printer in which the type slugs are carried by the links of a revolving chain. The print speed is usually in the range of 600–3 000 lines per minute.

Channel. A path along which signals can be sent. The portion of a storage medium that is accessible to a reading or a writing station, for example a track, band.

Chargeout systems. Methods of allocating costs to end user departments based on the information services rendered and information system resources utilized.

Check digit. A digit in a data field that is utilized to check for errors or loss of characters in the data field as a result of data transfer operations.

Client/Server network. A computing environment where end user workstations (clients) are connected to micro or mini LAN servers and possibly to mainframe *superservers.*

Clock. A device that generates periodic signals from which synchronism may be maintained. A device that measures and indicates time. A register whose content changes at regular intervals in such a way as to measure time.

COBOL (COmmon Business-Orientated Language). A programming language designed for business data processing.

Code. Computer instructions.

Communications satellite. Earth satellites placed in stationary orbits above the equator that serve as relay stations for communications signals transmitted from earth stations.

Compile. To prepare a machine language program from a computer program written in another programming language by making use of the overall logic structure of the program, or by generating one or more machine instructions for each symbolic statement.

Computer. (1) A data processing device that can perform substantial computation, including numerous arithmetic or logic operations, without intervention by a human operator during the processing. (2) A device that has the ability to accept data, internally store, and execute a program of instructions, perform mathematical, logical, and manipulative operations on data, and report the results.

Computer-Aided Design (CAD). The use of computers and advanced graphics hardware and software to provide interactive design assistance for engineering and architectural design.

Computer-Aided Manufacturing (CAM). The use of minicomputers and other computers to automate the operations systems of a manufacturing plant.

Computer-Aided Software Engineering (CASE). Same as computer-aided systems engineering, but emphasizing the importance of software development.

Computer Output Microfilm (COM). Miniature photographic images of output. Computer output is placed on magnetic tape which serves as the input to a microfilm processor.

Computer program. A series of instructions or statements, in a form acceptable to a computer, prepared in order to achieve a certain result.

Computer virus or worm. Program code that copies its destructive program routines into the computer systems of anyone who accesses computer systems which have used the program, or anyone who uses copies of data or programs taken from such computers. This spreads the destruction of data and programs among many computer users. Technically, a *virus* will not run unaided, but must be inserted into another program, while a *worm* is a distinct program that can run unaided.

Concentrator. A special-purpose mini- or microcomputer that accepts information from many terminals using slow-speed lines and transmits data to a main computer system over a high-speed line.

Concurrent processing. The generic term for the capability of computers to work on several tasks at the same time, that is, concurrently. This may involve specific capabilities such as overlapped processing, multiprocessing, multiprogramming, multitasking, parallel processing, and so on.

CPU. See *Central Processing Unit.*

Critical success factors. A small number of key factors that executives consider critical to the success of the enterprise. These are key areas where successful performance will assure the success of the organization and attainment of its goals.

Cursor. A movable point of light displayed on most video display screens to assist the user in the input of data. The cursor may look like a dot, short underline, or other shape that indicates the position of data to be entered or changed.

Cylinder. The group of data tracks accessed simultaneously by a set of read and write heads on a disk storage device.

Daisy-wheel printer. An output device resembling an office typewriter; it employs a flat disk with petal-like projections containing characters on the surfaces. Printing occurs one character at a time.

Data. A representation of facts, concepts or instructions in a formalized manner suitable for communication, interpretation, or processing by humans or by automatic means.

Data administration. Managing and developing the data bases and information resources of an organization.

Data base. A set of data, consisting of at least one file, that is sufficient for a given data processing system. A collection of data fundamental to a system.

Database administrator. A specialist responsible for maintaining standards for the development, maintenance, and security of an organization's databases.

Data Base Management Systems (DBMS). A set of programs that serves as an interface between the data base and three principal users — the programmer, the operating system, and the manager (or other information user); provides a method of arranging data to limit duplication, an ability to make changes easily and a capability of handling direct enquiries.

Data design. The design of the logical structure of databases and files to be used by a proposed information system. This produces detailed descriptions of the entities, relationships, data elements, and integrity rules for system files and databases.

Data dictionary. A file containing information about the content, relationships, and structure of one or more data bases. It may also refer to the software that supports the creation and maintenance of this file.

Data entry. The process of converting data into a form suitable for entry into a computer system. Also called data capture or input preparation.

Data flow diagram. A diagramming methodology that expresses the logical data flows in a system.

Data model. A conceptual framework which defines the logical relationships among the data elements needed to support a basic business or other process.

Decision Support System (DSS). An information system that utilizes decision rules, decision models, a data base, and a decision maker's own insights in an interactive computer-based process.

Desktop Publishing (DTP). The use of microcomputers, laser printers, and page-makeup software to produce a variety of printed materials, formerly done only by professional printers.

Digitizer. A device that is used to convert drawings and other graphic images on paper or other materials into digital data that is entered into a computer system.

Direct access. A method of storing data whereby it can be retrieved in any order, at random.

Direct Access Storage Device (DASD). A storage device that can directly access data to be stored or retrieved, for example, a magnetic disk unit.

Disk pack. A removable unit containing several magnetic disks that can be mounted on a magnetic disk storage unit.

Distributed data processing. Geographically distributed computers (usually minicomputers) connected in a network with each other and (usually) with a central computer. Local processing is carried out by the distributed computers, and the results are transmitted to the central computer for further processing.

Distributed processing. A form of decentralization of information processing made possible by a network of computers dispersed throughout an organization. Processing of user applications is accomplished by several computers interconnected by a telecommunications network rather than relying on one large centralized computer facility or on the decentralized operation of several independent computers.

Downtime. The time interval during which a device is malfunctioning or inoperative.

Dump. To write the contents of storage, or of a part of a storage, usually from an internal storage to an external medium, for a specific purpose such as to allow other use of the storage, as a safeguard against faults or errors, or in connection with debugging.

EBCDIC (Extended Binary-Coded Decimal Interchange Code). An alphanumeric coding system that uses eight bits to represent a character.

EDI (Electronic Data Interchange). The electronic transmission of source documents between the computers of different organizations.

Edit. The process of ensuring the syntactical correctness of data.

EFT (Electronic Funds Transfer). The development of banking and payment systems that transfer funds electronically instead of using cash or paper documents such as checks.

Electronic mail. The transmission of messages at high speeds over telecommunications facilities within an organization.

Encryption. A term describing the translation of data into a secret code for security reasons.

End user. Anyone who uses an information system or the information it processes.

End user computing systems. Computer-based information systems that directly support both the operational and managerial applications of end users. Also, the direct, hands-on use of computers by end users.

Enquiry. A request for information from a computer system.

Erasable Programmable Read Only Memory (EPROM). A memory unit that can be erased, but only by being subjected to a special process.

Execute. To perform a computer instruction or a set of instructions, such as a computer program.

Executive information systems. An information system that provides strategic information tailored to the needs of top management.

Expert system. A computer-based information system that uses its knowledge about a specific complex application area to act as an expert consultant to users. The system consists of a knowledge base and software modules that perform inferences on the knowledge, and communicate answers to a user's questions.

Facilities management. The use of an external service organization to operate and manage the electronic data processing facilities of an organization.

Facsimile. The transmission of images and their reconstruction and duplication on some form of paper at a receiving station.

Feasibility study. Part of the process of systems development that determines the information needs of prospective users and the objectives, constraints, basic resource requirements, cost/benefits, and feasibility of proposed projects.

Fibre optics. The technology that uses cables consisting of very thin filaments of glass fibres that can conduct the light generated by lasers at transmission frequencies that approach the speed of light

Field. In a record, specified area used for a particular category of data, for example a wage rate.

File. A set of related records treated as a unit; for example, in stock control, a file could consist of a set of invoices.

File label. A unique name assigned to a file to identify its contents. A magnetic tape file has two labels, a header at the start and a trailer at the end.

File maintenance. The activity of keeping a file up to date by adding, amending, or deleting data.

Floating-point representation. A representation of a real number in a floating-point representation system. For example, the floating-point representation of the number 0.0001234 is 0.1234^{-3}, where 0.1234 is the fixed point part and -3 is the exponent. The numerals are expressed in the variable-point decimal numeration system.

Floppy disk(ette). A flexible plastic platter with two iron-oxide-coated surfaces.

Flowchart. A graphical representation of the definition, analysis, or method of solution of a problem. Symbols are used to represent operations, data, flow, equipment, etc.

FORTRAN (FORmula TRANslation). A high-level programming language widely utilized to develop computer programs that perform mathematical computations for scientific, engineering, and selected business applications.

Fourth-generation languages. A very high-level language through which users or DP personnel can express their computing requirements.

Front-end processor. Typically a smaller, general-purpose computer that is dedicated to handling data communications control functions in a communications network, thus relieving the host computer of these functions.

Full duplex. A communications line (or a data transmission method) that permits the simultaneous transmitting and receiving of data.

Gigabyte. One million bytes. More accurately, 2 to the 30th power, or 1 073 741 824 in decimal notation.

GIGO. A contraction of 'Garbage In, Garbage Out,' which emphasizes that information systems will produce erroneous and invalid output when provided with erroneous and invalid input data or instructions.

Graphics. Pertaining to symbolic input or output from a computer system, such as lines, curves, and geometric shapes, using video display units or graphics plotters and printers.

Groupware. Software packages which support work activities by members of a work group whose workstations are interconnected by a local area network.

Hacking. The unauthorized access and use of computer systems.

Half duplex. A type of communication channel through which communication can occur in only one direction at a time, but that direction can change

Handshaking. Exchange of predetermined signals when a connection is established between two communications terminals.

Hard copy. A data medium or data record that has a degree of permanence and that can be read by people or machine.

Hardware. The physical equipment used in data processing; in electronic data processing the machine devices in a computer system, including the central processing unit devices for data preparation, data input, secondary storage, and output, and devices for intercommunication among hardware components.

Hash total. The sum of the numbers in a data field that are not normally added, such as account numbers or other identification numbers. It is utilized as a control total, especially during input/output operations of batch processing systems.

Head crash. The abrasive contact between a read/write head and the magnetizable surface due to contaminants breaking up the film of air on which the head rides above the surface.

Header label. A machine-readable record at the beginning of a file containing data for file identification and control.

Hexidecimal. Pertaining to the number representation system with a base at 16.

Hierarchical network. A design approach in which an organization's needs are divided into multiple levels which receive different levels of support.

High-level language. A programming language that utilizes macro instructions and statements that closely resemble human language or mathematical notation to describe the problem to be solved or the procedure to be used. Also called a compiler language.

HIPO (Hierarchy plus Input-Process-Output). A documentation technique used to describe the inputs, processing, and outputs of program modules.

Host computer. Typically a larger central computer that performs the major data processing tasks in a computer network.

Image processing. A computer-based technology which allows end users to electronically capture, store, process, and retrieve images that may include numeric data, text, handwriting, graphics, documents, and photographs. Image processing makes heavy use of optical scanning and optical disk technologies.

Impact printers. Printers that form images on paper through the pressing of a printing element and an inked ribbon or roller against the face of a sheet of paper.

Index. An ordered reference list of the contents of a file or document together with keys or reference notations for identification or location of those contents.

Indexed Sequential Access Method (ISAM). A file organization technique in which records are placed on a file in sequence and a multiple-level index is maintained, thus allowing both sequential and direct access processing.

Information. (1) Data that has been transformed into a meaningful and useful form for specific human beings. (2) The meaning that a human assigns to data by means of the known conventions used in its representation.

Information centre. A support facility for the computer users of an organization. It allows users to learn to develop their own application programs and to accomplish their own information processing tasks. The users are provided with hardware support, software support, and people support (trained user consultants).

Information system. A system that uses the resources of hardware (machines and media), software (programs and procedures), and people (users and specialists) to perform input, processing, output, storage, and control activities that transform data resources into information products.

Initialize. To set counters, switches, addresses, or contents of storage to zero or other starting values at the beginning of, or at prescribed points in, the operation of a computer program or module.

Input. Usually pertains to data that is to be fed into a computer program. In the English language, the adjective input may be used in place of input data, input signal, input terminal, etc when such usage is clear in the given context.

Installation. (1) The process of installing new computer hardware or software. (2) A data processing facility such as a computer installation.

Instruction. A grouping of characters that specifies the computer operation to be performed and the values or locations of its operands.

Intangible benefits. Benefits gained from a computer system which are not easily translated into monetary values.

Intangible costs. Costs of a system that are only indirectly measurable in monetary values.

Integrated circuit. A complex micro-electronic circuit consisting of interconnected circuit elements that cannot be disassembled because they are placed on or within a 'continuous substrate' such as a silicon chip.

Integrated packages. Software that combines the ability to do several general-purpose applications (such as word processing, electronic spreadsheet, and graphics) into one program.

Interactive. Describes the mode of entering data into the computers in a question, validation and answer sequence.

Interface. A shared boundary, such as the boundary between two systems; for example, the boundary between a computer and its peripheral devices.

Interpreter. A computer program used to interpret source program instructions prior to executing them.

Interrupt. A signal sent to the central processing unit to indicate the completion of an input/output transmission or the attempted execution of an illegal computer instruction.

Job. A set of data that completely defines a set of work for a computer. A job usually includes all necessary computer programs, linkages, files, and instructions to the operating system.

Job Control Language (JCL). A language that provides a set of short commands and identifiers used to describe a job to the computer.

Joystick. A small lever set in a box used to move the cursor on the computer's display screen.

K. An abbreviation for the prefix 'kilo', which is 1 000 in decimal notation. When referring to storage capacity it is equivalent to 2 to the 10th power, or 1 024 in decimal notation.

Key. One or more characters within an item of data that are used to identify it or control its use.

Keypunch. A keyboard-actuated device that punches holes in punched cards.

Key-to-disk(ette). Hardware designed to transfer data entered via a keyboard to magnetic disk or diskette.

Label. One or more characters used to identify a statement or an item of data in a computer program or the contents of the data file.

Language. A set of representations, conventions, and rules used to convey information.

Language translator program. A program that can convert the programming language instructions of computer programs into machine language instructions. Also called language processors. Major types include assemblers, compilers, and interpreters.

Large-Scale Integration (LSI). Refers to miniaturized circuits, each containing hundreds of electronic circuits on a single silicon chip.

Laser printing. A non-impact printing process which uses a low-power laser beam to print the mirror image of characters on a light sensitive surface covering a rotating drum in the form of dot images.

Librarian. Data processing personnel responsible for the control and maintenance of files, programs, and catalogues for subsequent processing or historical record-keeping.

Library. A collection of related files. For example, one line of any invoice may form a file, the collection of inventory control files may form a library, and the libraries used by organization are known as data bank. A repository for dismountable recorded media, such as magnetic disk packs and magnetic tapes.

Light pen. A photoelectronic device that allows data to be entered or altered on the face of a video display terminal.

Line number. The number that precedes each statement. Line numbers tell the computer the order in which the statements are to be executed.

Line printer. A device that prints a line of characters with one machine cycle.

Local Area Network (LAN). A communications network that typically connects computers, terminals, and other computerized devices within a limited physical area such as an office building, manufacturing plant, or other worksite.

Logical record. A record independent of its physical environment. Portions of the same logical record may be located in different physical records, or several logical records or parts of logical records may be located in one physical record.

Loop. A series of instructions that is executed repeatedly as long as specified conditions remain constant.

Machine instruction. An instruction that a computer can recognize and execute.

Machine language. A programming language where instructions are expressed in the binary code of the computer.

Magnetic bubble. An electromagnetic storage device that stores and moves data magnetically as tiny magnetic spots that look bubbles under a microscope as they float on the surface of a special type of semiconductor chip.

Magnetic core. Tiny rings composed of iron oxide and other materials strung on wires that provide electrical current that magnetizes the cores. Data is represented by the direction of the magnetic field of groups of cores. Widely used as the primary storage media in second- and third-generation computer systems.

Magnetic disk. A flat circular plate with a magnetic surface layer. Synonymous with 'disk'.

Magnetic Ink Character Recognition (MICR). The recognition of characters printed with ink that contains particles of magnetic material. Contrast with *Optical Character Recognition (OCR)*.

Magnetic tape. A tape with a magnetic surface on which data can be stored by selective magnetization of portions of the surface.

Mainframe. (1) Same as central processing unit. (2) A larger-size computer system, typically with a separate central processing unit, as distinguished from microcomputer and minicomputer systems.

Management Information System (MIS). An information system that provides information to support managerial decision making. More specifically, an information reporting system, executive information system, or decision support system.

Mass storage. Secondary storage devices with extra-large storage capacities such as magnetic or optical disks.

Master file. A file that is used as an authority in a given job and that is relatively permanent, even though its contents may change.

Matrix printing. An impact process by which the characters, made up of dots in a matrix, are printed on paper.

Megabyte. One million bytes. More accurately, 2 to the 20th power, or 1 048 576 in decimal notation.

Memory. A storage medium for binary data. Examples are main memory provided by core and secondary memory provided by disks.

Menu. A displayed list of items (usually the names of data processing jobs) from which a video terminal operator makes a selection.

Menu driven. A characteristic of most interactive processing systems that provides menu displays and operator prompting to assist a video terminal operator in performing a particular job.

Merge. To combine the items of two or more sets that are each in the same given order into one set in the same order.

Microcomputer. A very small computer; often a special-purpose or single-function computer on a single chip.

Microprocessor. The CPU of a microcomputer.

Microsecond. One millionth of a second.

Millisecond. One thousandth of a second.

Minicomputer. A small (for example, the size of a desk) electronic, digital, stored-program, general-purpose computer.

Mnemonic. The use of symbols that are chosen to assist the human memory, typically abbreviations or contractions such as 'MPY' for multiply.

Modem (MOdulator-DEModulator). A device that converts the digital signals from input/output devices into appropriate frequencies at a transmission terminal and converts them back into digital signals at a receiving terminal.

Module. A part of a whole, a program segment, a subsystem.

Monitor. Software or hardware that observes, supervises, controls, or verifies the operation of a system.

Mouse. A small device that is electronically connected to a computer and is moved by hand on a flat surface in order to move the cursor on a video screen in the same direction. Buttons on the mouse allow users to issue commands and make responses or selections.

Multiplexor. An electronic device that allows a single communications channel to carry simultaneous data transmission from many terminals.

Multiprocessing. A mode of operating a multiprocessor that provides for the parallel processing of two or more computer programs. Pertaining to the simultaneous execution of two or more computer programs or sequences of instructions by a computer or computer network.

Multiprogramming. A mode of operation that provides for the interleaved execution of two or more computer programs by a single processing unit. Pertaining to the concurrent execution of two or more computer programs or sequences of instructions by a computer or computer network.

Multitasking. The concurrent use of the same computer to accomplish several different information processing tasks. Each task may require the use of a different program, or the concurrent use of the same copy of a program by several users.

Nanosecond. One billionth of a second.

Natural language. A programming language that is very close to human language. Also called very high-level language.

Network. A group of computers connected by communication lines.

Non-impact printers. Printers that use specially treated paper that form characters by laser, thermal (heat), electrostatic, or electrochemical processes.

Non-procedural language. A highest level computer programming language designed to allow easy development of special purpose programs using relatively natural forms of language.

Non-volatile memory. Memory that retains its contents during power loss.

Object-Oriented Language. An object-oriented programming (OOP) language used to develop programs which create and use objects to perform information processing tasks.

Object program. A compiled or assembled program composed of executable machine instructions. Contrast with *Source program*.

Office Automation (OA). The use of computer-based information systems that collect, process, store, and transmit electronic messages, documents, and other forms of office communications among individuals, work groups, and organizations.

Offline. Pertaining to equipment or devices not under control of the central processing unit.

Online. Pertaining to equipment or devices under control of the central processing unit.

Operand. That which is operated upon. That part of a computer instruction that is identified by the address part of the instruction.

Operating system. The main control program of a computer system. It is a system of programs that controls the execution of computer programs and that may provide scheduling, debugging, input/output control, system accounting, compilation, storage assignment, data management, and related services.

Operation code. A code that represents specific operations to be performed upon the operands in a computer instruction.

Optical Character Recognition (OCR). The machine identification of printed characters through the use of light sensitive devices. Contrast with *Magnetic Ink Character Recognition (MICR)*.

Optical disks. A secondary storage medium using laser technology to read tiny pits on a plastic disk. The disks are currently capable of storing billions of characters of information.

Optical scanner. A device that optically scans printed or written data and generates their digital representations.

Output. The results (management information, custodial documents, or historical records) generated by processing input.

Output device. A device that places data from the central memory on to a storage medium such as magnetic tape or punched cards.

Pack. To compress data in a storage medium by taking advantage of known characteristics of the data in such a way that the original data can be recovered.

Packet switching. A data transmission process that transmits addressed packets such that a channel is occupied only for the duration of transmission of the packet.

Paging. A procedure for maximizing the memory capacity of a computer by swapping data between primary memory and a second storage device (see also *Virtual storage)*.

Parallel. Pertaining to the concurrent or simultaneous occurrence of two or more related activities in multiple devices or channels.

Parallel processing. Executing many instructions at the same time, that is, in parallel. Performed by advanced computers using many instruction processors organized in clusters or networks.

Parity bit. A bit appended to a byte to ensure correctness of data transmission. The addition of the parity bit to make the total number of bits (including the parity bit) odd is called 'odd parity'; if the total number of bits is made even by the addition of the parity bit, it is called 'even parity'.

PASCAL. A hierarchical computer language developed in Switzerland in the late 1960s and designed for structured programming.

Peripheral. An input, output or secondary-storage device attached to a CPU.

Personal computing. The use of microcomputers by individuals for educational, recreational, professional, and other personal applications.

PERT (Program Evaluation and Review Technique). A system used to find the most efficient scheduling of time and resources when producing a complex project or product.

Picosecond. One thousandth of a nanosecond.

Plotter. An output device that converts data emitted from the CPU into graphic form; produces hard copy output.

PL/1. A high-level programming language developed by IBM.

Point-of-sale (POS). A terminal that serves the same purpose as a cash register, but is also capable of relaying sales and inventory data to a central computer for immediate updating of records.

Pointer. A data element associated with an index, a record, or other set of data that contains the address of a related record.

Procedures. Sets of instructions used by people to complete a task.

Program. A sequence of instructions given in a computer language that will perform a specific function or series of functions.

Program flowchart. A step by step program showing each discrete procedure and element in the solution to the problem.

Programmable Read Only Memory (PROM). A read only memory whose contents can be changed by special procedures but not by the use of a standard programming process.

Programmer. A person mainly involved in designing, writing, and testing computer programs.

Programming. The design, writing, and testing of a program.

Programming language. A language used to prepare computer programs.

Project management. Managing the accomplishment of an information system development project according to a specific project plan, in order that a project is completed on time, within its budget, and meets its design objectives.

Prompt. Messages that assist the operator in performing a particular job. This would include error messages, correction suggestions, questions, and other messages that guide an operator.

Protocol. A set of rules and procedures for the control of communications in a communications network.

Prototyping. A 'quick and dirty' type of systems development where an actual working model (a prototype) of the information system needed by a user is quickly developed using an application generator and an interactive process between a systems analyst and a user.

Pseudocode. An informal design language used to represent the control structures of structured programming.

Punched card. A card punched with a pattern of holes to represent data.

Query. A request for specific data or information.

Query language. A high-level, English-like language provided by a data base management system that enables user to easily extract data and information from a data base.

Queue. (1) A waiting line formed by items in a system waiting for service. (2) To arrange in or form a queue.

Random access. Same as *Direct access*.

Random Access Memory (RAM). (1) A memory unit in which any location or group of locations may be obtained directly (that is, without the sequential reading of other data locations). (2) RAM is sometimes used as an abbreviation for semi-conductor memory.

Read. To acquire or interpret data from a storage device, a data medium, or any other source.

Read Only Memory (ROM). A device used to store data (or instructions) that are not alterable by computer instructions. The contents are thus protected against accidental destruction.

Read/write head. An electromagnet used as a component of a tape or disk drive; in reading, it detects magnetized areas and translates them into electrical pulses; in writing, it magnetizes appropriate areas, thereby erasing data stored previously.

Real time. Pertaining to the performance of data processing during the actual time a process transpires, in order that results of the data processing can be used in guiding the process.

Record. A collection of related data or words treated as a unit. For example in stock control, each invoice could constitute one record. See *Logical record, Variable-length record.*

Reduced Instruction Set Computer (RISC). A CPU architecture which optimizes processing speed by the use of a smaller number of basic machine instructions than traditional CPU designs.

Redundancy. In information processing, the repetition of part or all of a message to increase the chance that the correct information will be understood by the recipient.

Register. A device that can contain a computer word, character, or portion of a word. The register holds the information for manipulation by the computer. The arithmetic/logic unit of a computer will contain one or more registers.

Relational data structure. A logical data structure in which all data elements within the database are viewed as being stored in the form of simple tables. DBMS packages based on the relational model can link data elements from various tables as long as the tables share common data elements.

Remote access. Pertaining to communication with the data processing facility by one or more stations that are distant from that facility.

Report generator. A feature of database management system packages which allows an end user to quickly specify a report format for the display of information retrieved from a database.

Routine. An ordered set of instructions that may have some general or frequent use.

RPG. Report Program Generator — an example of a problem-oriented language originally designed to produce business reports.

Schema. An overall conceptual or logical view of the relationships between the data in a data base.

Secondary storage. Storage that supplements the primary storage of a computer. Synonymous with *Auxiliary storage*.

Sequential file. Data (records) stored in a specific order, one right after the other.

Serial processing. A method of processing where programs are executed one at a time, usually found in simple operating systems such as the earliest computer systems.

Server. A computer that supports telecommunications in a local area network, as well as the sharing of peripheral devices, software, and databases among the workstations in the network.

Service bureau. A firm offering computer and data processing services. Also called a computer service centre.

Service program. A program that provides general support for the operation of a computer system, such as input/output, diagnostic, and other 'utility' routines.

Silicon chip. Solid-logic circuitry used in the primary storage of third-generation computers.

Simplex. Pertaining to a communications link that is capable of transmitting data in only one direction. Contrast with *Duplex*.

Simulation. The representation of certain features of the behaviour of a physical or abstract system by the behaviour of another system. Contrast with *Emulation*.

Smart products. Industrial and consumer products, with 'intelligence' provided by built-in microcomputers or microprocessors that significantly improve the performance and capabilities of such products.

Software. Computer programs and procedures concerned with the operation of an information system. Contrast with *Hardware*.

Software package. A set of standardized computer programs, procedures, and related documentation designed to solve problems of a specific application, often acquired from an external supplier.

Solid state. Pertaining to devices whose operation depends on the control of electric or magnetic phenomenon in solids such as transistors and diodes.

Sort. To segregate items into groups according to some definite rules.

Source program. A computer program expressed in a source language.

Spooling. A process of writing output data on a temporary storage device (usually a magnetic drum) until an output unit is available.

Standards. Measures of performance developed to evaluate the progress of a system towards its objectives.

Statement. In a programming language, a meaningful expression that may describe or specify an operation.

Storage. Pertaining to a device into which data can be entered, in which they can be held, and from which they can be retrieved at a later time.

Structure chart. A design and documentation technique used in structured programming to show the purpose and relationships of the various modules in a program.

Structured programming. A modular approach to programming that emphasizes dividing a program into logical sections in order to reduce testing time, increase programmer productivity, and bring clarity to programming.

Structured Query Language (SQL). A query language that is becoming a standard for advanced database management system packages. A query's basic form is SELECT ... FROM ... WHERE.

Structured walk-throughs. A structured programming methodology that requires a peer review by other programmers of program design and coding to minimize and reveal errors in the early stages of programming.

Subschema. A subset or transformation of the logical view of the data base schema that is required by a particular user application program.

Subroutine. A routine that can be part of another program routine.

Synchronous. A characteristic in which each event, or the performance of any basic operation, is constrained to start on, and usually to keep in step with, signals from a timing clock. Contrast with *Asynchronous.*

System. (1) A group of interrelated or interacting elements forming a unified whole. (2) A group of interrelated components working together toward a common goal by accepting inputs and producing outputs in an organized transformation process. (3) An assembly of methods, procedures, or techniques united by regulated interaction to form an organized whole. (4) An organized collection of people, machines, and methods required to accomplish a set of specific functions.

Systems analysis. The analysis of an activity to determine precisely what must be accomplished and how to accomplish it.

Systems design. Deciding how a proposed information system will meet the information needs of end users. Includes logical and physical design activities, and user interface, data, and process design activities which produce system specifications that satisfy the system requirements developed in the systems analysis stage.

Systems development. (1) Conceiving, designing, and implementing a system. (2) Developing information systems by a process of investigation, analysis, design, implementation, and maintenance.

Systems flowchart. A group of symbols that represents the general information flow in a system. It focuses on inputs and outputs rather than on internal computer operations.

Systems implementation. The stage of systems development in which hardware and software are acquired, developed, and installed, the system is tested and documented, people are trained to operate and use the system, and an organization converts to the use of a newly developed system.

Systems maintenance. The monitoring, evaluating, and modifying of a system to make desirable or necessary improvements.

System specifications. The product of the systems design stage. It consists of specifications for the hardware, software, facilities, personnel, databases, and the user interface of a proposed information system.

Systems software. Programs that control and support operations of a computer system. System software includes a variety of programs such as operating systems, data base management systems, communications control programs, service and utility programs, and programming language translators.

Tangible benefits and costs. The quantifiable benefits and costs of a proposed solution or system.

Telecommunication. The transmission of signals over long distances, such as by telegraph, radio, or microwave.

Telecommunications monitors. Computer programs that control and support the communications between the computers and terminals in a telecommunications network.

Teleconferencing. The use of video communications to allow business conferences to be held with participants who are scattered across a country, continent, or the world.

Teleprocessing. The combined use of communication facilities, such as the telephone system and data processing equipment.

Terabyte. One trillion bytes. More accurately, 2 to the 40th power, or 1 009 511 627 776 in decimal notation.

Terminal. A device used to communicate data or information from the user to the computer or vice versa.

Throughput. The total amount of useful work performed by a data processing system during a given period of time.

Time-sharing. The apparent use of a computer by more than one user at the same time. Each user interacts actively with the computer by use of a remote terminal.

Top-down design. A method of defining a solution in terms of major functions to be performed, and further breaking down the major functions into subfunctions; the further the breakdown the greater the detail.

Touch-sensitive screen. An input device that accepts data input by the placement of a finger on or close to the CRT screen.

Track. The portion of a moving storage medium, such as a drum, tape, or disk, that is accessible to a given reading head position.

Transaction. An event that occurs as part of doing business, such as a sale, purchase, deposit, withdrawal, refund, transfer, payment, and so on.

Transaction file. A file that contains new records or modifications to existing records; used to update a master file.

Transaction processing cycle. A cycle of basic transaction processing activities including data entry, transaction processing, database maintenance, document and report generation, and inquiry processing.

Transcription. The process of transferring data from one medium to another prior to input into the computer.

Translator. A device or computer program that transforms statements from one language to another, such as a compiler or assembler.

Turnaround document. Output of a computer system (such as customer invoices and statements) that is designed to be returned to the organization as machine-readable input.

Turnaround time. The elapsed time between submission of a job to a computing centre and the return of the results.

Turnkey system. A DP system, including hardware and software, capable of performing the data functions of a business.

Universal Product Code (UPC). A code consisting of ten pairs of vertical bars that represent the manufacturer's identity and the identity code of the item.

Update. The process of accessing data in a file, changing its contents and writing the data either back to the file or (in the case of sequential processing) to a new file.

User friendly. A characteristic of human-operated equipment and systems that makes them safe, comfortable, and easy to use.

Utility program. A standard set of routines that assists in the operation of a computer system by performing some frequently required process such as sorting or merging.

Variable-length record. Pertaining to a file in which the records need not be uniform in length.

Verify. To determine whether a transcription of data or other operation has been accomplished accurately.

Very Large-Scale Integration (VLSI). Refers to miniaturized circuits, each containing thousands of electrical components on a single silicon chip.

Virtual machine. Pertaining to the simulation of one type of computer system by another computer system.

Virtual memory. A computer memory system that expands the primary memory beyond its physical limitations by means of additional secondary storage capacity and the use of paging.

Visual Display Terminal. A terminal capable of receiving output on a cathode ray tube (CRT) and, with special provisions, of transmitting data through a keyboard.

Voice recognition. Direct conversion of spoken data into electronic form suitable for entry into a computer system. Also called voice data entry.

Volatile memory. A memory whose contents are irretrievably lost during power loss.

Wand. A handheld optical character recognition device used for data entry by many transaction terminals.

Wide Area Network (WAN). A data communications network covering a large geographic area.

Window. One section of a computer's multiple section display screen, each of which can have a different display.

Word. A character string or a binary element string that is convenient for some purpose to consider as an entity.

Word processing. The manipulation of text data to achieve a desired output.

Word processor. An electronic device that performs text-editing functions, primarily used by secretaries.

Workstation. A computer terminal or micro- or minicomputer system designed to support the work of one person. Also, a high-powered computer to support the work of professionals in engineering, science, and other areas that require extensive computing power and graphics capabilities.

Write. (1) The transfer of data from the computer to an output device; for example, the writing of data on magnetic tape. (2) The placement of data from an output device into locations of main memory.

Index